LENIN

COLLECTED WORKS

18

THE RUSSIAN EDITION WAS PRINTED
IN ACCORDANCE WITH A DECISION
OF THE NINTH CONGRESS OF THE R.C.P.(B.)
AND THE SECOND CONGRESS OF SOVIETS
OF THE U.S.S.R.

ИНСТИТУТ МАРКСИЗМА-ЛЕНИНИЗМА при ЦК КПСС

В. И. ЛЕНИН

СОЧИНЕНИЯ

Издание четвертое

ГОСУДАРСТВЕННОЕ ИЗДАТЕЛЬСТВО
ПОЛИТИЧЕСКОЙ ЛИТЕРАТУРЫ

МОСКВА

V. I. LENIN

COLLECTED WORKS

VOLUME
18
April 1912 – March 1913

PROGRESS PUBLISHERS
MOSCOW

TRANSLATED FROM THE RUSSIAN BY STEPAN APRESYAN
EDITED BY CLEMENS DUTT

First printing 1963
Second printing 1968
Third printing 1973
Fourth printing 1975
Fifth printing 1978

Л $\frac{10102 - 038}{014(01) - 78}$ без объявл.

Printed in the Union of Soviet Socialist Republics

CONTENTS

ILLUSTRATIONS

PREFACE

Volume Eighteen contains works written by V. I. Lenin from April 1912 to March 1913, during the new revolutionary upswing in Russia.

The bulk of the volume is made up of writings in which Lenin analyses the socio-economic and political causes of the growth of a new revolution in Russia, elaborates the tactics to be followed by the Bolshevik Party in the conditions of the new revolutionary upswing, and exposes the counter-revolutionary nature of the liberal bourgeoisie and the treacherous part played by the Menshevik liquidators, Trotskyists and Vperyodists in the working-class movement. Among them are the articles "The Revolutionary Upswing" and "Political Parties in Russia", the pamphlet *The Present Situation in the R.S.D.L.P.*, "The Liquidators Against the Party", "How P. B. Axelrod Exposes the Liquidators", etc.

A large number of writings—"The Fourth Duma Election Campaign and the Tasks of the Revolutionary Social-Democrats", "The Platform of the Reformists and the Platform of the Revolutionary Social-Democrats", "Results of the Elections", "Concerning Certain Speeches by Workers' Deputies", etc.—are devoted to the Fourth Duma election campaign, and to appraising the election results and the activity of the Duma Social-Democratic group.

In "The Essence of the 'Agrarian Problem in Russia'", "A Comparison of the Stolypin and the Narodnik Agrarian Programmes", "The Last Valve" and other articles, Lenin reveals the essence of Stolypin's agrarian policy and demonstrates why it was bound to fail.

The resolutions of the "February" meeting of the C.C. R.S.D.L.P. and Party functionaries, published in this volume, give directives on all the major questions of Social-Democratic work in Russia.

The volume contains fifteen writings that are included in Lenin's *Collected Works* for the first time. They are concerned with the struggle against the liquidators and with the elaboration of tactical problems of the Bolshevik Party.

The document "Concerning the Workers' Deputies to the Duma and Their Declaration" is a draft declaration for the Social-Democratic group in the Fourth Duma.

In "The Illegal Party and Legal Work", "A Reply to the Liquidators", "Original Postscript to the Pamphlet *The Present Situation in the R.S.D.L.P.*", "Can the Slogan 'Freedom of Association' Serve as a Basis for the Working-Class Movement Today?", "Letter to the Swiss Workers", "On the Attitude to Liquidationism and on Unity. Theses", and "Original Postscript to the Article 'The Development of Revolutionary Strikes and Street Demonstrations'", Lenin criticises the views of the liquidators and of Trotsky, who fully supported the liquidators.

The articles "The Cadets and the Big Bourgeoisie" and "Constitutional Illusions Lost" expose the Duma tactics of the Cadets, the party of the counter-revolutionary liberal bourgeoisie.

The articles "Revolts in the Army and Navy', "The Workers and *Pravda*", and "Before and Now" analyse the upswing of the revolutionary movement and the development of the legal Bolshevik press.

The "Notification" on the February meeting of the C.C. R.S.D.L.P. and Party functionaries sums up the results of that meeting.

THE FOURTH DUMA ELECTION CAMPAIGN AND THE TASKS OF THE REVOLUTIONARY SOCIAL-DEMOCRATS

The political strikes and the first demonstrations over the Lena shootings[1] show that the revolutionary movement among the masses of workers in Russia is growing. This thickening of the revolutionary atmosphere casts a vivid light on the tasks of the Party and its role in the election campaign.

The crisis is growing in a new situation. The reactionary Duma,[2] which provides the landlords with power, the bourgeoisie with an arena for making deals, and the proletariat with a small platform, is a necessary factor in this situation. We need this platform, we need the election campaign, *for* our revolutionary work among the masses. We need the illegal Party to *direct* all this work as a whole—in the Taurida Palace, as well as in Kazanskaya Square,[3] at workers' mass meetings, during strikes, at district meetings of worker Social-Democrats, and at open trade union meetings. Only the hopelessly blind can fail even now to see the utter absurdity and perniciousness for the working class of otzovism and liquidationism,[4] those products of decay and disintegration during the period of the triumph of counter-revolution. The example of the Narodniks has shown us clearly the scandalous *zero* one gets as the result of adding the *liquidationism* of the "Trudoviks", as well as of the legally functioning writers of *Russkoye Bogatstvo*[5] and *Sovremennik*,[6] to the *otzovism* of the Socialist-Revolutionary "party".

Let us now sum up the facts brought to light during the pre-election mobilisation of political forces. *Three* camps stand out clearly: (1) The *Rights*—from Purishkevich to Guchkov—are pro-government. The Black-Hundred[7] land-lord and the conservative merchant are heart and soul for the government. (2) The *liberal* bourgeois—the "Progress-ists" and the Cadets, along with groups of various non-Russians—are against the government *and against* the revolution. The counter-revolutionary nature of the liberals is one of the main features of the present historical juncture. Whoever does not see this counter-revolutionary nature of the "cultured" bourgeoisie has forgotten everything and learned nothing, and takes the name of democrat, to say nothing of socialist, in vain. As it happens, the Trudoviks and "our" liquidators see poorly and understand things poorly! (3) The democratic camp, in which only the revo-lutionary Social-Democrats, the anti-liquidationists, united and organised, have firmly and clearly unfurled *their own* banner, the banner of revolution. The Trudoviks and our liquidators are vacillating *between* the liberals and the democrats, between legal opposition and revolution.

The class roots which brought about the division between the first two camps are clear. But the liberals have succeeded in leading astray many people, from Vodovozov to Dan, as to the class roots which divided the second camp from the third. The liberal "strategy", naïvely blurted out by Blank in *Zaprosy Zhizni*,[8] is very simple: the Cadets are the centre of the opposition, the thill-horse; the outrunners (the "flanks") are the Progressists on the right, and the Trudoviks and the liquidators on the left. It is on this "troika" that the Milyu-kovs, in their role of "responsible opposition", hope to "ride" to triumph.

The hegemony of the liberals in the Russian emancipation movement has *always* meant, and will always mean, defeat for this movement. The liberals manoeuvre between the monarchy of the Purishkeviches and the revolution of the workers and peasants, betraying the latter at *every* serious juncture. The task of the revolution is to *use* the liberals' fight against the government and to *neutralise* their vacilla-tions and treachery.

The policy of the liberals is to scare Purishkevich and Romanov a little with the prospect of revolution, in order to share power with them and jointly suppress the revolution.

And it is the class position of the bourgeoisie that determines this policy. Hence the Cadets' cheap "democracy"
and their *actual* fusion with the most moderate "Progressists" of the type of Yefremov, Lvov, Ryabushinsky and Co.

The tactics of the proletarian Party should be to use the
fight between the liberals and the Purishkeviches over the
division of power—without *in any way* allowing "faith"
in the liberals to take hold among the people—in order to
develop, intensify and reinforce the revolutionary onslaught
of the masses, which overthrows the monarchy and entirely
wipes out the Purishkeviches and Romanovs. At the elections, its tactics should be to unite the democrats *against*
the Rights *and against* the Cadets by "using" the liberals'
fight against the Rights in cases of a second ballot, in the
press and at meetings. Hence the necessity for a revolutionary platform that even now goes beyond the bounds of
"legality". Hence the slogan of a republic—as against the
liberals' "constitutional" slogans, slogans of a "Rasputin-
Treshchenkov constitution".[9] Our task is to train an
army of champions of the revolution everywhere, always,
in all forms of work, in every field of activity, at every
turn of events which may be forced on us by a victory of
reaction, the treachery of the liberals, the protraction of
the crisis, etc.

Look at the Trudoviks. They are Narodnik liquidators
sans phrases. "We are revolutionaries," Mr. Vodovozov
"hints", "*but*—we can't go against Article 129,[10]" he adds.
A hundred years after Herzen's birth, the "party" of the
peasant millions is unable to publish even a sheet—even a
hectographed one!—in defiance of Article 129!! While gravitating towards a bloc "first of all" with the Social-Democrats, the Trudoviks are unable to say clearly that the
Cadets are counter-revolutionary, to lay the foundations for
a *republican* peasant party. Yet that is exactly how the question stands after the lessons of 1905-07 and 1908-11: either
fight for a republic, or lick the boots of Purishkevich and
grovel under the whips of Markov and Romanov. There is
no other choice for the peasants.

Look at the liquidators. No matter how much the Marty-
novs, Martovs and Co. shift and shuffle, any conscientious
and sensible reader will recognise that R—kov[11] summed up

their views when he said: "Let there be no illusion. What is
in the making is the triumph of a very moderate bourgeois
progressism." The *objective* meaning of this winged phrase is
the following: revolution is an illusion, the real thing is to
support the "Progressists". Surely anyone who does not deliberately close his eyes must see now that it is *precisely this*
that the Dans and Martovs are saying, in slightly different
words, when they issue the slogan: "Wrest the Duma [the
Fourth Duma, a landlord-ridden Duma!]* from the hands of
the reactionaries"? Or when they make, again and again, the
slip of referring to two camps? Or when they shout, "Do not
frustrate" the progressive work of the liberal bourgeois?
Or when they fight against a "Left bloc"? Or when, writing
in *Zhivoye Dyelo*,[12] they smugly snap their fingers at "the
literature published abroad which nobody reads"? Or when
they *actually* content themselves with a legal platform and
legal attempts at organisation? Or when they form "initiating groups"[13] of liquidators, thus breaking with the
revolutionary R.S.D.L.P.? Is it not clear that this is also
the tune sung by the Levitskys, who are lending philosophical depth to the liberal ideas about the struggle for right,
by the Nevedomskys, who have lately "revised" Dobrolyubov's[14] ideas backwards —*from* democracy *to* liberalism —and
by the Smirnovs, who are making eyes at "progressism", and
by all the other knights of *Nasha Zarya*[15] and *Zhivoye Dyelo*?

Actually the democrats and the Social-Democrats, even
if they had wanted to, would never have been able to "frustrate" a victory of the "Progressists" among the landlords
and bourgeois! All this is nothing but idle talk. This is not
where the serious differences lie. Nor is this what constitutes the distinction between a *liberal* and a *Social-Democratic* labour policy. To "support" the Progressists on the
ground that their "victories" "bring the cultured bourgeois
nearer to power" is a liberal labour policy.

We Social-Democrats regard a "victory" of the Progressists as an *indirect* expression of a democratic upswing. It is
necessary to use the skirmishes between the Progressists and

---

* Interpolations in square brackets (within passages quoted by
Lenin) have been introduced by Lenin, unless otherwise indicated.—
Ed.

the Rights—the mere slogan of support for the Progressists
is no good. Our job is to promote the democratic upswing,
to foster the new revolutionary democracy that is growing
in a new way in the new Russia. Unless it succeeds in
gathering strength and winning in spite of the liberals, *no*
"triumph" of the Progressists and the Cadets in the elections
will bring about any serious change in the actual situation
in Russia.

The democratic upswing is an indisputable fact now.
It is progressing with greater difficulty, at a slower pace and
along a more arduous path than we should like, but it is
progressing nonetheless. It is *this* that we must "support"
and promote by our election work and every other kind of
activity. Our task is to organise the revolutionary democrats—by ruthless criticism of Narodnik liquidationism and
Narodnik otzovism to forge a republican peasant party—
but first of all and above all else to clean "our own house"
of liquidationism and otzovism, intensify our revolutionary
Social-Democratic work among the proletariat and strength-
en the illegal Social-Democratic Labour Party. The outcome of the growing revolutionary crisis does not depend
on us; it depends on a thousand different causes, on the revolution in Asia and on socialism in Europe. But it does depend
on us to conduct consistent and steady work among the
masses in the spirit of Marxism, and only this kind of work
is *never* done in vain.   .

Sotsial-Demokrat No. 26,   Published according
May 8 (April 25), 1912   to the text in *Sotsial-Demokrat*

THE LIQUIDATORS AGAINST THE PARTY

The liquidators of all shades, writing in the legal Russian press, are conducting a campaign of slander against the Party Conference[16] with an easy shamelessness which might well be envied by the Bulgarins and Burenins.[17] The articles in *Zhivoye Dyelo*, which openly question the delegates as to *who* sent them and, under the protection of the censorship, attack what cannot be defended in the legal press, exemplify such disregard for the elementary rules of literary decency that they are bound not only to evoke protests from the adherents of the Conference, but also to disgust any fair-minded political leader. As for the articles of the anonymous informer of *Vorwärts*,[18] they reek of shameless braggadocio and florid lying so overpoweringly as not to permit of any doubt that the liquidators' order for them found itself in experienced hands.*

Driven into a corner, the groups and circles of liquidators do not confine themselves, however, to a campaign of slander against the Party. They are trying to convene a conference of their own. Every measure has been taken, of course, to lend the Organising Committee,[19] which is to convene this conference, the semblance of a "pro-Party", "non-factional", "unity" body. After all, these are such convenient words—when the liquidators want to hook all those who for some reason are dissatisfied with the Party Conference. Trotsky

---

* To acquaint the German comrades with the actual state of affairs in the R.S.D.L.P., the editorial board of the Central Organ published a special pamphlet in German, exposing, among other things, the methods of the anonymous writer in *Vorwärts*. (See present edition, Vol. 17, pp. 533-46.—*Ed.*)

was entrusted with singing all the virtues of the Organising
Committee and of the forthcoming liquidationist conference;
nor could they have assigned the job to anyone fitter than
the "professional uniter". And he did sing them—in every
variety of type his Vienna printer could find: "The supporters of *Vperyod* and *Golos*, pro-Party Bolsheviks, pro-Party
Mensheviks,[20] so-called liquidators and non-factionalists—
in Russia and abroad—are firmly supporting the work..."
of the Organising Committee. (*Pravda*[21] No. 24.)

The poor fellow—again he told a lie, and again he miscal-
culated. The bloc under the hegemony of the liquidators,
which was being prepared in opposition to the Conference
of 1912 with so much fuss, is now bursting at the seams and
the reason is that the liquidators have shown their hand too
openly. The Poles refused to take part in the Organising
Committee. Plekhanov, through correspondence with a
representative of the Committee, established several interesting details, to wit: (1) that what is planned is a "constituent" conference, i.e., not a conference of the R.S.D.L.P.,
but of some new party; (2) that it is being convened on "anar-
chical" lines; (3) that the "conference is being convened
by the liquidators". After these circumstances had been
revealed by Comrade Plekhanov, there was nothing surprising to us in the fact that the so-called Bolshevik (?!) conciliators plucked up courage and resolved to convict Trotsky
of—having told a lie by listing them among the supporters
of the Organising Committee. "This Organising Committee,
as it is now constituted, with its obvious tendency to impose upon the whole Party its own attitude to the liquidators, and with the principles of organisational anarchy which
it has made the basis for increasing its membership, does
not provide the least guarantee that a really general Party
conference will be convened." That is how our emboldened
"pro-Party" people comment on the Organising Committee
today. We do not know where the most Leftist of our Left—
the *Vperyod* group, who at one time hastened to signify its
sympathy with the Organising Committee—stand today.
Nor is this of any importance. The important thing is that
the liquidationist character of the conference to be held by
the Organising Committee has been established by Plekhanov with irrefutable clarity, and that the statesmanlike

minds of the "conciliators" had to bow to this fact. Who remains, then? The open liquidators and Trotsky.

The basis of this bloc is obvious: the liquidators enjoy full freedom to pursue their line in *Zhivoye Dyelo* and *Nasha Zarya* "as before", while Trotsky, operating abroad, screens them with r-r-revolutionary phrases, which cost him nothing and do not bind them in any way.

There is one little lesson to be drawn from this affair by those abroad who are sighing for unity, and who recently hatched the sheet *Za Partiyu*[22] in Paris. To build up a party, it is not enough to be able to shout "unity"; it is also necessary to have a *political* programme, a programme of political action. The bloc comprising the liquidators, Trotsky, the *Vperyod* group, the Poles, the pro-Party Bolsheviks (?), the Paris Mensheviks, and so on and so forth, was foredoomed to ignominious failure, because it was based on an unprincipled approach, on hypocrisy and hollow phrases. As for those who sigh, it would not be amiss if they finally made up their minds on that extremely complicated and difficult question: With whom do they want to have unity? If it is with the liquidators, why not say so without mincing? But if they are against unity with the liquidators, then what sort of unity are they sighing for?

The January Conference and the bodies it elected are the only thing that actually unites all the R.S.D.L.P. functionaries in Russia today. Apart from the Conference there is only the promise of the Bundists[23] and Trotsky to convene the liquidationist conference of the Organising Committee, and the "conciliators" who are experiencing their liquidationist hang-over.

Sotsial-Demokrat No. 26,   Published according
May 8 (April 25), 1912   to the text in *Sotsial-Demokrat*

IN MEMORY OF HERZEN

One hundred years have elapsed since Herzen's birth. The whole of liberal Russia is paying homage to him, studiously evading, however, the serious questions of socialism, and taking pains to conceal that which distinguished Herzen the *revolutionary* from a liberal. The Right-wing press, too, is commemorating the Herzen centenary, falsely asserting that in his last years Herzen renounced revolution. And in the orations on Herzen that are made by the liberals and Narodniks abroad, phrase-mongering reigns supreme.

The working-class party should commemorate the Herzen centenary, not for the sake of philistine glorification, but for the purpose of making clear its own tasks and ascertaining the place actually held in history by this writer who played a great part in paving the way for the Russian revolution.

Herzen belonged to the generation of revolutionaries among the nobility and landlords of the first half of the last century. The nobility gave Russia the Birons and Arakcheyevs,[24] innumerable "drunken officers, bullies, gamblers, heroes of fairs, masters of hounds, roisterers, floggers, pimps", as well as amiable Manilovs.[25] "But," wrote Herzen, "among them developed the men of December 14,[26] a phalanx of heroes reared, like Romulus and Remus, on the milk of a wild beast.... They were veritable titans, hammered out of pure steel from head to foot, comrades-in-arms who deliberately went to certain death in order to awaken the young generation to a new life and to purify the children born in an environment of tyranny and servility."[27]

Herzen was one of those children. The uprising of the Decembrists awakened and "purified" him. In the feudal Russia of the forties of the nineteenth century, he rose to a height which placed him on a level with the greatest thinkers of his time. He assimilated Hegel's dialectics. He realised that it was "the algebra of revolution". He went further than Hegel, following Feuerbach to materialism. The first of his *Letters on the Study of Nature*, "Empiricism and Idealism", written in 1844, reveals to us a thinker who even now stands head and shoulders above the multitude of modern empiricist natural scientists and the host of present-day idealist and semi-idealist philosophers. Herzen came right up to dialectical materialism, and halted—before historical materialism.

It was this "halt" that caused Herzen's spiritual shipwreck after the defeat of the revolution of 1848. Herzen had left Russia, and observed this revolution at close range. He was at that time a democrat, a revolutionary, a socialist. But his "socialism" was one of the countless forms and varieties of bourgeois and petty-bourgeois socialism of the period of 1848, which were dealt their death-blow in the June days of that year. In point of fact, it was not socialism at all, but so many sentimental phrases, benevolent visions, which were the expression *at that time* of the revolutionary character of the bourgeois democrats, as well as of the proletariat, which had not yet freed itself from the influence of those democrats.

Herzen's spiritual shipwreck, his deep scepticism and pessimism after 1848, was a shipwreck of the *bourgeois illusions* of socialism. Herzen's spiritual drama was a product and reflection of that epoch in world history when the revolutionary character of the bourgeois democrats was *already* passing away (in Europe), while the revolutionary character of the socialist proletariat had *not yet* matured. This is something the Russian knights of liberal verbiage, who are now covering up their counter-revolutionary nature by florid phrases about Herzen's scepticism, did not and could not understand. With these knights, who betrayed the Russian revolution of 1905, and have even forgotten to think of the great name of *revolutionary*, scepticism is a form of transition from democracy to liberalism, to that toadying, vile, foul and brutal liberalism which shot down the workers in 1848, restored the shattered thrones and applauded Napoleon III, and which Herzen *cursed*, unable to understand its class nature.

With Herzen, scepticism was a form of transition from the illusion of a bourgeois democracy that is "above classes" to the grim, inexorable and invincible class struggle of the proletariat. The proof: the *Letters to an Old Comrade*—to Bakunin—written by Herzen in 1869, a year before his death. In them Herzen breaks with the anarchist Bakunin. True, Herzen still sees this break as a mere disagreement on tactics and not as a gulf between the world outlook of the proletarian who is confident of the victory of his class and that of the petty bourgeois who has despaired of his salvation. True enough, in these letters as well, Herzen repeats the old bourgeois-democratic phrases to the effect that socialism must preach "a sermon addressed equally to workman and master, to farmer and townsman". Nevertheless, in breaking with Bakunin, Herzen turned his gaze, not to liberalism, but to the *International*—to the International led by Marx, to the International which had begun to "*rally the legions*" of the proletariat, to unite "*the world of labour*", which is "abandoning the world of those who enjoy without working".[28]

Failing as he did to understand the bourgeois-democratic character of the entire movement of 1848 and of all the forms of pre-Marxian socialism, Herzen was still less able to understand the bourgeois nature of the Russian revolution. Herzen is the founder of "Russian" socialism, of "Narodism". He saw "socialism" in the emancipation of the peasants *with land*, in community land tenure[29] and in the peasant idea of "the right to land". He set forth his pet ideas on this subject an untold number of times.

Actually, there is *not a grain* of socialism in this doctrine of Herzen's, as, indeed, in the whole of Russian Narodism, including the faded Narodism of the present-day Socialist-Revolutionaries. Like the various forms of "the socialism of 1848" in the West, this is the same sort of sentimental phrases, of benevolent visions, in which is expressed the *revolutionism* of the bourgeois peasant democracy in Russia. The more land the peasants would have received in 1861[30] and the less they would have had to pay for it, the more would the power of the feudal landlords have been undermined and the more rapidly, freely and widely would capitalism have developed in Russia. The idea of the "right to land" and of "equalised division of the land" is nothing but a formulation of the revolutionary aspiration for equality cherished by the peasants who are fighting for the complete overthrow of the power of the landlords, for the complete abolition of landlordism.

This was fully proved by the revolution of 1905: on the one hand, the proletariat came out quite independently at the head of the revolutionary struggle, having founded the Social-Democratic Labour Party; on the other hand, the revolutionary peasants (the Trudoviks and the Peasant Union[31]), who fought for every form of the abolition of landlordism even to "the abolition of private landownership", fought precisely as proprietors, as small entrepreneurs.

Today, the controversy over the "socialist nature" of the right to land, and so on, serves only to *obscure* and cover up the really important and serious historical question concerning the difference of *interests* of the liberal bourgeoisie and the revolutionary peasantry in the Russian *bourgeois* revolution; in other words, the question of the liberal and the democratic, the "compromising" (monarchist) and the republican trends manifested in that revolution. This is exactly the question posed by Herzen's *Kolokol*,[32] if we turn our attention to the essence of the matter and not to the words, if we investigate the class struggle as the basis of "theories" and doctrines and not vice versa.

Herzen founded a free Russian press abroad, and that is the great service rendered by him. *Polyarnaya Zvezda*[33] took up the tradition of the Decembrists. *Kolokol* (1857-67) championed the emancipation of the peasants with might and main. The slavish silence was broken.

But Herzen came from a landlord, aristocratic milieu. He left Russia in 1847; he had not seen the revolutionary people and could have no faith in it. Hence his liberal appeal to the "upper ranks". Hence his innumerable sugary letters in *Kolokol* addressed to Alexander II the Hangman, which today one cannot read without revulsion. Chernyshevsky, Dobrolyubov and Serno-Solovyevich, who represented the new generation of revolutionary raznochintsi,[34] were a thousand times right when they reproached Herzen for these departures from democracy *to* liberalism. However, it must be said in fairness to Herzen that, much as he vacillated between democracy and liberalism, the democrat in him gained the upper hand nonetheless.

When Kavelin, one of the most repulsive exponents of liberal servility—who at one time was enthusiastic about *Kolokol* precisely because of its *liberal* tendencies—rose in arms against a constitution, attacked revolutionary agitation, rose against "violence" and appeals for it, and began to preach tolerance, Herzen *broke* with that liberal sage. Herzen turned upon Kavelin's "meagre, absurd, harmful pamphlet" written "for the private guidance of a government pretending to be liberal"; he denounced Kavelin's "sentimental political maxims" which represented "the Russian people as brutes and the government as an embodiment of intelligence". *Kolokol* printed an article entitled "Epitaph", which lashed out against "professors weaving the rotten cobweb of their superciliously paltry ideas, ex-professors, once open-hearted and subsequently embittered because they saw that the healthy youth could not sympathise with their scrofulous thinking". Kavelin at once recognised himself in this portrait.

When Chernyshevsky was arrested, the vile liberal Kavelin wrote: "I see nothing shocking in the arrests ... the revolutionary party considers all means fair to overthrow the government, and the latter defends itself by its own means." As if in retort to this Cadet, Herzen wrote concerning Chernyshevsky's trial: "And here are wretches, weed-like people, jellyfish, who say that we must not reprove the gang of robbers and scoundrels that is governing us."

When the liberal Turgenev[35] wrote a private letter to Alexander II assuring him of his loyalty, and donated two goldpieces for the soldiers wounded during the suppression of the Polish insurrection, *Kolokol* wrote of "the grey-haired Magdalen (of the masculine gender) who wrote to the tsar to tell him that she knew no sleep because she was tormented by the thought that the tsar was not aware of the repentance that had overcome her". And Turgenev at once recognised himself.

When the whole band of Russian liberals scurried away from Herzen for his defence of Poland, when the whole of "educated society" turned its back on *Kolokol*, Herzen was not dismayed. He went on championing the freedom of Poland and lashing the suppressors, the butchers, the hangmen in the service of Alexander II. Herzen saved the honour of Russian democracy. "We have saved the honour of the Russian name," he wrote to Turgenev, "and for doing so we have suffered at the hands of the slavish majority."

When it was reported that a serf peasant had killed a landlord for an attempt to dishonour the serf's betrothed, Herzen commented in *Kolokol*: "Well done!" When it was reported that army officers would be appointed to supervise the "peaceable" progress of "emancipation", Herzen wrote: "The first wise colonel who with his unit joins the peasants instead of crushing them, will ascend the throne of the Romanovs." When Colonel Reitern shot himself in Warsaw (1860) because he did not want to be a helper of hangmen, Herzen wrote: "If there is to be any shooting, the ones to be shot should be the generals who give orders to fire upon unarmed people." When fifty peasants were massacred in Bezdna, and their leader, Anton Petrov, was executed (April 12, 1861), Herzen wrote in *Kolokol*:

"If only my words could reach you, toiler and sufferer of the land of Russia!... How well I would teach you to despise your spiritual shepherds, placed over you by the St. Petersburg Synod and a German tsar.... You hate the landlord, you hate the official, you fear them, and rightly so; but you still believe in the tsar and the bishop ... do not belfeve them. The tsar is with them, and they are his men. It is him you now see—you, the father of a youth murdered in Bezdna, and you, the son of a father murdered in Penza.... Your shepherds are as ignorant as you, and as poor.... Such was another Anthony (not Bishop Anthony, but Anton of Bezdna) who suffered for you in Kazan.... The dead bodies of your martyrs will not perform forty-eight miracles, and praying to them will not cure a toothache; but their living memory may produce one miracle—your emancipation."

This shows how infamously and vilely Herzen is being slandered by our liberals entrenched in the slavish "legal" press, who magnify Herzen's weak points and say nothing about his strong points. It was not Herzen's fault but his misfortune that he could not see the revolutionary people in Russia itself in the 1840s. When *in the sixties* he came to see the revolutionary people, he sided fearlessly with the revolutionary democracy against liberalism. He fought for a victory of the people over tsarism, not for a deal between the liberal bourgeoisie and the landlords' tsar. He raised aloft the banner of revolution.

In commemorating Herzen, we clearly see the three generations, the three classes, that were active in the Russian revolution. At first it was nobles and landlords, the Decembrists and Herzen. These revolutionaries formed but a narrow group. They were very far removed from the people. But their effort was not in vain. The Decembrists awakened Herzen. Herzen began the work of revolutionary agitation.

This work was taken up, extended, strengthened, and tempered by the revolutionary raznochintsi—from Chernyshevsky to the heroes of Narodnaya Volya.[36] The range of fighters widened; their contact with the people became closer. "The young helmsmen of the gathering storm" is what Herzen called them. But it was not yet the storm itself.

The storm is the movement of the masses themselves. The proletariat, the only class that is thoroughly revolutionary, rose at the head of the masses and for the first time aroused millions of peasants to open revolutionary struggle. The first onslaught in this storm took place in 1905. The next is beginning to develop under our very eyes.

In commemorating Herzen, the proletariat is learning from his example to appreciate the great importance of revolutionary theory. It is learning that selfless devotion to the revolution and revolutionary propaganda among the people are not wasted even if long decades divide the sowing from the harvest. It is learning to ascertain the role of the various classes in the Russian and in the international revolution. Enriched by these lessons, the proletariat will fight its way to a free alliance with the socialist workers of all lands, having crushed that loathsome monster, the tsarist monarchy, against which Herzen was the first to raise the great banner of struggle by addressing his *free Russian word* to the masses.

Sotsial-Demokrat No. 26,
May 8 (April 25), 1912

Published according
to the text in *Sotsial-Demokrat*

LANDOWNERSHIP IN EUROPEAN RUSSIA

The famine that has affected thirty million peasants has again revived the question of the condition of the peasantry in Russia. In discussing this question people usually overlook the main point, namely, the interrelation between the existence of large landed estates, primarily in the hands of the nobility, and the condition of the peasantry. It is to this main point that we wish to draw the attention of the reader.

In 1907, the Ministry of the Interior published a volume of *Statistics of Landownership in 1905*. From these official data, which can under no circumstances be suspected of partiality for the peasants, we can obtain a fairly accurate idea of one of the main causes of the famines.

The government statistics put the amount of land in the fifty gubernias of European Russia at 395 million dessiatines. But this figure does not represent the real state of affairs, since it includes more than 100 million dessiatines of state land in the far north, in the Archangel, Olonets and Vologda gubernias. Most of this land is unsuitable for farming, being the tundra and forests of the far north. Reference to this land is usually made for the sole purpose of *obscuring* the actual distribution of the cultivable land.

If we deduct this land, we obtain a total of 280 million dessiatines (in round figures) of usable land. Out of this total 101 million dessiatines are listed as privately owned, and 139 million dessiatines as allotment land. It is necessary to distinguish between the land in the possession of the big landlords and that owned by small peasants.

As regards the large estates, government statistics provide the following data:

Privately-Owned Land in European Russia

Size of estates	Number of estates	Total land (dessiatines)	Average per estate (dessiatines)
Over 500 to 2,000 dessiatines	21,748	20,590,708	947
Over 2,000 to 10,000 dessiatines	5,386	20,602,109	3,825
Over 10,000 dessiatines . .	699	20,798,504	29,754
Total	27,833	61,991,321	2,227

These figures are incomplete, because they do not include the lands belonging to the crown, to big commercial companies, etc. Nevertheless, these figures give us an idea of the *main* feature of Russian landlordism. *Seven hundred* landlords own *21* million dessiatines, i.e., nearly *thirty thousand dessiatines each.*

Less than 28 thousand landlords own **62** million dessiatines of land, i.e., an average of *2,200 dessiatines per estate.* To this should be added the crown lands—their total is estimated to exceed *five* million dessiatines—and more than *three and a half* million dessiatines belonging to 272 "commercial, industrial, factory and other" companies. The latter are undoubtedly big estates, most of them in Perm Gubernia, where *nine* such companies own *nearly one and a half million* dessiatines of land (the exact figure is 1,448,902).

Consequently, the total land area in the hands of the biggest owners is certainly not less, and most likely more, than *70 million* dessiatines. The number of such big landlords is less than *30 thousand.*

Now take the land owned by the peasants. According to government statistics, the peasants with the smallest allotments had the following amounts of land:

Allotment Land

Size of allotments	Number of households	Total land (dessiatines)	Average per household (dessiatines)
Less than 5 dessiatines	2,857,650	9,030,333	3.1
5 to 8 dessiatines . .	3,317,601	21,706,550	6.5
8 to 15 " . .	3,932,485	42,182,923	10.7
Total	10,107,736	72,919,806	7.0

Consequently, *ten million* peasant families, out of a total of about 13 million, own *73 million dessiatines of land.* The average per household is *seven* dessiatines. To this should be added the small privately-owned estates. The number of owners of farms of less than 10 dessiatines each is placed at 409,864, and they own a total of 1,625,226 dessiatines of land, i.e., less than four dessiatines per household. Consequently, we have a total of *approximately ten and a half million* peasant families with *75 million* dessiatines of land.

Now we can place side by side these principal figures, which are very often forgotten or misrepresented in arguments about the peasant problem:

Large landed estates—*30 thousand* owners, 70 million dessiatines of land.

Small peasant farms—*ten and a half million* owners, 75 million dessiatines of land.

To be sure, these are the gross figures. For a more detailed study of the condition of the peasants and the role of the big estates, it is necessary to take the figures for the various regions or districts, sometimes even for the individual gubernias. But the economists of the government, the liberal and even, to a certain extent, the Narodnik camps very often *obscure the essence* of the land problem by referring to individual regions or to particular aspects of the problem. To get at the *root* of the land problem and of the condition of the peasants, we must not lose sight of the main figures cited above; we must not allow the main point to be obscured by particulars.

In our next article,* we shall cite instances of this kind of obscuring. For the present, we will make the first fundamental summary.

The land in European Russia is so distributed that the big landlords, those owning more than 500 dessiatines each, hold 70 million dessiatines, and the number of such landlords is less than 30 thousand.

On the other hand, the vast majority of the peasants, namely, ten and a half million families out of 13 million peasant families, own 75 million dessiatines of land.

---

* See pp. 73-77 of this volume.—*Ed.*

The average large landed estate is *2,200 dessiatines*. The average size of a small peasant farm is *seven* dessiatines.

If the land of the thirty thousand big landlords were transferred to ten million peasant households, the land held by these households would be *nearly doubled*.

In our next article, we shall discuss the economic relations between the landlords and the peasants resulting from this distribution of the land.

Nevskaya Zvezda No. 3,
May 6, 1912
Signed: *R. Silin*

Published according
to the text in *Nevskaya Zvezda*

THE TRUDOVIKS AND THE WORKER DEMOCRATS

The Fourth Duma election campaign has brought about some little revival of activity and has increased the interest in political issues. The broad movement stirred up by the events in the Lena gold-fields has lent importance to this revival and made this interest particularly urgent. More than ever, it is now appropriate to discuss the question of the attitude of the Trudoviks, i.e., of the peasant democrats, to the worker democrats.

In an article entitled "The Trudovik Group and the Workers' Party" (*Zaprosy Zhizni* No. 17), Mr. V. Vodovozov, answering my articles—"Liberalism and Democracy"* —in *Zvezda*,[37] sets forth the Trudovik view on this question. The controversy bears on the very essence of two political trends which express the interests of *nine-tenths* of Russia's population. It is therefore the duty of every democrat to pay the closest attention to the subject of the controversy.

I

The standpoint of the working-class democracy is the class struggle. The wage-workers constitute a definite class in modern society. The position of this class is radically different from that of the class of small proprietors, the peasants. That is why their association in one party is out of the question.

The aim of the workers is to abolish wage slavery by eliminating the rule of the bourgeoisie. The peasants' aim lies in democratic demands that could abolish serfdom, with all

---

* See present edition, Vol. 17, pp. 569-77.—*Ed.*

its social roots and in all its manifestations, but which could not even slightly affect the rule of the bourgeoisie.

In Russia today, the tasks which the workers and the peasants have in common are drawing the working-class democracy and the peasant democracy closer together. While necessarily following different paths, the two democracies can, and for the purpose of achieving success should, act jointly against all that is contrary to democracy. Unless there is such joint or common action, unless the peasant democrats get rid of the tutelage of the liberals (Cadets), any serious democratic reforms in Russia will be out of the question.

Those are the views of the working-class democrats, the Marxists, which I have developed in the two articles entitled 'Liberalism and Democracy".

The Trudoviks, whose views are expounded by Mr. Vodovozov, want to be a party standing "above classes". They are convinced that one party "could fully take care of the interests of three classes of society": the peasantry, the working class and the "working intelligentsia".

I said that this "conviction" contradicted (1) all the facts of economic science, (2) the entire experience of countries which went through epochs similar to the present epoch in Russia, and (3) Russia's experience during a particularly important and crucial period of her history, the year 1905. I derided the truly Cadet claim to "embrace" different classes, and recalled the fact that the Cadets describe the Maklakovs as "working intelligentsia".

Mr. Vodovozov, without citing these arguments of mine fully and coherently, seeks to disprove them by disjointed statements. In reply to the first argument, for instance, he says: "The peasantry is a mass of people living by their own labour; its interests are the interests of labour, and therefore it represents one contingent of the great army of labour, just as the workers represent another contingent of that army."

This is not Marxist, but bourgeois economic science: the phrase about the interests of labour here obscures the fundamental difference between the position of the small proprietor and that of the wage-worker. The worker owns no means of production and sells himself, his hands, his *labour-*

power. The peasant does own means of production —implements, livestock, and his own or rented land —and sells the *products* of his farming, being a small proprietor, a small entrepreneur, a petty bourgeois.

Even today in Russia peasants hire no less than *two million* agricultural wage-labourers to work on their farms. And if all the landed estates were transferred, without compensation, to the peasants, the latter would employ a much greater number of labourers.

Such a transfer of the land to the peasants is a common interest of the entire peasantry, of all wage-workers, of all democrats, because landlordism is the foundation of the landlords' political power of the type with which Purishkevich, followed by Markov the Second and other "men of the Third Duma"—nationalists, Octobrists, etc.—have made Russia so very familiar.

This shows that the common aim now before the peasants and the workers has absolutely nothing of socialism, despite the opinion of ignorant reactionaries, and sometimes of liberals. That aim is purely democratic. Its achievement would mean the achievement of freedom for Russia, but it would not at all mean the abolition of wage slavery.

If we want to put the joint action of different classes on a sound basis, and if we want to ensure the real and durable success of such action, we must be clear as to the points on which the interests of these classes converge and those on which they diverge. All delusions and "misconceptions" on this score, and any obscuring of the matter with meaningless phrases are bound to have the most ruinous effect, are bound to undermine success.

II

"Agricultural work is different from work in a factory; but then the work of a factory worker is different from that of a shop-assistant, yet *Zvezda* assiduously tries to prove to the shop-assistants that they belong to the same class as the workers, and that therefore they must regard Social-Democrats as their representatives...."

That is how Mr. Vodovozov tries to disprove the arguments regarding the profound class distinction between small proprietors and wage-workers! In this case too, Mr. Vodovozov's arguments are permeated with the usual spirit of bourgeois political economy. The small proprietor who is a farmer belongs to the same *class* as the manufacturer, or the small proprietor who is an artisan, and as the small proprietor who is a shopkeeper; there is no class distinction between them, they are distinguished only by their *occupations*. The wage-worker in agriculture belongs to the same class as the *wage*-worker in a factory or in a commercial establishment.

These are all elementary truths in terms of Marxism. And Mr. Vodovozov is mistaken if he thinks that by describing "my" Marxism as "extremely oversimplified" he can conceal the *essence of the matter*, namely, that the Trudoviks are constantly slipping from Marxist to bourgeois political economy.

Mr. Vodovozov slips into the same error, and along the same lines, when, in dealing with my reference to the profound class distinction between small proprietors and wage-workers as proved by the experience of all countries and by that of Russia, he tries to refute me by pointing out that sometimes one class is represented by several parties, and vice versa. In Europe the workers sometimes follow the liberals, the anarchists, the clericals, etc. The landlords are sometimes divided among several parties.

What do these facts prove? Only that, in addition to *class* distinctions, there are other distinctions, such as religious, national, etc., that affect the formation of parties.

That is true, but what has it got to do with *our* controversy? Does Mr. Vodovozov point to the existence in Russia of specific historical conditions—religious, national and otherwise—that *add themselves* in the *present instance* to the class distinctions?

Mr. Vodovozov did not, and could not, point to any such conditions at all. Our controversy turned entirely on whether it is possible to have in Russia a party "standing above classes", one "serving the interests of three classes". (Incidentally, it is ridiculous to call the "working intelligentsia" a class.)

Theory gives a clear answer to this question: it is impossible! An equally clear answer is provided by the experience of 1905, when *all* the class, group, national, and other distinctions stood out in bold relief in the most open and most massive actions at a highly important turning-point in Russian history. The Marxist theory was *confirmed* by the experience of 1905, which showed that a single party of peasants and workers is *impossible* in Russia.

All three Dumas have shown the same thing.

Why refer, then, to the fact that in various countries of Europe there have been instances of one class divided into several parties or of several classes united under the leadership of a single party? This reference is quite beside the point. By this reference Mr. Vodovozov is merely deviating —and trying to divert the reader—from the point at issue.

If the Russian democracy is to attain success, it is very important for it to know its own strength, to take a sober view of the state of affairs, and to realise clearly which *classes* it can count upon. It would be exceedingly harmful for it to cherish illusions, to cover up class distinctions with empty phrases, or to dismiss them with good wishes.

We must plainly recognise the profound class distinction between the peasants and the workers of Russia, a distinction which cannot be eliminated within the framework of capitalist society, within the framework of domination by the market. We must plainly recognise the points on which their interests coincide *at present*. We must unite each of these classes, cement its forces, develop its political consciousness and define the common task of both.

A "radical" (to use Mr. Vodovozov's term, although I do not think it a fortunate one) peasant party is useful and indispensable.

All attempts to found a party standing "above classes", to unite the peasants and the workers in one party, to represent a non-existent "working intelligentsia" as a class by itself, are extremely harmful and ruinous to the cause of Russian freedom, since such attempts can bring *nothing* but disillusionment, a waste of strength, and confusion in people's minds.

While fully sympathising with the formation of a *consistently* democratic peasant party, we are obliged to combat the above-mentioned attempts. The workers must also combat the influence of the *liberals* upon the democratic peasantry.

III

Concerning the attitude of the liberals towards the bourgeois democracy, and of the Cadets towards the Trudoviks,
the conference of the latter said nothing clear and definite.[38]
The Trudoviks do not seem to realise that it was the dependence of the democratic peasantry upon the liberals that was
one of the principal causes of the failure of the emancipation
movement in 1905-06, and that this movement *cannot* be
successful so long as wide and leading sections of the
peasantry are unaware of the difference between democracy
and liberalism, and do not free themselves from the tutelage and domination of the liberals.

Mr. Vodovozov touched upon this question of cardinal
importance in an extremely cursory and unsatisfactory manner. He says that "the Cadet Party serves primarily the interests of the urban population". This is not true. This
definition of the class roots and political role of the Cadet
Party is utterly worthless.

The Cadet Party is the party of the liberal-monarchist
bourgeoisie. The social basis of this party (as well as of
the "Progressists") is the economically more progressive (as
compared with the Octobrists) sections of the bourgeoisie,
but above all the bourgeois intelligentsia. However, a section of the urban and rural petty bourgeoisie still follows
the Cadets only by tradition (i.e., by mere habit, blind
repetition of what was done yesterday), and because they
are simply deceived by the liberals.

By calling themselves democrats, the Cadets are deceiving themselves and the people. Actually the Cadets are
counter-revolutionary liberals.

This has been fully *proved* by the entire history of Russia,
particularly in the twentieth century, and above all in 1905-
06. And the publication *Vekhi*[39] *demonstrated* it, exposed it,
particularly clearly and completely. Nor can any "reservations" of the Cadet diplomats in regard to *Vekhi* alter this
fact.

The first phase of the liberation movement in Russia, the
first decade of the twentieth century, revealed that the
mass of the population, while gravitating towards democracy, is not sufficiently class-conscious, *cannot distinguish*

between liberalism and democracy, and submits to the leadership of the liberals. So long and insofar as there is no change in this respect, all talk of democratic reform in Russia is pointless. It would be just idle talk.

How does Mr. Vodovozov counter these premises, on which I based my article? "In the present conditions," he writes, "the Trudoviks consider it extremely tactless [!!] to say too much about the counter-revolutionary nature of the Cadets...."

Well, well! What has "tact" got to do with it? And why "too much"? If it is true that the Cadets are counter-revolutionary liberals, this truth must be told. Whether we should say a lot or only a little about the counter-revolutionary Rights and the counter-revolutionary liberals is not a serious question at all. *Whenever* a publicist speaks of the Rights, and whenever he speaks of the liberals, he must tell the truth. The Trudoviks told the truth about the Rights. We praise them for this. As regards the liberals, the Trudoviks *themselves* began to speak of them, but they *did not speak the whole truth*!

That is the only thing for which we reproach the Trudoviks.

"Too much" or too little—that is quite beside the point. Let the Trudoviks devote a thousand lines to the Rights and five lines to the liberals—we shall have no objections to that. That is not the reason for our objections to the Trudoviks. What we objected to is that in those "five lines" (you must blame yourself, Mr. Vodovozov, for bringing into the controversy your unfortunate expression "too much"!) the truth about the liberals was *not* told.

Mr. Vodovozov avoided answering the real question: are the Cadets counter-revolutionary or not?

It is a big mistake on the part of the Trudoviks to evade this question, for that implies *in fact* that a section of the democrats and a section of the former Marxists are dependent *on* the liberals.

This question is inexorably posed by the entire history of the first decade of the twentieth century.

In Russia today, *new* democratic elements are growing up everywhere, among the most diverse sections of the population. That is a fact. As they grow these democratic elements must be educated in the spirit of *consistent* democracy. Such education will be impossible unless we explain the true nature of the liberals, who have at their disposal hundreds of press organs and a hundred seats in the Duma, thus constantly exerting an influence along *falsely* democratic lines upon an incomparably greater number of people than we can reach with our propaganda.

The democrats must rally their forces. We shall always praise the Trudoviks for their democratic speeches about the Rights. But theirs will be an inconsistent democracy if, *when* they speak of the liberals, they do so *in liberal fashion*, instead of using a language worthy of democrats.

It is not two, but three camps that are contending in the elections. Do not lump the second camp (the liberals) with the third camp (the democrats), Trudovik gentlemen. Do not obscure the distinction between them—the liberals are doing "*too much*" as it is towards that objectionable end.

Pravda Nos. 13 and 14,
    May 8 and 9, 1912
    Signed: *P.P.*

Published according
to the *Pravda* text

POLITICAL PARTIES IN RUSSIA

The Duma elections are compelling all the parties to intensify their agitation and rally their forces, so that they may return the greatest possible number of deputies of "their own" party.

In Russia, as in all other countries, the election campaign is attended by the most brazen self-advertisement. All the bourgeois parties, that is, those which uphold the economic privileges of the capitalists, are advertising themselves in the same way as individual capitalists advertise their goods. Look at the commercial advertisements in any newspaper—you will see that the capitalists think up the most "striking", bombastic and fashionable names for their merchandise, which they praise in the most unrestrained manner, stopping at no lie or invention whatever.

The general public—at any rate in the big cities and trade centres—has long since become used to commercial advertisement and knows its worth. Unfortunately, political advertisement misleads an incomparably greater number of people; it is much harder to expose and its deception much more lasting. The names of some parties, both in Europe and in Russia, are chosen with a direct eye to advertisement, and their "programmes" are quite often written for the sole purpose of hoodwinking the public. The greater the degree of political liberty in a capitalist country and the more democracy there is, i.e., the greater the power of the people and of their representatives, the more shameless, in many cases, is the self-advertisement of parties.

That being so, how is one to see what is what in the fight between the various parties? Does not this fight, with its fraud and advertising, indicate that representative institutions, parliaments, assemblies of people's representatives, are in general useless and even harmful, as rabid reactionaries, the enemies of parliamentarism make out? No. In the absence of representative institutions there is *much more* deception, political lying and fraudulent trickery of all kinds, and the people have much fewer means of exposing the deception and finding out the truth.

To see what is what in the fight between the parties, one must not take words at their face value but must study the actual history of the parties, must study not so much what they say about themselves as their *deeds*, the way in which they go about solving various political problems, and their *behaviour* in matters affecting the vital interests of the various classes of society—landlords, capitalists, peasants, workers, etc.

The greater the degree of political liberty in a country and the more stable and democratic its representative institutions, the easier it is for the mass of the people to find its bearings in the fight between the parties and to *learn politics*, i.e., to expose the deception and find out the truth.

The division of any society into different political parties is revealed most clearly of all in times of profound crises shaking the whole country. For at such times governments are compelled to seek support among the various classes of society; all phrase-mongering, all that is petty and extraneous, is brushed aside by the gravity of the struggle; the parties strain every nerve and appeal to the *masses*, and the masses, guided by their unerring instinct and enlightened by the experience of an open struggle, follow the parties that represent the interests of a particular class.

The epochs of such crises always determine the party alignment of the social forces of the country concerned for many years or even decades ahead. In Germany, for instance, such crises were the wars of 1866 and 1870[40]; in Russia, the events of 1905. We cannot understand the essence of our political parties, nor gain a clear idea as to which *classes* a particular party in Russia represents, unless we go back to the events of that year.

Let us begin our brief survey of the political parties in Russia with the parties of the extreme Right.

On the extreme right flank, we find the Union of the Russian People.

The programme of this party is set forth as follows in *Russkoye Znamya*, the Union's newspaper published by A. I. Dubrovin:

"The Union of the Russian People, which on June 3, 1907, was accorded the honour of being called upon from the height of the Tsar's throne to be its reliable bulwark, and to serve as an example of law and order to all and in everything, proclaims that the will of the Tsar can only be exercised: (1) if the Tsar's autocratic power, which is indissolubly and vitally bound up with the Russian Orthodox Church, canonically established, manifests itself in full measure; (5) if the Russian nationality is dominant not only in the inner gubernias, but also in the border regions; (3) if there is a Duma, composed exclusively of Russians, as the main assistant of the monarch in his work for building up the state; (4) if the principles of the Union of the Russian People with regard to the Jews are fully observed; and (5) if all officials who are opposed to the Tsar's autocratic power are removed from government service."

We have faithfully copied this solemn declaration of the *Rights*, on the one hand, so that the reader may be directly acquainted with the original and, on the other, because the fundamental motives stated in it are valid for all the parties of the majority in the Third Duma, i.e., for the nationalists and the Octobrists as well. This will be seen from what we say further on.

The programme of the Union of the Russian People in effect repeats the old slogan of the days of serfdom, that is, Orthodoxy, Autocracy, Nationhood. In regard to the question on which the Union is generally set apart from other kindred parties—namely, recognition or rejection of "constitutional" principles in the Russian political system—it is particularly important to note that the Union is *by no means* opposed to representative institutions in general. It is evident from the programme quoted above that the Union favours a Duma that will play the part of "assistant".

Moreover, the specific feature of the Russian Constitution—if we may call it that—is expressed by the Dubrovinite correctly, i.e., in keeping with the actual state of affairs. It is this stand that is taken by both the nationalists and the Octobrists in their practical policies. The controversy between these parties over the "Constitution" is largely a fight over words. The Rights are not opposed to a Duma; they only stress with particular zeal that it must be an "assistant", without specifying its powers in any way. The nationalists and the Octobrists, for their part, do not insist on any clearly specified powers of the Duma, let alone on real guarantees of its powers. The Octobrist "constitutionalists" fully agree with the "opponents of Constitution" on the basis of the June Third Constitution.

The programme of the Black Hundreds is straightforward clear and outspoken on the point of persecuting non-Russians in general and the Jews in particular. As always, they bring out more rudely, brazenly and incitingly what the other government parties more or less "bashfully" or diplomatically keep to themselves.

In reality, both the nationalists and the Octobrists have a hand in the persecution of non-Russians, as is well known to anyone who is at all familiar with the activity of the Third Duma or with such press organs as *Novoye Vremya*, *Svet*, *Golos Moskvy*[41] and the like.

The question is: What is the social basis of the party of the Rights? What class does it represent? What class does it serve?

That party's reversion to the slogans of serfdom, its upholding of all that is outdated, of all that is medieval in Russian life, its complete satisfaction with the June Third Constitution—the *landlords'* Constitution—and its defence of the privileges of the nobility and officialdom all provide a clear answer to our question. The Rights are the party of the semi-feudal landlords, of the Council of the United Nobility.[42] Not for nothing did that Council play such a prominent, indeed a leading, role in the dispersal of the Second Duma, the change of the electoral law and the coup d'état of June 3.[43]

To give an idea of the economic strength of this class in Russia, it is sufficient to cite the following basic fact, proved by the data of the *government* statistics of landownership in 1905, published by the Ministry of the Interior.

Less than 30,000 landlords in European Russia own 70,000,000 dessiatines of land; *the same amount* of land is owned by 10,000,000 peasant households with the smallest allotments. This makes an average of about 2,300 dessiatines per big landlord, and, in the case of the poor peasants, an average of 7 dessiatines per family, per household.

It is quite natural and inevitable that the peasant cannot live on such an "allotment" but can only die a slow death. The recurrent famines which affect millions, such as this year's famine, continue to dislocate peasant farming in Russia following each crop failure. The peasants are compelled to rent land from the landlords, paying for it by various forms of *labour service*. To pay for the use of the land, the peasant works for the landlord with his horse and his implements. This is nothing short of corvée, except that it is not officially called serfdom. With 2,300 dessiatines of land at their disposal, most of the landlords can run their estates only by keeping the peasants in bondage, by resorting to labour service, that is, the corvée system. They cultivate only part of these huge estates with the help of wage-labourers.

Further, that same class of the landed nobility supplies the state with the overwhelming majority of all higher and middle-ranking civil servants. The privileges of officialdom in Russia represent another side of the privileges and agrarian power of the landed nobility. It is therefore natural that the Council of the United Nobility and the "Right" parties should uphold the policy of adhering to the old feudal traditions not by accident, but because it is inevitable, and not because of the "ill will" of individuals, but under the pressure of the *interests* of a tremendously powerful *class*. The old ruling class, the survivals of landlordism, who remain the ruling class as in the past, has created for itself an appropriate party—the Union of the Russian People or the "Rights" in the Duma and in the Council of State.[44]

But, since there exist representative institutions, and since the *masses* have already come out openly in the political arena, as they did in our country in 1905, each party must necessarily appeal to the people, within certain limits. Now what can the Right parties appeal to the people about?

Of course, they cannot speak plainly in defence of the interests of the landlords. What they do speak of is preserving the old traditions in general, and they spare no efforts to foment distrust towards non-Russians, particularly towards the Jews, to incite the utterly ignorant, the utterly benighted, to pogroms, to "Yid"-baiting. They seek to conceal the privileges of the nobility, the bureaucrats and the landlords with talk about the "oppression" of Russians by non-Russians.

Such is the party of the "Rights". One of its members, Purishkevich, the most prominent spokesman of the Rights in the Third Duma, has worked a good deal, and successfully, to *show* the people *what* the Rights want, *how* they act, and *whom* they serve. Purishkevich is a gifted agitator.

Next to the "Rights", who have forty-six seats in the Third Duma, are the *"nationalists"* with ninety-one seats. There is hardly a shade of difference between them and the Rights. In fact, these are not two parties, but one party which has effected a division of "labour" in persecuting non-Russians, "Cadets" (liberals), democrats, etc. One lot acts more crudely, the other more subtly, but both *are doing* the same thing. Indeed, it is to the government's *advantage* to have the "extreme" Rights —who are capable of any sort of scandal, riot, the murder of people like Herzenstein, Yollos, Karavayev—standing somewhat apart, as if *they* were "criticising" the government from the right.... The distinction between the Rights and the nationalists cannot be of any serious importance.

The *Octobrists* in the Third Duma are 131 strong, including, of course, the "Right Octobrists". Essentially there is nothing in the present policy of the Octobrists to distinguish them from the Rights, except that the Octobrist Party serves not only the landlords, but also the big capitalists, the conservative merchants, and the bourgeoisie, which was so terrified by the awakening of the workers, and then also of the peasants, to independent political life, that it made a *volte-face* towards defence of the old order. There are capitalists in Russia—quite a few, indeed—who treat the workers not a bit better than the landlords treated the serfs of old; they look on workers and clerks as their menials, as servants. Nobody is better fitted to defend this old order than the Right parties, the nationalists and the Octobrists. There are also capitalists who at the Zemstvo[45] and municipal congresses in 1904 and 1905 demanded a "constitution", but are quite willing to make peace on the basis of the June Third Constitution *to oppose* the workers.

The Octobrist Party is the chief counter-revolutionary party of the landlords and the capitalists. It is the leading party in the Third Duma: the 131 Octobrists with the 137 Rights and nationalists constitute a solid majority in the Third Duma.

The electoral law ot June 3, 1907, *guaranteed* the land-lords and the big capitalists a majority: the landlords and electors of the first urban curia (i.e., the big capitalist curia) have a majority in *all* the gubernia assemblies electing deputies to the Duma. In twenty-eight gubernias the land-owners even by themselves have a majority in the election assemblies. The entire policy of the June Third Government has been carried out with the aid of the Octobrist Party, and this party bears the responsibility for all the sins and crimes committed by the Third Duma.

In words, in their programme, the Octobrists uphold a "constitution", and even liberties! In reality, this party supported all the measures taken against the workers (the Insurance Bill, for example—recall the conduct of the *Chairman* of the Duma Committee on Labour, Baron Tiesen-hausen!), against the peasants, and against any mitigation of tyranny and lack of rights. The Octobrists are just as much a government party as the nationalists. This situation is not in the least altered by the fact that from time to time —particularly on the eve of elections!—the Octobrists deliv-er "opposition" speeches. In all countries that have parlia-ments, the bourgeois parties have long been known to indulge in this *playing at opposition*—a harmless game as far as they are concerned, because no government takes it serious-ly, and a game which occasionally proves useful as a means of "soothing" the voter by a show of opposition.

However, the greatest expert, the virtuoso, at the game of opposition is the chief opposition party in the Third Duma— the Cadets, *Constitutional-"Democrats"*, the party of "peo-ple's freedom".

The very name of this party is part of the game, for in fact it is *not at all* a democratic party, and *by no means* a people's party; it is a party, not of freedom, but of half-freedom, if not of quarter-freedom.

In fact, it is the party of the liberal-monarchist bourgeoi-sie, which dreads the popular movement far more than reaction.

The democrat has faith in the people, in the movement of the masses, and he helps this movement in every way, although he fairly often has (as have the bourgeois demo-crats, the Trudoviks) a wrong notion about the significance of this movement within the framework of the capitalist system. The democrat sincerely strives to put an end to *all* medievalism.

The liberal is afraid of the movement of the masses; he tries to check it, and *deliberately* defends certain institutions of medievalism—in fact, the most important of them —as a bulwark against the masses, particularly the workers. What the liberals want is by no means to destroy all the foundations of the power of the Purishkeviches, but to share power with them. The democratic petty bourgeois (hence also the peasant and the Trudovik) says: everything for the people and through the people. He sincerely strives to uproot all the foundations of Purishkevichism, though he does not understand the significance of the wage-workers' struggle against capital. The real aim of the liberal-monarchist bourgeoisie, on the other hand, is to share power with Purishkevich and rule with him *over* the workers and *over* the small proprietors.

In the First and the Second Dumas, the Cadets had a majority or occupied a leading position. They used it for a senseless and inglorious *game*: when facing the Right, they played at loyalty and ability to serve as ministers (as if to say that they could solve all the contradictions by peaceful means, without spoiling the muzhik or offending Purishkevich); when facing the Left, they played at democracy. The result of this game was that in the end the Cadets got a kick from the right. And on the left they earned the just title of betrayers of people's freedom. In both the First and the Second Dumas, they fought all the time not only against the working-class democrats, but against the Trudoviks as well. We need only recall the fact that the Cadets *defeated* the plan for local land committees proposed by the Trudoviks (in the First Duma), a plan based on the elementary requirements of democracy, on the ABC of democracy. The Cadets thus upheld the *supremacy* of the landlords and the bureaucrats *over* the peasants in the land committees!

In the Third Duma the Cadets have been playing at a "responsible opposition", an opposition in the possessive case.[46] As such, they voted time and again for the government budgets ("democrats"!), explained to the Octobrists that there was nothing dangerous or harmful in their plan of

"compulsory" redemption payments (compulsory for the peasants) —remember Berezovsky the First; they sent Karaulov
to deliver "pious" speeches from the rostrum, renounced
the movement of the masses, appealed to the "upper strata",
and *silenced* the lower strata (the Cadets' fight *against*
the workers' deputies over workers' insurance), and so on
and so forth.

The Cadets are the party of counter-revolutionary liberalism. By their claim to the role of a "responsible opposition",
i.e., a recognised, lawful opposition *permitted* to compete
with the Octobrists, an opposition not to, but of the June
Third regime—the Cadets have committed suicide as "democrats". The shameless *Vekhi* propaganda of the Cadet ideologists—Struve, Izgoyev and Co., smothered with kisses by
Rozanov and Anthony of Volhynia—and the role of a
"responsible opposition" in the Third Duma, are two sides of
the same medal. The liberal-monarchist bourgeoisie, tolerated by the Purishkeviches, wants to seat itself by the side
of Purishkevich.

The bloc of the Cadets and the "Progressists" at the present time, for the elections to the Fourth Duma, has provided
additional proof of the profoundly counter-revolutionary
nature of the Cadets. The Progressists do not at all claim to
be democrats, they do not say a word about fighting the
entire June Third regime, and are far from so much as
dreaming of "universal suffrage". They are moderate liberals
who do not make a secret of their kinship with the Octobrists. The alliance of the Cadets and the Progressists should
open the eyes of even the blindest "yes-men of the Cadets"
to the true nature of that party.

The *democratic bourgeoisie* of Russia is represented by the
Narodniks of all shades, from the most Left Socialist-Revolutionaries to the Popular Socialists and Trudoviks. They all
readily mouth "socialist" phrases, but it would be impermissible for a class-conscious worker to be deceived as to the real
meaning of those phrases. Actually there is *not a grain of*
socialism in the "right to land", "equalised division" of
the land, or "socialisation of the land". This should be clear
to anyone who knows that the abolition of private landownership, and a new, even the "fairest" possible, division of
the land, far from affecting commodity production and the

power of the market, of money and capital, leads to their expansion.

However, the phrases about "the labour principle" and "Narodnik socialism" express the democrat's deep faith in the possibility and indispensability of destroying *all* medievalism in landownership and, at the same time, in the political system as well (just as they express his sincere desire to achieve this). Whereas the liberals (the Cadets) seek to share political power and political privileges with the Purishkeviches, the Narodniks are democrats precisely because they are striving, and are bound to strive at present, to abolish *all* the privileges of landed property and *all* privileges in politics.

The position of the great bulk of the Russian peasants is such that they cannot even dream of any compromise with the Purishkeviches (something quite possible, attainable and *near and dear* to the liberal). That is why the democracy of the petty bourgeoisie will have roots among the masses in Russia for a fairly long time to come, whereas Stolypin's agrarian reform,[47] an expression of the Purishkeviches' bourgeois policy against the muzhik, has so far produced nothing durable but—the starvation of thirty million peasants!

The millions of starving small proprietors cannot help striving for a *different* kind of agrarian reform, a democratic one, which cannot break out of the bounds of capitalism or abolish wage slavery, but *can* sweep *medievalism* from the face of the Russian land.

The Trudoviks are an extremely weak group in the Third Duma, but they represent the *masses*. The vacillation of the Trudoviks between the Cadets and the worker democrats is an inevitable result of the class position of the small proprietors, and the fact that it is particularly difficult to rally, organise and enlighten them accounts for the extremely indeterminate and amorphous character of the Trudoviks as a party. That is why the Trudoviks, with the aid of the stupid "otzovism" of the Left Narodniks, present the sad picture of a liquidated party.

The difference between the Trudoviks and our own near-Marxist liquidators is that the former are liquidators out of weakness, while the latter are liquidators out of malice.

The task of the working-class democracy is to help the weak petty-bourgeois democrats, wrest them from the liberals, and rally the democratic camp against the counter-revolutionary Cadets and not merely against the Rights.

Concerning the working-class democracy, which had its group in the Third Duma, we can say but little here.

Everywhere in Europe, the parties of the working class took shape by casting off the influence of general democratic ideology and learning to distinguish between the struggle of the wage-workers against capital and the struggle against feudalism, which they did, incidentally, in order to strengthen the latter struggle, to rid it of all wavering and timidity. In Russia, the working-class democracy completely dissociated itself both from liberalism and from bourgeois democracy (Trudovikism), to the great advantage of the democratic cause in general.

The liquidationist trend among the working-class democrats (*Nasha Zarya* and *Zhivoye Dyelo*) shares the weakness of Trudoviks, glorifies amorphousness, longs for the status of a "tolerated" opposition, rejects the hegemony of the workers, confines itself to *words* about an "open" organisation (while inveighing against the organisation that is not open), and advocates a liberal labour policy. The connection between this trend and the disintegration and decadence of the period of counter-revolution is evident, and its falling-away from the working-class democracy is becoming obvious.

The class-conscious workers, who are not liquidating anything and are rallying their ranks in opposition to liberal influences, organising as a class and developing all forms of trade union and other unity, are coming forward both as representatives of *wage*-labour against capital and as representatives of consistent democracy against the entire old regime in Russia and against any concessions to it.

———

By way of illustration, we give below the figures relating to the strength of the various parties in the Third Duma, which we borrow from the official Duma *Handbook* for 1912.

Parties in the Third Duma

Landlords

Rights	46
Nationalists	74
Independent nationalists	17
Right Octobrists	11
Octobrists	120
Total government parties	*268*

The Bourgeoisie

Progressists	36
Cadets	52
Polish Kolo[47a]	11
Polish-Lithuanian-Byelorussian group	7
Moslem group	9
Total liberals	*115*

Bourgeois Democrats

Trudovik group	14

Working-Class Democrats

Social-Democrats	13
Total democrats	*27*
Unaffiliated	27
Grand total	*437*

Thus there have been two possible majorities in the Third Duma: (1) the Rights and the Octobrists=268 out of 437; (2) the Octobrists and the liberals=120+115=235 out of 437. Both majorities are counter-revolutionary.

Nevskaya Zvezda No. 5,
May 10, 1912
Signed: *V. Ilyin*

Published according
to the text in *Nevskaya Zvezda*

A QUESTIONNAIRE ON THE ORGANISATIONS
OF BIG CAPITAL[48]

The Industry and Economics Department of the Imperial Russian Technical Society sent out a questionnaire on "public organisations of the commercial and industrial class in Russian", or rather on the organisations of big capital. The results of the questionnaire are now set forth in Mr. Gushka's[49] book *Representative Organisations of the Commercial and Industrial Class in Russia* (St. Petersburg, 1912). Both the material contained in the book and the conclusions, which the author indicates in fairly definite terms, deserve serious attention.

I

As a matter of fact, the questionnaire of the Technical Society dealt with the "representative" organisations of capitalists, which make up approximately 80 per cent of all the organisations. About 15 per cent of the organisations are cartels, trusts and syndicates, nearly 5 per cent are associations of employers, and the rest are stock-exchange committees, boards of congresses, etc. These latter organisations are very fond of calling themselves "representative". Their job is to influence government bodies.

The employers' associations, in Mr. Gushka's opinion, conduct a "direct" class struggle against the wage-workers, whereas the representative organisations conduct an "indirect" class struggle—a "struggle against other classes by exerting pressure on the state power and on public opinion".

That terminology is wrong, of course. It at once betrays one of the principal defects which Mr. Gushka has in common with most representatives of "professorial", bourgeois political economy. On the face of it, he accepts the concept of the class struggle; on the face of it, the class struggle serves as the basis of his investigation. Actually, however, that concept is narrowed down and distorted. Indeed, from what Mr. Gushka says, the struggle of the capitalists against the wage-workers within the framework of a given political system is a "direct" class struggle, while the struggle *for the political system itself* is an *"indirect"* class struggle! What about the struggle for "state power" itself—where does that belong?

But we shall have occasion to deal with this fundamental fault of Mr. Gushka's "world outlook" in the proper place. The value of his work is not in its theory, but in the summary of facts it offers. The data on organisations of the preponderant type are at any rate of considerable interest.

The total number of "representative" organisations of big capital in Russia in 1910 is given as 143. Seventy-one of them were stock-exchange societies with their committees. Then came 14 committees of commerce and manufacture, three merchants' boards, 51 organisations in the "combined" group (congresses and their boards, advisory bureaus, etc.), and four organisations of an indefinite type. The questionnaire was answered by only 62 organisations, or less than half the total. Out of the 51 organisations in the "combined" group, which is the most interesting, 22 answered the questionnaire.

The data on the time the organisations were founded are characteristic. Of the 32 stock-exchange committees which answered the questionnaire, 9 were founded in the last century, from 1800 to 1900, 5 in the four years 1901-04, 9 *in the two years of revolution*—1905-06—and 9 in the period 1907 to 1910.

"Here," writes Mr. Gushka, "we clearly see the effect of the impetus which the social movement of the stormy year 1905 lent the process of the self-organisation of the representatives of capital."

Of the 22 organisations in the combined group, only 7 came into being during the period 1870 to 1900, 2 from 1901 to 1904, 8 *in the two years of revolution*—1905-06—and 5 from 1907 to 1910. All those "congress boards" of representatives of industry in general—mine owners, oil industrialists, and so on and so forth—are a product chiefly of the period of revolution and counter-revolution.

The organisations are divided according to industries as follows. The group of stock-exchange committees is predominantly mixed: these committees usually unite all the branches of industry and commerce of the area concerned. In the group of committees of commerce and manufacture, the textile industry is in the forefront. In the main, combined, group, almost half the organisations represent not commerce, but industry—mining and metallurgy, to be specific.

"It is this group of industries (mining and metallurgy) that constitutes the economic basis of the organisations of Russia's modern industrial 'guard'," writes Mr. Gushka, who has a slight weakness for using a "lofty style" in speaking of the subject of his investigation.

Only in the case of a part of the organisations was it possible to establish the total turnover or output for the entire branch of commerce or industry to which the organisation in question belongs. The total thus obtained is 1,570 million rubles, of which 1,319 million rubles belongs to members of the organisations. Consequently, the organised represent 84 per cent of the total. The turnover of 3,134 members of organisations amounted to 1,121 million rubles, or an average of 358,000 rubles per member. The number of workers employed by 685 members of organisations is approximately 219,000 (on p. 111, the author mistakenly puts it at 319,000), or an average of more than 300 workers per member.

It is clear that we are dealing here with organisations of *big* capital, or even the *biggest* capital, to be exact. Mr. Gushka is fully aware of this, for he points out, for instance, that only the really big and biggest merchants and industrialists are admitted as members into the stock-exchange committees and the committees of commerce and manufacture, and that the congresses of representatives of industry and commerce are made up of the "biggest" capitalist undertakings.

That is why the author is wrong when he refers, in the title of his book, to organisations "of the commercial and industrial *class* in Russia." That is incorrect. Here again the author narrows down the concept of class. Actually, Mr. Gushka is dealing with a *stratum*, not with a class. Sure enough, the stratum of the biggest capitalists economically dominates all the other strata, which it unquestionably overwhelms by the size of its turnover. This is beyond doubt. Nevertheless, it is a stratum, and not a class. Thus, for instance, there is a vast distance between the political role of the representative organisations of this stratum and its political domination, as well as between its political domination and that of the commercial and industrial class.

In this connection, we must point out the following argument of Mr. Gushka's: "We in Russia," he writes, "are accustomed to applying a very large scale to define what is called a big or a small undertaking, in view of the well known extraordinary concentration of capital in our country, surpassing the concentration of capital even in Germany...."

The comparison with Germany is wrong. For instance, in the Urals there are very few small undertakings, if any, in the mining and metallurgical industries for reasons of an entirely distinctive nature—due to the absence of full freedom for industry and to the survivals of medievalism. And our official (or, what is the same thing, our Narodnik) distinction between factory and "handicraft" industries—does it not make our industrial statistics incomparable with the German statistics? Does it not very often mislead the observer by speaking of "extraordinary concentration" in Russia and obscuring the "extraordinarily" *scattered character* of the countless small peasant undertakings?

II

It is interesting to note some of the data provided by the questionnaire on the activity of the representative organisations of the biggest capital. For instance, the author gives a summary of the information about their budgets. The budgets of the 22 organisations in the combined group show a total income of 3,950,000 rubles, and the total income of all the organisations is 7.25 million rubles. "This annual budget of our 56 organisations," writes Mr. Gushka, "amounting to 7.25 million rubles, would probably be 50 or 100 per cent higher if the financial reports of the other organisations, those not covered by our questionnaire, were included."

However, more than a half of this budget, namely, 4.5 million rubles, is spent on business and on charity. On

purely representational functions, the 56 organisations spend
2.7 million rubles. "Most of the answers or financial reports
put at the head of this expenditure on representation the
salaries of the personnel, then the renting of premises. In
64.4 per cent of the organisations, the greatest part of the
expenditure goes for maintenance of personnel, and in 26.7
per cent of them it goes for premises."

These figures, in view of the turnover of 1,319 million
rubles in the capitalist associations covered by the investigation, show that the expenditure is very modest, so that
Mr. Gushka's pompous conclusion that the budget of expenditure is an *"index of the financial might* [author's italics]
of the representative organisations of the commercial and
industrial bourgeoisie in Russia" again betrays his inordi-
nate fondness for big words.

The author devotes Chapter IX of his book to the "third
element", i.e., the intelligentsia in the service of the capitalist associations. It appears that 29 stock-exchange committees listed 77 representatives of the third element as
their employees; the 22 organisations in the combined group
listed 180 such employees. Most of the answers speak of 2
to 4 representatives of the third element per organisation.
Since capitalist associations often understate this kind of
data, the author thinks it probable that "the representative
organisations of capital have in their service, holding key
posts, a host [!!] of intellectuals numbering *at least a thousand persons*"—secretaries, accountants, statisticians, legal
advisers, etc.

Really, it does not take much to set Mr. Gushka talking
about a "host".

The publishing activity of the capitalist associations is
characterised by the following figures. In addition to the
answers to the questionnaire, there accumulated a small
library of 288 volumes—the proceedings of congresses, reports, statutes and memoranda—which have never been on
sale.

Nine organisations publish periodicals: *Mining and
Smelting, Oil, Industry and Commerce, Bulletin of the Russian Association of Distillery Owners*, etc. The author gives
the total number of issues of these publications as 2,624
"volumes", to which he adds 452 volumes of "proceedings".

annual reports, etc., as well as 333 volumes of non-periodical publications. Mr. Gushka puts the total at 3,409 "volumes", which he describes as "impressive". The total number of publications probably amounts to 4,000-5,000 volumes.

"It may be said without exaggeration that a veritable treasure lies buried in that library," exclaims Mr. Gushka, "a wealth of material for the study of the anatomy and physiology, if we may say so, of the big bourgeoisie in Russia…. Unless we study this valuable material, we cannot form a proper idea of the balance of the dominant social forces in Russia, and more particularly of the social nature and role of Russian state power both before and after 1905."

Mr. Gushka makes very frequent excursions of this kind into the sphere of the social nature and role of Russian state power. They merit special consideration because of the importance of the question, and because it is misrepresented by the author, who exaggerates things beyond measure and for that very reason vows in passing that he speaks "without exaggeration".

III

"The centre of gravity of the activity of the organisations under survey," writes Mr. Gushka, "as representative organisations, i.e., organisations devoted to representing the interests of the industrial and commercial class, is naturally in the sphere of *formulating the position* of the representatives of this class on various questions concerning its interests, and of *defending this position* by various means."

Undoubtedly, that is exactly where the "centre of gravity" lies. The questionnaire allots much space to questions about the items discussed by the organisations of the capitalists and to the petitions they filed. In summarising the information obtained, the author singles out a long list of what, in his opinion, are "questions of a *general* nature". The most important questions are grouped as follows: (a) workers' insurance, public holidays, etc.; (b) income tax, taxes on enterprises, etc.; (c) tariff policy; (d) transport; (e) joint-stock companies, credit, etc.; (f) consulates abroad, statistics, the organisation of a mining department; (g) participation of the merchant class in the Zemstvo institutions, in the Council of State, in the preliminary discussion of government Bills, etc.

In this connection, Mr. Gushka draws the following conclusion: "In any event, as may be gathered from the enumerated groups of questions and petitions, our organisations have a very wide sphere of activity...." On reading such a conclusion, one cannot help stopping to see whether by any chance the word *not* has been omitted. For it is obvious that the sphere of activity indicated by the author is *not* wide at all. But it is certainly not a slip of the pen we have here; the trouble comes from the essential "pattern" of the author's mentality. "It would be difficult to name any more or less important field of the social and political life of the country that is outside the sphere of activity of the representative organisations of capital," he maintains.

Incredible, but true: Mr. Gushka in all seriousness presents us with this flagrant untruth, which he repeats in a dozen different ways!

"It would be difficult to name...." What about the electoral law? Or the agrarian question? Is it possible that these are not "important fields of the social and political life of the country"?

Mr. Gushka looks at "social and political life" from the narrow peep-hole of a *merchant's* standpoint. He cannot for the life of him understand that his absolute statements testify to narrowness, and certainly not to breadth. The questions raised by the merchants are narrow because they concern *only* the merchants. The capitalists do *not* rise to questions of *general political* importance. "Admission of representatives of industry and commerce" into local or central institutions of one sort or another is the limit of the "courage" they show in their petitions. As to how these institutions are to be organised *in general*, that is something they *are unable* to think of. They accept the institutions which have taken shape at someone else's bidding, and beg for a place in them. They slavishly accept the political basis created by some other class, and on this basis "petition" for the interests of *their* social-estate, *their* group, *their* stratum, unable even in this sphere to rise to a broad understanding of the interests of the whole of their *class*.

Mr. Gushka, who glaringly distorts the facts, slips into a tone of sheer praise. "The energetic and insistent pressure brought to bear upon government bodies," he writes. "Our

organisations" "perfectly [!!] understand this themselves."
... "The organisations of big capital have developed into a
regular *lobby* which actually exerts perhaps a greater influence upon legislation than the Duma, the more so"—the
author tries to be witty—"as Article 87[50] does not apply to the
capitalist parliament, and the organisations of capital have
never been purposely dissolved for three days."...

This witticism is an obvious indication of the boundless
conceited narrow-mindedness of the big-wigs of industry
and of their eulogist, Gushka. A minor detail, a mere trifle,
has been overlooked: the Duma raises questions concerning
the entire state administration and all classes, being an
institution of the whole state, while the organisations of the
merchant big-wigs consider it courageous to raise questions concerning *only* the merchants, *only* the rights of the merchants.

Mr. Gushka goes to the length of quoting the statement,
made by the Ufa Stock-Exchange Committee in its report
for 1905-06, that "the government itself, by a series of
fundamental measures to reform the stock-exchange institutions, is selecting ... *worthy assistants for itself*", and he calls
this statement "correct", puts the last phrase in italics, and
speaks of "real and active co-operation with the government".

On reading such stuff one cannot help thinking of the
German word *Lobhudelei*—grovelling adulation, or adula-
tory grovelling. To speak with a smug countenance—in
1905-06—of "fundamental measures to reform—the stock-
exchange institutions"! Why, this is the viewpoint of a
flunkey whom the master has permitted to "consult" with
the cook about arrangements for dinner, etc., calling the
two of them his "worthy assistants".

How close Mr. Gushka is to this point of view can be seen
from that subsection of Chapter XV dealing with the results
of the petitions of the organisations, which he has entitled
"Losing Positions". "It cannot be denied," we read there,
"that there are *several fields* in which the petitions and
demands of the representatives of capital do come up against
government resistance." Then follow examples in this se-
quence: (1) state-owned forests—the state is itself engaged
in the timber industry; (2) railway tariffs—the railways are
run by the state itself; (3) the question of representation in
the Zemstvos; and (4) the question of representation in the

Duma and in the Council of State. "In both cases," says
the author, referring to the last two questions, "the effect
of the close ties between the bureaucracy and the other ruling
class—the big landowners—·makes itself felt, of course."

"But if we leave out the few above-mentioned questions," continues the happy Mr. Gushka, "then it must be admitted that in all
the other fields ... the data furnished by our questionnaire show the
position of the commercial and industrial class to be a winning one."

Is this not a real gem? The losing position is the timber
business, railways, the Zemstvos and parliament. But "if we
leave out the few above-mentioned questions", we shall
have a winning position!

And in the "conclusion" of his book, where he takes up
the cudgels against the "traditional prejudice" about the
lowliness and lack of rights of the commercial and industrial class, Mr. Gushka rises to what may be called pathetic
Lobhudelei:

"It is not as a lowly class lacking rights that the commercial
and industrial bourgeoisie sits at the table of Russian statehood,
but as a welcome guest and collaborator, as a 'worthy assistant' of
the state power, occupying a prominent place both by established
custom and by law, by recorded right. Nor is it since yesterday that
it has occupied this place."

This would fit perfectly into an official speech delivered
by a Krestovnikov, an Avdakov, a Tiesenhausen or their like
at a dinner given by a Minister. It is this kind of speeches,
written exactly in this kind of language, that are familiar
to every Russian. The only question that arises is: how
are we to describe a "scientist" who, while laying claim to
a "scientific" analysis of a serious questionnaire, introduces
into his writings the after-dinner speeches of servile merchants as "the conclusion to be drawn from the questionnaire"?

"We have inherited from the 'good old times'," continues Mr.
Gushka, "a view which has acquired the stability of a prejudice,
namely, that capitalist Russia is characterised by the contradiction
that the big bourgeoisie, while dominating *economically*, remains
enslaved *politically*. The whole of the evidence supplied by our questionnaire deals a telling blow at this traditional notion."

It requires unbounded vulgarisation of Marxism, whose
terminology Mr. Gushka makes a show of using, to regard a
questionnaire on the organisations of capitalists as capable
of supplying "material" about the political enslavement of

the bourgeoisie by the autocracy and the landlords. The author hardly touches on the material which supplies the real answer to this question, nor could he have touched on it so long as he kept within the limits of the questionnaire.

The questionnaire, which touches on one aspect of the life of our bourgeoisie, *confirms*, in fact, that the latter is politically enslaved. It shows that the bourgeoisie is making economic progress, that certain particular rights of the bourgeoisie are being extended, that it is becoming ever more organised as a class and is playing an increasing role in political life. But the very fact that these changes are taking place makes *still more profound* the contradiction between the retention of 0.99 of the political power by the autocracy and the landlords, on the one hand, and the growing economic might of the bourgeoisie, on the other.

Mr. Gushka, who makes a show of using Marxist terminology, actually shares the standpoint of an ordinary social-liberal. It is one of Russia's specific features, or maladies if you will, that this liberalism is embellished with Marxist phrases. Adopting the standpoint of liberalism, Mr. Gushka came up against the question of the social nature of the state power in Russia. But he did not appreciate, even approximately, the vast scope and significance of this question.

The class nature of the state power in Russia has undergone a serious change since 1905. That change has been in a bourgeois direction. The Third Duma, *Vekhi* liberalism, and a number of other signs are evidence of a new "step in the transformation" of our old state power "into a bourgeois monarchy". But while taking one more step along this new path, it *remains the old power*, and this only goes to increase the sum total of political contradictions. Mr. Gushka, who came up against a serious question, revealed his inability to deal with it.

IV

In analysing the material of a rather special questionnaire, Mr. Gushka touched on another highly important question of principle, which is worth dwelling on specially. It is the question of "The Role of 1905", as the title of a subsection of Chapter XIII in Mr. Gushka's book reads.

Question 41 of the questionnaire, referring to the number of meetings of the executive body of each organisation during each of the past five years, was intended to ascertain the extent to which the activities of the organisations increased in 1905. The material provided by the answers to the questionnaire "has not"—to quote Mr. Gushka—"revealed any such phenomenon in the life of our organisations", that is, any appreciable increase in activity.

"And that is understandable," Mr. Gushka comments. Well, how does he explain this phenomenon?

The "employers'" associations, he argues, were bound to have increased their activity in 1905, in view of the increased strike movement.

> "The organisations of a purely representative type, however," continues Mr. Gushka, "were, to a certain extent, in an entirely different position: their chief contractor, the government, was on the defensive throughout 1905; it had very little faith in itself and inspired hardly any confidence in others. In that 'crazy' year, when the authorities withdrew', it seemed to all, including the industrialists (particularly at the end of the year), that the old 'authorities' would never come back.
>
> "That is why the representative organisations of capital had no reason in those days for intensifying their activity as representative bodies in dealing with the government authorities."

This explanation won't hold water. If the "authorities" had really "withdrawn", the withdrawal of the old political authorities would inevitably have resulted in the new economic authorities increasing their activity and becoming new political authorities. If the government was mainly on the defensive, how could the "collaborator and worthy assistant" of that government (as Mr. Gushka describes the commercial and industrial bourgeoisie) help increasing *its* activity to defend that government and itself? Our author has not at all thought out what he was saying. He confines himself to a mere collection of words—the most current and customary ones. Perhaps he feels that the question at issue is an extremely important one on the answer to which depends, or with the answer to which is closely linked, the answer to the more general question of the political role of the bourgeoisie, and he shrank from tackling an important question in earnest—fled from it, as it were.

Reflect on the following statement of the author on the same point—about the role of 1905:

"Neither did the organisations of capital feel inclined to meet often in order to formulate their attitude towards the social and political problems that preoccupied the whole country at the time. Pushed into the background by the sweeping tide of the popular movement, they preferred to bide their time, to wait for the results of the struggle seething around them. Towards the end, when the 'authorities' unmistakably revealed their inclination to 'come back', the organisations of the commercial and industrial class likewise began gradually to resume their representative activity in its usual form and degree of intensity."

"The organisations of capital" were "pushed into the background by the sweeping tide of the popular movement". Very well! Only, Mr. Gushka is again giving no thought to what he is saying. Against whom was the sweeping tide of the popular movement directed? Against the old regime. How then was it possible for the "collaborator and worthy assistant" of that regime to be pushed into the *back*ground? If it really were a collaborator and worthy assistant, then the greater its economic strength, which was independent of the old organisation of political power, the more vigorously it should have pushed into the *fore*ground.

How was it possible for the "collaborator and worthy assistant" of the old regime to find itself in a position where it "preferred to bide its time"?

Mr. Gushka set out to battle against the theory of the political enslavement of the economically dominating bourgeoisie, and got into a muddle the moment he tackled the job! Contrary to his view, the "theory" which he promised to demolish is reinforced by the course of events in 1905.

Both big commercial and industrial capital and the Russian bourgeois liberals, far from "biding their time" in 1905, took up a very definite counter-revolutionary position. The facts testifying to this are too well known. But there is no doubt that, compared with the forces of absolutism and the landlord class, the very big capital was to a certain extent *"pushed into the background"*.

But how could it happen that in a bourgeois revolution the peak of "the sweeping tide of the popular movement" pushed the bourgeoisie into the background more than any other class?

It happened because only by completely distorting the concept of "bourgeois revolution" can one arrive at the view that the latter declines when the bourgeoisie recoils from it. It was bound to happen, because the chief driving force of the bourgeois revolution in Russia is the proletariat and the peasantry, with the bourgeoisie vacillating. Being politically enslaved by the landlords and absolutism, the bourgeoisie, on the other hand, takes a counter-revolutionary stand when the working-class movement grows in intensity. Hence its vacillations and its retreat into the "background". It is both against and for the old order. It is willing to help the old regime against the workers, but it is perfectly capable of "establishing" itself, and even of strengthening and expanding its domination without any landlords and without any remnants of the old political regime. This is clearly shown by the experience of America and other countries.

It is easy to understand, therefore, why the peak of "the sweeping tide of the popular movement" and the greatest weakening of the old regime can cause the commercial and industrial bourgeoisie to retreat hurriedly into the "background". This bourgeoisie is precisely the class which can be neutralised in the struggle between the new and the old, between democracy and medievalism; for, while it feels more at home, at ease and comfortable by the side of the old, this class can also exercise its rule in the event of the most complete victory of the new.

V

In speaking of the questionnaire of the Imperial Russian Technical Society, we cannot pass over in silence an article by Mr. A. Yermansky in Nos. 1-2 and 3 of the liquidationist *Nasha Zarya*. Mr. Yermansky gives a most detailed account of Mr. Gushka's book, but not once does he indicate that he disagrees with him! As if a man who considers himself a Marxist could identify himself with the wishy-washy liberalism of a praiser of the commercial and industrial big-wigs!

Mr. Yermansky goes even further than Mr. Gushka in the direction of social-liberalism *à la* Brentano and Sombart,[51] slightly touched up to look like Marxism.

"The organisations of the representative type," writes Mr. Yermansky, "are organisations of class struggle in its full scope and on a national (partly even international) scale. The material provided by the questionnaire produces a picture of a practically boundless range of questions discussed by the organisations The activity of our organisations extends to almost all problems of state importance, as was justly stated by the Yekaterinoslav Stock-Exchange Committee." That is how Mr. Yermansky talks in a magazine that claims to be Marxist! This talk is blatantly false from beginning to end. It substitutes the *liberal* concept of class struggle for that of the class struggle in the Marxian sense. It proclaims as being of national and state importance the very thing which lacks the main feature of what concerns the *whole* nation and the *whole* state: the organisation of state power and the entire sphere of "state" administration, state policy, etc.

See the lengths to which Mr Yermansky goes in his misguided zeal. In disputing the view that "the capitalist bourgeoisie in Russia" (he means the big commercial and industrial bourgeoisie) is flabby, underdeveloped, and so on, he seeks a "contemporary formula" that would express "the actual position of the big bourgeoisie in Russia".

And what happens? It turns out that Mr. Yermansky sees this formula in the words uttered by Avdakov in the Board of Mining during a debate (mark this!) on the adoption of *a new organisation of mining congresses with an elected chairman*. The practice (in Russia) has been such, said Avdakov, "that so far no one has ever hampered us in anything".

"That," writes Mr. Yermansky, "is a formula which fits contemporary conditions to a T "

We should think so! As far as the organisation of mining congresses is concerned, no one has hampered the dull-witted merchants who are submissively bearing the yoke of the political privileges of the landlords! Instead of ridiculing the bombastic Kit Kitych[52] Avdakov, Mr. Yermansky strains every nerve in his zeal to assure people that Avdakov is not a Kit Kitych, that he has given a "contemporary formula" which expresses "the actual position of the big bourgeoisie in Russia"! As for Kit Kitych Avdakov, he is the perfect image of a portly butler who never dared even to think of becoming full master *in place of* his lord and who is touched by the fact that his lord permits him to confer in the servants' hall with the chambermaid, the cook, etc.

The following tirade in Mr. Yermansky's article shows that it is this difference between the status of the butler and the master that he refuses to understand:

"Here again," he writes, "it will not be superfluous to make one comparison. Everybody remembers how emphatically and with how much publicity, so to speak, the aspirations of the Zemstvo members 'to take part in the affairs of internal administration' were described as 'absurd dreams'. On the other hand, the St. Petersburg Stock-Exchange Committee, which declared, as early as the pre-constitution period, that it was necessary 'to extend as far as possible the right of the stock-exchange societies [note this!] to take part in administrative affairs', was fully justified in adding: 'Such a right of the stock-exchange societies would not constitute any innovation, for the stock-exchange societies already enjoy it in part.' What was 'an absurd dream' in the case of others, was no dream, but reality, an element of a real constitution, in the case of the representatives of big capital."

"Was", but not quite, Mr. Yermansky! Your "comparison" betrays your inability or unwillingness to distinguish between the aspiration (of the landlord class) to become *full* master itself and the aspiration (of the village elder who has grown rich) to consult with the master's *other servants*. There is a world of difference between the two.

It is only natural that Mr. Yermansky should arrive at conclusions entirely in the spirit of Larin. The representatives of big capital in Russia, says Mr. Yermansky, "long ago won the position of a ruling class in the full sense of the term".

This is false from beginning to end. Mr. Yermansky has forgotten *both* the autocracy *and* the fact that power and revenues are still in the hands of the feudal landlords. He is wrong in thinking that "*only* in the late nineteenth and the early twentieth century" did our autocracy "cease to be *exclusively* feudal". This "exclusiveness" no longer existed as far back as the epoch of Alexander II, compared with the epoch of Nicholas I. But it is absolutely impermissible to confuse a feudal regime which is shedding the quali ties that make it *exclusively* feudal, and which is taking steps towards a bourgeois monarchy, with "the complete domination of the representatives of big capital"

VI

The editors of *Nasha Zarya*, as usual, added a little "reservation" to Mr. Yermansky's article, saying that the author "underestimates the importance which direct participation in the exercise of political power has for it" (the big bourgeoisie).

The method of making little reservations has firmly established itself among the liquidators. In a series of articles, Yermansky expounds in great detail views on the class struggle that are inspired by liberalism. What the magazine preaches is liberalism. As for the "reminiscences of the glorious days" of Marxism, they are squeezed into two lines of a footnote! The readers of *Nasha Zarya* are being brought up in the spirit of liberalism, which is substituted for Marxism, and the editors wash their hands of it—by a little reservation, in just the same way as in the Cadet *Rech.*[53]

The point is not only that Mr. Yermansky "underestimates" a certain aspect of the issue. The point is that his view on the class struggle is wrong from beginning to end. The point is that he makes a fundamental mistake in appraising the social organisation of the autocracy. We pointed out long ago, and shall not cease to point out, that *this* question *cannot be evaded* by ridiculing "the answers of 1908" (or 1912), etc. This question *cannot* be evaded in any political writing that is at all serious.

The difference of opinion between Yermansky and Larin, on the one hand, and the editors of *Nasha Zarya*, on the other, is a difference between frank and, in their own way, honest liquidators and the diplomats of liquidationism. We should have no illusions on this score.

Larin wrote that the state power in our country has already become bourgeois. Therefore the workers must organise, not in expectation of a revolution (and not "for revolution", he added), but for taking part in the constitutional renovation of the country. Yermansky, who approaches the question

from a *different* angle, repeats in substance Larin's *first*
premise; but he only hints at the conclusions, without
stating them plainly.

Martov "corrected" Larin in the same way as the editors
of *Nasha Zarya* are correcting Yermansky, saying that the
state power is not bourgeois as yet, and it will be "enough"
for the workers to seize on the contradiction between constitutionalism and absolutism.

Thus the result is agreement between Martov (plus the
editors of *Nasha Zarya*) and Larin-Yermansky as regards
the conclusions, which is quite natural considering their
agreement on the fundamental premises of the liberal view
on labour policy.

We, however, still believe this view to be fundamentally
wrong. The point is not whether Yermansky "underestimates" or Martov "overestimates" the "leftward trend" of
the Guchkovs, Ryabushinskys and Co. It is not whether
Yermansky "underestimates" or Martov "overestimates" the
"importance which direct participation in the exercise of
political power has for the *bourgeoisie*". The point is that
both of them not only "underestimate", but simply do not
appreciate the importance which "direct participation in the
exercise of political power" has for the *working class*, and
for the bourgeois democracy that is following its lead and is
free from the present-day waverings of the liberals! Both of
them have in mind only *one* "political power" and forget
about the *other*.

Both of them are looking up to the top and do not see the
lower ranks. But if a dozen Ryabushinskys and a hundred
Milyukovs are grumbling and giving vent to liberal indignation, that *means* that tens of millions of petty bourgeois and
of "small folk" in all walks of life feel that their condition is
unbearable. And these millions, too, are a potential source
of "political power". Only the rallying of such democratic elements against the Rights and regardless of the vacillation of the liberals can "solve" the problems with which
history has confronted Russia since the beginning of the
twentieth century.

Prosveshcheniye No. 5-7.   Published according
   April-June 1912   to the text in *Prosveshcheni,*
   Signed· V. *Ilyin*

THE ESSENCE OF "THE AGRARIAN PROBLEM IN RUSSIA"

An "agrarian problem" — to use this common and accepted term — exists in all capitalist countries. In Russia, however, there exists, *alongside* the general capitalist agrarian problem, *another*, "truly Russian" agrarian problem. As a brief indication of the difference between the two agrarian problems, we may point out that no civilised capitalist country has any widespread democratic movement of small landowners for the transfer of big landed estates into their hands.

In Russia there *is* such a movement. Accordingly, in no European country, except Russia, do the Marxists put forward or support the demand for the transfer of the land to the small landowners. An inevitable effect of the agrarian problem in Russia is that *all* Marxists recognise this demand, despite disagreements over the *manner* in which tenure and disposal of the transferred land should be organised (division, municipalisation, nationalisation).

Why the difference between "Europe" and Russia? Is it due to the distinctive character of Russia's development, to the absence of capitalism in Russia, or to the special hopelessness and irremediability of our capitalism? That is what the Narodniks of various shades think. But this view is radically wrong, and events disproved it long ago.

The difference between "Europe" and Russia stems from Russia's extreme backwardness. In the West, the bourgeois agrarian system is fully established, feudalism was swept away long ago, and its survivals are negligible and play no serious role. The predominant type of social relationship in Western agriculture is that between the *wage-labourer* and the employer, the farmer or landowner. The small cultivators occupy an intermediary position, some of them passing into the class of those who hire themselves out, who sell their labour-power (the numerous forms of the peasant's so-called auxiliary work or subsidiary earnings), while others pass into the class of those who hire (the number of labourers hired by small cultivators is much greater than is generally believed).

Undoubtedly, a system of agriculture just as capitalist has already become firmly established and is steadily developing in Russia. It is in this direction that both landlord and peasant farming is developing. But purely capitalist relations in our country are still overshadowed to a *tremendous* extent by *feudal* relations. The distinctive character of the Russian agrarian problem lies in the struggle which the mass of the population, above all of the peasantry as a whole, are waging against these relations. In the West *this* kind of "problem" existed everywhere in olden days, but it was solved there long ago. In Russia, its solution has been delayed —the problem was not solved by the agrarian "Reform" of 1861, *nor can* it be solved under present conditions by the Stolypin agrarian policy.

In the article "Landownership in European Russia" (*Nevskaya Zvezda*[54] No. 3),* we cited the main data revealing the nature of the agrarian problem in present-day Russia.

About 70 million dessiatines of land owned by 30,000 of the biggest landlords, and about as much owned by 10 million peasant households—such is the main background of the picture. What are the economic relations to which this picture testifies?

The 30,000 big landlords represent chiefly the old landed nobility and the old feudal economy. Of the 27,833 owners of estates exceeding 500 dessiatines each, 18,102, or *nearly two-thirds*, are members of the nobility. The huge latifundia in their possession—each of these big landlords owns an average of more then 2,000 dessiatines!—cannot be cultivated with the implements, livestock and hired labour at the disposal of the owners. That being so, the old corvée system is largely inevitable, and this means small-scale cultivation, small-scale farming, on the big latifundia, the cultivation

---

* See pp. 32-35 of this volume.—*Ed.*

of the landlords' land with the implements and livestock of the small peasants.

This corvée system is especially widespread, as we know, in the central, traditionally Russian, gubernias of European Russia, in the *heart* of our agriculture. So-called labour rent is nothing but a direct continuation and survival of the corvée system. The farming methods based on impossible terms of bondage, such as winter hiring,[55] work for the cut-off land,[56] "composite labour service",[57] and so on and so forth, are also part of the corvée system. Under this system of farming, the peasant "allotment" is a means of supplying the *landlord* with farm hands, and not only with farm hands but also with implements and livestock, which, wretched though they are, serve to cultivate the landlords' land.

Dire poverty of the mass of the peasantry, who are tied to their allotments but cannot subsist on them, extremely primitive agricultural techniques, and the extreme inadequacy of the home market for industry—such are the results of this state of affairs. And the present famine affecting 30 million peasants is the most striking proof that at bottom, in substance, this state of affairs has remained unchanged to this day. Only the serf-like downtroddenness, distress and helplessness of the mass of small proprietors in bondage *can* lead to such frightful mass starvation in an epoch of rapidly developing agricultural techniques, which have already achieved a relatively high standard (on the best capitalist farms).

The fundamental contradiction leading to such terrible calamities, which have been unknown to the peasants of Western Europe since the Middle Ages, is the contradiction between capitalism, which is highly developed in our industry and considerably developed in our agriculture, and *the system of landownership*, which remains medieval, feudal. There is no way out of this situation unless the old system of landownership is radically broken up.

Not only the landed property of the landlords, but that of the peasants as well is based on feudal relations. In the case of the former, this is so obvious as to arouse no doubts. We need only note that the abolition of the feudal latifundia, say, of those exceeding 500 dessiatines, will not undermine large-scale *production* in agriculture but will,

indeed, increase and develop it For the feudal latifundia are
bulwarks of *small-scale* farming based on bondage, and not
of large-scale production. In most regions of Russia it is
practically impossible or, at all events, exceedingly difficult
to run *large farms* taking up as much as 500 or more dessiatines of land with the implements and livestock of the
owner and with wage-labour. A *reduction* in the size of such
estates is one of the conditions for small-scale farming on
terms of bondage going out of existence and for agriculture
passing to large-scale capitalist production.

On the other hand, the allotment form of peasant land
tenure in Russia also retains medieval, feudal features.
And it is not only a question of the juridical form, which is
now being changed, in sergeant-major fashion, through the
destruction of the village commune and the introduction
of private land ownership; it is also a question of the *actual*
nature of this ownership, which is unaffected by any break-
up of the commune.

The actual condition of the vast mass of peasants holding
small and dwarf "parcels" (=tiny plots of land), consisting
mostly of several narrow strips far removed from each
other and distinguished by soil of the poorest quality (due
to the delimitation of the peasant land in 1861 under the
supervision of the feudal landlords, and due to the ex-
haustion of the land), inevitably places them in a relation
of bondage to the hereditary owner of the latifundium, the
old "master".

Just keep clearly in mind the following picture: as against
30,000 owners of latifundia of 2,000 dessiatines each, there
are 10,000,000 peasant households with 7 dessiatines of land
per "average" household. It is obvious that no matter what
destruction of the village commune and creation of private
landownership takes place, this will *still not* be able to
change the bondage, labour rent, corvée, feudal poverty,
and feudal forms of dependence, stemming from this state
of affairs.

The "agrarian problem" resulting from such a situation
is the problem of doing away with the survivals of serfdom,
which have become an intolerable obstacle to Russia's capitalist development. The agrarian problem in Russia is one
of radically breaking up the old, medieval forms of land-

ownership, both that of the landlords and that of the allotment peasants—a break-up which has become absolutely
indispensable in view of the extreme backwardness of this
landownership, in view of the extreme disharmony between
it and the whole system of the national economy, which
has become capitalist.

It must be a radical break-up, because the disharmony is
too great, the old is too old, and "the disease too neglected".
In any event and in all its forms, this break-up is bound to
be bourgeois in content, since Russia's entire economic life
is already bourgeois, and the system of landownership is
certain to become subordinate to it, to adapt itself to the
dictates of the market, to the pressure of capital, which is
omnipotent in our society today.

But while the break-up cannot fail to be radical and
bourgeois, there is still this question to be answered: *which*
of the two classes directly concerned, the landlords or the
peasants, will carry out this change or direct it, determine
its forms? Our next article, "A Comparison of the Stolypin
and the Narodnik Agrarian Programmes",* will deal with
this "unsolved problem".

Nevskaya Zvezda No· 6.   Published according
    May 22, 1912   to the text in *Nevskaya Zvezda*
    Signed: *R S*.

See pp. 143 49 of this volume.—*Ed.*

SOME CONCLUSIONS TO BE DRAWN
FROM THE PRE-ELECTION MOBILISATION

Almost all the political forces taking part in the elections to the Duma are by now finally organised. At any rate, the main party alignments have taken such definite shape that there can be no question of any serious and material changes.

The government began the election campaign long ago. The Rights, the nationalists, and the Octobrists are "at work" with the obvious assistance of the authorities. *Rech* recently published, and many newspapers have reprinted, the circular sent by the governors to the police chiefs about the adoption of "measures" to prevent "Left" candidates from being elected as delegates (particularly from the peasants) or electors. This circular lifts the veil somewhat from the "election" machinery of the Ministry of the Interior. Everything possible—and impossible—will undoubtedly be done in this quarter against the opposition. Not for nothing did Premier Kokovtsov, in his speech to the Moscow merchants, lay so much stress on the perniciousness of "opposition for the sake of opposition".

But while there can be no doubt about the zeal of the government and the police in the elections, it is just as undoubted that a widespread "leftward" swing has taken, or is taking, place in the sentiments of the voters. No stratagems of the government can alter this fact. On the contrary, all that stratagems and "measures" can accomplish is to increase discontent. And it is easy to understand that while this discontent among the big bourgeoisie is expressed by Shubinsky's "opposition" speech, by Ryabushinsky's "cautious" allusion to the desirability of "cultured methods of administration", or by caustic digs at the Ministry on the part of the Cadet

Rech, there is much keener and more serious discontent in the large circle of the "small people" who are dependent on the Ryabushinskys, Golovins and others.

What are the political alignments that have taken definite shape in the camp of the opposition, which gives political expression to this discontent? One group that has taken shape is the "responsible", liberal-monarchist opposition of the Cadets and the Progressists. The bloc of these two parties clearly denotes that the Cadets are much more "to the right" than they seem to be.

Another group that has taken shape is that of the working-class democracy, which has undertaken the task, not of "supporting" the Cadet-Progressist opposition, but of *utilising* the latter's conflicts with the Rights (including the nationalists and the Octobrists) to enlighten and organise the democratic forces. Lastly, the group of the bourgeois democracy has also taken shape: at the conference of the Trudoviks it declared in favour of agreements "in the first place, with the Social-Democrats", but it did not put forward any definite slogan calling for a fight against the counter-revolutionary liberalism of the Cadets, which means that in practice it is wavering between the two.

What are the conclusions to be drawn from this pre-election "political mobilisation" of the parties? The first and principal conclusion, which the working-class democrats drew long ago, is that there are *three*, not two, camps engaged in the contest. The liberals are eager to make it appear that the contest is really between two camps; and the liquidators, as has been shown on many occasions, are constantly slipping into an acceptance of the same view. "For or against a constitution?" is how the Cadets formulate the difference between the two camps. Actually, however, this formulation defines nothing at all, because the Octobrists, too, avow that they are constitutionalists, and indeed, generally speaking, it should be a question not of what can or cannot be called a constitution, but of the exact content of certain liberal or democratic demands.

It is the content of the demands, the real distinctions between the class tendencies, that differentiates the three camps: the Right, or government, camp; the camp of the liberal, or liberal-monarchist, bourgeoisie, which takes a counter-revolutionary stand; and the democratic camp. Furthermore, it is not so much a question of "chances" under the existing electoral system, for the issue goes much deeper—it concerns the whole character of political propaganda during the elections, the whole ideological and political content of the election campaign.

In view of this state of affairs, the "strategy" of the liberals is daily directed towards taking the leadership of the "whole" opposition movement into their hands. The liberal *Zaprosy Zhizni* blurted out the "secret" of this strategy, so carefully kept by *Rech*. "The Progressists," writes Mr. R. B.[58] in *Zaprosy Zhizni* No. 13, "have opened their campaign by a promising move [!]—they formed the so-called 'non-partisan Progressist bloc', which proved from the first to have a strong appeal for the political opposition circles to the right of the Cadets." On the other hand, "the election platform of the Trudovik group, despite its vagueness—in part due to it, perhaps—meets the requirements of large sections of the democratic intelligentsia". "Under certain conditions, the Trudovik group to the left of the Cadets could perform a role similar to that undertaken by the Progressist group to the right of the Cadets. The opposition front would then be made up of mobile and wavering, but flexible extreme flanks, and an immobile but persistent centre, which strategically has its advantage in the political struggle as well."

What is in the thoughts of the Milyukovs and Shingaryovs is on R. B.'s tongue! It is precisely two "flexible" flanks that the Cadets need: the Progressists for netting the bourgeois June Third voter, and the "vague" democrats for netting the democratic-minded public. Indeed, this "strategy" follows from the very nature of the Cadet Party. It is the party of the counter-revolutionary liberals, which by fraudulent means has won the support of certain democratic strata, such as a section of the shop-assistants, office clerks, etc. What such a party needs is exactly the "non-partisan Progressist" as its real class bulwark, and the vague democrat as an attractive sales ticket.

The landlord Yefremov and the millionaire Ryabushinsky may be described as typical Progressists. The typical vague democrat is represented by the Trudovik in the Narodnik

camp and the liquidator in the Marxist camp. Take the whole
history of the Cadet Party, and you will find that its method
has *always* been democracy in words, and liberalism "of the
Yefremov brand and acceptable to Ryabushinsky" in deeds.
From the defeat of the plan for local land committees in 1906
to the vote for the budget in the Third Duma, or to Milyukov's[59] "London" slogans, etc., we see this very *nature* of
the Cadet Party and its sham-democratic *attire*.

Mr. R. B. of *Zaprosy Zhizni* is so very clumsy that he
inadvertently told the truth, which had been carefully kept
from the democrats and muddled by the liberals. The programme of the Progressists, he confesses, "puts the issue on
a firm and realistic basis!"And yet that programme has
nothing except general phrases in a purely Octobrist style
(as, for instance, "the complete realisation of the Manifesto
of October 17"[60]). What is described as a firm and realistic
basis is the basis of a bourgeois liberalism so moderate,
so mild and impotent, that it would be simply ridiculous
to pin any hopes on it. Those who were "Peaceful Renovators"[61] in 1907, those who in the Third Duma steered a
middle course between the Cadets and the Octobrists, are
described as a firm and realistic basis!

The millionaire Ryabushinsky is a Progressist. *Utro
Rossii*[62] is the mouthpiece of this and similar Progressists.
And none other than *Rech*, the paper of the Cadets, who have
formed a bloc with the Progressists, wrote: "*Utro Rossii*,
organ of the Moscow industrialists, is gratified [by Kokovtsov's speech] more than anyone else.... It echoes Krestovnikov: 'Commercial and industrial Moscow can feel satisfied.'"
And *Rech* added for its own part: "As far as *Golos Moskvy*
and *Utro Rossii* are concerned, they are willing not to pursue any line, and feel perfectly satisfied."

The question arises: where is the evidence that Yefremov
or other Progressists *have* a "line"? There is no such evidence. For democrats to support this sort of progressism,
whether it is called progressism or Cadetism, would mean
only surrendering their position. But using the conflicts
between the bourgeoisie and the landlords, between the
liberals and the Rights, is another matter. That is the only
way in which a democrat can formulate his task.

To fulfil this task, to politically enlighten and organise

the very wide masses that are economically dependent on the Yefremovs and Ryabushinskys, one has to be well aware of the counter-revolutionary nature of Cadet and Progressist liberalism. The lack of this awareness is the chief defect of both the Trudoviks and the liquidators. The Trudoviks say nothing at all about the class characteristics of liberalism. The liquidators utter phrases about "wresting the *Duma* from the hands of the reactionaries", about the Cadets and Progressists coming closer to power, and about the historically progressive work they are doing (see Martov and Dan). Taken as a whole, it adds up to that very role of a Cadet "flank" which pleases R. B. so much.

To be sure, these are not the subjective wishes of the Trudoviks and the liquidators and, indeed, it is not a question of their subjective plans, but of the objective alignment of the social forces. And in spite of all the adherents of the idea of two camps, in spite of the malicious shouts about disorganisation in the workers' democratic movement (see the same article by Mr. R. B.), this alignment clearly shows us that a third camp has formed. Its line is clearly presented and is known to all. The anti-liquidationist workers are pursuing this line, rallying all the democrats in the struggle *both* against the Rights *and* against the liberals. Without entertaining any illusions about the impotent liberalism of the Cadets, who are grovelling before the reaction in all fundamental questions, the workers are using clashes between that liberalism and the reaction to promote their own cause, their own class organisation, their own democracy, which is now quietly ripening in the broad mass of the people enslaved by the Yefremovs and Ryabushinskys.

Thanks to the anti-liquidationist tactics of the workers, the fight between the Rights and the "responsible" opposition must, and will, serve to develop the political consciousness and independent organisation of an "opposition" which lays no claim to the scarcely honourable title of "responsible".

Nevskaya Zvezda No. 6,   Published according
    May 22, 1912   to the text in *Nevskaya Zvezda*
    Signed: *B. G.*

ECONOMIC AND POLITICAL STRIKES

Ever since 1905 the official strike statistics kept by the Ministry of Commerce and Industry have subdivided strikes into economic and political. This subdivision was necessitated by reality, which has evolved *distinctive* forms of the strike movement. The combination of economic and political strike is one of the main features of these forms. And now that there is a revival of the strike movement, it is in the interest of a scientific analysis, of an intelligent attitude to events, that the workers should look closely into this distinctive feature of the strike movement in Russia.

To begin with, we shall cite several basic figures taken from the government strike statistics. For three years, 1905-07, the strike movement in Russia kept at a height *unprecedented in the world*. Government statistics cover only factories, so that mining, railways, building and numerous other branches of wage-labour are left out. But even in factories alone, the number of strikers was 2,863,000, or a little less than 3 million, in 1905, 1,108,000 in 1906, and 740,000 in 1907. In the fifteen years from 1894 to 1908, during which strike statistics began to be systematically studied in Europe, the greatest number of strikers for one year — 660,000 —was registered in America.

Consequently, the Russian workers were *the first in the world* to develop the strike struggle on the mass scale that we witnessed in 1905-07. Now it is the British workers who have lent a new great impetus to the strike movement with regard to economic strikes. The Russian workers owe their leading role, not to greater strength, better organisation or higher development compared with the workers in Western Europe, but to the fact that so far Europe has not gone through great national crises with the proletarian masses taking an independent part in them. When such crises do set in, mass strikes in Europe will be even more powerful than they were in Russia in 1905.

What was the ratio of economic to political strikes in that period? Government statistics give the following answer:

Number of strikers (thousands)

		1905	1906	1907
Economic	strikes	1,439	458	200
Political	strikes	1,424	650	540
Total		2,863	1,108	740

This shows the close and inseparable connection between the two kinds of strike. When the movement was at its highest (1905), the *economic* basis of the struggle was the broadest; in that year the political strike rested on the firm and solid basis of economic strikes. The number of economic strikers was *greater* than that of political strikers.

We see that as the movement declined, in 1906 and 1907, the economic basis *contracted*: the number of economic strikers dropped to 0.4 of the total number of strikers in 1906 and to 0.3 in 1907. Consequently, the economic and the political strike support each other, each being a source of strength for the other. Unless these forms of strike are closely interlinked, a really wide mass movement—moreover, a movement of *national* significance—is impossible. When the movement is in its early stage, the economic strike often has the effect of awakening and stirring up the backward, of making the movement a general one, of raising it to a higher plane.

In the first quarter of 1905, for instance, economic strikes noticeably predominated over political strikes, the number of strikers being 604,000 in the former case and only 206,000 in the latter. In the last quarter of 1905, however, the ratio was reversed: 430,000 workers took part in economic strikes, and 847,000 in political strikes. This means that in the early stage of the movement many workers put the economic struggle first, while at the height of the movement it was the other way round. But *all the time* there was a *connection* between the economic and the political strike. Without such a connection, we repeat, it is impossible to have a really great movement, one that achieves great aims.

In a political strike, the working class comes forward as the advanced class of the whole people. In such cases, the proletariat plays not merely the role of one of the classes of bourgeois society, but the role of guide, vanguard, leader. The political ideas manifested in the movement involve the whole people, i.e., they concern the basic, most profound conditions of the political life of the whole country This character of the political strike, as has been noted by all scientific investigators of the period 1905-07, brought into the movement all the classes, and particularly, of course, the widest, most numerous and most democratic sections of the population, the peasantry, and so forth.

On the other hand, the mass of the working people will never agree to conceive of a general "progress" of the country without economic demands, without an immediate and direct improvement in their condition. The masses are drawn into the movement, participate vigorously in it, value it highly and display heroism, self-sacrifice, perseverance and devotion to the great cause only if it makes for improving the economic condition of those who work. Nor can it be otherwise, for the living conditions of the workers in "ordinary" times are incredibly hard. As it strives to improve its living conditions, the working class also progresses morally, intellectually and politically, becomes more capable of achieving its great emancipatory aims.

The strike statistics published by the Ministry of Commerce and Industry fully bear out this tremendous significance of the economic struggle of the workers in the period of a general revival. The stronger the onslaught of the workers, the greater their achievements in improving their standard of living. The "sympathy of society" and better conditions of life are both results of a high degree of development of the struggle. Whereas the liberals (and the liquidators) tell the workers: "You are strong when you have the sympathy of 'society'," the Marxist tells the workers something different, namely: "You have the sympathy of 'society' when you are strong." What we mean by society in this case is all the various democratic sections of the population, the petty bourgeoisie, the peasants, and the intellectuals, who are in close touch with the life of the workers, office employees, etc.

The strike movement was strongest in 1905. And what was the result? We see that in that year the workers achieved the greatest improvements in their condition. Government statistics show that in 1905 *only* 29 out of every 100 strikers stopped their fight without having gained *anything*, i.e., were completely defeated. In the previous ten years (1895-1904), as many as 52 strikers out of 100 stopped fighting without having gained anything! It follows that the large scale of the struggle contributed immensely to its *success*, almost doubling it.

When the movement began to decline, the success of the struggle began to diminish accordingly. In 1906, 33 strikers out of 100 stopped fighting without having gained anything, or having been defeated, to be exact; in 1907 the figure was 58, and in 1908, as high as 69 out of 100!!

Thus the scientific statistical data over a number of years fully confirm the personal experience and observations of every class-conscious worker as regards the necessity of combining the economic and the political strike, and the inevitability of this combination in a really broad movement of the whole people.

The present strike wave likewise fully confirms this conclusion. In 1911 the number of strikers was double that in 1910 (100,000 against 50,000), but even so their number was extremely small; purely economic strikes remained a relatively "narrow" cause, they did not assume national significance. On the other hand, today it is obvious to one and all that the strike movement following the well-known events of last April had *precisely* *this* significance.[63]

It is therefore highly important to rebuff from the outset the attempts of the liberals and liberal labour politicians (liquidators) to *distort* the character of the movement. Mr. Severyanin, a liberal, contributed to *Russkiye Vedomosti*[64] an article *against* "admixing" economic or "any other [aha!] demands" to the May Day strike, and the Cadet *Rech* sympathetically reprinted in the main passages of the article.

"More often than not," writes the liberal gentleman, "it is unreasonable to link such strikes with May Day.... Indeed, it would be rather strange to do so: we are celebrating the international workers' holiday, and we use the occasion to demand a ten per cent rise for calico of such-and-such grades." (*Rech* No. 132.)

What is quite clear to the workers seems "strange" to the liberal. Only the defenders of the bourgeoisie and its excessive profits can sneer at the demand for a "rise". But the workers know that it is the *widespread* character of the demand for a rise, it is the *comprehensive* character of a strike, that has the greatest power to attract a multitude of new participants, to ensure the strength of the onslaught and the sympathy of society, and to guarantee both the success of the workers and the national significance of their movement. That is why it is necessary to fight with determination against the liberal distortion preached by Mr. Severyanin, *Russkiye Vedomosti* and *Rech*, and to warn the workers in every way against this kind of sorry advisers.

Mr. V. Yezhov, a liquidator, writing in the very first issue of the liquidationist *Nevsky Golos*, [65] offers a similar purely liberal distortion, although he approaches the question from a somewhat different angle. He dwells in particular on the strikes provoked by the May Day fines. Correctly pointing out that the workers are not sufficiently organised, the author draws from his correct statement conclusions that are quite wrong and most harmful to the workers. Mr. Yezhov sees a lack of organisation in the fact that while in one factory the workers struck merely in protest, in another they added economic demands, etc. Actually, however, this *variety* of forms of strike does not in itself indicate any lack of organisation at all; it is ridiculous to imagine that organisation necessarily means uniformity! Lack of organisation is not at all to be found where Mr. Yezhov looks for it.

But his *conclusion* is still worse:

"Owing to this [i.e., owing to the variety of the strikes and to the different forms of the combination of economics and politics], the principle involved in the protest (after all, it was not over a few kopeks that the strike was called) became obscured in a considerable number of cases, being complicated by economic demands...."

This is a truly outrageous, thoroughly false and thoroughly liberal argument! To think that the demand "for a few kopeks" is *capable* of "obscuring" the principle involved in the protest means sinking to the level of a Cadet. On the contrary, Mr Yezhov, the demand for "a few kopeks" deserves full recognition and not a sneer! On the contrary, Mr Yezhov, that demand, *far from* "obscuring" "the principle involved in the protest", *emphasises* it! Firstly, the question of a higher standard of living is *also* a question of principle, and a most important one; secondly, whoever protests, not against one, but against two, three, etc., manifestations of oppression, does not thereby weaken his protest but strengthens it

Every worker will indignantly reject Mr. Yezhov's outrageous liberal distortion of the matter.

In the case of Mr. Yezhov, it is by no means a slip of the pen. He goes on to say even more outrageous things:

> "Their own experience should have suggested to the workers that it was inadvisable to complicate their protest by economic demands, just as it is inadvisable to complicate an ordinary strike by a demand involving a principle."

This is untrue, a thousand times untrue! The *Nevsky Golos* has disgraced itself by printing such stuff. What Mr. Yezhov thinks inadvisable is perfectly advisable. Both each worker's *own experience* and the experience of a very large number of Russian workers in the recent past testify to *the reverse* of what Mr. Yezhov preaches.

Only liberals can object to "complicating" even the most "ordinary" strike by "demands involving principles". That is the first point. Secondly, our liquidator is sorely mistaken in measuring the present movement with the yardstick of an "ordinary" strike.

And Mr Yezhov is wasting his time in trying to cover up his liberal contraband with someone else's flag, in confusing the question of *combining* the economic and the political strike with the question of *preparations* for the one or the other! Of course, it is most desirable to make preparations and to be prepared, and to do this as thoroughly, concertedly, unitedly, intelligently and firmly as possible. That is beyond dispute. But, contrary to what Mr. Yezhov says, it is necessary to make preparations precisely for a *combination* of the two kinds of strike.

> "A period of economic strikes is ahead of us," writes Mr. Yezhov. "It would be an irreparable mistake to allow them to become inter-

twined with political actions of the workers. Such combination would have a harmful effect on both the economic and the political struggle of the workers "

One could hardly go to greater lengths! These words show in the clearest possible way that the liquidator has sunk to the level of an ordinary liberal. Every sentence contains an error! We must convert every sentence into its *direct* opposite to get at the truth!

It is not true that a period of economic strikes is ahead of us. Quite the reverse. What we have ahead of us is a period of something more than just economic strikes. We are facing a period of political strikes. The facts, Mr. Yezhov, are stronger than your liberal distortions; and if you could look at the statistical cards dealing with strikes, which are filed in the Ministry of Commerce and Industry, you would see that *even* these government statistics fully refute you.

It is not true that "intertwining" would be a mistake. Quite the reverse. It would be an irreparable mistake if the workers failed to understand the great singularity, the great significance, the great necessity, and the great fundamental importance of precisely such "intertwining" Fortunately, however, the workers understand this perfectly, and they brush aside with contempt the preaching of liberal labour politicians.

Lastly, it is not true that such intertwining "would have a harmful effect" on both forms. Quite the reverse. It *benefits* both. It strengthens both.

Mr. Yezhov lectures some "hotheads" whom he seems to have discovered. Listen to this:

"It is necessary to give organisational form to the sentiments of the workers...." This is gospel truth! "It is necessary to increase propaganda for trade unions, to recruit new members for them...."

Quite true, *but*—but, Mr. Yezhov, it is impermissible to *reduce* "organisational form" to the trade unions alone! Remember this, Mr. Liquidator!

"This is all the more necessary since there are many hotheads among the workers nowadays who are carried away by the mass movement and speak at meetings *against unions*, alleging them to be useless and unnecessary. "

This is a liberal slur on the workers. It is not "against unions" that the workers—who have been, and always will be, a thorn in the side of the liquidators—have been coming out. No, the workers have been coming out against the attempt to *reduce* the organisational form to "trade unions" alone, an attempt which is so evident from Mr. Yezhov's preceding sentence.

The workers have been coming out, not "against unions", but against the liberal distortion of the nature of the struggle they are waging, a distortion which pervades the whole of Mr. Yezhov's article.

The Russian workers have become sufficiently mature politically to realise the great significance of their movement for the whole people. They are sufficiently mature to see how very false and paltry liberal labour policy is and they will always brush it aside with contempt.

Published in *Nevskaya Zvezda*
No. 10, May 31, 1912
Signed: *Iv. Petrov*

Published according to
the newspaper text verified with
the text in the symposium
Marxism and Liquidationism,
Part II, St. Petersburg, 1914

THE PROBLEM OF RESETTLEMENT

As we know, the government and the counter-revolutionary parties had placed especially great hopes in the settlement of peasants on new land. All the counter-revolutionaries expected that if it would not solve the agrarian problem radically, then at least it would blunt it considerably and render it much less dangerous. That is why they advertised resettlement with particular zeal and encouraged it in every way at the imminent approach, and then during the development, of the peasant movement in European Russia.

What is in the thoughts of the government representatives and the more far-sighted politicians of, say, the Octobrist Party, is on the tongue of such undisguised reactionaries as Markov the Second, the diehard[66] from Kursk. During the debate on the resettlement problem in the Duma, this deputy declared frankly, with praiseworthy straightforwardness: "Yes, it is by means of resettlement that the government should solve the agrarian problem." (First Session.)

There is no doubt that resettlement, if properly organised, could play a role of some importance in Russia's economic development. To be sure, this role must not be overrated even today, when the condition of the Russian muzhik is so intolerable that he is willing to go anywhere, not only to Siberia, but to the end of the world; even today, when the peasants who own little or no land are encouraged in every way to migrate and settle as colonists, so as to keep them from the temptation of contemplating the landlords' latifundia, and when the decree of November 9[67] has greatly facilitated for the settlers the liquidation of the remnants of their farms at home; even today, as even the apologists of the theory of a natural population increase must

admit. It is only in the gubernias that provide the largest
percentage of emigrants (the South, West, and the black-
earth central area of Russia), that their number equals the
natural increase of the population, or slightly exceeds it

Nevertheless, there is still a substantial reserve of unoc-
cupied land in Siberia suitable for resettlement. True, very
little has been done so far to ascertain the extent of that
reserve even approximately. In 1896 Kulomzin set the reserve of land fit for resettlement at 130,000 per capita allotments Since then ten times as many allotments have been
apportioned, but the reserve has not yet been exhausted.
On the contrary, according to estimates of the Resettlement
Department, by 1900 the reserve of land suitable for resettlement amounted to three million per capita allotments,
sufficient to provide for six million settlers. As we see, the
figures differ considerably, and the range of the variation
between them is very great.

Be that as it may, even discounting a certain percentage
of the last-mentioned figures to allow for the usual bureaucratic complacency, it is certain that there is still a reserve
of land in Siberia and that, consequently, its settlement
could have a certain importance both for Siberia and Russia, provided it was properly organised.

It is just this *conditio sine qua non* that the present government does not comply with. The present organisation
of resettlement once again demonstrates and proves that
our "old order" is quite incapable of meeting even the most
elementary economic requirements of the population. The
bad organisation of resettlement is additional evidence that
the present masters of the situation are powerless to do
anything at all for the economic progress of the country.

An explanation of the trend, character and implementation of the resettlement policy was given by the Social-
Democratic deputies to the Duma in their speeches during
each year's discussion of budget appropriations for the Resettlement Department.

What is the government's aim in resettling the peasants?
That is the main question, the answer to which determines
the answer to all the others; for the aim of the government's
resettlement policy determines its entire character.

Deputy Voiloshnikov, who spoke for the Social-Democratic group at the Second Session of the Duma, described as follows the government's aims in resettling the peasants: "The resettlement policy is an element of the government's agrarian policy as a whole. When the landlords needed economically weak or insecure peasants as a source of cheap labour, the government did everything to impede resettlement and to keep the surplus population where it was. What is more, it strongly opposed voluntary migration, trying thereby to close that safety valve. But the natural growth of the population went on, and times changed. Storm clouds—the proletariat and the starving peasantry—loomed large, with all their consequences. The government and the landlords seized upon resettlement, which, together with the decree of November 9, they made the basis of their agrarian policy. However, in regard to implementing the decree, attention was centred on the economically strong and prosperous, on taking the land from the poor and transferring it to the prosperous peasants. But in regard to resettlement it is a matter of packing off the poor peasants to Siberia in as large numbers as possible; and while lately there has been evidence of a tendency to an increase in the average proportion of prosperous settlers, the bulk still consists of weak peasants, to use Stolypin's terminology. The land committees are also taking part, or, I should say, have been enlisted to take part in this business of packing off peasants in increased numbers.

"The land committees have been charged with assigning the settlers their plots and thus putting an end to the former agrarian disorders. It follows, gentlemen, that the decree of November 9, the vigorous advertisement of resettlement, the vigorous drive to pack off the weak peasants to Siberia, and the activities of the land committees are two closely connected aspects of the same problem and the same policy. It will be readily seen that the implementation of the decree of November 9 helps settlement of the prosperous and strong on the allotments at the expense of the weak peasants, and will thereby help to squeeze out these weak elements, who are not very suitable as settlers, into border regions that are alien to them. Both as regards the village commune and migration, the government's resettlement policy has been guided solely by the interests of a handful of semi-feudal landlords and of the ruling classes in general, who are oppressing the masses of workers and the labouring peasantry. The government shows no understanding of the elementary requirements of the country and of the needs of the national economy." (Second Session, 77th sitting.)

This aspect of the matter was disclosed most fully by Deputy Chkheidze (in his speech during the Second Session of the Duma), who drew a detailed picture of the resettlement policy in the Caucasus.

To begin with, the Social-Democratic deputy proved by facts and figures that all the official reports about vacant land in the Caucasus are in glaring conflict with the truth. It should be specially stressed that Deputy Chkheidze, in order to forestall any accusation of partiality or distortion, used only official data and the reports of government officials. According to the figures collected as long ago as the eighties by the former Minister of State Property, "among the state peasants alone, who have been settled on state land in the Caucasus, there were, in the four Transcaucasian gubernias, 22,000 persons who owned no land at all, 66,000 with allotments of less than one dessiatine per capita, 254,000 with allotments of from one to two dessiatines per capita, and 5,013 with allotments of from two to four dessiatines, a total of about 1,000,000 persons having smaller allotments than the minimum fixed for the settlers who have established themselves in the Caucasus. In Kutais Gubernia, 2,541 out of 29,977 household owned no land or less than one dessiatine per household, 4,227 owned from one to two dessiatines per household, 4,016 from two to three, and 5,321 from three to five. According to the latest data, 46 per cent of the villages in the four Transcaucasian gubernias had no state land at all or very little, and in Kutais Gubernia the number of unprovided households was approximately 33 per cent of the total. From the report of the Baku Committee on the needs of the agricultural industries we know that such villages insufficiently provided with land send the landless peasants to take up their residence with those owning large allotments and they remain for many years in this dependent position. And Senator Kuzminsky, in a report submitted to the Emperor, says the following: 'It has been noted that

sometimes the settlers consist of persons who have given
up farming and lease the land received for purposes of resettlement to fellow villagers or to native peasants in a
neighbouring village.' Thus even twenty-five years ago there
were in Transcaucasia hundreds of thousands of state peasants—who, one would think, should have been better provided than other categories of peasants, and whom one
could describe without exaggeration as farm labourers. As
far back as some twenty-five years ago the local peasants
were compelled to rent the land that was allotted to settlers".

Such are the data enabling us to judge of the extent to which
the state peasants in the Caucasus are provided with land.

"As for the so-called temporarily bonded[68] peasants," the speaker
went on to say, "we see from an examination of the verified   deeds
that in Tiflis Gubernia 1,444 households were left without any land
and 386 households received no land even for their dwelling-houses
and gardens. They comprise 13 per cent of the total number of landlords' peasants in Tiflis Gubernia. In Kutais Gubernia there was an
even greater number of peasants left without land after the Reform.
Even if we take the Tiflis ratio to apply to the former serfs in all the
gubernias, we get in Kutais Gubernia 5,590 households, representing
25,000 persons, who received not a single patch of land when the
peasants were emancipated in the Caucasus. Twenty years after the
Reform, in 1895, continues the author of the memorandum on the
abolition of obligatory relations, there were in Yelisavetpol Gubernia
5,308 landless households, or 25,000 persons of both sexes. In Baku
Gubernia there were 3,906 households, or 11,709 landless persons
of both sexes. And here are data on the amount of land held by the
peasants who were temporarily bonded and who have not redeemed
their allotments but have some kind of farm. In Tiflis Gubernia the per
capita amount is 0.9 dessiatine, and in Kutais Gubernia 0.6 dessiatine.
Among those who have redeemed their allotments, the per capita
holdings amount to 1.7 dessiatines in Tiflis Gubernia and to 0.7
dessiatine in Kutais Gubernia. That is the extent to which peasants
having some sort of farm are provided with land. We find a general
description of the economic position of the peasants in the Caucasus
in the report of the Kutais Gubernia Committee on the needs of the
agricultural industries. According to data culled from various official
investigations, the proportion of peasants suffering acute want in
Kutais Gubernia is as high as 70 per cent. Furthermore, it is also
pointed out that 25 per cent of the nobility in that gubernia are suffering acute want.

"Owners of such plots of land can retain their economic independence," the report goes on to say, "only if they have earnings outside
their farms, and they are in no position to spend anything at all on
improvements, implements and fertiliser. The big demand could not
but have an effect on the cost of renting allotments, which is as high

as 60 per cent of the gross income in the case of the share-cropping system, and sometimes, in years of a poor crop, payment in the form of a definite quantity of the produce of the land exceeds the gross income. Cases of land being leased for money are rare, and the rent amounts to 30 rubles per dessiatine a year. This is the situation in Kutais Gubernia. And now a few figures on the amount of land held by the peasants in four uyezds of Yelisavetpol Gubernia. According to data concerning all the peasants who live on the owner's land, the holdings in four uyezds of Yelisavetpol Gubernia, namely, Jibrail, Zangezur, Shusha and Jevanshir, are up to 0.6 dessiatine per person. Senator Kuzminsky has calculated that the average allotment per male person among the peasants settled on the owner's land in Len koran Uyezd of Baku Gubernia amounts to 0.5 dessiatine, and in Kuba Uyezd to 0.9 dessiatine. That, gentlemen," the speaker conclud ed, "is how the peasants in Transcaucasia are provided with land."

Since the condition of the Caucasian peasants as regards land-hunger differs but little from that of the peasants in Russia, where, one may ask, does the reserve of land for resettlement in the Caucasus come from, and why are people sent there as settlers, instead of resettlement of the local peasants being carried out?

The land for resettlement is obtained as a result of flagrant violation of the land rights of the native inhabitants, and the settlement of peasants from Russia is carried on for the glory of the old nationalist principle of "Russification of the outlying regions".

Deputy Chkheidze cited a number of facts, likewise culled from official sources, about how whole villages of natives were driven from their homes so that a reserve of land might be created for resettlement, how court trials were engineered to justify the expropriation of land held by mountaineers (report on the mountain village of Kiknaveleti, Kutais Uyezd, submitted by Prince Tsereteli, Marshal of the Nobility, to the Minister of the Interior), etc. Nor were all these isolated or exceptional facts but "typical cases", as was also established by Senator Kuzminsky.

The result is downright hostile relations between the settlers and the natives. Thus, for instance, when the Alar community was driven from its lands, "evicted", to quote Senator Kuzminsky, "without being provided with land, and left to its fate", the settlers who seized its land were armed at government expense: the uyezd rural superintendents[69] were ordered to "see to it that the peasants of the newly-established villages on the Mugan, including those from Pokrovskoye, were supplied with arms —ten Berdan rifles for each hundred households". This is an interesting illustration of the "nationalist course" of the present policy.

Nevertheless, Right-wing deputies to the Duma spoke triumphantly of the existence of a reserve for resettlement amounting to 1,700,000 dessiatines, citing the report of the Vice-Gerent of the Caucasus to this effect. However, according also to the testimony of the Vice-Gerent, nearly half of this reserve has already been taken over by settlers, while a considerable part of it is situated in areas where —according again to the Vice-Gerent's evidence —it is physically impossible for cultivators unaccustomed to the conditions to engage in farming.

Deputy Chkheidze also spoke of the way in which the government provides for the new settlers. "Inadequate water supply and lack of irrigation on the land set aside for resettlement," says the report of the Vice-Gerent, "particularly in the eastern areas of Transcaucasia, is one of the main reasons why many peasants already settled migrate back again. In the Black Sea region the new settlers are deserting their farms because of the absence of roads suitable for wheeled traffic not only between the various settlements, but even within each of the resettlement areas. To this it should be added that in their turn the unfavourable climatic conditions, to which the settlers are unaccustomed and which are attended in many parts of the Caucasus by malaria that affects not only people but livestock as well, no less than the lack of roads, cause the less sturdy of the new settlers to flee from the Caucasus. Due to the above-mentioned causes there is a continuous migration in evidence from the Yelisavetpol and Baku gubernias and from Daghestan Region, as well as from the Tiflis and Black Sea gubernias."

The upshot is that the results of the resettlement in the Caucasus are assessed by the Vice-Gerent himself as follows: "The attitude taken so far to the Caucasian population and its land affairs can no longer be tolerated, if only because it undoubtedly plays a rather prominent part in fostering revolutionary sentiments among the rural population."

The government and the ruling classes are pursuing very similar aims in settling peasants in Siberia; here, too, in view of the political objectives involved, no consideration whatever is given either to the interests of the settlers or to the rights of the old residents.

In the emigration areas, in Russia, resettlement matters have now been entrusted to the land committees, the rural superintendents and the governors. Vitally interested as they are in reducing the number of peasants with little or no land and in leaving only as many of them as are needed to provide for the requirements of the big landowners (as a source of supply of wage-labour), the land committees have shown such zeal in "moving" poor peasants as to shock even the Resettlement Department. "The land committees," complained one official of the Department, "form parties of completely destitude people who at the outset need an allowance for their travelling expenses, who need a loan not for setting up a home but for food; and even if, as an exception, a settler happens to have some little money, he spends it all on fares and food."

Swarms of these "weak" foster-children of the land policy which proclaimed as its motto "stake on the strong" are being sent off to Siberia in unaltered cattle wagons, packed chock-full with old men, children, pregnant women. In these cattle wagons (which bear the famous inscription: "40 men, 8 horses"), the emigrants have to cook their food and wash their linen; lying in them, too, are often persons afflicted with contagious diseases, whom the emigrants usually keep out of sight lest they be removed from the train and thus fall behind the party. At terminal points and stations the emigrants are at best provided with tents; in the worst cases they are left in the open, with no shelter from sun or rain. Deputy Voiloshnikov told the Duma that at Sretensk he had seen people stricken with typhus lying in the open, with no protection from the rain. And conditions such as those described above, under which the peasants have to travel, two Ministers (Stolypin and Krivoshein) find to be "tolerable". "The sanitary conditions provided for the settlers on their way are tolerable," they wrote in a report to the Emperor; "many of them even find conveniences en route to which they have not been accustomed." Truly, there is no limit to bureaucratic complacency!

After going through such ordeals on their way to "the

promised land", the poorest emigrants find no happiness in Siberia either. Here, for instance, is how Deputy Voiloshnikov described their condition in the new places of settlement by quoting from official reports.

One official (a special inspector of the Resettlement Department) writes: "Most of the lots are scattered among taiga forests without water, without ploughland, and without pastures." Another adds: "The granting of loans has entirely lost its significance as a means for setting up homes; the amount of the loans is in itself too small to be of real help in this respect. The established procedure of granting loans has turned the latter into a matter of charity pure and simple, for it is impossible to set up a home and live for two years on the 150 rubles granted as a loan."

And here, by way of example, is a description of the sanitary conditions of the new settlers, quoted from the same official reports:

"After the typhus," writes one official,* "scurvy has been raging here on a no lesser scale; practically in all the settlements and in every house there are people suffering from this disease or liable to contract it. In many homes there are cases of both diseases. In the Okur-Shask settlement I came across the following picture: the master of the house was ill with typhus in the period of peeling; his pregnant wife was extremely exhausted from undernourishment; their son, a boy of twelve, had swollen glands and scurvy; the wife's sister was sick with scurvy and could not walk; she had a breast-fed baby; her ten-year-old boy was sick with scurvy, was bleeding through the nose and could hardly move; her husband alone, of the whole family, was well.

"Scurvy and typhus are followed by night blindness. There are settlements in which literally all the settlers, without exception, suffer from this blindness. The groups of lots along the Yemna River are covered almost entirely with taiga forests, have no pastures or meadowland, and in the course of two or three years the new settlers barely managed to clear the ground to build wretched huts. There could be no question of the settlers having their own grain; they had to live entirely on the loans, and when these gave out there was a terrible scarcity of bread; many literally starved. The scarcity of bread was aggravated by the scarcity of drinking water."

Such reports are plentiful. Appalling as these official accounts are, they apparently do not tell the whole truth, and

---

* *Memorandum*, p. 8

4*

thus give too favourable a picture of the actual state of affairs. Here is, for instance, how Prince Lvov, a man, as we know, of moderate views, who visited the Far East as a representative of the Zemstvo organisation, describes resettlement in Amur Territory:

"Cut off from the world as if they were on an uninhabited island, amid marshy hummocks in the primeval taiga, amid swampy valleys and swampy hills, and forced to put up with barbaric conditions of life, labour and subsistence, the dispirited and indigent settler naturally feels crushed. He lapses into a state of apathy, having exhausted his small store of energy at the very beginning of his struggle against harsh natural conditions in setting up his wretched dwelling. Scurvy and typhus attack the wasted organism and carry it off to the grave. In many of the settlements founded in 1907, the death rate is simply incredible—25 to 30 per cent. There are as many crosses as there are households, and many settlements are doomed to be removed completely to new sites or to the grave-yard. Instead of resettlement, what rivers of bitter tears shed by unhappy families and what costly funerals at state expense in the remote borderland! It will be long before those who survived last year's great wave of resettlement will stand on their feet again after their defeat in the taiga. Many will die, and many others will flee back to Russia, where they will defame the territory by stories about their misfortunes, scaring off new settlers and holding up further resettlement. It is not accidental that this year we witness an unprecedented reverse movement from the Maritime Region, and an influx of new settlers that is one-fifth of the former proportion."

Prince Lvov is justly appalled by the isolation of the settler from the world and his desolation in the boundless Siberian taiga, particularly in view of the lack of roads in Siberia. We can imagine with what brilliant success the policy of setting up separate homestead farms and the apportionment of *otrubs* is now being put into effect there, for the very same men who direct the agrarian policy have proclaimed "the necessity for a decisive turn [!] in the land policy in Siberia", the necessity of "establishing and promoting private property", of "ensuring that individual peasants have their plots in accordance with the decree of November 9, 1906", "assigning lots for resettlement, with the land divided, as far as possible, into *otrub* holdings",* etc.

The conditions of resettlement being what they are, it is quite natural that, according to the Resettlement Depart-

---

* *Memorandum*, pp. 60, 61, 62.

ment, 10 per cent of the peasants settled in 1903-05 owned not a single draught animal, 12 per cent owned only one draught animal per household, 15 per cent owned no cow, and 25 per cent owned no plough (from the speech of Deputy Gaidarov during the First Session, when he spoke on behalf of the Social-Democratic group). Deputy Voiloshnikov, basing himself on the same official reports, was therefore fully justified when he summed up the results of the resettlement policy in 1906-08 as follows:

"In three years—1906, 1907 and 1908—1,552,439 persons of both sexes, half of them paupers, lured by the government's advertising, were sent across the Urals, into unknown parts, and there left to their fate. According to the Resettlement Department, 564,041 persons settled down, and 284,984 persons of both sexes went back. Thus the Resettlement Department provides information about 849,025 persons. But what has become of the rest? Where are the other 703,414 persons? The government, gentlemen, is perfectly well informed of their bitter lot, but it will say nothing about them. Some of them have gone to live in the villages of the old residents, and some others have swollen the ranks of the Siberian proletariat and are begging for alms.

"As for the vast majority, the government arranged a costly funeral for them, and that is why it keeps silent about them."

That is how the hopes of Markov the Second to "solve the agrarian problem" through resettlement are materialising. Faced with these facts, even the Octobrist spokesmen of big capital had to admit that there are "defects in the resettlement work". During the First Session the Octobrists called (and the Duma supported them) for "changing and improving the travelling conditions of the emigrants", for "creating in the resettlement areas the conditions necessary for their cultural and economic development", and for "respecting the interests and rights of the local peasantry and the non-Russian population when apportioning the land and settling the peasants". It goes without saying that these cautious and deliberately ambiguous wishes have to this day remained "a voice crying in the wilderness". And the Octobrist woodpeckers patiently repeat them year after year.

Nevskaya Zvezda No. 11,
June 3, 1912
Signed: *V. I.*

Published according
to the text in *Nevskaya Zvezda*

THE REVOLUTIONARY UPSWING[70]

The great May Day strike of the proletariat of all Russia and the accompanying street demonstrations, revolutionary leaflets, and revolutionary speeches before gatherings of workers have clearly shown that Russia has entered a period of revolutionary upswing.

This upswing did not come as a bolt from the blue. The way had been paved for it over a long period by all the conditions of Russian life, and the mass strikes over the Lena shootings and the May Day strikes merely marked its actual arrival. The temporary triumph of the counter-revolution was inseparably bound up with a decline in the mass struggle of the workers. The number of strikers gives an approximate yet absolutely objective and precise idea of the extent of the struggle.

During the ten years preceding the revolution, from 1895 to 1904, the average number of strikers was 43,000 a year (in round figures). In 1905 there were 2,750,000 strikers, in 1906—1,000,000, and in 1907—750,000. The three years of the revolution were distinguished by a rise in the strike movement of the proletariat *unprecedented anywhere in the world*. Its decline, which began in 1906-07, became definite in 1908, when there were 175,000 strikers. The coup d'état of June 3, 1907, which restored the autocratic rule of the tsar in alliance with the Duma of the Black-Hundred landlords and the commercial and industrial magnates, was an inevitable result of the flagging of the revolutionary energy of the masses.

The three years 1908-10 were a period of Black-Hundred counter-revolution at its worst, of liberal-bourgeois renegacy and of proletarian despondency and disintegration.

The number of strikers steadily dropped, reaching 60,000 in 1909 and 50,000 in 1910.

However, a noticeable change set in at the end of 1910. The demonstrations in connection with the death of the liberal Muromtsev, and of Leo Tolstoy, and also the student movement, clearly indicated that a fresh breeze had begun to blow, that the mood of the democratic masses had reached a turning-point. The year 1911 saw the workers gradually going over to an *offensive*—the number of strikers rose to 100,000. Signs from various quarters indicate that the weariness and stupor brought about by the·triumph of the counter-revolution are passing away, that once again there is an *urge* for revolution. In summing up the situation, the All-Russia Conference, held in January 1912, noted that "the onset of a political revival is to be noted among broad democratic circles, chiefly among the proletariat. The workers' strikes in 1910-11, the beginning of demonstrations and proletarian meetings, the start of a movement among urban bourgeois democrats (the student strikes), etc., are all indications of the growing revolutionary feelings of the masses against the June Third regime". (See the "Notification" of the Conference, p. 18.*)

By the second quarter of this year these sentiments had become so strong that they manifested themselves in actions by the masses, and brought about a *revolutionary upswing*. The course of events during the past eighteen months shows with perfect clarity that there is nothing accidental in this upswing, that it has come quite naturally and was made inevitable by the whole development of Russia in the previous period.

The Lena shootings led to the revolutionary temper of the masses developing into a revolutionary upswing of the masses. Nothing could be more false than the liberal invention, which Trotsky repeats in the Vienna *Pravda* after the liquidators, that "the struggle for freedom of association is the *basis* of both the Lena tragedy and the powerful response to it in the country". Freedom of association was neither the specific nor the principal demand in the Lena strike. It was not lack of the freedom of association that the Lena

---

* See present edition, Vol. 17, p. 467.—*Ed.*

shootings revealed, but lack of freedom from provocation, lack of rights in general, lack of freedom from wholesale tyranny.

The Lena shootings, as we have already made clear in *Sotsial-Demokrat*[71] No. 26, were an exact reflection of the *entire* regime of the June Third monarchy. It was not at all the struggle for one of the *rights* of the proletariat, even the most fundamental, the most important of them, that was characteristic of the Lena events. What was characteristic of those events was the complete absence of *any* kind of elementary legality. The characteristic feature was that an *agent provocateur*, a spy, a secret police agent, a menial of the tsar, resorted to mass shootings without any political reason whatever. It is this general lack of rights typical of Russian life, this hopelessness and impossibility of fighting for particular *rights*, and this incorrigibility of the tsarist monarchy and of its entire regime, that stood out so distinctly against the background of the Lena events as to *fire* the masses with *revolutionary* ardour.

The liberals have been straining every nerve to represent the Lena events and the May Day strikes as a trade union movement and a struggle for "rights". But anyone who is not blinded by liberal (and liquidationist) controversies will see in them something different. He will see the *revolutionary* character of the mass strike, which is especially emphasised by the St. Petersburg May Day leaflet of various Social-Democratic groups (and even of one group of worker Socialist-Revolutionaries!), which we reprint in full in our news section,[72] and which repeats the slogans advanced by the All-Russia Conference of the R.S.D.L.P. in January 1912.

And then, it is not really slogans that are the main proof of the revolutionary character of the Lena and May Day strikes. The slogans *formulated* what the facts showed. The mass strikes spreading from district to district, their tremendous growth, the speed with which they spread, the courage of the workers, the increased number of mass meetings and revolutionary speeches, the demand that the fines imposed for celebrating May Day be cancelled, and the combination of the political and the economic strike, familiar to us from the time of the first Russian revolution, are all obvious indications of the true nature of the movement, which is *a revolutionary upswing of the masses.*

Let us recall the experience of 1905. Events show that the *tradition* of the revolutionary mass strike *lives on* among the workers and that the workers at once took up and revived this tradition. The strike wave of 1905, unprecedented in the world, involved 810,000 strikers during the first, and 1,277,000 during the last quarter of the year, being a combination of the political and the economic strike. According to tentative estimates, the strikes over the Lena events involved about 300,000 workers and the May Day strikes about 400,000, and the strike movement continues to grow. Every day the newspapers, even the liberal ones, bring news of how the wildfire of strikes is spreading. The second quarter of 1912 is not quite over, and yet it is already becoming quite obvious that, as regards the size of the strike movement, the beginning of the revolutionary upswing in 1912 is not *lower, but rather higher* than the beginning in 1905!

The Russian revolution was the first to develop on a large scale this proletarian method of agitation, of rousing and uniting the masses and of drawing them into the struggle. Now the proletariat is applying this method once again and with an even firmer hand. No power on earth could achieve what the revolutionary vanguard of the proletariat is achieving by this method. A huge country, with a population of 150,000,000 spread over a vast area, scattered, oppressed, deprived of all rights, ignorant, fenced off from "evil influences" by a swarm of authorities, police, spies —the *whole* of this country is getting into a ferment. The most backward sections both of the workers and the peasants are coming into direct or indirect contact with the strikers. Hundreds of thousands of revolutionary agitators are all at once appearing on the scene. Their influence is infinitely increased by the fact that they are inseparably linked with the rank and file, with the masses, and that they remain among them, fight for the most urgent needs of *every* worker's family, and combine with this immediate struggle for urgent economic needs their political protest and struggle against the monarchy. For counter-revolution has stirred up in millions and tens of millions of people a bitter hatred for the monarchy, it has given them the rudiments of an understanding of the part played by it, and now the slogan of the foremost workers of the capital—long live the democratic republic!—spreads through thousands of channels, in the wake of every strike, reaching the backward sections, the remotest provinces, the "people", the "depths of Russia"!

Very characteristic are the comments made on strikes by Severyanin, a liberal, which were welcomed by *Russkiye Vedomosti* and sympathetically reprinted by *Rech*:

> "Have the workers any grounds for admixing economic or any [!] demands to a May Day strike?" asks Mr. Severyanin; and he answers: "I make bold to think that they have none. Every economic strike can and should be begun only after a serious weighing of its chances of success.... That is why, more often than not, it is unreasonable to link such strikes with May Day.... Indeed, it would be rather strange to do so: we are celebrating the international workers' holiday, and we use the occasion to demand a ten per cent rise for calico of such-and-such grades."

That is how the liberal reasons! And this piece of infinite vulgarity, meanness and nastiness is sympathetically accepted by the "best" liberal papers, which claim to be democratic!

The crudest self-interest of a bourgeois, the vilest cowardice of a counter-revolutionary—that is what lies behind the florid phrases of the liberal. He wants the pockets of the employers to be safe. He wants an "orderly" and "harmless" demonstration in favour of "freedom of association"! But the proletariat, instead of this, is drawing the masses into a *revolutionary* strike, which indissolubly links politics with economics, a strike which wins the support of the most backward sections by the success of the struggle for an immediate improvement in the life of the workers, and at the same time rouses the people *against the tsarist monarchy*.

Yes, the experience of 1905 created a deep-rooted and great tradition of mass strikes. And we must not forget the results that these strikes produce in Russia. Stubborn mass strikes are inseparably bound up in our country with *armed uprising*.

Let these words not be misinterpreted. It is by no means a question of a *call* for an uprising. Such a call would be most unwise at the present moment. It is a question of establishing the *connection* between strike and uprising in Russia.

How did the uprising *grow* in 1905? Firstly, mass strikes, demonstrations and meetings made clashes between the people and the police and troops more and more frequent. Secondly, the mass strikes roused the peasantry to a number of partial, fragmentary, semi-spontaneous revolts. Thirdly, the mass strikes very soon spread to the Army and Navy, causing clashes on economic grounds (the "bean" and similar "mutinies"), and subsequently insurrections. Fourthly, the counter-revolution *itself* started civil war by pogroms, by violence against democrats, and so on.

The revolution of 1905 was defeated not because it had gone "too far", or because the December uprising[73] was "artificial", as renegades among the liberals, and their like imagine. On the contrary, the cause of the defeat was that the uprising did *not* go *far enough*, that the realisation of its necessity was not sufficiently widespread and firmly assimilated among the revolutionary classes, that the uprising was not concerted, resolute, organised, simultaneous, aggressive.

Let us see now whether signs of a *gathering revolt* are in evidence at present. In order not to be carried away by revolutionary enthusiasm, let us take the testimony of the *Octobrists*. The German Union of Octobrists in St. Petersburg consists mainly of so-called "Left" and "constitutional" Octobrists, who are particularly popular among the Cadets, and who are most capable (in comparison with the other Octobrists and Cadets) of observing events "objectively", without making it their aim to frighten the authorities with the prospect of revolution.

Here is what the *St.-Petersburger Zeitung*, the newspaper of these Octobrists, wrote in its weekly political review on May 6 (19):

"May has come. Regardless of the weather, this is usually not a very pleasant month for the inhabitants of the capital, because it begins with the *proletarian 'holiday'*. This year, with the impression of the Lena demonstrations still fresh in the minds of the workers, May Day was particularly dangerous. The atmosphere of the capital, saturated with all sorts of rumours about strikes and demonstrations, portended a fire. Our loyal police were visibly agitated; they organised searches, arrested some persons and mobilised large forces to prevent street demonstrations. The fact that the police could think of nothing more clever than to raid the editorial offices of the workers' papers

and arrest their editors does not testify to a particularly intimate
knowledge of the wires by which the puppet regiments of the workers
were pulled. Yet such wires exist. This is evident from the disciplined
character of the strike and from many other circumstances. That
is why this May Day strike, the largest we have witnessed so far,
was so ominous—there were some 100,000 or perhaps even 150,000
workers of big and small workshops on strike. It was only a peaceful
parade, but the solid unity of that army was remarkable, all the
more because the recent unrest among the workers was accompanied
by other alarming facts. On various naval vessels, *sailors* were arrested for conducting revolutionary propaganda. Judging by all the
information that has got into the press, the situation is not very good
on our naval vessels, which are not numerous as it is.... The *rail-
waymen* are also giving cause for anxiety. True, matters nowhere
went so far as an attempt to call a strike, but arrests, including such
a conspicuous one as that of A. A. Ushakov, an assistant station master on the Nikolayevskaya Railway, show that there is a certain
danger there as well.

"Attempts at revolution on the part of immature worker masses
can, of course, have only a harmful effect on the outcome of the Duma
elections. These attempts are all the more unreasonable because the
Tsar has appointed Manukhin, and the Council of State has passed
the workers' Insurance Bill"!!

That is how a German Octobrist reasons. We, on our part,
must remark that we have received exact first-hand information about the sailors which proves that *Novoye Vremya*
has exaggerated and inflated the matter. The Okhrana[74]
is obviously "working" in *agent provocateur* fashion. Premature attempts at an uprising would be extremely unwise.
The working-class vanguard must understand that the support of the working class by the democratic peasantry and
the active participation of the armed forces are the main
conditions for a timely, i.e., successful, armed uprising in
Russia.

Mass strikes in revolutionary epochs have their objective
logic. They scatter hundreds of thousands and millions of
sparks in all directions—and all around there is the inflammable material of extreme bitterness, the torture of unprecedented starvation, endless tyranny, shameless and cyni-
cal mockery at the "pauper", the "muzhik", the rank-and-
file soldier. Add to this the perfectly unbridled, pogromist
Jew-baiting carried on by the Black Hundreds and stealthily fostered and directed by the Court gang of the dull-
witted and bloodthirsty Nicholas Romanov. "So it was, so
it will be"[75]—these revealing words were uttered by the

Minister Makarov, to his own misfortune, and to the misfortune of his class and his landlord tsar!

The revolutionary upswing of the masses imposes great and responsible duties on every working-class Social-Democrat, on every honest democrat. "All-round support for the movement of the masses that is beginning [we should say already: the *revolutionary* movement of the masses that *has begun*], and its expansion on the basis of full implementation of the Party slogans"—this is how the All-Russia Conference of the R.S.D.L.P. defined these duties. The Party slogans—a democratic republic, an eight-hour day, confiscation of all the landed estates—must become the slogans of *all* democrats, of the *people's* revolution.

To be able to support and extend the movement of the masses, we need *organisation and more organisation.* Without an illegal party we cannot carry on this work, and there is no point in just talking about it. In supporting and extending the onslaught of the masses, we must carefully take into account the experience of 1905, and in explaining the need for and inevitability of an uprising, we must warn against and keep off *premature* attempts. The growth of mass strikes, the enlistment of other classes in the struggle, the state of the organisations, and the temper of the masses will all suggest of themselves the moment when all forces must unite in a concerted, resolute, aggressive, supremely courageous onslaught of the revolution on the tsarist monarchy.

Without a victorious revolution there will be no freedom in Russia.

Without the overthrow of the tsarist monarchy by a proletarian and peasant uprising there will be no victorious revolution in Russia.

Sotsial-Demokrat No. 27,
June 17 (4), 1912

Published according
to the text in *Sotsial-Demokrat*

THE SLOGANS OF THE ALL-RUSSIA CONFERENCE OF THE R.S.D.L.P. IN JANUARY 1912 AND THE MAY DAY MOVEMENT

Elsewhere in this issue, the reader will find the full text of a leaflet printed and circulated by the St. Petersburg workers before the May Day action that will from now on be famous. That leaflet is very much worth dwelling on, for it is a most important document in the history of the working-class movement in Russia and in the history of our Party.

The leaflet reflects *a certain* state of disorganisation of the Social-Democratic Party in the capital, for the appeal is signed, not by the St. Petersburg Committee, but by individual Social-Democratic groups and even a group of worker Socialist-Revolutionaries. In most parts of Russia, the state of our Party is such that its directing committees and centres are constantly being arrested, and constantly re-establish themselves thanks to the existence of all kinds of factory, trade union, sub-district and district Social-Democratic groups—the very same "nuclei" that have always roused the hatred of the liberals and liquidators. In the latest issue of the magazine published by those gentlemen (*Nasha Zarya*, 1912, No. 4), the reader can see again and again how Mr. V. Levitsky, writing with impotent rage and *vomiting* abuse, hisses against the "rebirth of the Party through an artificial revival of politically dead nuclei".

What makes the leaflet under review all the more typical and noteworthy is the fact that, owing to the arrest of the St. Petersburg Committee, it was the *nuclei* that had to appear on the scene, nuclei deprived by the will of the police of the "directing centre" so hateful to the liquidators. Owing to this fact, which every revolutionary will find sad, the *independent* life of the nuclei came into the open. The nuclei had in all haste to rally their forces, establish contacts, and restore the *"underground"* in the face of fierce persecution by the police, who positively raged before May Day. The groups, representatives, etc., whose names appear under the leaflet, all constitute that very *underground* that is hateful to the liberals and the liquidators. While the same liquidationist leader, Mr. Levitsky, speaking on behalf of *Nasha Zarya* and *Zhivoye Dyelo*, of course assailed, foaming at the mouth, the *"cult of the underground"* (see p. 33 of the above-mentioned issue), we had, in the shape of the St. Petersburg leaflet, a precise and complete document revealing to us the existence of that underground, its vitality, the *content* of its work, and its significance.

The St. Petersburg Committee has been wiped out through the arrests, so now we shall see just what the underground nuclei are like in themselves, what they are doing or can do, what ideas they have actually made their own or evolved in their midst, and not merely borrowed from the supreme Party body, what ideas really enjoy the workers' sympathy.

The leaflet shows what the nuclei are doing: they are carrying on the work of the St. Petersburg Committee, which for the time being is shattered (to the delight of all the diverse enemies of the underground). They continue preparing for May Day. They hastily re-establish the contacts between *different* underground Social-Democratic groups. They enlist worker Socialist-Revolutionaries too, for they are well aware of the importance of uniting the proletariat round a living revolutionary cause. They rally these different Social-Democratic groups, and even a "group of worker Socialist-Revolutionaries", round *specific* slogans of the struggle. And this is when the real *character* of the movement, the real *sentiment* of the proletariat, the real *strength* of the R.S.D.L.P. and of *its January* All-Russia Conference, stands out.

As a result of the arrests, there happens to be no hierarchic body able to decree the advancing of particular slogans. Hence the proletarian masses, the worker Social-Democrats and even some of the Socialist-Revolutionaries can be united *only* by slogans that are really indisputable for the masses, only by slogans that derive their strength not from a "decree from above" (as demagogues and liquidators put it), but from the *conviction* of the revolutionary workers themselves.

And what do we find?

We find that, *after* the St. Petersburg Committee had been shattered, at a time when its immediate restoration was impossible, and when one group of workers influenced another group solely by ideological, and not by organisational, means, *the slogans adopted were those of the All-Russia Conference of the R.S.D.L.P. which was convened in January 1912* and which evokes a positively mad, savage hatred on the part of the liberals, the liquidators, Lieber, Trotsky and Co.!

"Let our slogans be," the St. Petersburg workers wrote in their leaflet, "a constituent assembly, an eight-hour working day, the confiscation of the landed estates." And further on the leaflet launches the call: "Down with the tsarist government! Down with the autocratic Constitution of June 3! Long live the democratic republic! Long live socialism!"

We see from this instructive document that *all* the slogans put forward by the Conference of the R.S.D.L.P. have been adopted by the St. Petersburg proletariat and have set their seal on the first steps of the new Russian revolution. All kinds of slanderers and detractors of the January Conference may carry on their dirty business as much as they like. The revolutionary proletariat of St. Petersburg has answered them. The work started long before the last Conference by revolutionary Social-Democrats, calling on the proletariat to assume the role of leader of the *people's* revolution, has borne fruit despite all police persecution, despite the reckless pre-May Day arrests and hounding of revolutionaries, despite the torrent of lies and abuse from the liberal and liquidationist press.

Hundreds of thousands of St. Petersburg proletarians, followed by workers throughout Russia, resorted to strikes and street demonstrations not as one of the separate classes of bourgeois society, not with "their own" merely economic slogans, but as the leader raising aloft the banner of the revolution *for* the whole people, *on behalf of* the whole people, and *with the aim of* awakening and drawing into the

struggle *all* the classes who need freedom and are capable
of striving for it.

The revolutionary movement of the proletariat in Russia
has risen to a higher level. Whereas in 1905 it began with
mass strikes and Gaponiads,[76] in 1912, despite the fact that
the police has smashed our Party organisations, the movement is beginning with mass strikes and the *raising of the
republican banner*! The separate "nuclei" and disconnected
"groups" of workers did their duty under the most difficult
and trying conditions. The proletariat set up its own "May
Day committees" and went into action with a *revolutionary*
platform worthy of the class which is destined to free mankind from wage slavery.

The May Day movement also shows what meaning some
words about "unity" have and how the workers unite *in
reality*. Rubanovich, a spokesman for the Socialist-Revolutionary Party, writes in *Budushcheye*,[77] Burtsev's Paris
newspaper, that "we must point out the following noteworthy feature of this May Day action: at the preparatory
meetings, St. Petersburg workers refused to recognise the
division existing among the various socialist groups; ...
the prevailing tendency was towards agreement". The leaflet
we have reprinted clearly shows what *fact* prompted such
an inference. The fact is that the Social-Democratic nuclei,
which had lost their guiding centre, re-established contact
with all the various groups by winning over workers regardless of the views they held and *advocating to them all* their
Party slogans. And precisely because these Party slogans
are correct, because they are in keeping with the proletariat's
revolutionary tasks and comprise the tasks of a revolution
of the whole people, they were accepted by *all* workers.

Unity materialised because the January Conference of
the R.S.D.L.P. gave up the idle game of bringing about
agreement among small groups abroad, gave up the idle
wooing of the liquidators of the revolutionary party, and
put forward clear and precise fighting slogans *at the right
time*. The proletariat's unity for revolutionary action was
achieved not by compromising between the proletarian
(Social-Democratic) and the non-proletarian (Socialist-
Revolutionary) parties, not by seeking agreement with
the liquidators who have broken away from the Social-

Democratic Party, but by rallying the workers of Russian Social-Democratic organisations and by these workers making a correct appraisal of the tasks of the moment.

A good lesson for those who, succumbing to the idle chatter of the liberals of the Bund and the Trotskys from Vienna, are still capable of believing in "unity"—with the liquidators. The vaunted "Organising Commission" of Lieber, Trotsky and the liquidators cried out from the house-tops about "unity", but in fact it could not, and did not, supply *a single* slogan actually uniting the revolutionary struggle of the workers. The liquidators supplied *their own*, non-revolutionary slogans, slogans of a liberal labour policy, but the movement disregarded them. That is what lies at the bottom of the Trotskyist fables about "unity"!

Swearing and vowing that he was "unifying", and cursing the Conference as hard as he could, Trotsky assured good souls in Vienna on April 23 (May 6) that "the struggle for freedom of association is the *basis*" (!!) of the Lena events and of their repercussions, that "this demand is, and will be, the *central* [!!] issue of the revolutionary mobilisation of the proletariat". Scarcely a week had passed when these pitiful phrases of the yes-man of the liquidators were swept away like so much dust—by the "representatives of all the organised workers of St. Petersburg", "the Social-Democratic Obyedineniye group", "the central Social-Democratic city group", "the group of worker Socialist-Revolutionaries", "the group of worker Social-Democrats" and "the representatives of May Day committees".

The Social-Democratic proletariat of St. Petersburg has realised that a new revolutionary struggle must be started, not for the sake of one right, even though it should be the most essential, the most important for the working class, but for the sake of *the freedom of the whole people*.

The Social-Democratic proletariat of St. Petersburg has realised that it must generalise its demands, and not break them up into parts, that the republic includes freedom of association, and not vice versa, that it is necessary to strike at the centre, to attack the source of evil, to destroy the whole system, the whole regime, of the Russia of the tsar and the Black Hundreds.

The Social-Democratic proletariat of St. Petersburg has realised that it is ridiculous and absurd to claim freedom of association *from* Nicholas Romanov, *from* the Black-Hundred Duma, that it is ridiculous and absurd to presume that Russia's present political system, our "autocratic Constitution of June 3", is *compatible with* freedom of association, that in a country where there is a general and indiscriminate lack of rights, where arbitrary rule and provocation by the authorities reign supreme, and where there is no "freedom" even for simply helping tens of millions of starving people—it is only liberal chatterers and liberal labour politicians that can put freedom of association as "the central issue of revolutionary mobilisation".

The Social-Democratic proletariat of St. Petersburg has realised that and unfurled the *republican* banner, demanding an eight-hour day and confiscation of the landed estates as the only guarantee of the truly democratic character of the revolution.

Sotsial-Demokrat No. 27,
June 17 (4), 1912

Published according
to the text in *Sotsial-Demokrat*

THE LIQUIDATORS
OPPOSE REVOLUTIONARY MASS STRIKES

The leading article of this issue had already gone to press when we received the first issue of the liquidationist *Nevsky Golos*. V. Yezhov, the well-known liquidator of *Nasha Zarya*, at once presented the new organ with such a gem that one is left gasping! Here it is, if you please:

"Owing to this [i.e., owing to the variety of the strikes, which in some cases did not go beyond a protest against the imposition of fines for celebrating May Day, while in other cases they supplemented the protest with economic demands, etc.], the principle involved in the protest (after all, it was not over a few kopeks that the strike was called) became obscured [!??!] in a considerable number of cases, being complicated by economic demands....

"Their own experience should have suggested to the workers that it was inadvisable [!!] to complicate their protest by economic demands, just as it is inadvisable to complicate [!?] an ordinary strike by demands involving principles.

"It is necessary to give organisational form to the sentiments of the worker masses. It is necessary to increase propaganda for trade unions, to recruit new members for them. This is all the more necessary since there are many hotheads among the workers nowadays who are carried away by the mass movement and speak at meetings *against unions*, alleging them to be useless and unnecessary.

"A period of economic strikes [only economic?] is ahead of us. It would be an irreparable mistake to allow them to become intertwined with political actions of the workers [!!!]. Such a combination would have a harmful effect [!!??] on both the economic and the political struggle."

Here you have the perfectly liberal Mr. Severyanin copied by the liquidator! Utter incomprehension of the fact that a *revolutionary* mass strike *necessarily* combines the economic with the political strike; narrow-mindedness, a monstrous distortion of the revolutionary character of the upswing and attempts to measure it by the yardstick of "ordinary strikes"; the most reactionary advice "not to complicate" politics with economics and not to "intertwine" them; and the using of the legally published press for an attack in the spirit of Struve and Maklakov against the revolutionary worker Social-Democrats, who are described as "hotheads" speaking out "against unions"!

A liberal *cannot* understand a revolutionary Social-Democrat except as one who is "against unions". But the workers at the meetings were, of course, not "against unions", but against *substituting* liberal slogans for revolutionary ones, which is what Mr. Yezhov and Co. are doing. Our slogan is not freedom of association, said the workers, and "trade unions" are not the only, nor the chief, means of "giving" our movement "organisational form". Our slogan is the demand for a republic (see the appeal of the St. Petersburg workers), we are building an *illegal* party capable of leading the revolutionary onslaught of the masses upon the tsarist monarchy. That is what the workers said at the meetings.

But the Liebers and Trotskys are assuring the workers that it is possible for the Social-Democratic proletariat and its Party to "unite" with liberals *à la* Yezhov, Potresov and Co.!

Sotsial-Demokrat No. 27,
June 17 (4), 1912

Published according
to the text in *Sotsial-Demokrat*

"UNITERS"

The liquidators are doing their utmost to "unite". The other day they almost "united" with the Polish Socialist Party[78] —with its Left wing (Lewica), which is a faction of Polish social-nationalism.

For more than ten years Polish Social-Democrats have been waging a struggle against the social-nationalism of the P.S.P. As a result, a section of the P.S.P. (the Left wing) had some of its nationalist prejudices knocked out of their heads. But the struggle continues. Polish worker Social-Democrats are *opposed* to unity with the above-mentioned faction of the P.S.P. as an organisation because they think it would be harmful to their cause. Individual workers and groups of the Left wing, who refuse to stop at a half-way revision of the nationalist principles of the P.S.P., are joining the ranks of the Social-Democratic Party. And this is the time when our liquidators are out to "unite" with the P.S.P. Left wing!

It is just as if the Russian Social-Democrats began, independently of the Bund, to "unite" with, say, so-called "Socialist-Zionists"[79] or, ignoring the Lettish Social-Democracy, with the so-called "Lettish Social-Democratic Union"[80] (actually a Socialist-Revolutionary organisation).

This is apart from the formal aspect of the matter. At the Stockholm Congress, the Polish Social-Democratic Party concluded an agreement with the R.S.D.L.P., by which any groups in Poland wishing to join the R.S.D.L.P. can do so only by joining an organisation of the P.S.D.[81] And at the All-Russia Conference of the R.S.D.L.P. held in December 1908, even a proposal to discuss the question of uniting with the Left wing was voted down by an overwhelming majority.

It is quite clear that, while constantly shouting about "unity", Trotsky and his liquidationist friends are actually *aggravating the split* in Poland. Fortunately for the R.S.D.L.P., this whole band of liquidators, together with the "conciliators" trailing behind them, is completely powerless to accomplish anything *in practice*, and this refers to Poland as well. Otherwise the amalgamation of the liquidators with the P.S.P. would certainly cause a very sharp split in Poland.

Why, then, have the liquidators embarked on this obviously adventurist policy? Certainly not because things are going well with them. The point is that they are in need of uniting with someone, of forming some sort of "party". Social-Democrats, the Polish Social-Democracy, refuse to go along with them, so, instead of Social-Democrats, they have to take members of the P.S.P., who have nothing in common with our Party. In the Russian towns, our old Party organisations refuse to go along with them, so they have to take, instead of the Social-Democratic nuclei, the so-called "initiating groups" of liquidators, who have nothing in common with the R.S.D.L.P.

"One does not fly from a good life." Is it not time, liquidator gentlemen, you started to unite with the Socialist-Revolutionaries (the Socialist-Revolutionary *liquidators*) as well? After all, these gentlemen, too, seem very anxious to "unite". What a "broad" party you would then have! Larin himself would be content.[82]

*   *

*

While "uniting" with "foreign powers", the liquidators continue to bargain with the "conciliators" over the terms of "uniting" the liquidator-conciliator camp. Mr. V. Levitsky contributed to *Nasha Zarya* an article which is a sort of manifesto addressed to "all trends" that are prepared to fight against the recent Conference of the R.S.D.L.P.

Mr. Levitsky entitled his article "For Unity—Against a Split". Quite like Trotsky, isn't it? Ever since the pro-Party elements thoroughly rebuffed the liquidators *in all* the spheres of activity, Levitsky and Co. have been using a very "conciliatory" language. Why, they are wholly in favour of "unity". They only advance the following four modest conditions for "unity":

(1) A fight against the Conference of the R.S.D.L.P., which has united all the Social-Democrats, except a handful of waverers.

(2) The formation, in place of the Party, of *"a central initiating group"* (Mr. Levitsky's italics, *Nasha Zarya* No. 4, p. 31). (What is meant by the liquidators' "initiating" groups has recently been explained in the press by Plekhanov — see his *Dnevnik Sotsial-Demokrata*[83] No. 16. Both the Bund and Trotsky, who are doing service for the liquidators, are concealing Plekhanov's explanation from their readers. But you can't conceal it, gentlemen!)

(3) No revival of the *"politically dead nuclei"* (ibid., p. 33).

(4) Acceptance of the slogan *"against the cult of the underground"* (ibid., p. 33).

The programme has been outlined clearly enough if not as frankly and confidently as in the past. And there and then Levitsky explains at great length to all the Trotskys: After all, gentlemen, you have no choice. You had better accept our terms, and in exchange we (i.e., Levitsky and Co.) will readily agree to the following: ·"to console yourselves", you (i.e., Trotsky and his like) can say that it is not you who have moved closer to the liquidators, but the other way round.

Martov, writing in the same issue of *Nasha Zarya*, threatens in advance the future Social-Democratic group in the Fourth Duma that if it turns out to be anti-liquidationist like its crafty predecessor, then "cases like the Belousov affair[84] will not be exceptions, but the rule", meaning, in plain language, that the liquidators will *split* the Duma group. Your bark, liquidator gentlemen, is worse than your bite. Had you had the strength to do so, you would long ago have formed your own liquidationist group in the Duma.

The cause of "unity" is in good hands, sure enough.

The miserable comedy of "unification" enacted by the liquidators and Trotsky is repellent to the least exacting people. Unity *is* being achieved, only it is not unity with the liquidators, but *against* them.

*　　*
*

As regards the incredibly Khlestakovian[85] role staged by Trotsky, Lieber (the Bund), and the liquidators, with their vaunted "Organising Commission", we think it sufficient to call the attention of the readers —those who prefer not to trust words but to verify the points at issue by a serious and careful study of the documents—to the following *facts*.

In June 1911, following the withdrawal of Lieber and Igorev from the meeting of the Central Committee members, the Organising Commission Abroad[86] was formed in Paris. The first organisation in Russia to be approached by it was the *Kiev* organisation. Even Trotsky admits that its status as an organisation is indisputable. In October 1911, the Kiev organisation took part in forming the Organising Commission in Russia. In January 1912 the latter convened the conference of the R.S.D.L.P.

In January 1912, a meeting was held by the representatives of the Bund, the Central Committee of the Letts and the Caucasian Regional Committee (all three being liquidationist groups). The Poles withdrew *at once*, declaring that the whole undertaking was a liquidationist affair. The "conciliators" and Plekhanov followed suit and *refused to join*, Plekhanov declaring in *Dnevnik Sotsial-Demokrata* No. 16 that *that* conference *was being called by the liquidators*. It is now June 1912, and yet neither the Bund nor Trotsky have succeeded in "uniting" *anyone*, except the *Golos* and the *Vperyod* groups; they have not won over a *single* serious and *indisputable* organisation in Russia, have not said a word to deny the substance of Plekhanov's statement, nor made the slightest change in the propaganda conducted by the liquidators in *Nasha Zarya* and similar press organs.

For all that, there is no end of phrase-mongering and bragging about "unity".

Sotsial-Demokrat No. 27,　　　　　Published according
　　June 17 (4), 1912　　　　　to the text in *Sotsial-Demokrat*

THE NATURE AND SIGNIFICANCE
OF OUR POLEMICS AGAINST THE LIBERALS

Mr. Prokopovich, a well-known advocate of revisionism and of a liberal labour policy, contributed to *Russkiye Vedomosti* an article entitled "Danger Ahead". The danger, according to this politician, is that the elections to the Fourth Duma will be shaped by the police chiefs. To combat this danger, he proposes "the unity of all the constitutionalist elements of the country", i.e., the Social-Democrats and the Trudoviks, as well as the Cadets and the Progressists.

The Right-Cadet *Russkiye Vedomosti* in an editorial note declares its *"satisfaction"* with Mr. Prokopovich's article. "Such unity of the opposition forces," it says, "we regard as an urgent requirement of the present moment."

The official-Cadet *Rech* gives a summary of Mr. Prokopovich's article and, quoting the opinion of *Russkiye Vedomosti*, comments for its own part:

"However, judging by the publications of the Social-Democratic trend, which bend all their energies mostly to fight the opposition, one can hardly attach any real importance to this appeal" (i.e., the appeal for "unity").

Thus the important question of the election tactics and the attitude of the workers to the liberals is being raised once more. Once again we see that the liberals pose this question not like serious politicians, but like matchmakers. Their aim is not to establish the truth, but to obscure it.

Indeed, ponder over the following circumstance. Do the liberals mean amalgamation of the parties when they speak of "unity"? Not in the least. Mr. Prokopovich, *Russkiye Vedomosti* and *Rech* are all agreed on this score.

Consequently, what they mean by unity is joint action against the Rights—from Purishkevich to Guchkov—is it not? It would seem that is so!

The question arises: does anyone among the "Lefts" reject such joint action?

No one does. That is common knowledge.

An agreement with the liberals to vote against the Rights is precisely what is meant by "unity" between the democrats and the liberals in the elections. Why, then, are the liberals dissatisfied? Why do they not say that the "Lefts" have quite definitely and explicitly declared in favour of agreements? Why are they so shy of mentioning the fact that *it is the liberals* who have *said nothing* clear, definite, explicit and official about agreements with the Lefts, with the democrats, with the Marxists? Why is it that, in speaking of the election tactics, they *do not say* a word about the well-known decision of the Cadet conference, which permitted of blocs with the "Left Octobrists"?

The facts are there, gentlemen, and no amount of dodging can alter them. It is the Lefts, the Marxists, that have declared, clearly, explicitly and officially, *in favour of* an agreement with the liberals (including both the Cadets and the Progressists) against the Rights. And it is *none other than the Cadets* who have evaded a quite explicit and official answer regarding the Lefts!

Mr. Prokopovich knows these facts very well, and it is therefore absolutely unpardonable on his part to distort the truth by keeping silent about the explicit decision of the Marxists and the evasiveness of the Cadets.

What is the reason for this silence? It is only too obvious from the quoted statement of *Rech* alleging that we "bend all our energies mostly to fight the opposition".

From the wording used by *Rech*, it follows inevitably that if they want to unite with the liberals, the democrats *must not* "bend all their energies" to fight the opposition. But in that case say so plainly, gentlemen! State your terms explicitly and officially. The trouble with you, however, is that you *cannot* do so. You would merely make everyone laugh if you tried to formulate such a condition. By putting forward such a condition you would refute yourselves, for you have all of you unanimously admitted that there are

"*profound differences*" between the liberals and the democrats (to say nothing of the Marxists).

And since there are differences, and profound ones at that,
how is it possible to avoid fighting?

The falsity of the liberals is precisely that, on the one
hand, they reject amalgamation, acknowledge the existence
of profound differences, emphasise that it is impossible
"for any of the parties to renounce the fundamental provisions of its programme" (*Russkiye Vedomosti*), and, on the
other hand, they *complain* of the "fight against the opposition"!!

But let us examine the matter more closely. To begin
with, is it true that the newspapers and magazines, to which
Rech refers, bend *all* their energies *mostly* to fight the opposition? No, far from it. The liberals cannot point to a single
question, not one, in which the democrats do not bend *all*
their energies *mostly* to fight the Rights!! Let anyone of you
who wishes to check this statement make a test. Let him
take any, say, three successive issues of any Marxist newspaper. Let him take three political questions as test cases and
compare the *documentary* data showing against whom the
fight of the Marxists on the questions selected is mostly
"directed" in those newspaper issues.

You will not make that simple and easy test, liberal gentlemen, because *any* such test will prove you wrong.

Nor is that all. There is another, and particularly important, consideration which refutes you even more strongly.
How do the democrats in general, and the Marxists in particular, *carry on* their fight against the liberals? They carry
it on in such a way, and only in such a way, that each —
positively and absolutely each—reproach or accusation
levelled at the liberals naturally involves an *even sharper*
reproach, an *even graver* accusation levelled at the Rights.

That is the gist of the matter, the crux of the issue! A few
examples will make our idea quite clear.

We accuse the liberals, the Cadets, of being counter-
revolutionary. Show us a *single* one of our accusations of
this kind that does not reflect with even greater force upon
the Rights.

We accuse the liberals of "nationalism" and "imperialism". Show us a single one of our accusations of this kind

that is not directed with even greater force against the Rights.

We have accused the liberals of being afraid of the movement of the masses. Now can you find in our newspapers a formulation of this accusation such as is not directed against the Rights as well?

We have accused the liberals of defending "certain" medieval institutions that are capable of "operating" against the workers. To accuse the liberals of *that* means accusing *thereby* all the Rights of the same thing, and of even more.

These examples can be multiplied indefinitely. You will find that always and everywhere, without any exception, the working-class democrats accuse the liberals exclusively for being close to the Rights, for the irresolute and *fictitious* nature of their fight against the Rights, for their half-heartedness, *thereby* accusing the Rights, not merely of "half a sin", but of a "whole sin".

"The fight against the liberals" waged by the democrats and the Marxists is more profound, more consistent and richer in content, and it does more to enlighten and rally the masses, than the *fight against the Rights.* That, gentlemen, is how matters stand!

And in order not to leave any doubts on this score, in order to forestall any absurd distortion of the meaning and significance of our fight against the liberals—to forestall, for example, the absurd theory of "one reactionary mass" (i.e., the lumping together of the liberals and the Rights in the single political concept of a reactionary bloc, of a reactionary mass)—we always take care, in our official statements, to speak of the fight against the Rights in terms *different* from those we use in speaking of our fight against the liberals.

Mr. Prokopovich knows this very well, as does every educated liberal. He knows, for instance, that in our definition of the social, class nature of the various parties, we always stress the medievalism of the Rights and the bourgeois nature of the liberals. And there is a world of difference between these two things. Medievalism can (and should) be destroyed, even keeping within the framework of capitalism. Bourgeois nature cannot be destroyed within this framework, but we can (and should) "appeal" from the bourgeois landlord to the bourgeois peasant, from the bourgeois liberal to the bourgeois democrat, from bourgeois half freedom to bourgeois full freedom. It is in such appeals, and only in such appeals, that our criticism of the liberals consists during the period Russia is passing through, i.e., the criticism which we are voicing from the standpoint of the immediate and next tasks of this period.

Take the following statement in Mr. Prokopovich's article. "The creation of sound conditions for the political life of the mass of the people—this is the immediate aim which at present unites the Lefts and the opposition."

Nothing could be more meaningless, more empty and misleading than this statement. Even an Octobrist, even an astute "nationalist", will subscribe to it, because it is so vague. It is a mere promise, sheer declamation, diplomatic concealment of one's thoughts. But if Mr. Prokopovich, like so many other liberals, has been given a tongue so that he may conceal his thoughts, we shall try to do our duty and reveal what is concealed behind his statement. To be on the safe side, let us take a minor example, something of rather little importance.

Is the two-chamber system a sound condition for political life? We do not think so. The Progressists and the Cadets think it is. For holding such views, we accuse the liberals of being anti-democratic, of being counter-revolutionary. And by formulating this accusation against the liberals, we level an even greater accusation at all the Rights.

Further, the question arises: How about "unity between the Lefts and the opposition"? Do we, on account of this difference of opinion, refuse to unite with a liberal against a Right? By no means. The counter-revolutionary views of the liberals on this question, as well as on all similar, *much more important* questions of political liberty, have been known to us for a long time—since 1905 or even earlier. Nevertheless, we repeat even in 1912 that both in a second ballot and at the second stage of the elections it is permissible to enter into agreements with the liberals against the Rights. For, despite its half-heartedness, bourgeois monarchist liberalism is not at all the same as feudal reaction. It would be very bad working-class politics not to take advantage of this difference.

But to proceed. *How* should we take advantage of it? *On what* terms is "unity between the Lefts and the opposition" possible? The answer of the liberal is: since the Lefts are waging a relentless fight against the opposition, there is no point in even talking of unity. And the liberal goes on to explain his idea as follows: the more modest the demand, the wider is the circle of those who agree with it, the more complete is the unity, and the greater the force capable of implementing that demand. A "tolerable" constitution providing for a two-chamber system (and other—how shall we put it mildly?—slight digressions from democracy) will have the support of all democrats and all liberals; that is a great deal. But if you insist on "pure" democracy, the Progressists will drop out, and you will also "alienate" many Cadets, with the result that the "constitutionalist elements" will be disunited and weakened.

That is how the liberal reasons. But we reason differently. Our main premise is that unless the masses are politically conscious there can be no change for the better. The liberal looks to the upper ranks, while we look to the "lower ranks". If we refrain from explaining the harm of the two-chamber system, or even relax ever so slightly the "fight" against all sorts of anti-democratic views on this question, we may "attract" the liberal landlord, merchant, lawyer, professor, who are all of a feather with Purishkevich, and can do nothing serious against the Purishkeviches. By "attracting" them, we alienate the masses—in the sense that the masses, to whom democracy is not just a diplomatic signboard, not a showy phrase, but their own vital cause, a question of life and death, would lose their confidence in the partisans of the two-chamber system; and also in the sense that relaxing the attacks on the two-chamber system implies inadequate political education of the masses, and unless the masses are politically conscious, wide-awake and full of determination, *no* changes for the better can be brought about.

The Cadets and the Prokopoviches tell us that by our polemics against the liberals we are driving a wedge between the Lefts and the opposition. Our answer is that consistent democracy repels the most wavering and unreliable liberals, those most tolerant to Purishkevichism—and they represent a mere handful; on the other hand, it attracts the millions now awakening to a new life, to a "sound political life", by which we mean something quite different from, something that is not at all the same as, that which Mr. Prokopovich means by it.

Instead of the two-chamber system, we might cite as an example the question of the composition of the land committees. Should influence in these committees be so divided as to give one-third to the landlords, one-third to the peasants and one-third to the bureaucrats, as the Cadets propose, or should they be elected quite freely, on the basis of a *fully* democratic electoral law? What, Mr. Prokopovich, are we to understand, in regard to this point, by "sound conditions for the political life of the mass of the people"? Whom will we repel and whom will we attract by adhering to a consistently democratic course on this question?

And let not *Russkiye Vedomosti* reply that "at present one point dominates over all the other points of the programme, a point common to all the progressive parties—the demand for political liberty". Precisely because this point *dominates*—and this is indisputable, it is gospel truth— there is a need for the widest masses, for millions upon millions of people, to distinguish between half freedom and freedom and to see the indissoluble connection between political democracy and democratic agrarian reform.

Unless the masses are interested, politically conscious, wide awake, active, determined and independent, absolutely nothing can be accomplished in either sphere.

Nevskaya Zvezda No. 12,
June 10, 1912
Signed: *V. I.*

Published according to
the text in *Nevskaya Zvezda*

CAPITALISM AND "PARLIAMENT"

The facts of democracy must not make us lose sight of a circumstance, often overlooked by bourgeois democrats, that in the capitalist countries representative institutions inevitably give rise to specific forms in which capital exercises its influence on the state power. We have no parliament, but then there is no end of parliamentary cretinism among the liberals and of *parliamentary licence* among all the bourgeois deputies.

The workers must thoroughly master this truth if they want to learn how to use representative institutions *for* promoting the political consciousness, unity, activity and efficiency of the working class. All the social forces hostile to the proletariat—the "bureaucrats", landowners and capitalists—are already using these representative institutions *against* the workers. One has to know how they are doing this if one wants to learn to uphold the independent interests of the working class and its independent development.

The Third Duma decided to award bonuses to home manufacturers of machinery. Who are these home manufacturers? The ones "operating" in Russia!

But upon examination we find that they are foreign capitalists who have transferred their plants to Russia. Tariff rates are high and profits immense, so foreign capital is moving *into* Russia. For instance, an American trust—a corporation of capitalist millionaires—has built a huge farm machinery works in Lyubertsi, near Moscow. In Kharkov, farm machines are made by the capitalist Melhose and in Berdyansk by the capitalist John Grieves. These manufacturers are very much of the "truly Russian", "home" variety, aren't they?

But, of course, unless they were helped in every way by Russian capitalists, they would have been *unable* to operate in Russia at all. One good turn deserves another. American, British and German capitalists rake in profits with the help of Russian capitalists, who get quite a big share. Take, for example, the Lena gold-fields or the mining enterprises in the Urals. How many millions foreign and Russian capitalists have shared between them there!

The Duma is very useful to the industrialists in this respect. Both in the Duma and in the Council of State, the capitalists have a goodly number of representatives. The landlords, too, would not amount to much nowadays without capital. For both the capitalists and the landlords, the Duma is a ready-made machinery for passing laws on "bonuses" (to be awarded *to themselves*), protective tariffs (i.e., another form of bonuses to themselves), concessions (a third form of bonuses to themselves), and so on, *without limit*.

The "Sceptic", a liberal writing in the liberal *Rech*, had some very apt comments to make on this matter. He writes with so much feeling against the "nationalists" (who awarded themselves "bonuses" to stimulate the "home" manufacture of machinery by Messrs. Grieves, Melhose, Elworthy, and other companies) that I, too, have become somewhat infected with scepticism.

Yes, the liberal "Sceptic" has not made a bad job of exposing the "nationalists". But why does he say nothing about the Cadets? When Golovin, for instance, was seeking a concession, did not his position as *member of the Duma* and former Chairman of the Duma stand him in good stead in that useful and lucrative pursuit?

When Maklakov was gobbling up his "Tagiyev" fees, did not his position as member of the Duma make it easier for him to get such "profitable" cases?[87]

And what about the numerous other Cadet landlords, merchants, capitalists, financiers, lawyers and brokers who extended their business, promoted their "connections", and put through their "affairs", thanks to their position as members of the Duma and to the benefits and advantages that position affords?

What if an inquiry were made into financial transactions

carried out by Duma members or with the aid of Duma members?

But no—in all capitalist countries measures have been taken to protect "trade secrets" and to guarantee that *not a single* "parliament" should permit such an inquiry.

However, the working-class deputies undoubtedly know a great deal about this matter; and if they took pains to look around, obtain additional information, collect material, look up newspaper files, inquire at the stock exchange, etc., they could themselves carry out a very instructive and useful "inquiry" into the *business* transactions carried out by Duma members or with the aid of such members.

In European parliaments, such transactions are well known, and the workers constantly expose them, naming the persons involved, so as to enlighten the people.

Nevskaya Zvezda No. 13,   Published according
June 17, 1912   to the text in *Nevskaya Zvezda*
Signed: *A Non-Liberal Sceptic*

———————

THE ELECTIONS AND THE OPPOSITION

Marxists long ago defined their fundamental attitude to the elections. The Right-wing parties—from Purishkevich to Guchkov—the liberal-monarchist bourgeoisie (Cadets and Progressists) and the democrats (worker democrats and bourgeois democrats, i.e., Trudoviks) are the *three* principal camps contesting the elections. The distinction between these camps is a basic one, for they represent different classes and have entirely different programmes and tactics. Correct practical conclusions regarding the election campaign can only be drawn if the principles on which each of the three camps bases its policy are clearly understood.

The Marxists fully established these points* about six months ago, and since then they have been proved correct above all by the utterances of the liberal opposition. Our "neighbours and enemies on the right", while by no means sharing our views, have with commendable zeal provided us with the best confirmation of the correctness of our points. We may proclaim the following *law*: the development of Cadet political activity and political views provides excellent evidence in support of Marxist views. Or, in other words: when a Cadet begins to speak, you may rest assured that he will refute the views of liberal labour politicians no less effectively than a Marxist.

That is why, incidentally, it is doubly useful for the workers to look closely into Cadet policy: first of all, they will get to know the liberal bourgeois very well and, secondly, they will learn to see more clearly the mistakes made by certain supporters of the working class.

---

* See present edition, Vol. 17, pp. 397-402.—*Ed.*

It is this doubly useful result that one may well expect
from the recent comments of *Rech* on the important pre-
election statements made by *Russkiye Vedomosti*. These are
statements by Mr. Akimov (V. Makhnovets), an old Economist, i.e., an opportunist of the period 1897-1902. They
amount to a straightforward defence of the "progressive
bloc", whose "platform" (a platform that, by the way, has
not been published!) Mr. Akimov, who chooses to call himself a Social-Democrat, considers "perfectly acceptable for
the Social-Democrats".

We have been, and are still being, told by numerous
political babes (from Paris to Krasnoyarsk) and seasoned
diplomats (from Vienna to Vilna),[88] that a liberal labour
policy is a "bogey". But take a look at Mr. Akimov, my
dear opponents! You will probably be unable to deny that
Akimov is an obvious embodiment of liberal labour policy.
Nor will you be able to say that he is unique, i.e., that he
is an isolated phenomenon and an inimitable rarity, the only
one of its kind. For, numerous though Mr. Akimov's inimitable qualities are, he is not an isolated phenomenon, and
it would be a downright untruth to say he is. He made his
statement after and in the same vein as Mr. Prokopovich.
He found for himself a widely circulated liberal paper,
a convenient rostrum from which his speeches carry far.
He obtained a "good press" among the liberal journalists.
Oh, no, he is not an isolated phenomenon. It does not matter that he ceased long ago to belong to any group. It does
not matter that his right to the name of Social-Democrat
is absolutely fictitious. But he represents a political *line*
which has roots, which is living and, though it often goes
into hiding, *invariably* comes into the open when there is
the slightest revival of political activity.

Rech "gives full credit to the sober realism" of Mr. Akimov's arguments, and stresses with especial pleasure his
opinion that "the Social-Democrats should at present put
forward those of their political aims that will have the support of sufficiently large, politically strong sections of the
people".

Rech certainly has good reason to rejoice. What *Nasha
Zarya* says with a thousand twists and turns, piling one little reservation on another, covering up its tracks, and flaunt-

ing pseudo-Marxist catchwords that have long become out-
worn, Mr. Akimov blurts out bluntly and rather brusquely,
rather simply, with a naïveté verging on innocence.

From a formal point of view, *Nasha Zarya* and *Nevsky
Golos* are perfectly in a position, of course, to disclaim
all responsibility for Mr. Akimov. But what actually happens is that the general reader, who is not versed in fine
points and is not interested in them, derives "Akimovism",
and nothing but "Akimovism", from these liquidationist
publications. "Don't wreck the Progressist cause," wrote
Martov. "Put forward those aims" that will have the support of the *Progressists*, writes Akimov, who, naturally,
makes the reservation that the non-partisanship of the Progressists makes it easier for any party to maintain its independence (on paper). *To put forward more* aims than are
acceptable to the Progressists means precisely to "wreck"
their cause—this is how Martov's slogan is interpreted by
the actual political struggle, by the *crowd* which Akimov
represents so well.

Akimov is convinced that the Cadets and Progressists
constitute "large and politically strong sections of the people". This is just the sort of liberal untruth about which
Nevskaya Zvezda wrote in a recent article on the nature and
significance of the Marxists' polemics against the liberals.*
In reality, however, the liberal-monarchist bourgeoisie,
taken as a whole, comprising the Cadets, the Progressists
and many others, is a very small section of the people and
one that is remarkably weak politically.

The bourgeoisie can never constitute a large section of
the people. As for being politically strong, it can be and is
that in a whole series of capitalist countries, but not in
Prussia or Russia. In these two countries, its amazing,
monstrous, all but incredible political impotence is fully
explained by the fact that the bourgeoisie here is far more
afraid of revolution than it is of reaction. Political impotence is an inevitable result of this. And all talk about the
"political strength" of the bourgeoisie is thoroughly false,
and consequently good for nothing at all, if it avoids this
fundamental feature of the state of affairs in Russia.

---

* See pp. 122-28 of this volume.—*Ed.*

Mr. Akimov has come out as a most outspoken and moderate liberal. We regard you as a force, Cadet and Progressist gentlemen, he says. We fully accept your platform (although there is no such platform!) and we ourselves are now putting forward *those* aims that have your support. All we ask of you is "that the list of the [Progressist] bloc should include the Social-Democrats". This is what Akimov wrote, word for word! I will accept everything, anything, he says, if only you include me in the liberal list!

It was truly ungracious of *Rech* to *decline* even so moderate a request. After all, it is a question of the June Third voters, the Cadets remind Akimov. And what do the Social-Democrats amount to among *them*? Nothing, "with the exception of the big cities, of which there is no question". And the official Cadet newspaper condescendingly teaches the humble and docile Akimov: "Apart from the border regions, they [the Social-Democrats] will almost everywhere else have to be guided, not by the hope of putting up candidates of their own, but by considerations making for the victory of the progressive bloc over the reactionary bloc of the oppressors of the people."

The liberal has brusquely declined to take the hand humbly proffered by the liberal labour politician! A well-deserved reward for refusing to fight in the big cities. The big cities belong to us because we are strong, say the Cadets, and the rest of Russia belongs to us because the June Third men and their June Third law, which guarantees our monopoly of opposition, are strong too.

Not a bad reply. The lesson which Akimov has been taught is a cruel but useful one.

Nevskaya Zvezda No. 14,
June 24, 1912
Signed: *K. F.*

Published according to
the text in *Nevskaya Zvezda*

THE SIGNIFICANCE
OF THE ST. PETERSBURG ELECTIONS

According to newspaper reports, the question of the date when the Fourth Duma should be convened and of the time when elections to it should be held has aroused some doubts among the ruling circles. Some were in favour of postponing the convening of the Duma until January, while others declared for October. Now the question is said to have been decided in favour of the latter opinion.

Thus the elections are quite near at hand—a mere seven to nine weeks. We must take steps to *redouble* our efforts with regard to all aspects of our pre-election work.

I should like to deal in this article with a special question, which, however, has acquired very great general importance for the worker democrats. I mean the role of the St. Petersburg elections.

The elections in St. Petersburg's second urban curia are the focal point of the *entire* Fourth Duma election campaign.

Only in St. Petersburg is there a tolerably well organised working-class press, one which, for all the fierce persecution it is subjected to, for all the fines and the arrests of its editors, for all the instability of its position, and for all that it is kept down by the censorship, is able to reflect, to some little degree, the views of worker democrats.

In the absence of a daily press, the elections remain an obscure matter, and their significance in terms of the political enlightenment of the masses is reduced by half, if not more.

For this reason, the St. Petersburg elections acquire the significance of a *model* of the election campaign which worker democrats have to undertake in the incredibly difficult conditions of Russian reality. Nowhere else are the workers in a position to hold an election campaign *visible* to everyone. To be sure, the elections in the worker curia are highly important, but there the workers cannot come up against the other classes of the population, and therefore cannot present on an *adequate* scale the *national* demands, and the views on the tasks involved in a *common policy*, which have been worked out by the progressive, proletarian democrats, so *that* they may serve all democrats in general as a guide.

In St. Petersburg the elections are direct. Hence the pre-election struggle here may take much more definite, more distinct and more partisan forms than elsewhere. The other big cities would have been as important as St. Petersburg, but administrative pressure in the provinces is *still* so much stronger than in the capital that it is difficult for worker democrats to force their way through, to get a hearing.

Lastly, in St. Petersburg the struggle in the second curia has to take place between the liberals and the democrats. The Cadets consider the second curia to be *their* domain. St. Petersburg is represented by Milyukov, Rodichev and Kutler.

Obviously, the fact that a fairly large number of democratic voters are represented by the liberals can by no means be considered normal. The elections to the Second Duma showed that Cadet "domination" among the democratic urban voters is very far from being solid. In St. Petersburg itself, the "Left bloc" in the Second Duma elections, i.e., the bloc of worker and bourgeois democrats (Narodniks), not only *could*, but *certainly would*, have won, if at that time Mensheviks like Dan and Co. had not split the workers' election campaign and thereby given rise, among the Narodniks, to wavering and vacillations that were exceedingly harmful to the success of the cause. One has only to recall that in the Second Duma elections even the "Socialist-Revolutionaries" followed the Mensheviks' lead to the last minute, defending their bloc with the Cadets!

The electoral law now in force permits of a second ballot, so that no blocs are required, or permissible, at the first stage.

The struggle in St. Petersburg will be between the worker democrats and the liberals. The Narodniks will hardly be strong enough to act independently—they have been "liquidating" themselves much too zealously by following our liquidators' line. The worker democrats are therefore almost certain to be supported by the bourgeois democrats (Trudoviks and Narodniks), if not at the first stage of the election, then at any rate when a second ballot is taken.

The liberals have their leader, Mr. Milyukov, from St. Petersburg. They have had a large following so far. The funds which the liberal-monarchist bourgeoisie supplies them with, the propaganda weapons in the form of two daily newspapers, and an organisation which is virtually tolerated and all but legalised *de facto*, all afford the Cadets tremendous advantages.

On the workers' side are the mass of the workers, consistent and sincere democracy, energy and devotion to the cause of socialism and working-class democracy. The workers *can* win if they rely on *these* forces and if they have a workers' daily newspaper. The workers' struggle for seats in the Duma for St. Petersburg is undoubtedly acquiring a vast and *country-wide* significance in the entire Fourth Duma election campaign.

Those who like to talk of "unity" of the whole opposition—from the Progressists and Cadets to the warily dodging liquidator Martov and the crudely simple-minded Prokopovich and Akimov—are all at pains to evade the issue of the St. Petersburg elections or to leave it out. They bypass the political centre but readily make their way into what may be called the political backwoods. They speak volubly, fervently and eloquently of what will be opportune at the second stage of the elections, i.e., when the principal, the chief, the decisive, part of the election campaign is over, and they "are eloquently silent" about St. Petersburg, which has been won by the Cadets and which has to be *won back* from them, has to be restored to the democrats.

There were no democratic deputies for St. Petersburg under the law of December 11,1905, nor under that of June 3, 1907,[89] so that "restored" would seem to be an unsuitable term. But St. Petersburg belongs to the democrats by virtue of the entire course of the entire emancipation movement in

First page of *Nevskaya Zvezda* No. 15, of July 1, 1912,
in which Lenin's articles "The Significance of the St.
Petersburg Elections" and "A Comparison of the Stolypin and
the Narodnik Agrarian Programmes" were published

Reduced

Russia, and at a certain stage of its development *even* the monstrously high dam of the June Third electoral law will be unable to stem the "democratic flood".

The majority of the voters in the second curia undoubtedly come from the democratic sections of the population. The Cadets induce them to follow their lead *by simply deceiving* them, by making themselves, a liberal-monarchist bourgeois party, out to be democrats. This kind of deceit has been, and is, practised by *all* liberals in the world in elections to every sort of parliament. And the workers' parties in all countries gauge their success by, among other things, the extent to which they succeed in freeing petty-bourgeois democrats from liberal influence.

The Russian Marxists, too, must set themselves this task clearly, specifically, and firmly. That is why, with regard to the big cities, they have said plainly in their well-known January decisions that blocs there are permissible, in view of the known absence of a Black-Hundred danger, *only* with the democrats, against the liberals.* This decision "takes the bull by the horns". It gives a straightforward answer to one of the most important questions of election tactics. It determines the *spirit*, the trend, and the character of the *entire* election campaign.

On the other hand, those liquidators who like to talk of the Cadets as of "representatives" of the "urban democracy" are committing a grave error. This kind of talk *distorts* matters by representing the *liberals'* election victories *over* the democrats, and the liberals' election tricks played *on* democratic voters, as proof of the Cadets' "democracy". As though Europe did not know of dozens of instances of *anti*-democratic parties for years keeping various democratic strata in leading strings, until real bourgeois democrats, but most often Social-Democrats, freed those strata from the influence of political parties that were *alien* to them in spirit.

The election struggle in St. Petersburg is a struggle for hegemony between the liberals and the worker democrats within the whole of Russia's emancipation movement.

This exceptionally important role of the St. Petersburg elections leads us, incidentally, to two practical conclusions.

---

* See present edition, Vol. 17, pp. 469-70.—*Ed.*

He to whom much is given, much shall be asked. The St. Petersburg workers will have to carry on the election campaign in the urban second curia on behalf of *all* the worker democrats of all Russia. It is a great and difficult task that they have to tackle. They must serve as a model. They must show the greatest initiative, energy and perseverance. They have done so in regard to the workers' daily newspaper. At the elections, too, they must continue the work they have begun so splendidly.

The attention of all Russia is riveted on the election struggle in St. Petersburg. All Russia should also *help* St. Petersburg. Unless the St. Petersburg workers receive the most varied aid from all parts of Russia, they will be unable to overcome the "enemy" by themselves.

Nevskaya Zvezda No. 15,
July 1, 1912
Signed: *F. F.*

Published according to
the text in *Nevskaya Zvezda*

A COMPARISON OF THE STOLYPIN
AND THE NARODNIK AGRARIAN PROGRAMMES

In previous articles (see *Nevskaya Zvezda* Nos. 3 and 6)*
we have cited the basic data on landownership in European
Russia and described the nature of the agrarian question in
Russia. The main point of this question is to abolish medievalism in *landownership*.

The contradiction between capitalism, which prevails
throughout the world, including Russia, and medieval
landownership, as embodied both in the landed estates and
in the peasant allotments, is irreconcilable. The old, medieval system of landownership is bound to be broken up, and
the more drastic, ruthless and bold this break-up, the better
for the entire development of Russia and the better for the
workers, and for the peasants, who are today crushed and
oppressed by innumerable survivals of medievalism, *as
well as* by capitalism.

The question may be asked: Such being the situation, how
can one compare the Stolypin and the Narodnik agrarian
programmes? Are they not in direct opposition to each
other?

Yes, they are, but this opposition does not remove the
one fundamental point which the two programmes have *in
common*, namely, the fact that *both* recognise the necessity
of *breaking up* the old system of landownership. The old
has to be broken up—as early and thoroughly as possible,
say those in charge of Stolypin's "land distribution"; but it
has to be broken up in such a way as to ensure that the whole
burden of it falls on the shoulders of the majority of the

---

* See pp. 32-35 and 73-77 of this volume.—*Ed.*

peasants —of the most ruined and most disinherited of them. The landlords should lose nothing in the process. If it is inevitable that they should lose part of their land, then the land should be alienated exclusively by the freely given consent of the landlords, and at a price considered "fair" by the landlords. The well-to-do peasants should be supported, and there is no reason to shrink from the ruin of the mass of "weak" peasants.

Such is the meaning of the Stolypin agrarian programme. The Council of the United Nobility, which entrusted Stolypin with drafting it, behaved as a true representative of the reactionaries —not of those who make fine speeches but of those who mean business. The Council was perfectly loyal to its class interests when it banked on the strong. And indeed, after 1905 it became obvious that the police and the bureaucracy alone were inadequate as a protection against the peasants.

Where else was the Council of the United Nobility to seek for allies? Only among the insignificant minority of the well-to-do peasants —the kulaks. It could not have found any other allies in the countryside. And to win over the "new landlords" to their side, the reactionaries did not shrink from delivering *the whole countryside* into their hands literally to be sacked and plundered.

If a break-up is inevitable, then let us break up *allotment* landownership in *our* favour and for the benefit of the *new landlords*—that is the gist of the agrarian policy which the Council of the United Nobility dictated to Stolypin.

But, speaking in purely theoretical terms, it has to be admitted that a break-up —a no less, and indeed much more, drastic one —is also possible *from the other side*. It cuts both ways. If, for instance, the 70 million dessiatines of land belonging to 30,000 landlords were to pass to 10 million peasant households in addition to the 75 million dessiatines they already own, and if the two categories of land were *merged* and then distributed among the well-to-do and middle peasants (the poor peasants could not use the land anyway, because they have nothing to plough, sow, fertilise and cultivate it with), what would be the result of the reform?

Pose this question from a purely economic standpoint. Consider this fundamental possibility from the angle of the general conditions of capitalist economy throughout the world. You will see that our suggested reform would result in a *more consistent*, drastic and ruthless break-up of *medieval* landownership than the Stolypin programme envisages.

Why medieval and none but medieval? Because *capitalist* landownership *cannot* be abolished, by its very nature, through any transfer of the land, not even through the transfer of all the land to the state (i.e., through what the science of political economy calls land "nationalisation"). Capitalist landownership is the holding of land by those who have capital and adapt themselves best to the market. Regardless of whether the land is still owned by the landlord, or by the state or the allotment peasant, it is bound to have a *master*, who can always rent it. The renting of land is increasing in *all* capitalist countries, under the most diverse forms of landownership. No bans whatever can prevent the capitalist, the master who has capital and knows the market, from laying his hands on the land, since the market dominates the whole of social production, i.e., since this production remains capitalist.

Nor is that all. The renting of land is *even more convenient* for pure capitalism, for the fullest, freest, and most "ideal" adaptation to the market, than is ownership of land. Why? Because private ownership of land *hampers* its transfer from hand to hand, *hinders* the adaptation of land tenure to the conditions of the market, *perpetuates* ownership of the land by a particular family or person and his heirs, even if they are bad farmers. Renting is a more flexible form, under which the adaptation of land tenure to the market takes place most simply, most easily and most rapidly.

That, incidentally, is why Britain is not an exception among the capitalist countries, but is the country that, from the point of view of capitalism, has the most perfect agrarian system, as Marx pointed out in his criticism of Rodbertus.[90] And what is Britain's agrarian system? It is the old system of landownership, landlordism, with the new, free, purely capitalist renting of land.

And what if that landlordism were to exist without land-lords, i.e., if the land were owned, not by landlords, but by the state? That, from the point of view of capitalism, would be a *still more* perfect agrarian system, with still greater freedom of adaptation of land tenure to the market, with still greater ease in the mobilisation of the land as an object of economy, with still greater freedom, breadth, clarity and definiteness in the class struggle characteristic of every form of capitalist landownership.

And the more a country is lagging behind world capitalism, the greater the effort it must make to overtake its neighbours, the more it has "neglected" its "disease", the disease of medieval landownership and small-scale bondage farming, and the more imperative that country's need for a *radical* break-up of *all* its relations of landownership, of all its agrarian system, the more natural will be the rise and wide dissemination in that country, among its agricultural population, of all sorts of ideas and plans of land national-isation.

Both the year 1905 and the two first Dumas proved beyond question—and the Third Duma confirmed it indirectly, through its "peasant" deputies (sifted through a landlord sieve)—that all sorts of ideas and plans for nationalising the land are extremely widespread among Russia's agricul-tural population. Before approving or condemning these ideas, one should ask oneself *why* they have become wide-spread and *what* economic necessity has evoked them.

It is not enough to criticise those ideas from the stand-point of their inner logic and harmony or of their theoretical correctness. They should be criticised from the standpoint of the economic necessity reflected in them, however "fan-ciful", inaccurate or "twisted" this reflection may some-times be.

The economic necessity which at the beginning of the twentieth century gave rise among the Russian peasantry to ideas of nationalising the land is the necessity of a drastic break-up of the old system of landownership. The ideas of "equalised division" of all the land are ideas of *equality*, necessarily born of the struggle against the survivals of serfdom and *inevitably* transplanted to the land in a sit-uation where 30,000 "residual serf-owners" possess 70 million dessiatines, while 10 million bond peasants possess 75 million dessiatines.

There is nothing utopian about the transfer of the first category of land into the second category, or rather to the owners of this second category. What *is* utopian is merely the dream of equality among the masters of the land while the market dominates; it is utopian to dream of the *"right to land"* for all "citizens, men and women" (including those who have no household) under capitalism. But the utopian character of *these* ideas should not allow us to forget the very true, living reality which is *actually* behind them.

There is nothing utopian about the abolition of *all* medieval distinctions of landownership—landlord, allotment, etc. There is nothing utopian about breaking up the old relations in regard to the land. On the contrary, the development of capitalism most imperatively demands *this* breakup. There *can* be *neither* "equalised division" of the land *nor* "socialisation" of it under capitalism. That is utopia.

Land nationalisation is quite feasible economically under capitalism, and its *real* significance would consist in any case—that is, no matter how it was effected, by whom and on what conditions, whether stably and for a long time or unstably and for a short time—in the maximum elimination of all that is medieval in Russian landownership and Russia's agrarian system; it would consist in the *freest* adaptation of the *new* system of land tenure and landownership to the new conditions of the world market.

Let us imagine for a moment that the Left Narodniks' plan was put into practice, say, through the equal division of all the lands among all citizens, men and women. Such division under capitalism is the greatest absurdity. Under capitalism, it would not and could not last even a year. But does this imply that its results would be zero or negative?

Not in the least! Its results would be of tremendous *advantage*—not the kind the Left Narodniks expect, but a most real advantage. That advantage would consist in all distinctions between the present social-estate and category forms of landownership being broken up. It would be a tremendous gain for the whole national economy, for capitalism, for the proletariat, because nothing could be more harmful to the development of Russia than our old, present-day, landownership. Both landlordism and allotment landownership are *thoroughly* feudal forms of landownership.

An equalised redivision of the land could not last, but it would be impossible to *go back to the old system*! No "restoration" could revive the boundaries once they had been removed. No political force on earth could prevent the establishment of such *new* boundaries, limits, and forms of land tenure as would correspond to the *new* requirements of the market.

"Departition the land," I recall a Left Narodnik saying in the Second Duma. He fancied that the result would be "equalised land tenure". He was mistaken. But speaking *through him* was, as the irony of history would have it, the most consistent and fearless radical *bourgeois*, who is aware of the absurdity of the *old*, medieval "partitions" of our "allotment", "nobility", "church", etc., etc., landownership, and is aware of the necessity of *breaking down all* those partitions to make way for a *new* distribution of the land. Only, this distribution would have to be not "per capita", which is the Narodnik's dream, but *per capital*, as *imposed by the market*.

The Narodniks' constructive plans are utopia. But their constructive plans have an element that is destructive in relation to medievalism. And that element is by no means utopia. It is the most living reality. It is the most consistent and progressive reality from the standpoint of capitalism and the proletariat.

Let us briefly sum up our views. The real similarity between the Stolypin and the Narodnik agrarian programmes lies in the fact that *both* advocate a radical *break-up* of the old, medieval system of landownership. And that is very good. That system deserves no better than to be broken up. The *most* reactionary *of all* are those Cadets of *Rech* and *Russkiye Vedomosti* who reproach Stolypin for causing a break-up, instead of proving the need for a still more consistent and resolute break-up. We shall see in a following article that the Stolypin type of break-up *cannot* do away with bondage and labour service, while the Narodnik type *can*.*

For the time being we shall note that the only entirely real result of the Stolypin break-up is a famine among 30 million people. And it remains to be seen whether the Stolypin break-up may not teach the Russian people *how* they *should* carry out a more thorough break-up. It is no doubt teaching that. But will it succeed in it? Time will tell.

Nevskaya Zvezda **No. 15,**
July 1, 1912
Signed: *R. S.*

Published according to
the text in *Nevskaya Zvezda*

---

* See pp. 248-53 of this volume.—*Ed.*

THE SITUATION IN THE R.S.D.L.P.
AND THE IMMEDIATE TASKS OF THE PARTY

The R.S.D.L.P. has passed through unprecedentedly hard years of rampant counter-revolution and is now on the right way to re-establishing its organisation and increasing its forces and its guiding influence on the Russian proletariat, which dealt powerful blows at the autocracy in 1905 and will destroy it in the coming revolution.

The hard years 1908-11 were years of division; it was in that period that the present Executive Committee of the Social-Democratic Party of Poland and Lithuania, which had joined our Party in 1906 and had marched with us Bolsheviks against the Menshevik opportunists, seceded from the R.S.D.L.P.

The worker Social-Democrats of Poland should make a critical appraisal of this secession of the present Executive from the R.S.D.L.P. Therefore I very gladly accept the proposal of the *Warsaw Committee* of the S.D.P. of Poland and Lithuania that I should briefly explain in *Gazeta Robotnicza*[91] the causes of the division in the Party and the sorry role which the present Executive played in it, and should point out the immediate tasks of the Social-Democratic proletariat of all Russia.

I

Our comrades, the Polish workers, are familiar with the differences existing between the Bolsheviks and Mensheviks during the revolution of 1905. A number of prominent representatives of the S.D.P. of Poland and Lithuania, such as Rosa Luxemburg, were on the Mensheviks' side at first, in 1904, but the revolution soon revealed their error, clearly demonstrating the Mensheviks' opportunism.

The counter-revolution of 1908-11 initiated a new stage in Russian history. The old autocracy moved a step closer to a bourgeois monarchy. The Duma of the landlords and the big bourgeoisie came into being. Tsarism had not yet lost its feudal character, but it was pursuing a bourgeois agrarian policy designed to institute private landownership as early as possible, at the price of unprecedented ruin and extermination of millions of peasants. Bourgeois liberalism made a sharp turn towards counter-revolution, and indulged in veritable orgies of renegacy.

Unparalleled division and dissension prevailed among the intelligentsia in general. The proletariat was subjected to persecution on the part of tsarism, which was taking its vengeance for the revolution, and to torrents of slander on the part of the renegades.

The task of the R.S.D.L.P. was to preserve the *revolutionary* Social-Democratic Party of the working class by *adapting itself to the new* conditions of work.

The very first steps towards accomplishing that task brought out new anti-proletarian trends in the R.S.D.L.P. that tended to undermine *the very existence* of the Party. They were engendered by the historical situation which our counter-revolution had created. These bourgeois trends are *liquidationism and otzovism.*

The liquidators, caught up by the wave of bourgeois desertion, repudiated the revolution. Giving up the illegal Party as a bad job, they sought only a legal basis for themselves in the allegedly "constitutional" regime of June 3 (16) and advocated its constitutional renovation. An "open workers' party" and slogans of *constitutional reform* were the gist of their policy. It was not a Social-Democratic, but a liberal labour policy.

Obviously, it would be simply ridiculous to compare the liquidators with the West-European opportunists within the Social-Democratic workers' parties (as the present Executive does under Tyszka's influence). Our liquidators refuse to recognise the Party in its illegal, i.e., its present, form, and are founding a *new*, legal party. It is not a trend inside the Party, but a withdrawal from the Party. The liquidators' obvious repudiation and destruction of the Party gave rise to sharp resistance from the Mensheviks themselves.

The worker Mensheviks in Russia *refused* to follow the liquidators, and outside Russia the Menshevik Plekhanov put himself at the head of the "pro-Party" Mensheviks (anti-liquidators). Plekhanov has now publicly and unequivocally admitted in the press that the liquidators are *founding a new* party.

We shall add, for the Polish workers' information, that the liquidators' main press organs are: abroad, *Golos Sotsial-Demokrata*[92] (Martov, Dan, Axelrod and other *Golos* supporters); in Russia, *Nasha Zarya* (Potresov, Levitsky, Cherevanin and others). The "otzovists" (from the word *otzvat*,* meaning the Social-Democratic deputies to the Third Duma) boycotted the Third Duma, for they did not realise the necessity of using the Duma rostrum and all "legal opportunities" for revolutionary Social-Democratic work. They reduced the slogans of the revolutionary tactics of 1905 to meaningless phrases. Experience soon showed that boycotting the Third Duma was an absurdity leading the Russian Social-Democrat boycotters to anarchism even against their will. In the summer of 1907 most Bolsheviks favoured a boycott; but as early as the spring of 1908 they had learned the lesson taught by experience and very sharply rebutted otzovist propaganda in St. Petersburg and Moscow. After being defeated so thoroughly in Russia, the otzovists and their defenders eked out a miserable existence abroad in the form of the absolutely impotent little group of *Vperyod* (Lunacharsky, Alexinsky and others).

Needless to add that, owing to the weakness of the majority of organisations in Russia and to the fact that the groups abroad were out of touch with the work going on in Russia, most of those groups were quite "freely" engaged in destroying and disrupting the Party, completely ignoring all discipline and holding no mandate from any organisation in Russia to direct a newspaper or publish pamphlets and leaflets. Besides the little groups holding different views on questions of principle, there sprang up, as usually happens, various little groups that had no principles at all, and strove to make some little political capital by brokerage, petty diplomacy, and intrigues under the guise of

---

* To recall.—*Tr.*

"reconciling" and "uniting" the Party. Past masters in this respect were Trotsky with the Vienna newspaper *Pravda* and Tyszka with the Executive Committee.

II

The R.S.D.L.P. was confronted with the question of how to re-establish the Party.

Clearly, it was impossible to re-establish the Party *jointly* with those who wanted to *liquidate* the Party or with those who boycotted the Duma and legal opportunities. Either the little groups abroad which were pursuing that bourgeois policy must abandon it in submission to the overwhelming majority of the organisations, groups and circles in Russia, or Russia must re-establish the Party *in spite of* those groups abroad.

In January 1910 the Central Committee of the R.S.D.L.P. held a plenary meeting for the last time; it made an attempt to save the liquidators and otzovists, who were breaking away from the Social-Democrats, and to guide them on to the path of Party work. The absurdity and un-Social-Democratic character of both deviations were so obvious that *no one* ventured to defend them. It was *unanimously* recognised that both were *bourgeois* trends, and that only by repudiating them could conditions be provided for the revival of the Party.

But unanimous decision is insufficient if it is not followed by united action. The liquidators and otzovists, contrary to the decisions of the Plenary Meeting of the Central Committee, did not relax but *intensified* their destructive work. It turned out that it was the Party's Central Organ, led by the Bolsheviks and the Poles, that fought *for the Party* during a year and a half (January 1910 to June 1911), with the Menshevik Plekhanov contributing vigorously to the struggle against the liquidators.

"Working" *against* the Party with might and main were the liquidators, the *Vperyod* group, Trotsky and the Bund. The Letts vacillated, most often siding with the liquidators.

The liquidators carried their destructive work to the point of destroying the Central Committee of the Party! The Plenary Meeting resolved to re-establish the C.C. in

Russia and to co-opt new members; but the liquidators would not even attend a single sitting, and declared that both the illegal Party and the illegal C.C. were "harmful". Under these circumstances, can anyone compare the liquidators with the West-European opportunists unless he is bent on intrigue?

The Party was left without a C.C., and its disintegration was unavoidable. Only the *Russian* organisations, i.e., those operating in Russia, could re-establish it. And that is when Tyszka displayed his hypocritical policy of intrigue in all its splendour by winning in the Executive Committee a majority over the adherents of a more principled policy and pushing the Executive to a break with the R.S.D.L.P., to the point where it found itself *between* the Party and the liquidators of the Party.

To explain that policy, which harms the Polish Social-Democratic movement, we shall first of all cite a fact of the *ideological* struggle in our Party.

The Plenary Meeting of the Central Committee unanimously condemned liquidationism, as we have pointed out above. But one section of the most important resolution (known as its Clause 1) was formulated in such a way as to have the directly opposite meaning; it played into the hands of the liquidators. This clause expressed the opinion that at present, i.e., at a time of counter-revolution, the Social-Democrats were *for the first time* making full use of the methods of the international Social-Democracy. This clause, which left a loophole for renegade theories, was proposed by Tyszka, who tried to manoeuvre between the liquidators and the Party. It is only natural that the liquidators should have enthusiastically supported the clause, helping Tyszka to "victory"; some of the Bolsheviks—the so-called group of "conciliators" (i.e., virtual Trotskyists) — also went over to the side of the liquidators.

After the Plenary Meeting Plekhanov superbly and scathingly ridiculed the clause (not knowing who its author was) for its "looseness", vagueness, and generality. I spoke after Plekhanov and told about my fruitless struggle against Tyszka's alliance with the "conciliators" and liquidators.*

---

* See present edition, Vol. 16, pp. 226-31.—*Ed.*

In two years, *not one* of the numerous writers of the Executive has spoken *a single word* in defence of that clause.

All that Tyszka's manoeuvring has resulted in is a liquidationist distortion of the views of the Party.

The results of this policy have been even more unfortunate in regard to the organisational question.

The Central Committee does not exist. The Party can be re-established only by a conference of the organisations in Russia. But how to convene such a conference? Obviously, it must be convened *not together* with those who are liquidating the Party, but *without them*.

Tyszka is walking the tight-rope, manoeuvring and playing at "unification" of the Party with those who are liquidating it. First Tyszka plus a small group of "conciliators" (a perfectly impotent little group abroad, which did not during a whole year receive a single order for its printed writings from any organisation in Russia) joined the Bolsheviks, assumed *control* over the convening of a conference, gave money to the agents who were to convene it, and dispatched those agents, asserting as they did so that they were "unifying" the Party (an assertion which brought Homeric laughter both from the liquidators and from us).

The agents began their tour *with Kiev*, with a Menshevik organisation whose status was so indisputable that even our sworn enemies, Trotsky and the Letts, admitted this in the press. In view of the furious attacks of the liquidators on our Conference, the Polish workers must know that it was with the participation of the above-mentioned organisation that the Russian Organising Commission for the convening of the Conference was formed (in October 1911). And it was a delegate from that organisation (Kiev) that was chairman of the Credentials Committee at the Conference!

It should be clear that the majority on the Russian Organising Commission consists of Bolsheviks and part of the "pro-Party" (i.e., anti-liquidationist) Mensheviks. The other little groups were not represented on it, being no more than fictitious units abroad having no connections in Russia.

That is when Tyszka, in despair because there was no possibility of mediating and intriguing, playing at unification with the liquidators, dissociated himself from the

Russian Organising Commission and did not attend the Conference even though he had been invited *three times*.

Instead, he attended a meeting of the *liquidators*[93] to discuss the convening of another (liquidationist) conference, and then left it, saying that there were liquidators there!! Is not a "conciliator" like that a buffoon?*

III

The January Conference of the R.S.D.L.P. united most of the organisations in Russia: St. Petersburg, Moscow, the Volga, the Caucasus, the South, the Western Territory. The Conference established that the liquidators (*Nasha Zarya*) had placed themselves outside the Party. It disclaimed all responsibility for the little groups abroad which were disrupting the Party by their actions.

At its twenty-three sittings, the Conference examined all the tactical questions in detail and adopted a whole series of resolutions in the spirit of the previous four years' work of the Central Organ and all the leading Party bodies. The Conference defined its terms of reference as the supreme Party body and elected the Central Committee.

It is quite understandable why the liquidators, and all the impotent little groups abroad along with them, attack the Conference, foaming at the mouth. The Conference condemned them. Every condemned person is entitled to abuse his judges all day long.

But there is *no* other Central Committee, *no* other Social-Democratic Party in Russia. Tyszka and the Executive who kept away from this Conference and assure the Polish workers that it is possible (with the help of brokers) to "unify" the Party with the liquidators, are deceiving the workers. As a result of this deceit, the Polish workers were unable to confer with their Russian comrades, to discuss with them tactics and slogans at such an important time

---

* The Executive Committee, writing in *Vorwärts*, calls Trotsky an agent of the liquidators, and in *Czerwony Sztandar*[94] it argues that there can be no unity, not only with the liquidationist Left wing of the Polish Socialist Party, but with the liquidationist Bund in Poland!! Tyszka, on the other hand, promises to unify the R.S.D.L.P. with the Russian liquidators.

as the revolutionary upswing in April and May, as well as the elections to the Fourth Duma.

The revolutionary upswing of the Russian proletariat is obviously growing stronger. To assist this strengthening, consolidate the illegal organisation, give the movement the correct revolutionary slogans, rebut the opportunism of the legalist liquidators, imbue the legal organisations with an anti-liquidationist spirit, and carry out the elections to the Fourth Duma along these lines—these are the immediate tasks which the R.S.D.L.P. is now carrying out in practice—tasks the theoretical attitude to which was defined at the All-Russia Conference in January.

As far as the trend of their work is concerned, the Polish revolutionary worker Social-Democrats are marching with us. I should therefore like to close by expressing confidence that the proletariat of Poland will be able to join us, the R.S.D.L.P., organisationally as well, despite the vacillation of the present Executive on matters of principle.

Published on July 16, 1912
in *Gazeta Robotnicza* No. 15-16
Signed: *N. Lenin*

Published according
to the newspaper text

A REPLY TO THE LIQUIDATORS[95]

The liquidators of *Nevsky Golos* are doing their utmost to *disrupt* the unity of the workers' elections in St. Petersburg. They will fail. Hypocritical shouts about "unity" (*coming from liquidators!!*) cannot deceive anyone.

The unity of the working-class democracy is certain.

The workers do not follow the lead of those who liquidate the workers' democratic Party and merely promise to replace it by an open "party" pursuing a liberal labour policy. Unity of the mass of the workers and not "agreement", to the detriment of this unity, with the circles of liquidationist splitters from among the intelligentsia—this is what the politically-conscious workers want. And *Pravda*[96] is following this slogan.

We are not put out by the unworthy sallies of the liquidators, who are *openly* asking *where* to "find" that which does not make a boast of being "open". Draw up your "open" platform, gentlemen, found your new, "open" party—and a good riddance to you!

P.S. I earnestly ask you to answer me immediately, or as soon as possible, on the matter I have raised here. *Keeping silent will not do.* You can spoil everything and evoke protests from the workers *on the left* by keeping silent about this. The liquidators must be rebuffed. We *cannot* conduct an election campaign without saying *for whom* we are doing it (people might think it is for the benefit of the liquidators).

If you do not want to aggravate and spoil *everything* "on the left", publish this "reply to the liquidators". If you do *not* publish it, send this sheet back to me *without delay*. It is *important* to me!

Written in July 1912

First published in 1933.
in *Lenin Miscellany XXV*

Published according
to the manuscript

IN SWITZERLAND

The local socialists call Switzerland a "republic of lackeys". This petty-bourgeois country, in which inn-keeping has long been a major industry, has depended too much on wealthy parasites squandering millions on summer travel in the mountains. A small proprietor toadying to rich tourists—such, until recently, was the most widespread type of Swiss bourgeois.

Things are changing now. A large-scale industry is developing in Switzerland. The use of waterfalls and mountain rivers as direct sources of electric power is playing a big part in this. The power of falling water, which replaces coal in industry, is often called "white coal".

The industrialisation of Switzerland, i.e., the development there of a large-scale industry, has put an end to the former stagnation in the working-class movement. The struggle between capital and labour is assuming a more acute character. The drowsy, philistine spirit which often in the past pervaded some of the Swiss workers' associations is disappearing to give way to the fighting mood of a class-conscious and organised proletariat that is aware of its strength.

The Swiss workers entertain no illusions about the fact that theirs is a bourgeois republic upholding the same kind of wage slavery as exists in all the capitalist countries without exception. At the same time, however, they have learned very well to use the freedom of their republican institutions to enlighten and organise the wide mass of the workers.

The fruits of their work were clearly revealed during the general strike in Zurich on July 12 (June 29, old style).

This is how it came about. The painters and fitters in Zurich had been on strike for several weeks, demanding higher wages and shorter hours. The enraged employers decided to break the resistance of the strikers. The government of the bourgeois republic, eager to serve the capitalists, came to their aid, and began to *deport* foreign strikers! (There are many foreign workers, particularly Italians, who go to Switzerland to work.) But the use of brute force did not help. The workers held their ground as one man.

Then the capitalists resorted to the following method. In Hamburg, Germany, there is a firm, owned by Ludwig Koch, which specialises in supplying strike-breakers. The Zurich capitalists—patriots and republicans, don't laugh!— had that firm send in strike-breakers, who they knew included all sorts of criminals convicted in Germany for pandering, brawling, etc. The capitalists supplied this riff-raff or gang of convicts (lumpenproletarians) with pistols. The brazen band of strike-breakers filled the taverns in the workers' district and there engaged in unheard-of hooliganism. When a group of workers gathered together to eject the hooligans, one of the latter *shot down* a worker who was on strike.

The workers' patience was exhausted. They beat up the murderer. It was decided to make an interpellation in the Zurich City Council on the hooligans' outrages. And when the city authorities, in defence of the capitalists, prohibited strike picketing, the workers resolved to protest by a *one-day general strike*.

All the trade unions declared unanimously for the strike. The printers were the only sad exception. They declared against the strike, and the meeting of 425 representatives of all the Zurich workers' organisations replied to the printers' decision with a stentorian cry of "Shame!" The strike was decided on, even though the leaders of political organisations were against it (the same old spirit of the philistine, opportunist Swiss leaders!).

Knowing that the capitalists and the management would try to wreck the peaceful strike, the workers acted according to the wise maxim, "In war as in war." In war-time one does not tell the enemy *when* an attack will take place. The workers purposely declared on Thursday that the strike would take place on Tuesday or Wednesday, whereas in reality they had fixed it for *Friday*. The capitalists and the management were taken by surprise.

The strike was a signal success. Thirty thousand leaflets in German and Italian were circulated early in the morning. Some 2,000 strikers occupied the tram depots. Everything stopped. Life in the city came to a standstill. Friday is a market day in Zurich, but the city seemed dead. The consumption of spirits (all alcoholic drinks) was prohibited by the strike committee, and the workers strictly obeyed this decision.

An imposing mass demonstration took place at 2 p.m. When the speeches were over, the workers dispersed peacefully, and without singing.

The government and the capitalists, who had hoped to provoke the workers to violence, saw their failure and are now beside themselves with rage. Not only strike picketing, but also open-air meetings and demonstrations have been prohibited by special decree throughout the Zurich Canton. The police occupied the People's House in Zurich and arrested a number of the workers' leaders. The capitalists announced a three-day lock-out by way of avenging themselves for the strike.

The workers are keeping calm; they scrupulously observe the boycott of spirits and wine, saying among themselves: "Why shouldn't a working man rest three days a year, since the rich rest all the year round?"

Pravda No. 63, July 12, 1912
        Signed: *B. Z.*

                                                Published according
                                                to the *Pravda* text

DEMOCRACY AND NARODISM IN CHINA

The article by Sun Yat-sen, provisional President of the Chinese Republic, which we take from the Brussels socialist newspaper, *Le Peuple*, is of exceptional interest to us Russians.

It is said that the onlooker sees most of the game. And Sun Yat-sen is a most interesting "onlooker", for he appears to be wholly uninformed about Russia despite his European education. And now, quite independently of Russia, of Russian experience and Russian literature, this enlightened spokesman of militant and victorious Chinese democracy, which has won a republic, poses purely Russian questions. A progressive Chinese democrat, he argues exactly like a Russian. His similarity to a Russian Narodnik is so great that it goes as far as a complete identity of fundamental ideas and of many individual expressions.

The onlooker sees most of the game. The platform of the great Chinese democracy—for that is what Sun Yat-sen's article represents—impels us, and provides us with a convenient occasion, to examine anew, in the light of recent world events, the relation between democracy and Narodism in modern bourgeois revolutions in Asia. This is one of the most serious questions confronting Russia in the revolutionary epoch which began in 1905. And it confronts not only Russia, but the whole of Asia, as will be seen from the platform of the provisional President of the Chinese Republic, particularly when this platform is compared with the revolutionary developments in Russia, Turkey, Persia and China. In very many and very essential respects, Russia is undoubtedly an Asian country and, what is more, one of the most benighted, medieval and shamefully backward of Asian countries.

Beginning with its distant and lone forerunner, the nobleman Herzen, and continuing right up to its mass representatives, the members of the Peasant Union of 1905 and the Trudovik deputies to the first three Dumas of 1906-12, Russian bourgeois democracy has had a Narodnik colouring. Bourgeois democracy in China, as we now see, has the same Narodnik colouring. Let us now consider, with Sun Yat-sen as an example, the "social significance" of the ideas generated by the deep-going revolutionary movement of the hundreds of millions who are finally being drawn into the stream of world capitalist civilisation.

Every line of Sun Yat-sen's platform breathes a spirit of militant and sincere democracy. It reveals a thorough understanding of the inadequacy of a "racial" revolution. There is not a trace in it of indifference to political issues, or even of underestimation of political liberty, or of the idea that Chinese "social reform", Chinese constitutional reforms, etc., could be compatible with Chinese autocracy. It stands for complete democracy and the demand for a republic. It squarely poses the question of the condition of the masses, of the mass struggle. It expresses warm sympathy for the toiling and exploited people, faith in their strength and in the justice of their cause.

Before us is the truly great ideology of a truly great people capable not only of lamenting its age-long slavery and dreaming of liberty and equality, but of *fighting* the age-long oppressors of China.

One is naturally inclined to compare the provisional President of the Republic in benighted, inert, Asiatic China with the presidents of various republics in Europe and America, in countries of advanced culture. The presidents in *those* republics are all businessmen, agents or puppets of a bourgeoisie rotten to the core and besmirched from head to foot with mud and blood—not the blood of padishahs and emperors, but the blood of striking workers shot down in the name of progress and civilisation. In those countries the presidents represent the bourgeoisie, which long ago renounced all the ideals of its youth, has thoroughly prostituted itself, sold itself body and soul to the millionaires and multimillionaires, to the feudal lords turned bourgeois, etc.

In China, the Asiatic provisional President of the Republic is a revolutionary democrat, endowed with the nobility and heroism of a class that is rising, not declining, a class that does not dread the future, but believes in it and fights for it selflessly, a class that does not cling to maintenance and restoration of the past in order to safeguard its privileges, but hates the past and knows how to cast off its dead and stifling decay.

Does that mean, then, that the materialist West has hopelessly decayed and that light shines only from the mystic, religious East? No, quite the opposite. It means that the East has definitely taken the Western path, that new *hundreds of millions* of people will from now on share in the struggle for the ideals which the West has already worked out for itself. What has decayed is the Western bourgeoisie, which is already confronted by its grave-digger, the proletariat. But in Asia there is *still* a bourgeoisie capable of championing sincere, militant, consistent democracy, a worthy comrade of France's great men of the Enlightenment and great leaders of the close of the eighteenth century.

The chief representative, or the chief social bulwark, of this Asian bourgeoisie that is still capable of supporting a historically progressive cause, is the peasant And side by side with him there already exists a liberal bourgeoisie whose leaders, men like Yüan Shih-kai, are above all capable of treachery: yesterday they feared the emperor, and cringed before him; then they betrayed him when they saw the strength, and sensed the victory, of the revolutionary democracy; and tomorrow they will betray the democrats to make a deal with some old or new "constitutional" emperor.

The real emancipation of the Chinese people from age-long slavery would be impossible without the great, sincerely democratic enthusiasm which is rousing the working masses and making them capable of miracles, and which is evident from every sentence of Sun Yat-sen's platform.

But the Chinese Narodnik combines this ideology of militant democracy, firstly, with socialist dreams, with hopes of China avoiding the capitalist path, of preventing capitalism, and, secondly, with a plan for, and advocacy of, radical agrarian reform. It is these two last ideological and political trends that constitute the element which forms *Narodism* — Narodism in the specific sense of that term, i.e., as distinct from democracy, as a supplement to democracy.

What is the origin and significance of these trends?

Had it not been for the immense spiritual and revolutionary upsurge of the masses, the Chinese democracy would have been unable to overthrow the old order and establish the republic. Such an upsurge presupposes and evokes the most sincere sympathy for the condition of the working masses, and the bitterest hatred for their oppressors and exploiters. And in Europe and America—from which the progressive Chinese, *all* the Chinese who have experienced this upsurge, have borrowed their ideas of liberation—emancipation *from* the bourgeoisie, i.e., socialism, is the immediate task. This is bound to arouse sympathy for socialism among Chinese democrats, and is the source of their *subjective* socialism.

They are subjectively socialists because they are opposed to oppression and exploitation of the masses. But the *objective* conditions of China, a backward, agricultural, semifeudal country numbering nearly 500 million people, place on the order of the day only one specific, historically distinctive form of this oppression and exploitation, namely, feudalism. Feudalism was based on the predominance of agriculture and natural economy. The source of the feudal exploitation of the Chinese peasant was his *attachment* to the land in some form. The political exponents of this exploitation were the feudal lords, all together and individually, with the emperor as the head of the whole system.

But it appears that out of the subjectively socialist ideas and programmes of the Chinese democrat there emerges in fact a programme for "changing all the juridical foundations" of "immovable property" *alone*, a programme for the abolition of feudal exploitation *alone*.

That is the *essence* of Sun Yat-sen's Narodism, of his progressive, militant, revolutionary programme for bourgeois-democratic agrarian reform, and of his quasi-socialist theory.

From the point of view of doctrine, this theory is that of a petty-bourgeois "socialist" reactionary. For the idea that capitalism can be "prevented" in China and that a "social revolution" there will be made easier by the country's backwardness, and so on, is altogether reactionary. And Sun Yat-sen himself, with inimitable, one might say virginal, naïveté, smashes his reactionary Narodnik theory by admitting what reality forces him to admit, namely that "China is on the eve of a gigantic industrial [i.e., capitalist] development", that in China "trade [i.e., capitalism] will develop to an enormous extent", that "in fifty years we shall have many Shanghais", i.e., huge centres of capitalist wealth and proletarian need and poverty.

But the question arises: does Sun Yat-sen, on the basis of his reactionary economic theory, uphold an actually reactionary agrarian programme? That is the crux of the matter, its most interesting point, and one *on* which curtailed and emasculated liberal quasi-Marxism is often at a loss.

The fact of the matter is that he does not. The dialectics of the social relations in China reveals itself precisely in the fact that, while sincerely sympathising with socialism in Europe, the Chinese democrats have transformed it into a reactionary theory, and *on the basis* of this reactionary theory of "preventing" capitalism are championing a *purely capitalist*, a maximum capitalist, agrarian programme!

Indeed, what does the "economic revolution", of which Sun Yat-sen talks so pompously and obscurely at the beginning of his article, amount to?

It amounts to the transfer of rent to the state, i.e., land nationalisation, by some sort of single tax along Henry George lines. There is absolutely nothing else that is *real* in the "economic revolution" proposed and advocated by Sun Yat-sen.

The difference between the value of land in some remote peasant area and in Shanghai is the difference in the rate of rent. The value of land is capitalised rent. To make the "enhanced value" of land the "property of the people" means transferring the rent, i.e., land ownership, to the state, or, in other words, nationalising the land.

Is such a reform possible within the framework of capitalism? It is not only possible but it represents the purest, most consistent, and ideally perfect capitalism. Marx pointed this out in *The Poverty of Philosophy*, he proved it in detail in Volume III of *Capital*, and developed it with particular clarity in his controversy with Rodbertus in *Theories of Surplus Value*.

Land nationalisation makes it possible to abolish absolute rent, leaving only differential rent. According to Marx's theory, land nationalisation means a maximum elimination of medieval monopolies and medieval relations in agriculture, maximum freedom in buying and selling land, and maximum facilities for agriculture to adapt itself to the market. The irony of history is that Narodism, under the guise of "combating capitalism" in agriculture, champions an agrarian programme that, if fully carried out, would mean the *most* rapid development of capitalism in agriculture.

What economic necessity is behind the spread of the most progressive bourgeois-democratic agrarian programmes in one of the most backward peasant countries of Asia? It is the necessity of destroying feudalism in all its forms and manifestations.

The more China lagged behind Europe and Japan, the more it was threatened with fragmentation and national disintegration. It could be "renovated" only by the heroism of the revolutionary masses, a heroism capable of creating a Chinese republic in the sphere of politics, and of ensuring, through land nationalisation, the most rapid capitalist progress in the sphere of agriculture.

Whether and to what extent this will succeed is another question. In their bourgeois revolutions, various countries achieved various degrees of political and agrarian democracy, and in the most diverse combinations. The decisive factors will be the international situation and the alignment of the social forces in China. The emperor will certainly try to unite the feudal lords, the bureaucracy and the clergy in an attempt at restoration. Yüan Shih-kai, who represents a bourgeoisie that has only just changed from liberal-monarchist to liberal-republican (for how long?), will pursue a policy of manoeuvring between monarchy and revolution. The revolutionary bourgeois democracy, represented by Sun Yat-sen, is correct in seeking ways and means of "renovating" China through maximum development of the initiative, determination and boldness of the peasant masses in the matter of political and agrarian reforms.

Lastly, the Chinese proletariat will increase as the number of Shanghais increases. It will probably form some kind of Chinese Social-Democratic labour party which, while criticising the petty-bourgeois utopias and reactionary views of Sun Yat-sen, will certainly take care to single out, defend and develop the revolutionary-democratic core of his political and agrarian programme.

Nevskaya Zvezda No. 17,
July 15, 1912
Signed: *Vl. Ilyin*

Published according to
the text in *Nevskaya Zvezda*

THE ITALIAN SOCIALIST CONGRESS

A few days ago the Thirteenth Congress of the Italian Socialist Party came to a close in the town of Reggio Emilia.

The struggle within the Italian Socialist Party has assumed particularly sharp forms in recent years. Originally there were two basic trends: revolutionary and reformist. The revolutionaries upheld the proletarian character of the movement and combated all manifestations of opportunism, i.e., the spirit of moderation, deals with the bourgeoisie, and renunciation of the ultimate (socialist) aims of the working-class movement. The cardinal principle of this trend and the basis of its views are the class struggle.

The reformists, in fighting for reforms, i.e., individual improvements of political and econqmic conditions, kept forgetting the socialist character of the movement. They advocated blocs and alliances with the bourgeoisie to the point of socialists entering bourgeois ministries, of renouncing consistently republican convictions (in monarchical Italy, republican propaganda in itself is not considered unlawful), of defending "colonial policy", the policy of seizing colonies, of oppressing, plundering and exterminating the natives, etc.

These two basic trends, which exist in one form or another in *all* socialist parties, gave rise in Italy to two further extreme trends that deviated completely from socialism and tended therefore to dissociate themselves from the workers' Socialist Party. One of these non-socialist extremes is *syndicalism*, which became "fashionable" in Italy at one time. The syndicalists inclined towards anarchism, slipped into revolutionary phrase-mongering, destroyed the discipline of the working-class struggle and opposed the use of the parliamentary platform by socialists, or upheld such opposition.

Anarchist influence is feeble everywhere, and the working-class movement is rapidly ridding itself of this sickness.

The Italian syndicalists (led by Arturo Labriola) are already *outside* the Socialist Party. Their role in the working-class movement is negligible. The Marxist revolutionaries in Italy, as in other countries, do not in the least indulge in anarchist sentiments and trends, which disrupt the proletarian movement.

The reformists are less staunch with regard to the extreme Right reformists who, by drifting to a liberal labour policy, pass completely into the liberal camp and desert to the bourgeoisie. That is why the removal of these traitors to the working-class cause from the Socialist Party seldom takes place without the Marxist revolutionaries having to wage a most bitter struggle against *all* reformists. This was the case in France, for example, where Millerand, an opportunist and reformist, ended by a deal with the bourgeoisie and entered a bourgeois Ministry.

The same is true of Italy. There the reformists have split into Left reformists (led by Turati) and Right reformists (led by Bissolati). The Reggio Emilia Congress marked the last act of this split.

There were three trends at the Congress: (1) the revolutionaries (they had about 12,500 votes at the Congress, according to the number of their supporters in the Party); (2) the Left reformists (about 9,000), and (3) the Right reformists (about 2,000). The revolutionaries moved for expelling Bissolati and another three extreme Right reformists from the Party. As for the Left reformists, one-third of them also favoured expulsion, but they wanted the reason for it to be expressed in "milder" terms, while two-thirds were against expulsion and for a mere censure.

The revolutionaries, who were in a majority, as the above figures show, gained the upper hand, and Bissolati and Co. were expelled.

What were Bissolati's views and actions which necessitated his expulsion from the Party? Bissolati, in the face of numerous decisions of the Party, went so far in backing the bourgeois Ministry as to almost become a "minister without portfolio" himself (that is, not being a minister, he behaved like a supporter and member of the bourgeois Ministry).

Despite republican convictions, which Italian socialists strictly adhere to, Bissolati began to make trips to the Quirinal, where he visited the king and held negotiations with him! He went as far as to defend Italy's present war against Turkey, although the *entire* Party has emphatically condemned the war as shameless bourgeois plundering and a dirty business—massacring African natives in Tripoli by means of improved deadly weapons.

Following the expulsion of Bissolati and Co., *all* the Right reformists left the Party and founded a party *of their own*, which they named the Socialist Reformist Party. Behind that façade is *in reality* a "party" of liberal-monarchist "labour" politicians.

A split is something distressing and painful. But sometimes it becomes indispensable, and then all weakness, all "sentimentality" (a term used in Reggio by a compatriot of ours, Balabanova), is a crime. The leaders of the working class are not angels, saints or heroes, but people like anyone else. They make mistakes. The Party puts them right. The German Workers' Party sometimes had to correct the opportunist errors of even such great leaders as Bebel.

But when someone persists in an error, when, to defend an error, a group is formed that spurns all the decisions of the party, all the discipline of the proletarian army, a split becomes indispensable. And the party of the Italian socialist proletariat has taken the right path by removing the syndicalists and Right reformists from its ranks.

Pravda No. 66, July 15, 1912
Signed: *I*.

Published according to
the *Pravda* text

"FREEDOM OF SPEECH" IN RUSSIA

The newspaper *At Your Service, Sir*, commonly known as *Novoye Vremya*, has reprinted a report received by its worthy colleague, *Peterburgskiye Vedomosti*, from Ivanovo-Voznesensk.

"In our industrial town," says the report, "foul language in the street has supplanted human speech. It is used by factory workers and cabbies and well-dressed people, and by policemen performing their official duties."

Commenting on this picture of mores, *Novoye Vremya* remarks:

"A lucky workers' town, where the most daring Social-Democratic expectations of completely unrestricted freedom of speech have been realised."

How very instructive, this caddish sally, isn't it?

Surely it is common knowledge, gentlemen of the editorial board of a newspaper loyally serving the government, that freedom of speech with regard to foul language has been "realised" in the Third Duma precisely by those Right-wing parties closest to the government. Surely everyone knows that the Purishkeviches, Markovs and *their* colleagues have become famous for this throughout Russia.

It is imprudent of *Novoye Vremya* to talk like that, very imprudent indeed. Why, it could have played its servant's role much more adroitly. Yet here is a paper, one sincerely devoted to the government, suddenly reminding us of the kind of "freedom of speech" that Purishkevich and Co.

practise and the kind practised by the Social-Democratic deputies to the Duma.

Freedom of speech for the Purishkeviches in a landlord Duma, and freedom of speech at workers' meetings.... It is an excellent pre-election topic brought up by *Novoye Vremya*, which is so clumsy in its zealous servility!

Pravda No. 66, July 15, 1912
Signed: *V.*

Published according
to the *Pravda* text

HOW P. B. AXELROD EXPOSES THE LIQUIDATORS

I

P. B. Axelrod is destined to play an original role in the development of the opportunist trend among the Marxists. His idea of a "labour congress", for example, once made quite a stir. A certain number of workers were attracted and carried away by his propaganda. But the more widespread that propaganda became and the nearer the idea drew to being put into effect, the clearer became the *spurious* character of the scheme, which fizzled out of itself. Experience confirmed what the Bolsheviks had pointed out more than once, namely, that Axelrod's "ideas" are an invention of the opportunist intelligentsia, a dream of how to "bypass" grim class and political struggles.

Exactly the same story has now been repeated with regard to the idea of a workers' publishing house and a "non-factional" workers' newspaper. Any St. Petersburg worker will recall how much the liquidators made of that idea until very recently, how they tempted the workers with the dream of "bypassing" all struggle among the worker democrats, and how comically they fumed against *Zvezda* because it showed that the issue of a liberal labour policy (think of the bakers' decision[97]) cannot be bypassed and that all talk about workers' control over a non-factional newspaper is sheer demagogy.

And now Axelrod, writing in the liquidationist *Nevsky Golos* No. 6, has excellently exposed —has had to expose— the demagogy of his own friends. Demagogy means lavishing promises that cannot be fulfilled. The idea of a broad labour congress, a legal workers' publishing house and a non-factional workers' newspaper is tempting. But the point is that these tempting things *cannot be achieved without* first waging a stubborn and difficult struggle for political liberty in general, for the victory of Marxism among the worker democrats, etc. Demagogic promises are easy to give. But life soon shows that they cannot be fulfilled, and exposes the opportunism of "rosy dreams".

In *Nevsky Golos* No. 6, Axelrod dishes up an amazing amount of empty declamation, asserting, for instance, that he and his friends are "progressive spokesmen of the Party", while their opponents are "reactionaries". Of course, Axelrod likes very much to think so, and the liquidators like to print what he thinks. Only, what cheap talk it is! Praising himself for his "progressive" attitude.... Would it not be better to *explain* the substance and meaning of the divergencies?

"The idea of a non-factional Social-Democratic (genuinely Social-Democratic, without inverted commas) organ is utopian at present and, moreover, a utopia that objectively runs counter to the interests of the Party's political development and the organisational unification of the proletariat under the banner of Social-Democracy. Drive Nature out of the door and she will fly in through the window and the cracks."

That is what Axelrod writes. Those are not bad ideas at all. They are perfectly sound in principle. They show that Axelrod's liquidationist friends were quite wrong when yesterday they were still putting out among the mass of the workers the very idea which Axelrod now condemns. Only, we cannot regard the lavishing of unrealisable promises as a "progressive" attitude.

"We may be said to have no factions that have taken shape organisationally," writes Axelrod. "Instead, we have various circles and small groups, of which some hold more or less definite political, tactical and organisational views, while the others waver in various directions, getting in the way of the former."

The first sentence is not entirely correct. Axelrod knows very well that there is something which has *fully* taken shape organisationally —as far as that is possible nowadays. But the second is correct: there *are* many small groups that are wavering and are getting in the way of the others. By stating this truth under the compulsion of events, Axelrod exposes his friends again. Everyone is aware that what Axelrod's friends are just now making a display of is ostentatious "unification" on paper of the wavering little groups. Do they not promise this fictitious "unification" of all the liquidators and all the waverers in the very same No. 6 of *Nevsky Golos*?

"The focal point and main source of the discord," Axelrod continues, "is, on the one hand, the difference in the attitude of the various Party circles to the new, open Social-Democratic labour movement [shouldn't you have said to the open *Party*, esteemed P. B. Axelrod? It is a bad thing to distort the essence of the divergency!] and, on the other hand, substantial differences over immediate political tasks and the political tactics of the Russian Social-Democratic movement. The requirements of both these categories are becoming particularly burning and topical issues just now when a new social and political movement is beginning. And it is over them that the Russian Social-Democrats have split into two main camps. The question arises whether the projected labour newspaper will be able to take a neutral position between these two opposed camps, and whether such a position is permissible in principle. Obviously not."...

A very correct conclusion. Axelrod has given a good thrashing not only to those of his friends who yesterday were clamouring for a neutral and non-factional newspaper, but also to those who today are assuring naïve people of their "agreement", "unity", solidarity, and so on, with the *neutral* little groups.

There are indeed two main camps. One of them has completely taken shape organisationally. Its answers to all the questions listed by Axelrod are quite formal, precise and definite, unlike the desultory and contradictory little articles of certain writers. As for the other camp, i.e., the liquidationist camp, to which Axelrod belongs, it has admittedly not taken shape organisationally (what we have instead is only hollow promises of an open labour *party*, only talk about open political societies of the workers, which are even less feasible than a labour congress would have been in 1906-07), nor can it answer, in specific and precise terms, the questions listed by Axelrod himself (what we have instead of specific answers is only the journalistic exercises of Yezhov, Levitsky, Klenov, Chatsky, and others).

"As soon as a working group of publishers and journalists makes up its mind to put forward a specific programme of action, to take a definite stand on questions relating, say, to the election campaign, to put particular tasks and slogans before the workers in the campaign and declare itself for a particular tactic towards the different political parties—as soon, I say, as a publishing association decides to lend its publication the character of an essentially proletarian political organ, it will be faced with the same vexed questions and differences that worry and rend asunder the Russian Social-Democracy. And then it may happen that that association itself will become a new source of the same kind of discord, unless its members come to terms and reach agreement on these questions beforehand."

Axelrod hits out at the liquidators very correctly and very well. What the "association" needs, *Nasha Zarya* and *Nevsky Golos* need still more badly. Then why cannot they *come to terms* on the *vexed questions and differences*? Why cannot they give *precise answers* at least to the more important questions listed by Axelrod (the attitude to different parties, the tasks, slogans and tactics)?

"Physician, cure thyself." Axelrod has so well explained to the *workers* the need for clear and precise answers to the "vexed questions" that the *writers* of *Nasha Zarya* and *Nevsky Golos* (and, perhaps, not only *Nevsky Golos*) ought to heed his words. One *cannot* do without precise and clear answers to the "vexed questions", cannot confine oneself to articles—that would indeed be the circle spirit. *Decisions*—precise, formal, well-considered, and definite decisions—are needed. After all, it is not for nothing that Axelrod speaks—and very aptly!—of a *specific programme of action, of tasks and slogans*, etc.

Incidentally, the reason why the liquidators are called liquidators is that, while they have rejected the old, they offer nothing new. That an open party is useful, and that open political societies are necessary, is something which all liquidators have been dinning into our ears. But this talk of theirs is not all that is required, and as for *action*, there is no evidence of it, none whatsoever. There is no evidence of precisely what Axelrod demands from the workers!

In the *Nevsky Golos* feuilleton, below the dividing line, Axelrod has given excellent evidence exposing the liquidators who write *above the dividing line*, in the editorial section of the paper. Read Axelrod's feuilleton carefully and you will see that it is deception and self-deception for the liquidators to shout about "agreement" concerning an election platform, a "single" platform, etc.

"A *Zvezda* Supporter" has already exposed this deception in *Nevskaya Zvezda* No. 16. But the exposure provided by Axelrod goes even deeper and is still more valuable because it comes from Axelrod.

We are entirely in favour of a *single* platform—namely, the one which the Bolsheviks and pro-Party Mensheviks adopted long ago, and are putting into effect, as "A *Zvezda* Supporter" justly points out. We are entirely in favour of a *single* election campaign precisely on that platform, on the basis of these same decisions, of definite and precise answers to *all* the "vexed questions".

By shouting about "unity", the liquidators seek to carry away ignorant workers by the mere sound of the word. "Unity" is agreeable, "non-factional newspapers" are more attractive! But read Axelrod *at least*, and he will make it clear to you that non-factionalism is *impossible*, that it is utopian; that there are *two camps* among the worker democrats, and that these two camps are *opposed*.

What now? Are the liquidators by any chance going to defend a "platform" *in order to conceal* their views?—a *diplomatic* platform, such as the bourgeoisie likes so much? — a platform that does not furnish any answers to the "vexed questions" but is "simply" and "merely" concerned with "getting into the Duma"?

That would be the height of unprincipledness. But the workers would never accept it. Such platforms, no matter how "open", could not hold their own even for a single day.

Yes, we have had enough of self-deception. It is time we faced up to the truth, which this time has also been plainly acknowledged by the leader of the liquidators, Axelrod. If you, liquidator gentlemen, choose to insist on a platform of your "own" (although you have yet to put it forward, and we do not believe in platforms concocted six weeks before elections!), if you choose to insist on tactics of your "own" (although so far you have nowhere stated them precisely, formally, in a manner befitting a party!), then you alone are to blame. Then it is *you* who violate the unity that is there *already*. Then it is *you* who will be held *entirely* responsible for that violation.

Yes, we have had enough of self-deception. Liquidationist cries about "unity" are no more than a blind. Knowing very well that the workers are against them, the liquidators are equally well aware what a complete, shattering defeat their separate action would bring them. That is why they are willing to promise anything as long as they are elected to the Duma.

That will not do. Only the bourgeois behave in that way. Worker democrats believe only in programmes, decisions, tactics and slogans that have been put into effect *for years* before the elections and are merely *repeated* for the hundredth time during the elections. As for those who make up meaningless "platforms" *without such decisions*, just for the elections, they deserve no confidence whatever.

Axelrod's feuilleton is useful as a means of destroying all self-deception, of enlightening the various concocters of "new", "open", "common" platforms.

II

The closing part of Axelrod's article, of which we spoke in *Nevskaya Zvezda* No. 18, has now appeared in *Nasha Zarya*. Taken as a whole, that final part has fully borne out our appraisal, and we can merely repeat that Axelrod's article is useful as a means of destroying all self-deception, of revealing the real nature of liquidationism, of appreciating the sheer inanity of the vaunted "non-factionalism" which today is being made so much of, and so very uselessly, in certain quarters.

Axelrod hits out at Trotsky, who is now in alliance (is it a stable one?) with the liquidators, in a particularly eloquent and convincing fashion. "The ideological and organisational union of the progressive elements into an independent faction," writes Axelrod, who amuses himself by calling the liquidators Party progressives and calling us Party reactionaries, "is—in view of the present state of affairs— their direct duty and pressing task." "In this situation in the Party, to talk of 'non-factionalism' as the sole remedy means behaving like the ostrich, which buries its head in sand at the approach of danger; it means deceiving oneself and others as to the actual state of affairs among the Social-Democrats." (*Nasha Zarya* No. 6, p. 15.)

Poor Trotsky! It is downright cruel and ungracious of Axelrod to inveigh against a true friend of the liquidators and a contributor to *Nasha Zarya* in this way. What are we to expect now? Will Trotsky come out with a devastating article against the factionalist Axelrod, or will Martov reconcile the conciliator Trotsky with the factionalist Axelrod by pasting together, as usual, what is falling apart with a dozen plastering reservations?

Really, how can anyone speak seriously now of the vaunted bloc* of Trotsky, and the Lettish and Jewish near-Marxists, etc., with Axelrod?

Axelrod's article contains a point that is worthy of serious analysis, namely, the one on the "Europeanisation" of our Social-Democratic movement. But before passing to that point, it is necessary to say a few words about one of the methods of the liquidators.

One page in Axelrod's article (16) is a collection of the strongest, most vicious and choicest terms of abuse, against the anti-liquidators in general and this writer in particular. It would not be worth replying to abuse at all (a person in Axelrod's position can do nothing but revile and curse) but for documentary evidence indicating that some deliberately use such abuse while others are embarrassed by it.

Mr. Chernov, for example, *replying* in *Zavety*[98] to what Kamenev says to prove that he, leader of the "Left" Narodniks, is drifting from democracy to liberalism, selects a bunch of the most abusive expressions of the liquidators and anti-liquidators, chuckling as he does so. Mr. Chernov's method is so despicable that it suffices to point to it and pass on.

No struggle over principles waged by groups within the Social-Democratic movement *anywhere in the world* has managed to avoid a number of personal and organisational conflicts. Nasty types make it their business deliberately to pick on "conflict" expressions. But only weak-nerved dilettanti from among "sympathisers" can be embarrassed by

---

* Axelrod's article is dated May 17, 1912, or *five months* after the solemn formation of the Trotskyist and liquidationist bloc to fight the anti-liquidators under the banner of "non-factionalism"!

these conflicts, can shrug them off in despair or in scorn, as if to say "it is all a squabble!" Those who take a serious interest in the working-class movement always learn—it is possible and necessary to learn it, if only by studying the historical role of the great leaders of the working-class movement—to distinguish between the "conflict" aspect of the struggle of *ideas*, of the struggle of trends, and that aspect of it which is a matter of principle. People will always be people, and no historical clash between the Marxist and the anarchist trends (Marx and Bakunin), between the Guesdist and the Jaurèsist, between the Lassallean and the Eisenach trends, etc., has ever managed to do without "conflict" material, without "squabbles".

There still exists a nasty type of writers who deliberately select "from those days" bunches of accusations of a thousand and one dishonesties, etc. But there are serious Social-Democrats who lay bare the *ideological* roots of the differences, which in the splits of particular groups, in the circumstances of political exile, etc., inevitably took the form of conflicts in the nature of desperate squabbles.

Let the reader not imagine that we want to frighten anyone away from studying the data to which Axelrod alludes—merely alludes—in the more abusive passages of his article. Quite the reverse. We *invite* those who want to know everything about the Social-Democratic movement to study those data. They are available in *complete* form abroad, and they include not only passionate accusations, but also documents and evidence by neutral persons. A study of those documents and that evidence will supply an answer to the question *why* the attempt to establish complete peace between the liquidators and the anti-liquidators, made in January 1910, ended in failure.

———

One of the more interesting passages of fundamental importance in Axelrod's article is the following:

"To organise and unite as a faction is a direct obligation and pressing task of the advocates of a reform, or rather [listen to this!] revolution, in the Party, for this is the only way in which they will be able to accomplish their task—to Europeanise, i.e., radically change the character of, the Russian Social-Democratic movement as it took shape in the pre-revolutionary period and developed further in the revolutionary period, and organise it on the same principles on which the European Social-Democratic party system is based."

And so, the liquidators advocate a revolution in the Party. This exceptionally truthful statement of Axelrod's is worthy of note, for the bitter truth is more useful than deceit that "uplifts us",[99] and more valuable than diplomatic quibbles and reservations. Try to carry out a revolution in the Party, esteemed P. B. Axelrod! We shall see whether you and your friends will be more successful than those "revolutionaries" who only a short time ago tried to accomplish a "revolution" (against the republic) in Portugal.[100]

But the chief thing in the statement just quoted is the vaunted "Europeanisation", which is being talked about in every possible tone by Dan and Martov and Trotsky and Levitsky and all the liquidators. It is one of the main points of their opportunism.

"To Europeanise, i.e., radically change the character of, the Russian Social-Democratic movement...." Think over these words. What determines the "character" of *any* Social-Democratic movement and *radical* changes in it? The general economic and political conditions of the country concerned, without a doubt. And there is no doubt that the character of the Social-Democratic movement of a people can be radically changed *only* if those conditions undergo *radical* changes.

These are all most elementary and indisputable truths. But it is these truths that expose Axelrod's opportunist error! The trouble with him is that he wants to *bypass* a stubborn and grim struggle for a *radical* change in Russian political conditions, which has not yet taken place, by dreaming of a *radical* change in the "character of the Russian Social-Democratic movement".

Just as the Cadets, who readily talk about Europeanisation (the liquidators have borrowed both the Cadets' catchword and their ideas), by means of this loose term push into the background an exact concept of the solid foundations of political liberty and "*play*" at "constitutional opposition", so the liquidators *play* at "European Social-Democracy", although—in the country where they amuse themselves with their game—there is *as yet no* constitution, *as yet no* basis for "Europeanism", and a stubborn struggle *has yet to be waged* for them.

A naked savage who put on a top-hat and imagined himself therefore to be a European would look rather ridiculous. Milyukov, a supporter of the bourgeoisie, reminds one of just such a savage when he asserts in the Third Duma that "we have a constitution, thank God", and so does Axelrod, a supporter of the workers, when he puts on a top-hat inscribed "I am a European Social-Democrat". Both of them —Milyukov as well as Axelrod —are ridiculous in their naïveté. They are both opportunists, for, by uttering dreamy phrases about "Europeanism", they evade the difficult and urgent question of how a particular class, in non-European conditions, ought to act *for* a stubborn struggle to secure a *basis* for Europeanism.

Axelrod has *proved* by his article that the result is evasion of a vital and urgent matter by means of dreamy phrases. Trotsky has prepared a perfectly European —yes, truly and perfectly European —plan for setting up a *"press committee"* as an "elected collective control body" of the workers for working-class newspapers (p. 18 of Axelrod's article). Trotsky probably even consulted "European Social-Democrats" about this and received their blessing as a gift —a blessing which he makes a great deal of.

And now the "European Social-Democrat" Axelrod, after waiting two months or so, during which Trotsky plagued all the St. Petersburg Social-Democrats with his letters about "elected collective control bodies", making everyone laugh, has at last taken pity on Trotsky and explained to him that a "press committee" is no good and is impossible, and that what is needed instead is an *"agreement"* between the workers and the liquidationist *Zhivoye Dyelo* (pp. 18 and 19 of Axelrod's article)!!

This is a small example, and we must unfortunately confine ourselves to it. But it is a very typical one. The laughable result produced by Trotsky's "European" plan for a "press committee" is also being produced by the "European" plans of all the liquidators for an "open workers' party" or "legal political societies of the workers", for a "campaign" for "freedom of association", etc.

The *only* result of Trotsky's "European" plans for a "press committee", an "elected collective control body" for the working-class newspaper, "of all the working-class organisations that have taken shape", etc., is that the legalist game of a "workers' publishing house" has taught the workers a special lesson, while the liquidators have in fact *failed to produce either* a "press committee" *or* a working-class press! These are the facts.

The "press committee" was a dream of the opportunist intellectual who, ignoring the difficult non-European conditions of the working-class movement in Russia, drew up a splendid European plan and took advantage of the occasion to boast of his "Europeanism" to the whole world.

This bitter lot of the liquidators is not accidental, it is inevitable. As soon as their "European" plans come near to being realised, they turn out to be soap bubbles, inventions of opportunist intellectuals. This was the case with the labour congress, the "press committee", the workers' legal political society (the confused little reservations by which Martov seeks to "rescue" that "plan" in *Nasha Zarya* No. 5 do not improve matters in the least) and the campaign for freedom of association.

The liquidators describe as "Europeanism" the conditions in which the Social-Democrats have been active in the principal countries of Europe *since 1871*, i.e., precisely at the time when the whole historical period of bourgeois revolutions was over and when the *foundations* of political liberty had taken firm shape for a long time to come. The "change in the character" of the Social-Democratic movement in those countries occurred, firstly, *after* a radical change in political conditions—after a definite constitutional system had been firmly established, comparatively speaking; secondly, that change was only a temporary one, for a definite period (which has lately been nearing its end, as is generally acknowledged by the most cautious Social-Democrats of Europe).

In these conditions of fully established bourgeois constitutionalism, a campaign for, say, freedom of association or universal suffrage, and for *constitutional reforms* in general, could be, under certain circumstances, a campaign of the working class, a real political campaign, a real struggle for constitutional reforms.

In our country, however, opportunist intellectuals transplant the slogans of such "European" campaigns to a *soil* lacking the *most elementary* foundations of European constitutionalism, in an attempt to *bypass* the specific historical evolution which usually *precedes* the laying of these foundations.

The difference between the reformism of our Axelrod and his friends, who pose as "European Social-Democrats", and the reformism of Bissolati, that genuine European, *is* that Bissolati sacrifices the principles of the class struggle and of consistent Marxist theory and practice *for the sake of reforms* which are really effected (with certain curtailments) by the really dominant liberal bourgeoisie. Axelrod, however, makes the same sacrifice as Bissolati *for the sake of reforms* which impotent, light-minded, dreamy liberals merely prattle about.

The liberal bourgeoisie here in Russia will become a real force only when the development of the country overcomes the liberals' timidity and their conciliatory, half-hearted slogans. That is how it has been everywhere. Liberals become a power only when the democracy has won *in spite of* the liberals.

Written late in July 1912

Published in *Nevskaya Zvezda* Nos. 18 and 19, July 22 and 29, 1912
Signed: *V. I.*

Published according to the newspaper text verified against the text in the collection *Marxism and Liquidationism*, Part II, St. Petersburg, 1914

THE RESULTS OF SIX MONTHS' WORK[101]

By founding a workers' daily newspaper, the workers
of St. Petersburg have accomplished a major feat, one that
without exaggeration can be called historic. The workers'
democratic movement has rallied together and consolidated
itself in incredibly difficult conditions. Of course, it is not
possible to talk of the *stability* of the workers' democratic
press in our country. Everyone knows very well the persecution to which working-class newspapers are subjected.

For all that, the founding of *Pravda* is an outstanding
proof of the political consciousness, energy and unity of
the Russian workers.

It is useful to look back and note some results of the six
months' work of the Russian workers for founding a press of
their own. Since January of this year the interest shown by
working-class circles of St. Petersburg in their press has
become fully evident and a number of articles dealing with
a workers' daily has appeared in newspapers of all shades
that come into contact with the world of labour.

I

Data on *who* founded a daily working-class press in Russia
and *how* it was founded are, fortunately, available in a
comparatively full form. They are the data on the *collection of funds* for a workers' daily newspaper.

Let us begin with the funds with which *Pravda* was
brought into being. We have the accounts of *Zvezda*, *Nevskaya
Zvezda* and *Pravda* for the period from January 1 to June
30, or exactly six months. Publicity ensured the absolute

accuracy of the accounts, accidental errors being corrected
immediately on indications from those concerned.

What is of the greatest importance and interest to us is
not the sum total of the funds collected, but the *composition
of the givers.* When, for example, *Nevskaya Zvezda* No. 3
gave the total contributions for a workers' daily newspaper
as 4,288 rubles 84 kopeks (from January to May 5, exclusive
of the donations which from April 22, the day when *Pravda*
first appeared, came directly to that newspaper), we were at
once prompted to ask: what was the role which the workers
themselves and groups of workers played in collecting this
sum? Does it consist of large donations by sympathisers?
Or did the workers themselves show in this case a personal
and active concern for the working-class press and make
up a large sum out of donations from a *large* number of
workers' groups?

From the point of view of the initiative and energy of
the workers *themselves,* it is much more important to have
100 rubles collected by, say, 30 groups of workers than
1,000 rubles collected by some dozens of "sympathisers".
A newspaper founded on the basis of *five-kopek pieces* collected by small factory circles of workers is a far more
dependable, solid and *serious* undertaking (both financially
and, *most important of all*, from the standpoint of the development of the workers' democratic movement) than a newspaper founded with tens and hundreds of rubles contributed
by sympathising intellectuals.

To obtain exact data on this fundamental and most
important matter, we have performed the following operation with regard to the figures on collections published in
the three newspapers mentioned. We have singled out *only*
the donations stated to have been made by *groups* of factory or office workers.

What we are interested in at the moment is the contributions made by the workers *themselves*—moreover, not by
individual ones, who may have come across a collector by
chance, not being linked with him ideologically, i.e., in
terms of their views and convictions; we mean *groups* of
workers, who must no doubt have *discussed* beforehand
whether they should donate any money, *whom* they should
give it to and for what purpose.

ПРАВДА

ЕЖЕДНЕВНАЯ РАБОЧАЯ ГАЗЕТА.

№ 80.   Среда, 1 Августа 1912 г.   ЦѢНА 2 коп.

First page of *Pravda* No. 80, of August 1, 1912,
in which Part III of Lenin's article "The
Results of Six Months' Work" was published

Reduced

Each report by *Zvezda*, *Nevskaya Zvezda* or *Pravda* which indicated that the money contributed for a workers' daily came from a *group* of factory or office workers, we assumed to be *a group contribution* by the workers themselves.

How many such group contributions by workers were there in the first half of 1912?

Five hundred and four group contributions!

More than five hundred times, groups of workers made contributions for the founding and maintenance of *their* paper, either donating what they had earned in one day, or making a single contribution, or contributing repeatedly from time to time. In addition to individual workers and sympathisers, *504 groups of workers* took a most active part in founding their newspaper. This figure is an unquestionable indication that a deep and conscious interest in a workers' newspaper has been aroused among the *mass* of the workers—and not just in any workers' paper, but in a workers' democratic paper. Since the masses are so politically conscious and active, no difficulties or obstacles can frighten us. There are not, and cannot be, difficulties or obstacles which the political consciousness, activity and interest of the mass of the workers would be unable to overcome in some way or another.

Those 504 group contributions break down by months as follows:

January 1912		14
February "		18
March "		76
April "		227
May "		135
June "		34
Six-month total		504

This little table makes clear, incidentally, the great importance of April and May as a *period of radical change*. From darkness to light, from passivity to activity, from action by individuals to action by the masses.

In January and February group contributions by the workers were as yet quite insignificant. Obviously, the activity was only just beginning. March showed a noticeable and substantial rise. Seventy-six group contributions by workers in one month—this indicates at all events a serious movement among the workers, a tenacious effort by the masses to have their way at all costs, undeterred by having to make donations. This speaks of the workers' deep confidence in their own strength and in the undertaking as a whole, in the trend of the projected newspaper, and so on. In March there was as yet no workers' daily, which means that groups of workers were collecting money and giving it to *Zvezda*, as it were, on credit.

April brought an *enormous* leap that decided the matter. Two hundred and twenty-seven group contributions by workers in one month, an average of over seven contributions a day! The dam had been broken, and the founding of a workers' daily paper was assured. Every group contribution means not merely the sum of five-kopek and ten-kopek pieces, but something far more important—the sum of combined, massed energy, the determination of *groups* to support a workers' newspaper, to disseminate and guide it, to bring it into being through their own participation.

The question may arise: were not the April contributions greatest *after* the 22nd, i.e., after *Pravda* had appeared? No, they were not. *Before* April 22, *Zvezda* reported *188 group contributions*. Between the 22nd and the end of April, *Pravda* reported 39 group contributions. This means that during 21 days of April, before *Pravda* had appeared, there was an average of *nine contributions* a day, while the last nine days of April saw only four contributions a day by groups.

Two important conclusions follow from this:

Firstly, the workers were particularly active *before* the appearance of *Pravda*. By giving money "on credit", showing their confidence in *Zvezda*, the workers expressed their determination to have their way.

Secondly, it is seen that *it was the April effort* of the workers that brought the workers' newspaper, *Pravda*, into being. There can be no doubt as to the closest connection between the general upswing of the working-class movement (not in a narrow guild, narrow trade union sense, but with a scope affecting *all the people*) and the founding of the daily newspaper of the St. Petersburg worker democrats. We need something more than trade union publications, we need a political newspaper of our own—this is what the

masses realised more and more in April; what we need is
not just any political workers' newspaper, but a newspaper
of the foremost worker democrats; we need a newspaper not
only to promote our working-class struggle, but also to
provide a model and a beacon for the whole people.

In May the upswing was still very marked. Group contributions averaged more than four a day. On the one hand,
it was an indication of the general upswing in April-May.
On the other, the mass of the workers realised that, although the publication of a daily newspaper had already
begun, its position would be particularly difficult at first
and group support particularly necessary.

In June the number of group contributions fell below the
March figure. Of course, the fact has to be taken into consideration that *after* the workers' daily newspaper had
begun to appear *another* form of assistance to the newspaper
arose and acquired decisive significance, namely, subscrip-
tion to it and its circulation among fellow-workers, acquaint-
ances, countrymen, etc. The politically-conscious friends
of *Pravda* do not limit themselves to subscribing to the paper
but pass it on or send it to others as a sample, to make it
known at other factories, in neighbouring flats or houses,
in the countryside and so on. Unfortunately, we have no way
of obtaining complete statistics on *this kind* of group assistance.

II

It will be most instructive to see how those 504 contributions by groups of workers are distributed among *towns*
and factory localities. In what parts of Russia and how readily did the workers respond to the appeal to help in founding a workers' daily newspaper?

Fortunately, data on this are available for all of the workers' group contributions reported by *Zvezda*, *Nevskaya
Zvezda* and *Pravda*.

In summing up these data, we must first of all single out
St. Petersburg, which naturally has taken the lead in the
matter of founding a workers' newspaper, then fourteen
towns and factory localities which sent in contributions
from more than one group of workers, and lastly, all the
other towns, thirty-five in all, which sent in only one group

contribution each during the six months. This is the picture
we obtain:

	Total of group contributions
St. Petersburg	412
14 towns with 2 to 12 group contributions each	57
35 towns with 1 group contribution each	35
Total for 50 towns	504

This shows that *almost the whole of* Russia took an active
part, to some extent or another, in founding a workers'
daily. Considering the difficulties which the circulation of
the workers' democratic press encounters in the provinces,
it is amazing that *so large a number* of towns should have
responded within six months to the appeal of the St. Petersburg workers.

Ninety-two group contributions by workers in forty-nine
towns of Russia,* besides the capital, is a very impressive
figure, at least for a beginning. There can be no question
here of chance, indifferent, passive givers; these are undoubtedly representatives of the proletarian masses, people
united by conscious sympathy for the workers' democratic
movement although scattered throughout Russia.

We note that the list of provincial towns is headed by
Kiev with 12 group contributions, then comes Yekaterinoslav with 8, while Moscow with 6 is only in the fourth place.
This lag of Moscow and its entire area can be seen still more
clearly from the following summary data on all the areas
of Russia:

---

* Here is a complete list of the towns and localities: **Vicinity of
St. Petersburg**: Kronstadt, Kolpino and Sestroretsk. **South**: Kharkov, 4 group contributions; Yekaterinoslav, 8; Ananyev, 2; Lugansk,
3; Kherson, Rostov-on-Don, Pavlograd, Poltava; Kiev, 12; Astrakhan,
4; Chernigov; Yuzovka, 3; Minakovo, Shcherba Mine, Rykov Mine,
Bélgorod, Yelisavetgrad, Yekaterinodar; Mariupol, 2; Nizhne-Dne-
provsk and Nakhichevan. **Moscow area**: Rodniki, 2; Ryazan; Tula,
2; Bezhetsk, 2. **North**: Archangel, 5; Vologda. **West**: Dvinsk, Vilna,
Gomel, Riga, Lepaya and Mühlgraben. **Urals**: Perm, Kyshtym, Mi-
nyar and Orenburg. **Volga region**: Sormovo and Balakovo Village.
Caucasus: Baku, 2; Grozny and Tiflis. **Siberia**: Tyumen and Blagovesh-
chensk. **Finland**: Helsingfors.

Number of group contributions by workers for a workers'
daily newspaper during six months — January to June 1912

St. Petersburg and vicinity	415
South	51
Moscow and its area	13
North and West	12
Urals and Volga region	6
Caucasus, Siberia and Finland	7
Total for Russia	504

These data may be interpreted as follows:

In terms of renewed activity of the worker democrats in Russia, proletarian St. Petersburg has already awakened and is at its glorious post. The South is awakening. Mother Moscow, however, and the rest of Russia are still asleep. It is time she awoke too.

The lag of the entire Moscow area becomes obvious when that area is compared with the other *provincial* areas. The South is farther from St. Petersburg, much farther away than Moscow. Nevertheless, the South, which has *fewer* industrial workers than the Moscow area, exceeds that area *almost fourfold* in the number of group contributions by workers.

Moscow seems to be lagging behind even the Urals and the Volga region, for the number of workers in Moscow and its area exceeds their number in the Urals and the Volga region not twice, but many times over. Yet Moscow and its area made only 13 group contributions against 6 in the Urals and the Volga region.

There are probably two special reasons for the lag of Moscow and its area. Firstly, the dominant industry here is the textile industry, in which the economic situation, i.e., market conditions and conditions for a more or less considerable increase in production, has been worse than, say, in metallurgy. That is why textile workers participated less in strikes and showed less interest in politics and in the workers' democratic movement. Secondly, in the Moscow area there are more factories scattered over out-of-the-way localities and therefore less accessible to newspapers than in the big city.

In any case, we must undoubtedly draw a lesson from the data cited above. The closest attention must be paid to the circulation of the workers' newspaper in Moscow. We cannot put up with the lag of Moscow. Every politically-conscious worker realises that St. Petersburg without Moscow is like one hand without the other.

The *bulk* of Russia's factory workers is concentrated in Moscow and its area. In 1905, for instance, according to government statistics, there were 567,000 factory workers here, i.e., *more than one-third* of Russia's total (1,660,000), and many more than in the St. Petersburg area (298,000). The Moscow area is therefore destined to take the *first* place for the number of readers and friends of a workers' newspaper, for the number of politically-conscious representatives of the workers' democratic movement. Moscow will, of course, have to have a workers' daily newspaper *of its own*.

Meanwhile St. Petersburg must help it. Every morning the readers of *Pravda* should tell themselves and their friends: "Workers, remember the Muscovites!"

III

The above data should draw our attention from yet another standpoint, one that is very important and urgent as regards our practical tasks. Everyone realises that a political newspaper is one of the basic conditions for the participation of any class of modern society in the political affairs of the country in general and in an election campaign in particular.

Thus, a newspaper is required by the workers in general, and for carrying out elections to the Fourth Duma in particular. The workers know very well that they can expect no good either from the Third or from the Fourth Duma. But we must take part in the elections, firstly, to rally and politically enlighten the mass of the workers during the elections, when party struggles and the entire political life will be stimulated and when the *masses* will *learn politics* in one way or other; and, secondly, to get our worker deputies into the Duma. Even in the most reactionary Duma, in a purely landlord one, worker deputies *have done*, and can do, a great deal for the working-class cause, provided they are true worker democrats, provided they are connected with the masses and the masses learn to direct them and check on their activity.

In the first half of 1912 *all* the political parties in Russia began, and virtually *completed*, what is known as the pre-election *mobilisation* of the party forces. Mobilisation is a military term. It means putting the army in a state of readiness for action. Just as an army is put in a state of readiness before a war, the reserves being called up and arms and ammunition distributed, so, before an election, all parties sum up their work, reaffirm their decisions on party views and slogans, rally their forces and prepare to fight all the other parties.

This work, we repeat, is virtually completed. The elections are only *a few weeks* off. During this time we can and must bend our energies to increase our influence on the voters, on the masses, but if a party (the party of any class) has not got ready in six months, nothing can help it any longer, for it is already a *zero* in the elections.

That is why the six months which our statistics cover are six months of *decisive* mobilisation of the workers' forces prior to the Fourth Duma elections. They have been six months of mobilisation of all the forces of the worker demo- crats—of course, not only with regard to the Duma campaign, but we are for the moment devoting our attention to the latter.

A question arises at this point, a question raised recently by *Nevskaya Zvezda* No. 16, and *Pravda* No. 61. It concerns the so-called liquidators, who since January 1912 have been publishing the newspapers *Zhivoye Dyelo* and *Nevsky Golos* in St. Petersburg. The liquidators, who have their own sep- arate newspapers, say that "agreement" has to be reached with them, the liquidators, if there is to be "unity" of the worker democrats in the elections, otherwise they try to frighten us with the prospect of "duplicate candidates".[102]

It seems that these attempts at intimidation have so far had very little success.

And this is quite understandable. How could anyone seriously take into account people who have rightly earned the name of liquidators and advocates of a liberal labour policy?

But perhaps there are, nevertheless, many workers who follow the erroneous, un-Social-Democratic views of this group of intellectuals? If so, ought we not to pay special attention to these workers? We now have objective, open and quite precise data for an answer to this question. As we know, throughout the first half of 1912 the liquidators showed particular vigour in attacking *Pravda*, *Nevskaya Zvezda*, *Zvezda*, and all opponents of liquidationism in general.

How successful were the liquidators among the workers? We can judge this from the contributions for a workers' daily newspaper published in the liquidationist newspapers *Zhivoye Dyelo* and *Nevsky Golos*. The liquidators recognised the need for a daily very long ago —in 1911 or perhaps even 1910—and advocated the idea most energetically among their supporters. In February 1912 *Zhivoye Dyelo*, which was first issued on January 20, began to carry reports on the contributions it received for this purpose.

Let us single out from those contributions (which totalled 139.27 rubles in the first half of 1912) *group contributions by workers*, just as we did in the case of the non-liquidationist papers. Let us sum up all the sixteen issues of *Zhivoye Dyelo* and the five issues of *Nevsky Golos* (its issue No. 6 appeared in July), and even add contributions for the benefit of *Zhivoye Dyelo* itself (although we did not take data on such contributions from the non-liquidationist papers). We obtain the following data on the total of group contributions by workers in six months:

Number of group contributions by workers for a workers' daily newspaper during the first half of 1912

	Non-liqui-dationist newspapers	Liquida-tionist newspapers
January	14	0
February	18	0
March	76	7
April	227	8
May	135	0
June	34	0
Total	504	15

And so, by dint of frantic effort, the group of liquidationist intellectuals succeeded in enlisting the support of *15 groups of workers in all*!

Could one imagine a more shattering defeat of the liquidators since January 1912? Could one imagine a more specific proof of the fact that we are in the presence of a group of liquidationist intellectuals who are capable of publishing a semi-liberal magazine and newspaper, but totally lack any serious support among the proletarian masses?

Here, in addition, are data on the territorial distribution of the donations sent to the liquidators by groups of workers:

Number of group contributions by workers for
a workers' daily newspaper during the first half of 1912

	Non-liqui-dationist newspapers	Liquida-tionist newspapers
St. Petersburg and vicinity . . .	415	10
South	51	1
Moscow and its area	13	2
North and West	12	1
Urals and Volga region	6	0
Caucasus, Siberia and Finland . .	7	1
Total	504	15*

And so, the liquidators' defeat in the South during the six-month period is even worse than in St. Petersburg.

These exact workers' statistics, which were published openly for as long as six months in newspapers of opposed trends, definitely settle the question of "liquidationism". One may revile the opponents of liquidationism and slander them as much as one pleases, but these exact data on group contributions by workers are irrefutable.

It is quite understandable now why neither *Nevskaya Zvezda* nor *Pravda* took the liquidators' threat of "duplicate candidates" seriously. It would be ridiculous to take seriously threats from people who in six months of open struggle revealed that they amount to little more than zero. All the defenders of liquidationism have united in *Zhivoye Dyelo*

---

* Moscow, 2; Nakhichevan, Novonikolayevsk and Archangel, 1 each.

and *Nevsky Golos*. And it took all of them together six months to win over fifteen groups of workers!

Liquidationism amounts to nil in the working-class movement; it is only strong among the liberal intelligentsia.

IV

The data in *Pravda* on all kinds of workers' contributions are, generally speaking, extremely interesting. They provide us, for the first time, with highly accurate data on the most diverse aspects of the working-class movement and the life of Russian worker democrats. We hope to return to the analysis of these data more than once.

At the moment, however, before we finish our survey of data on the contributions made by groups of workers for a daily newspaper, we must point out one practical conclusion.

Workers' groups made 504 contributions to *their* press, to *Zvezda* and *Pravda*. The workers had absolutely no other aim in view except the founding and maintenance of their workers' press. That is precisely why a simple truthful summary of these data for six months provides a most valuable picture of the life of worker democrats in Russia. The five- and ten-kopek pieces collected and marked "from a group of workers of such-and-such a factory" have made it possible also to appraise the workers' sentiments, their class-consciousness, their unity, and their readiness to promote the working-class cause.

That is why this custom of group collections by the workers, brought into being by the upswing in April and May, should by all means be continued, developed and expanded, and it goes without saying that accounts of the collections are necessary too, such as have always been published in *Pravda*.

This custom is of vast importance from the standpoint of both the stability of the working-class press and the common interests of the worker democrats.

The working-class press needs to be developed and strengthened. And this requires money. Workers' newspapers in Russia can be satisfactorily organised through persevering effort only on condition that the workers constantly arrange massive collections. There is a workers' paper in America (*Appeal to Reason*[103]) which has *over half a million* subscribers. That Russian worker, we would say, paraphrasing a well-known saying, is a poor worker indeed if he does not hope to overtake and surpass his American fellow-workers.

What is very much more important, however, is not the financial aspect of the matter, but something else. Let us assume that a hundred workers in different shops of a factory contribute *one kopek* each on pay-day to the workers' newspaper. That will add up to two rubles a month. Let us assume, on the other hand, that ten well-paid workers meeting by chance collect ten rubles at once.

The former two rubles are worth more than the latter ten. This is so obvious to any worker that it does not have to be explained at length.

It should be made a custom for *every* worker to contribute *one kopek* to the workers' newspaper *every* pay-day. Let subscriptions to the paper be taken as usual, and let those who can contribute more do so, as they have done in the past. It is very important, besides, to establish and spread the custom of *"a kopek for the workers' newspaper"*.

The significance of such collections will depend above all on their being regularly held every pay-day, without interruption, and on an ever greater number of workers taking part in these regular collections. Accounts could be published in a simple form: "so-and-so many kopeks" would imply that so many workers at the given factory had contributed to the workers' paper, and if there were any larger contributions, they could be stated as follows: "In addition, so-and-so many workers contributed so-and-so much."

If this custom of *a kopek for the workers' newspaper* becomes established, the workers of Russia will soon raise their papers to the proper standard. Workers' papers should give more information, and of a more varied nature; they should have Sunday supplements and so on, and should have their correspondents in the Duma, in all Russia's towns and in the major cities abroad. The workers' newspaper should develop and improve *steadily*, which cannot be done unless the greatest possible number of workers regularly collect money for their press.

Monthly reports on the *workers' kopek* will show everyone how the workers throughout Russia are shaking off their indifference and drowsiness, how they are awakening to an intelligent and cultured life—not in the official nor in the liberal sense of the term. It will be possible to see clearly how interest in the workers' democratic movement is growing, and how the time is drawing near when Moscow and the other big cities will have workers' papers of their own.

We have had enough of the domination of the bourgeois *Kopeika!*[104] That unscrupulous, huckster-minded newspaper has reigned long enough. In a matter of six months, the workers of St. Petersburg have shown how tremendously successful joint collections by the workers can be. May their example and their initiative not be in vain. May the custom of *a workers' kopek for the workers' newspaper* develop and gain strength!

Written on July 12-14 (25-27), 1912

Published in *Pravda* Nos. 78, 79, 80, 81,   Published according to
July 29 and 31, and August 1 and 2, 1912   the newspaper text
          Signed: *A Statistician*

THE PRESENT SITUATION IN THE R.S.D.L.P.[105]

The German comrades often have occasion to read reports of bitter struggles and fundamental divergencies inside the R.S.D.L.P. Unfortunately, such reports originate from particular groups of political exiles. In most cases they come from people who are either absolutely unfamiliar with the actual state of affairs in Russia at the present time or deliberately seek to mislead the German comrades by a one-sided presentation of party politics. Every such group of exiles has its own special "trend", but in reality it consists of people who have lost all living contact with the fighting Russian workers' Party or have never had such contact. Unfortunately, one of this kind of "informants" succeeded in winning the confidence of *Vorwärts*. The Central Organ of the German Social-Democratic Party in a series of articles opened its columns to a torrent of unheard-of slander against the Russian Party, poured out from the pen of that informant and supposed to be derived from "objective" sources.

Actually, those sources were "subjective" and false through and through. Since *Vorwärts* did not insert our *factual correction*, we had to issue a separate pamphlet entitled *The Anonymous Writer in* Vorwärts *and the State of Affairs in the R.S.D.L.P.*,* which was issued in several hundred copies and was sent to the executive committees of all the German Party organisations of any importance and to the editors of the major organs of the Party press.

As far as the factual evidence of the pamphlet is concerned, *Vorwärts* was unable to raise *a single objection*, and thereby tacitly accepted it.

---

* See present edition, Vol. 17, pp. 533-46.—*Ed.*

To enable our German Party comrades to appraise the authenticity of certain reports reaching them, we quote here a letter which the Central Committee of the R.S.D.L.P. sent to the Executive Committee of the German Social-Democratic Party. The Letts had suggested that the Executive should arrange a joint meeting of eleven "centres" on the question of material support for the election campaign, whereupon the Executive asked those centres about their attitude to the matter. The letter is the answer given by the Central Committee, and it reads as follows:

July 30, 1912*

TO THE EXECUTIVE COMMITTEE
OF THE GERMAN SOCIAL-DEMOCRATIC PARTY

Dear Comrades,

Recently we received a copy of the letter sent to you by the Committee of the Lettish Social-Democracy Abroad on June 24. We saw no point in explaining the queer plan of these Letts to you, as we did not think any well-informed person would take that plan seriously. But we were surprised to learn from your letter to us of July 22 that you intend to adopt that plan. This compels us to express our emphatic protest, which we hereby send you. Objectively, the intention of the Executive Committee is nothing short of an attempt to contribute to the split in our Party (the R.S.D.L.P.) and to the formation of a new party hostile to us. This is unprecedented in the history of the whole International. We shall furnish the German comrades with accurate data to bear out our assertion.

THE SITUATION IN THE R.S.D.L.P.
SINCE JANUARY 1912

In January 1912 the R.S.D.L.P. held its All-Russia Conference which was attended by delegates from the organisations of St. Petersburg, Moscow, the Moscow district,

---

* The letter is quoted here with minor stylistic changes.

Kazan, Saratov, Tiflis, Baku, Nikolayev, Kiev, Yekaterinoslav, Vilna and Dvinsk. This Conference restored the Party and elected a new Central Committee in place of the one destroyed by the liquidators; furthermore, the Conference was compelled to declare these liquidators to be outside the Party. (See pamphlet *The Anonymous Writer in* Vorwärts *and the State of Affairs in the R.S.D.L.P.*, which was sent to the Executive Committee; it mentioned the protest of the liquidators and of the national organisations—the Poles, the Letts, the Bund and the groups abroad.)

In January also a meeting took place with the aim of setting up an Organising Committee to convene a new conference—a "general Party conference", as the liquidators and their friends called it.

In their letter to the Executive Committee of June 24, the Letts affirmed that this "Organising Committee" involved the following organisations and trends: the Bund, the Lettish Social-Democrats, the Caucasian Regional Committee, the Menshevik *Golos Sotsial-Demokrata*, the Vienna *Pravda* and the *Vperyod* group.

And so, on one side there is the Central Committee of the R.S.D.L.P. elected at the Conference by Russian organisations, i.e., organisations working in Russia (the opponents call it the Leninist trend); on the other side there is the so-called Organising Committee, which promises to convene a "general" Party conference.

WHAT IS THE RELATION OF THE HITHERTO NEUTRAL RUSSIAN SOCIAL-DEMOCRATS TO THE SO-CALLED ORGANISING COMMITTEE?

Plekhanov, the best known of the Mensheviks, who had been waging a determined fight against the destruction of the Party by the liquidators, did not attend the January Party Conference, although he was invited. In April 1912 he published his correspondence with the representative of the Organising Committee (see his *Dnevnik Sotsial-Demokrata* No. 16).

Plekhanov refused to take part in the so-called Organising Committee because, he said, the Bund was convening not a conference of the existing Party organisations, but an *"inaugural" conference, i.e., one that was to found a new party*. The so-called initiating groups, which in reality are the only groups backing the Organising Committee, are, according to Plekhanov, liquidationist groups, which do not belong to the Party and want to form a new party. In April 1912 Plekhanov wrote: "The new conference is being called by the liquidators."

In July this Organising Committee published its *Listok* No. 3, which contains not a word, not a hint, of a reply to Plekhanov. One can judge from this how the Executive Committee is kept informed by the Letts, those very same Letts who complain that the "Leninist" Central Committee does not answer the letters of the Organising Committee.

Is it really so very strange that the Central Committee of the Party—of the old Party—should not reply to those who, according to the hitherto neutral Plekhanov, are founding a new party?

The Organising Committee must first of all prove to the neutral Plekhanov that it is not forming a new party and not liquidating the old one.

The Letts who are taking part in the Organising Committee and who appealed to the Executive Committee on June 24 should—after six months' struggle of this Organising Committee of the liquidators against the Party—have shown by facts and documents the results of this struggle; instead, they show the Executive Committee the **Potemkin villages**[106] **of the liquidators**.

The Letts proposed that the Executive should convene eleven "organisational" centres, organisations and factions of the Russian Social-Democrats. That is literally what they stated (see p. 4 of the Letts' letter to the Executive of June 24).

All over the world, parties have so far been formed of local organisations united by a single central body. But in 1912 the Russian and Lettish liquidators made a great discovery. From now on, a party may be formed of "centres, organisations and factions".

According to the Letts' latest liquidationist electoral geometry, the eleven organisational centres, organisations and factions include, firstly, the Organising Committee and, secondly, six factions, or organisations, or centres, *which form that Organising Committee.* The Letts' letter says in so many words: "Points 2 to 7 inclusive form the Organising Committee."

Thus the intellectualist groups that are liquidating the Party obtain a *treble* vote, like the aristocracy in the "rotten boroughs":

(1) The Caucasian Regional Committee, a fictitious organisation;

(2) Ditto, as represented by the Paris *Golos*, although *Golos* has no permanent mandate from the Caucasus;

(3) Ditto, as represented by the Organising Committee.

We maintain that the Russian workers will indignantly and contemptuously reject the idea of discussing the question of duplicate candidates, i.e., the attempt of the liquidators jointly with the insignificant groups abroad to cause a split, the more so since these groups represent only intellectualist disorganisers.

We wish to point out the fact that not a single one of the groups abroad that are fighting against the Party has during the past six months received a mandate from any organisation in Russia to publish its newspaper or issue leaflets. If the Letts are trying to prove the contrary to the Executive Committee, let them name in the Russian press at least one such mandate prior to July 22.

Golos Sotsial-Demokrata is not the organ of any Russian organisation.

Nor is Trotsky's Vienna *Pravda* the organ of any Russian organisation. Three years ago *Pravda* was the organ of the Ukrainian Spilka[107] (Southern Russia), but the Spilka cancelled its mandate long ago.

Neither *Vperyod*, nor Plekhanov, nor the "pro-Party Bolsheviks", publish any organs that are Party organs of any organisation in Russia.

It is very easy to refer to groups which do not exist in reality. Nor is it difficult to print reports expressing "sympathy". But to bring out, even for six months, the organ of an organisation operating in Russia, it is necessary to have regular contacts, the unqualified confidence of the mass of the workers in the localities, and unity of views on tactics, which can be achieved only through joint work over a long period. The tiny groups abroad which the Lettish and Bundist disorganisers are mobilising against the Party lack all this.

As regards the Polish Socialist Party, we shall say briefly: it is *no Social-Democratic* organisation. It has *never* been part of the Social-Democratic Labour Party. There is only one reason for inviting it, namely, it "promises" to become Social-Democratic and join the liquidators! For the disorganisers and lovers of splits, this, of course, is sufficient! If the Polish Socialist Party is to be invited to take part in meetings, why not also invite the Socialist-Revolutionaries, who take part in the Duma elections, the Zionist-Socialists, the Lettish Union of Socialist-Revolutionaries, and other similar "trends"?

THE SOCIAL-DEMOCRATIC GROUP IN THE THIRD DUMA

Among the organisational centres the Executive Committee has included the little groups abroad; on the other hand, *it has not invited the Social-Democratic group in the Duma.* This is incredible, yet it is a fact. It will be useful for the Russian workers to know how Trotsky and Co. are misleading our foreign comrades.

In their letter to the Executive Committee of June 24, the Letts wrote:

"As regards the Social-Democratic Duma group, there can be no question of its good offices in the matter of financial assistance to the election campaign, for the Duma session is drawing to a close and simultaneously the Duma group is thereby dissolving itself" (p. 2 of the repeatedly quoted letter).

This is either deliberate deception, or boundless political ignorance, indicating clearly enough how far the Letts in Brussels are informed about the elections in Russia.

The letter is dated June 24. On June 9, i.e., June 22, new style, the Third Duma was officially dissolved for an indefinite period, all the deputies, the Social-Democrats among them, retaining their mandates. The latter are therefore *still Duma deputies*, which is known to every literate worker in Russia. But this is unknown to the slanderers of the Party abroad.

The only legally existing Social-Democrats in Russia, who are the only official organisation in whatever part of the country they may be, are precisely the members of the Social-Democratic group in the Third Duma.

All the liquidators hate the group. The sheets of the liquidators (*Nasha Zarya*) heap abuse and insinuations upon it, and all the disorganisers abroad spread tittle-tattle about it. Why? Because the majority of the group, in which pro-Party Mensheviks have always predominated, have always fought with determination against the liquidators and helped to make them quite harmless in St. Petersburg.

In the pamphlet *The Anonymous Writer*, etc., we published an important fact. No one could say a word to refute it. Only *two* members of the group regularly contribute to the liquidationist papers. *Eight* members of the group regularly contribute to the anti-liquidationist papers.*

Both the Letts and Trotsky propose that the Executive Committee should exclude from the meeting this body, the only all-Russia body to have preserved unity! Even if the Letts were mistaken and on June 24 did not know what was known to all the workers in Russia, why did they not take the trouble prior to July 22, i.e., in the course of a whole month, to correct their mistake? Some mistakes are very useful to those who make them.

The intention of the Letts and the liquidators who have misled the Executive Committee is to impose liquidationist candidates on us, against the majority of the Party in Russia, of the Social-Democratic group in the Duma, by means of a bloc of fictitious little groups abroad and to obtain money by fraud from the German workers. Such is the gist of the long speeches (of the Letts, Bundists, Trotsky and Co.).

But this deception will not go unpunished.

OFFICIALLY VERIFIABLE DATA
ON THE INFLUENCE OF THE LIQUIDATORS COMPARED WITH THAT OF THE PARTY

Every sensible person knows that the empty phrases about what is alleged to be secret "organisations" sympathising with the liquidators are not to be trusted at all.

---

* See present edition, Vol. 17, p. 545.—*Ed.*

We maintain that all the liquidationist organisations in Russia are fictitious.

It is difficult for those who lack accurate information on the state of affairs in Russian Social-Democratic circles to establish the truth. But even they can ascertain it if they search the written records and examine their meaning, refusing to take anything on trust. We have already given the first commonly known and verifiable fact, namely, the division of the forces in the Social-Democratic Duma group between the liquidators and anti-liquidators.

But now, after six months' struggle between the liquidators and the Party, there are further entirely objective, and still more convincing, facts.

In the letter of June 24 (pp. 5 and 6), the Letts mentioned the legal Marxist papers in St. Petersburg. They named *Zhivoye Dyelo* and *Nevsky Golos*, which advocate a Menshevik trend (that of *Golos Sotsial-Demokrata*), and contrasted them with *Zvezda* and the St. Petersburg *Pravda* (not to be confused with Trotsky's liquidationist Vienna *Pravda*), which, according to the Letts, "*are owned and led by Lenin's group*" alone.

Even though this assertion is unfortunate, the Letts have in spite of themselves cited a valid fact against the liquidators.

While the term "open party" is no more than an empty, liberal phrase of the liquidators, open *activity* in the Duma and in the press is the principal activity of Marxist propaganda. It is here, and only here, that facts are to be found which objectively show the relative strength of the liquidators and the anti-liquidators.

There are no other all-Russia political organs except those named by the Letts. The liquidators have *Zhivoye Dyelo* and *Nevsky Golos*; the anti-liquidators, *Zvezda*, subsequently named *Nevskaya Zvezda*, and *Pravda* (St. Petersburg). There are no other trends or factions in Russia, either in the press or in the public mass arena; all the groups abroad named by the Letts are mere ciphers.

We now have the results of the six months' activities of both trends.

During these six months (January-June 1912) all the Russian parties began, and completed, their preparations for the elections. Only six or eight weeks now remain till the elections. Most of the electoral lists have been drawn up. The outcome of the elections is virtually predetermined by these six months' preparations.

"Points" 1-7 in the Letts' list declared for the liquidators (the Organising Committee, the Bund, the Lettish Social-Democracy, *Golos*, the Vienna *Pravda*, the Caucasian Regional Committee, *Vperyod*). The anti-liquidators were supported by the Central Committee, which unites the Russian organisations, i.e., those functioning in Russia (only the "Leninist trend", as the liquidators assert).

Now let us see what each of the two has done.

From January 1 to June 30 (old style), 1912, the liquidators published in St. Petersburg sixteen issues of *Zhivoye Dyelo* and five issues of *Nevsky Golos*, or twenty-one issues in all.

During the same six months, the anti-liquidators published thirty-three issues of *Zvezda*, fourteen issues of *Nevskaya Zvezda* and fifty-three issues of *Pravda*, or one hundred issues in all.

Twenty-one to one hundred.

Such is the balance of forces between the liquidators and the Party in Russia. The data on the newspapers are open data; anyone can check and substantiate them.

How do matters stand with the circulation of the papers? The Letts affirm that the liquidators have distributed 30,000 copies. Let us assume that this is not an overstatement. With regard to the anti-liquidationist papers, a person whom Comrade Haase and other members have seen gave the Executive Committee the figure of 60,000 copies. This ratio reduces the influence of the liquidators, as compared with that of the Party, to 1 : 10.

While information on circulation has not been published and may therefore seem exaggerated, other data have been published that are more important, and more convincing.

They are the information concerning the connection of the liquidators and of the Party with the mass of the workers in Russia.

OPEN AND VERIFIABLE DATA
ON THE LINKS OF THE LIQUIDATORS AND THE PARTY
WITH THE MASS OF THE WORKERS IN RUSSIA

The data on the number of newspaper issues and copies
published do not fully prove the superiority of the Party
over the liquidators. Even small groups of liberal intellectuals can publish newspapers. Any newspaper which is
"friendly to the workers", or even a liberal newspaper of
a radical shade, will always find many readers in Russia.
It will be read not only by workers, but by liberals and also
by petty-bourgeois democrats.

There are facts, however, which reveal much more simply
and clearly the links of the liquidators and the Party with
the mass of the workers in Russia.

They are the data on the funds collected for a workers'
press.

For a long time agitation has been carried on among the
workers in Russia for the collection of funds to publish a
workers' daily newspaper. Everyone realised that without
such a newspaper, participation in the elections would
almost be a fiction. A newspaper is the chief weapon in
an election campaign, the chief means of Marxist agitation
among the masses.

But where is the money for a newspaper to come from?

It is necessary to organise collections among the workers.
These collections form a fund and show the strength of the
links of this or that group. They are an indication of the
prestige of the groups, the confidence placed in them by the
workers, and their actual influence on the proletarian
masses.

Such collections for a workers' newspaper were begun in
St. Petersburg early in 1912. Six months—from January 1 to
June 30—is a long enough period. Data on the collections
are published in all the newspapers listed above, the liquidationist as well as the anti-liquidationist ones.

The conclusions which may be drawn from these data for
six months are best evidence, an open, complete, objective and final answer to the question concerning the balance
of the forces of the liquidators and the Party in Russia.
Therefore we have given in the appendix a full translation
of all the accounts of money collections for a daily workers'

newspaper, taken from all the five above-mentioned newspapers for six months.

Here we give only the totals.

During the six months, the anti-liquidationist newspapers published accounts of 504 money collections among groups of workers, i.e., those giving the name of the workers' groups which made the collections. These collections were made in fifty Russian towns and factory settlements.

During the same six months—from January 1 to June 30, 1912—the liquidationist newspapers published accounts of fifteen money collections among groups of workers. These collections were made in five Russian towns.*

Here are the precise accounts:

Money collections by groups of workers for a workers' daily newspaper
January 1 to June 30, 1912

	In liquidationist newspapers	In anti-liquidationist newspapers
January	0	14
February	0	18
March	7	76
April	8	227
May	0	135
June	0	34
	15	504

Ditto: According to the Main Areas of Russia

St. Petersburg	10	415
South Russia	1	51
Moscow	2	13
North and West Russia	1	12
Urals and Volga	0	6
Caucasus, Siberia and Finland	1	7
	15	504

---

* In spite of the gossip spread by the liquidators, it was these collections, which exceeded 12,000 marks, and the aid rendered earlier by the German comrades, that formed the basic fund of our Social-Democratic press in Russia. The full translation, mentioned in the text, of all the accounts of money collections published by the various Social-Democratic newspapers over the six months was sent to the Executive Committee, the Auditing Committee and Bebel.

After six months' struggle against the Party, the liquidators were completely routed.

The liquidators do not count at all in the Russian Social-Democratic labour movement. This is proved by the above-quoted data, which anyone can verify. Such are the facts published in Russia for a whole half-year, despite the bragging of Trotsky and the liquidators.

It should be noted that Trotsky is a contributor to *Zhivoye Dyelo*. Furthermore, the Letts themselves, in their letter of June 24, admit that all the six groups, including Trotsky, the Menshevik *Golos*, and the leaders of *Zhivoye Dyelo* and *Nevsky Golos*, form the so-called Organising Committee. Therefore, our data prove that not only the liquidators, but all their pretentious friends abroad are of no account in the Social-Democratic labour movement in Russia.

On the average, only one group of workers in Russia out of thirty sides with them.

We give here the addresses and the dates of publication of all the Social-Democratic papers in St. Petersburg.

Liquidationist

1. *Zhivoye Dyelo*. St. Petersburg, Bolshaya Moskovskaya, 16. No. 1—January 20, 1912; No. 16 (last issue)—April 28, 1912 (suppressed).

2. *Nevsky Golos*. St. Petersburg, Kolokolnaya, 3. No. 1—May 20, 1912; No. 5—June 28, 1912 (still exists—up to July 29, 1912).

Anti-Liquidationist

3. *Zvezda*. St. Petersburg, Razyezzhaya, 10, Apt. 14. No. 1 (37)—January 6, 1912; No. 33 (69)—April 22, 1912 (suppressed).

4. *Nevskaya Zvezda*. St. Petersburg, Nikolayevskaya, 33, Apt. 57. No. 1—February 26, 1912; No. 2—May 3, 1912; No. 14—June 24, 1912 (still exists).

5. *Pravda*. St. Petersburg. Nikolayevskaya, 37, Apt. 18. No. 1—April 22, 1912; No. 53—June 30, 1912 (still exists).

CONCLUSION

The candidates of the R.S.D.L.P. in the forthcoming Duma elections will be nominated by the local Party organisations without distinction of views and trends. The minority of the worker Social-Democrats will everywhere have to submit to the majority.

The notorious duplication of candidates is simply nonsense, serving merely to frighten the foreign comrades and extort money.

All that is wanting is for the notorious ten "trends" to raise the bogey of *ten* candidates and for money to be begged from foreigners for each of them.

There will be no duplicate candidates. The liquidators are so weak that they cannot put up duplicate candidates. We do not negotiate with a handful of liquidators who have betrayed the Party. Neither the Central Committee in Russia nor the local organisations take the liquidators seriously. Note, for example, the latest events in St. Petersburg. The liquidators reported in *Nevsky Golos* (No. 6) that meetings were held with them (the liquidators) in St. Petersburg in connection with carrying out the election campaign. Both *Nevskaya Zvezda* (No. 16) and *Pravda* (No. 61) of July 21 and 23 reported that they had *not* sent representatives to the meetings; moreover, one participant in the meetings announced in *Nevskaya Zvezda* that the workers all over Russia would carry out the decisions of the January Conference of the R.S.D.L.P.

"Union of the various trends," he said, referring to the liquidators, "is quite inconceivable in the Social-Democratic election campaign." (*Nevskaya Zvezda* No. 16, July 8 [21], 1912.)

No financial assistance in the world can win the sympathies of the Russian workers for the liquidators. But, of course, it is possible to put up fictitious duplicate candidates in various places with the money of the Executive Committee. In that case the responsibility for such candidates, who will virtually be candidates of the German Executive

Committee, will also fall on the Executive Committee. *The money handed out to the liquidators, who have no daily newspaper, will help them to found a competing organ. That money will be used to bring about a split by those who during long years of struggle have proved their insignificance; the money will be used for trips, etc., with the aim of founding a new party.*

If the Executive Committee now wants to help the liquidators in one way or another, then, much as we respect the fraternal German Party, we shall have to appeal to the International. Then we shall *prove* to the Vienna International Congress[108] *by documents* that the Executive Committee has expressed its readiness by means of financial support to help in bringing about a split in our Party, putting up duplicate candidates and galvanising that corpse—the defeated liquidators. If the German comrades want to help the R.S.D.L.P., they must transfer the money to the Central Committee of the old Party, not to those who are organising a new party.

Central Committee of the R.S.D.L.P.

After the Executive Committee had called off the proposed meeting, it informed us that it "cannot give money to any of the Party groups in Russia for the election campaign until all of them jointly indicate to us [the Executive Committee] a body enjoying universal confidence and authorised to receive and distribute funds".

This pretended neutrality of the Executive Committee amounts in reality to a refusal to support the workers' Party in Russia because of the calumny heaped upon it by the little groups abroad and by the "conference" of the liquidators.

Besides the comments made above, we regard it as our duty to add the following.

The Russian newspapers legally existing and published in a Marxist spirit are at the present time the most important legal mouthpiece of the mass of the Russian Social-Democratic workers in connection with the Party's agitation work.

The newspapers appearing abroad, which are illegal in Russia, cannot *really* claim to be as important as those mentioned above, although their *fundamental* importance for theoretically elucidating the movement is undoubtedly very great. For everyone knows how easily, and sometimes frivolously, such papers are founded by small groups of Russian exiles scattered abroad. Those newspapers have a precarious existence among the groups concerned, and hardly ever reach the Russian members of the Party. That is why they cannot really be said to exert any appreciable influence on Party life in Russia.

After six months' struggle of the anti-liquidationist newspapers (from January to June 1912) there is *only one* liquidationist paper—*Nevsky Golos*. This paper has almost ceased to exist as a political organ. During a month and a half (from June to mid-August), only *two* issues appeared (Nos. 6 and 7). Obviously, no such newspaper can withstand the police persecution that is raging in Russia against *all* workers' newspapers, and even against many quite moderate liberal ones, unless it draws its vital energy from close contact with the mass of the workers.

The weekly *Nevskaya Zvezda* and the daily *Pravda* are now workers' newspapers of this kind; they carry great political weight and are of immediate and topical importance. Both appear in St. Petersburg; our *political opponents* among the Lettish Social-Democrats have contemptuously dismissed them as organs of "Lenin's group". From the *objective* data cited above, which can be openly verified at any time, it should become obvious to our German comrades that this "Lenin's group" comprises, in fact, the overwhelming majority of the Russian worker Social-Democrats.

Hence it is quite understandable why the information coming from the liquidators and groups, or tiny groups, sympathising with them, is *not to be trusted in the least*. All the rumours spread by those little groups together with the Jewish (Bund) and Lettish Social-Democrats, who have no direct contact with the *Russian* movement, about the joint conference of all "trends"[109] that has been convened, or allegedly is about to be convened, turn out to be pure inventions. No such conference, even if it were to take place, could play *any serious part* in the struggle of the Russian proletariat. Basically, therefore, it is, if we reluctantly are to use a harsh word, a question of a swindle.

To make the relevant facts, which are undoubtedly of
great political importance, still clearer to our German Party
comrades, we shall quote in conclusion some extracts from
an article by Axelrod, one of the liquidationist leaders,
which appeared in the last issue of the monthly *Nasha Zarya*.
Axelrod wrote:

"The idea of a 'non-factional' Social-Democratic ... organ is
utopian at present and, moreover, a utopia that ... runs counter to
the interests of the Party's political development.... We may be
said to have no factions that have taken shape organisationally.
Instead, we have various circles and small groups, of which some
hold more or less definite political, tactical and organisational views,
while the others waver in various directions, getting in the way of
the former.... The focal point and main source of internal Party discord is, on the one hand, the difference in the attitude of the various
Party circles to the new, open Social-Democratic and labour movement and, on the other hand, substantial differences over the immediate political tasks and the political tactics of the Russian Social-
Democratic movement. The questions of both these categories ...
are becoming particularly burning and topical issues just now....
And it is over them that the Russian Social-Democrats have split
into two main camps.... The question arises whether the projected
labour newspaper [proposed by some workers in St. Petersburg and
by many intellectuals abroad] will be able to take a neutral position
between these two opposed camps, and whether such a position is
permissible on principle. Obviously not.... Such being the situation
in the Party, to talk about 'non-factionalism' as a panacea means
... deceiving oneself and others as to the real state of affairs in the
Social-Democratic movement.... Factional organisation and consolidation are a direct duty and urgent task of the advocates of a Party
reform, or rather revolution" (in the Party).

Axelrod's last words obviously refer to the liquidators.
We can only advise our German Party comrades, if they hear
from various quarters about "non-factionalism", or about a
non-factional conference with the liquidators participating,
to demand, for better orientation, a full translation of Axelrod's above-quoted article for the German Social-Democratic press. Then they will see certain fables for what they
are, and will be able to judge them.

Editorial Board of Sotsial-Demokrat,
Central Organ of the R.S.D.L.P.

Confidential! Only for the organised members of Social-Democratic parties!

POSTSCRIPT
TO THE PAMPHLET *THE PRESENT SITUATION IN THE R.S.D.L.P.*

Today, September 15, 1912, we have received *via* Paris the following letter from the Executive Committee, a letter which should make it particularly clear to the German comrades how right we were in protesting against the irresponsible private "informants" of the Executive who are afraid to act openly.

On the 10th inst., the Party Executive wrote:

Berlin, September 10, 1912

Dear Comrade Kuznetsov,

Will you be so kind as to inform us whether it is true that the constituencies in which all the Social-Democratic groups reached agreement during the elections to the State Duma include the following:

Yekaterinoslav, Kharkov, the city of Moscow and Moscow Gubernia, the Don region and Odessa. Kindly send your information as early as possible to H. Müller, *Chemnitz.*

If we have no news from you by September 17, we shall consider the above statement to be true.

With Party greetings, *H. Müller*

We answered the letter as follows:

Executive Committee of the Social-Democratic Party of Germany.

Dear Comrades, it goes without saying that all that has been reported to the Executive Committee is based on an untruth and is an invention pure and simple of the liquidators. We can affirm with confidence that that fable could have been told to the Executive only by the Letts, the Bundists, or even by Trotsky's adherents, who only a short time ago closed "their" conference, which they would have liked to call a "party conference", but which was in fact a liquidationist conference. In order not to state anything that could not be confirmed and not to quote our organisational correspondence, we shall limit ourselves here to pointing to a document published in St. Petersburg.

On August 28 (September 10, new style), 1912, the St. Petersburg Marxist daily, *Pravda* No. 102, carried a letter received from one of Kharkov's biggest factories and devoted especially to the Duma elections. The letter said openly and plainly that "the names of the liquidators' candidates *have so far not been announced*" and that the liquidators "*deny the necessity for a workers' party*" (*Pravda* No. 102, p. 4, col. 1).

From this alone the German comrades can see how shamelessly the Letts, the Bundists, Trotsky's adherents and all such private informants are deceiving them. The point is, evidently, that all of them, probably including the Caucasians, wanted to obtain money on behalf of pretended "organisations", whose existence cannot be confirmed or verified either by the Party Executive or by anyone else.

Is it possible that the German Party. which has ninety Social-Democratic dailies, cannot—that is, if it does not want to compromise itself by misinterpreting the state of affairs in the Russian Party—open a discussion on the R.S.D.L.P., and openly compel all the informants who are hiding from the light of day to present statements over their signatures and produce documents?

After all, Russia is not as far away as Central Africa, and it would not take much effort on the part of the German worker Social-Democrats to establish the truth and thereby also relieve the German members of the Executive Committee of the need to hear *unverifiable* private stories.

On behalf of the Central Committee of the R.S.D.L.P.

N. Lenin

Written between July 17 (30) and
August 20 (September 2) 1912,
the postscript September 2 (15), 1912

Published as a pamphlet
in German, Leipzig, 1912

First published in Russian
in 1924 in Volume XII, Part
One of the *Collected Works*
of N. Lenin (V. Ulyanov)

ORIGINAL POSTSCRIPT TO THE PAMPHLET
THE PRESENT SITUATION IN THE R.S.D.L.P.[110]

After the above lines had gone to press, we received *Nevsky Golos* No. 7, published in St. Petersburg on August 17, old style. Consequently, the liquidationist newspaper has resumed publication after an *interruption of one and a half months*. (The previous issue of this weekly —No. 6 — appeared on July 5, old style.)

The information published in *Nevsky Golos* No. 7 provides the best confirmation of the appraisal of the *actual* significance of the liquidators in Russia which was given in our Central Committee's letter to the *Vorstand*.*

Indeed, early in July the paper suspended publication. Needless to say, the liquidators and their friends bent all their efforts to revive it. The results of their efforts *during one and a half months* (July and half August) are reported by *Nevsky Golos itself* (No. 7) as follows:

"This newspaper has received, *for the replenishment of its funds*:

July. From 14 persons, 25 rubles each (I. F., P., G., M. I., K., L., K. F., L., B., Vsh., Lv., Vl., V. P., B. of Moscow); through R., 50 rubles; from M—i, 11 rubles; Shkh., 11 rubles; from 8 persons, 10 rubles each (E., I., Is., S., Rf., Avg., Ob., P. O.); from K. I., 8 rubles; from S., 7 rubles; from K., 5 rubles; B. B., 5 rubles; from F., 6 rubles; M. B., 5 rubles; from Lepaya 5 rubles; Gmp., 3 rubles. Total, 546 rubles.

---

* Executive Committee of the Social-Democratic Party of Germany.—*Ed.*

"*August.* From Wulfsohn (Zurich), 10 rubles; also from him, 3.57 rubles; Benzia (Zurich), 15 rubles; G—ya (Kishinev), 20 rubles; Az—v (Astrakhan), 3 rubles; Sp—y (Bogorodsk), 15 rubles; V. V., 6 rubles; Y.Y.F., 59 rubles; from Dubbeln, through S., 20 rubles; from B., Moscow, 25 rubles; from Y. L., 10 rubles; L. L., 12 rubles; M. Gr., 3 rubles; from Moscow init. group, 35 rubles; B. B., 5 rubles; B., 5 rubles; from An. Konst., St. Petersb., through L. L., 6 rubles; from a group of friends in Paris, 8.54 rubles; from B., Pavlograd, 20 rubles. Total, 281.11 rubles."

Such is the account published by the liquidators themselves. Their work and their *links with the masses* during the one and a half months present the following picture:

Collected in all . . . . *827.11 rubles*

Including:		
Initiating group, Moscow	35	rubles
A group of friends in Paris	8.54	"
Private contributions by individuals:		
35 contributions amounting to . . .	708	"
15 " " " . . .	75.57	"

Total . . . . 827.11 rubles

Everyone knows, as Plekhanov stated in print (*Dnevnik Sotsial-Demokrata* No. 16) as far back as April 1912, that the *"initiating groups"* are groups of *liquidators.*

And so, the liquidators were helped, at the most trying moment, when their paper had suspended publication, by:

one group of liquidators in Russia

one group of friends in Paris

35 well-to-do persons, each of whom contributed an average of 20 rubles (over 40 marks each)

15 private individuals, each of whom contributed an average of 5 rubles (over 10 marks each).

Was not our Central Committee justified in asserting that the liquidators in the Russian working-class movement were of no account at all?

The liquidators refer to the "Caucasian Regional Committee". *Not a single workers' group* in the Caucasus has sent them a single contribution during those one and a half months.

The liquidators would like to have the help of the Bund and the Lettish Social-Democratic organisation. *Not a single* workers' group, either in the Bund or among the Letts, has sent them a single contribution during one and a half months.

During the same period (July to August 14) *Pravda*, the St. Petersburg daily newspaper of the anti-liquidators, published accounts of *41 group collections by workers* in various parts of Russia, including oil-field workers (Grozny fields, Terek Region) (*Pravda* No. 60) and Jewish workers in Lepaya (*Pravda* No. 67). We venture to think that this aid from workers means more than all the talk and declamation of the "Caucasian Regional Committee", the Letts and the Bund.

No aid in the world, and no "conferences" with the Letts, the Bund, etc., can transform the liquidationist *nothing* in the Russian working-class movement into a something.

Let the German comrades undertake the not too arduous task of collecting the documents on the position of the R.S.D.L.P. and verifying them —after all, Russia is not Central Africa, about which any kind of "tall stories" can be told. The German comrades probably want to end this strange, *gelinde gesagt,** situation in which they get their information on the Italian, Swedish and any other socialist movement from openly published documents, while their information on the Russian socialist movement is obtained from privately communicated fables and gossip.

Written between August 20 and
24 (September 2 and 6), 1912
Published for the first time

Published according
to the manuscript

---

* To put it mildly.—*Ed.*

CAPITALISM AND POPULAR CONSUMPTION

Recently the French magazine *La Revue scientifique*[111] published data on the production of *margarine* in various countries. Those data were an additional reminder of the fact noticed long ago that the diet of the people deteriorates as capitalism develops.

As everyone knows, margarine is fat (from which stearine has been removed) processed by a special method. From it an artificial substance is made, known as margarine butter.

Margarine production in the principal European countries has assumed very large proportions. Germany produces 12.5 million poods of it per year, Britain, 7.5 million poods, and so on.

Margarine is cheaper than real butter. Butter is too costly for the vast majority of the population in the capitalist countries. The workers earn so little that they have to buy cheap, low-grade, substitute food products. And yet the workers are the chief consumers. There are millions of workers, and only hundreds of capitalists. And so the output of cheap substitutes is growing daily and hourly, along with the unheard-of luxury of a handful of millionaires.

The wealth of the bourgeoisie is growing. So are the poverty and want of the proletariat and of the mass of small proprietors, peasants, artisans and petty traders, who are being ruined.

Remarkably enough, margarine consumption is highest in the very countries which are particularly famous as producers of large quantities of the finest natural butter. To find out how great the consumption of margarine is, it is necessary to divide the whole amount of margarine produced in the country concerned (adding import and subtracting export) by the number of inhabitants.

It appears that the greatest consumer of margarine is Denmark —16,4 kilograms (about one pood) a year per inhabitant. Next comes Norway —15 pounds, Germany —7.5 pounds, etc.

Denmark is the richest country for butter output. Danish butter —real butter —ranks among the finest grades. The world's biggest and richest city, London (population, including that of the suburbs, about six million), prefers Danish butter to any other, and pays the highest price for it.

Danish well-to-do peasants, but above all the Danish capitalists, make a good deal of money from the butter trade. And yet Denmark is the world's biggest consumer of substitute butter, margarine!

What is the explanation?

It is very simple. The vast majority of the Danish population, like that of any other capitalist country, consists of workers and propertyless peasants. They cannot afford real butter. Even the middle peasants in Denmark, being in need of money, sell abroad the butter they produce on their farms and buy the cheap margarine for themselves. The wealth of the Danish capitalists is growing, and so are the poverty and want of the Danish workers and peasants.

The same thing is happening here in Russia. Very long ago, some forty years back, when it became fashionable to set up cheese dairies and artels in the countryside, Engelhardt, a democratic writer, noted that the peasants, being in need of money, sold their milk and butter while their children starved to death.

That fact has been noted many times since then. Cheese production is growing, the production of milk for sale is growing, and the few well-to-do peasants and the merchants are becoming rich, while the poor become poorer still. The children of poor peasants, left without milk, die in enormous numbers. Child mortality in Russia is incredibly high.

Fairly often milk is sold to cheese dairies, from which the peasants then get *skimmed milk* for their own consumption.

The rich have the profits from growing production and trade, while the workers and peasants have margarine and skimmed milk. Such is capitalist reality, which liberal and official scholars are at such pains to embellish.

Pravda No. 70, July 20, 1912
     Signed: *B. B.*

Published according
to the *Pravda* text

LIBERALS AND CLERICALS

The priesthood is about to flood the Fourth Duma.

How are we to react to this emergence of the priests on the political scene?

Democrats can never hold the view that priests should not participate in political affairs. It is an arch-reactionary view. It leads only to official hypocrisy and nothing more. In practice, all measures debarring a particular group or section of the population from politics and the class struggle are absolutely impossible and unrealisable.

Let us recall that Bebel and the German Social-Democrats were for freedom of Jesuit agitation in Germany We are against liberal phrases about "prohibiting" Jesuit agitation, said the Social-Democrats. We are not afraid of the Jesuits. Let the Jesuits enjoy *complete freedom* of agitation, but let the authorities guarantee that we Social-Democrats, too, shall enjoy complete freedom of agitation. That is how Bebel and the German Social-Democrats reasoned.

The worker democrats in Russia are fighting against the falsification of suffrage (and all other rights) in favour of the landlords or the priesthood, etc., and not at all against freedom of the priesthood to participate in political affairs. We stand for the class struggle, and we demand complete freedom for any class or social-estate, for either sex, for any people, any section or group of the population, to take part in politics.

The liberals' reasoning on this question is wrong and undemocratic. Prince Trubetskoi, for example, wrote not so long ago, to the applause of *Rech*:

"The transformation of the Church into a political instrument is achieved at the price of its internal destruction."

He described the plan of flooding the Duma with priests as "contrary to Christianity and the Church".

That is not true. It is hypocrisy. It is a thoroughly reactionary point of view.

Trubetskoi and other liberals take an *un*democratic stand in their struggle against clericalism. Under the guise of opposing participation of the priesthood in the political struggle, they advocate its more covert (and hence much more harmful) participation.

Worker democrats favour freedom of political struggle for all, including the priests. We are opposed, not to the priests taking part in the election campaign, in the Duma, etc., but *solely* to the medieval privileges of the priesthood. We are not afraid of clericalism, and will readily join issue with it—on a free platform on which all will be on an equal footing. The priesthood has always participated in politics *covertly*; the people stand to gain, and to gain a good deal, if the priesthood begins to participate in politics *overtly*.

Pravda No. 74, July 25, 1912
Signed: *A Layman*

Published according
to the *Pravda* text

CADETS AND DEMOCRATS

"We are accustomed to think," says the leading article in *Rech*, "that Marxists admit the Cadets to be a democratic party, although they affix the offensive label of 'bourgeois'" (i.e., bourgeois-democratic).

It would be hard to imagine crasser political ignorance on the part of "educated people" who read Marxist literature. The question inevitably arises: does not calculation sometimes make people simulate ignorance?

Since 1906 we have explained hundreds and thousands of times that the Cadets are *not* democrats but a liberal-monarchist bourgeoisie. In the spring of 1907 formal decisions adopted by Marxists from all parts of Russia and familiar to every politically-educated person confirmed this and stated for all to hear that the Cadets were a party of the liberal-monarchist bourgeoisie, that their democracy was "hypocrisy", and that the Cadets were followed by a section of the petty bourgeoisie "only by force of tradition [a blind habit of clinging to the customary, to the old] and because it was *simply deceived by the liberals*".[112]

These ideas have since been reaffirmed and elaborated hundreds and thousands of times.

But the Cadets assert, as if nothing had happened, that they are "in the habit of thinking" that Marxists consider them democrats! There is none so deaf as he who will not hear.

The liberals differ from the conservatives (Black Hundreds) in that they represent the interests of the bourgeoisie, which *needs* progress and a fairly well organised legal system, the observance of legality, of the constitution, and a guarantee of some degree of political liberty.

But this progressive bourgeoisie dreads the democracy and the movement of the masses even more than it dreads reaction. Hence the liberals' perpetual tendency to make concessions to the old, to compromise with it, to defend many fundamental mainstays of the old order. And all this makes for the complete impotence of liberalism, for its timidity, half-heartedness and eternal vacillations.

Democrats represent the broad mass of the population. A democrat is not afraid of the movement of the masses but believes in it. In Russia the democrats are represented by the Trudoviks and Left "Narodniks" in general. The Marxists call them *bourgeois* democrats, not at all because they want to "offend" them, but because no redivision of the land and no democratic changes in the state are *sufficient to remove* the rule of capital, of the bourgeois system.

The policy of the worker democrats is clear. We recognise agreements with the liberals against the Rights only at the second stage of the elections, and only where it is impossible together with the democrats to defeat the liberals. We fight side by side with all bourgeois democrats as long as they are true to their democratic principles.

Pravda No. 75 July 26, 1912   Published according
                                                  to the *Pravda* text

THE LIBERAL CAMPAIGN

The liberals have begun to get busy and have brought concerted pressure to bear on *Pravda*. Leading articles in the Cadet *Rech*, and the non-partisan progressive Mr. Prokopovich and Mr. R. Blank in *Zaprosy Zhizni* opened fire on the workers' newspaper for its decision to conduct an independent election campaign in St. Petersburg.

"The efforts of *Nevskaya Zvezda* and *Pravda* are completely useless," asserts *Zaprosy Zhizni*. "Surely they cannot seriously expect the candidate of the workers' party to win in the St. Petersburg city curia, where the workers' participation is negligible."

There you have a sample of the liberal arguments, and a method of intimidating the voter who has not yet risen above philistinism, has not worked out an entirely conscious policy for himself.

There was a time when the liberals tried to intimidate simply with the prospect of a Black-Hundred victory in the elections. But crude lies no longer "work". Everyone knows that there is not the slightest danger of the Black Hundreds winning in the St. Petersburg elections. So a different kind of intimidation is resorted to: "there is no reason to expect the workers to win".

Oh, no, liberal gentlemen, the democratic voter in general, and the worker in particular, has lived through many things, he has thought over and learned many things in the past difficult five years. That sort of intimidation will get you nowhere.

Nowhere in the world have the workers begun *their* election campaign in a big city without being *opposed* by strong liberal parties. Nowhere in the world have worker

democrats succeeded without a stubborn fight in wresting
from the liberals their influence on the mass of the lower-
grade office workers, shop-assistants, handicraftsmen, petty
traders, etc.

Whoever is against the St. Petersburg workers beginning
that fight here and now (or rather going on from where they
left off in 1906, 1907 and 1909), assumes the name of democrat in vain, and remains in fact a slave of the liberals.

Thousands upon thousands of new democratic voters will
now take part in the St. Petersburg elections.

The St. Petersburg workers' great achievement in founding
their own workers' daily newspaper fully entitles us to expect no lesser achievements in the election campaign.

Thousands of old voters are awakening to a new, more
class-conscious political activity. They are learning, with
the help of their workers' newspaper, to fight for a better
life for themselves, developing the habit of joint political
action, and growing increasingly aware of the great national
problems which the worker democrats are solving.

The liberals in St. Petersburg can be defeated. And from
the liberals' uneasiness and quarrelsome sallies, from their
shouting and their attempts at intimidation, democratic St.
Petersburg will derive added confidence that it is on the
right path to victory.

Pravda No. 77, July 28, 1912   Published according
                                                  to the *Pravda* text

REVOLTS IN THE ARMY AND NAVY

Recently a few reports have slipped even into our legal press about revolutionary unrest in the armed forces. We shall mention three chief reports.

Black Sea Fleet. On June 27 a naval court in Sevastopol tried behind closed doors Zelenin, an electrician of the battleship *Ioann Zlatoust*. Together with Karpishin and Silyakov, he was charged with writing and circulating an appeal for an armed revolt. Zelenin, Karpishin and Silyakov were sentenced to death and were shot on July 10.

On July 2 the same court tried the crew of the same battleship. It charged sixteen sailors with incitement to seize the battleship. Ten of the sailors were sentenced to death and five to penal servitude for six years. On July 4 official telegrams reported that the ten men condemned to death had appealed for pardon.

Baltic Fleet. On July 16 the naval court in Kronstadt harbour is to try *sixty-five sailors* of the training ship *Dvina*, the cruiser *Aurora* and the battleship *Slava*. On July 3 the Octobrist paper *Golos Moskvy* received a telephone report from St. Petersburg saying that there was much talk in the city about that sensational trial. The sixty-five sailors are said to be charged with membership of the Socialist-Revolutionary Party and of "a secret association which had planned an open revolt and the assassination of superior officers". The case goes back, according to the same report, to the arrest of a *Dvina* sailor on January 22, 1912.

It is known, furthermore, that during May arrests were made among the sailors of the Baltic Fleet in Helsingfors.

Lastly, on July 1, there was an attempt at revolt by engineering troops in the village of Troyitskoye, near Tashkent. The insurgents bayoneted Junior Captain Pokhvisnev. *The telegram reporting the incident was not released for publication* Not until July 10 did a reprint appear in St. Petersburg from *Turkestanskiye Vedomosti*, an official paper, which admitted that there *had been a battle* with the insurgents. Riflemen and Cossacks had smashed the insurgent engineers, alleged to have numbered in all 100 to 130 men. The revolt began in the evening and was over, according to the official report, by the morning. *Some 380 engineers* were arrested, of whom "more than one-half [the government paper asserts] undoubtedly [??] had no share" in the revolt. The insurgents killed, besides Pokhvisnev, two second lieutenants—Krasovsky and Koshchenets—and two privates, and wounded five officers and twelve privates. The official paper says nothing about the number of the insurgents killed.

Such is the scant information, clearly incomplete and clearly distorted and minimised by the police, that we now have at our disposal.

But what do these facts mean?

They fully confirm what was pointed out in the decisions of the All-Russia Conference of the R.S.D.L.P. in January 1912 and explained in greater detail in the Central Organ, *Sotsial-Demokrat* (No. .27), a month ago.*

A *revolutionary* upswing has begun in Russia. With the mass strikes in April and May the Russian proletariat began to pass to the offensive—against capital *and* against the tsarist monarchy, for a better life for the workers, worn out by counter-revolutionary persecution and tyranny in 1908-11, *and* for freedom for the whole people, for a democratic republic.

It is an idle tale the liberals are putting about (followed by the *Nevsky Golos* liquidators) when they say that the

---

* See pp 102-09 of this volume. —*Ed*

basis of the April-May movement was the struggle for freedom of association. The facts belie that tale. One cannot
fight for only one of the political rights in enslaved Russia,
nor can one fight for constitutional reforms under the tsarist
autocracy. The struggle of the proletariat swept over Russia
in a wave of strikes that were *both* economic *and* political.
The *strength* of the movement lay, and lies, in the combination of the two types of strike. They are not ordinary strikes,
they mark a *revolutionary* upsurge of the masses, the *beginning of an offensive* by the mass of the workers against the
tsarist monarchy.

The mass strikes were bound to kindle the flames of revolution *everywhere*. And the outbreaks of revolt among the
armed forces are a *proof* that those flames are flaring up —
there is inflammable material *everywhere*, and *everywhere*
a revolutionary mood is growing among the masses, including even those workers and peasants who are held down
by barrack drill.

The mass strikes in Russia are inseparably linked with
an armed uprising. Where strikes grow, the uprising grows
too.

That is what the events mentioned at the beginning of
this article have shown.

Those events provide a lesson which is pointed out in
the Central Organ, *Sotsial-Demokrat* No. 27. Appeals for
an uprising are most unwise now. An uprising would be
premature. Only a *combined* onslaught by the mass of the
workers, by the peasantry and the best section of the armed
forces can create conditions for a *victorious*, i.e., *timely*
uprising.

And the foremost workers must do their utmost to
strengthen, restore and develop the *illegal* party of the
working class, the R.S.D.L.P. *Only* a party such as this
will be in a position, by conducting revolutionary agitation and using every means of legal propaganda through
the working-class press and through the worker deputies
to the Duma, to keep the army of the proletariat from frittering away its forces in hopeless petty revolts and to train
it for the great victorious uprising

Long live the revolutionary soldiers and sailors!

Long live concerted, persevering, stubborn revolutionary

work to develop a wide revolutionary onslaught by the millions, to develop workers' strikes and peasant movements! It is only by being at the head of the onslaught of the millions, and only in the closest inseparable alliance with them, that the revolutionary section of Russia's armed forces can and will defeat the tsarist monarchy!

Rabochaya Gazeta No. 9,
July 30 (August 12),[113] 1912

Published according
to the text in *Rabochaya Gazeta*

ON THE EVE OF THE ELECTIONS
TO THE FOURTH DUMA

On the eve of the elections the Russian Social-Democratic Labour Party has come forward, despite cruel persecution, despite wholesale arrests, with a clearer, more distinct and more precise programme, tactics and platform than any other party.

In January 1912 the All-Russia Conference of the R.S.D.L.P. summed up the results of the ideological and political work carried out by the Party in the grim years of the counter-revolution. The Conference decisions gave answers to all the pressing questions of the movement. Thanks to those decisions, the election platform was simply a final statement. The platform was published by the Central Committee in Russia and was then reprinted by a whole series of local organisations.[114] The whole bourgeois press reported the Conference and published some of its decisions.

In the six months since the Conference, work has been going on through the Party press and dozens of reports, in hundreds of speeches in factory groups and at the meetings held in April and May, to explain the Conference decisions and to put them into effect. The Party's slogans—a republic, an eight-hour working day, confiscation of the landed estates—have spread throughout Russia and have been accepted by the foremost proletarians. The revolutionary upsurge of the masses, its expression ranging from strikes and meetings to revolts in the armed forces, has proved these slogans to be correct and vital.

Our Party has already made use of the elections, and very extensively too. No amount of "interpretation" by the police, no amount of falsification of the Fourth Duma (by the priesthood or otherwise) can nullify *this* result. Propaganda, organised strictly on Party lines, has already been carried out everywhere and has *set the tone* for the entire election campaign of the Social-Democrats.

The bourgeois parties in a hasty, slapdash manner are writing "platforms *for* the elections", for promises, for hoodwinking the voters. The liquidators, too, who are trailing behind the liberals, are now devising a *legal* "platform *for* the elections". The liquidators are making a fuss about platforms in the legal, censored press as they prepare to cover up their utter confusion, disorganisation, and lack of ideological principle, with a respectable, law-abiding "platform for the elections".

Not a platform "for the elections", but elections to implement the *revolutionary Social-Democratic* platform!—that is how the Party of the working class sees it. We have already used the elections to this end, and will use them to the hilt. We will use even the most reactionary tsarist Duma to advocate the revolutionary platform, tactics and programme of the Russian S.D. Labour Party. Truly valuable are only those platforms that complete the long work of *revolutionary* agitation, which has already given *full* answers to *all* the questions of the movement, and not those platforms (particularly the legal ones!) that are composed in all haste as a stop-gap and as a noisy advertisement, as in the case of the liquidators.

Six months have passed since the Party re-established itself. Overcoming incredible difficulties, suffering from fierce persecution and experiencing breaks in the work of this or that local centre or of the common centre—the Central Committee—the Party is definitely going forward, extending its work and its influence among the masses. This extension of the work is taking place *in a new form*: in addition to the illegal nuclei, which are secret and narrow, and better disguised than before, there is broader legal Marxist propaganda. It is just this distinctive character of the new preparations for revolution in the new conditions that has long been noted and acknowledged by the Party.

And we can now give a full answer to the noisy utterances of the liquidators, who threaten us with "duplicate candidates". Empty threats that scare no one! The liquidators are so badly beaten and impotent that *no amount of help* can revive them. They cannot so much as think of putting up "duplicate candidates"; if they did so, they would win a pitiful, ludicrously insignificant number of votes. They know this and will not try the experiment. They are making a noise merely to divert attention and conceal the truth.

We said "no amount of help" The liquidators are counting on help from abroad. Their friends—particularly the Letts, the Bund, and Trotsky—have announced the convocation of *ten* "centres, organisations and factions"! Don't laugh! The world abroad is rich, great and bountiful. As many as "ten centres"!! The methods used in this case are the same as with the government in the Fourth Duma: preparations for setting up a representative body, and the conversion of a number of ciphers into the semblance of "big numbers". First of all, Trotsky (in Russia he is a cipher, he is only a contributor to *Zhivoye Dyelo*, and his agents are only defenders of the liquidators' "initiating groups"). Secondly, *Golos Sotsial-Demokrata*, i.e., the selfsame impotent liquidators Thirdly, the "Caucasian Regional Committee", also a cipher, in a third garb. Fourthly, the "Organising Committee"—a fourth garb of the *very same* liquidators. Fifthly and sixthly, the Letts and the Bund, which is wholly liquidationist today. But enough!

Needless to say our Party is laughing at this game of nonentities abroad. They cannot resuscitate a corpse, for the liquidators in Russia are a corpse.

Here are the facts.

For six months the liquidators and *all* their friends have been waging a desperate struggle against the Party. There exists a legal *Marxist* press. It is fearfully handicapped, and does not dare utter a word about a republic, our Party, uprising, or the tsar's gang. It would be simply ridiculous to think of advocating the slogans of the R.S.D.L.P through that press.

But the worker in Russia is no longer what he used to be. He has become a force. He has paved a way for himself. He has *his own* press, which is handicapped but belongs to him and defends Marxism *theoretically*.

In this open arena, everyone can see the "successes" of the liquidators' struggle against the anti-liquidators. S. V [115] of *Vperyod* has already pointed out those successes in Trotsky's Vienna, liquidationist, *Pravda*. The fact is, he wrote, that the workers' *collections* go almost entirely to the anti-liquidators. But he sought to comfort himself, saying that it is not because the workers sympathise with the "Leninists".

Why, naturally "not because", dear friend of the liquidators!

But still, look at the facts.

Six months of open struggle for a *workers' daily newspaper.*

The liquidators have been shouting about it since 1910. What about their success? In six months—from January 1 to July 1, 1912—their papers, *Zhivoye Dyelo* and *Nevsky Golos*, carried the accounts of 15 (*fifteen*) collections made by groups of workers for a workers' daily newspaper! Fifteen groups of workers in six months!

Take the newspapers of the anti-liquidators. See their accounts of the collections made for a workers' daily during the same six-month period. Add up the number of collections by groups of workers. You will find that there were 504 *contributions by workers' groups!*

Here are exact monthly data for the various parts of Russia:

*Number of workers' group contributions for
a workers' daily newspaper during the first half of 1912*

	In anti-liquidationist newspapers	In liquidationist newspapers
January	14	0
February	18	0
March	76	7
April	227	8
May	135	0
June	34	0
Total	504	15
St. Petersburg and vicinity	415	10
South	51	1
The rest of Russia	38	4
Total	504	15

The liquidators have been thoroughly beaten in the eyes of the workers' groups in Russia. The liquidators are a corpse, and no number of terrible (oh, how terrible!) "associations of groups, centres, factions, trends and tendencies" abroad can revive this corpse.

No shrill manifestos abroad and no fake conferences between "initiating groups" and the liquidators can undo or alleviate this complete defeat of the liquidators in the eyes of *hundreds of workers' groups in Russia*.

The unity of the election campaign of the worker Social-Democrats in Russia is *assured*. It is assured not through "agreements" with the liquidators, but through the complete victory over the liquidators, who have already been reduced to their true role, the role of liberal intellectuals. See how well Savin, the Socialist-Revolutionary liquidator, fits into *Nasha Zarya*. See how warmly L. M. [116] praises, in *Listok Golosa Sotsial-Demokrata*, "the initiative" of the Socialist-Revolutionaries, who repeatedly stray (because of an otzovist hangover!) into liquidationism. Ponder on the significance of the fact that the same sheet holds up the well-known Socialist-Revolutionary "leader", Avksentyev, as an example for Plekhanov. Remember how *all* liquidators kiss the *non*-Social-Democratic Left wing of the Polish Socialist Party. Liquidators of all parties, unite!

Everyone finds his niche in the end. Groups of intellectualist liquidators from among former Marxists and former liberals with a bomb are being welded together by the course of events.

As for the Party of the working class, the R.S.D.L.P., it has, in the six months since it regained its freedom from the bondage of those who had liquidated it, made a huge stride forward, as can be seen from the facts cited.

Rabochaya Gazeta No. 9,
July 30 (August 12), 1912

Published according
to the text in *Rabochaya Gazeta*

CAN THE SLOGAN "FREEDOM OF ASSOCIATION"
SERVE AS A BASIS
FOR THE WORKING-CLASS MOVEMENT TODAY?

In the legal press, the liquidators headed by Trotsky argue that it can They are doing all in their power to *distort* the true character of the workers' movement. But those are hopeless efforts The drowning liquidators are clutching at a straw to rescue their unjust cause.

In 1910 little groups of intellectuals began a campaign of *petitions* for freedom of association. It was an *artificial* campaign The mass of the workers remained indifferent One cannot fire the proletariat with so futile an undertaking. It was fitting for liberals to believe in political reforms *under* the tsarist autocracy. The workers at once saw through the falsity of the undertaking and remained aloof.

The workers are not against the struggle for reforms — they fought for the Insurance Bill. Through their deputies they used every opportunity in the Third Duma to bring about at least slight improvements. But the point is that the Third Duma and the Insurance Bill are not fiction, but political facts, while "freedom of association" *under* the June Third monarchy of Romanov is an empty promise from rotten liberals.

The liberals are enemies of the revolution. Even now they are outspoken in their opposition to it —the Black-Hundred Third Duma has not taught them to throw off their fear of the revolution. Being afraid of the revolution, the liberals comfort themselves with the hope of *constitutional reforms* and advocate for the workers one of those reforms, freedom of association.

But the workers do not believe the fable about a "constitution" under the conditions of the Third Duma, general lack of rights, and unbridled tyranny. The workers demand freedom of association *in earnest* and *therefore* they are fighting for freedom for the whole people, for *the overthrow of the monarchy*, for a republic.

The strikes in April and May showed in point of fact that the proletariat had risen in a *revolutionary strike*. The combination of the economic and political strike, revolutionary meetings, and the slogan of a republic advanced by the St. Petersburg workers on May Day—all these facts were conclusive proof of the beginning of a *revolutionary upswing*.

The factual, objective situation in Russia is this: the proletariat has begun a revolutionary struggle of the masses to overthrow the tsarist monarchy, and unrest in the armed forces is growing—an indication that they have joined in the struggle. As for the peasant democrats, the best among them are turning away from the liberals to lend ear to the working-class vanguard.

Meanwhile the liberals, enemies of the revolution, uphold *only* the "constitutional" path and put forward, *against* the revolution, the promise (an empty and false promise) of "freedom of association" *under* Russia's tsarist monarchy!

Such is the actual political situation. And these are the real social forces: (1) the tsarist monarchy, which flouts all "constitution"; (2) the liberal-monarchist bourgeois, who out of fear of the revolution pretend that they believe in a combination of "freedom" and the tsarist regime, and (3) the revolutionary democrats; from the midst of the latter a leader has already risen—the mass of the workers, to whose appeal the sailors and soldiers, from Helsingfors to Tashkent, are responding.

How hopelessly stupid, under the circumstances, is the liquidators' talk about "freedom of association"! Of all "reforms", these sages of liberal labour policy have chosen an *impossible* constitutional reform, which is nothing but a promise, and they are amusing themselves by playing at "European" constitutionalism.

It won't do! The workers are casting aside the liberals and liberal labour policy. They will support, develop, and make an object of *their* campaigns, *every* reform that really becomes an immediate issue—both in the Third and in the

Fourth Duma—from insurance to increased salaries for those who slave in offices.

But the workers laugh contemptuously at the empty and absurd promise of a *constitutional* political reform *under* the autocracy. May the revolutionary struggle begun by the masses in order to overthrow the monarchy and win a republic grow in scale and intensity! The struggle will show what half-hearted constitutional reforms will result in if the new revolution is *defeated*, but to suggest to the masses a *non*-revolutionary road, a peaceful constitutional reform, now, at the beginning of a revolutionary onslaught, is something that only the "man in a muffler"[117] can do.

The revolutionary onslaught which has begun calls for revolutionary slogans. Down with the monarchy! Long live the democratic republic, the eight-hour working day, and the confiscation of all landed estates!

Rabochaya Gazeta No. 9,   Published according
July 30 (August 12), 1912   to the text in *Rabochaya Gazeta*

LETTER TO THE SWISS WORKERS[118]

Dear Comrades,

On behalf of the Russian Social-Democratic Labour Party, I confirm hereby for the benefit of all the Swiss comrades that the general Conference of this Party, held in January 1912, *disclaimed* by a special resolution *all responsibility for individual Russian groups abroad.*

I also confirm that the Central Committee of our Party *has so far recognised only one* Russian Social-Democratic organisation abroad, namely, *the Committee of Organisations Abroad* and *its Zurich section.* I enclose a pamphlet published by the Central Organ of our Party in German, which describes in detail the disorganising behaviour of the petty groups of Russians abroad.*

With Party greetings, *Lenin (V. Ulyanov)*

Representative of the Russian Social-Democratic Party in the International Socialist Bureau.[119]

Written in July 1912

Hectographed as a separate leaflet in German, August 1912

Published according to the leaflet text Translated from the German

---

* See pp. 203-20 of this volume.—*Ed.*

QUESTIONS OF PRINCIPLE

A slight increase in the election campaign activity, and the official-Cadet *Rech* has begun to speak (it has done so at last!) of the differences it has with the Lefts over questions of principle.

"We never intended, nor do we intend, to make peace with the June Third regime," writes *Rech.*

That is not true. You did intend and you do intend to, Cadet gentlemen. Evidence of it is your talk about a "responsible" opposition and an opposition in the possessive case. That is not merely "intending" peace. but a policy of "peace" with the June Third regime.

And what about Karaulov's pious speeches in the pious Third Duma? Or the Cadets' voting for the budget and for its more important items? Or the speeches of Berezovsky the First on the agrarian question? Or Gredeskul's recent statements, repeated in *Rech*? Does not all that amount to a policy of *peace* with the *foundations* of the June Third regime? It certainly does.

"Over a period of five years," writes *Rech,* "we have never seen any difference between the tactics of the Social-Democratic Party *within the framework of the Duma* and those of other opposition parties. Yet in this case it is a question of elections to the Duma "

There you have a specimen of sophistry and distortion of the truth! Not on a single question have Social-Democratic tactics in the Duma been akin to Cadet tactics. They have been fundamentally different on all questions: they have *not* been tactics of "peace" *or* of liberalism; they have *always* been tactics of *democracy* and the *class struggle*.

Does *Rech* really maintain that mere "voting against" can be described as *kinship* in tactics, instead of kinship in posing questions from the standpoint of *principle* in the Duma speeches and in the formulas of procedure?

Does *Rech* really venture to say that it is permissible to say one thing in the Duma and another outside it? But if it does, is it not because it wants to hush up the issue of the *un*democratic character of Cadet propaganda *outside the Duma*?

"We cannot deny the 'democratic' movement, which we serve ourselves, the right to independent aims and actions," writes *Rech*.

That is not true, educated liberal gentlemen! See if you can state your fundamental views on the distinction between liberalism and democracy. See if you can illustrate your views with examples from English, French or German history, even leaving out specifically working-class, proletarian, Marxist democracy. You will not be able to deny the distinction between bourgeois liberalism and bourgeois democracy as regards their attitude to the old order. And we shall always prove to you that you are a party of the liberal-monarchist bourgeoisie and not at all a democratic party.

Bourgeois democracy in Russia is represented by the Trudoviks and Narodniks of all types.

"Once you have set your hand to the plough you can't give up." You have set out to discuss the principles of the Cadets and the Lefts, so you must really explain those principles. That is the only way to raise election agitation somewhat above the question of how many lawless acts such-and-such a police officer, governor, or administrative body is guilty of.

Pravda No. 79, July 31, 1912

Published according to the *Pravda* text

THE LAST VALVE

We concluded our previous article on the agrarian question in Russia today (see *Nevskaya Zvezda* No. 15) as follows:

"The real similarity between the Stolypin and the Narodnik agrarian programmes lies in the fact that both advocate a radical break-up of the old, medieval system of landownership. And that is very good. That system deserves no better than to be broken up. The most reactionary of all are those Cadets of *Rech* and *Russkiye Vedomosti* who reproach Stolypin for causing a break-up, instead of proving the need for a still more consistent and resolute break-up. We shall see in a following article that the Stolypin type of break-up *cannot* do away with bondage and labour service, while the Narodnik type *can*.

"For the time being we shall note that the only entirely real result of the Stolypin break-up is a famine among 30 million people. And it remains to be seen whether the Stolypin break-up may not teach the Russian people *how* they *should* carry out a more thorough break-up. It is no doubt teaching that. But will it succeed in it? Time will tell."*

And so, the question now confronting us is: why is it that the Stolypin break-up of medieval landownership *cannot*, while the peasant-Trudovik or Narodnik break-up *can*, do away with bondage and labour service?

In starting to analyse this question, we shall note first of all that one of the fundamental defects of the most widespread arguments concerning this matter—arguments that are liberal, Narodnik and partly revisionist (P. Maslov)—

---

* See pp. 148-49 of this volume.—*Ed.*

is the abstract *presentation* of the question, ignoring the concrete historical "replacement" which is actually coming about. The replacement coming about in Russia has long since occurred in the advanced countries of the West: it is the replacement of a feudal by a capitalist economy.

It is, and can only be, a question of the forms, conditions, rapidity and circumstances of *this* replacement; all *other* considerations, which are not infrequently put in the forefront, are no more than an *unwitting* beating about the bush, the "bush" being precisely this replacement.

The predominant feudal form of modern Russian agriculture is bondage and labour service. The preservation of natural economy to a comparatively considerable degree, the existence of the small cultivator who cannot make both ends meet and farms on a tiny patch of poor land, using old, wretchedly inadequate implements and production methods, and the economic dependence of this small cultivator on the owner of the neighbouring latifundium, who exploits him not only as a wage-labourer (which marks the beginning of capitalism), but as a small cultivator (which is a continuation of the corvée system) —these are the conditions engendering bondage and labour service, or rather, characterising both the one and the other.

For the 30,000 big landlords in European Russia there are 10,000,000 households of the peasant poor. The average result is roughly the following: one landlord owning over 2,000 dessiatines is surrounded by some 300 peasant households, each owning approximately 7 dessiatines of poor and exhausted land and equipped with implements that are incredibly outdated and primitive (from the European point of view, to say nothing of the American).

Some of the well-to-do peasants "get on in the world", i.e., become petty bourgeois using wage-labour to cultivate their land. The landlords, many of whom yesterday were serf-owning lords or are their sons, resort to the same kind of labour on a certain part of their land and for certain farming operations.

But besides these capitalist relations, and pushing them into the background in all the purely Russian gubernias of European Russia, there is the cultivation of landlord land by peasants using their own implements and livestock, that is to say, labour service, a continuation of the former corvée, and there is also the "utilisation" of the desperate want of the small cultivator (precisely as a *cultivator*, as a small proprietor) for "service" on the neighbouring landed estate, that is to say, *bondage*. Money loans in exchange for work, grain loans, winter hire, land lease, permission to use the road, watering-place, meadows, pastures and woods, the lending of implements and livestock, and so on and so forth, are all infinitely varied forms of modern bondage.

Things are sometimes pushed to the length of obliging the peasant to fertilise the landlord's fields with manure from his own farm, while the "housewife" is obliged to provide eggs—and this not in the eighteenth, but in the twentieth century A.D.!

One has only to pose clearly and precisely the problem of these survivals of medievalism and feudalism in modern Russian agriculture to appreciate the significance of the Stolypin "reform". This "reform", of course, gave dying serfdom a new lease of life, just as the notorious, so-called "peasant" (in reality *landlord*), Reform of 1861, extolled by the liberals and Narodniks, *gave a new lease of life* to the corvée system, perpetuating it in a different guise right up to 1905.

The "new lease of life" given by Stolypin to the old order and old feudal agriculture lies in the fact that another valve was opened, the *last* that could still be opened without expropriating all the landed estates. That valve was opened to let off some of the steam—in the sense that some of the thoroughly impoverished peasants acquired a title to their allotments as personal property and sold them, thus being converted from proletarians with an allotment into proletarians pure and simple, and that, furthermore, some of the well-to-do peasants, having acquired their allotments, and in some cases having settled on *otrubs*, built up even more solid capitalist farms than before.

Lastly, the valve was opened and some of the steam let off in the sense that in some areas a particularly intolerable type of strip holding was abolished and the mobilisation of peasant land required under capitalism was made easier.

But did this new lease of life decrease or increase the overall number of contradictions in the countryside? Did it decrease or increase the tyranny of the feudal latifundia, or the total amount of "steam"? The answer to these questions can only be the second alternative.

The famine among 30 million peasants is factual proof that the only answer which can be given at present is the second alternative. It is a famine among small proprietors. It presents a picture of the crisis of *the same* old poverty-ridden peasant farming, shackled by bondage and crushed by the feudal latifundia. There are no such famines, nor can there be, in the case of the big *non*-feudal estates, of the capitalist latifundia, in Europe.

The plight of the mass of the peasantry, apart from the proletarians who have completely freed themselves from the land (who "acquired" their land in order to sell it) and a negligible minority of well-to-do peasants, is the same as before or has even become worse. No acquiring of holdings as personal property, no measures against strip holdings, can make the mass of the impoverished peasants — settled on poor, exhausted land and possessing only antiquated, thoroughly worn-out implements and starved draught animals and cattle — to any extent cultured, to any extent masters of their farms.

Around a landlord (of the Markov or Purishkevich type) owning 2,000 dessiatines of land, the owners of tiny seven-dessiatine plots will inevitably remain paupers in bondage, however much they may be resettled, however much they may be freed from the village commune, however much their paupers' plots may be "acquired" as their personal property.

The Stolypin reform *cannot* do away with the bondage and labour service of the mass of the peasants or with famines among them. Decades upon decades of similar periodical famines will be needed before the bulk of the present-day households dies out painfully and the Stolypin reform "succeeds", i.e., before the established bourgeois system of the general European type is introduced in our countryside. At present, however, after a six-year trial of the Stolypin "reform" and six years of "brilliant" progress in the number of those who have "acquired" their land, etc., there cannot be the slightest doubt that the reform has not removed the crisis and cannot remove it.

Both at the present time and for the immediate future, it is beyond all question that Russia confronts us with the old crisis of an economy which is feudal as regards a number of survivals, the old crisis of pauperised small farming held in bondage by the latifundia of the Markov or Purishkevich type.

And this crisis, so graphically documented by the famine of 30 million peasants, confronts us despite Stolypin having opened the *last* valve that the Markovs and Purishkeviches have. They (and the Council of the United Nobility along with them) could have thought up nothing else,* nor can anything else be thought up to enable the Purishkeviches to retain land and power, than the pursuit of a bourgeois policy by these same Purishkeviches.

This is actually what the contradictions of the modern Russian countryside amount to: the pursuit of a bourgeois agrarian policy by the former serf-owners, who fully retain their land and their power. In the agrarian sphere, this is also "a step towards transformation into a bourgeois monarchy".**

This step towards the new has been taken by the old, which has retained its omnipotence, its land, its general appearance and conditions. This is the last step that the old can still take. It is the last valve. There are not, and cannot be, any other valves at the disposal of the Purishkeviches, who are in command of a bourgeois country.

And precisely because this step towards the new has been taken by the old, which has retained its omnipotence, it could not produce, and will not produce, any lasting result. On the contrary, it is leading—as shown clearly by all the symptoms of the period we are passing through—to the growth of the old crisis at a different and higher stage of Russia's capitalist development.

---

* It goes without saying that the phrase "thought up" should be taken with a grain of salt: the imagination of the class in command was limited and determined by the entire course of the capitalist development of Russia and the world as a whole. With the given alignment of the classes in a Russia developing along capitalist lines, the Council of the United Nobility could not have acted otherwise if it wanted to retain its power.

** See present edition, Vol. 15, p. 347.—*Ed.*

The old crisis is growing in a new way, in a new situation, at a time when the class relations have become much more definite; but it *is* growing, and its social and economic (and not merely economic) nature remains essentially unchanged.

A negligible number of good, *otrub* farms of the peasant bourgeoisie, while the number of proletarians bound to allotments is declining, while the Purishkeviches retain their omnipotence, while the vast mass of the pauperised and starving middle peasants are in bondage, and while the number of proletarians not bound to allotments is increasing—such is the picture of the Russian countryside today.

Does it still have to be demonstrated that the Stolypin agrarian programme cannot, while the Narodnik (in the historical and class sense of the term) programme can, abolish bondage and labour service? Surely the present situation in the countryside must suggest that given full freedom of mobilisation of the land, good *otrub* farms would inevitably put an end at once to all medieval famines, to all bondage and labour service, if such farms were set up by the free choice of the peasants on all the seventy million dessiatines of landed estates which for the time being are outside the "land distribution system"? And will not the irony of history compel us to say that Stolypin's land surveyors have come in handy for a Trudovik Russia?

Nevskaya Zvezda No. 20,
August 5, 1912
Signed: *R. S.*

Published according
to the text in *Nevskaya Zvezda*

A LITTLE EXPLANATION

The question whether our Cadets are democrats or a party of the liberal-monarchist bourgeoisie is of great scientific interest.

Let us recall that even the Trudovik (bourgeois democrat) Vodovozov showed vacillation on this question.

Concerning this question, *Pravda* referred to *Mr. Gredeskul's recent statements, repeated in "Rech".**

Rech answers: "We do not know what statements by Mr. Gredeskul *Pravda* is talking about."

How very nice, isn't it? *Pravda* said in clear and precise terms that it was speaking of the statements *repeated* in *Rech* Well? Can it be that *Rech does not know* what is published in *Rech*?? Would it not be more natural to suppose that the liberals *want* to forget certain things in their recent past for the sake of their pre-election playing at democracy?

Be that as it may, I shall quote, with a view to clarifying an important scientific question, what Mr. Gredeskul said in a series of public lectures and what he *repeated* in *Rech* No 117 (2071), without the editors making a single reservation

"At the very end of my lecture," wrote Mr. Gredeskul, "in arguing against the contention of *Vekhi* that the Russian emancipation movement had failed (allegedly through the fault of the intelligentsia) and comparing it with the opinion of those who stand much further to the left than P. B. Struve but who likewise believe that the movement has brought us absolutely nothing, I upheld a thesis to the contrary, saying that a very great deal had been done, that the very foundations had been laid for the future constitutional edifice, and very deeply and solidly, too, in the very midst of the masses of

* See p 246 of this volume. —*Ed.*

the people. To provide a critical confrontation for these two assertions and at the same time to express an idea which I also consider of
the utmost political importance for our time, I brought both of them
into relation with the future and said that from the point of view of
the former (if nothing had been done in 1905-06), everything had to
be started from the beginning, or, in other words, a second movement
had to be organised, whereas from the point of view of the latter assertion (that 1905-06 had seen the laying of the foundations for a Russian constitution), the opposite was true—no second popular movement was needed but merely quiet; persevering and confident constitutional work.

"It was at this point that I was interrupted by the Lepaya chief of
police (it happened in Lepaya). In this manner there ensued in Lepaya
a police demonstration against a public denial of the need for a new
revolution in Russia" (*Rech*, 1912, No. 117 [2071])

Mr. Gredeskul has fully proved that the Lepaya chief
of police made a mistake. But besides this, Mr Gredeskul
has proved two important things: (1) that the polemics of
Mr. Gredeskul and Co. against *Vekhi* are so much pretence
and empty talk. Actually, in all essential respects, the
whole Cadet Party is a *Vekhi* party; (2) that the Marxist
characterisation of the Cadet Party according to its scientific, economic and political features is perfectly correct.

Pravda No. 85, August 8, 1912   Published according
    Signed: *N. B.*   to the *Pravda* text

WORKERS' EARNINGS
AND CAPITALIST PROFITS IN RUSSIA

A survey of factories in Russia was made in 1908.[120] There is no doubt that the survey gave exaggerated figures of the workers' earnings and understated the amount of production and the size of the capitalists' profits, for in our country all surveys of this kind are carried out on purely bureaucratic lines, inquiries being addressed only to the capitalists, while it is considered unnecessary to ask the workers any questions.

Let us see what these statistics, which are particularly advantageous for the capitalists, have revealed.

According to preliminary information—which is all that has been published so far—there were altogether nearly 20,000 factories in Russia (the exact figure is 19,983; we shall give the exact figures in parentheses but shall round them off in the text to make it easier for the reader to visualise and remember the principal data).

The total number of workers of both sexes was 2,250,000 (2,253,787), including mining workers and workers employed in the industries subject to excise duty.

The wages of all those workers totalled *more than 500 million* (555,700,000) rubles.

To find out the average pay per worker, we must divide the total of wages by the number of workers. We get the figure 246 rubles.

This means that in 1908 *two and a quarter million* Russian factory workers earned a mere *twenty* rubles fifty kopeks a month on the average!

Considering that with this sum the worker has to support his family, and this with the present high rents and high food prices, such pay must be described as meagre.

Let us now see what the profits of the capitalists are. To ascertain them, we must subtract all the outlays of the capitalists from the sum total of production, i.e., the gross receipts of all the factories.

The sum total of production exceeds 4,500 million (4,651 million) rubles, and all the outlays of the capitalists total 4,000 million (4,082 million) rubles.

It follows that the capitalists' profits *exceed 500,000,000 rubles* (568,700,000 rubles).

These profits average *28,500 rubles* per establishment. *Each* worker brings the capitalist a profit of *252 rubles a year*.

Let us now compare the workers' earnings and the capitalists' profits. Each worker receives, on the average; 246 rubles a year, but he brings the capitalist an average profit of 252 rubles a year.*

It follows that the worker works *the lesser part* of the day for himself and *the greater part of it* for the capitalist. If, for example, we take the working day to average 11 hours, we shall see that the worker is paid only for five and a half hours and even somewhat less than that. The other five and a half hours he works gratuitously, without receiving any pay, and the entire sum earned by him during this half day constitutes the capitalist's profit.

Pravda No. 85, August 8, 1912
Signed: *T.*

Published according to
the *Pravda* text

---

* Altogether the worker creates an annual 498 rubles' worth of new values.

THE STRIKE MOVEMENT AND WAGES

Everyone knows that the famous strike movement of the Russian workers in 1905 achieved very great successes not only in the political, but in the economic sphere as well. The data furnished by the reports of factory inspectors[121] now enable us to form a fairly accurate idea of the magnitude of those successes.

According to those data, the average earnings of a factory worker were:

in 1901 . . . . . . 201 rubles	in 1906 . . . . . . 231 rubles
" 1902 . . . . . . 202 "	" 1907 . . . . . . 241 "
" 1903 . . . . . . 208 "	" 1908 . . . . . . 242 "
" 1904 . . . . . . 213 "	" 1909 . . . . . . 236 "
" 1905 . . . . . . 205 "	" 1910 . . . . . . 242 "
average for five years 206 "	average for five years 238 "

This shows that the year 1905 was a turning-point. For it was after 1905 that wages rose *abruptly* from 205 to 231 rubles a year, i.e., *by 26 rubles*, or more than 10 per cent.

With regard to 1905, which shows a drop of 8 rubles in wages compared with 1904, the following must be borne in mind: firstly, 1905 was a year of economic depression, i.e., a slump in industry; secondly, according to data of the Ministry of Trade, the workers that year lost, through not receiving wages during strikes, *17,500,000 rubles*, or over 10 rubles per worker on the average.

Thus, we may assume that real wages in 1905 were 215 rubles a year, but out of these 215 rubles the workers contributed 10 rubles each to the strike movement, which in 1905 was distinguished by remarkable persistence and breadth, unprecedented anywhere else in the world.

The result is that as we now examine the data for a whole decade, 1901-10, we clearly see a *striking* difference between the *pre-revolutionary* and *post-revolutionary* epoch.

Until 1905 the Russian factory worker's wages averaged 206 rubles. After 1905, they averaged 238 rubles, i.e., *32 rubles more per year*—an increase of 15.5 per cent.

Within one year wages experienced such an upward leap that no subsequent efforts by the capitalists (who, it will be recalled, took away all the gains of 1905 one by one) were able to reduce the worker to his former low standard of living. The year 1905 improved the worker's living standard to a degree that normally is attained during several decades.

Through the strikes in 1905 the workers lost, according to official statistics, 17,500,000 rubles by not being paid wages during the strikes. According to the same source, the capitalists' drop in output in 1905 was 127,300,000 rubles.

The rise in wages after 1905, however, brought the workers an average gain of 32 rubles per worker in five years (1906-1910), i.e., a total of 57,600,000 rubles a year, or *286 million rubles in five years*, considering the number of workers to be 1,800,000.

Pravda No. 86, August 9, 1912

Published according to the *Pravda* text

9*

THE WORKING DAY IN THE FACTORIES
OF MOSCOW GUBERNIA

I. M. Kozminykh-Lanin, an engineer, has published a book on the length of the working day and working year in the factories of Moscow Gubernia.

The data collected by the author relate to the end of 1908 and cover 219,669 workers, or a little over seven-tenths of the total number of factory workers in Moscow Gubernia (307,773).

On the basis of these data, the author finds the average working day to be 9 $^1/_2$ *hours* for adults and juveniles and 7$^1/_2$ hours for those under age.

It should be noted that these data do not include overtime work (the author has prepared for the press a special book on overtime work) and, secondly, that the author's data are based solely on "obligatory regulations for employers and workers".

Whether these regulations are actually adhered to is a question our engineer does not raise. Only workers' unions, by compiling their own statistics, could collect data on this question as well.

This 9 $^1/_2$-hour day varies greatly from one establishment to another.

The author's tables show that *33,466 workers* work *over 10 hours a day*! This covers more than 15 per cent of the total number of workers surveyed.

There are *13,189 workers* who work *over 11 hours a day*, and 75 workers who work over 12 hours a day. The bulk of the workers crushed by this excessively long working day belongs to the textile industry.

If it is taken into account that approximately one-third of the workers are not included in the author's survey, the conclusion can be drawn that the working day of *more than 20,000* factory workers in Moscow Gubernia is monstrously long.

Lastly, Kozminykh-Lanin's data show that even the extremely obsolete Russian law of 1897, which permits an $11^{1}/_{2}$-hour (!!!) day, *is not observed by the factory owners*. Under that law, when working in two shifts, no worker may work more than 9 hours a day, calculated over a fortnight.

In reality, however, out of the 83,990 two-shift workers surveyed by the author, 14,376 worked *over 9 hours*. This comprises 17 per cent of the total number of those working in two shifts. And of the 3,733 two-shift workers engaged in repair and auxiliary jobs, 2,173, or *nearly three-fifths*, worked over 9 hours a day! A total of 16,500 workers who are compelled —even according to official data— to work longer than allowed by the law!

An eight-hour day existed in Moscow Gubernia in 1908 only for 4,398 workers —out of the 219,669 surveyed. This means that an eight-hour day is perfectly feasible even today; it is only necessary for 215,000 workers to overtake those 4,000.

Pravda No. 88, August 11, 1912
Signed: *V.*

Published according
to the *Pravda* text

THE WORKING DAY
AND WORKING YEAR IN MOSCOW GUBERNIA

The work bearing this title, from the pen of Kozminykh-Lanin, an engineer (Moscow, 1912, published by the Standing Commission of the Museum for the Promotion of Labour under the Moscow Branch of the Imperial Russian Technical Society. Price, 1 ruble 75 kopeks), is a summary of data relating to the end of 1908.

The data cover 219,669 workers, or 71,37 per cent of the total number of factory workers in the gubernia (307,773). The author says that he has "carefully studied the data on each industrial establishment in particular", and has "included in the summary only that part of it which left no room for doubt".

Such statistics would have been of outstanding interest, even though they come very late, had the data been tabulated more sensibly. Unfortunately, it is precisely this word that has to be used, for while Mr. Kozminykh-Lanin has compiled his tables most carefully, putting a very great deal of labour into the calculation of all sorts of totals and percentages, he has expended this labour irrationally.

The wealth of material seems to have overwhelmed the author. He has made hundreds and thousands of calculations that are absolutely superfluous and only encumbered his work, but he has not made some dozens of calculations that are absolutely necessary, since no general picture can be obtained without them.

Indeed, the author's principal tables, which almost fill the whole of his book, contain detailed figures, such, for instance, as that the workers who work from 9 to 10 hours a day are divided into 16 *categories* according to the number of working hours in two successive weeks (from 109 to 120 hours), and the average number of working hours is calculated for each category! And all this has been done twice: for the workers engaged in production and for the auxiliary workers.

It has to be admitted that such detailing is, first of all, absolutely unnecessary and that it looks like indulging in statistics for their own sake, a kind of game with figures, *to the detriment* of a clear picture and of material fit for study. Secondly, nine-tenths of these "averages", which the author has calculated to an accuracy of one per cent, are simply a waste of labour, for out of a thousand readers of the book (which will hardly find a thousand readers), only one reader will perhaps think this sort of "average" necessary (moreover, that one reader could have calculated *it for himself* if he had been so unfortunate as to need it!).

On the other hand, the book *completely lacks* absolutely indispensable summaries that the author *could* have drawn up with far less expenditure of labour and which one cannot do without if one wants to make a sensible study of the data of the survey. There are no summaries (1) giving totals, by production groups, of workers who work in one, two and three shifts; (2) classing workers according to production and auxiliary jobs; (3) giving average working hours according to production groups; (4) giving totals of working time of adults and juveniles; (5) singling out factories with various numbers of workers.

Let us dwell on this last point. The author seems so diligent—judging by the list he gives of the works which he has published or prepared for publication—and has such a wealth of interesting information at his disposal that a critical analysis of his methods may be not only of theoretical, but also of immediate practical use. We have already quoted the author where he says that he has "carefully studied the data on *each* industrial establishment *in particular*".

It follows that a summary of the material, if only by the factory groups used even by our official statistics (up to 20 workers, 21-50, 51-100, 101-500, 501-1,000, and over 1,000), was perfectly possible. Was it necessary?

Undoubtedly. Statistics should not give arbitrary columns of figures but should, by means of figures, throw light on those different social types of the phenomenon under study that have fully emerged, or are emerging, in reality. Can there be any doubt that establishments employing 50 and those employing 500 workers belong to essentially different *social types* of the phenomenon we are interested in, or that the entire social development of all the civilised countries increases the *difference* between these types and leads to one of them *superseding* the other?

Let us take the data on the working day. From the author's summary table of totals it can be concluded —provided we *ourselves* do a certain amount of necessary statistical work which we do not see in the book —that 33,000 workers (out of the 220,000 surveyed) work *longer than 10 hours a day*. The average duration of the working day of the 220,000 workers is $9^1/_2$ hours. The question arises: are not these workers, crushed by an excessive working day, employed in *small* establishments?

This question arises naturally and necessarily. It is by no means arbitrary. The political economy and statistics of all countries of the world *oblige* us to put precisely this question, for the prolongation of working hours by small establishments has been registered only too often. Capitalist economic conditions necessitate this prolongation in the case of small employers.

It turns out that the material at the author's disposal *did contain* data for answering this highly important question, but they have disappeared in his summary! In his summary, the author gives us very long and worthless columns of detailed "averages" but *does not give* the necessary division of factories according to the number of workers.

In the case of Moscow Gubernia, such a division is even more necessary (if we may here use the comparative degree) than elsewhere, for in Moscow Gubernia we see a comparatively large number of small establishments alongside a huge concentration of production. According to statistics for 1910, there were altogether 1,440 establishments in the gubernia, employing 335,190 workers. One-half of this number of workers (i. e., 167,199) was concentrated in *66 factories*, while at the other pole there were 669 establishments

employing a total of 18,277 workers. It is clear that we
have here entirely different social types and that statistics
which do not distinguish between them are no good at
all.

The author was so absorbed in his columns of figures
on the numbers of workers who work 94, 95, etc., to 144,
hours in two successive weeks, that he *left out altogether*
data on the number of establishments. The number is given
in the second part of his work, which deals with the length
of the working year; but the first part, which deals with the
working day, gives no information on the number of establishments, although this information was no doubt available
to the author.

The largest factories in Moscow Gubernia represent not
only distinctive types of industrial establishment, but also
distinctive types of population, with specific living and cultural (or rather cultureless) conditions. The singling out of
these factories, and a detailed analysis of the data for each
class of establishment, according to the number of workers,
are a necessary condition for rational economic statistics.

———

Let us cite the more important totals from Mr. Kozminykh-
Lanin's work.

As we have said, his survey of the length of the working
day covers 219,669 factory workers of Moscow Gubernia, or
71.37 per cent of their total number, the textile workers
being represented in his statistics more widely than workers
engaged in other industries. The survey covered 74.6 per
cent of all the textile workers and only 49-71 per cent of
the other workers. *Apparently*, the survey was less extensive
with regard to *small* establishments; in any case, the data
on the number of working days in the year cover 58 per cent
of the establishments (811 out of the 1,394 existing in 1908)
and 75 per cent of the workers (231,130 out of 307,773). It
is plainly the smaller establishments that have been left
out.

The author gives summary data on the length of the working day only for all the workers put together. The result is an average of $9^1/_2$ hours a day for adults and $7^1/_2$

hours for juveniles. The number of juveniles, it should be noted, is not great: 1,363 against 218,306 adults. This suggests that juvenile workers in particular may have been "hidden" from the inspectors.

Out of the total of 219,669 workers there were 128,628 (58.56 per cent) working in one shift, 88,552 (40.31 per cent) working in two shifts and 2,489 (1.13 per cent) working in three shifts. Two-shift work predominates over one-shift work in the textile industry, where there are 75,391 working in two shifts ("in production", i.e., exclusive of auxiliary workers) against 68,604 working in one shift. The addition of repair and auxiliary workers produces a total of 78,107 working in two shifts and 78,321 working in one shift. In the case of metalworkers, on the other hand, one-shift work predominates considerably (17,821 adult workers) over two-shift work (7,673).

Summing up the total of workers who work different numbers of hours a day, we obtain the following data:

Number of hours worked per day	Number of workers	
Up to 8 hours	4,398	
From 8 to 9 hours	87,402	
" 9 " 10 "	94,403	
" 10 " 11 "	20,202	} 33,466
" 11 " 12 "	13,189	
12 or more hours	75	
Total	219,669	

This shows how negligible still is the number of workers in Russia who do not work more than 8 hours a day —a mere 4,398 out of 219,669. On the other hand, the number of workers whose working day is excessively, scandalously long is very great: 33,466 out of 220,000, or over 15 per cent, work *more than 10 hours a day*! And this without considering overtime work.

To proceed. The difference in the length of the working day of one-shift and two-shift workers can be seen from the following data, which refer only to adult "production workers", i.e., exclusive of repair and auxiliary workers, who make up 8 per cent of the total.

Length of working day	Percentage of workers (working the indicated number of hours a day)	
	One-shift	Two-shift
Up to 8 hours	1.3	1.0
From 8 to 9 hours	13.3	81.9
" 9 " 10 "	60.7	14.7
" 10 " 11 "	15.2	1.4
" 11 " 12 "	9.5	1.0
" 12 or more hours	—	—
Total	100.0	100.0

This shows, among other things, that 17 per cent of the two-shift workers work *more than 9 hours* a day, or more than is permitted even by the law of 1897, which Mr. Lanin justly regards as exceedingly outdated. Under this law, when work is carried on in two shifts, the number of hours worked per day must not exceed nine, calculated over a fortnight. And Mr. Lanin in all his calculations and tables takes precisely a period of "two successive weeks".

Since a very definite and precise law is violated so openly, it is easy to imagine the fate of the other provisions of our factory legislation.

The average number of hours worked per day by a one-shift worker (only adult and only engaged in "production") is 9.89. This implies prevalence of a *ten-hour day* without any reduction even on Saturdays, and exclusive of overtime work. Needless to say such a long working day is certainly excessive and cannot be tolerated.

The average number of hours worked per day by a two-shift worker is 8.97, i.e., there predominates in practice the nine-hour day which the law requires in this case. Its reduction to eight hours is particularly imperative because in the case of two-shift work the time from 10 p. m. to 4 (!!) a.m. is considered "night", which means that in effect a very substantial portion of the *night* is considered to be "day" for the worker. A nine-hour day with night turned into *day*, and with constant night work—that is the situation prevailing in Moscow Gubernia!

In conclusion of our review of Mr. Kozminykh-Lanin's data, we wish to point out that he finds the average duration of the working year to be 270 days. For textile workers,

however, the figure is somewhat smaller —268.8 days —and
for metalworkers, a little greater —272.3.

The way in which Kozminykh-Lanin has analysed these
data on the length of the working year is also most unsatisfactory. On the one hand, excessive, utterly senseless detailing: we find as many as 130 horizontal rows in the overall
table on the length of the working year! Data on the numbers
of establishments, workers, etc., are given here *separately*
for each number of working days (per year) that occurs,
beginning with 22 and ending with 366. Such "detailing"
is more like complete failure to "digest" the raw material.

On the other hand, here too we do not find the necessary
summaries either on the numbers of workers in the factories
or on the difference in motive power (manual and mechanical
factories). Hence one cannot obtain a picture enabling one to
understand how various conditions affect the length of the
working year. The wealth of data collected by the author
has *gone to waste* through very bad handling.

We can ascertain —roughly and far from accurately —the
significance of the distinction between large-scale and small-
scale production even from the author's data, provided we
re-analyse them somewhat. Let us take the *four* main groups
of establishments according to length of the working year:
(1) those working up to 200 days a year; (2) from 200 to 250;
(3) from 250 to 270, and (4) 270 days or longer.

By summing up, for each of these categories, the number
of factories and that of the workers of both sexes, we obtain
the following picture:

Length of working year	Average number of working days per year	Number of		Average number of workers per factory
		factories	workers	
Up to 200 days	96	74	5,676	76
200 " 250 "	236	91	14,400	158
250 " 270 "	262	196	58,313	297
270 or more "	282	450	152,741	339
Total	270	811	231,130	285

This shows clearly that the larger the factory, the longer
(on the whole) the working year. Consequently, the social
and economic importance of small undertakings is much *less*

in reality than appears from their share in, say, the total number of workers. The working year in these undertakings is so much shorter than in the large ones that their share in production must be quite insignificant. Besides, with a short working year, these factories (the small ones) are incapable of forming a permanent body of proletarians, hence the workers here are more "bound" to the land, probably earn less, are less cultured, etc.

A large factory intensifies exploitation by prolonging the working year to the utmost and thus bringing into existence a proletariat which has completely severed its ties with the countryside.

If we were to study the differences in length of the working year depending on the technical organisation of factories (manual and mechanical motive power, etc.), we could undoubtedly derive a whole series of highly interesting indications of the living conditions of the population, the position of the workers, the evolution of our capitalism, etc. But the author, one can say, has not so much as touched on these questions.

All he has done is to give figures on the average duration of the working year in factories of the different groups of industries. The variations of the general average are very small: from 246 days in Group IX (processing of mineral substances) to 291 in Group XII (chemical industry).

These differences, as the reader will see, are far less than those in the duration of the working year in small and large factories in general, irrespective of the industry to which they belong.

Differences in the type of industry are *less* characteristic, and less important for social and economic statistics than differences in the *scale* of production. This does not mean, of course, that the former differences can be ignored. What it does mean is that sensible statistics are absolutely impossible unless the latter differences are taken into account.

Nevskaya Zvezda No. 21,
August 12, 1912
Signed: *V. I.*

Published according
to the text in *Nevskaya Zvezda*

IN BRITAIN

The British Liberals have been in power for six and a half years. The working-class movement in Britain is becoming stronger and stronger. Strikes are assuming a mass character; moreover, they are ceasing to be purely economic and are developing into political strikes.

Robert Smillie, the leader of the Scottish miners who recently showed such strength in mass struggle,[122] declares that in their next big fight the miners will demand the transfer of the collieries to state ownership. And this next big fight is approaching inexorably, because all the miners of Britain are perfectly well aware that the notorious Minimum Wage Act cannot bring about any appreciable improvement in their conditions.

And so the British Liberals, who are losing ground, have invented a new battle-cry in order once again to induce the mass of the electors to trust the Liberals for a while. "You can't sell without cheating" is the commercial slogan of capitalism. "You can't get seats in parliament without cheating" is the slogan of capitalist politics in free countries.

The "fashionable" slogan invented by the Liberals for this purpose is the demand for "land reform". It is not clear what the Liberals and their expert in humbugging the masses, Lloyd George, mean by that. Apparently, it is a question of increasing the land tax, and no more. But the idea that actually lies behind the resounding talk about "restoring the land to the people", etc., is to collect further millions for military adventures, for the Navy.

In Britain, agriculture is conducted wholly on capitalist lines. The capitalist farmers rent medium-sized plots of land from the landlords and cultivate them with the aid of wage-workers.

Under these circumstances, no "land reform" can in any way change the conditions of the agricultural workers. In Britain the buying-out of landed estates might even become a new method of fleecing the proletariat, since the landlords and the capitalists, who would retain state power, would sell their land at exorbitant prices. And the price would have to be paid by the taxpayers, i.e., the workers again.

The fuss made by the Liberals about the land question has done good in one respect: it has roused interest in organising the agricultural workers.

When Britain's agricultural workers wake up and join together in unions, the Liberals will no longer be able to get away with charlatan "promises of reform" or of allotments for farm-hands and day-labourers.

Recently a reporter of a British labour newspaper visited Joseph Arch, the veteran agricultural workers' leader who has done much to rouse the labourers to a class-conscious life. This could not be done at one stroke, and Arch's slogan — "three acres and a cow" for every agricultural worker — was a very naïve one. The union he founded fell to pieces, but the cause he fought for is not dead and the organisation of the agricultural workers in Britain is once again becoming an immediate issue.

Arch is now 83 years old. He lives in the same village and in the same house in which he was born. He told his interviewer that the agricultural workers' union had managed to raise wages to 15, 16 and 17 shillings a week. And now the wages of agricultural workers in Britain have again dropped — in Norfolk, where Arch lives — to 12 or 13 shillings a week.

Pravda No. 89, August 12, 1912
Signed: *P.*

Published according
to the *Pravda* text

CONCENTRATION OF PRODUCTION IN RUSSIA

In Russia, as in all capitalist countries, concentration of production is going on, i.e., its concentration to an ever greater extent in a small number of large and very large undertakings.

Under the capitalist system, every undertaking is entirely dependent on the market. In view of this dependence, the larger the undertaking, the more cheaply it can sell its product. A big capitalist buys raw materials more cheaply and expends them more economically; he uses better machinery, etc. Small proprietors, on the other hand, are ruined and go under. Production becomes more and more concentrated in the hands of a few millionaires. Millionaires generally increase their power still more through joint-stock companies, which put in their hands the capital of middle proprietors and "small fry".

Here are data, for example, on the factory industry in Russia for 1910 compared with 1901:[123]

Groups of establishments by number of workers	Number of establishments		Number of workers (thousands)	
	1901	1910	1901	1910
Up to 50	12,740	9,909	244	220
51 to 100	2,428	2,201	171	159
101 " 500	2,288	2,213	492	508
501 " 1,000	403	433	269	303
Over 1,000	243	324	526	713
Total	18,102	15,080	1,702	1,903

Such is generally the situation in all capitalist countries. The number of small establishments is *decreasing*; the petty bourgeoisie, the small proprietors, are ruined and go under;

they join the ranks of office employees, and sometimes of the proletariat.

The number of very large undertakings is growing fast, their share in production as a whole increasing still more.

From 1901 to 1910 the number of large factories employing over 1,000 workers each increased almost 50 per cent—from 243 to 324.

In 1901 they had about half a million (526,000) workers, or less than one-third of the total number, whereas in 1910 the figure *exceeded 700,000*, which is more than one-third of the total.

The bigger factories choke the small ones and concentrate production more and more. Ever greater numbers of workers are brought together in a few undertakings, but the whole profit from the labour of the combined millions of workers goes to a handful of millionaires.

Pravda No. 89, August 12. 1912
      Signed: *T*.

Published according
to the *Pravda* text

A CAREER

The life story of the millionaire A. S. Suvorin, the publisher of *Novoye Vremya*, who died not long ago, reflected and expressed a very interesting period in the history of Russia's bourgeois society as a whole.

At the start of his career he was a poor man, a liberal and even a democrat; towards the end of his career, he was a millionaire, a self-satisfied and brazen extoller of the bourgeoisie, who grovelled before every turn in the policies of the powers that be. Is this not typical of the *bulk* of the "educated" and "intellectual" members of so-called society? It is true, of course, that not all practise renegacy with such furious success as to become millionaires, but nine-tenths, or perhaps ninety-nine out of a hundred, practise the very same renegacy, *beginning* as radical students and *ending* up as holders of "cushy jobs" in some office or other, in some swindle or other.

A penniless student who could not enter university for lack of money; a teacher in an uyezd school, who also held the office of secretary to the Marshal of the Nobility or gave private lessons in the homes of aristocratic and wealthy serf-owners; a budding liberal and even democratic journalist sympathising with Belinsky and Chernyshevsky and hostile to reaction—this is how Suvorin *began* in the fifties and sixties of the last century.

The landlord Katkov, a liberal who sympathised with the British bourgeoisie and the British Constitution, turned during the first upsurge of the democratic movement in Russia (in the early sixties of the nineteenth century) to nationalism, chauvinism and rabid Black-Hundredism.

The liberal journalist Suvorin turned during the second upsurge of the democratic movement in Russia (in the late seventies of the nineteenth century) to nationalism, to chauvinism, to shameless fawning upon the powers that be. The Russo-Turkish War helped this careerist to "find himself", and to find his path of a flunkey rewarded by the huge profits of his newspaper *At Your Service, Sir*.

Suvorin's *Novoye Vremya* earned that nickname, *At Your Service, Sir*, for many decades to come. The newspaper became in Russia model example of the venal press. *Novoye Vremya* became an expression synonymous with the concepts of apostasy, renegacy and sycophancy. Suvorin's *Novoye Vremya* is a specimen of brisk trade, of how to sell stuff "for consumption off or on the premises". It deals in everything, from political convictions to pornographic advertisements.

And now, after the third upsurge of the democratic movement in Russia (in the early twentieth century), how many more liberals have taken the *Vekhi* path, turning to nationalism, to chauvinism, to the defamation of democracy, to sycophancy to the reaction!

Katkov—Suvorin—the *Vekhi* group are all historical stages of the turn taken by the Russian liberal bourgeoisie *from democracy to* the defence of reaction, to chauvinism and anti-Semitism.

The class-conscious workers become steeled in their convictions, realising the inevitability of this turn of the bourgeoisie, as well as of the turn of the working masses to the ideas of working-class democracy.

Pravda No. 94, August 18, 1912
    Signed: *I. V.*

Published according
to the *Pravda* text

TO THE SECRETARIAT
OF THE INTERNATIONAL SOCIALIST BUREAU

August 31, 1912

Dear Comrade,

I have received from you Circular No. 15 (July 1912) in which the Executive Committee of the Social-Democracy of Poland and Lithuania gives notice of a split in that organisation.

In my quality of representative of the R.S.D.L.P. in the International Socialist Bureau, I must emphatically protest against the notice for the following reasons:

1. The Executive of the S.D.P. and L. declares that the Warsaw Committee "is not affiliated to the R.S.D.L.P., of which the S.D.P. and L. is an autonomous section".

But the Executive of the S.D.P. and L. has no authority whatsoever either to decide or to declare who is affiliated to the R.S.D.L.P., which I represent.

Today the Executive of the S.D.P. and L. itself is not affiliated to our Party, for it maintains no organisational relations either with the Central Committee I represent, which was elected at the Conference in January 1912, or with the opposed liquidationist centre (the so-called "Organising Committee").

2. The assertion of the Executive of the S.D.P. and L. that the split occurred "unexpectedly just before the Duma elections" is not in accord with the facts.

I happen to know that the very same Executive of the S.D.P. and L. must have foreseen a split as early as two years ago, when it provoked a sharp conflict with its former members, Malecki and Hanecki, and removed Hanecki from the Board.

3. It is hypocritical of the Executive to declare:

firstly, that *agents provocateurs* have made their way into the Warsaw organisation "as into all the other revolutionary organisations in tsarist Russia";

secondly, that the split came about with "the active co-operation of the secret police", although the Executive cannot give a single name, and does not dare to express any specific suspicion!

How very hypocritical one has to be to make in public the dishonest accusation of "co-operation of the secret police", with the aim of morally destroying one's political opponents, even while lacking the courage to give a single name or express any specific suspicion!

I am confident that every member of the International will indignantly reject these unheard-of methods of struggle.

I have for a number of years known the two former members of the Executive of the S.D.P. and L., Malecki and Hanecki, who openly march shoulder to shoulder with the Warsaw Committee. I have received, precisely from the Warsaw Committee, an official notification confirming this fact.

In the present situation, I consider it my duty to convey to the International Socialist Bureau the enclosed protest from the Warsaw Committee of the S.D.P. and L.

As the statement of the Executive Committee has been circulated to all members of the International Socialist Bureau, I must ask you, dear comrade, to circulate also this statement of mine, together with the protest of the Warsaw Committee, to the representatives of all the parties affiliated to the International.

With Party greetings, *N. Lenin*

Published in *Gazeta Robotnicza*
No. 19, November 21, 1912

Published according
to the newspaper text
Translated from the Polish

THE CADETS AND THE AGRARIAN QUESTION

In their polemics against *Pravda*, the Cadets were unable, much as they tried, to evade the question whether they are a democratic or a liberal-monarchist party.

This is a highly important question. Its importance goes beyond that of a general question of principle which provides material for elucidating basic political concepts. Moreover, the question of the nature of the Cadet Party, which claims leadership of the entire opposition, is inseparably bound up with *all* the fundamental questions of the Russian emancipation movement in general. That is why anyone who takes an intelligent interest in the election campaign, and appreciates its significance for the political enlightenment of the masses, is bound to pay the greatest attention to this controversy on the nature of the Cadet Party.

The Cadet *Rech* is now trying to stifle this controversy, to shut out questions of principle by subterfuges and quarrelsome sallies ("a lie", "a distortion", etc.), to rake up some abuse or other which the liquidators flung at us when their personal annoyance, caused by sharp organisational conflicts, was at its highest. All these are familiar and battered methods used by people who realise their weakness in a controversy over principles. And for this reason our reply to the Cadets must be a repeated explanation of questions of principle.

What are the distinctions between democracy and liberalism in general? Both the bourgeois democrat and the liberal (all liberals are bourgeois liberals, but not every democrat is a bourgeois democrat) are opposed to the old order, to absolutism, serfdom, the privileges of the upper social-estate, etc; they are for political liberty and a constitutional "legal" system. That is the resemblance between them.

Now for the difference between them. The democrat represents the mass of the population. He shares their petty-bourgeois prejudices, expecting, for example, that a new, "equalised" redivision of all the land would not only abolish all vestiges of serfdom (he would be justified in expecting this), but would also undermine the foundations of capitalism (which is entirely unjustified, for *no* redivision of the land can do away either with the power of the market and of money, or with the power and omnipotence of capital). But the democrat believes in the movement of the masses, in its strength and justice, and has no fear at all of this movement. He advocates the abolition of *all* medieval privileges without exception.

The liberal does not represent the mass of the population but a minority of the latter, namely, the big and middle liberal bourgeoisie. The liberal is *more* afraid of the movement of the masses and of consistent democracy than of reaction. Far from seeking complete abolition of all medieval privileges, he frankly *defends* some privileges which are, moreover, very substantial ones, and strives to ensure that these privileges are divided between the Purishkeviches and the Milyukovs and not abolished altogether.

The liberal defends political liberty and the constitution—invariably in a curtailed form (such as the two-chamber system and many other things), each curtailment amounting to the preservation of a privilege of the serf-owners. Thus the liberal vacillates continuously between the serf-owners and the democrats; hence the extreme, almost incredible *impotence* of the liberals in all matters of any importance.

Russia's democrats are the working class (proletarian democrats) and the Narodniks and Trudoviks of all shades (bourgeois democrats). Russia's liberals are the Cadet Party, as well as the "Progressists" and most of the non-Russian groups in the Third Duma.

Russian democrats have important victories to their credit, Russian liberals none at all. The former have proved their ability to fight, and their defeats have always been great, historic defeats of the whole of Russia; moreover, even after a defeat some of the democrats' demands have invariably been met. The latter, i.e., the liberals, have proved *incapable* of fighting, and they have nothing to show in Russian history but a constant contemptuous treatment of the liberals by the serf-owners, comparable to the treatment of the serfs by their lords.

Let us test these general considerations and basic theoretical postulates by the Cadets' agrarian programme. *Pravda* told the Cadets that their undemocratic nature was evident from the speeches on the agrarian question made by the Cadet Berezovsky the Second in the Third Duma.*

The Cadet *Rech* answered, in its issue No. 208: "The speech of Berezovsky the Second was, as we know, a reaffirmation of the Cadet agrarian programme."

See how evasive this answer is! We said that the speech of Berezovsky the First** was a specimen of *un*democratic treatment of the question. *Rech* knows very well what we consider an indication of liberalism as distinct from democracy. But it has no intention of analysing the question seriously, of stating which precisely are the signs of the distinction between liberalism and democracy that it, i.e., *Rech*, considers correct, and of ascertaining whether these signs are evident in the speech of Berezovsky the First. *Rech* does nothing of the kind. It dodges the issue, thus betraying a fundamental weakness and a guilty conscience.

But even *Rech* could not bring itself to disclaim the responsibility of the *entire* Cadet Party for the speech delivered by Berezovsky the First. It admitted—it had to admit—this responsibility by describing the speech as a "reaffirmation of the Cadet agrarian programme".

Splendid. And now we shall quote the main passages from that indisputably and officially Cadet speech by a member of the Third Duma, the Simbirsk landlord A. Y. Berezovsky. We shall see, in analysing the speaker's arguments, whether his point of view is democratic or liberal. And we shall also see whether the Cadet gentlemen succeed in refuting us in their vast press or at their meetings.

---

* See p. 246 of this volume.—*Ed.*
** Both *Pravda* and *Rech* were mistaken in speaking of Berezovsky the Second. The Cadet is Berezovsky the *First*, Alexander Yeleazarovich, a Simbirsk landlord.

"It is my deep conviction," said A. Y. Berezovsky in the Third Duma in October 1908 (we are quoting from the verbatim report published in *Rossiya*[134]), "that this Bill [the Cadets' land Bill] is far more beneficial to the landowners as well [and not to the peasants alone], and I say this, gentlemen, because I am familiar with agriculture, having engaged in it all my life and being a landowner myself. For a cultured farming system, the Bill of the party of people's freedom would undoubtedly be more useful than the present system. One should not seize on the bare fact of compulsory alienation, become indignant about it, and say that it is violence, but should see and appreciate *what the things proposed in our Bill will amount to and how this compulsory alienation is to be effected....*"

We have emphasised these truly precious words of Mr. A. Y. Berezovsky's—precious because of their rare veracity. Anyone who recalls the speeches and articles of the Marxist Bolsheviks against the Cadets at the time of the First Duma, or who takes the trouble to read those articles now, will have to agree that in 1908 Mr. A. Y. Berezovsky brilliantly confirmed the Bolsheviks of 1906. And we venture to predict that any history that is at all impartial will confirm *their* policy three times over.

In 1906 we said: "Don't trust the *sound* of that phrase— 'compulsory alienation'." The point is, *who* will compel *whom*. If the landlords compel the peasants to pay for poor lands three times their worth, in the fashion of the notorious compensation of 1861, then this kind of "compulsory alienation" will be a *landlord* reform beneficial to the landlords and ruinous to the peasants.[*]

The liberals, the Cadets, in raising the question of compulsory alienation, *manoeuvred* between the landlords and the peasants, between the Black Hundreds and the democrats. In 1906, they addressed themselves to the democrats, trying to make their "compulsory alienation" pass for something democratic. In 1908, they addressed themselves to the diehards in the Third Duma, arguing that one should see "what this compulsory alienation will amount to and how it is to be effected".

Let us listen then to the official spokesman of the Cadet Party.

---

[*] See present edition, Vol. 10, pp. 414-17.—*Ed.*

"Take the Bill of the forty-two members of the First State Duma,"
said A. Y. Berezovsky. "It contained only [exactly, Mr. Berezovsky!]
the recognition of the necessity of alienating first of all those lands
which are not exploited by their owners themselves. Furthermore,
the party of people's freedom favoured the establishment of local
committees which would have to ascertain at a certain time which
lands are or are not subject to alienation and how much land the
peasants require to meet their needs. The committees were to be
constituted in such a manner as to ensure that half of the members
were peasants and the other half non-peasants."

Mr. A. Y. Berezovsky omitted a trifle from his statement.
Anyone who wishes to look into the agrarian Bill prepared
by Kutler (the Cadet Party's recognised authority on the
agrarian question) and published in Volume II of the Cadet
publication, *The Agrarian Question*, will see that, by the
terms of the Bill, the chairmen of the committees were to
be appointed by the government, i.e., they too were to be
representatives of the landlords.

But let us assume even that A. Y. Berezovsky expressed
the Cadet views more accurately than Kutler. Let us assume
that A. Y. Berezovsky said *everything* and that the Cadets
actually want committees made up of *equal numbers* of
peasants and "non-peasants", without representatives of
the class government. What then? Will anyone dare to assert that such a Bill is democratic?

Democracy is the rule of the majority. Only universal,
direct and equal elections can be called democratic. Only
such committees are democratic as have been elected by
the *entire* population on the basis of universal suffrage.
This follows from the general, basic, elementary truths of
democracy so indisputably that it even seems strange to have
to explain it to the Cadet gentlemen.

On paper, the Cadets recognise universal suffrage. But
in reality, with regard to one of the most important questions of the Russian emancipation movement, the agrarian
question, they do *not* recognise universal suffrage! No subterfuges or reservations remove this fact, which is of prime
importance.

And do not imagine that the Cadets merely depart here
from the principle of universal suffrage, from the principle
of democracy. No. They take as a basis a *different* principle,
the principle of "*agreement*" between the old and the new,

between the landlord and the peasant, between the Black Hundreds and the democrats. What the Cadets proclaim is: half to one side and half to the other.

This is a typical principle of the vacillating liberal-monarchist bourgeoisie. What this bourgeoisie wants is not the *abolition* of medieval privileges, but their *division* between the landlords and the bourgeoisie. Indeed, how can anyone deny that to grant the "non-peasants" (i.e., the landlords, to put it bluntly) *equality* with the peasants, who make up seven-tenths of the population, means *preserving* and *reaffirming* medieval privileges? What else did medieval privileges amount to but that the landlord meant as much in politics as hundreds and thousands of peasants?

From *equality* of the landlords and the peasants there can be no other outcome but a division of privileges between the landlords and the bourgeoisie. That was precisely the case in 1861, when the landlords ceded one-thousandth of their privileges to the nascent bourgeoisie, while the peasant masses were doomed to *half a century* (1861+50=1911) of the agony of disfranchisement, humiliation, slow starvation, extortion of taxes, etc. Besides, it should not be forgotten that in 1861 the landlords, ceding one-thousandth of their political privileges to the bourgeoisie (the Zemstvo, urban and judicial reforms, etc.), began themselves to develop economically into a bourgeoisie by setting up distilleries and sugar refineries, joining the boards of joint-stock companies, and so on.

We shall see in a moment the final outcome of this "equality" of a negligible number of landlords and a huge number of peasants, as pointed out by Mr. A. Y. Berezovsky himself. But first we must stress the great significance of Berezovsky's statement that the vaunted committees would have to "ascertain which lands *are* or *are not subject* to alienation and how much land the peasants *require* to meet their needs".

All the talk about various "norms" of allotment for the peasants, etc., is nothing but empty words with which, incidentally, our Narodnik intellectuals, including the most "Left" of them, often lull themselves and the peasants. The *only* important question is: will all the lands be subject to alienation or not? And, in the latter case, *who* is to decide *"which are not subject"*? (I do not speak of *who* is to deter-

mine the amount of the compensation, for the very idea of
compensation for medieval privileges is a liberal-bourgeois
principle, one that is radically, at bottom, absolutely undemocratic and anti-democratic).

All the clauses of the Cadets' land Bills—clauses which
have been drafted in detail and bureaucratically polished
—are a useless bureaucratic undertaking. The only important question is: *who* is to determine *which* lands are to be
alienated and *on what terms*? The most ideal Bill is no more
than chicanery if it evades this question.

But how does Mr. Berezovsky decide this sole important
question? For it should be clear that, given equality of
the peasants and "non-peasants", there will be no agreement in most cases, nor, indeed, is it necessary to draft
Bills for an amicable settlement between the serf-owners
and the serfs of yesterday. The serf-owners are always
agreeable to an *"amicable* settlement" with them, even
without any laws.

And Mr. Berezovsky gave a clear answer to the burning
question, in speaking to the Third Duma diehards. Listen
to what he said next:

"In view of this, that general concrete work on the spot would,
of course, bring to light both the amount of land '*available*' [listen
to this!] for alienation and the amount of land required for the peasants [required for what? Would it be for performing services? But
that is something the serf-owners have always agreed to!], and finally,
the peasants themselves would see to what extent it was possible
to meet their fair [ahem! God save us from lordly anger, lordly love
and the landlord's "fairness"] demands. Then it would all go through
the Duma and [mark this well!] the Council of State and, after being
recast [ahem!], would be sanctioned in final form [i.e., made law].
This methodical work [it certainly could not be more "methodical"!]
would no doubt result in really meeting the true needs of the population and thereby in pacifying and preserving the cultural farms,
which *the party of people's freedom has never wanted to demolish unless strictly necessary.*"

This was said by a spokesman of the "party of people's
freedom", which it would be fair to call the party of landlord
pacification.

It is perfectly clear from this that the "compulsory alienation" proposed by the Cadets implies *compulsion of the
peasants by the landlords.* Whoever sets out to deny this
must prove that in the Council of State the peasants predomi-

nate over the landlords! "Equality" of the landlords and the peasants to begin with, and in the end—unless an amicable settlement is reached—a *"recasting"* of the draft by the Council of State.

"The party of people's freedom has never wanted to demolish the cultural farms unless strictly necessary," said the landlord A. Y. Berezovsky, who probably considers his farm "cultural". But we will ask: *who* is to decide *whose* farm is "cultural" and in what sense, and where does "strict necessity" begin? Answer: this will be decided, first by a committee made up of *equal numbers* of landlords and peasants, and then by the Council of State.

Well then? Are the Cadets a democratic party or a counter-revolutionary party of the liberal-monarchist bourgeoisie? Are they a party of "people's freedom" or of landlord pacification?

Russia's bourgeois democrats, i.e., the Trudoviks and Narodniks of all shades, have grievously erred in expecting the transfer of the landed estates to the peasants to bring about "equalisation", the spread of "labour principles", and so on; they have also erred by obscuring, with empty talk about various "standards" of landownership, the question whether there is to be medieval land tenure or not, but these democrats have helped the new to force out the old and have not drafted Bills to enable the old to *retain* a number of privileges.

Really, to deny that the Cadets are not a democratic party but a party of the counter-revolutionary, liberal-monarchist bourgeoisie, means simply flying in the face of well-known facts.

———

In conclusion we shall briefly examine a question which might well be asked by certain naïve Cadets. If the "compulsory alienation" suggested by the Cadets implied compulsion of the peasants by the landlords, why did the majority of the landlords reject it?

This question was answered unintentionally by Mr. Milyukov, in his speech in the Third Duma on October 31, 1908, when he spoke *as a historian*. Milyukov the *historian* had to admit that until the end of 1905 both the government and the *landlords* had regarded the peasantry as a *conservative* *force.* At the Peterhof meeting on July 19-26, 1905—that meeting paved the way for the Bulygin Duma[125]—A. A. Bobrinsky, Naryshkin and other pillars of the future Council of the United Nobility were *in favour of giving the peasants a predominant position in the Duma.* At that time Witte held that the mainstay of the autocracy should be (and could be) the "peasant democrats", *not* the nobility *or* the bourgeoisie.*

"Gentlemen," said Mr. Milyukov, "this is an interesting moment because it is at this moment that the government has conceived the idea of compulsory alienation. (*Voices:* "It's Kutler's idea.") Yes, Kutler's, gentlemen.... *Kutler is drafting a Bill on compulsory alienation....*

"He has been working on it, gentlemen; *his work continued for a month or two*—I cannot say exactly—*until the end of 1905.* It went on unhampered until the well-known Moscow events took place, after which there was a noticeable change in sentiment."

On January 4, 1906, the Marshals of the Nobility met in congress. The congress rejected Kutler's draft, which it knew from hearsay and private reports. It adopted an agrarian programme of its own (the future "Stolypin" programme). In February 1906 Minister Kutler resigned. On March 30, 1906, the Witte Cabinet (with its "peasant" programme) was succeeded by the Gurko-Goremykin Cabinet (with its "Stolypin" programme, a programme of the nobility and the bourgeoisie).

These are the facts which Milyukov the *historian* had to admit.

The inference from them is obvious. The "Cadet" Bill on compulsory alienation was a Bill prepared by Kutler, *Minister* in the Witte Cabinet, who dreamed of an autocracy supported by the peasantry! When the peasants' democratic movement was on the rise, attempts were made to bribe the movement, to corrupt it, to deceive it with a Bill for "peaceful", "compulsory alienation", a "second emancipation", a Bill for a bureaucratic "compulsion of the peasants by the landlords".

---

* See *Report of the People's Freedom Group* on the Second Session of the Third Duma (St. Petersburg, 1909), p. 43. It is unfortunate—very unfortunate—that the Cadets did *not* publish Berezovsky's speech.

This is what the facts of history tell us. The Cadets' agrarian Bill is a Witte Minister's plan for "playing" at peasant Caesarism.

The peasant democrats did not live up to expectations. They showed—probably more clearly in the First Duma than in 1905—that since 1861 they had become *politically conscious*. With a peasantry *such as this*, the Kutler-Cadet Bill became an absurdity: the peasants, far from letting themselves be hoodwinked in the old fashion, would have used even the Cadets' local land committees to organise a new onslaught.

On January 4, 1906, the Marshals of the Nobility correctly decided that the Bill prepared by the liberal landlords (Kutler and Co.) was a hopeless affair, and cast it aside. The civil war had *outgrown* liberal-bureaucratic scheme-making. The class struggle had dispelled the vision of "social peace" and raised the issue squarely: "either the Stolypin way or the Trudovik way".

Nevskaya Zvezda No. 22,
  August 19, 1912
  Signed: *W. Frey*

Published according
to the *Nevskaya Zvezda* text

A POOR DEFENCE

In "The Strike Movement and Wages", an article published in *Pravda* No. 86 on August 9,* we cited official statistical data on the average wages of Russian factory workers in the first decade of the twentieth century.

It appeared that by their famous strike movement in 1905 the workers had raised their wages from 206 rubles (the annual average per worker) to 238 rubles, i.e., by 32 rubles, or 15.5 per cent.

Our conclusion did not please the official newspaper *Rossiya*. It devoted the leading article in its August 15 issue to a detailed restatement of the data cited by us (withholding for some reason the name of the newspaper from which it had borrowed the data), and tried to refute our conclusions.

"It is true, of course, that wages rose abruptly in 1906," wrote *Rossiya*. "But it is just as true that the prices of all commodities and food rose simultaneously with them...." And *Rossiya* went on to present its calculations, according to which wages have risen by 20 per cent, while the cost of living has gone up by 24 per cent. *Rossiya*'s calculations are inaccurate in every respect. In reality the rise in wages is not so large, while the rise in the cost of living is more considerable.

But we shall not now correct the mistakes of *Rossiya*. Let us take its figures.

"They do not at all suggest that the workers have gained anything," wrote *Rossiya*. "Indeed, judging by their frequent complaints of hard times, one could rather draw the reverse conclusion, namely, that they have scarcely gained anything."

---

* See pp. 258-59 of this volume.—*Ed.*

A strange way to reason, isn't it? If wages have risen to a lesser extent than prices of the prime necessities of life, it is necessary to raise wages to a *still greater extent!* Surely this is obvious.

But how can the workers achieve a rise in wages without an economic struggle and without strikes? Has *Rossiya* ever seen capitalists offer the workers a pay rise *of their own accord*, in view of the rising prices of the prime necessities of life?

Rossiya admits that wages rose abruptly in 1906—thanks to a widespread mass strike movement unprecedented in the world for tenacity. But food prices began to climb *before 1905*. The price of bread, for example, has never dropped in Russia *since 1903* but has only risen. The prices of livestock products have never dropped since 1901 but have only risen.

It follows that solely by their strike movement did the workers ensure that wages, *too*, began to rise following the rise in the prices of bread and other foodstuffs. Since the wage rise is inadequate, as is admitted *even* by *Rossiya*, it is necessary to raise wages further.

Pravda No. 96, August 21, 1912
Signed: *W.*

Published according
to the *Pravda* text

THE LIQUIDATORS AND "UNITY"[126]

The seventh issue of *Nevsky Golos*, which appeared a few days ago, can only be described as hysterical. Instead of a labour chronicle, nearly two pages of it contain choice abuse against *Pravda* and *Nevskaya Zvezda*. Curiously enough, this abuse is offered under the slogan of "unity" of the working class, of "unity" in the election campaign.

Gentlemen—we shall reply to the liquidators—unity of the working class is a great principle. But, really, you make yourselves ridiculous if, while shouting about "unity", you try to impose on the working class the platform and the candidates of a group of liberal liquidationist intellectuals.

Pravda has proved by means of *accurate* figures that "liquidationism is nothing in the working-class movement, and that it is strong only among the liberal intelligentsia" (*Pravda* No. 80, August 1, 1912*). *Nevsky Golos* No. 7, of August 17, now reviles those articles of *Pravda*, calling them "feuilleton-like", "Khlestakovian", and so on. And yet it does not even try to question the simple fact that in the course of six months *Pravda* drew *504* contributions from groups of workers, while the liquidationist papers drew only *15*.

What is the conclusion to be drawn from this but that all the shouting and noise and abuse and clamour about unity are merely intended to cover up the extreme and total impotence of the liquidators within the working class?

No matter how much *Nevsky Golos* may abuse us, we shall calmly point out the incontrovertible facts to the workers. Look at the collections listed in *Nevsky Golos* No. 7, and at those made in July and August "to replenish the funds

---

* See pp. 196-200 of this volume.—*Ed.*

of the newspaper" (i.e., in plain language, to restore the liquidationist paper suspended for lack of support from the mass of the workers). The report on those collections lists 52 contributions totalling 827.11 rubles. Of these, only two were group collections: one by *"the Moscow initiating group"*, amounting to 35 rubles, and the other by a *"group of friends in Paris"*—8.54 rubles. Of the remaining 50 individual contributions, 35 added up to 708 rubles, i.e., *over 20 rubles per contribution on the average.*

Nevsky Golos may fume and abuse—the facts will be no less true for that. It is common knowledge that the "initiating groups" are groups of liquidators who have *broken away* from the working-class party. Even Plekhanov admitted this openly and plainly as long ago as April 1912.

A group of break-away liquidators has resumed—with the donations of bourgeois liberal intellectuals—the publication of its newspaper to fight the working-class press! And yet this group is shouting about "unity". Now how can anyone help laughing at that?

Pravda No. 99, August 24, 1912

Published according to the *Pravda* text

A TALK ON "CADET-EATING"

Pravda and *Nevskaya Zvezda* have administered a stern but well-deserved rebuttal to Messrs. Blank, Korobka, Kuskova and Co. for their foul liberal attacks against the working-class press.

Nevertheless, however good the answers given to "the gentlemen boycotting the workers" may have been, there is still a most important question of principle to be examined. The Blanks and Kuskovas sought by their crude lies to hush it up, to obscure it. But we must not allow questions of principle to be obscured; we must reveal their full significance, bringing to light the roots of the differences, which are of interest to every class-conscious worker, from beneath the heap of Blank-Kuskova distortions, calumnies and abuse.

One of these roots may be described by the term "Cadet-eating". Listen to the solitary but persistent voices of the liquidators, to the remarks of people whose party views are somewhat indefinite, and you will often encounter, if not an accusation against *Pravda* and *Nevskaya Zvezda*, at least head-shaking on account of their "Cadet-eating".

Let us, therefore, examine the question of "Cadet-eating", which is a question of principle.

There are two circumstances which explain first of all, and most of all, the occurrence of such an accusation against *Pravda*: (1) failure to understand the essence of the question of "two and three camps" in the election campaign and in present-day politics in general; (2) lack of consideration for the special conditions in which the Marxist press—the newspapers of the worker democrats—has now been placed.

Let us begin with the first question.

All the liberals adhere to the theory of two camps: *for* a constitution and *against* a constitution. They are all agreed on this, from Milyukov to Izgoyev, and from Prokopovich to M. M. Kovalevsky. Nor must we forget that the theory of two camps necessarily follows from the *class nature* of our liberals.

What is this nature from the economic point of view? It is the fact that the liberals are a party of the bourgeoisie, which is afraid of the movement of the peasant masses, and still more of the workers' movement, for this movement is capable of *limiting* (at present, in the immediate future, without changing the capitalist system as a whole) the extent and forms of the bourgeoisie's *economic* privileges. And the economic privilege of the bourgeoisie is ownership of capital, an ownership which in Russia yields twice or three times as much profit as in Europe.

To uphold this "Russian" superprofit, it is necessary to prevent the third camp from gaining independence.

For example, the bourgeoisie can rule quite well even if the working day is eight hours. In fact, its rule will then be fuller, purer, wider and freer than with a ten- or eleven-hour day. But the dialectics of the class struggle are such that, unless there is an extreme need, unless it is the last remedy, the bourgeoisie will never replace the tranquil, habitual, profitable (from an Oblomov[127] point of view) ten-hour day by an eight-hour one.

What we have said about an eight-hour day applies to the upper chamber, to landlordism and many other things.

The bourgeoisie will not relinquish the tranquil, convenient, profitable, old-Russian forms of exploitation to replace them *only* by European, *only* by democratic forms (for democracy, let it be said without offence to the ardent heroes of *Zavety*, is *also* a form of bourgeois rule); it will not do so, we say, unless there is an extreme need, and unless it is the last remedy.

This need can arise only from the movement of the masses achieving a certain system and strength. And the bourgeoisie, which upholds its economic interests, is fighting against this movement, *that is to say*, against the independence of the third camp.

What is the class nature of liberalism from the political point of view? It is fear of the movement of these same social elements, for that movement is capable of undermining political privileges which the bourgeoisie values. Liberalism dreads democracy more than reaction. This was proved in 1905, 1906 and 1907.

To retain *any part* of the political privileges, it is necessary to prevent the independence of the third camp, to keep *all* opposition in *none but* the position expressed by the formula *"for* or *against* a constitution".

This formula expresses an *exclusively* constitutional position. It does *not go beyond* constitutional reforms. The essence of this formula was excellently and accurately expressed by Mr. Gredeskul—who inadvertently blurted out more than he had meant to—in those statements of his which *Rech* repeated without a single reservation and which *Pravda* reproduced not long ago.*

The essence of this formula is quite in the spirit of *Vekhi*, for *Vekhi* wants nothing better and has, in fact, never preached anything else. *Vekhi* is not at all against a constitution or constitutional reforms. It is *"only"* against the democrats, with their criticism of any sort of constitutional illusions.

The Russian liberals have proved to be sufficiently "adroit" politicians to call themselves "democratic" with a view to fighting the democrats and suppressing the latter's independence. Such is the usual and normal method used by every liberal bourgeoisie in all capitalist countries: deceiving the masses with a democratic façade in order to *deflect* them from a truly democratic theory and truly democratic practice.

But the experience of all countries, including Russia, has shown beyond question that only such practice is capable of ensuring real progress, whereas liberalism inevitably dooms itself to impotence by its fear of democracy, and its *Vekhi*-Gredeskul theories: the impotence of Russian liberalism in 1861-1904, and of German liberalism in 1849-1912.

The third camp, that of democracy, which understands the narrowness of liberalism and is free from its half-hearted-

---

* See pp. 254-55 of this volume.—*Ed.*

ness and flabbiness, from its vacillation and timid backward looks, cannot take shape, cannot exist, without systematic, undeviating, day-by-day criticism of liberalism.

Those who scornfully or with ill-will dub this criticism "Cadet-eating" are thereby advocating precisely *liberal* views—deliberately or unwittingly. For, in practice, *all* criticism of Cadetism is *thereby*, by its very presentation of questions, a criticism of reaction, of the Rights. Our polemic against the liberals, said *Nevskaya Zvezda* (No. 12)* very justly, "is *more profound and richer in content* than the fight against the Rights".**

In reality there is hardly one Marxist newspaper for every hundred liberal papers in Russia, so that it is simply ridiculous to talk about our "exaggerated" criticism of the Cadets: we are not yet doing even one-hundredth of what is necessary in order that the sentiment of "general opposition" prevailing in society and among the people may be replaced by an anti-liberal, definitely and consciously democratic sentiment.

Without such a "replacement", nothing sensible and useful has ever come about, or will come about in Russia.

Accusations of "Cadet-eating", or scornful smiles at "Cadet-eating", are no more than a *façon de parler*, a way of advocating liberal views, or the views of a liberal labour policy when there is a discussion before or about workers.

From the standpoint of liquidationism that is at all consistent and thought out, accusations of "Cadet-eating" are understandable and *necessary*. They express the essence of liquidationism.

---

* See pp. 124-26 of this volume.—*Ed.*

** *Rech* objects to this, saying: if that is so, why do the Rights sympathetically *quote Pravda* against *Rech*? *Rech* makes an overstatement here: if the Rights were to give *Pravda* more *freedom* than to *Rech*, it would be a forcible argument against the Social-Democrats. But everyone knows that the reverse is the case. Our press has a hundred times less freedom than *Rech*; it is a thousand times less firmly established and enjoys 10,000 times less "constitutional" protection. Any literate person realises that *Rossiya and Novoye Vremya* are *teasing Rech* with *Pravda* and that, moreover, they are strangling *Pravda* while merely grumbling at or chiding *Rech*. These are two entirely different things.

Look at the liquidationist views as a whole—at their inner logic, at their interconnection and the interdependence of the various theses: "freedom of association" is a constitutional reform; economic strikes are supplemented with a "political *revival*", no more; a far-reaching election platform is declared to be "lunacy"; the task is formulated as one of fighting for the open existence of the *Party*, i.e., is also formulated as a constitutional reform; the regime in Russia is declared to be bourgeois *already* (Larin); the commercial and industrial bourgeoisie is declared to be already a ruling class; the workers are told that it is "sufficient" to seize on the contradiction between absolutism and constitutionalism (Martov).

Taken as a whole, this is *reformism*, it is the system of views of a liberal labour policy. It makes no difference at all that some Ivan or Pyotr, in defending these views (*some part or other of them*, for liquidationism is going through a "process of growth of growing tasks"), *himself* thinks he is a Marxist.

The point at issue is not their good intentions (of those who have any), but the objective significance of their policy, i.e., what its results are, *cui prodest*—whom it benefits, to whose mill it actually brings grist.

This is defence of the workers' interests *on the basis* provided by the "struggle" (or is it bickering?) between the *liberals* and the Rights; it is not a struggle *for* a democratic, anti-liberal *basis* of sapping the strength of the Rights. The liquidators are supporters of the workers, there is no doubt of that. But they *understand* the interests of the workers in such a way that they uphold these interests *within the framework of the* Russia which the liberals promise to build, not of the Russia which the *democrats* were building yesterday, and will be building tomorrow (and which they are invisibly building even today), *in spite of* the liberals.

That is the crux of the matter. So far there is no new Russia. It has yet to be built. Should the workers build themselves a nest of a "class" (in effect a craft) nature in the Russia of the kind which the Milyukovs are building in common with the Purishkeviches, or should the workers *themselves*, in their own way, build a new Russia entirely without the Purishkeviches and in spite of the Milyukovs?

That new Russia will in any case be bourgeois, but there is quite a big difference between the bourgeois (agrarian and non-agrarian) policy of Stolypin and the *bourgeois* policy of Sun Yat-sen.

The chief feature of the present epoch in Russia is determination of the size of that difference.

"In spite of the Milyukovs", we said. It is this "in spite of" that is "Cadet-eating". That is why, being unafraid of words, we remain, and shall remain, *"Cadet-eaters" as a matter of principle*, without forgetting for one moment the special tasks of the working class, *both* against Milyukov *and* against Sun Yat-sens.

The accusation of "Cadet-eating" is merely a longing (whether conscious or unconscious, makes no difference) to see the workers, in building a new Russia, trail after the Milyukovs and not show the way to our own little Sun Yat-sens in spite of the Milyukovs.

It remains for us to say a few words about a second circumstance, which those who talk about "Cadet-eating" overlook.

It is said: why cannot we develop our views *constructively*? Why engage in excessive *polemics*? Those who say that argue, as it were, in the following way: we are not against a special line entirely different from the Cadet line, nor are we against three camps; we are only against the "substitution of polemics for politics", to use the biting phrase of a friend of the liquidators.

It is easy to answer those who talk like that: in the first place, one cannot develop new views other than through polemics (and Marxist views are new, both as regards the time of their emergence and the extent to which they have spread, in comparison with liberal views). Secondly, the arena in which *Nevskaya Zvezda* and *Pravda* are operating, is an arena of *purely theoretical* Marxist propaganda. It would be wrong to regard this arena as something more: it is *only* a theoretical ABC, a theoretical first step, an indication of the direction of the work, but not yet the work itself.

In this arena, Marxists cannot present their practical conclusions in a "constructive" form, for "reasons beyond our control". It would therefore be a *liquidationist* error to exaggerate the importance of this arena. The most that can be done here is to indicate the *direction*, and that *only* in the form of a criticism of the Cadets.

Novoye Vremya and *Zemshchina*,[128] in *teasing* the Cadets, draw a picture of the Cadets being *eaten*, and that is all. *Rech*, for obvious reasons, *pretends* to accept this "interpretation". The Korobkas and Kuskovas make the same pretence—some from sheer stupidity, and others from sheer "pro-Cadet flunkeyism".

But every politically literate person sees very well that Marxist "Cadet-eating", on absolutely *every* point of its criticism of the Cadets, indicates the *direction* of a *different* "opposition", if I may use this unsuitable term.

When "eating" a Cadet because of Karaulov's "pious" speeches, a Marxist is not in a position to develop his point of view constructively. But any literate person understands that democracy cannot remain true to the name if it is pious.

When "eating" a Cadet because of Gredeskul's speeches, a Marxist is not in a position to develop his point of view constructively. But any literate person realises that democracy cannot remain true to the name if it shares Gredeskul's views.

When a Marxist—but we should never finish if we undertook to list in this manner all the questions and points of our "Cadet-eating". The two examples are enough to make our thesis on the *second* circumstance perfectly clear: *accusations of Cadet-eating are a form of expressing the philistine, harmful, bad prejudice that a certain arena is an adequate arena.*

We shall remain "Cadet-eaters", incidentally with the very aim of combating that harmful prejudice.

Nevskaya Zvezda No. 23,   Published according
     August 26, 1912   to the text in *Nevskaya Zvezda*
     Signed: *K. S.—y*

THE WORKERS AND *PRAVDA*

Pravda has already summed up some of the results of its six months' work.

These results showed first of all and above all that *only* through the efforts of the workers themselves, *only* through the tremendous upsurge of their enthusiasm, their resolve and stubbornness in the struggle, and *only* after the April-May movement, was it possible for the St. Petersburg workers' newspaper, *Pravda*, to appear.

In its summing up, *Pravda* confined itself for a start to the data on group donations made by workers to their daily newspaper. These data reveal to us only a *small part* of the workers' support; they do not tell us about the much more valuable and difficult direct support—moral support, support through personal participation, support for the policy of the newspaper, support through contributing materials, discussing and circulating the paper, etc.

But even the limited data at the disposal of *Pravda* showed that a very impressive number of workers' groups had *directly* linked themselves with it. Let us cast a general glance at the results.

Number of contributions to Pravda *made by groups of workers*

January 1912	14
February "	18
March "	76
April "	227
May "	135
June "	34
July "	26
August (up to 19th) 1912	21
Total	551

Altogether *five hundred and fifty-one* groups of workers supported *Pravda* by their donations.

It would be interesting to sum up the results of a whole number of other collections and donations by workers. We have constantly seen in *Pravda* reports on contributions in support of various strikes. We have also seen reports on collections for the victims of repressions, for the Lena goldfields victims, for individual *Pravda* editors, collections for the election campaign, for relief of the famine-stricken, and so on and so forth.

The varied nature of these collections makes it much more difficult to assess the results here, and we are not yet in a position to say whether a statistical summary can give a satisfactory picture of the matter. But it is obvious in any case that these varied collections take up a very substantial part of the *workers' life.*

As they look through the reports on workers' collections *in connection* with letters from factory and office workers in all parts of Russia, *Pravda* readers, most of whom are dispersed and separated from one another by the severe external conditions of Russian life, gain *some* idea how the proletarians of various trades and various localities are fighting, how they are awakening to the defence of working-class democracy.

The chronicle of workers' life is only just *beginning* to develop into a permanent feature of *Pravda*. There can be no doubt that subsequently, in addition to letters about abuses in factories, about the awakening of a new section of the proletariat, about collections for one or another field of the workers' cause, the workers' newspaper will receive reports about the views and sentiments of the workers, election campaigns, the election of workers' delegates, what the workers read, the questions of particular interest to them, and so on.

The workers' newspaper is a workers' forum. Before the whole of Russia the workers should raise here, one after another, the various questions of workers' life in general and of working-class democracy in particular. The workers of St. Petersburg have made a beginning. It is to their energy that the proletariat of Russia owes the workers' first daily newspaper after the grim years of social stagnation. Let us, then, carry their cause forward, unitedly supporting and developing the workers' paper of the capital, the harbinger of the spring to come, when the whole of Russia will be covered by a network of workers' organisations with workers' newspapers.

We, the workers, *have yet* to build *this* Russia, and we *shall build* it.

Pravda No. 103, August 29, 1912
    Signed: *St.*

Published according
to the *Pravda* text

BEFORE AND NOW

Eighteen years ago, in 1894, the working-class movement in St. Petersburg was just being born in its modern, mass form illumined by the light of the Marxist teaching.

The seventies had affected a quite insignificant top section of the working class. The foremost representatives of the working class revealed themselves even then as great leaders of the workers' democratic movement, but the masses were still slumbering. Only in the early nineties did *they* begin to awaken, and at the same time there began a new and more glorious period in the history of the entire democratic movement in Russia.

Unfortunately, we must confine ourselves here, in our small parallel, to one aspect of one manifestation of the working-class movement, namely, the economic struggle and economic "exposures".

At that time, in 1894, a very few circles of the foremost workers were heatedly discussing plans for organising factory exposures. A weighty statement by the workers themselves, addressed to their fellow-workers and pointing out the more glaring abuses of power by capital, was an exceedingly rare occurrence at the time. Speaking of such things publicly was out of the question.

But the awakening mass of the workers was able to take up the factory exposures addressed to it, despite all difficulties and in the face of all obstacles. The strike movement was growing, and the *connection* between the economic struggle of the working class and other, higher forms of struggle was developing irresistibly. The vanguard of Russia's democratic movement was awakening, and *ten* years later it showed itself in its full stature. It is to this force alone that Russia owes the rupture of the old shell.

Those who recall the first factory exposures which the advanced workers of St. Petersburg addressed to the masses in 1894 will find it most interesting and instructive to compare them with the factory exposures made by *Pravda*. This little comparison of one manifestation of the workers' struggle clearly shows the growth of its *entire* scope, its breadth and depth, its strength, etc.

At that time there were a mere five or six factory exposures, secretly circulated by workers in several dozen copies.

Today there are tens of thousands of copies of the daily *Pravda*, each making several exposures relating to the most diverse fields of labour.

At that time there were a mere five or six so-called "circles", which discussed—in secret, of course—the state of affairs in the factories, with some Marxist intellectual or other participating, and decided on the subject of the points to be "published".

Today there are hundreds and thousands of workers' groups springing up spontaneously, discussing their vital needs and taking their letters, their exposures, their appeals for resistance and unity, to *Pravda* of their own accord.

In a matter of eighteen years, the workers have advanced from the first signs of activity, from a most timid beginning, to a movement that is a *mass* movement in the most exact sense of the term.

We must unfortunately limit ourselves *only* to parallels of factory exposures. But they, too, show the great path travelled, and the goal to which this path leads.

Eighteen years are a short span in the history of a whole class which is destined to accomplish the greatest task in the world—the emancipation of mankind.

The greater part of this path has been travelled in the dark. But now the road has been reached. Forward with courage and determination!

Pravda No. 104, August 30, 1912

Published according to the *Pravda* text

THE INTERNATIONAL CONGRESS OF JUDGES

The First World Congress of Judges is now in session in Vienna, and so is the Thirty-First Congress of German Lawyers.

The speeches of the high-ranking delegates are dominated by an extremely reactionary spirit. The bourgeois lawyers and judges have launched a campaign against the participation of the people in legal procedure.

Two principal forms of such participation are customary in the modern states: (1) the jury, which decides only the question of culpability, while the punishment to be meted out is determined and the procedure directed only by judges of the crown; (2) the court of assessors, who, like our own "social-estate representatives", participate in the decision of *all* questions on a par with the judges of the crown.

And so, the "enlightened" judges of constitutional states are fulminating against all participation of people's representatives in legal procedure. One of the delegates, Elsner, inveighing against the jury and the court of assessors, which he said led to "anarchy in the application of laws", defended instead the principle of the *irremovability* of judges.

We shall remark in this connection that a liberal demand is being put forward here instead of a democratic one and as a disguise for a complete departure from democracy. The participation of people's representatives in a court of justice is undoubtedly a democratic principle. The consistent application of this principle requires, in the first place, that the election of jurors should not be made conditional on *qualifications*, i.e., the right to be chosen should not be restricted by educational, property, residential or any other conditions.

At present, because of the exclusion of workers, most of the jurors are often particularly reactionary petty bourgeois. This evil should be remedied by developing democracy to its consistent and integral form, and not by basely repudiating democracy. It is well known that the election of judges by the people is recognised in all civilised countries as the second condition for consistent democracy in the judicial system.

The irremovability of judges, however, which the liberal bourgeois in general and those of Russia in particular make so much of, is no more than a *division* of medieval privileges between the Purishkeviches and the Milyukovs, between the feudal lords and the bourgeoisie. In *reality* it is impossible fully to put irremovability into practice, and indeed, it is absurd to defend it with regard to unfit, careless, bad judges. In the Middle Ages, judges were appointed exclusively by feudal lords and absolute monarchs. The bourgeoisie, which has now obtained ample access to the judiciary, is *defending itself* against the feudal lords by means of the "principle of irremovability" (for most of the appointed judges will necessarily be—since most of the "educated" lawyers belong to the bourgeoisie—people of bourgeois origin). By defending itself in this way *against the feudal lords*, the bourgeoisie at the same time defends itself *against the democrats* by upholding the principle of the appointment of judges.

It is interesting to note, furthermore, the following passages in a speech by Dr. Ginsberg, a judge from Dresden. He enlarged on *class justice*, i.e., on the manifestations of class oppression and the class struggle in modern legal procedure.

"Anyone who imagines that the participation of people's representatives in legal proceedings removes class justice is sorely mistaken," exclaimed Dr. Ginsberg.

Quite so, Your Honour! Democracy in general does not remove the class struggle but merely makes it more conscious, freer and more open. But this is no argument against democracy. It is an argument in favour of its consistent development all the way through.

"Class justice no doubt exists in reality," continued the judge from Saxony (and Saxon judges have made a name for themselves in Germany by their ferocious sentences against workers), "but not at all in the Social-Democratic sense, not in the sense of preference given to the rich as against the poor. On the contrary, class justice exists precisely in the reverse sense. Once I had the following case. There were three of us judging—two assessors and myself. One of them was an overt Social-Democrat and the other something of the sort. The defendant was a striker who had thrashed a blackleg ['a worker willing to work'—to quote the exact words used by the Saxon judge], seized him by the throat and shouted: 'We've got you at last, you damned scoundrel!'

"Normally this entails from four to six months imprisonment, which is the least punishment that should be meted out for deeds as savage as that. And yet I had the greatest difficulty in preventing the acquittal of the defendant. One assessor, the Social-Democrat, said that I didn't understand the psychology of the workers. But I told him that I understood very well the psychology of the beaten man."

The German papers which carried the text of Judge Ginsberg's speech inserted *"Laughter"* at the end of the above passage. The lawyers and judges laughed. To tell the truth, had we chanced to hear that Saxon judge, we, too, should have burst out laughing.

The doctrine of the class struggle is something against which one can conceivably make an effort to argue in terms of (would-be) science. But one has only to approach the matter from a practical standpoint, to look closely at everyday realities, and behold! the most violent opponent of this doctrine can prove to be as gifted an advocate of the class struggle as the Saxon judge, Herr Ginsberg.

Pravda No. 104. August 30. 1912
Signed: *I. V.*

Published according to the *Pravda* text

IN SWITZERLAND

In *Pravda* No. 63, on July 12,* we told the reader about the general strike in Zurich on June 29 (July 12, new style). It may be recalled that the strike was decided *in defiance of* the leaders of political organisations. The meeting of 425 representatives of all the workers' organisations of Zurich, which declared for the strike, greeted the statement of the printers, who were against the strike, with shouts of *"Shame!"*

By now the press has published data exposing that opportunism.

It appears that the political leaders of the Swiss workers in their opportunism have gone so far as direct *betrayal of the Party*. It is this scathing but justified phrase that the best organs of the Swiss and German working-class press use in describing the conduct of the Social-Democratic members of the Zurich Magistracy (Town Council). The Zurich Town Council, *defending the capitalists*, prohibited strike picketing (and then the workers decided to protest by a one-day general strike).

There are nine members on the Zurich Magistracy, including four Social-Democrats—Erismann, Pflüger, Fogelsanger and Klöti.

And now it has become known that the prohibition of picketing was decided on by the Town Council *unanimously*, that is to say, Erismann and his three Social-Democratic colleagues voted *for* it!!! The Zurich Cantonal Government

---

* See pp. 160-62 of this volume.—*Ed.*

had insisted that the Town Council should prohibit *all*
picketing, but the four sapient minnows,[129] that is, Zurich
Social-Democrats, made a *"compromise"* proposal to prohibit picketing only in the area of the two mechanical shops
where work had been stopped.

Of course, it was just this partial prohibition of picketing that the bourgeoisie was demanding, and the "Social-
Democrats'" (?!) proposal was adopted by the bourgeois
majority of the Town Council!

What is more, the Zurich Town Council recently published an account of the events occasioned by the general
strike. The capitalists declared a three-day lock-out by way
of revenge. The Zurich Town Council decided *unanimously*,
with *all its four* Social-Democratic members participating,
that it was necessary to *call in troops* to reinforce the police
in maintaining public order.

Nor is that all. The bourgeois Town Council of Zurich
furiously attacked, by a series of repressive measures, those
manual and office workers in the town's establishments
who had joined in the strike. It sacked 13 workers and
imposed disciplinary punishments (demotion, pay cuts) on
another 116. These decisions of the Town Council were
likewise adopted *unanimously*, with Erismann and his two
colleagues participating.

The conduct of Erismann and Co. can only be described
as betrayal of the Party.

It is not surprising that the anarcho-syndicalists enjoy
a certain success in Switzerland, since it falls to them to
criticise before the workers a socialist party which tolerates
such opportunist traitors in its ranks. The reason why the
treachery of Erismann and Co. is of major international
significance is that it shows us *clearly from what quarter*
and *in what manner* the working-class movement is threatened with *internal* corruption.

Erismann and Co. are by no means common deserters to
the enemy camp; they are simply peaceful petty bourgeois,
opportunists who are accustomed to parliamentary "vermicelli" and who have succumbed to constitutional democratic
illusions. The moment the class struggle took a sharp turn,
all illusions about constitutional "order" and a "democratic
republic" were dispelled at once, and our philistines holding

the office of Social-Democratic members of the Town Council lost their heads and slid into the marsh.

Class-conscious workers can see from this sad example the consequences which the spread of opportunism in a workers' party is *bound* to have.

Pravda No. 105, August 31, 1912
Signed: *P. P.*

Published according
to the *Pravda* text

THE PRIESTHOOD AND POLITICS

As is known, the most desperate efforts are being made at present to *arouse* the entire priesthood for the elections to the Fourth Duma and to organise it as a solid Black-Hundred force.

It is most instructive to see that the *whole* Russian bourgeoisie—governmental, Octobrist, and oppositional Cadet alike—with equal zeal and agitation is exposing and condemning these plans of the government.

The Russian merchant and the Russian liberal landlord (or rather the landlord playing the liberal) fear the strengthening of an irresponsible government which desires to "cull" for itself the votes of obedient priests. It goes without saying that the democrats' opposition (to use a mild and inexact term) on this point is far more resolute than that of the liberals.

We have already pointed out in *Pravda* the undemocratic approach to the question of the priesthood by the liberals, who either frankly defend the arch-reactionary theory of "non-interference" of the priesthood in politics, or reconcile themselves to this theory.*

A democrat is absolutely hostile to the slightest *falsification* of suffrage and elections, but he is absolutely *in favour* of the widest masses of any priesthood being directly and openly drawn into politics. Non-participation of the priesthood in the political struggle is the most harmful hypocrisy. In reality the priesthood has *always* participated in politics covertly, and the people would only benefit if it were to pass to overt politics.

---

* See pp. 227-28 of this volume.—*Ed.*

Of outstanding interest in this respect is the article published in *Rech* a few days ago by Bishop Mikhail, an adherent of the old rites.[130] That writer's views are very naïve. He is under the impression, for example, that "clericalism is unknown [to us] in Russia", that prior to the revolution it (the priesthood) concerned itself only with heavenly matters, and so on.

But the instructive thing is the actual appraisal of events by this apparently informed man.

"It seems indisputable to me that the triumph of the elections will not be a triumph of clericalism," wrote Bishop Mikhail. "United, if artificially, and at the same time, of course, offended by this lording it over their votes and their conscience, the priesthood will see themselves standing between two forces.... Hence the need of a radical change, a crisis, a return to a natural alliance with the people. If the clerical and reactionary trend ... succeeded in growing strong and maturing by itself, this perhaps would not come about. Now that the priesthood has been roused from its quiescence while still with remnants of its former confusion, it will continue its history. And the democracy of the priesthood is the inevitable and closing stage of this history, which will be linked to the priesthood's struggle in its own behalf."

Actually it should be a question of a distribution between the contending classes, and not of "a return to a natural alliance", as the author naïvely believes. If the priesthood is drawn into politics, this distribution will certainly gain in clarity, breadth and political consciousness.

As for the fact that informed observers acknowledge the existence, vitality and force of the "remnants of the former confusion" even in such a social stratum of Russia as the priesthood, it is well worth putting on record.

Pravda No. 106, September 1, 1912
Signed: *I. V.*

Published according to the *Pravda* text

YET ANOTHER ANTI-DEMOCRATIC CAMPAIGN

That ill-famed publication, *Vekhi*, which was a tremendous success in liberal-bourgeois society, a society thoroughly imbued with renegade tendencies, was not adequately countered, nor appraised deeply enough, in the democratic camp.

This was partly due to the fact that the success of *Vekhi* occurred at a time of almost complete suppression of the "open" democratic press.

Now Mr. Shchepetev comes forward in *Russkaya Mysl*[131] (August) with a refurbished edition of *Vekhi* ideas. This is perfectly natural on the part of a *Vekhi* organ edited by Mr. P. B. Struve, leader of the renegades. But it will be just as natural for the democrats, particularly the worker democrats, to make up now for at least a little of what they owe the *Vekhi* people.

I

Mr. Shchepetev's utterances take the form of a modest "Letter from France"—*about the Russians in Paris*. But behind this modest form there is actually a very definite "discussion" of the Russian revolution of 1905 and the Russian democracy.

"That disturbing [Oh! Disturbing *to whom*, esteemed liberal?], troubled and thoroughly confused year 1905 is fresh in everyone's memory...."

"Troubled and thoroughly confused"! What dirt and dregs a person must have in his soul to be able to write like that! The German opponents of the revolution of 1848 called that year the "crazy" year. The same idea, or rather the same dull, base fright, is expressed by the Russian Cadet writing in *Russkaya Mysl*.

We shall counter him only with a few facts, the most objective and most "unpretentious" ones. That year wages were rising as they had never done before. Land rent was dropping. All forms of association of workers, including even domestic servants, were making unprecedented progress. Millions of inexpensive publications on political subjects were being read by the people, the masses, the crowd, the "lower ranks", as avidly as no one had ever read in Russia until then.

Nekrasov exclaimed, in times long past:

> *Ah, will there ever be a time*
> *(Come soon, come soon, O longed-for day!)*
> *When people will not buy the books*
> *Of Blücher or some silly lord,*
> *But Gogol and Belinsky's works*
> *From market stalls bring home.*[132]

The "time" longed for by one of the old Russian democrats came. Merchants stopped dealing in oats and engaged in more profitable business—the sale of inexpensive democratic pamphlets. Democratic books became goods for the *market*. The ideas of Belinsky and Gogol—which endeared these authors to Nekrasov, as indeed to any decent person in Russia—ran through the whole of that new market literature.

How "troublesome"! cried the liberal pig, which deems itself educated, but in fact is dirty, repulsive, overfat and smug, when *in actual fact* it saw the "people" bringing home from the market—Belinsky's letter to Gogol.[133]

And, strictly speaking, it is, after all, a letter from an "intellectual", announced *Vekhi*, to thunderous applause from Rozanov of *Novoye Vremya* and from Anthony, Bishop of Volhynia.

What a disgraceful sight! a democrat from among the best Narodniks will say. What an instructive sight! we will add. How it sobers up those who took a *sentimental* view of democratic issues, how it *steels* all the living and strong democratic elements, mercilessly sweeping aside the rotten illusions of the Oblomov-minded!

It is very useful for anyone who has ever been enchanted with liberalism to be disenchanted with it. And he who wishes to recall the early history of Russian liberalism will certainly see in the liberal Kavelin's attitude towards the democrat Chernyshevsky the exact prototype of the attitude adopted by the Cadet *Party* of the liberal bourgeoisie towards the Russian democratic *movement of the masses.* The liberal bourgeoisie in Russia has "found itself", or rather its tail. Is it not time the democrats in Russia found their head?

It is particularly intolerable to see individuals like Shchepetev, Struve, Gredeskul, Izgoyev and the rest of the Cadet fraternity clutching at the coat-tails of Nekrasov, Shchedrin and others. Nekrasov, who was weak as a person, wavered between Chernyshevsky and the liberals. but all his sympathy went to Chernyshevsky. Out of the very same personal weakness, Nekrasov occasionally sounded the false note of liberal servility, but he himself bitterly deplored his "falsity" and *repented* of it in *public*:

> *I never sold my lyre, although at times,*
> *When pressed by unrelenting fate,*
> *False notes would sound among my rhymes.*

"*False notes*" is what Nekrasov himself called the liberal servility he was occasionally guilty of. As for Shchedrin, he mocked mercilessly at the liberals, whom he branded for ever by the formula "conformably to villainy".[134]

How outdated this formula is as applied to Shchepetev, Gredeskul and the other* *Vekhi* people! The point now is by no means that these gentlemen must *conform* to villainy. Not by a long shot! They have created *their own theory* of "villainy" on their own initiative and in their own fashion, proceeding from Neo-Kantianism and other fashionable "European" theories.

---

* The objection will probably be raised that Gredeskul, as well as Milyukov and Co., *argued* with *Vekhi.* So they did, but they *remained* Vekhists for all that. See, inter alia, *Pravda* No. 85. (See pp. 254-55 of this volume.—*Ed.*)

II

"The thoroughly confused year 1905," writes Mr. Shchepe-tev. "Everything was mixed up and tangled in the general confusion and muddle."

On this point, too, we can raise only a few theoretical objections. We believe that historical events should be judged by the movements of the *masses* and of classes as a whole, not by the moods of individuals or small groups.

The overwhelming majority of Russia's population consists of peasants and workers. What indication is there of a "general confusion and muddle" among this majority of the population? Quite on the contrary, the objective facts testify irrefutably that it was among the mass of the population that a sorting out unprecedented in breadth and effectiveness was going on, a sorting out which *for ever* did away with "confusion and muddle".

Until then, the elements of patriarchal oppression and those of democracy had really been "confused and mixed up" among the "common people", making up a "general muddle". Evidence of this is to be found in such objective facts as that Zubatovism[135] and the "Gaponiad" proved possible.

It was the year 1905 that for ever put an end to that "muddle". No previous epoch in Russian history had *untangled* with such extreme clarity, by deeds not by words, relations tangled by age-long stagnation and age-old survivals of serfdom. In no other epoch had so distinctly and "efficiently" the *classes* become demarcated, the attitude of the *mass* of the population defined, and the theories and programmes of the "intellectuals" tested by the *actions* of millions.

How was it, then, that indisputable historical facts could be so greatly distorted in the mind of the educated and liberal writer of *Russkaya Mysl*? The explanation is very simple: this *Vekhi* spokesman seeks to impose his subjective sentiments on the whole people. He himself and his entire group—the liberal-bourgeois intelligentsia—found themselves at that time in a particularly "muddled", "thoroughly confused", position. And the liberal shifts his discontent—a natural result of this muddle and of the fact that the masses had exposed the utter worthlessness of liberalism—

to the *masses*, thus laying his own fault at someone else's door.

Indeed, was not the liberals' position a muddled one in June 1905? Or after August 6, when they called for participation in the Bulygin Duma but the people went *in fact* past and beyond the Duma? Or in October 1905, when the liberals had to "trail along behind" and call the strike "glorious" although only the day before they had fought against it? Or in November 1905, when the pitiful impotence of liberalism fully came to light, being demonstrated by so striking a fact as Struve's visit to Witte?

If the Vekhist Shchepetev cares to read the Vekhist Izgoyev's little book about Stolypin, he will see that Izgoyev *had* to admit that "muddle" in the Cadets'position "between two fires" in the First and Second Dumas. And this "muddle" and impotence of liberalism were an inevitable development, for the liberals had no *mass* support either among the bourgeoisie above or among the peasantry below.

Mr. Shchepetev closes his argument on the history of the Russian revolution with the following gem:

"However, all that muddle was very short-lived. The upper ranks freed themselves little by little from the almost panic terror that had gripped them and, having arrived at the fairly simple conclusion that a good company of soldiers was more effective than all revolutionary verbiage, equipped 'punitive expeditions' and set rapid-firing justice into motion. The results exceeded all expectations. In a matter of two or three years, the revolution was destroyed and eradicated to such an extent that certain security institutions were compelled to stage it in some places...."

While we could provide at least some theoretical commentary for the author's previous discourses, now we have not even this possibility. We must confine ourselves to fastening this glorious discourse to the pillory in as high a position as possible, so that it can be seen for as long a time and from as far off as possible.

However, we can also ask the reader: is it surprising that the Octobrist *Golos Moskvy*, as well as the nationalist, Judas-like[136] *Novoye Vremya*, quoted Shchepetev with the greatest delight? In fact, what is the difference between the "historical" appraisal given by the "Constitutional-Democratic" magazine and that given by the above-mentioned two publications?

III

Mr. Shchepetev devotes most space to sketches of life in exile. To find an analogy of these sketches, one would have to dig up *Russky Vestnik*[137] of Katkov's day and take from it novels portraying high-minded Marshals of the Nobility, good-natured and contented muzhiks, and disgruntled brutes, scoundrels and monsters called revolutionaries.

Mr. Shchepetev has observed Paris (assuming that he has) with the eyes of a philistine embittered against the democratic movement, who could see nothing but "unrest" in the appearance in Russia of the first democratic pamphlets for the masses.

It is known that everyone sees abroad what he chooses to. Or, in other words, everyone sees in new conditions *his own self*. A member of the Black Hundreds sees abroad splendid landlords, generals and diplomats. A secret police agent sees there the noblest policemen. A liberal Russian renegade sees in Paris well-meaning concierges and "efficient"* shopkeepers who teach the Russian revolutionary that among them "humanitarian and altruistic sentiments had too much suppressed personal requirements, often to the detriment of the general progress and cultural advancement of the whole of our country".**

A lackey in spirit is naturally keen above all else on the gossip and petty scandals prevailing in the servants' room. It goes without saying that a shopkeeper or a lackey-minded concierge takes no notice of the ideological issues discussed at Paris meetings and in the Paris Russian-language press. How can he see, indeed, that this press raised, as early as 1908, for example, the very same questions concerning the social nature of the June Third regime, the class roots of the new trends among the democrats, and so on,*** as found their way much later, and in much narrower and more distorted (and curtailed) form, into the press "protected" by reinforced security measures?

Shopkeepers and lackeys, however "intellectual" the garb in which people with such a mentality array themselves,

---

* See Mr. Shchepetev's article, p. 139 (*Russkaya Mysl* No. 8, 1912).
** Ibid., p. 153.
*** See present edition, Vol. 15, pp. 266-79.—*Ed.*

cannot notice and grasp these questions. If a particular lackey is called a "publicist" contributing to a liberal magazine, he, that "publicist", will pass over in complete silence the great ideological questions which are posed openly and clearly nowhere but in Paris. On the other hand, this "publicist" will tell you in detail all that is well known in the servants' rooms.

He, this noble Cadet, will tell you in the magazine of the most noble Mr. Struve, that a hapless emigrant-prostitute was evicted from "the flat of a very well-known woman revolutionary in Paris", "not without help from the police"; that the "unemployed" again made a row at a charity ball; that a copyist in a house familiar to Mr. Shchepetev "had rather a considerable sum of money advanced to him and then began to absent himself"; that the exiles "rise at noon and go to bed after 1 or 2 a.m., and there are visitors and noise and arguments and disorder all day long".

All this the lackey magazine of the Cadet Mr. Struve will tell you in detail and with illustrations, with gusto and spiced with pepper—just as well as Menshikov and Rozanov of *Novoye Vremya* do it.

"Give me money or I'll punch you on the jaw—this is the unambiguously hostile form which the relations between the upper and lower ranks of the exiles have taken. True, this formula has not become widespread, and 'the extreme trend among the lower ranks' has become represented [this is how the educated Cadet writes in Mr. Struve's magazine!] by a mere couple of dozens of very doubtful elements that are perhaps even guided by a skilful hand from outside."

Pause at this statement, reader, and think of the difference between an ordinary lackey and a lackey-minded publicist. Ordinary lackeys—meaning the bulk, of course, which does not include those politically-conscious elements that have already adopted a class point of view and are seeking a way out of their lackey's position—are unsophisticated, uneducated, and often illiterate and ignorant; it is pardonable for them to have a naïve passion for relating whatever reaches them more easily than anything else, and is closest and clearest to them. Lackey-minded publicists, on the other hand, are "educated" persons who are well received in all the finest drawing-rooms. They are aware that the number of common blackmailers among the exiles is very insignificant ("a couple of dozens" for *thousands* of exiles). They even realise that these blackmailers "are perhaps *guided*" by a *"skilful hand"*—from the tea-room of the Union of the Russian People.

And because he realises all this, the lackey-minded publicist operates as befits the "educated". He certainly knows how to cover up his tracks and make the most of his goods! He is not a venal hack of the Black Hundreds—nothing of the kind. He *"himself"* has even pointed out that *perhaps* someone is guiding the dozen or two of blackmailers, but at the same time it is *precisely* and *solely* those blackmailers rows and the absenteeism of copyists that he tells about!

The *Novoye Vremya* school for *"writers"* of *Russkaya Mysl* has not gone to waste. Suvorin of *Novoye Vremya* boasted that he had never received any subsidies—he *merely* "knew himself" how to hit the right tone.

Russkaya Mysl receives no subsidies—God forfend! It *merely* "knows itself" how to hit the right tone, a tone pleasing to the ear of the *Novoye Vremya* people and Guchkov's "stalwarts".

IV

Yes, there is much that is painful in the life of the exiles. It is exiles, and they alone, who in the years of social stagnation and lull raised major questions of principle concerning all Russian democrats. There is more poverty and want among them than elsewhere. The proportion of suicides is particularly great among them, and the proportion of those among them whose whole being is one bundle of sick nerves is incredibly, monstrously great. Indeed, how could things be different with tormented people?

Different people will take interest in different things when they find themselves among exiles. Some of them will be interested in the open discussion of major political questions of principle. Others will be interested in stories about a row at a ball, about an unscrupulous copyist, or about the distaste which concierges and shopkeepers have for the exiles' way of life. Everyone to his taste.

Nevertheless, when you experience all the hardships of a tormented, drab, morbidly nervous life in exile and think of the life of the Shchepetevs, Struves, Golovins, Izgoyevs and Co., you cannot help saying: what an immense happiness not to belong to this society of "respectable people", to the society where these individuals are received and where people shake hands with them!

Probably, rows do not occur in this "respectable society". Prostitutes do not find themselves in the position of all but room-mates of these gentlemen. Oh, no. They stay in other quarters.

The unemployed raise no rows at dances arranged by these people. For those dances are perfectly decorous. They keep these things apart: the prostitutes (from among the unemployed) live in one flat, while the dances are held in another. And if they take on a copyist, they never allow any depravity, such as letting the copyist take his pay in advance and then dare to absent himself.

Rows over money are out of the question with them. Near them are no starving, tormented, unnerved people, ready to commit suicide. And if "the millions fraternise"— today with "science" in the persons of Messrs. Struve and Co., tomorrow with the title of deputy in the persons of Messrs. Golovin and Co., and the day after with the titles of deputy and lawyer in the persons of Messrs. Maklakov and Co.[138]—where do rows come in here?

Those are all noble acts. If the writings of the Struves, Gredeskuls, Shchepetevs and Co. against the democrats give pleasure to the Ryabushinskys, etc., what is wrong with that? After all, Struve receives no subsidies—he "himself" hits the right tone! No one can say that *Russkaya Mysl* is a kept woman of the Ryabushinskys. It will occur to no one to compare the pleasure which the Ryabushinskys derive from certain "publicists" with the pleasure which serf girls gave the landlords in the old days by scratching their heels for them.

Indeed, what blame attaches to Mr. Struve or Mr. Gredeskul or Shchepetev, etc., because their writings and speeches, which express their own convictions, are a sort of heel-scratching for the Russian merchants and landlords, who are embittered against the revolution?

What is so shocking about the fact that Mr. Golovin, an ex-deputy, has got himself a profitable concession? After all, he has relinquished the title of deputy!! That means that when he was a deputy there was no concession as yet— it was only just in the making. And when he obtained a concession, he ceased to be a deputy. Is it not clear that there is no dirty business here?

Is it not obvious that only slanderers can point a finger at Maklakov? Did he not defend Tagiyev—as he himself stated in a letter published in *Rech*—"according to his convictions"? There can be no doubt whatever that no Paris concierge or shopkeeper will find anything—anything at all— reprehensible, awkward or shocking in the way of life or in the actions of all these respectable Cadet people.

V

Mr. Shchepetev's general statement of principle is worth reproducing in full:

"Hitherto, and above all in the circles taking part in the revolution, humanitarian and altruistic sentiments have suppressed personal requirements to an excessive degree, often to the detriment of the general progress and cultural advancement of the whole of our country. Too often the desire for the 'public good' and for the 'welfare of the whole people' made people forget about themselves, about their personal needs and requirements, so much so that the social sentiments and aspirations themselves could not be translated into reality in the form of positive [!!], creative, entirely conscious work, and fatally led to passive forms of self-sacrifice. Indeed, not only in this particular sphere, but also in the sphere of the most ordinary relations, the requirements of the individual were constantly suppressed in every manner—by a 'guilty conscience' which often swelled this thirst for heroism and self-sacrifice to hypertrophic proportions, on the one hand, and by an inadequate appraisal of life itself due to the low standard of our culture, on the other hand. The result is a constant split personality, a constant sense of the wrongness and even 'sinfulness' of one's life, a constant desire to sacrifice oneself, to come to the aid of the propertyless and disinherited, and, finally, to go into 'the camp of the perishing'—a fact which has found so full and vivid an expression in our literature.

"Nothing of the kind is met with in the views and moral principles of the French people."

This is a commentary on Mr. Gredeskul's political and programmatic statements which *Rech* published without a single reservation and which *Pravda* (No. 85) recalled when *Rech* chose to forget them.

This is a continuation and repetition of *Vekhi*. Once again we can and must see from the example of this discourse that *Vekhi* is merely making a show of fighting against the "intelligentsia" and that it is in fact *fighting against democracy*, which it completely renounces.

It is particularly necessary to stress the unity of *Vekhi*, Gredeskul and *Rech* today, during the elections, when the Cadets, playing at democracy, are doing their utmost to obscure and side-track all the truly important and vital political questions of principle. One of the urgent practical tasks facing the democrats is to raise these questions at election meetings, to explain to as large an audience as possible the meaning and significance of the talk of the Shchepetevs and all the Vekhists, and to expose the hypocrisy of *Rech* and the Milyukovs when they try to disclaim responsibility for *Russkaya Mysl*, although those who write for it are Cadet *Party members*.

The "arguments" with the Vekhists, the "polemics" of the Gredeskuls, Milyukovs and other such gentlemen against them, are no more than eyewash, nothing but a hypocritical disguise for the deep fundamental solidarity between the entire Cadet Party and *Vekhi*. Indeed, how can anyone "argue" against the basic propositions of the passage quoted above? How can he remain in the same party with people who hold such views, without bearing *full* responsibility for this advocacy of an emphatic repudiation of the elementary principles of all democracy?

The issue is obscured by those who are willing to present it *à la Vekhi*, in terms of contrasting "individualism" with "altruism", and so on. The political meaning of these phrases could not be clearer—they are a *volte-face against* democracy, a *volte-face* in favour of *counter-revolutionary* liberalism.

We must realise that this *volte-face* is no accident, but a result of the class position of the bourgeoisie. And we must draw from this the necessary political conclusions as regards the clear demarcation of democracy from liberalism. Unless we are aware of these realities, and unless we bring them home to the mass of the population, there can be no question of any real step forward.

Nevskaya Zvezda Nos. 24 and 25,   Published according to
    September 2 and 9, 1912   the text in *Nevskaya Zvezda*
        Signed: *V. I.*

THE UNITY OF THE CADETS
AND *NOVOYE VREMYA*

People in our country are only too often prone to regard the election campaign as a struggle for mandates, i.e., for cosy seats in the Duma.

As far as the class-conscious workers are concerned, this campaign is primarily, and more than anything else, a struggle for principles, i.e., for fundamental views, for political convictions. This struggle, which is being waged before the masses and which draws the masses into politics, is one of the principal advantages of the representative system.

Our Cadets, in reply to our posing fundamental questions about liberalism and democracy, about the policy of "peace" and that of the class struggle, dodge all polemics on the substance of the matter, merely hissing right and left over our alleged "Cadet-eating".

And yet facts indicating a touching unity between the Cadets and the *Novoye Vremya* people in the appraisal of the cardinal issues of life in Russia strike the eye.

The eighth issue of *Russkaya Mysl* has appeared. This magazine is edited by the Cadet Struve, and contributors to it are Izgoyev, Severyanin, Galich and many other Cadets.

In that issue Mr. A. Shchepetev printed, under the title "Russians in Paris", a foul Black-Hundred lampoon against the revolution and revolutionaries. *Novoye Vremya imme-diately* caught up the tune struck up by *Russkaya Mysl*; it quoted a whole series of "gems" from it, and exclaimed gleefully: "To think that those wretched representatives of mankind [i.e., the revolutionaries as portrayed by *Russkaya Mysl*] claimed the role of renovators of Russian life."

What will the official Cadet *Rech* say to that? Will it be that that "has no bearing" on the elections, i.e., on the struggle for cosy seats? Or that *Rech* "cannot be held responsible" for *Russkaya Mysl*, i.e., the party cannot be held responsible for its members whom *no* Cadet conference has ever so much as condemned?

Let *Rech* twist and turn, and let unprincipled and spineless people shrug their shoulders at our "Cadet-eating"—we shall never tire of saying to the citizens of Russia: look into the *principles* of the Cadets and don't remain disgracefully indifferent when the "Constitutional-Democrats" are slinging mud at the democrats.

Here are a few passages from the article of Mr. Shchepetev, the Black-Hundred Cadet; although few, they are the most prominent and, moreover, are concerned with questions of principle, not gossip.

"Hitherto, and above all in the circles taking part in the revolution, humanitarian [i.e., man-loving] and altruistic sentiments [i.e., disinterested sentiments not limited to the effort to keep one's skin whole] have suppressed personal requirements to an *excessive degree*, often to the detriment of the general progress and cultural advancement of the whole of our country. Too often the desire for the 'public good' and for the 'welfare of the whole people' [the ironical inverted commas were put in by *Russkaya Mysl*] made people forget about themselves, about their personal needs and requirements.... The result is a constant split personality, a constant sense of the wrongness and even 'sinfulness' of one's life, a constant desire to sacrifice oneself, *to come to the aid of the propertyless and disinherited*, and, finally, to go into 'the camp of the perishing'—a fact which has found so full and vivid an expression in our literature" (*Russkaya Mysl* No. 8, pp. 152-53).

How contemptible is a party pretending to be democratic that tolerates in its ranks these gentlemen who sling mud at the most rudimentary, the most elementary premises, convictions and principles of *the whole of democracy*!

The liberal bourgeoisie has developed a hatred for democracy, as has been proved by the issue of *Vekhi*, as is proved monthly by *Russkaya Mysl*, and as has been proved by the Karaulovs and Gredeskuls.

The liberals themselves are placing a bar between themselves and the democrats.

Pravda No. 109, September 5, 1912
Signed: *I. V.*

Published according
to the *Pravda* text

CONCERNING N. S. POLYANSKY'S LETTER

N. S. Polyansky's letter from the countryside, published in this issue of *Pravda*, poses a very interesting question. It would be desirable for the peasants themselves to comment on this question as often as possible.

For our part, we consider it necessary to point out the following.

N. S. Polyansky is perfectly right in saying that only an "idle parasite" would regard the volost meeting as a gathering of fools. Only the peasants *themselves* can decide which form of land tenure and landownership is to be preferred in a particular locality. All interference on the part of the law or the administration in the unfettered use of the land by the peasants is a survival of the serf-owning system. Such interference can only do harm; it can only humiliate and insult the peasant.

A worker-peasant vividly showed, in his letter published in *Pravda* No. 38, the absurd red tape resulting from such interference.

Let us now see what view the tens of millions of people who are for ever working and are for ever being exploited should take of the question: *khutor* or village commune?

What these people have to worry about is not at all the choice between the *khutor* and the village commune. They must worry about who is exploiting them and how they can lighten or do away with this exploitation.

In European Russia, for example, 30,000 of the big landlords own 70,000,000 dessiatines of land, and 10,000,000 poor peasants own as much. Whether these peasants are settled on *khutors* or in communes, their paupers' living conditions will not be changed in the slightest. If you have seven dessiatines of bad land for your whole family, while your landlord neighbour has 2,000 dessiatines of excellent land, the result will be almost the same as under serfdom, no matter whether you live on a *khutor* or in a commune.

Hungry people are being deluded with talk about *khutors* or communes, about a buckwheat pie or a cabbage pie. Meanwhile they have to eat turnip tops and live on marshy or sandy land; they have to do corvée for using the watering-place, the pastures and ploughlands.

By means of *khutors* attempts are being made to create "small landlords" to defend the big ones. But millions and tens of millions of peasants will starve even more in consequence.

In Western Europe, a really rapid and successful development of agriculture occurred *only where* all survivals of feudal oppression had been completely abolished.

In the genuinely free countries, where agriculture is well organised, there remains only one force that is crushing the peasant and the worker: the force of capital. There is only one way of countering this force—a free alliance of the wage-workers and ruined peasants. Such alliances will develop into a new social system under which cultivated lands, efficient machinery, steam and electricity will serve to improve the life of the working people themselves, and not to enrich a handful of millionaires.

Pravda No. 118, September 15, 1912
          Signed: *Fr.*

Published according
to the *Pravda* text

THE POLITICAL LINE

It is beyond doubt that the character of *Nevskaya Zvezda* and *Pravda* has been fully established, and is familiar not only to the workers, but also to all the political parties of Russia —thanks to the attacks made on *Pravda* and *Nevskaya Zvezda* by the Black Hundreds and the Octobrists (*Rossiya, Novoye Vremya, Golos Moskvy*, etc.), as well as by the liberals (*Rech, Zaprosy Zhizni*, etc.).

An appraisal of the political line followed by the two newspapers is of particular interest in the light of the election campaign, for this appraisal is the inevitable touchstone of views on basic questions of principle. That is why we propose to dwell on N. Nikolin's article in *Nevsky Golos* No. 9, about the line of *Pravda* and *Nevskaya Zvezda*. The article contains not a few exceedingly angry words, as the reader will see; but we can (and must) disregard that in view of the author's attempt to touch on the essence of important questions.

"I must admit," wrote N. Nikolin, "that in many respects *Pravda* fulfils rather satisfactorily its task of being an exponent of the desires, needs, requirements and interests of the Russian proletariat. Unfortunately, it considerably depreciates this useful work of its by a perfectly absurd presentation of political realities that is far from the truth and extremely harmful in its consequences."

We shall leave the angry words aside and take the important thing: the presentation of political realities. We readily forgive the writer his annoyance for this straightforward approach to the question, which is really fundamental. Let us argue on the substance of the matter. It is, in fact, impossible to take a single step in the field of practical work unless one has firm views as to *what* our "political realities" actually are.

N. Nikolin answers his straight question as follows:

> "*Pravda*—which in this case follows the example of *Nevskaya Zvezda*—assures its readers that the working class must build a new Russia despite the liberals. This sounds proud, of course, but it contains nothing but nonsense. Nobody is building a new Russia—she is *being built* [italics by N. Nikolin himself] in the complicated process of the struggle of different interests, and the task of the working class is not to make chimerical plans for building a new Russia *for others and in spite of all these others*, but to create, within the latter, the most favourable conditions for its further development."

Here, too, we readily forgive the writer his "spleen", his extreme irritation, because he tries to take the bull by the horns. N. Nikolin is more frank, sincere and thoughtful than many liquidators in touching here on one of the deepest sources of our deep differences.

"Nobody is building a new Russia—she is *being built* in the process—" Anyone will recognise in this wonderful argument the basic and invariable keynote of the entire liquidationist (or broader still, entire opportunist) music.

Let us, therefore, analyse this argument carefully.

If a new Russia is being built in the process of the struggle of different interests, this means that the *classes* which have *different* interests are *building* a new Russia in different ways. This is as clear as daylight. What sense is there, then, in N. Nikolin's *contrast*: "nobody is building a new Russia— she is *being built*, etc."?

No sense whatever. It is nonsense from the point of view of the most elementary logic.

But this nonsense has a logic of its own, the logic of opportunism, which inevitably, and not accidentally, slips into Nikolinist errors as it tries to defend its position "in Marxist fashion". It is on this "logic of opportunism" that we must dwell.

Whoever says that a new Russia *is being built* by such-and-such classes stands so firmly on the basis of Marxism that not only N. Nikolin's angry words, but even—even "unity-liquidationist" conferences and all their verbal "thunderbolts" cannot shake him.

Whoever says that "nobody is building a new Russia—she is *being built*, etc.", slips from the objectivism of the class struggle (i.e., from Marxism) to the "objectivism" of a bourgeois justification of reality. Herein lies the source of that sinful fall from Marxism into opportunism which Nikolin (unwittingly) commits.

If I say: a new Russia *has to* be built *in such-and-such a way* from the standpoint of, say, truth, justice, equalised labour, and so on, it will be a subjectivist approach that will land me in the sphere of chimeras. In practice, it is the class struggle, and not my very best wishes, that will determine the building of a new Russia. My ideals of building a new Russia will not be chimerical only if they express the interests of an actually existing class, whose living conditions compel it to act in a particular sense. By thus adopting a stand for the objectivism of the class struggle, I do not in the least justify reality, but, on the contrary, indicate in this reality *itself* the deepest sources (though they are invisible at first sight) and the forces that can transform it.

But if I say: "nobody is building a new Russia—she is *being built* in the struggle of interests", I at once throw a certain veil over the clear picture of the struggle of *such-and-such* classes, and make a concession to those who see only those actions of the ruling classes, i.e., particularly the bourgeoisie, that are on the surface. I slip involuntarily into justifying the bourgeoisie; instead of the objectivism of the class struggle, I adopt as a criterion the bourgeois trend that is most conspicuous, or that is successful for the time being.

We shall illustrate this by an example from history. New Germany (the Germany of the second half of the nineteenth century) was "built" in the process of the struggle of different interests. No educated bourgeois will question this, nor will he go farther than that.

But here is how Marx reasoned during the most "critical" period of the building of *new* Germany.

"The upper bourgeoisie," wrote Marx in 1848, "ever anti-revolutionary, concluded a defensive and offensive alliance with the reactionaries for fear of the people, that is to say, the workers and the democratic bourgeoisie."

"The French bourgeoisie of 1789 did not for a moment leave its allies, the peasants, in the lurch. It knew that its rule was grounded in the destruction of feudalism in the countryside, the creation of a free landowning peasant class.

"The German bourgeoisie of 1848 is, without the least compunction, betraying the peasants, who are its most natural allies, the flesh of its flesh and without whom it is powerless against the aristocracy.

"The continuance of feudal rights ... such is the result of the German revolution of 1848. The mountain brought forth a mouse."[139]

In Marx, the *classes* which *built* new Germany stand out at once as if they were living.

A bourgeois scholar who justifies reality in the name of "objectivism" says: Bismarck defeated Marx, Bismarck took into account how "new Germany was *built* in the complicated process of the struggle between different interests". Marx, however, "made chimerical plans for building" a Great-German democratic republic in spite of the liberals, with the aid of the workers and the democratic bourgeoisie (that bourgeoisie which does not enter into alliance with reaction).

That is what bourgeois scholars say in a thousand variations. In examining this question from a purely theoretical standpoint, let us ask ourselves what their mistake is. It is that they cover up and obscure the class struggle. It is that (by means of the would-be profound turn of speech, "Germany was *built* in the process, etc.") they gloss over the circumstance that Bismarck Germany was built by the bourgeoisie, who by its own "betrayals and treachery" made itself "powerless against the nobility".

Marx, however, was enabled by the objectivism of the class struggle to understand *political reality* a hundred times more deeply and accurately, without justifying it at all but, on the contrary, indicating and singling out in it the classes which were building a democratic Germany, and were able to become the bulwark of democracy and socialism even when events had taken a turn exceptionally favourable to Bismarck.

Marx understood political reality so correctly and so deeply that he was able in 1848, half a century in advance, to appraise the *essence* of Bismarck Germany as the Germany of a bourgeoisie "powerless against the nobility". At the elections in 1912, sixty-four years after Marx had made his appraisal, the liberals fully confirmed it by their behaviour.

Marx and the Marxists, who had been waging a ruthless struggle against the liberals since 1848—a struggle that was unprecedented in acuteness and evoked a universal howl from the liberals (excuse me for using this sharp phrase, esteemed Nikolin!)—were by no means advocates of a "chimera" when they upheld the "plan" for a Great-German democratic state.

On the contrary, by upholding their "plan", propagating it steadfastly and lashing the liberals and democrats who were betraying it, Marx and the Marxists were educating the very class which embodied the *vital* forces of "new Germany" and which, thanks to Marx's consistent and whole-heartedly resolute propaganda, now stands fully armed, ready to fulfil its historic role of grave-digger, not only of the Bismarckian bourgeoisie, but of all bourgeoisie in general.

*   *
*

The example from German history reveals to us the *logic of opportunism* in the views of Nikolin, who angrily abuses us for our "violent Cadet-eating" *precisely because* he is *unaware* that he himself is drifting to the liquidationist ideas of a liberal labour policy.

The more N. Nikolin (who is not alone!) flies into a rage and tries to brush us aside, the more explicitly and circumstantially will we, who are publicists, repeat to him that our struggle against the Cadets and the liquidators is prompted by considerations which have been deeply thought out and which for more than five years (for more than ten years, to be exact) have been reaffirmed many times by the official decisions of all Marxists. The trouble with N. Nikolin, as well as with the liquidators whom he defends, is that they have *nothing* even approximately formulated, definite and clear with which to counter these numerous, precise, formal tactical decisions adopted long ago.

It is not just a "proud" phrase to say that "the workers must build a new Russia in spite of the liberals". N. Nikolin knows very well that this idea is expressed in a number of tactical decisions recognised by most Marxists. This is, in effect, a simple *summing up* of Russia's political experience during at least the past decade. It is an absolutely indisputable historical fact that during the last ten years the Russian working class has been *building* a new Russia "in spite of the liberals". Such "building" work is *never* wasted, whatever the temporary "successes" of the Russian pretenders to the role of a Bismarck.

Russian opportunism—vague, indistinct, and eel-like, as it is in other countries—is unable to express its views definitely and clearly, to state formally that the working class must *not* build a new Russia in spite of the liberals but must do this, that and the other. Opportunism would not be opportunism if it were capable of giving clear and straightforward answers. But it expresses its discontent over the workers' policy, and the fact that it gravitates towards the bourgeoisie, by saying: "Nobody is building a new Russia—she is *being built* in the process of the struggle of interests."

And of what is *being built*, it is the "building" which the nobility and the bourgeoisie are doing, with the liberals *correcting* it, that is most conspicuous and striking, and enjoys momentary success and the admiration of the "crowd" more than anything else. "Why try to analyse which classes are building and how—that is all a chimera; we must take what is *being built*"—this is the true meaning of Nikolin's argument, and the "logic of opportunism".

This is indeed forgetting the class struggle. This is what constitutes the main principle of a liberal labour policy. It is through this sort of "logic" that the role of the working class is reduced from leadership of a genuine, consistent, whole-hearted democratic movement to spade-work for the liberals.

Hence the fact, only too familiar to us Russians, that *in words* the opportunists acknowledge that the party of the proletariat, too, should have an "independent" line, which, of course, is acknowledged by Nikolin as well. But *in fact* he defends a line that is *not independent*, but is the line of a liberal labour policy.

Nikolin tries to explain and to show us how very

immaterial it is to *proclaim* the independence of the working class.

The liquidators' platform, reported in *Nevsky Golos* No. 8, also proclaimed it as did Nikolin himself. But even as he *proclaims* "independence", he is advocating a *non-independent* policy.

By rejecting the idea of the working class pursuing a line of its own in present-day politics and in all questions of democracy (or, *in other words*, the idea of the working class "building a new Russia") in spite of the liberals, Nikolin virtually calls on the working class to trail behind the liberals.

That is the crux of the matter. That is the "logic of opportunism". As regards arguments to the effect that the working class should not be "isolated", that "the brunt of the struggle for political liberty should not be borne by the workers", that what is needed is "co-ordination and not division of forces", and so on, all that is meaningless rhetoric. In fact, they are all descriptions and paraphrases of one and the same thing: don't isolate yourselves (*from the liberals*), "co-ordinate your forces" (*with liberal policy*), recognise liberal policy to be an effective struggle for political liberty and not for a deal with the Purishkeviches, and so on and so forth.

We did not dwell on that rhetoric because one who wants to argue on the substance of the matter should take the real starting-points, the roots of the differences, and not the rhetorical flourishes of a basically wrong line.

Nevskaya Zvezda No. 26,   Published according
    September 16, 1912   to the text in *Nevskaya Zvezda*
    Signed: *M. M.*

THE SUCCESSES OF THE AMERICAN WORKERS

The latest issue of the American labour weekly, *Appeal to Reason*, received in Europe reports that its circulation has increased to 984,000 copies. The letters and demands coming in—writes the editor (No. 875, September 7, new style)—indicate beyond doubt that we shall exceed one million copies in the next few weeks.

This figure—a million copies of a socialist weekly which American courts harass and persecute shamelessly and which is growing and gaining strength under the fire of persecution—shows more clearly than long arguments the kind of revolution that is approaching in America.

Not long ago the sycophantic *Novoye Vremya*, a mouthpiece of venal hacks, wrote about the "power of money" in America, relating with malicious joy the facts about the monstrous venality of Taft, Roosevelt, Wilson and, indeed, *all* Presidential candidates put up by the bourgeois parties. Here is a free, democratic republic for you, hissed the venal Russian newspaper.

The class-conscious workers will reply to that calmly and proudly: we have no illusions about the significance of broad democracy. No democracy in the world can eliminate the class struggle and the omnipotence of money. It is not this that makes democracy important and useful. The importance of democracy is that it makes the class struggle broad, open and conscious. And this is not a conjecture or a wish, but a fact.

At a time when the membership of the German Social-Democratic Party has grown to 970,000 and when the circulation of an American socialist weekly has climbed to 984,000 copies, anyone who has eyes to see must acknowledge that a proletarian is powerless when alone but that millions of proletarians are all-powerful.

Pravda No. 120, September 18, 1912
                   Signed: *M . N.*

Published according
to the *Pravda* text

THE END OF THE ITALO-TURKISH WAR

Representatives of Italy and Turkey have signed preliminary terms of peace, according to telegraphic reports.

Italy has "won" the war, which she launched a year ago
to seize Turkish possessions in Africa. From now on, Tripoli
will belong to Italy. It is worth while taking a look at this
typical colonial war, waged by a "civilised" twentieth-
century nation.

What caused the war? The greed of the Italian moneybags and capitalists, who need new markets and new achievements for Italian imperialism.

What kind of war was it? A perfected, civilised blood-
bath, the massacre of Arabs with the help of the "latest"
weapons.

The Arabs put up a desperate resistance. When, at the
beginning of the war, the Italian admirals were incautious
enough to land 1,200 marines, the Arabs attacked them
and killed some 600. By way of "retaliation", about 3,000
Arabs were butchered, whole families were plundered and
done to death, with women and children massacred in
cold blood. The Italians are a civilised, constitutional
nation.

About 1,000 Arabs were hanged.

The Italian casualties exceeded 20,000, including 17,429
sick, 600 missing and 1,405 killed.

The war cost the Italians over 800 million lire, or over
320 million rubles. It resulted in terrible unemployment
and industrial stagnation.

The Arabs lost about 14,800 lives. Despite the "peace",
the war will actually go on, for the Arab tribes in the heart

of Africa, in areas far away from the coast, will refuse to submit. And for a long time to come they will be "civilised" by bayonet, bullet, noose, fire and rape.

Italy, of course, is no better and no worse than the other capitalist countries. All of them alike are governed by the bourgeoisie, which stops at no carnage in its quest for new sources of profit.

Pravda No. 129, September 28, 1912
Signed: *T*.

Published according
to the *Pravda* text

A GAME OF CHANCE

Novoye Vremya fully discloses the plans of the Russian nationalists. When reading this newspaper, which is "influential" in nationalist quarters, as well as among the Octobrists, the plan that they are firmly pursuing for robbing Turkey becomes obvious.

As usual, the policy of chauvinism and seizure of foreign territory is being carried out first and foremost by inciting the general public against Austria. "The Balkan peoples," writes *Novoye Vremya*, "have rallied together for a holy war of independence. The Austrian diplomat is on the look-out for the moment when they can be plundered."

Austria has torn off a chunk (Bosnia and Herzegovina) and Italy has torn off another (Tripoli); it is now our turn to enrich ourselves—such is the policy of *Novoye Vremya*. "A holy war of independence" is merely a phrase to deceive simpletons, for no one in our own Russia has so flouted the truly democratic principles of genuine independence of *all* peoples as have the nationalists and the Octobrists.

But why do the nationalists consider the time favourable for a policy of plunder? This, too, can be clearly seen from *Novoye Vremya*. Italy will not fight—it says in effect; as for Austria, it would be risky for her to start a war against the Balkan Slavs because she has a kindred population of many millions, and Germany would not venture a European war to defeat Turkey.

The nationalists' calculation is frank and shameless to the last degree. While mouthing pompous words about "a holy war of independence" of the peoples, they gamble with the lives of millions in the most cold-blooded way by inciting the peoples to a carnage for the profit of a handful of merchants and industrialists.

The Triple Alliance (Germany, Austria and Italy) is weak at the moment, for Italy has spent 800 million francs on the war against the Turks, and the "interests" of Italy and Austria do not coincide in the Balkans. Italy wants to snatch another morsel —Albania —but Austria will not let her. Our nationalists, who count on this, are playing a reckless game of chance, relying on the strength and wealth of two powers in the Triple Entente (Britain and France) and on the fact that "Europe" will not want a general war over the Straits or over the "rounding off" of "our" territories at the expense of Asiatic Turkey.

In a society of wage slavery, every merchant and every proprietor plays a game of chance, saying as it were: "I shall either be ruined or make a profit and ruin others." Every year hundreds of capitalists go bankrupt and millions of peasants, handicraftsmen and artisans are ruined. The capitalist countries play a similar game of chance with the blood of millions, whom they send into a carnage now here, now there with the aim of seizing foreign territory and plundering their weaker neighbours.

Pravda No. 134, October 4, 1912

Published according
to the *Pravda* text

THE PRIESTHOOD IN THE ELECTIONS,
AND ELECTIONS WITH THE PRIESTHOOD

According to reports in the press, the congresses of small landowners and deans of churches in 46 gubernias of European Russia have elected 7,990 delegates, including 6,516 priests. The latter make up 82 per cent.

The complete returns for the fifty gubernias cannot much alter this result.

Let us, therefore, see what these elections signify.

The law provides that the small landowners and the parishes shall elect one delegate *per electoral category* established for participation in the landowners' congress. This means that the number of delegates must be proportional to the amount of land owned by the electorate.

Statistics for 1905 give the following data for the fifty gubernias of European Russia:

Church estates	1,900,000	dessiatines
Lands privately owned by priests	300,000	"
Total owned by the priesthood	2,200,000	"
Lands privately owned by townspeople	3,700,000	"
Lands privately owned by peasants	13,200,000	"
Lands privately owned by other categories	2,200,000	"
Total of small holdings owned by "laymen"	19,100,000	"

These data probably take account of small holdings to a lesser extent than of the lands owned by the priesthood. Nevertheless, it follows that the small private holdings total 21,300,000 dessiatines, of which priests own 2,200,000 dessiatines, or *a little over* one-tenth. Yet the priesthood has elected upwards of *eight-tenths* of the total number of delegates!!

How could that come about? It was simple enough. The fact is that small landowners seldom go to elections —they lack the means and take little interest in the matter; besides, the police put a thousand obstacles in the way of free elections. The priests, however, have all been "induced" to attend.

The priests will vote for the candidates who suit the government. This explains why *even the landlords* are murmuring, to say nothing of the bourgeoisie. The Octobrists and the nationalists are murmuring too. They all accuse the government of *"engineering"* the elections. But the landlords and the big bourgeoisie *themselves* would like *to engineer the elections.*

Thus there is a clash between absolutism, on the one hand, and the landlords and the bourgeois bigwigs, on the other. The government wanted to secure the backing of the landlords and the top strata of the bourgeoisie; as is known, this idea underlies the whole law of June 3, 1907.

As it happens, however, the government cannot get along *even* with the Octobrists. It has *not succeeded* in organising *even* a feudal-bourgeois monarchy of a kind "satisfactory" to these classes.

Unquestionably, this failure has in fact been acknowledged by the government, which has set about organising *its own officials* in the shape of the subordinate, dependent priesthood!

In the science of history, this device of a government which retains the essential features of absolutism is called Bonapartism. In this case, it is not definite classes that serve as a support, or not they alone, and not chiefly, but hand-picked elements, mostly from among various dependent sections of the population.

How is the possibility of this phenomenon to be explained in "sociological" terms, i.e., from the standpoint of the class struggle?

It is due to a balance between the forces of the hostile or rival classes. If, for example, the Purishkeviches are competing with the Guchkovs and Ryabushinskys, the government may—provided there is a certain balance between the forces of these rivals—gain *greater* independence (within certain, rather narrow limits, of course) than when either of these classes has a decisive superiority. If, on the other hand, this government is historically linked by continuity and so on with especially "vivid" forms of absolutism, and if militarist and bureaucratic traditions in the sense of non-electivity of judges and officials are strong in the country, then the limits of that independence will be still greater, its manifestations still more open, the methods used in "picking" voters, and electors voting on orders from above, still more crude, and tyranny still more tangible.

It is something like this that contemporary Russia is passing through. The "step towards transformation into a bourgeois monarchy"* is made more difficult by the borrowing of Bonapartist methods. Whereas in France the bourgeois monarchy and the Bonapartist empire differed clearly and sharply from each other, in Germany Bismarck gave models of a "combination" of the two types, with those features which Marx called "military despotism"[140]—to say nothing of Bonapartism—obviously predominating.

It is said that the carp likes to be fried in sour cream. We don't know whether the philistine likes to be "fried" in a bourgeois monarchy, in old feudal absolutism, in the "latest" type of Bonapartism or in military despotism, or, lastly, in a certain blend of all these "methods". But while the distinction may seem very small from the point of view of the philistine and so-called "legal order", i.e., from a *purely* juridical, formally constitutional point of view, it is substantial from the point of view of the class struggle.

It won't make things easier for the philistine to know that he is being beaten not only in the old way but in the new as well. But the *stability* of a regime pressing down the philistine, the *conditions of development* and disintegration of this regime, and its capacity to suffer a rapid fiasco

---

* See present edition, Vol. 15, p. 347.—*Ed.*

all depend to a large degree on whether we are confronted with more or less evident, open, solid and direct forms of rule of definite classes, or with various indirect, unstable *forms* of their rule.

The rule of *classes* is harder to eliminate than the unstable forms of the superstructure steeped in the shabby spirit of old times and supported by a picked "electorate".

The experiment of Sabler and Makarov in "organising" the priesthood for the Fourth Duma elections should be of considerable interest to everyone, both "sociologically" and in terms of practical politics.

Nevskaya Zvezda No. 27,
October 5, 1912

Published according
to the text in *Nevskaya Zvezda*

MR. MILYUKOV'S "POSITION"

The leader of the Cadet Party has lost his way in a wood of three trees. He has been writing articles as long as Menshikov's about "three positions" and "one position". The more he writes, the more evident it becomes that he is trying to *fool* the reader with his talk, to *cover up* the point at issue with his dull and empty verbiage.

Poor learned historian! He has to *pretend* that he does not see the difference between liberalism and democracy. For the whole point is this difference, gentlemen! The Duma votes in general, the attitude towards "reforms", the votes on the budget, and the issue of "extra-parliamentary tactics" all bring out in different *forms* one and the same *point*, the profound difference between the liberal-monarchist bourgeoisie and the democrats.

For the thousand and first time, we shall briefly repeat what this difference is, for the benefit of the Milyukovs who "don't understand".

The liberals are defending a number of feudal-absolutist privileges (an upper chamber, etc.). The democrats are waging an uncompromising struggle against all privileges.

The liberals are for agreement with the forces of the old in social life; the democrats' tactics are to eliminate these forces.

The liberals are afraid of the independent activity of the masses, they do not trust it, they reject it; the democrats sympathise with it, believe in it, support and encourage it.

That is enough for the moment.

Does Mr. Milyukov really "not understand" this difference, which is familiar even from textbooks of history?

Does he really "not understand" that the very *programme* of the Cadets is a *programme* of the liberal-monarchist bourgeoisie, not of the democrats, and that only liberals (and bad ones at that) could have voted for the budget in the Third Duma, could have declared themselves a loyal opposition, etc.?

Mr. Milyukov understands this perfectly well, and he is trying to fool people with his talk, pretending that he has forgotten the ABC of the difference between liberalism and democracy.

To register in print this pitiful dodging of the Cadets, we shall remark to Mr. Milyukov that in all the *official* Social-Democratic press (except, of course, that of the liquidators, whom we will gladly give up to Mr. Milyukov), in *all* the resolutions of the guiding Social-Democratic bodies, and in the whole policy of the Social-Democrats in the Third Duma, we always and invariably meet, in thousands of forms, with the defence of the old tactics which Mr. Milyukov says the Social-Democrats have abandoned.

It is an indisputable historical fact, esteemed learned historian!

We must register in print how low the Cadets must have fallen if they try to deceive the public on questions which are so elementary and have been made perfectly clear by the history of the political parties in Russia.

In conclusion, a little question to Mr. Milyukov —to sum up and recapitulate what we have said: when you Cadet gentlemen agreed to bar Voiloshnikov from five sessions,[141] were you acting as liberals or as democrats?

Pravda No. 136, October 6, 1912   Published according
        Signed: *V. I.*   to the *Pravda* text

DEPUTY OF THE ST. PETERSBURG WORKERS

The proletariat of the capital is sending one of its elected representatives into the reactionary Duma of the landlords and priests. It is a glorious position this representative will hold. He will have to speak and act on behalf of millions; he will have to unfurl a great banner; he will have to voice the views that for years have been expressed in formal, specific, precise terms by the responsible spokesmen of Marxism and working-class democracy.

The election of someone to that position is a matter of such vast importance that it would be petty, cowardly and disgraceful to be afraid to speak of it straightforwardly, without beating about the bush, to be afraid of "offending" a particular individual, a particular circle, etc.

The election should accord with the will of the majority of the class-conscious, Marxist workers. That is obvious. Nobody would venture to deny this *outright*.

Everyone knows that from 1908 to 1912 a fight was waged among the St. Petersburg workers between the opponents of liquidationism and the liquidators at hundreds and thousands of meetings, discussions and talks, and in various press organs. It would be unseemly for anyone to bury his head in the sand like an ostrich and try to "forget" this fact.

Things are being muddled up by those who today are shouting about "unity" over the election of *one* deputy, for they are raising the wrong issue and *obscuring* the essential point by their shouting.

What has "unity" to do with it when it is necessary to elect *one* person and all are agreed that he must express the will of the majority of the class-conscious worker Marxists??

The liquidators are afraid to say plainly that they would like the choice to be a liquidator or a "non-factionalist" (i.e., a waverer). And since they are afraid to defend their views *openly*, they are trying to smuggle them through by *deceit*, by shouting about "unity".

It is our duty to expose this confusion. If the liquidators are in a majority among the class-conscious workers, no one on earth can prevent them from electing a liquidator. We must establish as accurately, calmly, firmly, prudently and certainly as possible which side has the majority, without bothering about the outcries of people who, *after five years of struggle*, are advocating "unity" (a few days before the elections!) in order to conceal their views.

The workers are not children to believe a fairy-tale like that. Only one of three possible decisions can be adopted: (1) to choose a liquidator; (2) to choose an opponent of liquidationism; (3) to choose a waverer. There have been no others among the Social-Democrats during the five years between 1908 and 1912, nor are there any today!

Workers who want to act as adult and independent people must not tolerate political strike-breakers in their midst. They must see to it that the will of the majority of class-conscious workers is respected and executed.

The workers need a deputy who will express the will of the majority and will know for certain *what* work he will carry out in and outside the Duma.

The will of the majority has been stated, and the deputy for St. Petersburg should be a determined opponent of liquidationism and a supporter of consistent working-class democracy.

Pravda No. 144, October 16, 1912
Signed: *I*.

Published according
to the *Pravda* text

THE BALKAN PEOPLES
AND EUROPEAN DIPLOMACY

Public attention is fixed on the Balkans just now, and understandably so. For the whole of Eastern Europe, the hour is perhaps striking when the peoples themselves will have their free and decisive word to say. There is no longer room for the game of the bourgeois "powers" and their diplomats who are past masters of intrigue, scheming and selfishly tripping up one another.

The Balkan peoples might say, as our serfs used to in the old days: "Save us from lordly anger and lordly love, the worst of all misfortunes."[142] For the Balkan peasants and workers, both hostile and would-be friendly intervention by the European "powers" means only adding all sorts of fetters and hindrances to free progress to the general conditions of capitalist exploitation.

That is one reason why it is essential to fight against both bureaucratic-governmental and liberal "diplomacy". *Rech*, for example, was false through and through when, a few days ago, it invited "Russian society" (i.e., the bourgeoisie) to remember the statement of a British ministerial organ which said that Europe would not permit "misgovernment" in the Balkans! "Let our diplomats not sit back idly," shouted *Rech*.

Even the most "liberal" bourgeois Europe, we say in reply, can bring the Balkans nothing but support for decay and stagnation, nothing but bureaucratic obstacles to freedom. It is "Europe" that is hindering the establishment of a federal republic in the Balkans.

The foremost workers in the Balkans, and all Balkan democrats, pin their hopes solely on the development of the political consciousness, democratic spirit and independent activity of the *masses*, and not on the intrigues of bourgeois diplomats, whatever liberal phrases they adorn themselves with!

Pravda No. 144, October 16, 1912
Signed: *V*.

Published according
to the *Pravda* text

THE FOX AND THE HEN-COOP

The issue of a Balkan war and of "Europe's" attitude to it is the most burning political issue today. It is important for all democrats in general and for the working class in particular to *understand* the class interests guiding this or that party in this matter.

The policy of the Octobrists, nationalists and unaffiliated "patriots", from *Novoye Vremya* to *Russkoye Slovo*, is clear and simple. The badgering of Austria, incitement to war against her, and shouts about the "Slav tasks" of Russia are a poorly disguised endeavour to divert attention from Russia's domestic affairs and to "grab a piece" of Turkey. Support for reaction at home and for colonial, imperialist plunder abroad—such is the essence of this crude "patriotic" "Slav" policy.

The Cadets' policy is couched in more subtle and diplomatic terms, but in effect their policy is *also a reactionary great-power* policy of *imperialism*. It is particularly important to understand this, for the liberals cunningly veil their views with democratic-sounding phrases.

Look at *Rech*. At first—prior to the "love tryst" of Milyukov and Sazonov[143]—it accused Sazonov of "readiness to bargain" and reproached the nationalists with weakening the "great idea" of capturing Constantinople. But now, after the tryst, *Rech* agrees with *Rossiya*, vigorously censuring the "foolish enthusiasm" of *Novoye Vremya*.

But what is the policy of *Rech* today?

We must not begin with proud demands, for if we do we shall lose support (from France and Britain), and shall "end by becoming, in spite of ourselves, *even more modest than we should be*" (No. 278)!!

And so, *Rech* is against the chauvinists *because* they "will end by being more modest than they should be". It is as much as to say: you chauvinists are bragging and you'll get nothing. But we are in favour of grabbing a big chunk quietly and peacefully, with the support of the French and British bourgeoisie!

"We need" support (from the Triple Entente) "in the interests of our own Balkan *protégés*", writes *Rech*. Mark this: *Rech, too, favours* the idea of Russia *"protecting"* the Slavs, of the fox protecting the hen-coop, except that it wants this done more cunningly!

"All that can be achieved has to be achieved only in this way— through the joint efforts of European diplomacy," declares *Rech*.

It is clear enough: the essence of Cadet policy is the same kind of chauvinism and imperialism as that of *Novoye Vremya*, only more cunning and subtle. *Novoye Vremya* roughly and stupidly threatens war on behalf of Russia alone. *Rech*, "subtly and diplomatically", *likewise* threatens *war*, but only on behalf of the Triple Entente, for to say "we must not be more modest than we should be" means precisely threatening war. *Novoye Vremya* is in favour of the Slavs being protected by *Russia*, while *Rech* favours their protection by the Triple Entente. In other words, *Novoye Vremya* wants to see only our fox in the hen-coop, while *Rech* favours an agreement among three foxes.

Democrats in general and workers in particular are opposed to all "protection" of the Slavs by foxes or wolves, and advocate the complete self-determination of nations, complete democracy, and the liberation of the Slavs from *all* protection by the "Great Powers".

The liberals and nationalists are arguing about *different ways* of plundering and enslaving the Balkan peoples by the European bourgeoisie. Only the workers are pursuing a genuinely democratic policy, for freedom and democracy everywhere and completely, against all "protection", plunder and intervention!

Pravda No. 146, October 18, 1912   Published according
          Signed: *V. I.*   to the *Pravda* text

A DISGRACEFUL RESOLUTION

The resolution adopted by the St. Petersburg City Council on October 10 has attracted public attention.

The resolution concerns the Balkan war, the most important event in world politics, and it comes from an influential public body—influential among the bourgeoisie. It was adopted *unanimously* by avowed reactionaries and by liberals.

Falbork, a liberal, and all but a "democrat" (!?) and Cadet, urged the necessity of that kind of resolution in an "ardent speech"; he was a member of the drafting commission, and voted for the resolution.

This resolution is a specimen of bourgeois chauvinism, of the bourgeoisie's abject servility to "the powers that be", of bourgeois support for a policy which turns the peoples into cannon fodder.

"St. Petersburg," says the resolution, which is addressed to the capitals of the belligerent Balkan powers, "shares your hope of a bright future of independent liberty for the oppressed peoples, a liberty in whose name you are shedding your blood."

This is the sort of phrases that chauvinism hides behind! Never and nowhere has "liberty" been won by the oppressed peoples through one people waging *war* against another. Wars between peoples merely increase the enslavement of peoples. Real *liberty* for the Slav peasant in the Balkans, as well as for the Turkish peasant, can be ensured *only* by complete liberty inside *every* country and by a federation of completely and thoroughly democratic states.

The Slav and the Turkish peasants in the Balkans are brothers who are equally "oppressed" by their landlords and their governments.

That is where real oppression lies, and the real obstacle to "independence" and "liberty".

The reactionary and liberal chauvinists, who are openly making common cause in the St. Petersburg City Council (just as they are covertly making common cause in the press, for the arguments of *Rech* and *Novoye Vremya* on this point are *at bottom* identical, differing only in tone and detail) — these chauvinists advocate turning the peoples into cannon fodder!

Pravda No. 146, October 18, 1912   Published according
          Signed: *T.*   to the *Pravda* text

TWO UTOPIAS

Utopia is a Greek word, composed of *ou*, not, and *topos*, a place. It means a place which does not exist, a fantasy, invention or fairy-tale.

In politics utopia is a wish that can never come true — neither now nor afterwards, a wish that is not based on social forces and is not supported by the growth and development of political, class forces.

The less freedom there is in a country, the scantier the manifestations of open class struggle and the lower the educational level of the *masses*, the more easily political utopias usually arise and the longer they persist.

In modern Russia, two kinds of political utopia have been most persistent and they exert a certain influence on the masses owing to their appeal. They are the liberal utopia and the Narodnik utopia.

The liberal utopia alleges that one could bring about appreciable improvements in Russia, in her political liberty, and in the condition of the mass of her working people, peacefully and harmoniously, without hurting anyone's feelings, without removing the Purishkeviches, without a ruthless class struggle fought to a finish. It is the utopia of *peace* between a free Russia and the Purishkeviches.

The Narodnik utopia is a dream of the Narodnik intellectuals and Trudovik peasants who imagine that a new and just division of the land could *abolish* the power and rule of capital and do away with wage slavery, or that a "just", "equalised" division of the land could be *maintained* under the domination of capital, under the rule of money, under commodity production.

What is it that gives rise to these utopias? Why do they persist rather strongly in present-day Russia?

They are engendered by the interests of the classes which are waging a struggle against the old order, serfdom, lack of rights—in a word, "against the Purishkeviches", and which do not occupy an independent position in this struggle. Utopia, or day-dreaming, is a product of this lack of independence, this *weakness*. Day-dreaming is the lot of the *weak*.

The liberal bourgeoisie in general, and the liberal-bourgeois intelligentsia in particular, cannot but strive for liberty and legality, since without these the domination of the bourgeoisie is incomplete, is neither undivided nor guaranteed. But the bourgeoisie is *more* afraid of the movement of the masses than of reaction. Hence the striking, incredible *weakness* of the liberals in politics, their absolute impotence. Hence the endless series of equivocations, falsehoods, hypocrisies and cowardly evasions in the entire policy of the liberals, who *have to* play at democracy to win the support of the masses but at the same time are deeply anti-democratic, deeply hostile to the movement of the masses, to their initiative, their way of "storming heaven", as Marx once described one of the mass movements in Europe in the last century.[144]

The utopia of liberalism is a utopia of impotence in the matter of the political emancipation of Russia, a utopia of the self-interested moneybags who want "peacefully" to share privileges with the Purishkeviches and pass off this noble desire as the theory of "peaceful" victory for Russian democracy. The liberal utopia means day-dreaming about how to beat the Purishkeviches without defeating them, how to break them without hurting them. Clearly, *this* utopia is harmful not only because it is a utopia, but also because it *corrupts* the democratic consciousness of the masses. If they believe in *this* utopia, the masses will never win freedom; they are not worthy of freedom; they fully deserve to be maltreated by the Purishkeviches.

The utopia of the Narodniks and Trudoviks is the day-dreaming of the petty proprietor, who stands midway between the capitalist and the wage-worker, about abolishing wage slavery without a class struggle. When the issue of economic emancipation becomes as close, immediate and *burning* for Russia as the issue of political emancipation is today, the utopia of the Narodniks will prove *no less* harmful than that of the liberals.

But Russia is still in the period of her bourgeois and not proletarian transformation; it is not the question of the economic emancipation of the proletariat that has *most completely* matured, but the question of political liberty, i.e. (in effect), of complete bourgeois liberty.

And in this latter question, the Narodnik utopia plays a peculiar historical role. Being a utopia in regard to the economic consequences that a new division of the land should (and would) have, it is an accompaniment *and symptom* of the great, mass *democratic* upsurge of the peasant masses, i.e., the masses that constitute the *majority* of the population in bourgeois-feudal, modern, Russia. (In a purely bourgeois Russia, as in purely bourgeois Europe, the peasantry will not form the majority of the population.)

The liberal utopia corrupts the democratic consciousness of the masses. The Narodnik utopia, which corrupts their *socialist* consciousness, is an accompaniment, a symptom, and in part even an expression of their democratic upsurge.

The dialectics of history is such that the Narodniks and the Trudoviks propose and promote, as an anti-capitalist remedy, a highly consistent and thoroughgoing capitalist measure with regard to the agrarian question in Russia. An "equalised" new division of the land is utopian, yet a most complete rupture—a rupture indispensable for a *new* division—with the whole of the old landownership, whether landlord, allotment or "crown", is the most necessary, economically progressive and, for a state like Russia, most urgent measure towards bourgeois democracy.

We should remember Engels's notable dictum:

"What formally may be economically incorrect, may all the same be correct from the point of view of world history."[145]

Engels advanced this profound thesis in connection with utopian socialism: that socialism was "fallacious" in the formal economic sense. That socialism was "fallacious" when it declared surplus value an *injustice* from the point of view of the laws of exchange. The theoreticians of bour-

geois political economy were right, in objecting to *that*
socialism, in the formal economic sense, for surplus value
results from the laws of exchange quite "naturally", quite
"justly".

But utopian socialism was *right* from the point of view of
world history, for it was a symptom, an expression, a harbinger of the class which, born of capitalism, has by now, in
the beginning of the twentieth century, become a mass force
which can put an end to capitalism and is irresistibly advancing to this goal.

Engels's profound thesis must be borne in mind when
appraising the present-day Narodnik or Trudovik utopia
in Russia (perhaps not only in Russia but in a number of
Asiatic countries going through bourgeois revolutions in the
twentieth century).

Narodnik *democracy*, while fallacious from the formal
economic point of view, is correct from the *historical* point
of view; *this* democracy, while fallacious as a socialist
utopia, is *correct* in terms of the peculiar, historically
conditioned democratic struggle of the peasant masses which
is an inseparable element of the bourgeois transformation
and a condition for its complete victory.

The liberal utopia discourages the peasant masses from
fighting. The Narodnik utopia expresses their aspiration to
fight, and promises them a million blessings in the event of
victory, while this victory will in fact yield them only a
hundred blessings. But is it not natural that the millions
who are marching to battle, who for ages have lived in
unheard-of ignorance, want, poverty, squalor, abandonment
and downtroddenness, should magnify tenfold the fruits of
an eventual victory?

The liberal utopia is a veil for the self-seeking desire
of the new exploiters to share in the privileges of the old
exploiters. The Narodnik utopia is an expression of the
aspiration of the toiling millions of the petty bourgeoisie
to put an end *altogether* to the old, feudal exploiters, but it
also expresses the false hope that the new, capitalist exploiters can be abolished along with them.

———

Clearly, the Marxists, who are hostile to *all and every* utopia, must uphold the independence of the class which can fight feudalism *with supreme devotion* precisely because it is not even one-hundredth part involved in property ownership which makes the bourgeoisie a half-hearted opponent, and often an ally, of the feudal lords. The peasants are involved in small commodity production; given a favourable conjuncture of historical circumstances, they *can* achieve the most complete abolition of feudalism, but they will *always*—inevitably and not accidentally—show a certain vacillation between the bourgeoisie and the proletariat, between liberalism and Marxism.

Clearly, the Marxists must carefully extract the sound and valuable kernel of the sincere, resolute, militant democracy of the peasant masses from the husk of Narodnik utopias.

In the old Marxist literature of the eighties one can discover systematic effort to extract this valuable democratic kernel. Some day historians will study this effort systematically and trace its connection with what in the first decade of the twentieth century came to be called "Bolshevism".

Written in October 1912   Published according
                                            to the manuscript
   First published in
   Zhizn No. 1, 1924
   Signed: *V. I.*

DEBATES IN BRITAIN
ON LIBERAL LABOUR POLICY

It is well known that in Britain there are two workers' parties: the British Socialist Party, as the Social-Democrats now call themselves, and the so-called Independent Labour Party.

This split in the British workers' socialist movement is no accident. It originated long ago. It arose out of the specific features of British history. Capitalism developed in Britain before it did in any other country, and for a long time Britain was the "workshop" of the world. This exceptional, monopoly position created relatively tolerable conditions of life for the *labour aristocracy*, i.e., for the minority of skilled, well-paid workers in Britain.

Hence the petty-bourgeois, craft spirit in the ranks of this labour aristocracy, which has been divorcing itself from its class, following in the wake of the Liberals, and treating socialism contemptuously as a "utopia". The Independent Labour Party is a party of liberal labour policy. It is justly said that this Party is "independent" only of socialism, but very dependent on liberalism.

In recent times Britain's monopoly has been thoroughly undermined. The previous relatively tolerable conditions of life have given way to extreme want as a consequence of the high cost of living. The class struggle is becoming immensely intensified, and along with this the basis for opportunism, the former basis for the spread of the ideas of liberal labour policy among the working class, is being undermined.

So long as these ideas persisted among considerable numbers of British workers, elimination of the split among the workers was out of the question. Unity cannot be *created* by phrases and desires, so long as the Social-Democrats have to fight against liberal labour policy. *At the present time*, however, this unity is really becoming possible, because the *protest* against liberal labour policy is *growing* in the Independent Labour Party *itself*.

Before us lies the official report of the latest, Twentieth, Annual Conference of that Party, held at Merthyr on May 27 and 28, 1912. The debate on parliamentary policy given in the report is extremely interesting; essentially it was a debate on a deeper issue, that of Social-Democratic and liberal labour policies, although the speakers did not use these terms.

The Conference debate was opened by Jowett, M.P. He moved a resolution against supporting the Liberals, of which we shall speak in greater detail below, and a fellow-thinker, Conway, who seconded the motion, said plainly: "The average worker is asking the question whether the Labour Party in Parliament has a view of its own." Suspicion is growing among the workers that the Labour Party is "tied" to the Liberals. "A feeling is growing in the country that the Labour Party is simply a wing of the Liberal Party." It should be observed that the Parliamentary Labour Party consists *not only* of I.L.P. M.P.s, but also of M.P.s sponsored by trade unions. These call themselves Labour M.P.s and Labour Party members, and *do not belong* to the I.L.P. The British opportunists have succeeded in doing what the opportunists in other countries are frequently inclined to do, namely, in combining opportunist "socialist" M.P.s with the M.P.s of allegedly non-party trade unions. The notorious "broad labour party", of which certain Mensheviks spoke in Russia in 1906-07, has materialised in Britain, and only in Britain.

To give practical expression to his views, Jowett moved a resolution, drawn up in the truly "British" manner, that is, without any general principles (the British pride themselves on their "practicality" and their dislike for general principles; this is just another expression of the craft spirit in the labour movement). The resolution called on the Labour group in the House of Commons *to ignore all threats* that the Liberal government might find itself in a minority and so be compelled to resign, and *to vote steadfastly on the merits of the questions brought before them*.

Jowett's motion "took the bull by the horns". The Liberal Cabinet in Britain, like the entire Liberal Party, is doing its utmost to persuade the workers that all forces must be united against reaction (i.e., against the Conservative Party), that the Liberal majority must be preserved, for it may melt away if the workers do not vote with the Liberals, and that the workers must not isolate themselves but must support the Liberals. And so Jowett puts the question clearly: vote "steadfastly", ignore the threat that the Liberal government may fall, do not vote as the interests of the Liberal Party require it, but on the merits of the questions, i.e., in Marxist language —pursue an independent proletarian class policy and not a liberal labour policy.

(In the ranks of the Independent Labour Party, Marxism is rejected *on principle*, and that is why Marxist language is not used at all.)

The opportunists, who predominate in the Party, immediately attacked Jowett. And—characteristically—they did it exactly as opportunists, in a roundabout way, by an evasion. They did not want to say *plainly* that they were *in favour* of supporting the Liberals. They expressed their idea in *general phrases*, and, of course, did not fail to mention the "independence" of the working class. Just like our liquidators, who always shout especially loudly about the "independence" of the working class whenever they are *in fact* preparing to replace its independence by a liberal labour policy.

Murray, the representative of the opportunist majority, moved an amendment, i.e., counter-resolution, as follows:

"That this Conference recognises that the Labour Party, in order to effectually carry out its object, must continue to regard all the possible consequences and effects, immediate and otherwise, of any line of action before adopting it, bearing in mind that its decisions must be guided solely by consideration for its own interest as a party, and by desire to increase its opportunities for attaining its ends."

Compare the two motions. Jowett's motion clearly demanded a break with the policy of supporting the Liberals. Murray's consisted of meaningless commonplaces, quite plausible and at first sight indisputable, but *in fact* serving to disguise *precisely* the policy of supporting the Liberals. Had Murray been acquainted with Marx, and had he been speaking to people who respected Marxism, he would have thought nothing of sweetening his opportunism with Marxist turns of speech and saying that Marxism demands that all the concrete circumstances of each particular case should be taken into consideration, that we must not tie our hands, that while preserving our independence we "take advantage of conflicts", "seize at the Achilles heel of the contradictions" in the present regime, and so on and so forth.

Opportunism can be expressed in terms of *any* doctrine *you like, including Marxism.* The peculiarity of the "destiny of Marxism" in Russia lies precisely in the fact that not only opportunism in the workers' party, but also opportunism in the liberal party (Izgoyev and Co.), likes to dress itself in Marxist *"terms"*! But that is by the way. Let us return to Merthyr.

Jowett was supported by McLachlan.

"What are the interests of a political party?" he asked. "Are the interests of the party merely to be served by retaining men in the House of Commons? If the interests of the party are to be considered, then the men and women who are outside Parliament have as much right to be considered as the men in Parliament. As a socialist organisation we should try to give effect to our principles in our political activities."

And McLachlan referred to the vote on the Heswell Reformatory case. A boy inmate of the reformatory had been tortured to death. A question was asked in Parliament. The Liberal Cabinet was threatened with defeat: Britain is not Prussia, and a Cabinet that is in the minority must resign. And so, to save the Cabinet, the Labour M.P.s voted in favour of whitewashing the torturer.

The Labour Party, said McLachlan, keeps on taking into account the effect which their vote might have on the fate of the government, thinking that should the Cabinet fall, Parliament would be dissolved and a new general election announced. But that was nothing to be afraid of. The fall of the Cabinet and the announcement of new elections would result in a *combination of the two bourgeois parties* (McLachlan simply said: the "other two parties", without the word "bourgeois". The British do not like Marxist terms!), *and the sooner that happened, the better for our movement.* The words of our propagandists should be carried into effect by the work of our men in the House. Until that was done, the Tory (i.e., Conservative) workman *would never believe there was any difference between the Liberal and Labour Parties*. Even if we lost every seat in the House through upholding our principles, it would do more good than attempts to coax a Liberal government into making concessions!

Keir Hardie, M.P., the Party leader, twists and turns.

"It is not true to say that the Labour Party upholds the balance of power. The Liberals and Irishmen in the House can outvote the Tory and Labour members.... In the case of the Heswell Reformatory I voted for the government purely on the merits of the case, and not in support of the government. The superintendent had been guilty of harshness and cruelty, and every Labour member went to the House determined to vote against the government. But during the debate the other side was put, and it showed that although the superintendent had been guilty of cruel treatment, the record of the School was the best in the Kingdom. Under those circumstances it would have been wrong to vote against the government.... [Such is the pass to which the British opportunists have brought the Labour Party: the leader was not howled down for that sort of speech, but was listened to calmly!]

"The real trouble is not with the I. L. P. members, but that when the Labour Party took over the Miners' Federation, and the miners' members joined the Labour group, *they were Liberals*, and they have not changed their opinions, since they gave a *purely nominal* adherence to the Party....

"Jowett's resolution reduces Parliamentary government to absurdity. The consequences of any vote must be considered....

"I would advise the previous question as regards both the resolution and the amendment." (!!!)

Lansbury, supporting Jowett's resolution, said:

"It is not so foolish as Keir Hardie would have us suppose. It does not mean that in voting upon a question every consideration should be ignored but *only* the consideration as to what effect it would have on the government. I got into the socialist movement through sheer disgust with political caucuses and bosses, and the control of the House of Commons by such people. My experience has been that every question that comes up for discussion has to be discussed in regard to its probable effect on the fortunes of the government of the day.

"It makes it almost impossible for the Labour Party to differentiate itself from the Liberal Party. I do not know of any particular piece of legislation in connection with which the Labour Party has in any kind of way differentiated itself from the Liberals. We as a party were part and parcel of the government in regard to the Insurance Act.... The Labour Party voted steadily for the Bill, and stood by the government all the way through.

"I was ashamed of the vote over the Heswell Reformatory. When a man poured boiling water over a boy until he died I felt ashamed of ... voting for the whitewashing of that man. On that occasion the Labour Party whips ran about the House bringing up their men to prevent the government being defeated.... To accustom men ... to voting against their consciences is deadly for the future of democracy in this country...."

Philip Snowden, M.P., one of the most rabid opportunists, wriggled like an eel. He said:

"My fighting instinct inclines me to support the resolution, but my common sense, judgement, and experience induce me to vote for the amendment. I agree that the present Parliamentary system has a demoralising effect upon those who went to the House moved by idealism and political enthusiasm. But I do not believe the adoption of Jowett's resolution will make much difference. The merits of a question are not confined to the particular question itself. There are certain issues which the Labour Party considers of greater importance than any possible consequences of voting for the government —Women's Suffrage is one—but are we to disregard consequences on every paltry issue? This policy would necessitate repeated General Elections and nothing is more irritating to the public than such contests.... Politics means compromise."

When a vote was taken, 73 voted for the resolution and 195 *against*.

The opportunists carried the day. That is not surprising in an opportunist party like the British I.L.P. But it is now a fully established fact that opportunism is giving rise to an opposition in the ranks of this very Party.

The opponents of opportunism acted far more correctly than their like-minded colleagues in Germany frequently do when they defend rotten compromises with the opportunists. The fact that they came out openly with their resolution gave rise to an extremely important debate on principles, and this debate will have a very strong effect on the British working class. Liberal labour policy persists owing to tradition, routine and the agility of opportunist leaders. But its bankruptcy among the mass of the proletariat is inevitable.

Written in October 1912
  First published in
Prosveshcheniye No. 4,
    April 1913
    Signed: *W.*

Published according
to the magazine text

A CADET PROFESSOR

Professor Tugan-Baranovsky, a candidate of the Cadet Party, is one of those Russian economists who were near-Marxists in their youth but later quickly "grew wiser", "corrected" Marx with shreds of bourgeois theories, and by their great services as renegades secured university chairs from which to bamboozle students in erudite fashion.

A few days ago Mr. Tugan, who has developed from a Marxist into a liberal, dished up in the newspaper *Rech* the following argument concerning the burning issue of the high cost of living:

"In my [?] view, the main [aha!] reason for the increased cost of living is perfectly clear. It is due to the enormous growth of the population, chiefly in the towns. The increased population necessitates a change to the use of more intensive cultivation methods, which, *in accordance with the well-known law of declining productivity* of agricultural labour, leads to a higher labour cost per unit of product."

Mr. Tugan likes to shout "I" and "my". But in fact he merely repeats shreds of bourgeois doctrines refuted long ago by Marx.

The "well-known law of declining productivity" is a bit of old bourgeois rubbish, which ignoramuses and the hired scholars of the bourgeoisie use *to justify capitalism*. Marx long ago disproved this "law", which puts the blame on *nature* (as if to say, productivity of labour is dropping, and there's nothing to be done about it!), whereas in fact the blame lies with the *capitalist social* system.

The "law of declining productivity of agricultural labour" is a bourgeois lie. The law of the growth of *rent*, i.e., of the income of the *owners* of land, under capitalism is a reality.

One reason for the high cost of living is land monopoly, i.e., the fact that land is held as private property. The landowners are therefore taking an ever greater contribution from *growing* productivity of labour. Only the organisation of the workers to defend their interests, only the abolition of the capitalist mode of production, can put an end to the high cost of living.

None but hangers-on of the bourgeoisie, such as the Cadet Mr. Tugan, are capable of trying to defend the fable about the "law" of declining productivity of agricultural labour.

Pravda No. 147, October 19, 1912
Signed: *V. I.*

Published according to the *Pravda* text

A NEW CHAPTER OF WORLD HISTORY

Even the bourgeois press throughout Europe, which for reactionary and selfish reasons defended the notorious *status quo* in the Balkans, is now unanimous in acknowledging that a new chapter of world history has begun.

The defeat of Turkey is beyond question. The victories won by the Balkan states united in a quadruple alliance (Serbia, Bulgaria, Montenegro and Greece) are tremendous. The alliance of these four states is a fact. "The Balkans for the Balkan peoples" is something that has *already* been achieved.

What, then, is the significance of the new chapter of world history?

In Eastern Europe (Austria, the Balkans, Russia), the powerful survivals of medievalism, which terribly hamper social development and the growth of the proletariat, have not yet been abolished. These survivals are absolutism (unlimited autocratic power), feudalism (landlordism and feudal privileges) and the suppression of nationalities.

The class-conscious workers of the Balkan countries are the first to put forward the slogan of a consistently democratic solution of the national problem in the Balkans. That slogan calls for a Balkan federal republic. The weakness of the democratic classes in the present-day Balkan states (where the proletariat is small in number and the peasants are downtrodden, disunited and illiterate) has resulted in an economically and politically indispensable alliance becoming an alliance of Balkan monarchies.

The national question in the Balkans has taken a big stride towards its settlement. Of all the states of Eastern Europe, *Russia alone* remains the most backward today.

Although the alliance which has come into being in the Balkans is an alliance of monarchies and not of republics, and although this alliance has come about through war and not through revolution, a great step has nevertheless been taken towards doing away with the survivals of medievalism throughout Eastern Europe. And you are rejoicing prematurely, nationalist gentlemen! That step is *against* you, for there are *more* survivals of medievalism in Russia *than anywhere else*!

As for Western Europe, the proletariat there is still more vigorously proclaiming the slogan: No intervention! The Balkans for the Balkan peoples!

Pravda No 149, October 21, 1912

Published according to the *Pravda* text

CADETS AND NATIONALISTS

When we pointed out that the Cadets were essentially national-liberals in their outlook and that their approach to the national question was *anything but democratic*, we got an angry and haughty retort from *Rech*, which accused us of not knowing the facts or misrepresenting them.

Here is a record —one of many. Let the readers and voters judge for themselves.

On October 18 a "circle of persons interested in the Slav question" held a second meeting at Mr. M.M. Kovalevsky's. An appeal to society was read, signed by Y. Anichkov. Kareyev, L. Panteleyev (Cadet ex-candidate), G. Falbork. Mr. Kovalevsky (of course) and others.

Will *Rech* try to dodge responsibility for Kareyev, Panteleyev and Co.?

The gist of the liberals' appeal to society is that

"amidst general enthusiasm, the hearts of the Russians... are beating in sympathy for the Slavs and with the hope that Russian national consciousness will help to ensure that they retain the fruits of their victories".

In what way does this differ from the nationalism and chauvinism of *Novoye Vremya* and Co.? Only in that it has white gloves on and that the turns of speech used in it are more diplomatically cautious. But chauvinism is abominable even when wearing white gloves and using the most refined turns of speech.

Democrats will never speak of "general enthusiasm" when beside (and above!) them are Russian nationalists ruthlessly oppressing a number of peoples.

Democrats will never stand for the Slav as such being contrasted with the Turk, whereas one should contrast the

Slav and Turkish peasants, *together*, with the Slav and Turkish landlords and bashi-bazouks.

Democrats will never allow "Russian national conscious-ness" to be substituted for the *political consciousness* of the partisans of freedom and enemies of oppression in *all* na-tionalities—at a time when Poles, Jews, and "non-Rus-sians" in general are oppressed and persecuted.

No fair-minded democrat, no sincere supporter of the oppressed nationalities, should vote for the Cadets!

Pravda No. 151, October 24, 1912
Signed: *V. I.*

Published according
to the *Pravda* text

THE HORRORS OF WAR

The belligerents are doing their utmost to conceal from "outsiders", i.e., from the whole world, what is going on in the Balkans. Correspondents are deceived and held up, and are not allowed on the battlefield until long after battles have come to an end.

That is why only exceptional circumstances enable one at rare intervals to learn the truth about the war. Apparently, such exceptional circumstances helped Mr. Donohoe, a correspondent of the British *Daily Chronicle*. He succeeded in being with the Turkish Army during the battle at Lule Burgaz; then he drove by car to Constantinople, and from there went by sea to Constanta in Rumania. From Constanta he was able to wire London without hindrance.

The Turks suffered a terrible defeat. Up to 40,000 (!) of them fell in battle. A catastrophe not less than that at Mukden,[146] wrote the British correspondent. Three-quarters of the Turkish artillery passed into Bulgarian hands. The Bulgarians would let the Turks come up very close and engage in a hand-to-hand combat, and then would swiftly withdraw while their *machine-guns* mowed the Turks down in hundreds and thousands.

The Turks' retreat became a disorderly flight of stupefied, starving, exhausted and maddened mobs. The correspondent's car got stuck in a crowd of fugitives. The starving Turks begged him for bread. They had to bandage their own wounds. Doctors were few. There were no dressings and no supplies. I have witnessed many a military campaign, wrote the correspondent, but I could never have imagined so appalling a disaster, such a wholesale massacre of starving, exhausted, tormented, helpless peasants from Anatolia (Asiatic Turkey).

Pravda No. 155, October 28, 1912
Signed: *V. Fr.*

Published according
to the *Pravda* text

THE CADETS AND THE BIG BOURGEOISIE

The Cadet victories in the first city curias of Moscow and St. Petersburg, then in the elections to the Council of State from the industries, and lastly, the *reactionaries'* aid to the Cadets against the Social-Democrats—a fact established beyond question—are all signs of a very interesting political development of *all* the classes of our society.

Let us recall the Social-Democrats' main decision on the nature of the Cadet Party, adopted in 1907: "The parties of the liberal-monarchist bourgeoisie, and the most important of them—the Cadet Party—have already turned definitely away from the revolution and aim at stopping it through a deal with the counter-revolution; the social basis of these parties is made up of the economically more progressive sections of the bourgeoisie, above all the bourgeois intelligentsia, while a section of the urban and rural petty bourgeoisie is still following these parties only by force of tradition [blind habit] and because it is simply deceived by the liberals."

The correctness of this description has been fully borne out by events. The democrats are ousting the Cadets from the second city curia (where there are *many* democratic voters). The Cadets are ousting the Octobrists from the first urban curia.

The more the reaction rages and the more openly the elections are rigged, the more big capital goes over to the side of liberalism. The class nature of the Cadet Party, indicated by the Marxists in 1906 and 1907, is now *being revealed* clearly before the masses.

The error of those who considered the Cadets a party of urban *democrats* is becoming obvious. The alliance of the Cadets and the reactionaries is gradually turning from a secret into an *open* one: it is the reactionaries who are voting the Cadet Mansyrev in against the Social-Democrat Priedkalns, and the Cadet Nikolayev against the Social-Democrat Pokrovsky.

The strength of Social-Democratic policy, the invincibility of this policy, is due to the fact that the *entire* development of capitalist society is increasingly proving it correct. The Cadets are rallying to the big bourgeoisie, which *cannot* be content for all that it is counter-revolutionary. The democrats are moving to the *left*, away from the Cadets.

Pravda No. 157, November 1, 1912   Published according to the *Pravda* text

TRULY RUSSIAN MORALS

A few days ago the newspaper *Zemshchina* carried, along with verses by Purishkevich, a little article concerning the "famous" official publicist Guryev of *Rossiya* (who from now on will be famous without inverted commas). *Zemshchina* assures its readers that he is a "publicist of a Jewish-liberal shade". How strange! Is it possible that the official *Rossiya*, too, is a Jewish-liberal organ?

But what is the point? It is that Guryev has been unanimously expelled from the board of a St. Petersburg spinning mill by the general meeting of its shareholders. In addition, the meeting resolved to request the procurator to start proceedings against Guryev for his irregular practices.

It appears that Guryev contributed 1,000 rubles and acquired the right to *one-third* of the profits, although two co-owners of the mill had contributed 100,000 rubles! Why this generous treatment of Guryev by the capitalists?

Because that gentleman is a councillor of state, a contributor to the official newspaper *Rossiya*, and so on and so forth. He was Witte's private secretary. He has "exceptional connections". He promised *government subsidies*!

And so, the capitalist gentlemen "valued" those government "connections" fairly highly: 49,000 rubles exactly. You have the goods, we have the money. You have "connections in government quarters", an opportunity of obtaining subsidies, we have money. Sale and purchase. "Connections in government quarters", so-and-so many thousands; a promise of subsidies, so-and-so much; contributions to the official *Rossiya*, so-and-so much. Collect your money, Mr. Guryev!

Guryev collected it —and fooled them. He did not keep his promises but claimed over one-third of the profits and, what is more, resorted to blackmail, i.e., to extorting money under threat of undermining the credit of the establishment.

A characteristic affair. A typical affair. An everyday occurrence. An illustration to the theme, "Government connections and subsidies, and their relation to capital".

Only, where does the "Jewish-liberal shade" come in, gentlemen of *Zemshchina*? It is a truly Russian, truly conservative shade! Don't be so modest, friends of Purishkevich!

Pravda No. 160, November 4, 1912
Signed: *T.*

Published according
to the *Pravda* text

THE PLATFORM OF THE REFORMISTS
AND THE PLATFORM OF THE REVOLUTIONARY
SOCIAL-DEMOCRATS

The revolutionary upswing in Russia made itself clearly felt in the first half of 1912. The number of political strikers, as calculated by the factory owners, reached 515,000 for five months. A particularly important document, reprinted in full in No. 27 of the Central Organ, namely, the May Day appeal of the St. Petersburg workers, provides evidence as to the nature of the strikers' slogans, their demands, the political content of their demonstrations, meetings, etc.

The slogans with which the St. Petersburg workers came forward in those memorable days were not reformist but revolutionary Social-Democratic slogans: a constituent assembly, an eight-hour working day, confiscation of the landed estates, the overthrow of the tsarist government, and a democratic republic.

The revolts and attempted revolts of soldiers and sailors—in Turkestan, in the Baltic Fleet and on the Black Sea—supplied fresh *objective* evidence that after long years of rampant counter-revolution and of a lull in the working-class movement, a new revolutionary upswing had begun.

This upswing coincided with the period of the elections to the Fourth Duma, when all parties and all political trends *had* to present, in one form or another, their *general* appraisal of the political situation. Now, if we want to analyse our political tasks seriously, as the tasks of the working class and not the pious wishes of little groups, and if we want to test programmes and platforms in a Marxist way by comparing them with the facts of the mass struggle and with the actions of *all* the classes of this society, we must also test the various election platforms on the touchstone of *this revolutionary upswing* of the masses. For, as far as the Social-Democrats are concerned, elections are not a special political operation, not an attempt to win seats through all sorts of promises and declarations, but merely a special occasion for advocating the basic demands and the principles of the political world outlook of the class-conscious proletariat.

The programmes and platforms of all the government parties, from the Black Hundreds to Guchkov, leave no room for doubt. They are plainly and openly counter-revolutionary. It is common knowledge that these parties lack a foothold of any real importance not only among the working class and the peasantry, but *even* among wide sections of the bourgeoisie. These sections have almost completely turned away from the Octobrists.

The programmes and platforms of the liberal bourgeois parties have been published in part almost officially (the platform of the Moslem group) and are partly known quite accurately through the "big" political press (the platforms of the "Progressists" and of the Cadets). The *essence* of all these programmes and platforms has been inimitably expressed in the declarations of the garrulous Cadet, Gredeskul, which were reprinted in *Rech* and from there found their way into the Marxist press.

"A public *denial of the need* for a new revolution in Russia" is how Gredeskul himself formulated his views (cf. *Sotsial-Demokrat* No. 27, p. 3). It was he, too, who contrasted the *real* platform of the liberals (with the Cadets at their head) with that of the revolutionaries, saying that "what we need is *merely* quiet, persevering and confident *constitutional* work".

We stress the words "real platform", for in Russia, as in all bourgeois countries, most platforms are mere *window dressing*.

The crux of the matter is what was admitted (in a rare fit of truthfulness) by Mr. Gredeskul. The liberal monarchist bourgeoisie is *opposed* to a new revolution and advocates *only* constitutional reforms.

The Social-Democrats consistently, and the bourgeois democrats (Narodniks) hesitantly, uphold the "need" for a new revolution, and are carrying on propaganda in favour of such a revolution. The upswing of the *mass* struggle *has begun*. The revolutionary Social-Democrats are trying to extend and strengthen it, helping it develop to a still higher plane, to the stage of *revolution*. The reformists, however, regard the upswing as a mere "revival"; their policy is a policy aimed at obtaining constitutional concessions, constitutional reforms. It follows that the bourgeoisie and proletariat have entered, at this "stage" of Russian history as well, into a struggle for influence over the "people", over the masses. No one can foretell the outcome of this struggle, but neither can anyone entertain any doubts as to the position which the R.S.D.L.P. must occupy in *this* struggle.

It is in this way, and only in this way, that one can start to appraise the election platform of the *Party* and the election platform issued the other day by the "Organising Committee" elected by the liquidationist conference.

The election platform of the Party, published by the Central Committee after the January Conference, was drafted *before* the events of April and May. These events *proved* it correct. A single theme runs through the whole platform — criticism of constitutional reforms in *present-day* Russia as hopeless and utopian, and the propaganda of revolution. The slogans of the platform have been framed *precisely* in such a way as to express the revolutionary tasks with perfect clarity and make it absolutely impossible to mistake them for promises of constitutional reforms. The platform of the Party represents a direct *appeal* of the revolutionary Social-Democrats to *hundreds of thousands* of political strikers, to those who are in the front ranks of the millions of the muzhik armed forces, to whom it *explains* the tasks of an uprising. A revolutionary party could not even dream of a better test for its platform, of a better confirmation of it by experience, than this direct response to the explanations of the Party—the May strikes and the attempted military revolts in June and July.

Look at the platform of the liquidators. Its liquidationist essence is artfully concealed by Trotsky's revolutionary phrases. This camouflage may sometimes blind naïve and altogether inexperienced people, and may even appear to be "reconciliation" between the liquidators and the Party. But the most cursory examination will rapidly dissipate this self-deception.

The platform of the liquidators was written *after* the May strikes and the attempted revolts in the summer. And in seeking a real practical answer to the question of the essence of this platform, the first thing we ask is: *how* does it appraise those strikes and those attempts?

"The economic upswing...", "...by the growth of its strike movement, the proletariat has signalled the coming new social upswing...", "...the powerful April movement of the proletariat demanding freedom of association"—that is *all* the liquidators' platform says about the April and May strikes.

But this is indeed an untruth! It is a crying distortion of the issue! The *main* thing is omitted here, namely, the *revolutionary* character of the political strike, which is not aimed at winning a constitutional reform, but at *overthrowing* the government, i.e., at revolution.

How could such an untruth come to be written in an illegal, revolutionary leaflet full of "red" phrases? It *had* to be, because *such* is the *view* of the liberals and the liquidators. They see in strikes what they wish to see—a struggle for constitutional reforms. They do not see what they do not wish to see, namely, a revolutionary upswing. We liberals want to fight for reform, but not for revolution— there you have the *truth* of the class position that found expression in the *untruth* of the liquidators.

With regard to the attempted revolts we read, "...the soldiers in the barracks are driven by violence, humiliation and starvation to *outbursts of desperate protest*, then they are suppressed with bullets, the rope", etc.

This is a liberal appraisal. We revolutionary Social-Democrats regard the attempted revolts as the *beginning of an uprising of the masses*, even if an unsuccessful, untimely, incorrect beginning. And we know that the *masses learn* how to make a successful uprising only from the experience of unsuccessful ones, just as the Russian workers, by a series of unsuccessful, and sometimes particularly unsuccessful, political strikes in 1901-04 learned to organise the successful strike of October 1905. We say that the workers and peasants who are most downtrodden by the barracks *have begun* to rise in revolt. Hence the plain and obvious conclusion: we must *explain* to them how and for what purpose they should prepare for a *successful* uprising.

The liberals take a different view. The soldiers *are* "driven" to "outbursts of *desperate* protest", they say. To a liberal, an insurgent soldier is not the subject of the revolution, not the forerunner of the masses rising in revolt, but an *object* of governmental evil ("driven to desperation"), serving to demonstrate that evil.

See how bad our government is—it *drives* the soldiers to *desperation* and then suppresses them with bullets, says the liberal (the inference being: if we liberals were in power, there would be no soldiers' mutinies).

See how deeply and widely revolutionary energy is maturing among the masses—says the Social-Democrat—even the soldiers and sailors who are downtrodden by barrack drill are beginning to rise in revolt, and by rising badly they teach how to rise successfully.

As you see, the liquidators have *"interpreted"* (in the senatorial sense of the word interpret) the revolutionary upsurge in Russia during the spring and the summer.

After which they "interpreted" the programme of our Party.

The Programme of the R.S.D.L.P. says:

"The R.S.D.L.P. sets itself the *immediate* political task of overthrowing the tsarist autocracy and replacing it by a democratic republic, whose constitution *would ensure*: (1) the sovereignty of the people" ... etc., and then comes a list of "liberties" and "rights".

One would think that this could not be misunderstood; the "immediate" task is the overthrow of the autocracy and its replacement by a republic, which would *ensure* liberties.

The liquidators have revised all this.

In their platform we read: "The Social-Democrats call on the people to fight for a democratic republic....

"Striving for this aim, which the people will be able to *achieve only as a result of revolution*, the Social-Democrats *in the present election campaign* [listen to this!] call on the working masses to rally to the following *current* demands: (1) universal, etc., suffrage ... *in the elections to the Duma*", etc.

Mr. Peshekhonov, a Socialist-Revolutionary liquidator, wrote in the autumn of 1906, when he was founding an "open party" (and almost succeeded in founding it, but the police stepped in and put him in quod!), that the republic was a *"remote* prospect", that "the question of a republic requires extreme caution", that the *immediate* demands now were reforms.

But the Socialist-Revolutionary liquidator was naïve, simple, clumsy and blunt. Do the "European" opportunists ever act in that way? No. They are more cunning, more clever, more diplomatic.

They do not renounce the slogan of a republic—what a libel! They only "interpret" it in a suitable fashion, being prompted by considerations obvious to every philistine. It is a moot point whether there will be a revolution or not, says the man in the street simply, and Trotsky repeats it in a scholarly fashion in *Nasha Zarya* (No. 5, p. 21). A republic *"only* as a result of revolution", but the *"current"* issue "in the present election campaign" is constitutional reforms!

Everything went off so smoothly: the republic is both recognised and relegated to the distant future. Heaps of r-r-revolutionary words were spoken, but in reality the demands put forward "in the present election campaign" (the whole platform is written only for this *present campaign!*) as "current" are those for reforms.

Yes, it was certainly great "masters of diplomacy" who were present at the liquidators' conference. But what puny masters they are! While they may delight the group diplomatists and mislead the simple-minded "conciliators" the Marxists will talk to them in a different strain.

The philistine is satisfied with the undoubted, holy and *empty* truth that it is impossible to say in advance whether there will be a revolution or not. A Marxist is not satisfied with that; he says: our propaganda and the propaganda of all worker Social-Democrats is *one of the factors determining* whether there will be a revolution or not. Hundreds of thousands of political strikers and the foremost men of various units of the armed forces ask us, our Party, what they should strive for, for the sake of what they should rise, what they should try to achieve, whether they should expand the upsurge that has begun into a revolution, or whether they should direct it towards a struggle for reforms.

The revolutionary Social-Democrats have given their answer to these questions, which are more interesting and important than the philistine-Trotskyist attitude of uncertainty: will there be a revolution or not, who can tell?

Our answer is—criticism of the utopia of constitutional reforms, explanation of the futility of the hopes placed in them, the utmost all-round promotion of the *revolutionary* upsurge, utilisation of the election campaign *for this purpose*. Whether or not there will be a revolution does *not* depend on us *alone*. But we shall do *our* work, and this work will never be in vain. It will sow the seeds of democracy and proletarian independence deep among the masses, and these seeds will *certainly* sprout and produce either a democratic revolution tomorrow, or a socialist revolution the day after.

Those, however, who preach to the *masses* their vulgar, intellectualist, Bundist-Trotskyist scepticism —"we don't know whether there will be a revolution or not, but the '*current*' issue is reforms"—are *already* corrupting the masses, preaching liberal utopias to them.

Instead of *permeating* the election campaign with the spirit of the present, real, "*actual*" political situation, in which half a million workers are engaged in revolutionary strikes, and the foremost men in the muzhik armed forces are firing on their aristocrat officers—instead of this they *dismiss* from their would-be "European" (they are so European, so European, are our liquidators!) "parliamentary" considerations this real situation (in which there is very little of the "European", but very much of the "Chinese", *that is to say*, of the democratic-revolutionary), and having dismissed it by means of a few non-committal phrases, they declare the reformist election campaign to be the *real* thing.

The Social-Democratic Party needs a platform for the elections to the Fourth Duma in order once more to explain to the masses—in connection with the elections, on the occasion of the elections, *and* in debates on the elections — *the need for, and the urgency and inevitability of*, the revolution.

They, the liquidators, need a platform "*for*" the elections, i.e., a platform enabling them politely to dismiss considerations about a revolution as an uncertain eventuality and to declare the election campaign for a list of constitutional reforms to be the "real" thing.

The Social-Democratic Party wants to use the elections in order again to drive home to the masses the idea of the need for revolution, and the fact of the revolutionary upswing which has begun. That is why the Social-Democratic Party, in its platform, says briefly and plainly to those voting in the elections *to the Fourth Duma*: *not* constitutional reforms, but a republic, *not* reformism, but revolution.

The liquidators are using the elections to the Fourth Duma to preach constitutional reforms and *weaken* the idea of revolution. It is *for* this purpose and because of this that they depict soldiers' revolts as "outbursts of desperate protest" to which soldiers are "driven", and not as the *beginning* of a mass uprising which will grow or subside according, among other things, to whether or not *all* the Social-Democratic workers of Russia at once begin to support it with all their might, with all their energy, with all their enthusiasm.

It is for this purpose that the May strikes have been "interpreted" from being revolutionary into being reformist.

It is for this purpose that the Party programme has been "interpreted", and instead of the "immediate" task of establishing a republic that will *ensure* liberties, it has been decreed to regard as *current* in the "present election campaign"—for the Fourth Duma, don't laugh!—the demand for various liberties.

How much that is old Chinese there is in Russian life! What an amount of old Chinese practices there is in our tsarism, and also in our liquidators, who wish to fit the "ceremonials" of parliamentary struggle and reformism into a setting which has the Purishkeviches and Treshchenkovs on top and revolutionary attempts of the masses below! How much that is old Chinese there is in these vain efforts of intellectuals to defend themselves against the Khvostovs and Makarovs by producing a letter of recommendation from MacDonald and Jaurès, from Bissolati and Bernstein, from Kolb and Frank!

The diplomatic "reconciliation" of liquidationist views with those of the Party that was staged by Trotsky at the liquidationist conference does not in reality "reconcile" anything at all. It does not remove the greatest political fact, which determines the entire social and political situation in present-day Russia. That fact is the struggle between the reformist and the revolutionary Social-Democratic platforms; it is the pronouncement of the bourgeoisie, as represented by its liberal party leaders, against the need for a new revolution in Russia and in favour of purely constitutional "work", in opposition to the revolutionary strike of hundreds of thousands of proletarians, which is a call to the masses to begin a real struggle for freedom.

To make one bow to the reformists and another to the revolutionary Social-Democrats does not do away with this objective political fact, does not weaken its force and weight in the slightest degree. Good intentions to smooth over differences arising from this fact —even assuming that these intentions are indeed perfectly "good" and sincere —are powerless to alter the irreconcilably hostile political tendencies arising from the entire counter-revolutionary situation.

The proletariat has risen with its revolutionary Social-Democratic banner, and on the eve of the Fourth, Black-Hundred, Duma, it will not lower it before the liberals, will not furl it to please the reformists, will not consent to blunt or tone down its platform for reasons of group diplomacy.

The platform of revolutionary Social-Democracy versus the platform of reformism—this was the watchword under which the May strikes took place. Under it, too, the R.S.D.L.P. is entering the elections to a landlord and priest Duma, and under it the Party will carry on its entire work in that Duma and among the masses.

Sotsial-Demokrat No. 28-29, November 5 (18), 1912

Published according to the text in *Sotsial-Demokrat*

THE ILLEGAL PARTY AND LEGAL WORK

The question of the illegal party and of legal work of the Social-Democrats in Russia is one of the cardinal Party questions. It has been the concern of the R.S.D.L.P. *throughout* the post-revolutionary period, and has given rise to the bitterest struggle within its ranks.

The struggle over this issue has been going on chiefly between the liquidators and the anti-liquidators, and its bitterness is due in full measure to the fact that it *amounted* to the question whether our old, illegal Party was to be or not to be. The Conference of the R.S.D.L.P. in December 1908 emphatically condemned liquidationism and, in a special resolution, clearly formulated the Party's view on the organisational question: the Party is made up of illegal Social-Democratic nuclei, which must establish for themselves "strong-points for work among the masses" in the form of as wide and as ramified a network of various legal workers' societies as possible.

Both the decision of the Plenary Meeting of the Central Committee in January 1910 and the All-Russia Conference in January 1912 fully confirmed this view of the Party. The thoroughly definite and stable character of this view is perhaps most clearly described in Comrade Plekhanov's latest *Dnevnik* (No. 16, April 1912). We say "most clearly" because it was Plekhanov who at that time took a neutral stand (on the significance of the January Conference). And from his neutral standpoint, he fully confirmed this established Party view, saying that the so-called "initiating groups"—which had broken away from the Party organisation or had deserted it or arisen independently of it—could

not be considered as belonging to the Party without a special decision taken by a congress or conference of the illegal
nuclei. It is anarchism in regard to principle, and support for and legitimation of liquidationism in regard to
practice, wrote Comrade Plekhanov, to allow the "initiating groups" to decide *for themselves* whether they belong
to the Party.

It would seem that, in view of this last explanation by
the neutral Plekhanov, the question which has been quite
definitely decided by the Party on so many occasions should
be regarded as finished with. But the resolution of the latest liquidationist conference makes us return to it in view
of the fresh attempts to tangle what had been untangled
and to obscure things that are clear. *Nevsky Golos* (No. 9),
along with the most furious abuse of the anti-liquidators,
declared that the new conference was not liquidationist.
Yet the conference resolution on one of the most important
issues, that of the illegal Party and legal work, shows most
plainly that the conference was liquidationist through and
through.

It is necessary, therefore, to analyse the resolution in
detail and to quote it in full for this purpose.

I

The resolution of the liquidators' conference is headed
"Organisational *Forms* of Party *Building*", yet its very first
clause reveals that it is not a question of "forms" of building, but of the *kind* of party—old or new—that they want
to "build" in this case. Here is that first clause:

"This Conference, having discussed the forms and methods of
building the Party, has reached the following conclusion:
"1. The transformation of the Social-Democratic Party into a
self-governing organisation of the Social-Democratic proletariat can
be effected only insofar as the Social-Democratic organisation takes
shape in the course of drawing the mass of the workers into open
social and political activities in all their manifestations."

Thus the very first word used in the resolution on *building* the Party is an unqualified recognition of the neces-

sity for a *transformation* of the Social-Democratic Party.
This is strange, to say the least. To be sure, every member of
the Party has a right to seek its "transformation", but then
the question has *admittedly* been, for four years already,
whether the *old* Party should be recognised! Anyone knows
that!

The Party resolution (December 1908) spoke in the clearest possible terms of condemning the liquidators, who
wanted to *"replace"* the old Party by a new one. In April
1912 Plekhanov asked point-blank the defenders of the
"initiating groups" which planned to (and did) call a liquidationist conference: "Does our old Party exist or not?"
(*Dnevnik Sotsial-Demokrata* No. 16, April 1912, p. 8).

This question cannot be evaded. It is posed by a four
years' struggle. It fully expresses the gravity of the so-
called Party "crisis".

When a question *such as this* is answered by saying:
"the *transformation* of the Social-Democratic Party ... can
be effected only —", we see at once that it is a meaningless evasion and not an answer.

None but members of the *old* Party may speak of transforming the *Party*. *By evading* the question whether there
is an old Party or not, and decreeing without further ado
(with *non*-Party "initiating groups" co-operating) what you
call a "transformation", you do no more, gentlemen, than
fully confirm that your standpoint is liquidationist! This
becomes still more evident when the resolution, after the
perfectly meaningless, declamatory phrase about a "self-
governing organisation of the Social-Democratic proletariat", reduces the issue to the proposition that the "transformation" *"can* be effected *only* insofar as the Social-
Democratic organisation takes shape [we will not dwell on
the ridiculous, inflated and stupid phraseology used] in
the course of drawing the mass of the workers into *open
social and political* activities"!!

What does that mean? Do the authors of this amazing
resolution call strikes and demonstrations "drawing the
masses into open", etc., activities? Logic suggests that
they *do*! In that case the resolution is sheer nonsense, for
anyone knows very well that an "organisation *takes shape*"
even without strikes and demonstrations. The organisation,

wise gentlemen, is always there, while the masses resort to *open* action only from time to time.

By "open social and political activities" (the bureaucrat-ic-liberal style those people use—just like that of *Russkiye Vedomosti* thirty years ago!) the liquidators mean the *legal* forms of the working-class movement, and not at all strikes, demonstrations and so on. Splendid. In that case, too, the resolution is nonsense, because it is by no means "only" in the course of drawing the masses into the legal movement that in our country the organisation "takes shape", and has taken shape. We *have* organisations in many places where *no* forms of legal movement are allowed.

Thus the main clause of the resolution (the organisation takes shape *"only insofar"*) is definitely worthless. It is nothing but a muddle.

But there is an obvious liquidationist *content* to this muddle. A transformation is possible *only* in the course of draw-ing the masses into the *legal* movement—that is what the gibberish of Clause 1 boils down to. And this *is* the sheerest liquidationism.

For four years the Party has been saying: our organisa-tion consists of illegal nuclei surrounded by as wide and as ramified a network of legal societies as possible.

For four years the liquidators have been denying that they are liquidators, and for four years they have been asserting: a transformation *can be effected only* in the course of drawing the masses into the legal movement. They evade the question of what our Party *consists* of and *what* this *old* Party *is like*, doing it in exactly the way that suits the legalists. It is very much the same old story; in April 1912 Plekhanov asked: does our old Party exist or not? The liquidators' conference replies: "a transformation can be effected *only insofar as* the masses are drawn into the legal movement"!

This reply comes from the legalists, who have broken away from the Party and who yesterday were strong and goaded the Party, but today (having been defeated) are timid and defend themselves by eloquence.

II

Clause 2 of the resolution reads:

"2. In view of the changed social and political conditions compared with the pre-revolutionary epoch, the illegal Party organisations already existing or coming into existence must adapt themselves to the new forms and methods of the open working-class movement."

Fine logic again. A *change* in social conditions necessitates only a *change* in the form of organisation, but the resolution in no way substantiates the *direction* of this change.

Why does the resolution refer to "the changed social and political conditions"? Evidently to prove, substantiate and draw the practical conclusion: it is necessary for the illegal organisation to adapt itself to the legal movement. But the premise does not warrant this conclusion. "In view of the changed conditions", the legal must adapt itself to the illegal—such a conclusion would be just as legitimate!

Why this confusion of the liquidators?

Because they are afraid to tell the truth and want to sit on two stools at once.

The truth is that the liquidators stand for a *liquidationist* appraisal (made by Levitsky, Larin, Yezhov and others) of the "present situation", for explaining *how* "social and political conditions have changed" *is* an appraisal of the present situation.

But they are afraid to state that appraisal in plain terms. Indeed, the conference could not bring itself even to raise this question. Tacitly, stealthily, in a smuggling fashion, it upholds the view that there have come about (*some kind of*) changes which necessitate "adapting" the illegal to the legal.

This is a view which in no way differs from the Cadet view, as the Social-Democratic Party press has repeatedly pointed out. The Cadets fully admit that their party "as a whole is compelled to remain illegal" (see Clause 3 of the liquidators' resolution) and that, in view of changed conditions, the illegal party must adapt itself to the legal movement. As far as the Cadets are concerned, this is enough. To them prohibition of their party, its illegality, is an accident, an "abnormality", a survival whereas the main, essential and basic thing is their legal work. This view of theirs follows *logically* from the "appraisal of the situation" formulated by Mr. Gredeskul: what is needed is not a new revolution, but only "constitutional work".

The illegality of the Cadet Party is an accident; it is an exception from the general rule of "constitutional work". Hence the logical conclusion that the illegal organisation must "adapt itself to the legal movement". And that is how matters actually stand with the Cadets.

But the Social-Democratic Party takes a different view. The main conclusion to be drawn from our appraisal —the Party appraisal —of the situation is that *the revolution is necessary and is coming*. The *forms* of the development leading to the revolution have changed, but the *old tasks* of the revolution remain. Hence the conclusion: the forms of organisation must change, the forms of the "nuclei" must be flexible, their expansion will often occur through the expansion, not of the nuclei themselves, but of their legal "periphery", etc. All this has been stated many times in Party resolutions.

But this change in the *forms* of the illegal organisation is not at all covered by the formula: "adaptation" to the legal movement. It is something entirely different! Legal organisations are *strong-points* for propagating the ideas of *illegal nuclei* among the masses. In other words, we change the form of exerting influence to ensure that former influence continues along *illegal* lines.

In terms of the *form* of the organisations, the illegal "adapts itself" to the legal. But in terms of the *content* of the work of our Party, legal activity *"adapts itself"* to illegal ideas. (Hence —it may be said in passing —the war which "revolutionary Menshevism" has been waging against the liquidators.)

Now judge how profound our liquidators must be to have accepted the *first* premise (on the form of the work) and forgotten the second (on the *content* of the work)!! And they have headed their piece of Cadet wisdom by an argument about the organisational forms of Party *building* that runs as follows:

"We must build the Party in such a way as to reorganise [it] by drawing the masses into the legal movement and to adapt the illegal organisation to that movement."

The question arises: does this look like the answer of the Party? (To build the Party means strengthening and increasing the number of illegal nuclei, surrounding them by a network of legal strong-points.)

Or does it look like legalising a loophole for the liquidators, since it repeats the ideas of the Cadets and the Popular Socialists? It was *precisely* these ideas that Mr. Peshekhonov, a Popular Socialist, was defending in August 1906, when he tried to found an "open party"—see *Russkoye Bogatstvo*, 1906, No. 8, and *Proletary* No. 4, the article "Socialist-Revolutionary Mensheviks".*

III

Clause 3 of the resolution reads:

"3. The Social-Democratic Party even at the present time, when its organisation as a whole is forced to remain illegal, must endeavour to carry on various parts of its Party work openly and to establish appropriate bodies for this purpose."

We have already pointed out that this is a literally exact description of the *Cadet* Party, correct from the first to the last word. But the term "Social-Democratic" is out of place here.

It is true that the Cadet Party "as a whole" is "forced" to remain illegal, and that "even" at the present time (when we have a constitution, thank God) they endeavour to carry on parts of their party work openly.

The implicit premise which shows through every line of this liquidationist resolution is its recognition of "constitutional work" as the sole work or, at the least, as the chief, fundamental and lasting work.

That is radically wrong. It is precisely a liberal labour policy outlook.

The Social-Democratic Party is illegal both "as a whole" and in its every nucleus, and —*most important of all*—in the entire content of its work, which is to propagate and

---

* See present edition, Vol. 11, pp. 197-206.—*Ed.*

pave the way for the revolution. Therefore the *most* open work of the most open nucleus of the Social-Democratic Party can*not* be regarded as "openly conducted Party work".

For example, the most "open" nucleus of the R.S.D.L.P. in 1907-12 was the Social-Democratic Duma group. It was in a position to speak more "openly" than anyone else. It *alone* was legal, and could speak legally *of a great many things.*

But not of everything! And not only, generally speaking, "not of everything", but not, in particular, even of its own Party and its Party work — "not of everything" nor of the most important thing. That is why, *even* in respect of the Social-Democratic Duma group, we cannot accept Clause 3 of the liquidationist resolution, not to speak of the remaining "various parts" of the Party.

The liquidators advocate an "open", legal party. They are now afraid (the workers have made them afraid, and Trotsky advises them to be afraid) to say so plainly. They now say the *same* thing *using little disguises.* They say nothing about legalising the Party. But they advocate its legalisation *by parts!*

The "initiating groups" of the legalists who have broken away are anti-Party, the neutral Plekhanov told the liquidators in April 1912. The "initiating groups" of the breakaway legalists are precisely the open conduct of various parts of "Party work", the liquidationist conference replies; they are precisely the "open movement" *to which* the illegal Party must "adapt" itself; they are the "open activities", the "drawing" of the masses into which is the yardstick and guarantee of the necessary "transformation" of the Party.

What simpletons the liquidators must have found if their story is true that these views were approved by the "anti-liquidators" brought by Trotsky!

IV

The last clause of the resolution reads:

"4. Being unable, on account of the illegal conditions of its existence, to draw into its sphere large sections of the workers to whom its influence extends, the Social-Democratic organisation must link itself with the politically active sections of the proletariat and through them with the masses, by establishing various kinds of more or less developed legal or illegal political organisations and various kinds of legal cover (election committees, political societies founded under the law of March 4, municipal companies, societies for combating the high cost of living, and so on), as well as by co-ordinating its actions with non-political working-class organisations."

Here, too, indisputable arguments about legal covers *disguise* what is not merely disputable but downright liquidationist.

Establishing *legal political organisations* is precisely what Levitsky and N. R—kov advocated; it is legalisation of the Party part by part.

For more than a year we have been telling the liquidators: stop talking and start founding your "legal *political* societies", such as the "society for the defence of working-class interests", and so on. Stop phrase-mongering and get down to work!

But they cannot get down to work because it is impossible to realise a liberal utopia in *present-day* Russia. All they can do is to *defend* in this covert fashion their "initiating groups", which are engaged in useful talk and mutual encouragement, in suggestions and considerations about "legal political organisations".

They defend their "initiating groups", officially declaring in their resolution that the illegal organisations *must* "link themselves with the *politically-active sections of the proletariat* and through them with the masses"!!! That is to say, it is *outside* the nuclei that the "politically-active" are to be found! Is this not a mere rewording of the well-known phrases and exclamations to the effect that all the active *have fled* from the "dead Party" into the "initiating groups"?

Trotsky and the liquidators expelled from the Party are putting more "mildly" what *Nasha Zarya* and *Dyelo Zhizni*[147] said plainly in *reviling* the illegal Party: in their view, it is outside the narrow illegal Party that the most *"active"* are, and it is with these that one must "link oneself". We—the liquidators who have broken away—are the active element; through us the "Party" must link itself with the masses.

The Party has said in no uncertain terms: in leading the economic struggle, the Social-Democratic Party nuclei must co-operate with the trade unions, with the Social-Democratic nuclei in them, and with individual leaders of the trade union movement. Or, in the Duma election campaign, it is essential that the unions should march abreast of the Party. This is clear, precise and easy to understand. What the liquidators are advocating *instead* is a hazy "co-ordination" of the Party's work in general with the "non-political", i.e., non-Party, unions.

P.B. Axelrod supplied Trotsky with liquidationist ideas. Trotsky advised Axelrod after the latter's sad reverses in *Nasha Zarya*, to cover up those ideas with phrases that would muddle them up.

Nobody will be deceived by this company. The liquidationist conference will teach the workers to look more closely into the meaning of evasive phraseology. That conference has nothing to give the workers apart from this lesson, which is bitter and uninteresting but not useless in bourgeois society.

We have studied the ideas of liberal labour policy attired in Levitsky's everyday clothes; it is not difficult to recognise them in Trotsky's gaudy apparel as well.

The Party's views on the illegal organisation and its legal work stand out more and more impressively when compared with all that hypocritical masquerading.

Sotsial-Demokrat No. 28-29,
November 5 (18), 1912

Published according
to the text in *Sotsial-Demokrat*

THE SOCIAL SIGNIFICANCE
OF THE SERBO-BULGARIAN VICTORIES

"Macedonia's conquest by Bulgaria and Serbia means for her a bourgeois revolution, a kind of 1789 or 1848." These words of Otto Bauer, the Austrian Marxist, reveal at a stroke the meaning of the events now taking place in the Balkans.

The revolution of 1789 in France and that of 1848 in Germany and other countries were bourgeois revolutions, because the liberation of the country from absolutism and from landlord, feudal privileges in fact provided freedom for the development of capitalism. But it goes without saying that such revolutions were most urgently required by the interests of the working class; in 1789 and 1848 even "non-Party" workers, who were not organised as a class, were leading fighters of the French and German revolutions.

Macedonia, like the other Balkan countries, is economically very backward. She still retains exceedingly strong survivals of the feudal system and of medieval dependence of the peasants on their feudal landlords. Among those survivals are quit-rent (in money or kind), share-cropping (the Macedonian peasant usually gives the landlord one-third of the harvest, that is, less than the Russian peasant does), and so on.

The landlords in Macedonia (known as *spahijas*) are Turks and Mohammedans, while the peasants are Slavs and Christians. The class antagonism is therefore aggravated by a religious and national antagonism.

Thus, the victories gained by the Serbians and Bulgarians denote the undermining of feudal rule in Macedonia, the formation of a more or less free class of peasant land-owners, and a guarantee for the entire social development of the Balkan countries, which has been checked by absolutism and feudal relations.

Bourgeois newspapers, from *Novoye Vremya* to *Rech*, are talking of *national* liberation in the Balkans, leaving out *economic* liberation. Yet in reality it is the latter that is the chief thing.

Given complete liberation from the landlords and from absolutism, national liberation and complete freedom of self-determination of the peoples would be an inevitable result. On the other hand, if the tyranny of the landlords and the Balkan monarchies over the peoples remains, national oppression, too, is bound to persist in some measure or another.

If the liberation of Macedonia had been accomplished through a revolution, that is, through the Serbian and Bulgarian and also the *Turkish* peasants fighting against the landlords of *all* nationalities (and against the landlord governments in the. Balkans), liberation would probably have cost the Balkan peoples a hundred times less in human lives than the present war. Liberation would have been achieved at an infinitely lower price and would have been infinitely more complete.

One may ask what are the historical causes of the issue being settled by war and not by revolution. The main historical cause is the weakness, disunity, immaturity and ignorance of the peasant masses in all the Balkan countries, as well as the small number of the workers who had a clear understanding of the state of affairs and demanded a Balkan federal (union) republic.

This brings out the radical difference between the European bourgeoisie and the European workers in their attitude to the Balkan problem. The bourgeoisie, even the liberal bourgeoisie, similar to our Cadets, shouts about the "national" liberation of the "Slavs". Thereby it plainly misrepresents the meaning and historic significance of the events now taking place in the Balkans, and thus *hampers* the real liberation of the Balkan peoples. It thus *contributes* to the preservation of landlord privileges, political tyranny and national oppression in some measure or another.

On the other hand, the worker democrats are the only ones to champion the real and complete liberation of the Balkan peoples. Nothing but economic and political liberation of the *peasants* of all the Balkan nationalities, carried through to the end, can eliminate all possibility of any sort of national oppression.

Pravda No. 162, November 7, 1912
Signed: *T.*

Published according
to the *Pravda* text

REGENERATED CHINA

Progressive and civilised Europe shows no interest in the regeneration of China. Four hundred million backward Asians have attained freedom, and have awakened to political life. *One quarter* of the world's population has passed, so to say, from torpor to enlightenment, movement and struggle.

But civilised Europe does not care. To this day even the French Republic has not officially recognised the Republic of China! A question on this subject is to be asked shortly in the French Chamber of Deputies.

Why this indifference on the part of Europe? The explanation is that throughout the West power is in the hands of the imperialist bourgeoisie, which is already three-quarters decayed and willing to sell all its "civilisation" to any adventurer for "stringent" measures against the workers, or for an extra five kopeks' profit on the ruble. To this bourgeoisie, China is *only* booty, and now that Russia has taken Mongolia into her "tender embrace", the Japanese, British, Germans, etc., will probably try to tear off a piece of this booty.

But China's regeneration is making speed nevertheless. Parliamentary elections are about to be held—the *first* in what was a despotic state. The Lower House will have 600 members and the "Senate", 274.

Suffrage is *neither* universal *nor* direct. It is granted only to persons above the age of 21 who have resided in the constituency for at least two years and who pay direct taxes amounting to about two rubles, or own property worth about 500 rubles. They will first vote for electors, who will elect the members of parliament.

This kind of suffrage indicates in itself that there is an alliance of the well-to-do peasantry and the bourgeoisie, there being no proletariat at all or one that is completely powerless.

The same circumstance is evident from the nature of China's political parties. There are three main parties:

(1) The Radical-Socialist Party, which in fact has *nothing at all* to do with socialism, any more than our own Popular Socialists (and nine-tenths of the Socialist-Revolutionaries). It is a party of petty-bourgeois *democrats*, and its chief demands are political unity of China, development of trade and industry "along social lines" (just as hazy a phrase as the "labour principle" and "equalisation" of our Narodniks and Socialist-Revolutionaries), and preservation of peace.

(2) The second party is that of the liberals. They are in alliance with the Radical-Socialists and together with them constitute the *National Party*. This party will in all likelihood win a majority in China's first parliament. Its leader is the well-known Dr. Sun Yat-sen. He is now drawing up a plan for a vast railway network (Russian Narodniks will please note that Sun Yat-sen is doing this *in order that* China may "avoid" a capitalist fate!).

(3) The third party calls itself the Republican League, an example of how deceptive political signboards can be. Actually it is a *conservative* party, backed chiefly by government officials, landlords and the bourgeoisie of *northern* China, which is the most backward part of the country. The National Party, on the other hand, is predominantly a party of the more industrially-developed and progressive *southern* part of the country.

The peasant masses are the mainstay of the National Party. Its leaders are intellectuals who have been educated abroad.

China's freedom was won by an alliance of peasant democrats and the liberal bourgeoisie. Whether the peasants, who are not led by a proletarian party, will be able to retain their democratic positions *against* the liberals, who are only waiting for an opportunity to shift to the right, will be seen in the near future.

Pravda No. 163, November 18, 1912
Signed: *T*.

Published according to the *Pravda* text

THE RESULTS AND SIGNIFICANCE
OF THE U.S. PRESIDENTIAL ELECTIONS

Wilson, a "Democrat", has been elected President of the United States of America. He has polled over six million votes, Roosevelt (the new National Progressive Party) over four million, Taft (Republican Party) over three million, and the Socialist Eugene Debs 800,000 votes.

The world significance of the U.S. elections lies not so much in the great increase in the number of Socialist votes as in the far-reaching *crisis* of the *bourgeois* parties, in the amazing force with which their decay has been revealed. Lastly, the significance of the elections lies in the unusually clear and striking revelation of *bourgeois reformism* as a means of combating socialism.

In *all* bourgeois countries, the parties which stand for capitalism, i.e., the bourgeois parties, came into being a long time ago, and the greater the extent of political liberty, the more solid they are.

Freedom in the U.S.A. is most complete. And for a whole *half-century* —since the Civil War over slavery in 1860-65 — *two* bourgeois parties have been distinguished there by remarkable solidity and strength. The party of the former slave-owners is the so-called Democratic Party. The capitalist party, which favoured the emancipation of the Negroes, has developed into the Republican Party.

Since the emancipation of the Negroes, the distinction between the two parties has been diminishing. The fight between these two parties has been mainly over the height of customs duties. Their fight *has not had* any *serious* importance for the mass of the people. The people have been deceived and diverted from their vital interests by means of spectacular and meaningless *duels* between the two bourgeois parties.

This so-called bipartisan system prevailing in America and Britain has been one of the most powerful means of preventing the rise of an independent working-class, i.e., genuinely socialist, party.

And now the bipartisan system has suffered a fiasco in America, the country boasting the most advanced capitalism! What caused this fiasco?

The strength of the working-class movement, the growth of socialism.

The old bourgeois parties (the "Democratic" and the "Republican" parties) have been facing towards the past, the period of the emancipation of the Negroes. The new bourgeois party, the National Progressive Party, is facing towards the *future*. Its programme turns entirely on the question whether capitalism is to be or not to be, on the issues, to be specific, of protection for the workers and of "trusts", as the capitalist associations are called in the U.S.A.

The old parties are products of an epoch whose task was to develop capitalism as speedily as possible. The struggle between the parties was over the question *how* best to expedite and facilitate this development.

The new party is a product of the present epoch, which raises the issue of the very existence of capitalism. In the U.S.A., the freest and most advanced country, this issue is coming to the fore more clearly and broadly than anywhere else.

The entire programme and entire agitation of Roosevelt and the Progressives turn on how to *save capitalism* by means of *bourgeois reforms*.

The bourgeois reformism which in old Europe manifests itself in the chatter of liberal professors has all at once come forward in the free American republic as a party four million strong. This is American style.

We shall save capitalism by reforms, says that party. We shall grant the most progressive factory legislation. We shall establish state control over *all* the trusts (in the U.S.A. that means over *all* industries!). We shall establish state control over them to eliminate poverty and enable everybody to earn a "decent" wage. We shall establish "social and industrial justice". We revere *all* reforms —*the only "reform"* we don't want is *expropriation of the capitalists!*

The national wealth of the U.S.A. is now reckoned to be 120 billion (thousand million) dollars, i.e., about 240 billion rubles. Approximately *one-third* of it, or about 80 billion rubles, belongs to *two* trusts, those of Rockefeller and Morgan, or is subordinated to these trusts! Not more than 40,000 families making up these two trusts are the masters of 80 million wage slaves.

Obviously, so long as these modern slave-owners are there, all "reforms" will be nothing but a deception. Roosevelt has been *deliberately* hired by the astute multimillionaires to preach this deception. The "state control" they promise will become —if the capitalists keep their capital —a means of combating and crushing strikes.

But the American proletarian has already awakened and has taken up his post. He greets Roosevelt's success with cheerful irony, as if to say: You lured four million people with your promises of reform, dear impostor Roosevelt. Very well! Tomorrow those four million will see that your promises were a fraud, and don't forget that they are following you *only* because they feel that it is *impossible* to go on living in the old way.

Pravda No. 164, November 9, 1912
Signed: *V. I.*

Published according
to the *Pravda* text

THE "VEXED QUESTIONS" OF OUR PARTY

THE "LIQUIDATIONIST" AND "NATIONAL" QUESTIONS

In August 1912 the Executive Committee of the Social-Democracy of Poland and Lithuania convened a "territorial conference"[148] of the Polish Social-Democrats. It will be recalled that at present the Executive of the Polish Social-Democracy is an executive *without* a party. In Warsaw, the Polish capital, the local Social-Democratic organisation emphatically condemned the disorganising policy of the Executive, which replied by resorting to vile anonymous accusations of provocation, set up a fictitious Warsaw organisation and hastened to convene a suitably rigged territorial conference "of its own".

Subsequent elections to the Duma by the Warsaw worker curia fully revealed the spurious character of the supporters of the Executive: among the 66 delegates there were 34 Social-Democrats, including only 3 (doubtful) supporters of the Executive.

This introductory remark is necessary for the reader to regard the resolution of the territorial conference of the S.D.P. and L. that we are going to discuss *only* as a resolution of the *Tyszka* Executive, and under no circumstances as a decision of the Polish worker Social-Democrats.

I

The question of the Polish Social-Democrats' attitude towards the R.S.D.L.P. is an unusually important and burning one. Therefore the *decision* adopted by the Tyszka conference on this question, however hard it may be to take it *seriously*, deserves closer study.

It is hard to take seriously the Tyszka resolution, which is full of abuse, if only because of its attitude to the *fundamental* question, that of liquidationism.

This has been a fundamental question in the R.S.D.L.P. during 1908-1912. The Party has been terribly broken up by the counter-revolution. It is making every effort to re-establish its organisation. And *throughout the four years* of counter-revolution, it has been waging a *continuous* struggle against the little groups of Social-Democrats who want to liquidate the Party.

Does it not follow clearly from this that one who has not settled the issue of liquidationism explicitly *has no right* to call himself a Party member?

The Tyszka conference, too, in its resolution on the attitude to the R.S.D.L.P. allotted more space to liquidationism than to anything else. The conference admitted that liquidationism was "a most serious obstacle to the development of the R.S.D.L.P. and a grave danger to its very existence".

"Overt and consistent liquidationism and revolutionary Social-Democracy are mutually exclusive," said the resolution.

As you see, Tyszka and Co. tackled the problem with a bold and firm hand —and dodged solving it!

Who are, then, the "overt and consistent" liquidators? And what is the practical conclusion that follows from the *experience of four years of struggle* against liquidationism?

These natural and necessary questions were answered in clear, precise and convincing terms by the January 1912 Conference of the R.S.D.L.P., which said that the liquidators were the group associated with the publications *Nasha Zarya* and *Zhivoye Dyelo*. This group had placed itself outside the Party.

One may consider this answer right or wrong, but one cannot deny that it is quite clear, one cannot evade making a clear statement of one's attitude!

But the Tyszka conference sought precisely to evade the issue, twist and turn like a petty thief. If it is not true that *Nasha Zarya* represents open and consistent liquidators, as we said clearly in January 1912, then why did Tyszka and Co. not disclose our error to the Polish worker Social-Democrats in August 1912? If it is not true that *Nasha Zarya* has placed itself *outside* the Party, and if you, Messrs. Tyszka, Rosa Luxemburg and Warski, consider it *to be in the Party*, why did not you say so plainly? It was your direct duty to the Polish worker Social-Democrats!

And however much you may abuse and curse and revile "Lenin's" conference in January 1912, the racket you are raising will not enable you to deceive anyone but people who want to be deceived. For, after the January Conference, one cannot be a politically-conscious and honest Social-Democrat, nor speak of the state of affairs in the R.S.D.L.P., without giving a clear and explicit answer to the question: is *Nasha Zarya* liquidationist or not, and does it belong in or outside the Party?

II

The spate of varied and wordy abuse which the Tyszka conference slung at the "Leninists" boils down to one thing —an accusation of *splitting* the Party.

The January Conference of the R.S.D.L.P. considered only the *Nasha Zarya* group to be outside the Party. This is a fact known to all. From this fact even Tyszka and his friends could have drawn the simple and obvious conclusion that the accusation of splitting the Party means regarding the *Nasha Zarya* group as a *Party* group.

Even a child would see that this conclusion is inevitable. And Tyszka and Co. are long past childhood years.

Anyone who accuses us of splitting the Party should have sufficient elementary courage and elementary honesty to say plainly: "The *Nasha Zarya* group is not liquidationist", "it *ought not* to be outside the Party, but belongs *inside* the Party", "it is a *legitimate shade of opinion* in the Party", and so on.

This is the heart of the matter, that the gentlemen who accuse us of splitting the Party, such as Tyszka, say this *in undertones*, shyly, in a roundabout way (for this *naturally* follows from the howls about a split) but they are *afraid* to say it plainly!

It is not easy to say and *prove* that *Nasha Zarya* ought to be in the Party. Anyone who says so assumes a certain responsibility, decides a certain question of principle, and plainly *defends* the chief liquidators. One may (and should) regard such a person as a supporter of the liquidators, but one must admit that he has his convictions and it cannot be denied that he is politically honest, if only within the limits of the narrow question whether or not a definite group of liquidators should be in the Party.

But when an entire organisation, if one may call it that, or a sum total of the organisations of a whole territory, dodgingly and stealthily, shamefacedly and without speaking straight out, defends the liquidators and accuses those who have expelled the liquidators from the Party of causing a split, but does not dare to say plainly, "This group of liquidators ought to be in the Party", the conclusion inevitably suggests itself that what we have before us is not an organisation of Social-Democrats who share such-and-such views, but a *circle of plotters* who want to make political capital out of "utilising" the struggle between the liquidators and the anti-liquidators.

To those who are familiar with the internal affairs of the R.S.D.L.P. since 1907, it has long been an open secret that Tyszka and Co., like the Bundists who preceded them, are specimens of this type of intriguer, "Marxists by weight", or "Tushino turncoats",[149] as Social-Democrats call such people. Tyszka, like some of the Bundists, bases his entire "stand" in the Party on a *game* between the liquidators and the anti-liquidators, on mediation, on profiting from being the extra "weight in the scales", without which neither the liquidators nor the anti-liquidators can have a majority!

In the autumn of 1911, when this old "game" of Tyszka's, of which everyone had grown tired, resulted in his collapse, he was openly called a plotter by the press of *both* opposed trends—the liquidators and the anti-liquidators.

Indeed, place yourself in the position of an extra "weight in the scales", and then the illogical, childishly naïve, ludicrously feeble and helpless resolutions of the Tyszka conference will at once become *perfectly* intelligible to you. This is just the way a plotter should speak: I condemn liquidationism—but I don't say plainly who are the overt and consistent liquidators! I admit that liquidationism endangers the very existence of the Party—but I don't say plainly whether or not such-and-such a group ought to be in the Party! I can *always*, under all circumstances, derive an advantage from a "position" such as this, can make "political capital" out of it, for *without me* the anti-liquidator cannot defeat the liquidator, *without me* the liquidator cannot have an assured place in the Party!!

"Tyszka" politics are not an accidental or isolated phenomenon. When there is a split and, in general, when there is a bitter struggle between trends, it is *inevitable* that groups should appear which base their existence on a continuous darting from one side to the other, and on petty intrigue. This is a sad and unpleasant feature of the life of our Party, a feature accentuated by the conditions of revolutionary work in exile. Groups of intriguers, and features of intrigue in the policy of certain groups, particularly those lacking strong ties with Russia, are phenomena one has to be aware of if one does not want to be fooled and to fall victim to various "misunderstandings".

III

The slogan of "unity" is "popular", of course, among wide sections of the workers, who do not know *with whom* that unity should be established, *what concessions* to a particular group that *unity* implies, and *on what basis* the policy of including the liquidators in the Party or expelling them from it is shaped.

To be sure, nothing could be easier than demagogically taking advantage of this *incomprehension* of the essence of the matter to howl about a "split". Nothing could be easier than disguising diplomacy by a demand for the "unity" of trends that have irrevocably drifted apart.

But however "popular" the slogan of "unity" among politically-ignorant people, and however convenient it is now for various demagogues, intriguers and group diplomats to hide behind it, we shall never stop demanding from every politically-conscious Social-Democrat a clear and explicit answer to the question decided by the January 1912 Conference of the R.S.D.L.P.

The conference which the liquidators convened in August 1912 showed clearly that all the controversies turn on the question of liquidationism, on whether the liquidators' groups are pro-Party or non-Party (or even anti-Party). Whoever evades this cardinal issue mystifies himself and others.

As a matter of fact, talk about the "factionalism" of the January Conference, and so on, is just such an *evasion* of the cardinal issue. All right, gentlemen, we might answer the talkers, let us assume that the January Conference was arch-factionalist and disruptive, that it was not duly authorised, and so on. But are you not using these "terrible words" merely *to clear yourselves in your own eyes*? A section of the Social-Democrats —it makes no difference which —declared in January that *Nasha Zarya* consisted of anti-Party liquidators who were outside the Party. That opinion is substantiated in a resolution —a detailed, well-grounded resolution prompted by four years of Party history.

Anyone who sincerely wishes to explain and refute the error of these, let us say, "January" Social-Democrats must analyse and refute this resolution. He must say and prove that *Nasha Zarya* should be in the Party, that its ideas are not ruinous to the Party, that such-and-such concessions should be made to that group, that such-and-such obligations should be demanded of it, that the guarantees of the fulfilment of these obligations should consist in this or that, and that the extent of the influence of the group within the Party should be established in such-and-such a way.

To put the question *in this way* would mean conscientiously and honestly refuting the convictions of the January Social-Democrats, would mean *explaining* to the workers what you think wrong. But the point is that *not one* of those who now engage in cheap clamour about a split has taken a single step towards putting the question in this way!!

That is why, contemptuously brushing aside the demagogues and intriguers, we calmly repeat: our resolution expelling the liquidators has not been refuted and is irrefutable. New facts, such as the publication of the liquidationist *Luch*,[150] which has made Trotsky's phrase-mongering its own, merely increase the force of our resolution a hundred-fold. The facts—the May Day action, the rallying of hundreds of workers' groups around the anti-liquidationist newspaper, the elections to the Fourth Duma by the worker curia—are *conclusive* proof of the correctness of our stand against the liquidators.

No amount of howling about a "split" can shake this conviction, because this howling is a cowardly, covert, hypocritical *defence* of the liquidators.

IV

The January 1912 Conference of the R.S.D.L.P. posed yet another serious question of principle, that of the *structure* of our Party with regard to nationalities. For lack of space, I shall only briefly touch on this question.

Complete or incomplete federation, "federation of the worst type" or complete unity? That is the question.

The Tyszka conference replies to this problem, too, with nothing but abuse and shouts about "fraud", "distortion of the facts", and so on. What senseless shouters they are, this Tyszka and his retinue!

The complete separateness of the Lettish, Polish and Jewish (Bund) Social-Democrats is a fact. Every Polish Social-Democrat knows that there is *not*, and has never been, *anything* like unity with the Bund in Poland. The same is true of the Russians and the Bund, etc. The non-Russians have their own special organisations, their central bodies, congresses, etc. The Russians lack *these things*, and *their* Central Committee cannot decide Russian questions without the participation of the Bundists, Poles and Letts who are fighting one another and who are unfamiliar with Russian matters.

This is a fact, one that no amount of abuse can suppress. *Everyone* in our Party has seen it since 1907. Everyone has sensed the falsity of this situation. That is why our Conference dubbed it *"a federation of the worst type"*.*

---

* See present edition, Vol. 17, pp. 464-65.—*Ed.*

All honest and sincere Social-Democrats must give a pertinent answer to this presentation of the question.

The correctness of this presentation of the question was *borne out* most convincingly by the August conference, which, as *even* Plekhanov admits, "adapted socialism to nationalism" by its notorious resolution on "national cultural" autonomy.

The Bund and Tyszka's Executive are alike in swearing by all the saints that they stand for unity, while in Warsaw, Lodz and elsewhere there is a *complete split between them*!!

The connection between the "liquidationist question" and the "national question" is not an invention of ours but has been revealed by the realities of life.

Let, then, all serious-minded Social-Democrats raise and discuss the "national question" as well. Federation or unity? Federation for the "nationalities", with separate centres and *without* a separate centre for the Russians, or complete unity? Nominal unity with a virtual split (or secession) of the Bund's local organisations, or real unity from top to bottom?

Anyone who thinks he can get away from these questions is sorely mistaken. Anyone who counts on a simple restoration of the "federation of the worst type" of 1907-11, *mystifies himself and others*. It is already *impossible* to restore that federation. That misbegotten child will never rise from the dead. The Party has moved away from it for good.

Where has it moved to? Towards an "Austrian" federation?[151] Or towards a *complete* renunciation of federation, to actual unity? We are for the latter. We are opposed to "adapting socialism to nationalism".

Let everyone give full thought to this question and finally decide it.

Written in November 1912

First published in *Pismo Dyskusyjne* (*Discussion Sheet*) No. 1, August 1913 Signed: *N. Lenin*

Published according to the text in *Pismo Dyskusyjne* Translated from the Polish

CONCERNING CERTAIN SPEECHES
BY WORKERS' DEPUTIES[152]

What are the basic ideas that should underlie the *first* speech of a workers' spokesman in the Duma?

Naturally, the workers will look forward to the *first* speech with particular eagerness and particular attention. Naturally, it is in the first speech that they expect to find the important and fundamental thing, a concise exposition of the view taken on issues that are of especial concern to everyone and come particularly into the forefront in the country's policies in general and in the practice of the working-class movement (both political *and economic*) in particular.

Among these issues are the following:

(1) *Continuity* of the activity of the Social-Democratic group in the Fourth Duma. Continuity implies the preservation of an *inseparable connection* with the former Social-Democratic groups of all the former Dumas, it being particularly necessary to stress the connection with the Social-Democratic group in the Second Duma—in view of the well-known attack which the counter-revolution made upon it.

It is important to lay stress on continuity, for, unlike the bourgeois parties, the worker democrats see something *integral* and *common* in *their* work in the First, Second, Third and Fourth Dumas, and will not let themselves be distracted by any turn in events (or by any development like the coup d'état of June 3) from fulfilling their tasks, from pursuing their invariable aims.

(2) The second thesis which should go into the first speech of a workers' deputy is socialism. Strictly speaking, it

consists of two subjects. One is the fact that Russia's Social-Democratic Party is a contingent of the international army of the socialist proletariat. That, in fact, is exactly what Pokrovsky said in the Third Duma (see his declaration in the verbatim reports, p. 328 of the official publication, Seventh Sitting, November 16, 1907). It is, of course, absolutely indispensable to make this point.

But there is another point which is highly important in our day. It is a reference to the *present* situation and the tasks of socialism *throughout* the world. What are the characteristics of this situation? (a) An extreme aggravation of the struggle between the working class and the bourgeoisie (high cost of living, mass strikes, the *imperialism* of the Powers, their fierce competition over markets and their nearness to war), and (b) the nearness of the realisation of socialism. The working class of the world is fighting not for recognition of its right to have a socialist party, but *for power*, and for the organisation of society along new lines. It is highly important to say so from the Duma platform, to tell the workers of Russia about the beginning of the great battles for socialism in Europe and America, about the *nearness* of the triumph (inevitable triumph) of socialism in the civilised world.

(3) The third thesis concerns the Balkan war and Russia's international position and foreign policy.

It is impossible to omit this subject, which is the most topical. It may be subdivided into the following questions:

(a) The Balkan war. The slogan of a Balkan federal republic should also be proclaimed by the Russian workers' deputy. Against Slav-Turkish enmity. *For* freedom and equal rights for *all* the peoples of the Balkans.

(b) Against the interference of other Powers in the Balkan war. It is absolutely necessary to side with the demonstration for peace which took place in Basle, at the International Socialist Congress.[153] War against war! Against all interference! For peace! Such are the slogans of the workers.

(c) Against the foreign policy of the Russian Government in general, with particular mention of the "lust" to seize (and of the seizure already begun) the Bosphorus, Turkish Armenia, Persia, Mongolia.

First page of Lenin's manuscript "Concerning Certain Speeches by Workers' Deputies". November 1912

Reduced

(d) Against the nationalism of the government, with reference to the oppressed nationalities: Finland, Poland, the Ukraine, the Jews, etc. It is highly important to put forward in precise terms the slogan of the *political self-determination* of all nationalities, in contrast to all hedging (such as *only* "equality").

(e) Against liberal nationalism, which is not so crude but is particularly harmful because of its hypocrisy and its "refined" deception of the people. What are the signs of this liberal (Progressist-*Cadet*) nationalism? Chauvinist speeches about the tasks of the "Slavs", speeches about the tasks of Russia as a "Great Power", speeches about Russia reaching an agreement with Britain and France so as to be able to *plunder* other countries.

(4) The fourth thesis is the political position of Russia. The essential thing here is to describe the existing tyranny and lack of rights, and reveal the *compelling* necessity of political liberty.

Special note should be made here of:

(a) The necessity of mentioning the prisons—Kutomara, Algachi, etc.[154]

(b) A reference to the rigging of elections, Bonapartist methods, the fact that the government is no longer trusted even by those classes (the landlords and the bourgeoisie) on which the coup d'état of June 3 counted.

The priests were made to vote against their conscience.

The Duma has moved to the right, while the country has moved to the left.

(c) It is particularly important to state correctly the relationship between the notorious liquidationist slogan of "freedom of association" and the objectives of *political liberty* in general. It is highly important to point out that freedom of the press, association, assembly and strikes is *absolutely* indispensable to the workers, but that it is *precisely* in order to bring it about that we must realise the *inseparable connection* between it and the general foundations of political liberty, a *radical* change in the entire political system. Not the liberal utopia of freedom of association *under* the June Third regime, but a struggle *for* freedom in general, and for freedom of association in particular, *against this regime* all along the line, against the *foundations* of this regime.

(5) Fifth thesis: the intolerable plight of the peasantry. The starvation of 30 million peasants in 1911. The ruin and impoverishment of the countryside. The government "land distribution system" only makes things *worse*. Financial prosperity is so much tinsel, a pretence of prosperity achieved by extorting dues and befuddling the people with drink. Even the modest land Bill of the **Right-wing** peasants (the "forty-three peasants") submitted to the Third Duma[155] has been shelved. The peasants need deliverance from the oppression of the landlords and of landlordism.

(6) Sixth thesis: three camps in the elections to the Fourth Duma, and three camps in the country:

(a) The government camp. It is impotent. Rigs elections.

(b) The liberal camp. It is highly important to point out, if only very briefly, the counter-revolutionary nature of the liberals, who are *against* a new revolution. One may quote word for word Gredeskul's statement which *Pravda* reprinted in its issue No. 85 (August 8).* "No second popular movement [in other words, no second revolution] was needed but merely quiet, persevering and confident constitutional work". These were Gredeskul's exact words, and *Rech* published them.

Liberal hopes of constitutional *reform with the foundations* of the present system retained, and *without* a broad movement of the people, are *utopia*.

(c) The third camp, the democrats. It is led by the working class. One may say, speaking of the past in the third person, what was said *even* by *Golos Moskvy*, namely, that the working class advanced *three* slogans during the elections: (1) a democratic republic; (2) an eight-hour working day; (3) confiscation of all the landed estates in favour of the peasantry.

(7) Seventh thesis: a reference to the political movement and strikes in 1912.

(a) It is highly important to point out that the number of *political* strikers rose to a million. Resurgence of the entire emancipation movement.

---

* See pp. 254-55 of this volume.—*Ed.*

(b) It is highly important to stress that the workers by their political strikes set themselves objectives affecting *the whole people*, that they did not raise particular problems but problems affecting *the whole people*.

(c) It is necessary to point out that it is the *connection* between political and economic strikes that lends strength and vitality to the movement.

(d) Mention the workers' protest against the execution of sailors.

(8) The eighth thesis, an important one following from the whole of the foregoing and closely linked with it, is the hegemony of the proletariat, its guiding role, its role as leader. It leads the whole people, the entire democratic movement. It demands freedom and leads into the battle for freedom. It sets an example, provides a model. It raises morale. It arouses a new mood.

(9) The ninth and final thesis: recapitulation and summary. It should be said, speaking of the class-conscious workers in the third person, that they are "unshakably loyal" to *three* principles: first, socialism; second, "the principles of the old, battle-tested Russian Social-Democratic Labour Party"—the workers are loyal to it. This *fact* should be conveyed; third, the workers are loyal to "their republican convictions". It is not a question of an appeal or slogan, but of loyalty to one's convictions. (There exist legal republican parties in a number of monarchies — Britain, Sweden, Italy, Belgium and other countries.)

———

P.S. The question may also arise of the need to put forward *separately* "freedom of association". It should be borne in mind that the liquidators advocate under this flag the liberal demand for a constitutional reform *while* keeping intact the *foundations* of the June Third —*

Written in November 1912

First published in Lenin's *Collected Works*, Second and Third editions, Vol. XVI, 1930

Published according to the manuscript

———

* The manuscript breaks off at this point.—*Ed.*

CONCERNING THE WORKERS' DEPUTIES
TO THE DUMA AND THEIR DECLARATION[156]

The Social-Democratic group, speaking from the platform of the Fourth Duma, declares that there is an inseparable continuity between its activity and that of the Social-Democratic groups in the previous Dumas, particularly the one in the Second Duma, a group against which the counter-revolutionaries committed an act of unprecedented political vengeance. The Russian Social-Democratic Party is a contingent of the great international liberation army of the socialist proletariat. This army is now growing rapidly throughout the world. The universal high cost of living, the oppression of capital grouped in associations, cartels, trusts and syndicates, and the imperialist policies of the Powers make the condition of the working masses intolerable and aggravate the struggle between capital and labour. The time is fast approaching when an end will be put to capitalism, when millions of united proletarians will establish a social system in which there will be no poverty of the masses, nor exploitation of man by man.

The Social-Democratic group joins its voice to that of the workers of all countries, who at the International Congress in Basle expressed an emphatic protest against war. The workers demand peace. They protest against all interference in Balkan affairs. Only complete freedom and independence of the Balkan peoples, and only a federal Balkan republic are capable of providing the best way out of the present crisis and a real solution to the national question through the recognition of complete equality and an absolute right to political self-determination for all nationalities without exception.

The Social-Democratic group in the Fourth Duma protests above all against the foreign policy of the Russian Government. It condemns the hidden intention to enlarge our state by seizing foreign territories on the Bosphorus, in Turkish Armenia, in Persia and China, and condemns the seizure of Mongolia, which disrupts good relations with the great, fraternal Chinese Republic.

All chauvinism and nationalism will find an implacable enemy in the Social-Democratic group—whether the crude, brutal nationalism of the government which crushes and strangles Finland, Poland, the Ukraine, the Jews and the other non-Great-Russian nationalities, or the hypocritically disguised, refined nationalism of the liberals and Cadets, who are willing to talk about the tasks of Russia as a Great Power and about an agreement between her and other Powers with the aim of plundering foreign lands.

The ruling classes resort to noisy nationalist speeches in a vain effort to divert the attention of the people from the intolerable domestic position of Russia. The unheard-of rigging of the Fourth Duma elections, which is reminiscent of the Bonapartist methods of that adventurer, Napoleon III, has shown for the hundredth and thousandth time that the government cannot rely for support upon any one class of the population. It cannot even maintain its alliance with the landlords and the big bourgeoisie, for the sake of which the coup d'état of June 3, 1907, was carried out. The Duma has swung to the right while the whole country has moved to the left.

The whole of Russia is suffocating under the yoke of oppression and tyranny. The entire civilised world hears with startled indignation of the tortures and the suffering of political prisoners in the Kutomara, Algachi and other prisons, where the finest people of our country are languishing in torment. Russia needs political liberty as badly as man needs air to breathe. Russia cannot live and develop unless there is freedom of the press, assembly, association and strikes, and, more than to any other class, these liberties are indispensable to the proletariat, which the lack of rights typical of Russian reality binds hand and foot in the fight it must carry on for higher wages, shorter working hours and better living conditions. The oppression of capital, the high cost of living, unemployment in the towns and the impoverishment of the countryside make it all the more necessary for the workers to associate in unions and fight for their right to live, while lack of political liberty keeps the worker in the position of a slave or serf. The workers will stop at no sacrifice in their struggle for freedom, well knowing that only a radical change in all the political conditions of Russian life, only the fullest provision of the foundations and pillars of political liberty, can guarantee the freedom of their struggle against capital.

The elections to the Fourth Duma and the workers' mass political strikes in 1912, which involved up to a million workers, showed that the time is drawing near when the workers will again march at the head of all democrats to win freedom. Three camps tested their strength in the election struggle. The camp of government counter-revolution proved so impotent that it had to rig the elections even under the law of June 3, compelling the downtrodden rural priests to vote against their conscience and convictions. The liberal camp moved still further from the democrats towards the big bourgeoisie. The Cadets demonstrated their counter-revolutionary nature by an alliance with the Black Hundreds against the Social-Democrats in Riga and Yekaterinodar, in Kostroma and the first St. Petersburg curia. The liberal utopia of constitutional reform, with the foundations of the present political system unchanged and without a powerful movement of the people, is more and more losing favour among the democrats. The slogan of the liberals is: "There is no need for a second revolution, what is needed is merely constitutional work." Being fully aware of the spuriousness of this slogan, the working class waged its struggle in the elections, rallying all the democratic forces to itself.

Everyone knows, and even the government press said so, that the working class had three slogans in the election campaign: a democratic republic, an eight-hour working day, and confiscation of all the landed estates in favour of the peasants.

The Social-Democratic proletariat is convinced that these three demands are the necessary culmination of the demands shared by every democrat, such as universal suffrage, freedom of the press, assembly, association and strikes, the election of judges and government officials by the people, abolition of the standing army and introduction of a people's militia, disestablishment of the Church and separation of the school from the Church, etc.

The condition of the peasant masses in Russia is becoming more and more intolerable. The government's so-called "land distribution system" merely worsens the plight of the majority by ruining the countryside, leading to famine such as affected 30 million peasants last year, and bringing no lasting improvement of agriculture in general. The pretence of financial prosperity is kept up by extorting taxes and befuddling the population with drink, while the government delays its bankruptcy by contracting more and more loans. Even the modest land Bill submitted to the Duma by the forty-three Right-wing peasants has been shelved. No wonder the better section of the peasantry is looking more and more to the working class as the only leader of the people in the struggle for freedom. No wonder all democrats regard the political strikes of 1912, which are inseparably linked with the economic movement of the working class, as the dawn of a new life, of a new more powerful emancipation movement.

The Social-Democratic group in the Fourth Duma will champion the interests and needs of this movement. It considers that it has no right to conceal from the majority in the Fourth Duma what all the class-conscious workers of Russia are thinking and feeling. The class-conscious workers remain unshakably loyal to socialism. They remain unshakably loyal to the principles of the old, battle-tested Russian Social-Democratic Labour Party. In the name of these principles, they remain unshakably loyal to their republican convictions.

Written in mid-November 1912

Published for the first time

Published according to
a copy made by N. K. Krupskaya

CONCERNING THE EVENT OF NOVEMBER 15

AN UNDELIVERED SPEECH

On November 15 the Fourth Duma opened. And on November 15 there was a demonstration of workers in St. Petersburg.[157] In view of previous political strikes, and because of them, this demonstration had the importance of a major historical event. The strikes led up to demonstrations. The movement of the masses rose to a higher plane—from strikes of a political nature to street demonstrations. This is a great step forward, which should be stressed, noted and estimated at its true worth by all politically enlightened leaders of the proletariat.

The significance of this step forward is all the greater because it coincided with the opening of the Fourth, landlord, Black-Hundred, June Third Duma. A perfectly timed demonstration! Wonderful proletarian instinct, the ability to counter and contrast the opening of the Black-Hundred "parliament" with red banners in the streets of the capital!

Wonderful proletarian instinct, the ability to counter the sycophantic, slavish, Cadet-Octobrist "demonstration" (over Rodzyanko's wretched phrase-mongering about a "constitution"[158]) inside the Palace by a demonstration of the real kind, a truly popular, truly democratic, purely labour demonstration (the intelligentsia, unfortunately, was absent, if we are to trust the newspapers).

Sycophantic chatter about a "constitution" (or pie in the sky à la Rodzyanko) inside the Black-Hundred Duma, and a specimen of the incipient struggle for freedom and a people's representative assembly (without inverted commas), fór a republic, outside the Duma—this contrast revealed the deep and unerring instinct of the revolutionary masses.

The fact that the liberal and liquidationist *Luch* "warned" against such a demonstration is worthy of traitors to the working-class cause.

But how could the Social-Democratic group "warn"? How could it stoop to the level of Cadets—to a slavish level? How did it happen that individual members of it submitted, and accepted such infamy?

The supposition arises—one that is sometimes put forward "in private"—that perhaps there were fears of a provocation in one of the groups "calling for" the demonstration?

Let us assume for a moment that this supposition *was* made. Does it exonerate the Social-Democratic group? No. Or, to be exact, it justifies the group's move from a *personal* point of view, but not *politically*. It exonerates the Social-Democratic Duma group from the suspicion of betrayal of the workers' cause, but not from the accusation of a political error.

Indeed, what would a *workers'* deputy, a real workers' deputy, have done had he, after three days of news about preparations for a demonstration of this kind, heard on the last day the "rumour" (which might have been provocative *too*): "Is there some provocation here?"

The workers' deputy would have found his way to several influential workers. He would have realised that at *such* a time his place was alongside the prominent workers, that it was a hundred times more important to be there with the workers than at the meetings of the Duma group. He would have learned from the prominent workers, from two or three (or perhaps four or five) *influential* workers of the capital, *how matters stood*, what the workers *thought* about it, and *what the mood* of the masses was.

The workers' deputy would have made inquiries about these things—he would have *known how* to make inquiries about them, and would have learnt that there was to be a strike (15 to 50 *thousand!!* according to the bourgeois press), that there was to be a demonstration, that the workers were not thinking of violence and disorders, and that, *consequently*, the rumour about a provocation was no more than a silly rumour.

The workers' deputy would have found out these things,

and would not have let himself be deceived by the terrified petty liberal intellectuals of the infamous "initiating group".

Rumours of a provocation. All right. But were there no rumours during the Gaponiad? A fine worker or workers' leader one would have been had one been unable to distinguish between the incipient peculiar awakening of the masses during the Gaponiad and the *agent provocateur* Gapon, or the police *agents provocateurs* who urged Gapon on!!

Let us assume that the police and *agents provocateurs* had a hand in the preparations for the demonstration on November 15. Let us (although it has not been proved and is incredible; it is more likely that what was a *provocation* was the *rumours* about a provocation).

But let us assume it was so. What of it? One must not resort to violence when there has been no question of it. One must warn against violence. But to warn against a peaceful strike at a time when the masses are *seething*? To warn against a *demonstration*??

It is a very, very sad mistake the Social-Democratic Duma group as a whole has made. And it would be gratifying to learn that this mistake was not made by all, and that many of those who did make it realise their mistake and will not repeat it.

The movement of the proletariat in Russia (whatever the police tricks anywhere) has risen *to a higher plane*.

Written in the latter half   Published according
   of November 1912   to the manuscript

First published in Lenin's
   Collected Works. Second
and Third editions, Vol. XVI, 1930
   Signed: *A Non-deputy*

A LETTER TO J. V. STALIN[159]

Dear friend, local Polish papers report that Jagiello has been admitted into the group, and has been granted a voice but no vote.[160] If that is true, it is a definite victory for the Party principle. In view of the agitation carried on by *Luch*, it is necessary: (1) To publish an article in *Dyen*[161] (I am sending a draft today), ... in the Collegium[162] (we must by all means teach them —doing so while they are with us here —to respond to everything with resolutions and immediately send copies of them here). Here is a tentative draft of such a resolution: "Having examined all the circumstances of Jagiello's admission into the Social-Democratic group, having studied the articles about it in the Marxist organ, *Pravda*, and in the newspaper of the liquidators, *Luch*, and taken into account So-and-So's report on the debate about it in the Social-Democratic Duma group and on the opinions of the various Social-Democratic organisations of Russia, the Collegium resolves: to recognise that the refusal to admit Jagiello with the right to vote was the only proper way out from the point of view of Party principle, since Jagiello is not a member of the Social-Democratic Party and was elected to the Fourth Duma against the will of the majority of the electors in the worker curia of the city of Warsaw. The Collegium condemns the anti-Party agitation carried on by the Bund and the liquidators in favour of admitting Jagiello into the group and expresses the hope that the granting of a consultative voice to Deputy Jagiello may help in rallying all the class-conscious Polish workers closer around the Polish Social-Democrats and in merging them completely with the workers of all nationalities into integral organisations of the R.S.D.L.P."

If, contrary to expectations, the liquidators have won and Jagiello has been admitted, it is still necessary, and doubly so, to have a resolution similar in content, expressing regret and appealing to the Party as a whole.

It is highly important, furthermore, for the Collegium to "correct itself" on the well-known resolution of November 13 and adopt a new one. Something like this: "Having examined all the circumstances of the strike of November 15, the Collegium finds that the warnings against the strike both from the Social-Democratic group and from the St. Petersburg Committee were prompted solely by the fact that part of the organisation was not ready to go into action on that day. However, events showed that nonetheless the movement of the revolutionary proletariat assumed a large scale and developed into street demonstrations in the name of a republic, an eight-hour working day, and confiscation of the landed estates, thus raising the entire working-class movement in Russia to a higher plane. Therefore the Collegium emphatically condemns the propaganda against revolutionary strikes which the liquidators, their ... group and *Luch* are carrying on, and recommends the workers to devote all their efforts to more extensive, thorough and concerted preparations for street demonstrations and political protest strikes, which should be made as short as possible (one-day) and concerted. The Collegium will try to develop a campaign for a strike and demonstration on January 9, 1913, with a special protest against the 300th anniversary of the House of Romanov, which enslaves Russia and drenches her in blood."

Next, it is highly important and essential for the five (curia) deputies to draft a well-grounded resolution on the Badayev case. Something like this: "The five deputies from the worker curia, having considered the baiting of Comrade Badayev by the liquidators in *Luch* and among the St. Petersburg workers, have resolved: (1) not to submit this matter to the Duma group, since the latter has admitted Badayev and no objection was raised in the group to his admission; (2) to investigate the conditions of Badayev's election, provided he abstains from voting on this matter; (3) the fact, established and verified by the five deputies, that (a) the anti-liquidationist mandate was printed beforehand, and was adopted unanimously by the delegates' meeting, all the electors and delegates who backed Badayev acting in concert and unity and as staunch fellow-thinkers, at the request of the St. Petersburg Committee of the R.S.D.L.P.; (b) that at the meeting of the Social-Democratic delegates fifteen persons voted for the St. Petersburg Committee's list and nine for the liquidators and that not all of the delegates and electors of *Luch* behaved as fellow-thinkers of the liquidators, some of them (Sudakov and others) vacillating; (c) that when three electors had been elected from each side, Badayev's supporters did their duty by moving that the matter be settled by drawing lots to prevent the dispute from being revealed to the bourgeoisie; (d) that the very fact that Badayev's supporters tabled this motion and the fact that the liquidators refused ... the question of P. and M.[163] (a liquidator)—therefore we have resolved: to recognise that Badayev is undoubtedly the elected representative of the majority of the worker Social-Democrats of St. Petersburg and is in fact a candidate at the request of the St. Petersburg Committee; that the entire responsibility for the disorganisation of the Social-Democratic Party elections in the St. Petersburg worker curia falls on the liquidators, who sought to frustrate the will of the majority, knowing themselves to be in a minority; and that the liquidators' refusal to draw lots was an outrageous violation of what is the duty of every Social-Democrat,[164] a violation unheard of in the working-class movement. We have resolved to publish this resolution in the press and to take concerted action among the workers for Badayev and against liquidationist agitation."

This resolution is essential. The Badayev case has already got into the world press. Steklov has printed evasive but foul things in *Die Neue Zeit*. And what is contained in the pamphlet which the liquidators have published in the German language for the International Congress is simply preposterous. We cannot keep silent. It is for the curia deputies to check the facts and exonerate Badayev, with Badayev himself abstaining, of course.

Written December 11. 1912
Sent from Cracow to St. Petersburg
Published for the first time

Published according
to a copy found in Police
Department archives

A LETTER TO J. V. STALIN[165]

For Vasilyev

December 6.

Dear friend, with regard to January 9, it is highly important to think things over and make preparations in advance. A leaflet must be prepared in advance calling for meetings, a one-day strike, and demonstrations (the latter should be decided on the spot, where it will be easier to decide).[166] We must "correct" the mistake of November 15—correct it against the opportunists, of course. The slogans in the leaflet must be the three main revolutionary ones (a republic, an eight-hour working day, and confiscation of the landed estates), with special emphasis on the 300 years' "infamy" of the Romanov dynasty. If there is no complete and absolute certainty that we can have the leaflet in St. Petersburg, we must prepare it here beforehand and take it there. The liquidators' impudence over Jagiello is unparalleled. If all of our six representatives have been elected by the worker curia, we must not tacitly submit to any Siberians. The six must by all means voice the most emphatic protest if they are outvoted; they must print their protest in *Dyen* and declare that they are appealing to the rank and file, to the workers' organisations. The liquidators want to inflate their majority and force through a split with the Polish Social-Democrats. Is it possible that the workers' representatives from six working-class gubernias will submit to the Skobelevs and Co. or to a chance Siberian[167]? Write more often and in greater detail.

The *Luch* articles against strikes are the height of villainy. We must come out sharply against them in the illegal press. Let me know as soon as possible which of the plans made by you for such action you have chosen.

Best regards.

P.S. Return the document—it is inconvenient to use it, its holder may be in St. Petersburg.

Written December 6, 1912
Sent from Cracow to St. Petersburg

First published in the book
The Period of Zvezda *and*
Pravda, *1911-14*, Issue III, 1923

Published according
to a copy made
by N. K. Krupskaya

THE DISEASE OF REFORMISM

"What ails us?" was the question asked in a recent issue of *Luch* by the author of an instructive feuilleton under that heading, written under the influence of the strike of November 15.

The answer is evident from the following two quotations:

"It would appear to be obvious to those who lay claim to the role of leaders that the demand for the abolition of emergency regulations and for freedom of association is one thing, and is an object of the struggle now and in the near future, while the alteration of the existing system, which the appeal speaks of, is something else. This can be brought about not by playing at strikes, which is what we see at present, but by stubborn, methodical work, by winning one position after another, by straining every nerve, by achieving perfect organisation and drawing into this struggle the mass of the people, and not merely the working class....

"If we take an intelligent attitude towards our tasks, methodically defend our interests and do not flare up today only to subside tomorrow, we shall create for ourselves both strong trade union organisations and an open political party that no one will dare encroach upon."

These passages are enough for us to say to the author: you would do better, my dear fellow, to ask "what ails" you yourself. And we will answer you: you are clearly suffering from reformism. You are obsessed with a fixed idea, the idea of a Stolypin workers' party. It is a dangerous disease, and the *Luch* doctors' cure will finish you off altogether.

The author very explicitly and deliberately advocates an "open political party" in contrast to the general demand for political liberty. A comparison of the two passages quoted leaves no room for doubt on this score. All evasion would be useless here.

We would ask the author: why is it that the "open party"
of the opportunists among the petty-bourgeois democrats
(the Popular Socialists of 1906) and the big-bourgeois
liberals (the Cadets in 1906-07 and later) turned out to be
a utopia while *your* "open" workers' party is not utopian?

You admit (or, at any rate, the "open" action in the
elections *made* you admit) that the Cadets are counter-
revolutionary, that they are not democrats, not a party of
the masses at all, but a party of the well-to-do bourgeoisie,
a party of the first curia. And yet here are you, a "sober-
minded, realistic politician", an enemy of "flare-ups and
fist-shaking", putting forward, allegedly on behalf of the
workers, an "immediate" demand which turned out to be
utopian, unattainable for the Cadets!! You are a great
utopian, but your utopia is small, petty, and wretched.

You have unwittingly contracted a fashionable disease—
there is such an epidemic just now!—the disease of dejec-
tion, faint-heartedness, despair and lack of faith. And
that disease is pushing you into the pitfall of opportunism,
for which Popular Socialists and Cadets alike have already
paid the price of universal ridicule.

You consider the demand for abolishing the emergency
regulations and for freedom of association to be topical
and realistic, "methodical" and "conscious". You are
at variance with the Social-Democrats radically, for they
understand the general conditions for achieving (and the
seriousness of) such reforms. You are substantially at one
with the Progressists and the Octobrists, for these are the
people who deceive themselves and others with meaningless talk about reforms and "liberties" under existing conditions. The Italian reformist Bissolati betrayed the working class for the sake of the reforms promised by Giolitti, a
liberal Minister, with the partiés of *all* classes existing
"openly". But you are betraying the working class for the
sake of reforms that *even* the Izgoyevs and Bulgakovs do
not expect from Makarov!

You speak contemptuously of "playing at strikes". I am
not in a position to answer you properly on that point
here. I shall merely point out briefly that it is not really
clever to describe a profound historical movement as "playing". You are *angry* at strikes just as *Novoye Vremya* (see

Neznamov's article in the issue of November 17), the Izgoyevs and the Bulgakovs are. And the reason why you are
angry is that reality mercilessly shatters your liberal illusions. The mass of the workers fully recognise the need
of organisation, system, preparation, and method, but your
statements they treat with contempt, and will continue to
do so.

The serious disease that has poisoned your system is due
to a very widespread bacillus. It is the bacillus of liberal
labour policy, or, in other words, of liquidationism. It is
in the air. But however angry you may be at the course of
events in general and at November 15 in particular, that
course is proving deadly to the bacillus.

Pravda No. 180, November 29, 1912
        Signed: *V. Ilyin*

                                        Published according
                                        to the *Pravda* text

IMPOVERISHMENT IN CAPITALIST SOCIETY

Bourgeois reformists, who are echoed by certain opportunists among the Social-Democrats, assert that there is no impoverishment of the masses taking place in capitalist society. "The theory of impoverishment" is wrong, they say, for the standard of living of the masses is improving, if slowly, and the gulf between the haves and have-nots is narrowing, not widening.

The falsity of such assertions has lately been revealed to the masses more and more clearly. The cost of living is rising. Wages, *even* with the most stubborn and *most* successful strike movement, are increasing· much more slowly than the necessary expenditure of labour power. And side by side with this, the wealth of the capitalists is increasing at a dizzy rate.

Here are some data on Germany, where the workers' condition is far better than in Russia, thanks to a higher standard of culture, to *freedom of strikes* and association, to political liberty, to the millions of trade unionists and the millions of readers of workers' newspapers.

According to data furnished by *bourgeois* sociologists, who draw on official sources, wages in Germany have increased by an average of 25 per cent during the past 30 years. In the same period, the cost of living has gone up by *at least* 40 per cent!!

Food, clothing, fuel and rent have all become more expensive. The worker is becoming impoverished *absolutely*, i.e., he is actually becoming poorer than before; he is compelled to live worse, to eat worse, to suffer hunger more, and to live in basements and attics.

But the *relative* impoverishment of the workers, i.e., the diminution of their *share* in the national income, is still more striking. The workers' *comparative* share in capitalist society, which is fast growing rich, is dwindling because the millionaires are becoming ever richer.

There is no income tax in Russia, and no data are available on the growing wealth of the well-to-do classes of society. Our reality, which is even sadder, is shut off by a veil—the veil of ignorance and lack of publicity.

In Germany there are exact data on the wealth of the propertied classes. In Prussia, for example, the *first* 10,000 million marks (5,000 million rubles) of taxable property belonged to 1,853 persons in 1902 and to 1,108 in 1908.

The number of the very rich has diminished. Their wealth has increased—in 1902 each of them owned property worth 5,000,000 marks (2,500,000 rubles) on the average and in 1908, as much as 9,000,000 marks (4,500,000 rubles)!

People speak of the "upper 10,000". In Prussia the "upper 21,000" rich owned property valued at 13,500 million marks, while the taxable property of the remaining 1,300,000 owners was worth only 3,000 million marks.

Four of the wealthiest millionaires in Prussia (one prince, one duke and two counts) owned property worth 149 million marks in 1907 and 481 million marks in 1908.

Wealth in capitalist society is growing at an incredible rate—side by side with the impoverishment of the mass of the workers.

Pravda No. 181, November 30, 1912
Signed: *V.*

Published according
to the *Pravda* text

THE WORKING CLASS
AND ITS "PARLIAMENTARY" REPRESENTATIVES

This is not the first time that Russia's class-conscious workers have had to deal with a collective body of representatives of the working class in the Duma. And each time such a body was formed in the Second, Third or Fourth Duma (we do not mention the First, which most of the Social-Democrats boycotted), there was a *discrepancy* between the views and trend of the *majority* of Social-Democrats and those of their representatives in the Duma.

There are exact data on this discrepancy as regards the Second Duma. In the spring of 1907 it was established officially and beyond question what were the views, tendencies and trends or groups predominating in the Social-Democratic Party and those in the Social-Democratic Duma group.

It was found that, by sending one delegate from every 500 worker Social-Democrats, the Bolsheviks at that time had 105 delegates, the Mensheviks 97 and those not belonging to either group 4.[168]

The Bolsheviks had an obvious superiority.

Among the non-Russian Social-Democrats, the Poles had 44 delegates, the Bundists 57 and the Letts 29. As opponents of opportunism, Menshevism and the Bund strongly predominated among the Letts at that time, the ratio of the "trends" among the non-Russians in general was similar to that among the "Russian" Social-Democrats.

Yet in the Duma group of the Social-Democrats at that time there were 36 Mensheviks and 18 Bolsheviks, with 12 Mensheviks and 11 Bolsheviks among the deputies elected by the worker curia.[169] It is obvious that the Mensheviks predominated.

Thus the balance of the "trends" in the Duma group was not the same as in the Social-Democratic movement but the direct opposite.

Is that an accident?

No. As a general rule, in all countries of the world the parliamentary representatives of the workers' parties have a *more opportunist* composition than that of the workers' parties themselves. The reason is easy to see: firstly, all the electoral systems of the bourgeois countries, even the most democratic, in practice *restrict* suffrage for the workers, either by making it conditional on age (in Russia it has to be 25 years), or on residence and permanence of work (six months in Russia), etc. And it is the young, more politically-conscious and resolute sections of the proletariat that these restrictions generally hit hardest of all.

Secondly, under *any* suffrage in bourgeois society, the non-proletarian elements of the workers' parties —officials of workers' unions, small proprietors, office employees, and particularly the "intelligentsia"—specialise more readily in the "parliamentary" profession (owing to their occupations, social standing, training, etc.).

What are the conclusions to be drawn from this fact, and how did matters stand in the Third and Fourth Dumas compared with the Second? We shall devote our next article to these questions.

Pravda No. 191, December 12, 1912   Published according
          Signed: *V. I.*   to the *Pravda* text

THE "RECONCILIATION"
OF THE NATIONALISTS AND CADETS

The most important political result of the Duma debate on the declaration of the government is the touching unity of the *nationalists*, Octobrists and *Cadets*. Our Russian so-called "society" yields so readily to high-sounding and cheap phrases that we have to lay particular emphasis on this *real* result of the action of *all* parties, with their criticism of political questions of principle.

"The parties disappeared," wrote the nationalist *Novoye Vremya* (No. 13199). "Deputy Maklakov's excellent speech (at the December 7 sitting) united the entire Duma, which applauded him, forgetful of all party calculations and differences of opinion."

This comment by a *nationalist* paper, the chief organ of all toadyism, of persecution of Jews and non-Russians in general, should be remembered and pondered by all who take a serious interest in politics.

It was not because they were "forgetful" of party differences of opinion that the Octobrists and nationalists, the Guchkovites and the *Novoye Vremya* people applauded Maklakov, but because they appreciated the profound *unity of opinion* of the liberal bourgeoisie and the nationalist landlords.

Maklakov revealed that unity of opinion on the fundamental issues of home and foreign policy. "While Russia does not seek war, neither does she dread it," exclaimed this Cadet, to prolonged applause by the *nationalists*. How could they help applauding? Any politically literate person realises that these words expressed the Cadets' *acceptance* of the policy of resorting to the threat of war, the policy of militarism, of armaments by land and by sea that oppress and ruin the mass of the people.

The liberals, who support militarism, are not feared by the reactionaries, who very correctly argue that support for militarism is *action*, whereas liberal exclamations are *mere words* which simply cannot be made a reality so long as the reactionaries are in power. "Give us millions to spend on armaments, and we will clap and applaud your liberal talk"—this is what every clever semi-feudal landlord says, and should say, to the Duma Balalaikins.[170]

And what about Maklakov's stand on home policy? Is it accidental that the Right-wing priests are highly satisfied, as *Rech* itself testifies, or that *Novoye Vremya* gleefully reprints Maklakov's "keynote": "Let there be no division of Russia into two camps—the country and the government"?

No, it is not accidental, because by his whining about the desirability of "reconciliation" Maklakov *in fact* echoes Kokovtsov. For Kokovtsov, too, desires "reconciliation"!

Kokovtsov desires *no* change in the balance of the social forces. Maklakov did *not* show *the slightest* understanding of the *kind* of change that is necessary or *how* it can be brought about. "Reconciliation" is precisely the term which *obscures* the only serious question, that of the conditions and means of achieving this change—obscures it with rotten phrases that say nothing, that blunt the civic consciousness of the masses and lull them.

A "society" which is capable of applauding the speeches of a Maklakov about "reconciliation" deserves nothing but contempt.

As for the speech of Malinovsky, the workers' representative, on the Ministerial declaration, both the nationalists and the Cadets took pains not to notice that in it the democrats were *posing* questions. But then Malinovsky's speech was *not* intended for their like at all.

Pravda No. 194, December 15, 1912

Published according to the *Pravda* text

THE NATIONAL-LIBERALS

Recent years have seen a definite differentiation taking place among the Russian liberals. The "genuine" bourgeoisie has been setting itself apart from the general liberal camp. Liberal capital is forming its *own* special party, which is to incorporate (and is incorporating) many bourgeois elements which in the past made common cause with the Octobrists and which, on the other hand, is being joined by the most moderate, big-bourgeois, "respectable" elements of the Cadet Party.

The "Progressist" group in the Third and Fourth Dumas, as well as the one in the Council of State are on the verge of becoming the official party representatives of this national-liberal bourgeoisie in the parliamentary arena. Indeed, the recent congress of the "Progressists" virtually outlined the national-liberal programme which *Russkaya Molva*[171] is advocating.

What do the so-called "Progressists" want? Why do we call them national-liberals?

They do *not* want full and undivided rule of the landlords and the bureaucrats. They seek—and they say so plainly—a moderate constitution with narrowly-restricted rights based on a bicameral system and an anti-democratic suffrage. They want a "strong authority" that would pursue the "patriotic" policy of conquering with sword and fire new markets for "national industry". They want the bureaucrats to heed them as much as they heed the Purishkeviches. And then they would be willing to forget their "old accounts" with the reactionaries and work hand in glove with them to establish a "great" capitalist Russia.

What separates these people from the Octobrist Party is that the landlords constitute too strong an element in that party and that it is tractable to the point of impotence. From the Cadet Party they are separated by their distaste for the Cadets' demagogical flirting with the democrats. The Cadets' hypocritical talk about universal suffrage and compulsory alienation of the land (even with compènsation) seems to these "respectable" constitutionalists quite unnecessary and impermissible.

The national-liberals go straight to the point: one must not be afraid of accusations of "pandering to the reactionary forces" but must fight openly against "appeals for seizing the landed estates" and against "fomenting hatred of the propertied classes"; as regards "military might", there should be neither Right nor Left.

"We are back in our country.... The Russian army is ... *our own* army.... The Russian court of justice is not Shemyaka's[172] but *our own*.... Russia's world standing is not a vainglorious whim of the bureaucracy but *our own* strength and joy" (see the policy statements of *Russkaya Molva*).

The national-liberals undoubtedly have a certain "future" in Russia. They will be a party of the "genuine" capitalist bourgeoisie, such as we see in Germany. The purely intellectual, liberal elements who have few "roots" will remain with the Cadets. The national-liberals will gain such ideologists as Struve, Maklakov, Protopopov, Kovalevsky and others, who have long had one foot in the reactionary camp. They will no doubt be joined also by the exceedingly moderate "Shipovite" Zemstvo-landlord elements, who likewise favour a constitution with narrowly-restricted rights, a "constitution" for the rich. (It is not for nothing that Mr. Struve has recently recalled Mr. Shipov in such kind terms.)

The "Progressists'" dreams of a "strong authority" pursuing a liberal policy cannot, of course, materialise in the near future. And so the Khvostovs and Purishkeviches are still sitting pretty. It may be that the national liberal party will not take final shape just yet and that their newspaper will cease to exist as *Slovo*,[173] a paper which on the whole had set itself the same aims, did three years ago. (In the Duma, however, the "Progressists" have become relatively stronger than the Cadets.) In any case, the coming into the open of the national-liberal bourgeoisie indicates a considerable maturing of the class antagonisms in Russia.

The workers must counter the self-determination of the capitalist bourgeoisie by putting ten times greater energy into *their own* organisation and *their own* self-determination as a class.

Pravda No. 200, December 22, 1912

Published according to the *Pravda* text

ON THE ATTITUDE TO LIQUIDATIONISM
AND ON UNITY

THESES

1. Four years' struggle against liquidationism.

   The Party defined liquidationism in *December* 1908. Liquidationism condemned for destroying the Party, not for legal work. Anti-liquidationism wins in the legal arena, 1912. ("**Pravda**" and **the elections**.)

2. The liquidators caused a split. The liquidators broke away from the Party. Their initiating groups are a product and manifestation of the split.

3. The August 1912 conference was anti-Party in composition, as even the conciliators had to admit.

   It is impermissible for little groups abroad, having no direct mandate from any Social-Democratic organisation in Russia, and not operating by agreement with it, to act in the name of the Social-Democratic Party.

4. The resolutions of the August conference on basic issues of the movement, above all on the fundamental issue of recognition—complete and sincere recognition—of the illegal Party, are, to put it as mildly as possible, "diplomacy", i.e., evasion of a straightforward answer to the question. They are in effect liquidationist resolutions.

5. The political behaviour of the liquidationist group in *Nasha Zarya* and *Luch* after the (August) conference revealed the absolutely anti-Party character of this group, which found expression (a) in advocacy of an open Party; (b) in scoffing at "underground" work in the legal press; (c) in a struggle against revolutionary strikes and revolutionary mass struggle in general.

A resolute struggle must be waged against this group as anti-Party.

6. The advocacy of unity in the legal press—evading and obscuring the essence of the matter, namely, the question of *recognising* the illegal Party *in practice*—is deception of the workers.

7. The unity of all trends and shades in the illegal organisation is absolutely necessary. Appeal for such unity.

Written in December 1912

First published in *Bolshevik*
No. 1, 1939

Published according
to the manuscript

NOTIFICATION AND RESOLUTIONS OF THE CRACOW MEETING OF THE CENTRAL COMMITTEE OF THE R.S.D.L.P. AND PARTY FUNCTIONARIES[174]

Published in pamphlet form
by the C.C. R.S.D.L.P. in Paris,
February 1913

Published according
to the text of the pamphlet,
which was checked:
for the "Notification",
against the manuscript
and for the "Resolutions",
against the hectographed
edition

NOTIFICATION

A meeting of the C.C. R.S.D.L.P. and Party functionaries was held in February this year. The Central Committee succeeded in securing the attendance of members of the illegal Party organisations of St. Petersburg (five persons), the Moscow Region (two), the South (two), the Urals and the Caucasus. Elections from the local organisations could not be held, and the meeting was therefore not constituted a conference. Some of the members of the Central Committee were unable to attend because of police measures.

Nearly all the participants in the meeting had been playing a prominent role in various legal workers' societies and in the use of so-called "legal opportunities". Thus the composition of the meeting ensured an accurate picture of the whole of Party work in all the principal areas of Russia.

The meeting held eleven sittings, and drafted resolutions on the following items of the agenda: (1) The revolutionary upswing, the strikes and the tasks of the Party. (2) Building the illegal Party organisation. (3) The Duma Social-Democratic group. (4) The Party press. (5) The insurance campaign. (6) The attitude to liquidationism. The issue of unity. (7) The non-Russian Social-Democratic organisations.

The resolutions were adopted unanimously, the only exception being the abstention of one comrade on two clauses of the "insurance" resolution, and of another on particulars of the resolution on the non-Russians.

Endorsed by the Central Committee, the resolutions of the meeting provide a summary of Party experience and a guiding line on all the major questions of Social-Democratic work in present-day Russia.

*   *
*

Taking systematic stock of the experience of 1912 is a most important task of the Social-Democrats, for that year saw a great, a historic change in Russia's working-class movement. The point is not merely that decline and disintegration are giving way to a revival. The working class has gone over to a massive offensive against the capitalists and the tsarist monarchy. The wave of economic and political strikes has surged so high that in this respect Russia is once more *ahead of all* the countries of the world, including the most developed of them.

This fact will not, of course, make any class-conscious worker forget how very far ahead of us are the proletarians of the free countries in regard to organisation and class education of the masses. But this fact has proved that Russia has entered a period of the growth of a *new revolution*.

The working class is faced with the great task of bringing about the revolutionary awakening of all the democratic masses and of educating them in the struggle, of leading them to the powerful onslaught which must bring Russia freedom and a republic by destroying the Romanov monarchy. The fundamental task of the moment is to give the utmost support to the open revolutionary struggle of the masses, to organise, extend, deepen and intensify it. Anyone who has failed to realise this task, who does not work in an illegal organisation, group or nucleus promoting the cause of the revolution, is not a Social-Democrat.

*   *
*

The revolutionary upswing of the proletariat in 1912 was the main cause of the universally recognised change in the mood of the democrats. Both in the elections to the Fourth Duma and in the matter of founding a legal working-class press that advocates at least the basic elements of Marxist theory, the Social-Democrats achieved important

[Handwritten manuscript in Russian — Lenin's hand]

First page of Lenin's manuscript
"Notification" on the meeting of the C.C. R.S.D.L.P.
and Party functionaries. January 1913

Reduced

victories. The tsarist government was unable to prevent these achievements solely because the open revolutionary struggle of the masses had altered the entire social and political situation. While continuing its steadfast, persevering and systematic work of using absolutely all "legal opportunities"—ranging from the platform of the Black-Hundred Duma to a simple temperance society—the R.S.D.L.P. does not for one moment forget that only he is worthy of the lofty name of Party member who really carries on his entire work among the masses in the spirit of the Party decisions that were thought out and adopted from the standpoint of the growing revolution and not of June Third "legality". Our task is not to succumb to the disorder and disintegration left over from the period of 1908-11, but to fight against them. Our job is not to swim with the stream of chaotic and unprincipled legalism, but to use every legal possibility for gradually grouping all live elements around the illegal Party. Our slogan is: no peace with those who misuse legalism to sow scepticism and indifference to the revolutionary struggle of the masses or even to hamper it outright.

We cannot guarantee the realisation of our demands by reducing them, by curtailing our programme, or by adopting the tactics of attracting unenlightened people with the deceptive promise of easy constitutional reforms under Russian tsarism. We can guarantee it only by educating the masses in the spirit of consistent democracy and awareness of the falsity of constitutional illusions. The guarantee lies in the revolutionary organisation of the foremost class, the proletariat, and in the great revolutionary enthusiasm of the masses.

The period of rampant counter-revolution has left us a heritage of ideological disorder and disruption, organisational disintegration in many centres of the working-class movement, primitive methods and forced isolation from the Party on the part of some, and a scornful, or even malicious, attitude to the "underground" that preserves the behests of the revolution and elaborates revolutionary tactics, on the part of others. The liquidators' break-away from the Social-Democratic Party, their virtual isolation, and in some cases departure from Social-Democratic principles and disintegration of the non-Russian Social-Democratic organisations have all accentuated the demand for *unity* to the utmost degree.

Unity of the Social-Democratic proletariat is a necessary condition for its victories.

Unity of the Social-Democratic proletariat is impossible without the unity of *its* Party, the R.S.D.L.P.

And here we see at once that we cannot decide the question of unity without deciding—not merely in words but by deeds as well—the question of the need for an illegal Party. Anyone who speaks of unity and yet advocates an "open workers' party" deceives himself and the workers. Anyone who speaks of unity, pretending that this question can be decided, cleared up, or at least raised, within the bounds of legality, deceives himself and the workers.

What will solve the problem of unity is certainly not meaningless phrases about "unity" in the legal press, nor agreements with various "straggling" little groups of intellectuals, nor yet the diplomacy of negotiations abroad, but *solely unity* in the localities, the actual *fusion* of *all* worker members of the R.S.D.L.P. into an integral illegal organisation.

The workers have already started of their own accord, from below, on the solution of the problem of unity, the only solution that is serious and realistic. This meeting calls on all Social-Democrats to take the same path.

Worker Social-Democrats everywhere are re-establishing integral illegal organisations of the R.S.D.L.P. in the form of factory nuclei and committees, district groups, town centres, Social-Democratic groups in *all kinds* of legal institutions, etc. Let all who do not wish to doom themselves to the role of powerless individuals join these organisations, where the recognition of the illegal Party and support for the revolutionary struggle of the masses take place under the control of the workers themselves.

*   *

*

The period of disintegration is passing. The time has come to gather our forces. Let us, then, rally in the illegal organisations of the R.S.D.L.P. They do not close the door to any Social-Democrat who wishes to work in them, who wishes to help the organisation of the proletariat, its struggle against capital, and the revolutionary onslaught against the tsarist monarchy that it has begun.

A nation-wide political crisis is slowly but steadily maturing in Russia. The June Third system was the last attempt to rescue the tsar's Black-Hundred monarchy, to renovate it by an alliance with the upper ranks of the bourgeoisie, and that attempt fell through. The new democratic forces are growing and gathering strength daily and hourly among Russia's peasantry and town bourgeoisie. The number of proletarians in town and country is growing faster than ever, they are becoming more organised, more united, and more confident of their invincibility, and their confidence is strengthened by the experience of mass strikes.

The R.S.D.L.P., in organising the foremost contingents of this proletariat into an integral whole, must lead it into revolutionary battle in the name of our old revolutionary demands.

Central Committee of the R.S.D.L.P.

February 1913

RESOLUTIONS

THE REVOLUTIONARY UPSWING, THE STRIKES, AND THE TASKS OF THE PARTY

1. The outstanding fact in the history of the working-class movement and the Russian revolution in 1912 was the remarkable development of both the economic and the political strike movement of the proletariat. The number of political strikers reached one million.

2. The character of the strike movement of 1912 deserves special attention. The workers in a number of cases put forward economic and political demands simultaneously; the period of economic strikes was succeeded by a period of political strikes and vice versa. The struggle against the capitalists for the gains of 1905 taken away by the counter-revolution, and the growing cost of living, aroused more and more sections of the workers, confronting them with political issues in the sharpest form. All these forms of combination and intertwining of the economic and political struggle are a condition for and an earnest of the might of the movement, giving rise to revolutionary mass strikes.

3. The beginning of outbursts of discontent and of revolts in the Navy and the Army, which marked the year 1912, was undoubtedly linked with the revolutionary mass strikes of the workers, and indicated the growing ferment and indignation among large sections of the democrats, in particular among the peasantry, who supply the bulk of the troops.

4. All these facts, combined with the general swing to the left in the country, which had its effect on the elections to the Fourth Duma despite the most shameless rigging

of them by the Black-Hundred tsarist government, showed beyond all doubt that Russia had once more entered a period of open revolutionary struggle by the masses. The new revolution, the beginning of which we are experiencing, is an inevitable result of the bankruptcy of the June Third policy of tsarism. This policy was unable to satisfy even the most compliant big bourgeoisie. The mass of the people has become still more enslaved, particularly in the case of the oppressed nationalities, and the peasantry has again been reduced to a state where millions upon millions are starving.

5. Under these circumstances, revolutionary mass strikes are of exceptional importance also because they constitute one of the most effective means of overcoming the apathy, despair and disunity of the agricultural proletariat and the peasantry, rousing them to independent political activity and drawing them into the most concerted, simultaneous and extensive revolutionary actions.

6. The Party organisations, in extending and intensifying their agitation for the immediate demands of the R.S.D.L.P.—a democratic republic, an eight-hour working day, and confiscation of all the landed estates for the benefit of the peasantry—must make it one of the prime objects of their activity to give all-round support to revolutionary mass strikes, and to develop and organise all forms of revolutionary action by the masses. In particular, an essential current task is to organise revolutionary street demonstrations both in combination with political strikes and as independent actions.

7. The fact that some capitalists resort to lock-outs (mass dismissals) against the strikers confronts the working class with new tasks. It is necessary to take careful account of the economic conditions of strikes in every area, every industry and every particular case, find new forms of struggle (such as stay-in strikes) to counteract the lock-outs, and replace political strikes by revolutionary meetings and revolutionary street demonstrations.

8. Some legal press organs are carrying on general agitation against revolutionary mass strikes, irrespective of their appraisal of this or that strike. Besides the liberal press, such agitation is being carried on, for example, by

the group of liquidators in the newspaper *Luch*, against the will of a substantial section of those workers who support the newspaper in one form or another. In view of this, the task of all pro-Party worker Social-Democrats is: (1) to wage a determined struggle against that group; (2) systematically and perseveringly to explain the harm of the above-mentioned agitation to all workers, irrespective of their leanings, and (3) to rally all proletarian forces for the furtherance of revolutionary agitation and revolutionary action by the masses.

BUILDING THE ILLEGAL ORGANISATION

1. In summing up the working-class movement and the Party's work in 1912, this meeting finds that—the new wave of revolutionary actions by the masses that has begun has fully borne out the previous decisions of the R.S.D.L.P. (particularly those of the January 1912 Conference) as regards building the Party. The course of the strike movement in 1912, the Social-Democrats' campaign in the elections to the Fourth Duma, the course of the insurance campaign, etc., have shown beyond doubt that the only correct type of organisational structure in the present period is an illegal party as the sum total of Party nuclei surrounded by a network of legal and semi-legal workers' associations.

2. It is absolutely obligatory to adapt the organisational forms of illegal building to local conditions. A variety of forms of cover for illegal nuclei and the greatest possible flexibility in adapting forms of work to local and general living conditions guarantee the vitality of the illegal organisation.

3. The chief immediate task in the field of organisational work at the present time is to establish in all factories purely Party illegal committees consisting of the most active elements among the workers. The tremendous upswing of the working-class movement creates conditions in which factory Party committees can be restored and the existing ones strengthened in the vast majority of localities.

4. The meeting points out that it has now become essential in every centre to form a single leading organisation out of the disconnected local groups.

In St. Petersburg, for example, a leading City Committee, formed by combining the principle of election by district nuclei and the principle of co-option, has emerged as a type of city-wide organisation.

This type of organisation makes it possible to establish a very close and direct connection between the leading body and the primary nuclei, and at the same time to create a small, mobile, particularly well disguised executive body, authorised to act at any moment on behalf of the entire organisation. The meeting recommends this type for other centres of the working-class movement as well, with such modifications as may be prompted by local and general living conditions.

5. With a view to establishing close links between local organisations and the Central Committee, as well as to guiding and unifying Party work, this meeting deems it imperative to organise regional centres in the principal areas of the working-class movement.

6. A system of authorised nominees is proposed as a most important practical factor in establishing a permanent living link between the Central Committee and local Social-Democratic groups, as well as in devising flexible forms of directing local work in the major centres of the working-class movement. Nominees should be recruited among workers in charge of local work. Only advanced workers can by themselves strengthen and consolidate the central apparatus of the Party locally, and throughout Russia.

7. This meeting expresses the wish that the Central Committee should confer as frequently as possible with local Party functionaries active in various fields of Social-Democratic work.

8. This meeting stresses the repeated Party decisions to the effect that the workers' party cannot exist unless there are regular membership dues and contributions by workers. In the absence of such contributions, particularly in present conditions, the existence of a central (local or

all-Russia) Party body, however modest, will be absolutely impossible.

9. (Not to be published.)

THE SOCIAL-DEMOCRATIC GROUP IN THE DUMA

1. This meeting notes that despite unheard-of persecution and the rigging of the elections by the government, and despite the Black-Hundred and liberal bloc against the Social-Democrats that in many places assumed a very definite character, the R.S.D.L.P. won tremendous victories in the elections to the Fourth Duma. The Social-Democrats polled an increased number of votes almost everywhere in the second urban curia, which they are wresting more and more from the liberals. In the worker curia, which is the most important for our Party, the R.S.D.L.P. retained its undivided supremacy, the working class emphasising with particular unanimity, by electing none but Bolshevik deputies in the curia, its unshakable loyalty to the old R.S.D.L.P. and its revolutionary behests.

2. This meeting hails the vigorous activity of the Social-Democratic deputies to the Fourth Duma, which found expression in a number of speeches in the Duma, the submission of interpellations and the reading of a declaration which in general correctly expressed the fundamental principles of Social-Democracy.

3. This meeting recognises that our Party's established tradition, by which the Duma Social-Democratic group is a body subordinate to the Party as a whole, in the shape of its central bodies, is the only correct one, and finds that in the interests of the political education of the working class and the proper organisation of the Party's work in the Duma, careful attention should be paid to every step of the Social-Democratic group, and in this way Party control exercised over the group.

4. This meeting cannot but regard the resolution concerning Jagiello as a direct violation of Party duty by the Social-Democratic group. That resolution backs the disruptive move of the Bund, which entered into an agreement with a non-Social-Democratic party (the P.S.P.) against

the Polish Social-Democrats and elected Jagiello, a non-Social-Democrat, in opposition to all the Social-Democratic electors, who were in the majority among the working-class electors. The group thereby aggravated the split among the workers in Poland and hampered the cause of unity in the Party as a whole.

5. Comrade Chkhenkeli's defence, on behalf of the group, of cultural national autonomy under the guise of "establishing the necessary institutions for the free development of each nationality" is a direct violation of the Party Programme.[175] The Second Congress of the Party, which adopted the Programme,[176] rejected by a special vote what was in effect an identical formulation. Concessions to nationalist sentiment, even in this disguised form, are impermissible for a proletarian party.

6. The Social-Democratic group's vote in favour of the Progressist (in reality Octobrist) formula of procedure with regard to the declaration of the Minister, and the failure to introduce an independent Social-Democratic formula are a blunder which should be noted by the Party in view of the malicious comments of the liberal press.[177]

7, 8 and 9. (Not to be published.)[178]

ILLEGAL LITERATURE

Having discussed the necessity for all-round development of illegal publishing and worked out a number of concrete instructions on the matter, this meeting insistently calls upon all local organisations of the Party, all workers' nuclei and individual workers to show greater independence and initiative in the matter of transport and contacts with the Bureau of the Central Committee[179] for the distribution of illegal literature.

THE INSURANCE CAMPAIGN

Noting that the working class and its Party, despite all persecution, have displayed great energy in upholding proletarian interests in connection with the introduction of the insurance law, this meeting considers:

1. It is necessary to wage the most determined and concerted struggle against attempts by the government and the capitalists to make the workers elect their delegates to the sick benefit funds blindly, without allowing workers' meetings.

2. Despite the prohibition, workers should everywhere try to hold spontaneous meetings for the preliminary nomination of the candidate delegates they want.

3. Workers should organise revolutionary meetings to protest against the violence and outrages accompanying the introduction of the insurance laws.

4. It is at all events necessary to draw up beforehand a workers' list of candidate delegates from among the more influential worker Social-Democrats and by concerted effort to champion the list also where no meetings can be held.

5. This meeting considers it inadvisable and harmful to boycott the election of delegates. At present the capitalists are devoting their main efforts to preventing the workers from gaining ascendancy in certain proletarian factory nuclei, such as the workers' sick benefit funds should become. A boycott, which at the present time would disunite the workers, would only assist the above-mentioned efforts of the capitalists.

6. The struggle for the proper election of delegates to sick benefit funds must not cease for one moment. While using every opportunity in every way and with the utmost energy, not for a moment allowing the employers to consider the normal course of production assured, and extending and developing the workers' struggle, we must not refrain from securing that the Social-Democratic list is adopted despite all obstacles. Elections do not preclude further development of the struggle. On the contrary, by securing the election of staunch worker Social-Democrats as delegates, we shall facilitate the further struggle for proper elections, in which the delegates will give the utmost assistance to the workers.

7. Wherever elections take place without meetings, it is necessary to carry on agitation for the re-election of delegates through genuinely free elections, with the workers holding meetings by every means available.

8. The Social-Democratic Duma group must immediately make a new interpellation on the banning of workers' election meetings.

9. All agitation on the introduction of insurance must be closely combined with a description of the entire state of affairs in tsarist Russia, explaining our socialist principles and revolutionary demands.

THE ATTITUDE TO LIQUIDATIONISM, AND UNITY

1. The Party's four years of struggle against liquidationism have proved the absolute correctness of the definition given by the December 1908 Party Conference of the R.S.D.L.P., which said:

"Attempts by a certain section of intellectuals in the Party to abolish the existing organisation of the R.S.D.L.P. and replace it by an amorphous association within the framework of legality at all costs, even at the price of a downright repudiation of the programme, tactics and traditions of the Party."

Consequently, the liquidators are condemned not for stressing the necessity of legal work, but for renouncing and destroying the illegal Party.

The founding of the first Marxist workers' daily newspaper in Russia and the election of none but Bolshevik deputies in the worker curia proved beyond all doubt that the Party was able to cope with legal activity, having pushed aside the liquidators.

2. By withdrawing from the illegal Party and grouping themselves separately from the local organisations, the liquidators brought about a split, which they confirmed by setting up so-called initiating groups in a number of localities, above all in St. Petersburg. The January 1912 Conference of the R.S.D.L.P., which decided that the liquidationist group of contributors to *Nasha Zarya* and *Dyelo Zhizni*—a group forming the core of the initiating groups—had "definitely placed itself outside the Party",* thereby merely registered the split effected by the liquidators.

---

* See present edition, Vol. 17, p. 481.—*Ed.*

3. The August 1912 conference, which named itself a "conference of organisations of the R.S.D.L.P.", proved in fact to be a liquidationist conference, since its principal and leading section was the literary group-of liquidators which had broken away from the Party and was cut off from the mass of the Russian workers.

4. The devotion of the overwhelming majority of the foremost workers to the illegal Party compelled the August conference to make seeming concessions to Party principle and profess recognition of the illegal Party. In reality, however, all the resolutions of that conference are permeated through and through with liquidationism, and immediately after the conference *Nasha Zarya* and *Luch*, which announced its adherence to the August decisions, intensified their liquidationist propaganda—

(a) for an open party;

(b) against the underground;

(c) against the Party Programme (defence of cultural national autonomy, revision of the agrarian laws enacted by the Third Duma, shelving the slogan of a republic, and so on);

(d) against revolutionary mass strikes;

(e) for reformist, exclusively legalist tactics.

Hence one of the Party's tasks is still to wage a determined struggle against the liquidationist group of *Nasha Zarya* and *Luch*, and to make clear to the mass of the workers the great harm of the liquidators' propaganda.

5. The "unity" campaign launched by the liquidators in the legal press evades and obscures the main issue, that of joining the illegal Party and working in it; thus it misleads the workers, for this issue cannot even be raised in the legal press. In reality the liquidators still behave as splitters, which became only too obvious during the elections in St. Petersburg, for when the electors were divided into two equal groups, it was the liquidators who rejected the proposal for drawing lots, the only means of doing away with the disunity of the workers in the face of the bourgeois parties.

6. Provided the illegal organisation of the R.S.D.L.P. is recognised and joined, the unity of worker Social-Democrats of all trends and shades is an absolute necessity dictated by all the interests of the working-class movement.

Unification on these very principles has already been effected in the Narva district organisation of St. Petersburg and in a number of provincial organisations.

7. This meeting most emphatically supports such unification and recommends that the same thing should immediately be begun everywhere from below, in factory committees, district groups, etc., the worker comrades verifying whether the recognition of the illegal organisation and readiness to back the revolutionary struggle of the masses and revolutionary tactics are really put into effect. Only to the extent that this unity from below is actually established will the final unification of the Party and complete consolidation of unity on an all-Russia scale be accomplished.

NON-RUSSIAN SOCIAL-DEMOCRATIC ORGANISATIONS

1. The experience of 1912 fully confirmed the correctness of the decision which the January (1912) Conference of the R.S.D.L.P. adopted on this question.* The Bund's support of the nomination of Jagiello, a non-Social-Democrat, against the Polish Social-Democrats, and the violation of the Party Programme in favour of nationalism by the August (1912) conference of the liquidators, the Bund and the Lettish Social-Democrats revealed with particular clarity the complete bankruptcy of the federalist principles of organising the Social-Democratic Party and the great harm which the isolation of the non-Russian Social-Democratic organisations does to the proletarian cause.

2. This meeting therefore calls earnestly on the workers of all the nationalities of Russia to rebuff the militant nationalism of the reactionaries with the utmost determination, to combat all manifestations of a nationalist spirit among the working masses. It calls on the worker Social-Democrats locally to display the closest solidarity, and to merge into integral organisations of the R.S.D.L.P. working in all the languages spoken by the local proletariat and achieving real unity from below, as has long been done in the Caucasus.

---

* See present edition, Vol. 17, pp. 464-65.—*Ed.*

3. This meeting expresses deep regret at the split in the ranks of the Polish Social-Democrats, which greatly weakens the struggle of the worker Social-Democrats of Poland. The meeting is compelled to state that the Executive of the Polish Social-Democrats, which today does not represent the majority of the Social-Democratic organisations of the Polish proletariat, resorts to impermissible methods in combating that majority (for example, groundlessly suspecting the entire Warsaw organisation of provocation). The meeting calls on all the Party organisations which come in contact with the Polish worker Social-Democrats to help them in establishing genuine unity among the Polish Social-Democrats.

4. This meeting points out in particular the extreme opportunism and liquidationism of the decisions adopted by the latest (ninth) conference of the Bund, which withdrew the slogan of a republic, pushed illegal work into the background and was oblivious of the revolutionary tasks of the proletariat. Equally reprehensible is the Bund's resistance to the unification of all worker Social-Democrats in the localities (Warsaw, Lodz, Vilna and elsewhere), a unification which the R.S.D.L.P. has repeatedly urged at its congresses and conferences since 1906.

5. This meeting greets the revolutionary worker Social-Democrats of the Lettish organisation, who perseveringly carry on anti-liquidationist propaganda, and expresses regret that the Central Committee of the Lettish Social-Democrats is inclined to support the anti-Party moves of the liquidators.

6. This meeting expresses firm confidence that the revolutionary upswing which has begun, and the mass economic and political strikes, street demonstrations and other forms of open revolutionary struggle by the masses will help in completely unifying and merging the worker Social-Democrats in the localities without any distinction between the nationalities, thereby strengthening the onslaught against tsarism, which oppresses all the peoples of Russia, and against the bourgeoisie of all the nations of Russia, which is in the process of uniting.

THE BRITISH LABOUR MOVEMENT IN 1912

The miners' strike was the outstanding event of the past year. While the railway strike in 1911 showed the "new spirit" of the British workers, the miners' strike definitely marked an epoch.

Despite the "war" preparations of the ruling classes, and despite the strenuous efforts of the bourgeoisie to crush the resistance of the rebellious slaves of capital, the strike was a success. The miners displayed exemplary organisation. There was not a trace of blacklegging. Coal-mining by soldiers or inexperienced labourers was out of the question. And after six weeks of struggle the bourgeois government of Britain saw that the country's entire industrial activity was coming to a standstill and that the words of the workers' song, "All wheels cease to whir when thy hand wills it",[180] were coming true.

The government made concessions.

"The Prime Minister of the most powerful empire the world has ever seen attended a delegate meeting of the mine-owners' striking slaves and pleaded with them to agree to a compromise." That is how a well-informed Marxist summed up the struggle.

The British Government, which year after year usually feeds its workers with promises of reform "some day", this time acted with real dispatch. In *five days* a new law was rushed through Parliament! This law introduced a *minimum wage*, i.e., regulations establishing rates of pay *below* which wages cannot be reduced.

It is true that this law, like all bourgeois reforms, is a miserable half-measure and in part a mere deception of the workers, because while fixing the lowest rate of pay,

the employers keep their wage-slaves down all the same.
Nevertheless, those who are familiar with the British labour
movement say that since the miners' strike the British proletariat *is no longer the same*. The workers have learned
to fight. They have come to see the *path* that will lead them
to victory. They have become aware of their strength. They
have ceased to be the meek lambs they seemed to be for so
long a time to the joy of all the defenders and extollers of
wage-slavery.

In Britain a change has taken place in the balance of
social forces, a change that cannot be expressed in figures
but is felt by all.

Unfortunately, there is not much progress in Party affairs
in Britain. The split between the British Socialist Party
(formerly the Social-Democratic Federation) and the Independent (of socialism) Labour Party persists. The opportunist conduct of the M.P.s belonging to the latter party
is giving rise, as always happens, to *syndicalist* tendencies
among the workers. Fortunately, these tendencies are not
strong.

The British trade unions are slowly but surely turning
towards socialism, in spite of the many Labour M.P.s who
stubbornly champion the old line of liberal labour policy.
But it is beyond the power of these last of the Mohicans
to retain the old line!

Pravda No. 1, January 1, 1913
Signed: *W.*

Published according
to the *Pravda* text

BETTER LATE THAN NEVER

I have had to be very late in coming out with a denial of what L. Martov wrote in *Luch* (No. 37, October 28, 1912). But how can it be helped? It is easy to tell an untruth, but sometimes it takes a long time *to find out* the truth.

In *Luch* No. 37, L. Martov heaped upon me the choicest abuse seasoned with the sort of "obscure" innuendoes that are usual with that writer. Having become accustomed in ten years to these methods of struggle used by L. Martov, I did not even read his article to the end. But some colleagues pointed out to me that L. Martov alleges that Comrade Haase, a member of the Central Committee of the German Social-Democrats, has said: "Lenin is *deceiving* the International."

To get at the truth, I had to find the *source* of Martov's allegation. He referred to a certain *Miners' Newspaper* No. 225. I could not find it. *Vorwärts* (central organ of the German Social-Democratic Party) contains no such words. I only found them in the *Bremer Bürger-Zeitung*[181] (the organ of the Bremen Social-Democrats).

I was faced with the necessity of questioning Haase himself if I did not want to imitate L. Martov's frivolous attitude.

I sent a written inquiry to the Central Committee of the German Social-Democrats.

Here is Haase's reply:

Central Committee
of the German Social-Democratic Party
Berlin, December 31, 1912

Dear Comrades,

In reply to your inquiry, I wish to inform you that the wording which, according to you, *Luch* used in reporting my speech in the International Socialist Bureau, is not in accord with the facts. The question discussed at the meeting was whether the Organising Committee can claim representation on the International Socialist Bureau. I said this was impermissible because, even according to its own statement, the Organising Committee is not an organisation but merely wants to be a union of groups for restoring the unity of the organisation. In this connection, I raised the question of who specifically was entitled to represent the Russian party in its present state, and remarked that if it was true that in its relations with the International Bureau the Central Committee acted as the "R.S.D.L.P.", this name might give rise to misunderstandings.

Thus there was no attack on Lenin here, and in general, the remark was not an insulting one at all. I wanted only to ascertain the state of affairs in view of the above-mentioned assertion, and primarily to raise the question whether the time had not come to take steps towards unifying all the Russo-Polish groups. I was very sorry Lenin was absent.

For the sake of completeness only, I wish to point out that the word "deceit" never passed my lips.

With comradely greetings, *Haase*

And so, in order to heap abuse on me for the thousandth time, L. Martov has repeated (echoing someone else) an *untruth* about Haase.

Haase was *against* the Organising Committee being represented, but he *did not dispute* the representation of the Central Committee.

Haase does not consider that the Central Committee represents the *entire* R.S.D.L.P., including the non-Russians and the liquidators; but then, as far as I know, the Central Committee itself has *never* claimed that it represented either of these.

The non-Russians (the Poles, the Bund, the Letts) have special representatives of their own.

I confine myself to this factual denial.

N. Lenin

Written on January 6 (19), 1913

Published in *Pravda* No. 8,   Published according
January 11, 1913   to the newspaper text

THE DEVELOPMENT OF REVOLUTIONARY STRIKES AND STREET DEMONSTRATIONS

It has long since been pointed out, and recognised by all, that the year 1912 was an outstanding landmark in the development of the strike movement. But not all have realised and taken proper account of it.

Let us take the data on political strikes in the first eleven months of the year. The result is as follows:

1905	1 052,000
1906	642,000
1907	540,000
. . . .	. . . .
1912 . . . . about	900,000

The number of political strikers in the first nine months was 700,000, according to the most conservative estimates. Strikes in connection with clearing up the matter of the delegates in St. Petersburg[182] involved up to 50,000 persons; the strike in protest against the Sevastopol executions and the strike on November 15, the day when the Duma opened, involved 188,000 persons, according to the Moscow *Manufacturers' Society*. These data are for the period before November 20. Obviously, 900,000 is a minimum figure. Even subtracting 100,000 that are hardly comparable with 1905-07 (factories *outside* the province of the factory inspectorate), we get 800,000.

In any case, the movement definitely surpassed that in 1906 and 1907, and fell but *slightly short* of that in 1905! What does this mean?

The national scale of the movement at present is, of course, much smaller than in 1905. Consequently, the *beginning* of the revolutionary upswing is *incomparably higher* today than it was before the first revolution. Consequently, the coming second revolution even now reveals a *much greater* store of revolutionary energy in the proletariat. The proletariat has grown in numbers—by a minimum of 20 per cent. Its concentration has increased. The purely proletarian mainstay of the movement has become stronger due to accelerated dissociation from the land. The size of the proletarian and semi-proletarian population in "domestic" industry, handicrafts and agriculture has grown to an enormous extent defying calculation.

Lastly, there has been an increase in the political consciousness, experience and determination of the foremost democratic class. This is admitted by all, but not all can bring themselves to think out all the implications. Not all can bring themselves to face the truth and admit that we are witnessing *revolutionary* mass strikes, the beginning of a *revolutionary* upsurge.

This is indicated first and foremost by the fundamental and most objective fact, one least of all permitting of subjective interpretation, namely, the scope of the movement. In no country of the world would it be possible, unless there were a revolutionary social situation, to rouse hundreds of thousands of workers to political action for the most varied reasons several times a year. But in our country this rise is taking place spontaneously, because tens of millions of the semi-proletarian and peasant population are passing on, if one can use this expression, to their vanguard a sentiment of concentrated indignation, which is surging up and overflowing.

The Russian workers' revolutionary strike in 1912 was national in the fullest sense of the term. For what should be understood by a national movement is not at all one with which—in the conditions of a bourgeois-democratic revolution—the whole bourgeoisie, or at least the liberal bourgeoisie, is in agreement. Only opportunists hold that view. On the contrary, a national movement is one which expresses the objective needs of the whole country, and aims its heaviest blows at the central forces of the enemy opposing the country's development. A national movement is one which has the sympathy of the vast majority of the population.

Such precisely is the workers' political movement this year, a movement which has the sympathy of all working and exploited people, of all democrats, however weak, downtrodden, disunited and helpless they may be. The more definite demarcation between liberalism and democracy (achieved not without a struggle against those who aspired to "wrest the Duma from the hands of the reactionaries") is a tremendous advantage of the new movement. If the revolution is to succeed, it must know as exactly as possible with whom it can go into battle, which of its allies is unreliable and who is its real enemy.

That is why the direct actions of the liberals (Cadets) against the new revolution are so very significant. And that is why the slogan of a republic, which clears the minds of all democrats willing to fight from the monarchist (as well as "constitutional") illusions which sapped so much the strength of the onslaught in 1905, is of the most exceptional importance (by comparison with Europe) in Russia just now. Of historic importance in the process of growth of the new revolution in Russia are two factors: firstly, the April and May strikes during which the St. Petersburg workers—in spite of the arrest of their leading organisation, the St. Petersburg Committee—put forward the slogan of a republic, an eight-hour working day, and confiscation of the landed estates. Secondly, the November strikes and demonstrations (see letters from Riga and Moscow[183]; the same thing happened in St. Petersburg, but the arrests swept away our correspondents). The slogans of those demonstrations were not only "Down with the death penalty! Down with war!", but also "Long live the revolutionary working class and the revolutionary army!"

In the streets of St. Petersburg, Riga and Moscow, the proletariat held out its hand to those foremost fighters of the muzhik armed forces who had risen heroically against the monarchy.

* *

*

The liberal bourgeoisie is against a new revolution, against revolutionary mass strikes. But the liberals are by no means opposed to political strikes in general, that is,

if these are only evidence of a "revival" and support merely
the liberal slogan of constitutional reform. And objectively,
irrespective of their "good" intentions, our liquidators
are mere servants of the counter-revolutionary bourgeoisie;
they marked both historic moments of the upswing by "pro-
nouncements" against revolutionary strikes!! In *Nevsky
Golos* No. 1, on May 20, 1912, the unforgettable and incomparable V. Yezhov rebelled against "complicating" economic strikes by political strikes and vice versa, against their
"harmful lumping together" (cf. *Sotsial-Demokrat* No. 27,
p. 4).*

In November 1912 the liquidationist *Luch*, too, was up
in arms against strikes. Afterwards it tried to put inattentive people "on a false scent" by referring to the fact that
the Social-Democratic group, too, was against the November 15 strike. But anyone who looks at all into the meaning
of the event will easily see through *Luch*'s trickery.

Yes, both the Social-Democratic group and the St. Petersburg Committee found the November 15 strike inoppor-
tune. They sounded a warning against that particular strike
on that particular day. It was the duty of the working-
class press to report this. And *Luch* and *Pravda* did.

But *Luch* did something besides.

After the event of November 15 (when the most zealous
in striking was the very same Vyborg District which until
then had been most of all linked with the Mensheviks), and
after the movement had grown to the dimensions of a demonstration, the sagacious *Luch* carried articles (an editorial
and, following the editorial of November 17, a *feuilleton*
on November 21) crying out against the "dangerous frittering
away of forces", declaring that "if strikes are used frequently, people will stop sympathising with them", advancing
the slogan "Let us seek a different path" and "Nothing is
to be gained by outbreaks" (!?!), and howling against "playing at strikes".

That is the kind of "philosophy", advocated by you
liquidator gentlemen, and long familiar to the St. Petersburg workers, both from *Nevsky Golos* and from speeches
by members of your "initiating group", that has gained

_____
* See pp. 116-17 of this volume.—*Ed.*

you the legitimate hatred and contempt of the St. Petersburg workers. A particular strike may be unfortunate or take place at an unfortunate moment. But only liberals and counter-revolutionaries are free to describe as "playing at strikes" one of the world's greatest movements, which brought into action almost a million proletarians!

Frequent strikes are apt to exhaust the workers. It may well be, therefore, that we shall have to call for shorter strikes and for demonstrations that have been better prepared. But the event of November 15 was remarkable precisely as a new step forward in the demonstration movement!

Instead of honestly admitting your mistake (for you were plainly mistaken as to the significance of November 15), you liquidators began to talk, like the most brazen liberals, about the "political illiteracy" of the revolutionary appeal, you who are repeating the ABC of liberal politics!

Let the workers judge the worth of the liquidators' smoothspoken talk about their "unity" with the Party when it happens that, at the time of the rise and development of revolutionary strikes and demonstrations, the liquidators launch a struggle against them, using the legal press to revile illegal appeals!!

* *
*

However, there is a more profound reason for the liquidators' campaign against strikes. The liquidators are slaves of the liberals. And the liberals have really begun to feel ill at ease because of the stubborn character of revolutionary strikes. The "Progressist" factory owner has begun to grumble and even to rage. The Milyukovs now fear lest their "bloc" with Rodzyanko should be disturbed.

Liquidationist policy serves to subject the workers to the liberals. Marxist policy raises the workers to the role of leaders of the *peasantry*. One cannot speak of this legally, liquidator gentlemen, but one must think of it and tell about it to those who want to be revolutionary Social-Democrats.

In free, constitutional Europe, political strikes for the time being (so long as the *socialist* revolution has not yet begun) serve the struggle for individual reforms. In slave, Asiatic, tsarist Russia, which is drawing near her next *bourgeois-democratic* revolution, political strikes are the only serious means of stirring up the peasantry and the better part of the peasant army, of shaking them up and rousing them to a revolutionary struggle! The time is past— fortunately for Russia—when there was no one to "go among the people" but heroic solitary Narodniks. The time is passing when solitary terrorists could speak of "rousing" the people by terrorism. Russia has left those sad times behind. In 1905 the revolutionary proletariat found for itself a different way "to go among the people", and a different means of drawing the masses into the movement.

That means is revolutionary strikes, stubborn strikes shifting from place to place, from one part of the country to another, recurrent strikes, strikes which rouse the backward to a new life of struggle for economic improvements, strikes which brand and lash every salient act of violence or tyranny, every crime of tsarism, strike-demonstrations which unfurl the red banner in the streets of the capital cities and bring revolutionary speeches and revolutionary slogans to the *crowd*, to the mass of the people.

Such strikes cannot be called forth artificially, but neither can they be stopped once they have begun to involve hundreds and hundreds of thousands.

Let the liberal, who is moved by being given a seat beside Rodzyanko "himself", tell the workers: "Brothers, no more outbreaks, seek a different path, take up the peaceful trade union movement, prepare yourselves earnestly for an open European party, don't incite the muzhik to rebellion, don't waste your energy on strikes or 'we' shall stop sympathising with you!"

The workers will know how to assess such talk, and will see through it even in the garb of the "near-Marxist" expressions of any of the *Luch* writers.

The workers will concentrate on *deliberately* supporting, strengthening, developing and consolidating the spontaneously growing revolutionary strike to prepare the peasants and the armed forces for a rising. If strikes exhaust the workers, they should be carried out intermittently, enabling some of the forces to rest while the forces that are rested or "fresh" are roused to take up the struggle. Shorter strikes should be called. Occasionally strikes should be replaced by demonstrations. But the important thing is that strikes, meetings and demonstrations should take place continuously, that the whole peasantry and the armed forces should know of the workers' stubborn fight, and that the countryside —even the most out-of-the-way corners of it —should see that there is unrest in the towns, that *"their"* people have risen in revolt, that they are waging a life-and-death struggle, that they are fighting for a better life, for higher pay, for an end to the outrages and tyranny of the authorities, for the transfer of the landed estates to the peasants, for the overthrow of the tsar's landlord monarchy, for a republic. It is essential that the smouldering resentment and subdued murmurings of the countryside should, along with the indignation in the barracks, find a centre of attraction in the workers' revolutionary strikes. We must work on this indefatigably, and we shall live to see the day when the proletariat, jointly with the peasantry and the armed forces, brings down the landlords and overthrows the tsarist monarchy by a people's uprising.

P.S. *Luch* is making progress: after the unsophisticated V. A. (No. 56) comes the diplomatic F. D.[184] (No. 65). But for all his "diplomacy", the meaning of F.D.'s statements is the same—he is *against* revolutionary strikes! We are faced with an out-and-out liberal to whom it *never occurs* that strikes awaken the peasants and lead them to insurrection, that strikes develop *revolutionary* agitation among the masses and awaken the armed forces, and that it is necessary to pass from strikes (insofar as they are exhausting) to street demonstrations, etc.

F.D.'s. vulgar liberal phrases about the "struggle for the right to organise" as the "immediate task"—a constitutional reform "on the order of the day" under Treshchenko! — is the sole cover for *Luch*'s fight against revolutionary strikes. It is not enough, liquidator gentlemen!

Sotsial-Demokrat No. 30,
January 12 (25), 1913

Published according
to the text in *Sotsial-Demokrat*

ORIGINAL POSTSCRIPT TO THE ARTICLE
"THE DEVELOPMENT OF REVOLUTIONARY STRIKES
AND STREET DEMONSTRATIONS"[185]

We call on Social-Democrats to pay particular attention to F.D.'s "Tactical Notes" in *Luch*. How rapidly the coating of showy conciliationism and "unification" phrase-mongering in the spirit of Trotsky has disappeared! How clearly the *real* trend of *Luch*—barefaced liquidationism—has been revealed!

In a legal organ, F.D. is waging a regular war not only against revolutionary mass strikes (to say nothing of an uprising), but also against all revolutionary agitation among the masses. In point of fact, F.D. goes much further than V.A. (*Luch* No. 56), betraying his complete ideological kinship with the Bund's "deletion" of the revolution. That is what comes of the liquidators' refusal to make a straightforward, clear and formal "appraisal of the situation": it is in fact Larin's appraisal that F.D. upholds by denying the *objective* conditions which make it *imperative* for the workers to organise *for revolution*, for drawing the masses in general and the peasantry in particular into the *revolutionary* movement.

We shall come back to F.D.'s articles again.

Written in January 1913

Published for the first time

Published according
to the manuscript

THE SPLIT AMONG THE POLISH SOCIAL-DEMOCRATS

The present split among the Polish Social-Democrats is the fruit of a conflict that began several years ago. At the Sixth Congress of the Party, in 1908, such a sharp antagonism was shown between the Executive Committee, on the one hand, and the Warsaw and Dombrowa area organisations, on the other, that the Congress rejected a motion of confidence in the Executive. The conflict was organisational but had great political significance. The two local organisations insisted on the opportunity to influence the political position of the Party, and claimed widespread discussion of all its steps by the organisations.

The Executive has remained, nevertheless, in the hands of the same people. And its majority, headed by the notorious Tyszka, sticks to its tactics, profiting by the weakening of the Party, by failures and by the conditions of counter-revolution. In the R.S.D.L.P., Tyszka played the master and plotted in the name of the Social-Democracy of Poland and Lithuania, without paying the slightest attention to the will of the latter. In the policy of the Party, an era of unprincipledness and vacillation began, on such questions, for example, as the trade unions, the attitude to the P.S.P., and the tactics of the Polish Social-Democrats within the R.S.D.L.P. Comrades who laid bare the contradictions in the policy of the Executive and demanded a consistently principled line had their mouths shut by the Executive, which would not allow any discussion in the press and, worse still, *constantly* promised to open a discussion "in the near future", when it would also publish the comrades' protests against its tactics. Tyszka's opponents on the Executive itself, who were all old functionaries, well known to the whole Party, were ousted one by one. One of them refused to stand for re-election at the Sixth Congress, saying that it was impossible to work with Tyszka, another was ousted in 1909, and a third refused to enter the Executive in 1911.

But as the movement grew and became more active, from early 1911 onwards, discontent began to show in local organisations as well. The "rebellion" was led by the Warsaw organisation, which is the most important and powerful, and above all the most consistent in the revolutionary sense, and which, ever since 1905, has been in the Left wing among the Polish Social-Democrats.

The Executive, of course, became uneasy and made ready to "nip it in the bud". The December 1911 inter-district conference in Warsaw served as the signal for the attack. That conference made bold to insist that the "terri-tory" should be represented more strongly at the next *Party* conference, i.e.—the impious idea!—that the influ-ence of the Executive at the conference should thereby be weakened. But that would have been half the trouble, for a similar resolution was adopted by the Lodz conference as well. Warsaw did something more criminal: it showed that it demanded this not haphazardly, but with a *political aim* in view. It adopted several political resolutions that Tyszka did not like; among other things, it expressed dis-pleasure at the fact that the Executive had submitted no report to Warsaw on its activity, and demanded that the Executive should acquaint the Party with its activity inside the R.S.D.L.P., that it should not make a "Russian" policy secretly from the Polish workers, and so on.

An open struggle began. Tyszka gave vent to a series of "circulars" and "explanations". He "explained" that (1) the Warsaw organisation had trampled the Party Rules underfoot and resorted to a split; (2) that its resolutions were an indication of boycottism, otzovism and anarchism; (3) that it had no ideological differences with the Exec-utive and hence the split had no political basis; (4) that the Warsaw organisation did not exist, the conference had been fictitious, and consequently there was and had been no split; (5) that the Warsaw organisation had been un-able to publish a single sheet on its own and had left all literary work to the Executive; that it had unlawfully devised a disruptive technique of its own and was publishing its own sheets. He also gave a personal description, complete with family details, of a couple of Warsaw "intellectualist *warchols*",* and explained that they had brought about a split but did not work in the organisation and never had.

Finally, seeing that the Warsaw organisation held its ground, Tyszka made up his mind to take "heroic"measures. He decided to call a *fictitious* conference and not to allow it to be attended by the opposition, i.e., the vast majority of the comrades active in the territory. To that end he announced the "dissolution" of the strongest organisation — Warsaw—and formed a separate "Warsaw organisation" of splitters out of two or three agents of his own.

But the most outrageous thing is the "grounds" on which Tyszka "dissolved" the Warsaw organisation. He announced that the organisation, which refused to submit to him, was nothing but a tool of police provocation. So far he has not cited a single serious fact, even of the very smallest kind, to support his allegation. Nor has he published *the name of a single* person he suspects. What is more, to leave the way to retreat open, he wrote like a coward, in a statement to the International Bureau, that provocation could very easily have ensconced itself in Warsaw *as in any other* organisation functioning under the present conditions.

Nevertheless, Tyszka saw fit to "dissolve" the Warsaw organisation, and even to declare it to be outside the R.S.D.L.P. The reader will see that this is no longer a factional struggle but in fact something of a criminal nature.

Needless to say this reckless step by Tyszka's caused indignation ten times as great. The committee which he himself had appointed to inquire into the provocation came out against him. Tyszka replied by expelling from the Party three leaders of the Polish Social-Democracy who had been members of the Party for many years and who enjoyed universal confidence. Forty-four veteran functionaries published a most emphatic protest against the

---

* Trouble-makers.—*Ed.*

Executive's actions, which are humiliating to any revolutionary. Both in the territory and abroad, people insist that the "Executive" should be called to account. It goes without saying that the Warsaw organisation did not dissolve itself to please Tyszka but continues its work, which is so difficult under present conditions. It was the "opposition" that achieved signal success in the elections for the worker curia of Warsaw. The elections gave the Social-Democrats an absolute majority over all the other parties. Of the 34 Social-Democratic delegates, 31 support the opposition, 2 are vacillating, and only one backs Tyszka. On the other hand, in the provinces, where the "work" is carried on by the Executive and its supporters, the election campaign was lost *everywhere*.

It is to be hoped that the petty and unseemly squabble caused by Tyszka's conduct will soon be a thing of the past and that differences of principle will stand out more clearly. The Polish worker Social-Democrats' desire to establish closer organisational links with their Russian comrades will also find a more specific expression. Tyszka's conduct in the R.S.D.L.P. has resulted in the Executive becoming completely divorced from the life of the Party as a whole and having not a single ally in the R.S.D.L.P., and both sides (the liquidators and anti-liquidators) alike are shrugging their shoulders over the strange and unprincipled "tactics" of Tyszka and his "Executive".

The Polish Social-Democrats are passing through hard times. But already there are signs of a way out. All the sound elements of the Polish Social-Democratic movement are rallying together. And the time is already near when the Polish Social-Democracy will be an organisation of pro-Party worker Social-Democrats who have principles and tactics of their own and are not a plaything in the hands of an unscrupulous plotter.

———

We think it necessary to complete the report on the split among the Polish Social-Democrats with certain data on the subsequent history of the accusation of "provocation". Here is what we have been told:

Rosa Luxemburg (member of the International Socialist Bureau from the Polish Social-Democracy) wrote a note to the I.S.B. alleging that the Warsaw Committee was made up of splitters and was *in the hands of the secret police*, stating that this was not to be published!

Yet Tyszka *himself* published this abomination in the Polish Social-Democratic press!!

Lenin, upon receiving a copy of Tyszka's note from Huysmans, Secretary of the International Socialist Bureau, sent a letter to Huysmans, of course, saying that it was a "most perfidious" act of vengeance, that Malecki and Hanecki, ex-members of the Central Committee, were known to all in the Party; that the committee of inquiry appointed by Tyszka himself had *discovered no* provocation; that to publish anything about provocation among political opponents, without giving names, was a most foul and mean thing to do.*

The Executive replied with mere abuse.

The Basle Congress met. The delegation of the Warsaw Committee was *unanimously* recognised by *all* R.S.D.L.P. delegates—liquidators, Letts, Vperyodists, Bundists and Trotskyists alike!

The Warsaw election resulted in *both* electors being worker Social-Democrats who *supported the Warsaw Committee* and were opposed to Tyszka and Co.

The fictitious nature of Tyszka's parallel organisation has been demonstrated to all. The honest course—of withdrawing the accusation of provocation—is more than Tyszka and his Executive can adopt.

But best of all are our liquidators and their Organising Committee, who love "unity". *Luch,* which officially *adheres* to the August conference, has *twice printed* Tyszka's foul lie!!

On the first occasion it was done by a gentleman who hid behind initials. The second time it was done by Mr. *Avgustovsky*.[186]

And see how brave they are! They put about a foul story —and take cover behind the back of the Executive. We've got nothing to do with it, they seem to say, we cannot be

---

* See pp. 276-277 of this volume.—*Ed.*

held responsible, we aren't putting about any foul story, we are *"only"* reporting the *fact* that something (a foul story) was *printed* on behalf of the Executive!!

Martov, Trotsky, Lieber, the Letts and Co. are *anonymously* putting about Tyszka's foul story—in the legal press, where documents cannot be quoted—hiding behind Tyszka's back!!

Sotsial-Demokrat No. 30,
January 12 (25), 1913

Published according
to the text in *Sotsial-Demokrat*

ON BOLSHEVISM[187]

The origin of Bolshevism is inseparably linked with the struggle of what is known as Economism (opportunism which rejected the political struggle of the working class and denied the latter's leading role) against revolutionary Social-Democracy in 1897-1902. Economism, supported by the Bund, was defeated and eliminated by the well-known campaign of the old *Iskra*[188] (Munich, London and Geneva, 1900-03), which restored the Social-Democratic Party (founded in 1898 but later destroyed by arrests) on the basis of Marxism and revolutionary Social-Democratic principles. At the Second Congress of the R.S.D.L.P. (August 1903), the Iskrists split: the *majority* stood for the principles and tactics of the old *Iskra*, while the *minority* turned to opportunism, and was backed by the one-time enemies of *Iskra*, the Economists and the Bundists. Hence the terms Bolshevism* and Menshevism* (Bolsheviks and Mensheviks). In 1903-04 the struggle was mainly over the Mensheviks' opportunism in questions of organisation. From the end of 1904 on, tactical differences became the most important. The "plan for the Zemstvo campaign"[189] put forward (autumn 1904) by the *new Iskra*, which had deserted to the Mensheviks, took up the defence of the tactics of "not intimidating the liberals". The year 1905 saw the tactical differences take final shape (the Bolshevik Congress, Third Congress of the R.S.D.L.P. in London, May 1905, and the Menshevik "conference" held in Geneva at the same time). The Mensheviks strove to adapt working-class tactics to liberalism. The Bolsheviks, however, put forward as the aim of the working class in the bourgeois-democratic revolution: to carry it through to the end and

---

* From the Russian words for *majority* and *minority*.—Tr.

to lead the democratic peasantry despite the treachery of the liberals. The main practical divergencies between the two trends in the autumn of 1905 were over the fact that the Bolsheviks stood for boycotting the Bulygin Duma while the Mensheviks favoured participation. In the spring of 1906, the same thing happened with regard to the Witte Duma. First Duma: the Mensheviks stood for the slogan of a Duma (Cadet) Ministry; the Bolsheviks, for the slogan of a Left (Social-Democratic and Trudovik) Executive Committee that would organise the actual struggle of the masses, etc. This could be set forth in greater detail only in the press abroad. At the Stockholm Congress (1906) the Mensheviks won the upper hand, and at the London Congress (1907), the Bolsheviks. In 1908-09 the *Vperyod* group (Machism[190] in philosophy and otzovism, or boycotting the Third Duma, in politics—Bogdanov, Alexinsky, Lunacharsky and others) broke away from the Bolsheviks. In 1909-11, in fighting against them (cf. V. Ilyin, *Materialism and Empirio-Criticism*, Moscow, 1909*), as well as against the liquidators (Mensheviks who denied the need for an illegal Party), Bolshevism came close to the *pro-Party Mensheviks* (Plekhanov and others), who had declared a resolute war on liquidationism. The Bolshevik organs were: *Vperyod* and *Proletary* (Geneva, 1905), *Novaya Zhizn* (St. Petersburg, 1905), *Volna*, *Ekho*, etc. (St. Petersburg, 1906), *Proletary* in Finland (1906-07), Geneva (1908) and Paris (1909), *Sotsial-Demokrat* in Paris (1909-12). Some of the principal writings of Bolshevism are collected in V. Ilyin's[191] *Twelve Years*, St. Petersburg, 1908, which also gives a more detailed bibliography. The main Bolshevik writers: G. Zinoviev, V. Ilyin, Y. Kamenev, P. Orlovsky and others. In recent years Bolsheviks have been the main contributors to the newspapers *Zvezda* (1910-12), *Pravda* (1912), St. Petersburg, and to the periodicals *Mysl* (1910), Moscow, and *Prosveshcheniye* (1911-13), St. Petersburg.

Written in the first half of January 1913

First published in 1913, in the book: N. A. Rubakin, *Among Books*, Vol. II, Second Ed., Moscow

Published according to the text in the book

---

* See present edition, Vol. 14.—*Ed.*

THE SIGNIFICANCE OF POINCARE'S ELECTION

The new President of the French Republic is being effusively congratulated. Take a look at the Black-Hundred-pogromist *Novoye Vremya* and the liberal *Rech*: how touchingly unanimous they are in congratulating President Poincaré and expressing their delight!

The appraisal of foreign policy issues and of the state of affairs in the Western countries is particularly indicative of the profound inner kinship of our Black Hundreds and our liberals. The fact that both of them hail the "national" President, Poincaré, who has been elected by an alliance of the big bourgeoisie and clerical and feudal reaction in France, makes it clear to anyone that the Black Hundreds and liberals disagree only over *methods* of combating socialism.

But Poincaré's election is of greater interest than the zealous "congratulators" think. Class-conscious workers, in pondering on the significance of this election, note three circumstances.

Firstly, Poincaré's election means another step forward in aggravating the class struggle confronting France. Poincaré was Premier in a Chamber having a *Radical* majority. But he has been elected President *against* the Radical candidate, Pams, with the aid of *clerical and feudal* reaction, and by the *Right bloc*.

What does that mean? Power in France is in the hands of the *last* bourgeois party, the Radicals.[192] It is becoming less and less distinguishable from "reaction". The *whole* bourgeoisie—from radical to reactionary—is uniting ever more closely against the socialist proletariat, and the boundary between the two sections of the bourgeoisie is becoming more and more obliterated. This was revealed all the more vividly by the election of Poincaré. This sort of unity is an unmistakable sign of the extreme aggravation of class antagonisms.

Secondly, Poincaré's career is worthy of note, being that of a typical bourgeois businessman who sells himself in turn to all parties in politics, and to all rich men "outside" politics. Poincaré has been a lawyer by profession since the age of twenty. At twenty-six he was a *chef de cabinet* and at thirty-three, a Minister. Rich men and the big-wigs of finance in all countries think highly of the political connections of such dexterous careerists. A "brilliant" lawyer-deputy and a political trickster are *synonyms* in the "civilised" countries.

Worthy of note, thirdly, is the demonstration made by the French Socialists during Poincaré's election. The vote in favour of Vaillant was a demonstration in honour of the Commune. Vaillant is a living memory of it. One has only to see the welcome which Parisian workers give the white-haired Vaillant when he appears on the platform to realise this.

And now, in the very same Versailles where bourgeois France in 1871 sold its country to Bismarck in order to crush the revolt of the proletariat, and in the very same hall where forty-two years ago was heard the beastly howling of the reactionary landlords of France who were longing for a king, the working-class deputies voted for a veteran Communard.

Pravda No 11, January 15, 1913   Published according
         Signed: *V. I.*   to the *Pravda* text

FRANKLY

This newspaper has already noted the failure, in the Council of State, of the Duma Bill to introduce a Zemstvo in Archangel Gubernia. But it is well worth dwelling once more on the importance of this fact, which, for all its insignificance, is highly characteristic.

For almost half a century there has existed a Zemstvo of the nobility, one which guarantees the absolute preponderance of the feudal type of *landlord*. And only in some gubernias, such as Vyatka Gubernia, where there is hardly any landed nobility, the Zemstvo has more of a muzhik character. However, there it is enmeshed even more in all kinds of bureaucratic bans, impediments, restrictions and specifications. It would seem that it is this sort of harmless, curtailed Zemstvo that Archangel Gubernia, too, has been seeking for over a half century.

And now the resolution of the Black-Hundred, landlord and bourgeois Third Duma to introduce a Zemstvo in Archangel Gubernia has been *rejected* by the Council of State. What a glaring light this "trifle" sheds on the *essence* of our "renovated" system! What a splendid lesson on the class roots of politics!

The arguments of the opponents of the Zemstvo on the Council of State are frank—there is no nobility there, you see. "Private" landownership in the whole gubernia amounts to a mere 2,660 dessiatines, exclaimed Mr. Stishinsky, the reporter in the Council of State.

It follows that where there is no landed nobility, the "people" are not mature enough even to deal with the repair of roads and the building of hospitals. But if there are no landlords, they should be implanted, directly or indirectly.

Implanted from where? From central Russia, where they are numerous enough. The landlords of the black-earth central region where the vestiges of serfdom are freshest, where more is left of the corvée (labour service) system than anywhere else, and where diehards like those in Kursk Gubernia rule and reign and govern—those are the ones to rely on where government and public affairs are concerned. In this sense, the attitude of the Council of State to the question of a Zemstvo in Archangel Gubernia is a most instructive and graphic lesson in our statehood.

Pravda No. 13, January 17, 1913   Published according
        Signed: *V.*   to the *Pravda* text

THE BRIAND CABINET

The well-known renegade Briand, once an extreme revolutionary and an advocate of the "general strike", finds himself again at the head of the French Ministry. Like John Burns in Britain, he has betrayed the working class and sold himself to the bourgeoisie.

The composition of his new Cabinet is of interest. It is dominated by the trio of Jonnart, Etienne and Baudin. What sort of men are they?

Take a look at the liberal papers, such as *Rech* No. 11. You will find there a most detailed account of where the Ministers were educated and where they were employed. You will find shameless advertising and the desire to curry favour: Jonnart is said to be a friend of King Edward, and Baudin, the nephew of a Communard!

"Zhomini this, Zhomini that—and not a word about vodka."[193] *Rech* says nothing about the *crux* of the matter. And the crux of the matter is very simple: this trio is a most arrant and shameless band of financial sharks and swindlers. Etienne has had a hand in all the dirty scandals involving millions, *from Panama onwards*. He is an old hand at financial transactions in the colonies, like the one concerning our own Bashkir lands. Jonnart took part in what was a no less "clean" business—securing the rich iron ore deposits of Ouenza, Africa, as a concession. His kith and kin sit on the boards of some of the largest joint-stock companies. Baudin is a lieutenant of capitalists, contractors and shipyard owners. The Naval Ministry is just the place for him—it is so much closer to contracts and to deliveries for the Navy!

Marx's statement that bourgeois governments are the lieutenants of the capitalist class[194] has nowhere been confirmed more clearly than in France. And the great progress made by France is that the working class has torn off all sham coverings, that it has made the unclear clear, and "cast off from the chains the false flowers adorning them— not in order that mankind might continue to bear those chains in their form, bare of all joy and all delight, but in order that it might cast off the chains and reach for the living flower".[195]

Pravda No. 14, January 18, 1913
Signed: *I*.   Published according
to the *Pravda* text

RESULTS OF THE ELECTIONS

The Fourth Duma election campaign has confirmed the appraisal of the historical situation that Marxists have been giving since 1911. The gist of that appraisal is that the first period of the history of Russian counter-revolution is over. The second period has begun, a period characterised by the awakening of "light contingents" of bourgeois democrats (the student movement), by the aggressive economic, and still more non-economic, movement of the working class, and so on.

Economic depression, the vigorous offensive of the counter-revolution, the retreat and disintegration of the democratic forces, and the spate of renegade, *Vekhi*, liquidationist ideas in the "progressive camp"—these are the distinguishing features of the first period (1907-11). As for the second period (1911-12), it is distinguished—economically, politically and ideologically—by the opposite features: an upswing in industry, the inability of the counter-revolution to press forward its offensive with the same force or vigour as before, etc., and the revival of the democratic movement, which forced *Vekhi*, renegade, liquidationist sentiments *to conceal themselves*.

Such is the general background of the picture, which has to be borne in mind if the election campaign of 1912 is to be appraised accurately.

I. MANIPULATING THE ELECTIONS

The most striking characteristic of the elections to the Fourth Duma is their systematic rigging by the government. It is not our aim here to sum up the results of "manipulating the elections". This has been commented on quite sufficiently by the *entire* liberal and democratic press, and the Cadets' detailed interpellation in the Fourth Duma speaks of the same thing. We shall probably be able to devote a special article to this question when the vast and increasing documentary evidence has been collated.

For the time being we shall only note the principal results of manipulating the elections, and the chief political significance of this manipulation.

The priesthood mobilised against the liberal and Octobrist landlords; repressive measures increased tenfold, and the law most unceremoniously violated to prejudice the rights of the bourgeois democracy in town and country; attempts made to wrest the worker curia from the Social-Democrats by the same means—these are the principal methods used in manipulating the 1912 elections. The purpose of this policy, which is reminiscent of Bonapartist policy, was to form a Right-wing and nationalist majority in the Duma, and this aim, as we know, has not been achieved. But we shall see below that the government has succeeded in "upholding" the former, Third Duma, situation in our parliament, if we may call it that: there remain two possible majorities in the Fourth Duma, a Right-wing and Octobrist and an Octobrist-Cadet one.

The electoral law of June 3, 1907, "built" the state system of administration—and, indeed, not only of administration—on a bloc of the feudal landlords and the top strata of the bourgeoisie, with the first-named social element retaining a tremendous preponderance in this bloc, while above *both* elements stood a virtually uncurtailed old authority. There is no need now to say what the specific nature of that authority, brought into being by the age-long history of serfdom, etc., has been and still is. At all events, the shift in 1905, the collapse of the old state of affairs, and the open and powerful actions of the masses and classes, necessitated the search for an *alliance* with particular social forces.

The hopes pinned on the "uneducated" muzhik in 1905-06 (the Bulygin and Witte electoral laws) were shattered. The July Third system "banked on the strong", on the landlords and the bourgeois big-wigs. But in the course of a mere five years the experience of the Third Duma has begun to break this gamble as well! It would be hard to imagine greater servility than the Octobrists showed in 1907-12, and yet even they did not prove servile enough. The old authority (the "bureaucracy"), which is closely akin to them in character, was unable to get along even with them. The bourgeois policy in the countryside (the law of November 9[196]) and full assistance to capitalism were both directed by the very same Purishkeviches, and the results proved to be deplorable. Purishkevichism—refurbished, repaired, and freshened up with a new agrarian policy and a new system of representative institutions—continued to crush everything and hamper progress.

The June Third system developed a crack. "Manipulation" of the elections became inevitable, just as Bonapartist methods are historically inevitable when there is no solid, durable and tested integral social basis, and when there is a need to manoeuvre among heterogeneous elements. If the democratic classes are powerless, or have been greatly weakened for temporary reasons, such methods may be attended by "success" over a number of years. But even the "classical" examples of Bismarck in the sixties of the last century, or of Napoleon III, bear witness that things do not work out without the most drastic changes (in Prussia it was a "revolution from above"[197] and several exceptionally successful wars).

II. THE NEW DUMA

To ascertain the results of the elections, let us take the official data on the party composition of the Fourth Duma and compare it with that of the Third Duma, not only at the end of its existence (1912), but also at the beginning (1908). We obtain the following instructive picture*:

---

* The data are taken from the following Duma publications: *Ukazatel (Directory)* for 1908, *Spravochnik (Reference Book)* for 1912 and *Spravochny Listok [IV] Gosudarstvennoi Dumy (Reference Sheet of the Fourth State Duma)* No. 14, December 2, 1912—corrected data as of December 1, 1912. The three national groups are the Poles, Byelorussians and Moslems.

	Third Duma		Fourth Duma
	1908	1912	
Rights	49	46	65
Nationalists and moderate Rights . .	95	102	120
Octobrists	148	120	98
Progressists	25	36	48
Cadets	53	52	59
The three national groups	26	27	21
Trudoviks	14	14	10
Social-Democrats	19	13	14
Unaffiliated	—	27	7
Total	429	437	442

The first conclusion to be drawn from these data is that in the Fourth Duma the former two possible majorities remain—the Right-wing and Octobrist majority of 283 votes (65+120+98) and the Octobrist-Cadet majority of 226 votes (98+48+59+21).

As far as the autocratic government is concerned, the most important thing for practical purposes is to have "its own" majority in the Duma. The distinction between the Third and Fourth Dumas is negligible in this respect. In the Third Duma, the Right-wing and Octobrist majority was 292 votes at the beginning and 268 at the end. What we have now is 283, a figure midway between those two.

But the drop in the Right-wing majority between the beginning and the end of the Third Duma was so considerable that the government, being an autocratic one, could not but resort to extraordinary measures of manipulating the elections. That manipulation is neither an accident nor a departure from the system, as the Meyendorfs, Maklakovs and Co. like to make out, but a measure indispensable for maintaining the "system".

You, liberal gentlemen headed by Maklakov, talk of "reconciling the government and the country" (i.e., the bourgeoisie). But if that is true, there are two alternatives. Either your *talk about reconciliation* is not meaningless words, and then you must also accept "manipulating the elections", for such is the real condition for reconciliation with the real government. After all, you are so fond of "realistic policy"! Or *your protests* against "manipulating the elections" are not meaningless words, and then you should speak not of reconciliation, but of something entirely unlike reconciliation.

The second majority of the June Third system, the Octobrist-liberal one, was 252 votes in the early period of the Third Duma and 235 at its end, and it has dropped to 226 in the Fourth Duma. Consequently, the government's "election campaign" was in effect a success; the government had its way, once again confirming its autocratic character in practice. For the cries about a Right-wing and nationalist majority were merely haggling. In reality, the government needs both majorities, *both* of which have a counter-revolutionary basis.

It is impossible to lay too much stress on the last circumstance, which the liberals gloss over in order to fool the democrats, while the liberal labour politicians (liquidators) do the same thing from lack of intelligence. The bloc of the Cadets and Octobrists, which came to light so strikingly during Rodzyanko's election (and was perhaps even more strikingly revealed by the unseemly, slavish words of *Rech* about Rodzyanko's speech), is by no means just a "technical" matter. This bloc expresses the community of the counter-revolutionary sentiments of the bourgeoisie in general, from Guchkov to Milyukov; it is made possible only by these sentiments.

On the other hand, the government, too, needs the liberal-Octobrist majority from the point of view of the entire system of the June Third regime. For the Third (and Fourth) Duma is not at all a "cardboard" institution, as it is often made out to be by the claptrap of the "Left" Narodniks, who are bogged down hopelessly in Ropshin-like experiences and "otzovist" phrases.[198] No, the Third and Fourth Dumas are a stage in the development of the autocracy and in that of the bourgeoisie; they are an attempt really to bring them closer together, a necessary attempt after the victories and defeats of 1905. And the failure of this attempt would be the failure not only of Stolypin and Makarov, or of Markov the Second and Purishkevich, *but also of the "conciliator" Maklakov and Co.!*

The government needs a liberal-Octobrist majority in order to try to lead Russia forward while preserving the omnipotence of the Purishkeviches. As regards instruments for curbing or moderating unusually fast-moving over-zealous liberal-Octobrist "Progressism", the government has plenty of them—the Council of State and many many more.

III. CHANGES WITHIN THE JUNE THIRD SYSTEM

The data quoted above provide interesting evidence of the evolution of the political parties, groupings and trends among the landlords and the bourgeoisie in the period of counter-revolution. The composition of the Third and Fourth Dumas hardly tells us anything about the bourgeois (peasant) or worker democrats, for the simple reason that the June Third system was devised with the express aim of ruling out the democrats. In the same way, the non-Russian parties, i.e., those not representing the "dominant" nationality, have been specially oppressed and stifled by the June Third system.

We shall therefore pick out only the Rights, the Octobrists and the Russian liberals—parties which have made themselves thoroughly comfortable within the June Third system and are protected by it against the democrats—and look at the changes that have occurred in these parties.

| | Third Duma | | Fourth Duma | Comparison of Fourth Duma and beginning of Third Duma |
	1908	1912		
Rights	144	148	185	+41, i. e., +28 per cent
Octobrists	148	120	98	−50 " −34 " "
Liberals (Progress- ists and Cadets)	78	88	107	+29 " +37 " "

This shows clearly how the so-called "Centre" is dwindling among the privileged strata and how their Right and liberal wings are gaining strength. It is interesting to note that the number of liberals among the landlords and the bourgeoisie is growing *faster* than that of the Rights, despite the emergency measures taken by the government to rig the elections in favour of the Rights.

There are those who, in view of these facts, like to talk pompously about the aggravation of the contradictions of the June Third system, about the coming triumph of moderate bourgeois progressism, and so on. They forget, firstly, that while the number of liberals is growing among the landlords, and above all among the bourgeoisie, it is the Right wing of the liberals, which bases its policy entirely on "conciliation" with the Rights, that is growing fastest of all. We shall deal with this in detail in a moment. Secondly, they forget that the vaunted "move to the left of the bourgeoisie" is merely a symptom of the real move to the left of the democrats who *alone* are capable of providing the motive forces for a serious change in the regime. Thirdly, they forget that the June Third system is specially intended to take advantage, within very broad limits, of the antagonism between the liberal bourgeoisie and the reactionary nature of the landlords, there existing an even more profound *common* antagonism between these and all democrats, particularly the working class.

To proceed. Our liberals like to pretend that the Octobrists' defeat was due to the "manipulation of the elections", which took away support from this "party of the latest government orders", and so on. Of course, in so doing the liberals themselves pose as an honest opposition, as independent people and, indeed, "democrats", while the distinction between a Maklakov and the Octobrists is in fact perfectly illusory.

Look at the changes that have occurred between the Third and Fourth Dumas compared with those between the beginning and end of the Third Duma. You will see that in the Third Duma the Octobrist Party lost a greater number of its members (28) than in the Fourth Duma elections (22). This, of course, does not mean that there was no "manipulation of the elections", for it was done on the most reckless scale, especially against the democrats. What it does mean is that despite manipulation of the elections in every sort of way, and even despite government pressure and "politics" in general, a process of party demarcation is going on among the propertied classes of Russia, the feudal-reactionary Right wing of the counter-revolution becoming demarcated from the liberal-bourgeois wing of *the same* counter-revolution.

The distinctions between the various groups and factions of the Right-wing and Octobrist Duma majority (Rights, nationalists, moderate Rights, the "Centre", Right Octobrists, and so on) are as unstable, indefinite, accidental, and often artificially constructed, as the distinctions within the Octobrist-liberal majority (Left Octobrists, Progressists, Cadets). What characterises the period we are passing through is not at all that the allegedly independent (Maklakov, of all people!) Constitutional-Democrat is forcing out the Octobrists who are dependent on the government. This is a silly liberal tale.

The characteristic thing is that genuine class parties are in course of formation and that, in particular, the party of counter-revolutionary liberalism is becoming consolidated under cover of noisy oppositional exclamations and honeyed talk about "reconciliation of the government and the country".

The liberal press, which is the most widespread in Russia, is doing its utmost to gloss over this process. We shall therefore turn once more to the precise data of the Duma statistics. Let us remember that we must judge parties, as well as individuals, by their deeds and not by their words. As far as *deeds* are concerned, the Cadets and Progressists make common cause on all the more important issues, and both groups made common cause with the Octobrists in the Third and Fourth Dumas, and in the recent elections (Yekaterinoslav Gubernia: the Rodzyanko-Cadet bloc!) on a whole series of issues.

Let us now look at the data concerning the three parties.

	Third Duma		Fourth Duma	Comparison of Fourth Duma and beginning of Third Duma
	1908	1912		
Octobrists	148	120	98	—50. i. e., —34 per cent
Progressists	25	36	48	+23 " +92 " "
Cadets	53	52	59	+ 6 " +11 " "

We see an enormous and steady decrease of the Octobrists; a slight decrease, and then a small increase, of the Cadets; and *an enormous and steady increase of the Progressists*, who have *almost doubled their numbers* in five years.

If we take the data for 1908 reported by Mr. Milyukov in *Yezhegodnik Rechi** for 1912, p. 77, we shall see the picture in even bolder relief. Mr. Milyukov considers that in the Third Duma in 1908 there were 154 Octobrists, 23 Progressists and 56 Cadets. Comparing the Fourth Duma with this, the increase in the number of Cadets is quite negligible and the number of Progressists is *more than double*.

In 1908 the numerical strength of the Progressists was less than half that of the Cadets. Today it is over 80 per cent of that of the Cadets.

Thus we arrive at the indisputable fact that the *most characteristic* feature of Russian liberalism during the counter-revolution (1908-12) is the tremendous growth of Progressism.

And who are the Progressists?

Both by composition and ideology, they are a *cross-breed of Octobrists and Cadets*.

In the Third Duma the Progressists still called themselves Peaceful Renovators, and one of their leaders, the counter-revolutionary nobleman Lvov, was a Cadet in the First Duma. The number of Progressists in the Third Duma increased, as we have seen, from 25 to 36, i.e., by 11; of these 11 deputies, 9 came over to the Progressists from other parties, namely, 1 from the Cadets 2 from the moderate Rights, 1 from the nationalists and 5 from the Octobrists.

The rapid growth of the Progressists among the political exponents of Russian liberalism, and the success of *Vekhi* in "society" are two sides of the same medal. The Progressists did in practical politics what *Vekhi* advocated in theory as it spat at the revolution, repudiated democracy, extolled the dirty enrichment of the bourgeoisie as God's work on earth, and so on and so forth.

In orating about reconciliation of the government and the country, the Cadet Maklakov merely sings the praise of what the Progressists are doing.

---

* *Rech Yearbook.—Tr.*

The further we move away from 1905 and 1906, the more obvious it becomes how very correct the Bolsheviks were at that time in exposing the Cadets when they were most exultant over their "victories", and in showing the true nature of the Cadet Party* which is now being more and more glaringly revealed by the whole course of events.

The Russian democrats cannot win a single victory unless they drastically undermine the Cadets' "prestige" among the masses. Conversely, the virtual fusion of the Cadets with *Vekhi* and the Progressists is a condition for, and a sign of, the strengthening and consolidation of the democratic movement under the leadership of the proletariat.

IV. WHAT WAS THE ISSUE IN THE ELECTIONS?

In most of the statements and articles on the elections, this question is pushed into the background more than any other, or is even obscured altogether. Yet it is the question of the ideological and political content of the election campaign, the most important question, one which has to be elucidated, or all other questions, and all the usual data on "opposition percentages" and so on, will completely lose their value.

The most widespread reply to this question is that the issue was whether there was to be a constitution or not. That is how the Rights see it. That is how the liberals see it. The view that there were in effect two warring camps, one of them fighting for and the other against a constitution, runs through the entire Right-wing and liberal press. Mr. Milyukov, the Cadet Party leader, and *Rech*, the official organ of that party, put forward this theory of two camps in no uncertain terms, doing so, moreover, on behalf of the conference of the Cadet Party.

But look at this "theory" from the standpoint of the outcome of the elections. How did it stand the test of reality?

The first step of the new Duma was marked by a bloc of the Cadets and the Octobrists (and even some of the Rights) around the "constitutional" candidature of Rodzyanko,

---

* See present edition, Vol. 10, pp. 199-276.—*Ed*

whose speech, alleged to contain a constitutional programme, was enthusiastically acclaimed by the Cadets.*

The Octobrist leader Rodzyanko, who, as we know, is regarded as a Right Octobrist, considers himself a constitutionalist, as does Krupensky, the leader of the "Centre faction", or conservative constitutionalists.

To say that the issue was over the constitution means saying nothing, for the question at once arises as to *what kind of* constitution is meant. Is it a constitution in the spirit of Krupensky or Rodzyanko or Yefremov-Lvov or Maklakov-Milyukov? And then comes an even more important question, one that does not concern wishes, statements or programmes—all of which remain on paper—but the real *means* of achieving the desired objective.

With regard to this cardinal point (the only serious one), Mr. Gredeskul's statement—reprinted by *Rech* (No. 117) in 1912—that there is no need for a new revolution, and that what is needed is "merely constitutional work", remains unrefuted and irrefutably correct. *Ideologically and politically*, that statement unites the Cadets and Octobrists much more closely and thoroughly than the assurances of devotion to a constitution, and even to democracy—assurances repeated a thousand times—are supposed to divide them.

Probably some 90 per cent of all the newspapers read in Russia are Octobrist or liberal. This press, by suggesting to the reader the idea of two camps, one of which favours a constitution, exerts an immensely corrupting influence on the political consciousness of the masses. One has only to think that all this campaign culminates in Rodzyanko's "constitutional" declaration which Milyukov has accepted!

In view of this state of affairs, one cannot insist sufficiently on repeating old truths of political science, truths that are forgotten by many people. In Russia, the *urgent* question is: what is a constitution?

A constitution is a deal between the historical forces of the old society (nobiliary, serf-owning, feudal, absolutist)

---

* In addition to the *Rech* articles of the time, see Mr. Milyukov's statement in the Duma on December 13, 1912: "The Chairman [Rodzyanko] delivered a speech ... he made his declaration, *which we recognised to be our own*" (*Rech* No. 343, December 14)!! There you have the Cadets' constitutional (don't laugh!) *declaration!*

and the liberal bourgeoisie. The actual terms of this deal, and the extent of the concessions made by the old order, or of the victories won by the liberal bourgeoisie, will depend on the victories of the democrats, of the broad mass of the people (primarily the workers), over the forces of the old.

Our election campaign could have its culmination in Milyukov's acceptance of Rodzyanko's "declaration" only because what the liberals are *actually* seeking is not abolition of the *privileges* (economic, political, etc.) of the old society, but *their division* between (to put it briefly) the landlords and the bourgeoisie. The liberals are more afraid of the democrats' popular, mass movement than they are of reaction; this accounts for the liberals' *impotence* in politics, which is amazing from the standpoint of the economic strength of capital.

In the June Third system, the liberals have a monopoly as a tolerated, semi-legal opposition, and the beginning of a political revival (to use a much too weak and inaccurate term) brings large sections of the new, rising generation of democrats under the influence of these monopolists. That is why the *essence* of the issue of political liberty in Russia today amounts to making it clear that there are three and not two warring camps, for it is only the latter camp, the one glossed over by the liberals, that really *has the strength* to achieve political liberty.

The issue in the elections of 1912 was not at all a "constitution", for the Cadets—the chief liberal party, which mainly attacked the Octobrists and defeated them—identified themselves with Rodzyanko's declaration. The battle, held fast in the police grip of the June Third system, was fought over the awakening, strengthening and unification of an *independent democratic movement* free from the vacillation and "Octobrist sympathies" of the liberals.

That is why it is a fundamental mistake to see the real ideological and political content of the election campaign *only* from the "parliamentary" standpoint. What is a hundred times more real than all "constitutional" programmes and platforms is the question of the attitude of the various parties and groups towards the political strike movement which marked the year 1912.

One of the surest ways of distinguishing between the bourgeois parties of any country and its proletarian parties is to examine their attitude to economic strikes. A party which in its press, its organisations and its statements in parliament does *not* fight together with the workers in economic strikes is a bourgeois party, no matter how much it may avow that it is "popular", "radically socialist", and so on. In Russia, *mutatis mutandis* (the appropriate changes having been made), the same must be said about parties that wish to pass for democratic: don't invoke the fact that you have written on a certain slip of paper: "constitution, universal suffrage, freedom of association, equality of nationalities", and so on, for these *words* are not worth a *copper* but show me your *deeds* in connection with the political strike movement of 1912! Even this criterion is *not quite* complete, but it is a serious criterion nevertheless, and not an empty promise.

V. THE ELECTION SLOGANS TESTED BY EXPERIENCE

An election campaign is of outstanding interest to any intelligent political leader because it furnishes *objective* data on the views and sentiments, and consequently interests, of the different *classes* of society. Elections to a representative body are comparable in this respect to a census of the population, for they provide political statistics. To be sure, these statistics may be good (in the case of universal, etc., suffrage) or bad (in the case of elections to our parliament, if one may call it that). To be sure, one must learn to criticise these statistics—just as any statistics—and to use them critically. To be sure, these statistics should be taken in connection with all social statistics in general; and strike statistics, for example, will often turn out—for those who are not affected with the disease of parliamentary cretinism—to be a hundred times more serious and profound than election statistics.

Despite all these reservations, it is beyond question that elections supply *objective* data. Testing subjective wishes, sentiments and views by taking into account the vote of the *mass* of the population representing different classes should always be of value to a politician who is at all worthy of the name. The struggle of parties—in practice, before the electorate, and with the returns summed up—invariably furnishes data *serving to test* our conception of the balance of the social forces in the country and of the significance of particular "slogans".

It is from this standpoint that we shall try to look at the election returns.

Regarding political statistics, the chief thing that needs to be said here is the obvious worthlessness of the greater part of them owing to the shameless application of administrative "measures": "clarifications", pressure, arrests, deportation, and so on and so forth—without limit. Mr. Cherevanin, for example, who in *Nasha Zarya* No. 9-10 sums up data on several hundred electors in different curias, is compelled to admit that it *"would be ridiculous"* to take the drop in the percentage of opposition electors (compared with the elections to the Third Duma) in the second urban curia and in the peasant curia as proof of a swing to the right. The only curia in respect of which the Mymretsovs, Khvostovs, Tolmachovs, Muratovs and Co. *were unable* to carry out any rigging was the first urban curia. That curia showed an increase in the proportion of "opposition" electors from 56 to 67 per cent, with that of the Octobrists dropping from 20 to 12 per cent, and that of the Rights from 24 to 21 per cent.

But while "clarifications" nullified the significance of election statistics regarding the electors, and while the democratic classes, *excluded* altogether from those privileged by the June Third system, personally experienced all the delights of those clarifications, nevertheless the liberals' *attitude* to the democrats became manifest in the elections. On this point objective data came to light which make it possible to test, by the experience of life, what the different "trends" thought and said *prior to* the elections.

The question of the liberals' attitude to the democrats is by no means "only a party" question, i.e., one that is important *only* in terms of one of the strictly party lines. It is the most important question for *anyone* striving for political liberty in Russia. It is a question of *how* to achieve, after all, the object of the common aspirations of all that is decent and honest in Russia.

The Marxists, in starting on the election campaign of 1912, put in the very forefront the slogans of *consistent* democracy as a counterpoise to liberal labour policy. These slogans can be tested in two ways: firstly, by the view and experience of other countries and, secondly, by the *experience of the campaign* of 1912. Whether the Marxists' slogans are correct or not should now be evident from the relationship which has *actually* come into being between liberals and democrats. What makes this test of slogans objective is that it is not we who tested them but the *masses*, and not merely the masses in general, but *our opponents* in particular.

Did the relations between liberals and democrats during and as a result of the elections develop as the Marxists expected or as the liberals expected or as the liquidators expected?

To get at the root of this matter, let us first recall those "expectations". At the very beginning of 1912, when the question of elections had only just been raised and when the Cadets (at their conference) unfurled the banner of a single opposition (i.e., *two camps*) and the permissibility of blocs with the Left Octobrists, the working-class press raised the question of slogans through the articles of Martov and Dan in *Zhivoye Dyelo*, of F. L—ko[199] and others in *Zvezda* (Nos. 11 [47] and 24 [60], and in *Zhivoye Dyelo* Nos. 2, 3 and 8).

Martov put forward the slogan: "Dislodge reaction from its Duma positions", and Dan, "Wrest the Duma from the hands of the reactionaries". Martov and Dan accused *Zvezda* of *threatening* the liberals and of striving to *extort* Duma seats from the liberals.

Three positions stood out clearly:

(1) The Cadets were for a single opposition (i.e., for two camps) and for the permission of blocs with the Left Octobrists.

(2) The liquidators favoured the slogan: "Wrest the Duma from the hands of the reactionaries" and facilitate the Cadets' and Progressists' "advance to power" (Martov in *Zhivoye Dyelo* No. 2). No *extorting* of seats from the liberals for the democrats.

(3) The Marxists were against the slogan: "Wrest the Duma from the hands of the reactionaries", for that would

mean wresting the *landlord* from the hands of the reactionaries. "The practical task that faces us at the elections is by no means to 'dislodge reaction from its Duma positions', but to strengthen the forces of democracy in general and of working-class democracy in particular" (F. L—ko in *Zvezda* No. 11 [47]).* We must *threaten* the liberals, *extort* seats from them, and go to war against them, undaunted by attempts at intimidation through cries about the Black-Hundred danger (same author, No. 24 [60]**). The liberals "advance to power" *only when* the democrats win *despite* the vacillation of the liberals.

The divergency between the Marxists and the liquidators is most profound and irreconcilable, however easy various good souls may think a verbal reconciliation of the irreconcilable. "Wrest the Duma from the hands of the reactionaries" is a whole range of ideas, a whole system of policy that *objectively* means transferring hegemony to the liberals. "Wrest the democratic movement from the hands of the liberals" is the opposite system of policy, one based on the fact that only a democratic movement which has ceased to be dependent on the liberals *is capable of actually* undermining reaction.

Now see what became in reality of the fight which was so much talked about *before* it began.

Let us take Mr. V. Levitsky of *Nasha Zarya* (No. 9-10) as a witness to the results of the fight—certainly no one will suspect *this* witness of partiality towards *Zvezda* and *Pravda*.

Here is how this witness assesses the results of the fight in the second urban curia, the only curia, as is known, where there was at least a remote resemblance to "European" elections and where it is possible, at least to some slight degree, to sum up the results of the "encounters" between liberals and democrats.

The witness speaks of as many as 63 actions by the Social-Democrats, including 5 cases of *forced* renunciation of nomination, 5 agreements with other parties and 53 independent actions. Of these 53 cases, 4 were in four big cities and 49 during the election of electors.

---

* See present edition, Vol. 17, p. 490.—*Ed.*
** Ibid., p. 561.—*Ed.*

In 9 cases out of these 49, it was not known whom the Social-Democrats were fighting against, in three it was against the Rights (whom they defeated in all three cases), in one against the Trudoviks (the Social-Democrats winning), and *in the other 36 cases, against the liberals* (21 victories of the Social-Democrats and 15 defeats).

Picking out the *Russian* liberals, we have 21 cases in which the Social-Democrats fought them. Here are the results:

	S. D.	Winners, opponents of S. D.	Total number of cases
S. D. versus Cadets	7	8	15
" " other liberals*	4	2	6
Total	11	10	21

And so, the chief opponents of the Social-Democrats were *liberals* (36 cases against 3); the Social-Democrats suffered their *chief* defeats at the hands of the *Cadets*.

Furthermore, out of five cases of agreement two were general agreements of the opposition against the Rights; *in three* "it may be a question of a Left bloc against the Cadets" (my italics; *Nasha Zarya* No. 9-10, p. 98). In other words, the number of agreements was less than one-tenth of the total number of actions. Sixty per cent of the agreements were against the Cadets.

Lastly, the returns in four big cities were the following:

	Votes cast (maximum figures)			
			Riga	
	St. Petersburg	Moscow	First ballot	Second ballot
For Cadets	19,376	20,310	3,754	5,517
" Social-Democrats . .	7,686	9,035	*4,583*	4,570
" Octobrists	4,547	2,030	3,674	—
" Rights	1,990	1,073	272	—
" Trudoviks	1,075	—	—	—

---

* Progressists and Cadets *together* with Progressists or Trudoviks

And so, *in-all* the four big cities the Social-Democrats fought *against the Cadets*, who in one case won in the second ballot *with help from the Octobrists* (considering these to include the candidate of the Baltic Constitutional Party).

The conclusions drawn by the witness himself are:

"The Cadet monopoly of representation of the urban democrats is coming to an end. The Social-Democrats' immediate task in this field is to win representation from the liberals in all the five cities represented independently. The psychological [??] and historical [what about economic?] preconditions for this—a 'swing to the left' of the democratic voter, the untenability of the Cadet policy, and the reawakening of proletarian initiative—already exist" (*Nasha Zarya*, op. cit., p. 97).

VI. "END" OF THE ILLUSIONS ABOUT THE CADET PARTY

1. The facts have shown that the real meaning of the Cadet slogan of a "single opposition" or "two camps" was deception of the democrats, the liberals' fraudulent appropriation of the fruits of a democratic awakening, and the liberals' *curtailment*, *blunting* and *frustration* of this awakening of the only force capable of pushing Russia ahead.

2. The facts have shown that the only election struggle that was at all like the "open", "European" type consisted *precisely* in wresting the democratic movement from the hands of the liberals. This slogan was a *living reality*, it expressed the awakening of a new democratic movement, an awakening that is actually taking place. As for the liquidators' slogan "Wrest the Duma from the hands of the reactionaries", it was a rotten invention of a circle of liberal intellectuals.

3. The facts have shown that only the "furious" struggle against the Cadets, and only the "Cadet-eating" of which the liberals' spineless servants, the liquidators, accused us, expressed the real need of the real mass campaign, because the Cadets actually turned out to be *even worse* than we had painted them. The Cadets turned out to be outright allies of the Black Hundreds against the Social-Democrat Priedkalns and the Social-Democrat Pokrovsky![200]

It is a historic turning-point in Russia: the Black Hundreds, who had gone to the length of blind hatred of the Cadets, whom they saw as their chief enemy, were impelled by the course of events to back the Cadets against the Social-Democrats. This seemingly minor fact denotes a very great shift in party policies, showing how superficial in fact were the Black-Hundred attacks on the Cadets and *vice versa*, and how easily in fact Purishkevich and Milyukov *found their bearings*, and came to their unity against the Social-Democrats.

Experience has shown that we Bolsheviks, far from underestimating the possibility of blocs with the Cadets (at the second stage and so on), rather continued to *overestimate* it, for what *actually* occurred in a number of cases was the formation of blocs between the Cadets and the Octobrists against us! This, of course, does not mean that we *refused* (as certain over-zealous otzovists of yesterday and their friends would have liked us to do) in a number of cases, such as at gubernia election meetings, to resort to blocs between ourselves and the Cadets against the Rights. What it does mean is that our *general line* (three camps; democrats against Cadets) was borne out and strengthened still further by experience.

Incidentally, Levitsky, Cherevanin and other contributors to *Nasha Zarya* collected valuable data for our election statistics with the most commendable zeal and diligence. It is a pity they did not sum up the data—which they evidently had—on the number of cases of direct and indirect blocs of the Cadets with the Octobrists and Rights *against* the Social-Democrats.

Priedkalns and Pokrovsky are not isolated cases, for there were many other cases of a similar nature at the gubernia election meetings. They should not be forgotten. They are worthy of serious attention.

To proceed. Our "witness", who had to draw the above conclusions about the Cadets, gave no thought at all to the appraisal of the Cadet Party that these conclusions *bore out*. Who called the Cadets a party of urban democrats? And who had argued *since March 1906*, or even earlier, that this liberal party kept itself alive by deceiving the democratic voter?

Now the liquidators have begun to chant like so many Forgetful Ivans: "The Cadet monopoly is coming to an end." Consequently, there was a "monopoly". What does this mean? Monopoly is the removal of competition. Was Social-Democratic competition against the Cadets in 1906-07 removed to a greater extent than in 1912?

Mr. V. Levitsky repeats a common phrase *without thinking* of the meaning of the words he is uttering. As he understands it, monopoly means "simply" that the Cadets predominated and that this is over now. But if you claim to be Marxists, gentlemen, you should really ponder, if only a little bit, on the class character of parties, and not treat so flippantly your own statements of yesterday.

If the Cadets are a party of urban democrats, then their predominance is not a "monopoly", but a product of the *class* interests of the urban democrats! If, however, their predominance turned out, a couple of years later, to be a "monopoly", i.e., something accidental and abnormal from the standpoint of the general and fundamental laws of capitalism and relations between the classes in capitalist society, it follows that those who took the Cadets for a party of urban democrats were opportunists, that they were carried away by a short-lived success, bowed down before the fashionable splendour of Cadetism, and abandoned Marxist criticism of the Cadets for liberal servility to them.

Mr. V. Levitsky's conclusion bears out *entirely, word for word*, the resolution on the class character of the Cadet Party adopted by the Bolsheviks in London in 1907, a resolution which the Mensheviks vehemently disputed. If the urban democrats followed the lead of the Cadets "*by force of tradition and because they were simply deceived by the liberals*", as the resolution has it, then it is perfectly logical that the severe lessons of 1908-11 dispelled "constitutional illusions", undermined "tradition", exposed the "deceit" and thereby ended the "monopoly".

Wilful or involuntary oblivion of the past, and an extremely thoughtless attitude towards precise, straightforward and clear answers to all important political questions and to verifying these answers by the ample experience of 1905-07 and 1908-12, is a much too widespread phenomenon nowadays. Nothing could be so ruinous to the awakening democratic movement as this oblivion and this attitude.

VII. CONCERNING AN "ENORMOUS DANGER
TO THE LANDOWNERSHIP OF THE NOBILITY"

Mr. Cherevanin, summing up the results of the election campaign, holds that the opposition had "49 seats wrested. from it in a purely artificial manner, solely through recourse to quite exceptional measures". In his opinion, adding these seats to those that were really won would raise the total to 207, which is only 15 short of an absolute majority. The conclusion he draws is: "On the basis of the June Third system, barring artificial emergency measures, nobiliary-feudal reaction would have been fully and decisively [??!] defeated in the elections."

"In the face of this enormous danger to the landownership of the nobility," he goes on to say, clashes between priests and land-lords are unimportant (op. cit., p. 85).

There you have the effects of the slogan of wresting the Duma from the hands of the reactionaries! Cherevanin has sorely punished Martov by reducing the latter's slogan to an absurdity and confirming, so to say, the results of liqui-dationist illusions along with the "results of the election campaign".

A Progressist and Cadet majority in the Fourth Duma would have represented an *"enormous danger to the landown-ership of the nobility"*! This is a real gem.

It is not a slip of the pen, however, but an inevitable result of the entire ideological content which the liberals and liquidators tried to impart to the election campaign.

The tremendous growth of the role of the Progressists compared with the Cadets, the Progressists' embodiment in politics of the entire renegacy (Vekhism) of the Cadets, and the virtual transition to a Progressist position which the Cadets themselves effected tacitly and secretly, are all facts which the liquidators *refused* to see and which brought them to the "Cherevanin" gem. "One should not talk too much about the counter-revolutionary character of the Cadets" is what, or approximately what, the Trudovik (Narodnik liquidator) Mr. Vodovozov wrote at one time. Our liquidators took the same view.

They even forgot the lesson of the Third Duma, where the Cadet Berezovsky in an official speech "interpreted" the

Cadets' agrarian programme, and proved it to be *beneficial* to the landed nobility. Think of expecting now, in 1912, an "enormous danger to the landownership of the nobility" from the "opposition" Duma of the landlords, or from the Progressists, those slightly repainted Octobrists.

Look here, Mr. Cherevanin, indulge in your fantasies, but have a sense of proportion!

We have an excellent illustration of the election results in connection with the Cherevanin summary of liquidationist tactics. The Fourth Duma approved, by 132 votes to 78, the Progressist formula of procedure.

None other than the Octobrist Antonov officially expressed his complete satisfaction with this most commonplace, empty formula as being an Octobrist one! Mr. Antonov is right, of course. The Progressists submitted a purely Octobrist formula. They played their role, that of reconciling the Octobrists with the Cadets.

Octobrism has been defeated, long live Octobrism! It is Guchkov Octobrism that has been "defeated" and the one that lives on is Octobrism of the Yefremov and Lvov brand.*

VIII. COVERING UP THE DEFEAT

It remains for us to examine the election returns for the worker curia, which is the most important.

No one has had, or has, any doubt that this curia is on the side of the Social-Democrats. The fight waged here was not against the Narodniks, among whom resistance to Narodnik liquidationism (*Pochin*[201] in Paris and the Popular Socialists in St. Petersburg) or Narodnik otzovism *did not occur*, and this lack of resistance to decadent trends reduced the Left Narodniks to *nil*.

The fight in the worker curia was waged only between the Marxists and the liberal labour politicians, the liquidators. In January 1912 the Marxists proclaimed frankly and clearly, openly and without any despicable evasions,

---

* *Rech* asserted on December 16 that the Social-Democrats had joined in voting for the Progressists' vile formula. That is incredible. *Pravda* says nothing about it. Perhaps the Social-Democrats who were sitting (or who rose to leave?) were "registered" as voting *for*.

that agreements in the *worker* curia (and in it alone) with the *destroyers* of the workers' Party were impermissible.*

This fact is common knowledge. It is also common knowledge that the liquidators' August conference was described even by the conciliator Plekhanov as "pitiful" and liquidationist (despite the vows of *Nasha Zarya*), and its resolutions as *"diplomacy"*, or deceit, to put it plainly.

What did the election returns show?

Did they, or did they not, provide *objective* data as to the relation of the January and August statements to reality? Whom did the working-class electors prove to be supporting?

There are very precise statistical data on this, which the liquidators are trying (in vain!) to obscure, to hide, to drown with outcries and abuse.

Beginning with the Second Duma (the First Duma was boycotted by most of the Social-Democrats), there are exact data on the number of deputies to the Duma from the worker curia, distributed among the various "trends" in the Social-Democratic Party. Here they are:

Deputies elected to the Duma from the worker curia:

	Mensheviks	Bolsheviks	Percentage of Bolsheviks
Second Duma (1907) . .	12	11	47
Third " (1908-12)	4	4	50
Fourth " (1912) . .	3	6	67

These figures speak for themselves!

In 1907 the Bolsheviks had a majority, registered officially, in the Party (105 Bolshevik and 97 Menshevik delegates). This means that the 47 per cent in the worker curia (the entire group comprised 18 Bolsheviks+36 Mensheviks=54) made up about 52 per cent in the workers' Party.

In 1912, for the first time, *all* the six *curia* deputies were Bolsheviks. It is known that those six gubernias are the principal industrial gubernias. It is also known that a far greater proportion of the proletariat is concentrated in them than in the other gubernias. It is obvious, therefore, and has

---

* See present edition, Vol. 17, p. 469.—*Ed.*

17*

been fully proved by a comparison with 1907, that 67 per cent in the worker curia mean more than 70 per cent in the workers' Party.

During the Third Duma, when the intelligentsia deserted the workers' Party and the liquidators justified this, the workers abandoned the liquidators. The liquidator Belousov's flight from the Social-Democratic group in the Third Duma, and the turn of the whole group (three-quarters Menshevik) from Menshevism to anti-liquidationism* were signs and sure indications of the fact that *the same* process was going on among the workers. And the elections to the Fourth Duma proved this.

That is why Oskarov, Martov, Cherevanin, Levitsky, etc., are incredibly indignant in *Nasha Zarya*, flinging hundreds of the most Purishkevichist "compliments" at an alleged circle that is alleged to be sectarian and Leninist.

Sectarian circle indeed! A "circle" that in 1908-12 got from the worker curia steadily increasing support—reaching 67 per cent of that curia in the Fourth Duma! They are clumsy polemicists, are the liquidators. They abuse** us as strongly as they can, but the result is the most flattering compliment for us.

Settling controversial issues by an abundance of outcries, abuse and groundless assertions is just like a circle of intellectuals. The workers prefer something different, namely, *objective* data. And in Russia, her present political position

---

* The liquidator Oskarov admits this indisputable fact in an amusing manner, saying that the Bolsheviks *"had their way*: they split the group at the critical moment, in fact if not in form" (*Nasha Zarya*, op. cit., p. 3)—meaning the Third Duma group. What he calls a "split" is either the liquidator Belousov's flight, or the fact that *two* members of the group were on a liquidationist newspaper and eight on an anti-liquidationist one, while the rest were neutral.

** The liquidators most readily raise a hullaballoo about St. Petersburg, bypassing the results of the elections for the worker curia, as if to say, "For shame!" It is a shame, of course, gentlemen! The shame is on those against whom a *mandate* was adopted that had been *printed* beforehand, i.e., approved by the organisation. It is disgraceful to back a *person* against a *mandate*. And it was still more disgraceful to refuse to cast lots when the result turned out to be 3 : 3. P., a *Pravda* man well known in St. Petersburg, plainly suggested casting lots to the liquidator M., but the latter rejected it!! Shame on the liquidators for the St. Petersburg elections!

being what it is, there is not, and cannot be, an *objective* measure of the strength and influence of a particular trend among the mass of the workers other than the working-class press and the worker curia of the Duma.

Therefore, liquidator gentlemen, the more you clamour and rail in *Nasha Zarya* and *Luch*, the more calmly we shall ask the workers to point out an objective criterion of connection with the masses other than the working-class press and the worker curia in the Duma.

Let the readers who are being deafened with cries about the "sectarian" "Lenin circle" and so on ponder calmly these objective data on the working-class press and the worker curia in the Duma. These objective data show that the liquidators are shouting to cover up their complete defeat.

But it is particularly instructive to compare the coming into being of *Luch*, which appeared *on the day of elections* owing to private initiative, and the coming into being of *Pravda*. The April surge of the working-class movement was one of the greatest historic surges of the workers' mass movement in Russia. Even according to estimates made by factory-owners, hundreds of thousands of workers joined in the movement. And *that movement itself created "Pravda"* as its by-product—first by strengthening *Zvezda* and converting it from a weekly into a newspaper appearing every two days, and then by increasing workers' money collections for *Pravda* to 76 in March and 227 in April (taking into account only group contributions by workers).

We have here a classical example of how a movement that has absolutely nothing to do with reformism, brings as a by-product either reforms or concessions, or an extension of bounds, and so on.

The reformists are betraying the working-class movement when they restrict its great scope by reformist slogans (as do our liquidators). The opponents of reformism, however, not only prove loyal to the uncurtailed slogans of the proletariat, but also turn out to be the better "practical workers", for it is precisely broad scope and uncurtailed slogans that ensure the strength which yields, as a by-product, either a concession or a reform, or an extension of bounds, or at least a temporary necessity for the upper ranks to tolerate a disagreeable increase in the activity of the lower ranks.

In 1908-12, while the liquidators were busy reviling the "underground", justifying "flight" from it and chattering about an "open party", the *entire* worker curia left them, and they were unable to use the first, and great, upsurge of the April-May tide!

Mr. Martov in *Nasha Zarya* admits this circumstance which is so sad for him, couching his admission in particularly amusing terms. He reviles and describes as nonentities the Plekhanov and *Vperyod* groups, which *the liquidators themselves* were depicting only yesterday as "centres" and trends, in defiance of our demand that only Russian organisations should be taken into account. And Martov admits bitterly and angrily, amid a torrent of venomous (venomous in a Burenin style) words, that "Lenin's" "sectarian circle" "stood its ground "and "is even taking the offensive", "having entrenched itself in fields that have nothing in common with the underground" (*Nasha Zarya*, op. cit., p. 74).

But this whole admission of Martov's evokes a smile. It is human nature that when the enemy makes a mistake we rejoice maliciously, but when he takes the right step we sometimes get into a childish temper.

Thank you for the compliment you were *forced* to pay us, liberal liquidator! Since the end of 1908 we have been insisting on the use of open forms of the movement, and in the spring of 1909 we broke with a number of friends[202] over it. And if in these "fields" we proved to be a force, it was only because we did not sacrifice content for form. To use the form in good time, to seize hold of the April upsurge, and to win the sympathy, so precious to a Marxist, of the worker curia, it was essential not to renounce the old, not to treat it in a renegade fashion, but firmly to uphold its ideas, its traditions, its material substrata. It was *those* ideas that imbued the April upsurge, it was they that predominated in the worker curia in 1912, and only those who were loyal to them in all fields and all forms could advance in step both with that upsurge and with that curia.

Written in January 1913

Published in *Prosveshcheniye* No. 1,
January 1913
Signed: V. *Ilyin*

Published according
to the magazine text

EXPERIENCE TEACHES

Anyone who is sincerely interested in the fortunes of the emancipation movement in our country cannot fail to be interested primarily in our *working-class* movement. The years of upswing, as well as those of counter-revolution, showed beyond all doubt that the working class is marching *at the head of all* the liberation forces and that therefore the fortunes of the working-class movement are most closely interwoven with those of the Russian social movement in general.

Take the curve indicating the workers' *strike movement* during the past eight years! And try to draw a similar curve showing the growth and decline of Russia's entire emancipation movement in general during these years. The two curves will coincide perfectly. There is a very close, an inseparable connection between the emancipation movement as a whole, on the one hand, and the working-class movement, on the other.

Look closely at the data on the strike movement in Russia since 1905.

Year	Number of strikes	Number of strikers (thousands)
1905	13,995	2,863
1906	6,114	1,108
1907	3,573	740
1908	892	176
1909	340	64
1910	222	47
1911	466	105
1912	approximately 1,500,000, strikers (economic and political)

Surely these data show most clearly that the Russian workers' strike movement is the best barometer of the entire nation-wide emancipation struggle in Russia.

There were about three million strikers in the peak year (1905). In 1906 and 1907 the movement ebbed but continued at a very high level, averaging one million strikers. Then it headed downwards and kept on declining to 1910 inclusive: the year 1911 was the turning-point, for the curve began to rise, even though timidly. The year 1912 saw a new major upswing. The curve rose confidently and steadily to the 1906 level, making plainly for the year when, at the figure of three million, it established a *world* record.

A *new epoch* has come. This is now beyond all question. The beginning of 1913 is the best evidence of it. The *mass* of the workers is advancing from individual *partial* issues to the point where it will raise the *general* issue. The attention of the widest masses is now centred on something more than particular defects in our Russian life. It is now a question of the *totality* of these defects, taken as a whole: it is now a question of reform, not reforms.

Experience teaches. The actual struggle is the best solver of the problems which until recently were so debatable. Take a look now, after 1912, at, say, our disputes over the "petitioning campaign" and the slogan "freedom of association". What has experience shown?

It turned out to be impossible to collect even a few tens of thousands of workers' signatures to a very moderate petition. On the other hand, it is a fact that *political* strikes alone involved a *million* people. The talk that one should not go beyond the slogan "freedom of association", because if one did the masses would allegedly not understand us and would refuse to mobilise, turned out to be meaningless and idle talk by people isolated from the realities of life. The living, real millions of the masses, however, mobilised precisely in support of the broadest, the old, uncurtailed formulas. It was only these formulas that fired the masses with enthusiasm. It has now been shown convincingly enough who has actually been advancing with the masses and who without or against them.

A fresh, vigorous and mighty movement of the masses themselves is sweeping aside as worthless rubbish the artificial formulas hatched in government offices, and marches on and on.

That is what constitutes the historic significance of the great movement taking place under our own eyes.

Pravda No. 15, January 19, 1913

Published according to the *Pravda* text

NEW DEMOCRATS

In his "Motley Encounters" published in the New-Year issue of *Rech*, Mr. Tan touched on an important question to which the workers should pay serious attention. It is the question of the growing numbers of new democrats.

"For about a year or perhaps more," wrote Mr. Tan, "the river of life has been changing and shifting again. Instead of the water decreasing, there has been an increase, coming from God knows where, probably from the bowels of the earth and from distant springs. All was quiet and empty for three years. Now there are people appearing, crawling one after another out of various crevices and dark corners....

"People of peasant stock who have come up from below are the most interesting. Their name is legion. They have flooded the middle walks of life and are even aiming at the higher ones, especially in the provinces. Technicians, accountants, agronomists, teachers, all sorts of Zemstvo clerks. They are all alike—grey-faced, broad-boned, uncouth-looking; they are not liable to reflexes, and are, indeed, as tough as cats.... Life must have taken yet another step upwards, for we commoners compared with them are as the nobility were compared with us."

This is very apt and true, although we should not forget that the old as well as the new commoners, those "of peasant stock", the democratic intelligentsia and semi-intelligentsia, represent the bourgeoisie as distinct from the semi-feudal nobility.

But the bourgeoisie consists of different strata having different historical possibilities. The upper ranks of the bourgeoisie and of the wealthy bourgeois intelligentsia—lawyers, professors, journalists, deputies, etc.—almost invariably gravitate towards an alliance with the Purishkeviches. Thousands of economic threads link *this* bourgeoisie to them.

On the other hand, the peasant bourgeoisie and the new intelligentsia "of peasant stock" are linked by a thousand threads to the *mass* of the disfranchised, downtrodden, ignorant, starving peasantry, and by virtue of all their living conditions are hostile to *all* Purishkevichism, to any alliance with it.

This new democratic element, which is more numerous and stands closer to the life of the millions, is rapidly learning, gaining strength and growing. It is for the most part full of vague opposition sentiments and feeds on liberal trash. One of the great and responsible tasks of the politically-conscious workers is to help these democrats to get rid of the influence of liberal prejudices. Only in so far as they overcome these prejudices, cast off the wretched burden of liberal illusions, break with the liberals and hold out their hand to the workers are they, Russia's new democrats, destined to do something real for the cause of freedom.

Pravda No. 15, January 19, 1913
Signed: *T.*

Published according
to the *Pravda* text

ON NARODISM

Mr. A. V. P.[203] has contributed to *Russkoye Bogatstvo* No. 12 a "leading" article on a "current" subject, headed "Socialism—Popular or Proletarian?"

The article is quite shallow and pointless in itself. It is quite a long time since we encountered in the "leading" articles of a Narodnik publication that considers itself important, such a meaningless set of words, such a spate of evasive, bald phrases, or such a hotchpotch of (eclectic) views.

But the characteristic thing about the article is that it raises the highly important and topical question of the disintegration of Narodism. Narodism is the ideology of Russia's peasant democrats. That is why every class-conscious worker should carefully watch the changes this ideology is undergoing.

I

Narodism is very old. It is considered to have been founded by Herzen and Chernyshevsky. Effective Narodism reached its peak when, in the seventies, revolutionaries began to "go among the people" (the peasantry). The Narodniks' economic theory was developed in its more integral form by V. V. (Vorontsov) and Nikolai —on,[204] in the eighties of the last century. In the early twentieth century, the views of the Left Narodniks were expressed in the most definite form by the Socialist-Revolutionaries.

The revolution of 1905, which showed *all* the social forces of Russia in an open, mass action of the classes, made a general test of Narodism and defined its place. The only real content and social significance of Narodism is peasant democracy.

The Russian liberal bourgeoisie is compelled, by virtue of its economic position, to strive not for the *abolition*, but for the *division* of the privileges of Purishkevich and Co. between the feudal landlords and the capitalists. On the other hand, the bourgeois democrats in Russia—the peasants—are compelled to strive for the *abolition* of all these privileges.

For the Narodniks, phrases about "socialism", "socialisation of the land", equalised tenure, and so on, are mere words covering up the fact that the peasants are striving for complete equality in politics and for the complete abolition of feudal landownership.

The revolution of 1905 finally revealed this social essence of Narodism, this class nature of it. The movement of the masses—in the form of the peasant unions of 1905, the local peasant struggles in 1905 and 1906, and the elections to the first two Dumas (the formation of "Trudovik" groups)—all these great social facts, which showed us millions of peasants *in action*, swept aside Narodnik, professedly socialist, phrase-mongering like so much dust and revealed the core: a peasant (bourgeois) democratic movement with an immense, still unexhausted store of energy.

Those whom the *experience* of the greatest epoch in new, modern, Russia has not taught to distinguish between the real content of Narodism and its verbal trappings are hopeless and cannot be taken seriously, they may be writers playing with words (like A. V. P. of *Russkoye Bogatstvo*), but not politicians.

In our next article we shall look more closely at the disintegration of Narodism and at that writer.

II

The experience of 1905 is vastly important precisely because it *compelled* the testing of Narodnik theories by the *movement* of the masses. And that test at once brought about the decay of Narodism and the collapse of Narodnik theories.

At the very first congress of the Socialist-Revolutionaries, in December 1905, the Popular Socialists began to break away from them, and they had seceded completely by the autumn of 1906.

Those Popular Socialists forestalled our liquidators. They chanted in exactly the same way about an "open party", and in the same way they abolished the slogans of consistent democracy and made renegade speeches (see, for example, Mr. Peshekhonov's articles in *Russkoye Bogatstvo* No. 8, 1906). Those were peasant Cadets, and the Second Duma (which was *not* boycotted by the Narodniks, nor even by the Socialist-Revolutionaries) *proved* that the majority of the peasant deputies followed the opportunists of *Russkoye Bogatstvo*, with the minority following the Socialist-Revolutionaries. The Second Duma finally confirmed what was evident already from the Narodnik newspapers of the "days of freedom" (autumn 1905 and spring 1906), namely, that the Socialist-Revolutionaries could be nothing but the Left wing of Russia's peasant democrats and that outside it they were nothing.

The disintegration of Narodism is bearing this out more and more clearly. While the counter-revolution was rampant, this disintegration progressed rapidly: the Left Narodniks "recalled" themselves from the ranks of the Duma Trudoviks. The old party was virtually liquidated but no new one was founded. Renegacy (which went as far as Ropshin's disgraceful writings "The Pale Horse" and "That Which Was Not") obtained a wide path for itself even to the "Left" Narodniks. Some of them (the *Pochin* group) are abandoning the boycott. Others gravitate towards Marxism (N. Sukhanov, for example, although he is still exceedingly muddled). Still others gravitate towards anarchism. All in all, the break-up is far greater than among the Social-Democrats, for while there are official centres, there is *no* clear, consistent, principled line capable of *combating* decadence.

And now Mr. A. V. P. presents us with an example of this ideological decadence. Once the Narodniks had a theory of their own. What is left now is nothing but "reservations" on Marxism picked up at random. Any unprincipled feuilleton-writer for a glib bourgeois sheet could subscribe to Mr.

A. V. P.'s article in defence of "popular" socialism without risking anything, without committing himself in any way, and *without professing anything*. For "popular" socialism is a meaningless phrase serving to *evade* the question of *which* class or social stratum is fighting for socialism throughout the world.

It suffices to quote two specimens of Mr. A. V. P.'s twaddle.

"It appears," he wrote, "that the party which has made the doctrine of proletarian socialism its own is in reality prepared to develop its forces also at the expense of other, 'semi-proletarian', or even 'bourgeois', strata."

An objection fit for a fourth-year schoolboy, isn't it? Both semi-proletarians and bourgeois are to be found in the socialist parties of the whole world, so *what follows?* It follows, Mr. A. V. P. concludes, that one may side-step the fact that *only* the proletariat all over the world (1) wages a sustained struggle against the capitalist class and (2) provides a *mass* support for the Social-Democratic parties.

Another example:

"Take the students," wrote the glib Mr. A. V. P. "Why, they are the most genuine bourgeoisie, and yet the socialists among them—I cannot say how it is now—until recently were almost a majority."

Now isn't that inimitable? Isn't that an argument worthy of a naïve Socialist-Revolutionary schoolgirl? He does not notice, after 1905-07, how tens of millions of peasants and millions of workers took sides in the arena of all political actions, while attaching importance (*as if it were an argument against* "proletarian socialism"!) to the fact that the liberal and democratic student youth in Russia sympathises with the Socialist-Revolutionaries and Social-Democrats! Look here, Mr. A. V. P., have a sense of proportion!

Class-conscious workers must follow a straightforward and clear policy with regard to the Narodniks. They must ruthlessly ridicule would-be socialist phrases and *not allow* the only serious question, that of consistent *democracy*, to be *hidden behind them*.

"Popular" socialism, equalised tenure, socialisation of the land, co-operation, the labour principle? All that is not even worth refuting. Experience and the revolution have long since *swept* it altogether out of the sphere of serious political issues. You are merely hiding the *serious* question, that of *democracy*, behind that sort of twaddle. You must say clearly and plainly whether you are loyal to the slogans of *consistent* democracy. Are you willing and able to transform these slogans into *regular* work among the *masses* of a clearly specified social stratum? If so, the worker democrat will be your ally and friend against all enemies of democracy. If not, go away, you are just a twaddler.

Pravda Nos. 16 and 17, January 20 and 22, 1913 Signed: *V. I.*

Published according to the *Pravda* text

TO THE SOCIAL-DEMOCRATS[205]

We reprint in full the leading article of the latest issue of the St. Petersburg newspaper *Luch* (January 19, 1913, No. 15—101):

"THE MASS OF THE WORKERS AND THE UNDERGROUND

"The authorities have again refused to register the metalworkers' union. Despite all the concessions which the workers were willing to make, the department found every single clause unacceptable. It makes no difference whether the force operating here was the association of factory-owners, which insisted, as the newspapers once reported, that the metalworkers should not be allowed to set up a new trade union, or whether the department itself decided to prevent the rise of such a union. The most progressive and most cultured section of the St. Petersburg workers is being deprived even of the miserable right they enjoyed under the provisional regulations on unions and associations! How much energy has been spent, how many lives have been lost in the struggle to win this bit of a right, which is now reduced to nought with a wave of the hand!

"Strangest of all is the fact that the wide mass of the workers do not at all react to this disfranchisement. Indeed, as a result of the latest persecution of legal organisations, sympathy for the 'underground' is reviving and growing here and there among the workers. We are far from shutting our eyes to this fact, which we find deplorable. But not being accustomed to worship spontaneity, we are trying to realise the meaning of this fact.

"The present talk about the 'underground' is largely reminiscent of the old disputes—now thoroughly forgotten, it seems—about terrorism. Terrorism, too, was 'worshipped' by many who wanted to mask their own worthlessness. It is well, they seemed to say, that there exist heroes; as for us, we'll trail somehow behind them. The same thing is happening now. We are too lazy to think, to seek new paths, and we are waiting for the underground to decide for us, and then we shall act at other people's risk. If we succeed, well and good, and if not, we shall know who is to blame.

"It is exactly this psychology—which, we admit, is rooted in our present political situation and is sufficiently explained by the neavy sacrifices already made for the sake of an open movement—

this psychology of irresponsibility, of a subconscious desire to prove one's absence in the event of failure, that inspires certain sections of the mass of the workers with a resurgent respect for the underground. We say respect for the underground, not flight into it, because it is always single individuals alone who have actually been underground—the masses have nothing to do underground— and those individuals, who are accountable to no one, have had command over mass actions.

"But, it is said, 'legal opportunities' have all been exhausted, resulting in an almost complete destruction of the legal organisations. And it is this that is wrong, to say that *all* opportunities have been exhausted. Actually, the *main* opportunity, without which any victory of the working class is unthinkable, has been used very little so far. We have spoken of the masses' methodical participation in upholding their organisations. What has been done so far has been done neither *methodically* enough nor with the *masses* participating in sufficient measure. Thousands of signatures put to a petition for freedom of association are nothing compared with the hundreds of thousands of factory workers. The dozens and rarely hundreds of members of our trade union, educational and various other associations are but a drop in the bucket compared with the huge numbers of workers engaged in a given trade, living in a given district, and so on. And the fact is that those who take a real interest in unions and work in them are still fewer.

"The masses, who assign the pick of the working-class intelligentsia the most dangerous posts in legal organisations, readily give up, and are willing to abandon the cause itself, when those foremost champions have been snatched out of their ranks. Herein lies the root of the weakness of the working-class movement today, and it is here that there is a virgin field for stubborn and persevering Social-Democratic work."

———

It would be hard to imagine a more complete, more exact and more eloquent document shedding light on the vexed questions of our Social-Democratic Party than this article. The leading article in *Luch* No. 101 with remarkable accuracy summed up all the hundred issues of *Luch* and all the five years' propaganda of the liquidators, P. B. Axelrod, F. Dan, V. Yezhov, Levitsky, Potresov, Martov, Martynov and others.

To comment on this leader in detail, one would have to write a whole volume repeating what Marxists of *all* trends have said against the liquidators in the press during 1909-12.

Let us only point out certain things. Sympathy for the underground is reviving and growing among the mass of the workers, and respect for it is resurgent. He who considers this fact deplorable is a liberal and not a Social-Democrat, a counter-revolutionary and not a democrat.

Comparing the underground with terrorism is an unheard-of affront to revolutionary work among the masses. Only the underground poses and solves problems of the growing revolution, directing revolutionary Social-Democratic work and attracting the mass of the workers precisely by this work.

The underground has been and is today drawn from the finest and most class-conscious of the foremost workers, those dearest to the masses. The link between the underground and the masses now can be, and often is, even broader and closer than before, chiefly owing to the greater class-consciousness of the masses, and in part also to "legal opportunities". The talk of an open party is stupid and base, but as far as our Social-Democratic Party nuclei are concerned, "legal opportunities" for *their* work among the masses have by no means been exhausted, and *cannot be* "exhausted".

Is it possible that the leading article in *Luch* No. 101 will not rouse the ire of *all* Social-Democrats? Will there be even a single "trend" among the Social-Democrats tolerant of such propaganda?

Can this summarising leading article fail to assist in settling the *vexed* question of the *unity* of the Social-Democratic Party?

The diplomats of liquidationism have been completely exposed in *Luch* No. 101. They stand unmasked. From now on, only hypocrites can talk about unity with the liquidationist group of *Luch* and *Nasha Zarya*.

It is time those Social-Democrats who so far have wavered for various reasons, who have given no explicit answer to the question under discussion, who have in an evasive form permitted "agreement" with *Luch* and sought to cloak their solidarity with *Luch* by talk about "unity"—it is high time they stopped wavering and spoke out plainly.

Unity with *Luch* is impossible, while unity *against Luch* is perfectly possible and urgently necessary. For the point at issue is unity of the *"underground"*, of the illegal Social-Democratic Party, the R.S.D.L.P., and of its revolutionary work among the masses.

Written on January 22
(February 4), 1913

Hectographed in leaflet form
in Cracow, late January, 1913

Published according
to the leaflet text

IN THE WORLD OF THE AZEFS[206]

The nationalist press raised a terrible clamour over the Alyokhin "incident". What! The Austrians had insulted Russia by arresting an innocent Russian engineer on a charge of espionage and by outraging the arrested man! There were endless "patriotic" sallies against Austria.

And now the whole background has come to light—the simple, old, long-familiar background of the affair. Mr. Alyokhin was a victim of Weissmann, an Austrian police agent, who had been shadowing Russian spies in Austria for 2,000 kronen (800 rubles) a month.

The Russian engineer, who knows no German and is evidently a semi-savage as well, naïvely fell for the bait of the *agent provocateur*, who showed him round the arsenals.

Novoye Vremya and our other papers of a Black-Hundred and government trend defend *Russian* Azefs with all their might. But when an Azef turned out to be in the Austrian service, those well-intentioned Russian patriots were fired with "righteous" indignation.

But it turned out, in addition, that Weissmann is a former *Russian* spy and *agent provocateur*. The career of this Weissmann is most instructive.

His father kept a brothel. The son, after this sort of sohooling, became a Russian spy in Vienna, Austria, where he also spied on Russian political exiles. Thus, from 1901 to 1905, Weissmann was in the service of the Russian police, being simultaneously a military and a political spy.

Subsequently Weissmann fell out with the Russian police and passed into the service of the Austrian police.

All very simple.

Poor Alyokhin was the victim of a former Russian spy. Now how can the servile Russian newspapers help being indignant at this "treachery" on the part of Austria?

Pravda No. 20, January 25, 1913
Signed: *W.*

Published according
to the *Pravda* text

THE BOURGEOISIE AND REFORMISM

The arguments of *Rech* concerning the urgent issue of strikes deserve the greatest attention on the part of the workers.

That liberal paper cited the following official data on the strike movement:

Year	Strikes	Workers (thousand)
1905	13,995	2,863
1906	6,114	1,108
1907	3,573	740
1908	892	176
1909	340	64
1910	222	47
1911	466	105
1912	1,918	683

We would note in passing that the figures for 1912 are plainly understated, since the number of political strikers is given as only 511,000. Actually their number was about twice as great. We would also recall that as late as May 1912 *Rech* denied the political character of our working-class movement, asserting that the whole movement was only economic. But we intend to deal now with another aspect of the matter.

How does our liberal bourgeoisie assess this fact?

"The main requirements of the political consciousness [why only *consciousness*??] of Russian citizens have yet to be met," wrote *Rech*.

"The working class everywhere is the most mobile and most sensitive section of the urban democrats ... the most active section of the people.... Given constitutional conditions ... given a normal political situation ... there would not have been the loss of tens of thousands of working days [because of the Putilov strike] in an industry which today is of extreme importance in view of external complications" (No. 19).

The point of view of the bourgeoisie is clear. "We" want an imperialist policy, the conquest of foreign territory. "We" are handicapped by strikes. "We" lose surplus value because of the "lost" working days. "We" want to exploit the workers as "normally" as they do it in Europe.

Splendid, liberal gentlemen! Your desire is legitimate, and we are willing to support your effort if—*if* it is not futile and dead!

Rech continued: "It was not out of sympathy for liberties that Prussian statesmen [it ought to have said "Prussian landlords"] granted '*the legalisation of the Social-Democratic Party*'. Reforms bear proper fruit when granted in good time."

Such is the consummate reformism of our bourgeoisie. It confines itself to wistful sighs; it wants to persuade the Purishkeviches without hurting their feelings, to make peace with them without removing them. It should be clear to any intelligent person that by virtue of its *objective* meaning (that is, regardless of the good intentions of individual little groups), the slogan of "legalisation of the Social-Democratic Party" is an inseparable component of this wretched and impotent bourgeois reformism.

We would make only one remark. Bismarck succeeded in his reforms only because he went further than reformism. As we know, he carried out a series of "revolutions from above"; he robbed one of the world's richest countries of five thousand million francs, and he *was in a position* to give universal suffrage and genuine legality to a people intoxicated with a stream of gold and unprecedented military successes.

Do you imagine, liberal gentlemen, that something of the kind could happen in Russia?? Why, then, did you declare reforms in Russia to be hopeless even in the case of the Archangel Zemstvo (a "reform", indeed!)??

Pravda No. 23, January 29, 1913
Signed: *T.*

Published according
to the *Pravda* text

APROPOS OF THE OPEN PARTY

Luch, a newspaper which succeeds in making the more "clamour" among circles of the intelligentsia the less the workers read it, continues its advocacy of *an open workers' party* with a zeal worthy of a better cause.

In the New-Year leading article of the paper we read an old untruth, namely, that the year 1912 "put forward, as its current slogan and as the militant banner of the Russia of the workers, the struggle for freedom of association and the struggle for the open existence of the Social-Democratic Labour Party".

Anyone who really came into contact with the workers' mass movement in 1912 and carefully observed its political character knows very well that the liquidators of *Luch* are telling an untruth. What the workers did put forward as their current slogan and militant banner was *something else.* This was particularly evident, for example, in May, when the foremost workers of different trends (even with a Narodnik minority participating along with the Social-Democratic majority) *themselves* put forward a *different* slogan and unfurled a different "militant banner".

The intellectuals of *Luch* know that, but they are trying to impose *their* want of faith, *their* narrow understanding and *their* opportunism on the workers. A familiar picture with nothing new about it! In Russia, however, the authors of this distortion are able to put it forward all the more easily because it has the monopoly of "open" expression in certain fields.

For all that, the untruth of *Luch* remains an untruth. And it becomes worse when *Luch* continues:

"It is this slogan that will form the pivot of the political mobilisation of the mass of the workers in 1913...."

In other words, *in defiance of* the mass of the workers, who have already advanced a *different* slogan, the intellectuals of *Luch* are going to dock and curtail it! You are free to do that, gentlemen, but what you are promoting is a liberal and not a Social-Democratic cause.

Let the reader recall the recent controversy between *Luch* and *Pravda* over an open party. Why is it that even the Cadets were unable to found an open party?—*Pravda* asked.* And F. D., writing in *Luch*, replied:

"The Cadets recognised that their desire was utopian" when they failed to get their Rules approved; as for the liquidators, they carried on "stubborn methodical work, winning one position after another" (see *Luch* No. 73).

You see: F. D. evaded giving a reply! The Cadets, too, carried on stubborn work and they, too, were "winning positions" in legal publications and legal unions. But even the Cadets have *no* open *party*.

Why, then, do the Cadets continue to dream and talk of an open party? Because they are the party of the counter-revolutionary liberal bourgeoisie, which is willing to *make peace* with the Purishkeviches for certain little concessions to the liberals, for the little concession of a "peaceful" open Cadet party.

That is the objective significance—which does not depend on good wishes and fine words—of the talk about an open party under the June Third regime. This talk is a *repudiation* of consistent democracy, and an advocacy of *peace* with the Purishkeviches.

It is unimportant what *aims* the liquidators pursue by their advocacy of an open party, or what their intentions and expectations are. That is a subjective question; it is well known that the road to hell is paved with "good" intentions. What is important is the objective significance of the advocacy of an open workers' party under the June Third regime, with a non-open liberal party, etc.

---

* See pp. 432-34 of this volume.—*Ed.*

This objective significance of the liquidators' talk about
an open party is a repudiation of the popular and fundamental conditions and demands of democracy.

That is why every politically-conscious worker reacts
adversely to the liquidators' propaganda, for the issue of
an "open party" is a *fundamental* question, one that concerns the *very existence* of the working-class Party. It is the
very existence of a genuine workers' party that is being
radically undermined by liquidationist propaganda.

Pravda No. 24, January 30, 1913
          Signed: *T*.

                                                  Published according
                                                  to the *Pravda* text

MOBILISATION OF PEASANT LANDS

Mobilisation of land is the transfer of landownership from one person to another. With regard to our peasants, both our legislation and our "public" opinion (even liberal opinion, as expressed by the Cadets) still maintain the *feudal* view that mobilisation of peasant lands is harmful and should be prohibited or restricted.

From the democratic point of view, the very assumption that peasants—adult persons and full-fledged citizens—may be prohibited from or impeded in selling their land is a most shameless affront to the peasantry. Only in a country like Russia, where all government officials and the bulk of the liberals still cling to the old, feudal view of the "muzhik" as being slow-witted, underprivileged and requiring tutelage, can this attitude to mobilisation persist.

From the economic point of view, the harm caused by all prohibition and restriction of mobilisation is enormous. Given living conditions that are at all tolerable, the peasant will *never* sell his land. On the other hand, when want or other conditions (resettlement, death of the breadwinner, and so on) *compel* a peasant to sell his land, *no law* can stop him. The law will *always* be bypassed, and bans will merely worsen the terms of sale of the land.

In the January issue of *Russkaya Mysl*, the mouthpiece of the extreme Right-wing Cadets, a cross-breed of liberals and Black Hundreds, a certain Prince V. Obolensky, who apparently shares the usual Black-Hundred and liberal view on mobilisation, was compelled to cite *facts* proving the stupidity and harm of all restrictions on it. Non-peasants are prohibited from buying allotments. So they register as peasants! Or a person is prohibited from buying more than six per capita allotments. So he signs fictitious, fraudulent deeds in the name of his relatives, and so on! Or he is prohibited from mortgaging allotment land. This makes speculative deals all the easier and the purchase of land by middle peasants all the more difficult!

Only feudal-minded people and hypocrites can expect restrictions on mobilisation to "relieve" the peasantry. As far as the politically-conscious peasants are concerned, they seek an entirely different solution.

Pravda No. 26, February 1, 1913
Signed: *T*.

Published according to the *Pravda* text

A WORD ABOUT STRIKES

Luch has carried a number of articles against mass strikes. It is obvious that we cannot reply to *Luch* here in the way it deserves.

We shall limit ourselves to a few purely theoretical comments on the *nature* of the arguments of *Luch*. Those who write for *Luch* and who diligently cite examples from Western countries, repeating the catchword "anarcho-syndicalism" and so on in a thousand variations, thereby betray their complete incomprehension of the historical peculiarity of the strikes in Russia in 1912.

Nowhere in Europe have strikes in the twentieth century had, and nowhere do they have or can they have, such importance as in the Russia of the period we are passing through. Why?

For the simple reason that while the period of radical democratic changes has long been absolutely over throughout Europe, in Russia it is just such changes that are on the order of the day—in the historical sense of the phrase.

Hence the nation-wide character of the economic, and still more of the non-economic, strikes in Russia. Strikes in Europe, where they herald entirely different changes, *do not possess* such a nation-wide character (from the standpoint of democratic changes in the country). Moreover, the relation between the strikes in Russia and the position of the agricultural small producers (peasants) is quite unlike what it is in the Western countries.

Putting all this together, we shall see that the arguments of *Luch* leave out of account precisely the national, democratic significance of the economic and non-economic strikes in the Russia of 1912. The most important and historically distinctive feature of our strikes is the fact that the proletariat comes forward as the leader *despite* the anti-democratic sentiments of the liberals. And it is just this that the *Luch* writers do not understand, and cannot understand from their liquidationist standpoint.

Of course, the point is not at all to appraise the advisability of any particular strike. It is not at all that the most methodical preparations are necessary and sometimes even the replacement of a strike by an action of *the same kind*. The point is the liquidators' *general* incomprehension of *this particular* significance of strikes in general which makes the slogan of "freedom of association" or of an "open party" unsuitable, out of keeping with the existing situation.

What the liquidators see as a disadvantage is the entire character of the movement and not particular cases, while the Marxists and all class-conscious workers see it as an advantage. That is why the workers have been incensed, and continue to be incensed, by *Luch*'s propaganda.

Pravda No. 27, February 2, 1913
Signed: *I.*

Published according to the *Pravda* text

RUSSIANS AND NEGROES

What a strange comparison, the reader may think. How can a race be compared with a nation?

It is a permissible comparison. The Negroes were the last to be freed from slavery, and they still bear, more than anyone else, the cruel marks of slavery—even in advanced countries—for capitalism has no "room" for other than legal emancipation, and even the latter it curtails in every possible way.

With regard to the Russians, history has it that they were "almost" freed from *serf* bondage in 1861. It was about the same time, following the civil war against the American slaveowners, that North America's Negroes were freed from slavery.

The emancipation of the American slaves took place in a less "reformative" manner than that of the Russian slaves.

That is why today, half a century later, the Russians still show *many more* traces of slavery than the Negroes. Indeed, it would be more accurate to speak of institutions and not merely of traces. But in this short article we shall limit ourselves to a little illustration of what we have said, namely, the question of literacy. It is known that illiteracy is one of the marks of slavery. In a country oppressed by pashas, Purishkeviches and their like, the majority of the population cannot be literate.

In Russia there are *73 per cent of illiterates*, exclusive of children under nine years of age.

Among the U.S. Negroes, there were (in 1900) *44.5 per cent* of illiterates.

Such a scandalously high percentage of illiterates is a disgrace to a civilised, advanced country like the North

American Republic. Furthermore, everyone knows that the position of the Negroes in America *in general* is one unworthy of a civilised country—capitalism *cannot* give either *complete* emancipation or even complete equality.

It is instructive that among the whites in America the proportion of illiterates is not more than 6 per cent. But if we divide America into what were formerly slave-holding areas (an American "Russia") and non-slave-holding areas (an American non-Russia), we shall find 11-12 per cent of illiterates *among the whites* in the former and 4-6 per cent in the latter areas!

The proportion of illiterates *among the whites* is *twice as high* in the former slave-holding areas. It is not only the Negroes that show traces of slavery!

Shame on America for the plight of the Negroes!

Written late January-early
        February 1913
    First published in
Krasnaya Niva No. 3, 1925
      Signed: *W*.

Published according
to the manuscript

A DISCOVERY

Bourgeois society lives and subsists exclusively by the wage labour of the millions. Failing this, neither the incomes of the landlords, nor the profits of the capitalists, nor yet the various "derivative" sources of a life of plenty, such as royalties, salaries, etc., would be possible. And the force which drives the millions into the ranks of wage labourers is hunger.

This is an old, universally known, hackneyed fact. The bourgeois public gets used to it and "does not notice" it. But from time to time glaring cases of want and poverty side by side with luxury compel "discoveries" to be made, particularly if the health and well-being of the bourgeois gentlemen are endangered! Once in a while they "discover", in every big city and any rural backwoods, appalling, abominable squalor, want and neglect unworthy of human beings. They "discover" them, inform the public through the "big" newspapers, comment on the fact for a day or two, and then forget it. The sated do not understand the hungry.

Recently in St. Petersburg a Dr. Kozlovsky, who inspected 251 lodging rooms in Rozhdestvensky District, acquainted the public with a "discovery" of this kind.

"Dark, damp rooms, suffocating air, squalor, people sleeping on trunks or on the floor, horrible overcrowding (3,578 tenants in 251 lodging rooms), crushed bugs on the walls—an appalling picture" (*Novoye Vremya*, No. 13236).

The public health society which heard the report resolved to study the problem, to make representations ... to ask for an investigation—i.e., it did all it could.

A few figures from St. Petersburg statistics for 1911. The Special Department for the Investigation and Accommodation of Paupers had 16,960 paupers entrusted to its care. Of these, 1,761 were *handed over to the courts*—next time they will know better than to disturb clean people!—1,371 were sent back to their native parts (the countryside is "accustomed" to having paupers on its hands), 1,892 remained to be cared for in the institutions of the Department, and 9,694 were *released.*

People did work hard in the Department, after all— they "investigated"; they do not get their salaries for nothing.

The same year 1911 saw 43,156 unskilled workers apply for employment to the city labour exchange (beyond Moskovskaya Zastava). Work was found for 6,076 men.

The "released" (those freed from "care" in the case of the paupers and from jobs in the case of unskilled labour) spend the night in the street, in doss-houses, in lodging rooms.... They are material for discoveries.

Pravda No. 29, February 5, 1913
Signed: *V. I.*

Published according
to the *Pravda* text

THE BRITISH LABOUR PARTY CONFERENCE

The Thirteenth Conference of the British Labour Party was held in London from January 29 to 31 (new style). It was attended by 500 delegates.

The Conference passed a resolution against war, and by a considerable majority passed another resolution calling on the Party's representatives in Parliament to vote against any electoral reform Bill that does not extend the franchise to women.

The British Labour Party, which exists *side by side* with the opportunist Independent Labour Party and the Social-Democratic British Socialist Party, is something in the nature of a *broad labour party*. It is a compromise between a socialist party and non-socialist trade unions.

This compromise resulted from the peculiarities of British history and the segregation of the labour *aristocracy* in non-socialist, liberal trade unions. These unions have begun to turn towards socialism, and this gives rise to a host of intermediate, confused situations.

On Party discipline, for example, a resolution was adopted threatening expulsion from the Party for violation of the decisions of the Party or of the *Parliamentary group*.

Disputes arose that would be impossible in any other country—as to whether this resolution is directed against the Liberals or against the Socialists?

The fact is that out of forty Labour M.P.s, 27 are *non-Socialists*!! In opposing the resolution, the Socialist Will Thorne said they wanted to *tie the hands* of the thirteen Socialists by subordinating them to the *non-Socialists*. Even Bruce Glasier, of the I.L.P., while supporting the resolution, admitted that there are about *half a dozen* Labour M.P.s whose place is among the Conservatives.

The resolution was carried.

A resolution that not only the posters of the opportunist *Daily Herald*[207] be displayed in Party premises was defeated by 643,000 votes to 398,000. The voting here is calculated according to the number of members which each delegation represents.

The majority at the Conference consisted of non-Socialists and extremely bad Socialists. But definite voices were heard indicating that the mass of the workers are dissatisfied with such a party and they demand that their M.P.s should do less playing at legislation and more socialist propaganda.

Pravda No. 30, February 6, 1913

Published according to the *Pravda* text

CONSTITUTIONAL ILLUSIONS SHATTERED

"We have a constitution, thank God!" exclaimed Mr. Milyukov after June 3, 1907. The leader of the liberal bourgeoisie sought comfort in amusing assertions of this kind, while concealing its distrust of the people and its reluctance, its fear, to depart from the "constitutional" path.

Most characteristically, it is just now, when the same Mr. Milyukov or his prim, official-minded liberal *Rech* acknowledges the "beginning of a social upswing" (No. 26), that the collapse of these constitutional illusions is becoming obvious. Underlying these illusions is the desire to dismiss an unpleasant reality (and the unpleasant necessity of taking a path that does not resemble the "constitutional" one), the desire to lull oneself and others with "constitutional" catchwords.

And now look what the liberals have to say of the present situation!

"It is dull in the Duma because there is no struggle going on" (No. 25).

Well, gentlemen, it was you who said we had a constitution!

"All the words have been spoken. What is needed now is deeds, *but there is no faith in them*. Hence the apathy" (ibid.).

You lulled yourselves with faith in *words*, which you addressed chiefly to the Octobrists. Now you admit that you spoke those words to cover up lack of *faith in deeds*.

You have condemned yourselves, liberal gentlemen.

Democrats in general, and workers in particular, have had no faith in words (about the constitution)—*

Written late January-early
February 1913
Published for the first time

Published according
to the manuscript

---

* Part of the MS. has been lost.—*Ed.*

THANK YOU FOR YOUR FRANKNESS

We wish to thank the Black-Hundred *Novoye Vremya* for publishing a frank statement by Kobylinsky, leader of the Rights on the Council of State. We also wish to thank the "leader" himself.

"Every now and again," Mr. Kobylinsky exclaimed, "members of the Duma betray ignorance and inability to legislate.... *Only shopkeepers draft laws like that....*

"We have been attacked for rejecting the Bill to introduce the Zemstvo in Archangel Gubernia.... The Duma did not stop for a moment to think that owing to the absence of cultured elements and the sparse population in Archangel Gubernia, people there would have to elect, as a wit put it, *a muzhik*, a reindeer and a bear to the Zemstvo council....

"Be that as it may, *we shall not allow* the establishment of a *muzhik* Zemstvo, as the Third Duma envisaged it."

Well, how can we help thanking the leader of the Rights on the Council of State, i.e., the leader of the Council of State, for being so frank?

We wholeheartedly recommend to the reader this clear and truthful argument *for* the Council of State instead of the hackneyed, non-committal liberal phrases *against* the Council of State.

Shopkeepers in the Duma ... muzhiks and bears in the Zemstvo ... we shall admit no shopkeepers or muzhiks. There you have the plain language of a feudal-minded landlord.

And mind you, he is right, is this feudal lord, in saying that there is *no* majority in the Duma without the "shopkeepers", i.e., without the *bourgeoisie*, to use the language of a class-conscious worker (and not of a wild landlord[208]). He is right, is this feudal lord, in saying that self-government would in fact be *peasant* self-gevernment (the class-conscious workers prefer the term *peasant* to *muzhik*, which is current among wild landlords). The peasants are a majority.

The Council of State is by no means an accidental political institution but a *class* organ—this is what Kobylinsky's truthful speech implies. The class in question is that of the big landlords. They *will admit no* "shopkeepers or muzhiks".

Really, Russian liberal "shopkeepers", and Octobrist and Cadet gentlemen, you must learn from Kobylinsky how to pose political questions seriously!

Pravda No. 35, February 12, 1913

Published according to the *Pravda* text

THE QUESTION OF UNITY

The letter which Shagov, the Kostroma workers' deputy, wrote to *Pravda* (No. 22—226) indicated very clearly the terms on which the workers think Social-Democratic unity feasible. Letters from a number of other deputies for the worker curia (*Pravda* Nos. 21-28) confirmed this view. The workers themselves must bring about unity "from below". The liquidators should not fight the underground but should form part of it.

It is amazing that after the question has been posed so clearly and squarely we come across Trotsky's old, pompous but perfectly meaningless phrases in *Luch* No. 27 (113). Not a word *on the substance* of the matter! Not the slightest attempt to cite *precise facts* and analyse them thoroughly! Not a hint of the *real terms* of unity! Empty exclamations, high-flown words, and haughty sallies against opponents whom the author does not name, and impressively important assurances—that is Trotsky's total stock-in-trade.

That won't do, gentlemen. You speak "to the workers" *as though they were children*, now trying to scare them with terrible words ("the shackles of the circle method", "monstrous polemics", "the feudal-serf-owning period of our Party history"), now "coaxing" them, as one coaxes small children, without either convincing them or explaining matters to them.

The workers will not be intimidated or coaxed. They *themselves* will compare *Luch* and *Pravda*; they will read, for example, the leading article in *Luch* No. 101 ("The Mass of the Workers and the Underground"), and simply shrug off Trotsky's verbiage.

"In practice the question of the underground, alleged to be one of principle, is decided by all Social-Democratic groups absolutely alike...," Trotsky wrote in italics. The St. Petersburg workers know from experience that that is not so. Workers in any corner of Russia, as soon as they read the *Luch* leading article mentioned above, will see that Trotsky is departing from the truth.

"It is ridiculous and absurd to affirm," we read in his article, "that there is an irreconcilable contradiction between the political tendencies of *Luch* and *Pravda*." Believe us, my dear author, that neither the word "absurd" nor the word "ridiculous" can frighten the workers, who will ask you to speak to them *as to adults on the substance of the matter*: just expound those tendencies and prove that the leading article in *Luch* No. 101 can be "reconciled" with Social-Democracy!

You cannot satisfy the workers with mere phrases, no matter how "conciliatory" or honeyed.

"Our historic factions, Bolshevism and Menshevism, are purely intellectualist formations in origin," wrote Trotsky.

This is the repetition of a liberal tale. In fact, however, the whole of Russian reality confronted the workers with the issue of the attitude to the liberals and the peasantry. Even if there had been no intelligentsia, the workers *could not* have evaded the issue of whether they should *follow* the liberals or lead the peasantry *against* the liberals.

It is *to the advantage* of the liberals to pretend that this fundamental basis of the differences was introduced by "intellectuals". But Trotsky merely disgraces himself by echoing a liberal tale.

Pravda No. 39, February 16, 1913   Published according
                                                      to the *Pravda* text

WHAT GOES ON AMONG THE NARODNIKS
AND WHAT GOES ON IN THE COUNTRYSIDE

The magazine *Russkoye Bogatstvo* shows us the two streams of the Narodnik or Trudovik current or trend in Russian life that can also be traced by drawing on other, more direct and immediate sources of political knowledge.

Let us recall, for example, the debates in the First and Second Dumas. Unfortunately, the verbatim reports of both have been withdrawn from sale. Nevertheless, the immense political material they provide for studying the views and aspirations of the Russian peasantry and Russian Trudoviks has in part already become, and in part will in the future become, known to every educated person. The chief conclusion to be drawn from this material is that the Trudovik *intellectuals* (including the Socialist-Revolutionary intellectuals) and the *peasant* Trudoviks represent essentially distinct political trends.

The intellectual Narodniks gravitate towards conciliatory or "philanthropic" phrases. One always senses the liberal in them. The standpoint of the class struggle is wholly foreign to them. They are·given to moralising. They are pulling the democratic peasantry *back* from the real and direct struggle against its class enemy to vague, forced, impotent, quasi-socialist phrase-mongering.

The peasant Narodniks in both of the early Dumas were full of fire and passion. They were eager for direct and resolute action. They were ignorant, uneducated and unsophisticated, but they rose against their class enemy so straightforwardly, uncompromisingly and implacably that one *sensed* what an impressive social force they were.

In other words, the Narodnik intellectuals are very bad socialists and lukewarm democrats. The peasant Trudoviks are far from playing at socialism, which is quite alien to them, but they are honest, sincere, ardent and strong democrats. No one can foretell whether peasant democracy will win in Russia, for this depends on much too complicated objective conditions. But it is beyond doubt that the Trudovik peasantry *could* win only *in spite of* the tendencies which the Narodnik intelligentsia brings into the movement of the Trudovik peasantry. A vigorous, fresh and sincere democratic movement *can* win, given a favourable historical situation, whereas "socialist" *phrase-mongering* and Narodnik moralising can never win.

I consider this conclusion to be one of the most important lessons of the Russian revolution, and I cherish the hope that some day I may be able to substantiate it by a detailed analysis of Narodnik speeches in the first two Dumas and by other political evidence from the 1905-07 period. For the time being I should like to note the remarkable confirmation of this conclusion to be found in the latest issue (No. 12, 1912) of *Russkoye Bogatstvo*, the chief and most authoritative Narodnik organ.

Two articles in that issue produce an impression that is undoubtedly typical. Mr. A.V.P.'s article ("Socialism—Popular or Proletarian?") is a specimen of the intellectualist arguments of the "Popular Socialists" and Socialist-Revolutionaries.

If it had been inevitable for the massive force of the Russian peasantry to be directed in the way that "results" from the *arguments* of Messrs. A.V.P. and Co., the cause of Russia's bourgeois democrats would have been hopelessly lost. For phrase-mongering and moralising *can never* result in history-making *action*. The impotence of *this kind* of Narodism is complete.

In Mr. Kryukov's article, "Without Fire", the peasantry and peasant life and psychology are described by a honey-tongued little priest, who portrays the peasantry in just the way it *itself* has acted, and continues to act. If this portrayal is accurate, Russia's bourgeois democrats— in the shape of the peasantry—are destined to carry out a major historical action that has every chance of success provided the situation is at all favourable.

To make this point clear, we shall briefly describe Mr. A. V. P.'s "ideas" and quote a few passages from the portrayal of the Russian peasantry given by the little priest.

Mr. A. V. P. defends the foundations of Narodism against Sukhanov, a writer for *Zavety*, who *surrenders* a whole series of cardinal theoretical premises of Narodism to Marxism, advocating a kind of unity between Marxists and Narodniks.

Mr. A. V. P. has no objection to unity but does not propose to "surrender" the principles of Narodism. And it is precisely this *defence* of the purity of the principles and of the solidity of Narodism by such an unquestionably competent and noted Narodnik as Mr. A. V. P. that shows most clearly that his position is quite *hopeless* and that *this kind* of Narodism *is absolutely lifeless.*

Mr. Sukhanov went as far as to say that the proletariat was the only class which was socialist by nature. Of course, if we were to reason with any degree of consistency, this means recognising Marxism and completely giving up Narodnik *socialism* as a bad job.

Mr. A. V. P. is up in arms against Mr. Sukhanov, but his arguments are exceptionally lame. They are nothing but so many little reservations, rectifications, question marks, and eclectic comments to the effect that revisionism "overemphasises" life's corrections to theory, while orthodoxy wastes its time disputing them. The hotchpotch dished up by Mr. A. V. P. exactly resembles the objections of the "humanitarian" bourgeois to the class struggle and class socialism—objections common in all European countries.

Mr. A. V. P. does not venture to deny the fundamental and well-known fact that throughout the world it is only the proletariat that wages a systematic, daily struggle against capital, and that it alone constitutes the mass bulwark of the socialist parties. And Mr. A. V. P. cannot but know that *the freer* a country is politically, *the less* the peasantry shows even feeble socialist leanings. And he simply *plays* on fragments of ideas expressed by European bourgeois professors and opportunists in order to *confuse* the issue,

without even trying to set against Marxism anything at all
like an integral, straightforward and clear social theory.

That is why nothing could be more boring than Mr.
A. V. P.'s article. And nothing could be more indicative of
the total ideological death of Narodnik *socialism* in Russia.
It is dead. You can find Mr. A. V. P.'s "ideas" in full in
any bourgeois social-reformist publication in the West, so
there is no point in refuting them.

But while Narodnik *socialism* is dead in Russia, having
been killed by the revolution of 1905 and buried by people
like A. V. P., and while nothing is left of it but rotten
phrases, Russia's peasant democracy—a democracy that is
by no means socialist but as bourgeois as was democracy in
America in the 1860s, in France at the close of the eighteenth century, in Germany in the first half of the nineteenth
century, etc., etc.—is *alive*.

The honey-tongued priest's story of the countryside, recorded by Mr. Kryukov, fully confirms this. And let us
note in passing that what Kryukov reports perhaps stands
out even more vividly and precisely from the observations
which the *Vekhi*-minded Bulgakov, an admitted enemy of
democracy, published in *Russkaya Mysl* (No. 11, 1912—"At
the Elections").

"Servility and cowardice have always been there!" says Kryukov's little priest, speaking of the Russian clergy. "But the difference now is that there has never been so *appallingly calm* and tacit
a falling-away from the church as today. It is as if the spirit of life
were dead in the church. I repeat that it isn't the intellectuals alone
who have left—so have the people.... I must admit it—after all,
I've been a country priest for two years."

The honey-tongued priest recalled the year *1905*. At
that time he was busy explaining the manifesto to the peasants.

"I had looked forward," he wailed, "to understanding, close
unity, *love*, sobriety, a sound mind, an awakening, vigour.... But
while understanding did seem to come, we had hatred and internecine
strife instead of solidarity and unity. And I was the very first man
to be hit by the countryside, and pretty roughly, too. Why, didn't
I stand for it heart and soul? I told them all about those liberties
and all that sort of thing. And you should have seen how they listened! I imagined you just couldn't make things any clearer than
I did, but no—there were other ideas that found their way into the

countryside. Besides, the new explainers made a much spicier stew—they talked about the land and equality and the landlords. *Of course, the muzhiks saw it and swallowed it at once.* First of all they came to tell me that they would pay me for tithes not two hundred rubles but one hundred....

"However, what *vexed* me particularly wasn't that fact—about that hundred rubles—but the totality of the things which so unexpectedly reshaped the countryside. Didn't they all try to open its eyes for it, to rid it of its ignorance, to lighten its darkness! And to tell the truth, they succeeded too. A bit of light did dawn on the blind, and they have no longer been blind since then, even though they haven't really recovered their eyesight. But with that half-vision came only the most sorrowful knowledge and the most choking hatred.... Some day they may sigh regretfully thinking of their past ignorance. There's so much hatred in the countryside that you'd say the very air is saturated with it nowadays.... They are quick with the knife and the cudgel and the fire-brand. There's a feeling of helplessness, the sting of unavenged grievances, internecine quarrels, indiscriminate hatred, envy of all who are better off, who live more comfortably and own more. To be sure, there was envy and hatred and sorrow and vile sin in the past as well, but people had faith in the divine will and realised the futility of worldly benefits. They had faith and *were therefore able to bear it,* hoping to be rewarded in the hereafter. That faith is no more. What people there believe in today is that we are oppressors and they are the oppressed. Weeds and thornapples have sprouted in the countryside from all that talk about freedom.... And now this new law about the land—brother has risen up against brother, son against father and neighbour against neighbour! The hatred and discord now are such that the countryside will choke with it, it certainly will."

We have underlined certain particularly characteristic words in this characteristic description of the countryside by the mealy-mouthed little priest (a genuine Narodnik intellectual!).

The priest is a partisan of "love" and an enemy of "hatred". In this respect he fully shares the Tolstoyan (we may also say Christian), thoroughly reactionary point of view which our Cadets and Cadet-like people are constantly promoting. Such a priest would hardly mind dreaming of some sort of "socialisation of the land" or prattling about the "socialist" significance of co-operation and about "standards of landownership". But when it came to hatred instead of "love", he at once recoiled, went limp and whimpered.

There is any amount of verbal, loud-mouthed "socialism" ("popular and not proletarian"), and in Europe too any literate philistine approves of it. But when it comes to "hatred" instead of "love", that is the end. Socialism as humane phrase-mongering—yes, we are for it; revolutionary democracy—no, we are against it.

What the honey-tongued little priest says on the hackneyed subject of "hooliganism" in the countryside is absolutely nothing new from the factual point of view. But it is evident from his own story that "hooliganism" is a concept introduced by the *feudal landlords*. "Burning, unavenged grievances" is what the sugary priest notes. And this, of course, is a very far cry from "hooliganism".

———

In the struggle against Narodism, Marxists have long regarded it as their task to smash Manilovism, cloying phrases, a sentimental supra-class point of view, and vulgar "popular" socialism worthy of a French "Radical Socialist" skilled in shady business deals. But, at the same time, Marxists have long considered it just as much their indispensable task to extract the *democratic* core of Narodnik views. Narodnik socialism is a putrid and evil-smelling corpse. Peasant democracy in Russia is a living force, if Kryukov's honey-tongued priest has depicted it accurately. Indeed, it cannot help being a living force so long as the Purishkeviches are in the saddle, and so long as there are some thirty million who are starving.

"Indiscriminate hatred", we are told. First of all, this is not the whole truth. It is the Purishkeviches and government officials and amiable intellectuals who see no "discrimination". Secondly, even at the beginning of the working-class movement in Russia there was a certain element of "indiscriminate hatred", such as that, for instance, which took the form of destroying machinery during the strikes of the sixties, seventies and eighties of the last century. That did not last. Nor was that the point. It would be banal to demand that people in this situation who were losing their patience should use "kid gloves".

The important thing is the far-reaching break with the old, hopelessly reactionary world outlook, the thorough assimilation of just that doctrine about the "enslaved" that is an earnest of real life and not of the sleep of death.

Narodnik socialism is rotten even in its most Left-wing section. What is alive and vital is the task of purifying, enlightening, arousing and unifying the democratic movement through a deliberate break with doctrines of "love", "patience", and so on. The honey-tongued little priest is sad. We, however, have every reason to rejoice in the ample opportunities for vigorous work.

Prosveshcheniye No 2.
February 1913
Signed: *V. I.*

Published according
to the text in *Prosveshcheniye*

AN INCREASING DISCREPANCY

NOTES OF A PUBLICIST

I

Recently the Cadet deputies conferred again with local leaders of that party.

As might have been expected, they discussed the features of the present political situation. The liberals appraised the situation as follows:

"Attention was drawn to the increasing discrepancy between the country's requirements for basic legislation and the impossibility of meeting them under the present system of legislative institutions and in view of the present attitude of the authorities towards popular representation."

The style is as tangled as a ball of wool with which a kitten has been playing for a long time. Our poor liberals— they have nowhere to express their ideas clearly!

But take a closer look: the trouble is not so much that the liberals have *nowhere* to talk as that they have *nothing* to say. The discrepancy is growing not only between the country's requirements and the hopelessness of the "present system", etc., but also between the country's requirements and the liberals' *helplessness*.

Why is it impossible for you, liberal politicians, to meet the requirements of the country? The Cadets reply: because the present system of legislative institutions and the present attitude of the authorities towards popular representation hinder it.

Consequently, we need a different system and a different attitude of the authorities. We shall see in what way they must be different when we analyse in subsequent articles the "four theses" of the Cadet meeting.

But we must first put the main question: What is the reason for the "present" "system and attitude"? Where could anything *different* come from? The Cadets did not even think of it! Their reticence on this *fundamental* question amounts to hardened, Asiatic philistinism, like saying that there were bad advisers but there can be good advisers.

Is there no connection, Cadet gentlemen, between the "present" and the *interests* of some *class*, such as the class of the big landlords? Or the richest section of the bourgeoisie? Is not there complete *accord* between the "present" and the interests of *definite classes*? Is it not clear that any one who sets about discussing the political situation without taking into account the relations between all the classes engages in useless talk?

Alas! The Cadets have nothing but empty talk to cover up the "increasing discrepancy" between their policy and the requirements of the country.

II

Our liberals in general—and they are followed by the liberal labour politicians (liquidators)—like to talk at length about the "Europeanisation" of Russia. A tiny little truth serves here as a cover for a big untruth.

There can be no doubt that Russia, speaking generally, is becoming Europeanised, i.e., reorganised in the image of Europe (moreover, in "Europe" we should now include Japan and China, in spite of geography). But this Europeanisation has been going on since Alexander II, or perhaps even since Peter the Great; it went on not only during the upswing (1905), but also *during reaction* (1908-11); it has been going on in the police and among the Markov-type landlords, who are "Europeanising" their methods of fighting the democratic movement.

The catchword "Europeanisation" turns out to be so general that it serves to obscure matters, to obscure urgent political issues.

The liberals want a Europeanised Russia. But the Council of the United Nobility, too, sought Europeanisation by *its* law of November 9, 1906 (June 14, 1910).

The liberals want a European constitution. But the constitutions established in various countries of Europe were the result of long and strenuous class struggles between feudalism and absolutism, on the one hand, and the bourgeoisie, the peasantry and the workers, on the other. Written and unwritten constitutions, with which the liberals "shame" our reactionaries, are merely a record of the *results* of struggle obtained through a series of hard-won victories of the new over the old and a series of defeats inflicted on the new by the old.

The liberals want the results to make their appearance in our country *without* the sum total of advantages and disadvantages of which the results consist! The liberal programme and liberal tactics amount to this: let a European way of life take shape in our country *without* the hard struggle which brought it into being in Europe!

It is understandable that our Kobylinskys greet the liberals' wishes and arguments with contemptuous sallies against "shopkeepers" and "muzhiks". "You want, liberal gentlemen," say the Kobylinskys, "to register on paper victories that you have not yet won in reality."

III

The Cadet meeting approved four theses on tactics. The first reads:

"The tactic of united action by the entire opposition front, while being a necessary condition for the execution of the Duma's current business, does not, however, guarantee either the securing of a solid and lasting majority in the Duma for the Bills of the opposition or the actual realisation of the Bills whose adoption in the Duma the opposition could secure, with the aid of the Duma Centre."

Translated into plain Russian, this gibberish means the following:

It is only with the Octobrists that the liberals can form a majority in the Duma. Such a majority is not permanent and its decisions are not put into effect.

Quite so. But this leads to the conclusion that to call those decisions "necessary", "current" and "business" (!??) is to deceive oneself and the people.

In defeating the Rights by voting with the Octobrists, we must not adopt the standpoint of legislating in the Fourth Duma, must not sow constitutional illusions—that is what the Cadets should have said to the people had they wanted to be democrats, not in words alone.

The first "thesis" of the Cadet meeting is strikingly illogical. It describes as "business" the approval by an inconstant and unstable majority in the Fourth Duma of Bills that are not put into effect!! The Cadets themselves have on a hundred occasions described this as "vermicelli" and a nuisance, and justly so.

But the Cadet tactics, extremely stupid from the standpoint of logic, become comprehensible from the standpoint of class interests. Let us recall what the Social-Democrats have been saying in the Third and Fourth Dumas ever since 1907. "There are two possible majorities in the Duma," they said, "a Right-wing and Octobrist and an Octobrist-Cadet one. Both take a counter-revolutionary stand" (cf. *Prosveshcheniye*, 1913, No. 1, p. 13).*

The Cadets' February 1913 meeting confirmed what we had been saying in our official decisions since 1907.

"The tactic of united action by the entire opposition front ... with the aid of the Duma Centre" is *indispensable* to the Cadets precisely because, like the Octobrists, they take a counter-revolutionary stand. In view of the inner kinship of the Cadets and Octobrists, it is understandable that they gravitate towards joint 'business', despite its hopelessness today.

The Octobrists are always whimpering in their press, railing at the revolution, railing at the government, the Rights and the Council of State, but in the Duma they confine themselves to a desire for reforms and follow the government.

The Cadets whimper even more in their press, railing at the revolution, railing at the government, the Rights, the

---

* See pp. 496-97 of this volume.—*Ed.*

Council of State and the Octobrists, but in the Duma they confine themselves to a desire for reforms and try to adapt their opposition to the Octobrists.

IV

The second thesis of the Cadet meeting reads:

"The Duma can be substantially strengthened as a legislative and political factor only by fulfilling three fundamental conditions: democratisation of the electoral law (universal suffrage), a radical reform of the Council of State, and a responsible Ministry."

The gist of the tactics set out here may be expressed by one word: reformism.

Historical science tells us that the distinction between a reformist and a non-reformist change in a given political form is, generally speaking, that in the former case the old ruling class retains power, while in the latter case power is transferred from the old class to a new one. The Cadets do not understand the class basis of historical changes. This is their basic error from the point of view of theory.

From the point of view of practice, the above theoretical distinction depends on whether the particular is changed while the general and basic is left unchanged, or whether it is the latter that is changed.

In different countries and in different periods of history, the bourgeoisie has been reformist or has gone further than that. On the other hand, the working class, which has never considered reforms capable of bringing about radical changes, under certain conditions by no means refrains from advancing immediate demands in the shape of reforms.

The point is, consequently, that the Cadets regard the retention of power by the present ruling class, i.e., the big feudal-type landowners, as indisputable. The Cadets persist in their standpoint of an opposition in the possessive case, continuing to hold the view that "there is a constitution in Russia, thank God".

In other words, the Cadets' "three basic conditions" are those proposed by the liberal bourgeoisie for an *amicable* division of economic and political privileges between the feudal landowners and the capitalists.

The Octobrists have the same standpoint ("reconciliation of the government and the country", as phrased by Maklakov, who is half Octobrist and half Cadet), except that the Octobrists propose conditions for division that are more "*subservient*" with regard to the landowners.

The big subservience of the Octobrists has proved a fiasco. What reasons are there for expecting a different result from the little subservience of the Cadets? From the point of view of reformism, the Octobrists are much more consistent, for those who adopt this point of view must take into account the *acceptability* of reforms, and the Octobrist "reforms" are much more "acceptable".

The only conclusion to be drawn is that the discrepancy between liberal reformism and the requirements of the country is growing.

V

The third thesis of the Cadet meeting reads:

"Preparing these conditions should become the main tactical task of the Constitutional-Democrats, and current legislative activity, jointly with the other opposition groups and with the Centre, should be utilised as far as it proves feasible but should not run counter to the realisation of these main tasks" (*Rech* No. 34, February 4).

The previous "thesis" was a concession to the Left Cadets, or rather a bait for the democrats, as if to say: support us Cadets, for we are "democrats" and are for universal suffrage!

After the nod to the left comes a serious turn to the right; the third thesis, translated from gibberish into plain Russian reads: we Cadets recognise *joint* current legislative activity *with the Progressists and Octobrists*!

But does not this "current" legislation produce *unrealisable* Bills, as the first thesis admits? The Cadets make a little reservation: "as far as feasible". Speaking more plainly, this is equivalent to saying: we shall busy ourselves with vermicelli, but the responsibility for it falls on the Octobrists! Really, they are good jokers, are our Cadets.

To proceed. Neither the Progressists, nor the Octobrists, who are more consistent than the Cadets in their adherence to the *reformist* point of view, agree to such "excessively" liberal demands as universal suffrage, radical reform of the Council of State, etc. That being so, how can the Cadets, who continue to pose as democrats, proclaim *joint* current legislative activity with these admitted *opponents* of democracy?

Here, too, the Cadets have a little reservation—to the effect that they, the Cadets, are busy *preparing* for universal suffrage, *preparing*, *jointly* with the Octobrists, for activity that "should not run counter to the realisation" of universal suffrage!

It is a simple loophole—they declare Rodzyanko's speech to be "constitutional", and they vote (not by mistake, as do the Social-Democrats, but by conviction) for the Octobrist formula of procedure with regard to the declaration of the Minister, for all this *does not run counter* to "preparing" for universal suffrage!!

Here we cannot say that the Cadets are good jokers In this case we should have to use a *different* word.

In all European countries, the counter-revolutionary liberal bourgeoisie, which has turned its back on the democratic movement, continues to assert that it is busy *preparing* (jointly with the national-liberals in Prussia and with all the Progressists in France) for "basic" democratic reforms.

The bourgeoisie which has definitely taken the reformist path is a rotten bourgeoisie, impotent in its liberalism, hopeless in the matter of democratic changes, and hostile to the workers, a bourgeoisie which has deserted *to* the Rights *from* the people.

VI

The fourth, and last, thesis of the Cadet meeting reads:

"This meeting considers it opportune, along with advancing the three slogans mentioned above, to raise the question of adopting more active tactical measures of parliamentary struggle."

Only parliamentary? And only "to raise the question"? Just what is meant by "more active tactical measures of parliamentary struggle", Allah alone knows. One might think the Cadet meeting had deliberately formulated its theses in the most incoherent terms.

In speaking of more active measures, the Cadets clearly want to show that they are moving to the left. But it is nothing more than a *show*, for nothing definite can be read into it.

What are the kind of "measures" of parliamentary struggle that can, generally speaking, be called more active?

Refusal to vote for the Octobrist and Progressist formulas of procedure.

Refusal to make speeches about "reconciliation of the government and the country".

Refusal to be silent whenever a Right-wing and Octobrist majority puts through anti-democratic measures.

Refusal to agree to the closure or curtailment of general debates on matters of principle.

We advise anyone who comes into contact with the Cadets to make a point of asking them whether they have "raised" the question of more active measures, how they have decided this question since they are going to raise it, and how they actually adopt "more active measures".

The country is moving to the left. The new democratic movement is awakening to life. The Cadets' show of a slight swing to the left has a very definite political meaning, namely, to deceive this new democratic movement, to impose its leadership upon it, to make themselves out to be its spokesmen.

The urgent task of the democrats is to prevent this deceit. Anyone who has not drawn from the hard lessons of the past the conclusion that even partial leadership of the democratic elements by the Cadets inevitably results in vacillation, betrayals, and inglorious defeats without struggle, has learned nothing. He should be regarded as an enemy of democracy.

VII

Taken as a whole, the Cadet meeting was an interesting document of the political activity of our "Centre". Normally the press in our country pays little attention to such documents, to the precise and formal decisions of organised parties. It has a distaste for "resolutions". It prefers interviews and gossip.

But those who take a serious view of politics must carefully analyse party decisions, and Marxists will do all in their power to make such an analysis.

We have described the Cadets as the "Centre". It is *customary*, however, to apply this term to the Octobrists, who stand midway between the Rights and the opposition.

However, both from the point of view of the class basis of the political parties and from that of the nature of *contemporary* politics in general, we must not limit ourselves to the Duma in analysing the parties, must not consider the Octobrists alone to be the "Centre".

Look at the class basis of our parties—the Rights and nationalists, in general, are semi-feudal landlords. They stand *for* the preservation and "aggravation" of the present regime.

Among the Octobrists, Progressists and Cadets, we see landlords of an undoubtedly more bourgeois type, and then the bulk of the big bourgeoisie. All these parties want *reforms*. They all form a *real* centre between the semi-feudal landlords and the democrats (peasants and workers).

The bourgeoisie is more afraid of democracy than of reaction; this applies both to the Progressists and to the Cadets. The oppositional nature of these two parties has, of course, to be taken into account in the practical tasks of everyday politics, but this oppositional nature should not make us close our eyes to the class kinship of these parties and the Octobrists.

The semi-feudal landlords rule both by themselves and in a bloc with the upper ranks of the bourgeoisie. The feudal landlords are against reforms. The bourgeoisie in general is in favour of reforms, and it confines itself to a reformist stand, which is more than we can say of the peasant, let alone of the worker, democrats.

The Cadet meeting clearly showed us the Cadets' *reformism* as their exclusive tactics. The most important thing is to see the *connection* between these tactics and the class interests of the bourgeoisie, and the *inadequacy* of these tactics, the "increasing discrepancy" between them and the requirements of the country. The most important thing is

to see the fundamental kinship of the Cadets and the Octobrists, and the absolute impossibility of any democratic
successes whatever under Cadet leadership.

VIII

This article was finished when I received *Golos Moskvy*
No. 30, with an editorial under the heading "What Next?",
devoted to the Cadet meeting.

Taken in conjunction with the Duma votings on February
6 (adoption of the formula of procedure with regard to Kasso's
explanation[209]), that editorial is so important and sheds
so vivid a light on the Cadets' attitude to the Octobrists
that it is absolutely necessary to comment on those votings.

The official Octobrist organ, *Golos Moskvy*, represents
the Cadet meeting (for some reason the paper calls it a "conference") as a victory of the Left Cadets, headed by Milyukov, over the Right Cadets.

"Legislative activity," said *Golos Moskvy*, expounding the Cadet
resolution, "can be utilised only insofar as it does not run counter
to these main tasks [i.e., universal suffrage, a reform of the Council
of State, and a responsible Ministry].

"To put it more simply, the adoption of this formula is tantamount
to renouncing all legislative work within the bounds of what can
actually be accomplished, and the Cadet opposition is henceforward
assuming a frankly irresponsible character."

Golos Moskvy infers that there is nothing for it but to
dissolve the Duma, for the Octobrists will never adopt the
Cadets' attitude, which is so "uncompromising" (don't
laugh!), there is no majority in the Duma, things are "utterly
hopeless"....

See how history is written!

That brings out remarkably well the profound kinship of
the Cadets and the Octobrists, and the true nature of their
"quarrel": a lovers' quarrel.

On February 6, in Moscow, the official Octobrist organ
announced, as we have seen, the complete break-up of the
Octobrist-Cadet bloc following the Cadet meeting, which
took place *before February 4* (when *Rech* reported the meeting).

On the very same day, February 6, the Octobrists and
Cadets in the Fourth Duma, in St. Petersburg, *together*

adopted by 173 votes to 153 the *Octobrist-Cadet* formula of procedure with regard to Kasso's explanation, a formula subsequently rejected by chance when a confirmatory vote was taken!!

That's good, isn't it?

We have here a classical example of how the Octobrists and the *Cadets* fix their political "affairs". They have nothing to do with any "bloc", God forbid! But they distribute the roles among themselves—to fool the public—so "skilfully" that no formal bloc could provide them with anything so "convenient". The Cadets see that the country is moving to the left, that a new democratic movement is arising, and so they play at leftism by putting in circulation, through their meeting, several phrases which say absolutely nothing and are completely meaningless, but which *sound like Left* phrases. The Octobrists *support* this feeling or impression among the public that the Cadets have gone left; they bolster it up by *officially* declaring, in the *Golos Moskvy* editorial, that the Cadets' attitude is uncompromising and that it is impossible to form a majority in the Duma by an alliance of the Octobrists and Cadets; they fulminate against the Cadets for their leftism, clamour for the dissolution of the Duma, and so on and so forth.

But in reality under cover of this clamour they haggled with the Cadets, and at the very time when they were making their sharpest attack on the Cadets' leftism they *struck a bargain* with them on a common formula!!

"The wolves had their fill and the sheep kept their skins." The democrats were hoodwinked, they were deceived and decoyed into the Cadet fold (the Cadets are so Left-wing—see how the Octobrists rail at them for their leftism!), and the Octobrist-Cadet bloc in the Black-Hundred Duma was preserved, strengthened and expanded.

One feels very much like exclaiming: O God, when will the Russian democrats see through this simple stratagem of liberal Cadet bamboozling! For liberal bourgeois politicians in all European countries use, in one form or another, the very same trick: when facing the people, they shout and swear in their official election speeches that they are democrats and radicals (the German "freethinkers", Lloyd George and Co. in Britain), and even socialists (the Radical

Socialists in France). But *in reality*, in their *actual* policy, they make *common* cause with unquestionably anti-democratic governments and parties, with the Octobrists of various shades and various nationalities.

How old this story is and how infinitely often the Cadets repeat it!

IX

Golos Moskvy asserts that prior to the elections the Cadets

"carried on. bitter polemics against the Lefts, trying to prove the need for legislative work within the bounds of the actual conditions. It was this that warranted the hope that agreement could be reached between the Duma Centre and the opposition. But after the elections the views of the leaders of the Cadet Party underwent an important change. The resolution on Duma tactics proposed by Milyukov and adopted by the conference is entirely at variance with all that was said during the elections—evidently to win the votes of the big urban bourgeoisie. The latter would scarcely have agreed to back the Cadets on the platform which the conference has now put forward."

In this specimen of reasoning, you wonder which is the more astounding—its naïve cunning or naïve ignorance.

The views of the Cadets have not changed *in the least*. The Cadets have always been, and remain, a liberal party leading the democratic movement by fraud. At the 1912 elections, too, they showed the big bourgeoisie their "true" face, their "solidarity" of smart dealers, their "sobriety" as servants of the capitalist class. But at the same time, in front of the democratic voters, they took great pains to suggest that they were democrats and that their Duma tactics did not differ in any essential from Social-Democratic tactics.

These two aspects of the Cadet policy are an indispensable "adjunct of the attire" of every liberal party in any civilised country. To be sure, individual party members often specialise, some in playing at democracy, others in sobering up the "over-zealous" and pursuing a "respectable" bourgeois policy. But then this is true of all countries. For example, Britain's well-known liberal charlatan, Lloyd George, poses in his speeches to the people as a regular revolutionary and all but a socialist, but in reality this Minister follows the policy of his leader, Asquith, who is no different from a Conservative.

The fact that the article in *Golos Moskvy* describes Mr. Milyukov as a representative of the Left Cadets can only call forth a smile. Mr. Milyukov in fact represents official Cadet diplomacy, which is trying to reconcile the undemocratic nature of the party with democratic phrase-mongering.

Golos Moskvy said:

"This new 'post-election' attitude of Mr. Milyukov's was approved by the conference anything but unanimously. A considerable number of participants insisted on the tactic of agreement with the Duma Centre for the purpose of securing the adoption of various Bills and cultural reforms. The advocates of this point of view argued that in discussing various Bills the group should compromise, trying to have them adopted in a liberal spirit, and by no means making them unacceptable." There followed a sally against "the famous Cadet discipline" and "unquestioning submission" of the Cadets to Mr. Milyukov's "autocratic will".

The game is obvious. It is transparent. The Octobrists "tease" the Right Cadets, whom they are trying to represent as defeated and provoke to a more determined struggle against the Left Cadets. But this Octobrist game (which would have been impossible had the Cadets and Octobrists not been members of one and the same little family) does not eliminate the indisputable fact that there are differences of shade between the Left and the Right Cadets, between the Lloyd Georges and the Asquiths of our liberalism.

Look at *Russkaya Molva*. This Progressist organ, which advocates a compromise between the Octobrists and the Cadets, is attracting an increasing number of *official* members of the Cadet Party. Mansyrev and Maklakov and Obolensky and Gredeskul and Alexandrov proved to be contributors—not all at once, but gradually, following the *Vekhi* leader, Struve. It is beyond doubt that these people urged closer links with the Octobrists. Nor could it have been otherwise. But it is just as doubtless that Milyukov is trying to reconcile them with the "Left Cadets" on a platform with a democratic façade and an Octobrist essence.

X

The various parties' Duma formulas of procedure with regard to Kasso's explanation are very interesting. They supply us with accurate material for political analysis, material officially confirmed by the deputies of the various parties. It is analysis that this material usually lacks most of all. It gets lost amid the comments of the daily press or in the pile of the Duma's verbatim reports. Yet it is well worth dwelling on if we want to understand the true nature of the various parties.

A leading article in *Rech* declared on the day following the adoption of the formula of no-confidence: "Thus Russian society has obtained from the Duma what it was entitled to expect" (No. 37, February 7). This sounds as though all that "society" had to know was whether the Duma trusts Mr. Kasso!

That is not true. The people and the democrats have to know the *motives* of no-confidence so as to *understand* the causes of a development considered abnormal in politics, and be able to find a *way out* to the normal. Unity of the Cadets, Octobrists and Social-Democrats on just the phrase "we have no confidence" is too little as far as these very serious issues are concerned.

Here is the Octobrists' formula of procedure:

"The Duma ... considers: (1) all involvement of secondary school pupils in political struggles is ruinous to the spiritual development of Russia's young forces and harmful to the normal course of the life of society; (2) it is necessary, whenever the authorities are informed in good time of undesirable developments in secondary schools, to take preventive measures and not to wait until developments assume an abnormal character*; (3) emphatically declares against the application to pupils of police measures, such as were adopted on December 10, 1912, without the knowledge of the school authorities, instead of natural educational influence; (4) considers anti-educational the slowness with which the fate of pupils removed from schools is decided on, and expecting this incident to be dealt with immediately in a sense benevolent to the pupils, proceeds to the next business."

What are the political ideas of this vote?

---

* This text was introduced at the January 25 sitting. At the sitting of February 1, Clause 2 was edited as follows: "It is noted with reference to this particular case that a formal and indifferent attitude to pupils prevails in secondary schools, that teaching staffs are estranged from the families, and that it is necessary to establish a general benevolent view on the rising generation."

Politics are harmful at school. The pupils are to blame. But it is their teachers who should punish them and not the police. We are dissatisfied with the government for its lack of "benevolence" and its slowness.

These are anti-democratic ideas. This is liberal opposition, for it implies: let the old system of authority remain, but *it* should be applied more mildly. You may flog, but within reason, and without publicity.

Look at the Progressist formula of procedure:

"The Duma finds that (1) the Ministry of Education, being informed of what had lately taken place in the secondary schools of St. Petersburg, adopted an impassive attitude to its duties and failed to protect the secondary schools against incursion by the police; (2) the methods used by police officers, methods which were resorted to without protest on the part of the Ministry of Education and consisted in searching the schools, seizing children and holding them under arrest at police-stations, and in applying impermissible methods of investigation, were utterly unjustifiable, all the more since in this case it was a matter not of safeguarding state security, but of restoring order in the secondary schools; (3) the whole set of measures adopted by the Ministry of Education, measures directed towards estranging the school from the family, creates, through its callous formalism which hampers the moral and intellectual growth of the young generation, conditions favourable to developments that are abnormal in school life. The Duma considers the explanation offered by the Minister of Education to be unsatisfactory and proceeds to the next business."

This formula was introduced on January 30, and the Progressists declared there and then that they would vote for the Octobrists provided the latter added no-confidence. We have seen above the results of this haggling.

On what basis *could* that haggling take place? On the basis of agreement in the main.

The Progressists, too, consider politics in the schools abnormal and they, too, call for "restoring order" (feudal order). They, too, are in opposition in the possessive case— opposition not to the old system of authority but to its application—"impassive, callous", and so on. In the 1860s Pirogov agreed that there must be flogging, but he insisted on the flogging *not* being done impassively or callously. The Progressists have no objection to the present social elements "restoring order", but they advise the latter to do it more "sympathetically". What progress has been made in our country in five decades!

The Cadets' formula of procedure:

"Having heard the explanation offered by the Minister of Education and considering: (1) that it shows a complete confusion of the educational point of view with that of the police; (2) that this explanation is a complete denial of the normal foundations on which relations of friendly co-operation can be established between school and family; (3) that the policy of the Ministry, by giving rise to deep resentment among the pupils and to legitimate annoyance in society, itself promotes the creation of an atmosphere making for the early involvement of school youth in political pursuits and hence itself creates conditions which it should prevent from arising; (4) that treating pupils as being guilty of crimes against the state cripples the lives of the most gifted among the rising generation, snatches numerous victims from its ranks and constitutes a threat to the future of Russia, the Duma considers the explanation offered by the Minister to be unsatisfactory and proceeds to the next business."

Here, *too*, "early" involvement in politics is condemned but in much milder terms and in a form veiled by phrases. This is an anti-democratic point of view. Octobrists and Cadets alike condemn police measures only because they want *prevention* instead. The system should prevent meetings, not disperse them. Obviously, such a reform would only embellish the system but not change it. "We are dissatisfied with the policy of the Ministry," say the Cadets, and from what they say it follows, exactly as with the Octobrists, that *it is possible to wish* for a change in this policy without something much more radical.

The Cadets pronounce themselves against the government much more sharply than the Octobrists, and because of the sharp language politically immature elements overlook the complete identity of the liberal, anti-democratic, *presentation of the issue* by the Cadets and the Octobrists.

The Duma should earnestly teach the people politics. Those who learn their politics from the Cadets are corrupting and not developing their political consciousness.

It is not an accident that the Octobrists, Progressists and Cadets haggled and struck a bargain on a common formula; it is a result of their ideological and political solidarity in the main. Nothing could be more paltry than the policy of the Cadets, who agree to a direct condemnation of

politics in the schools for the sake of finding the explanation offered unsatisfactory. But the Cadets agreed to this
because they themselves condemn "early" involvement.
The formula of the Trudovik group:

"Whereas: (1) the brute force used on December 9, 1912, against
secondary school pupils, which shocked society by the disgraceful
participation of the secret police in educational supervision over
pupils of secondary schools, was fully approved in the explanation
offered by Mr. Kasso, the Minister of Education, who sneered maliciously at public opinion; (2) the system of secret police and spying,
which is a result of the entire policy of the combined Ministry, and
in particular of Kasso, the Minister of Education, leads to complete
havoc, and threatens in the future to cause a severe shock to the rising generation, the Duma insists that all those discharged on December 9 should be immediately reinstated and, considering the explanation offered by Kasso, the Minister of Education, to be unsatisfactory, demands his immediate resignation, and proceeds to the next
business."

This formula is, strictly speaking, a markedly liberal
one; but it does not contain what a democrat, *as distinct*
from a liberal, should have said. A liberal, too, may find
it disgraceful to enlist the assistance of the secret police
in educational supervision, but a democrat should say (and
teach the people) that *no* "supervisors" have a right to encroach on the free organisation of political circles and talks.
A liberal, too, may condemn "the entire policy of the combined Ministry", but a democrat in Russia should make
clear that there are certain general conditions by virtue of
which any other Ministry would have had to pursue practically the same policy.

The democracy of the Trudovik formula shows *only* in
its tenor, in the sentiment of its authors. There is no denying
that sentiment is a political symptom. But it would not be
amiss to insist that the formula of procedure should contain
a well-thought-out idea and not merely "heart-warming"
sentiment.

The Social-Democrats' formula of procedure:

"Having heard the explanation offered by the Minister of Education and considering that it indicates: (1) a determination to combat the natural and encouraging desire of school youth to extend
their mental horizons through self-education and to hold comradely
intercourse; 2) a justification of the system of official formalism,
spying and police investigation that is being implanted in the higher,

secondary and elementary schools, a system which cripples youth mentally and morally, ruthlessly stamps out all signs of independence of thought and character, and results in an epidemic of suicides among pupils, the Duma considers the explanation unsatisfactory. Considering, at the same time, that (1) there is an inseparable connection between the domination of the police standpoint in the matter of public education and the domination of the secret police over the whole of Russian life, the suppression of all forms of organised and independent activity by the citizens, and the latter's lack of rights, and that (2) only a radical change in the political organisation and the system of state administration can free the citizens from police fetters and also free the school from them, the Duma proceeds to the next business."

This formula, too, can hardly be considered impeccable. One cannot help wishing it had presented the matter in more popular language and in greater detail, and regretting that it does not stress the legitimacy of engaging in politics, and so on and so forth.

However, our criticism of *all the formulas* is by no means aimed at details of formulation, but exclusively at the *fundamental political ideas* of their authors. A democrat should have said the important thing, namely, that political circles and talks are *natural and to be welcomed*. That is the point. All condemnation of involvement in politics, even if only of "early" involvement, is hypocrisy and obscurantism. A democrat should have raised the level of the question *from* the "combined Ministry" *to* the political system. He should have pointed out the "inseparable connection", firstly, with the "domination of the secret police" and, secondly, with the domination of the class of big landlords of the feudal type in the economic sphere.

Written on February 6-9 (19-22), 1913

Published in *Prosveshcheniye*
Nos. 3 and 4, March and April 1913
Signed: *V. Ilyin*

Published according
to the magazine text

SOME RESULTS OF THE "LAND DISTRIBUTION" POLICY

What are the results of the new agrarian policy? All workers take an interest—a very legitimate one—in this question. Government statistics are kept so poorly and are so biassed that they are not to be trusted. The new land policy is no doubt a *bourgeois* policy, but it is wholly managed by the Purishkeviches, Markovs and Co., i.e., feudal landlords of the old type. One could hardly expect anything but failure from this kind of "management".

We wish to note the conclusions drawn by Mr. V. Obolensky in the latest issue (No. 2, 1913) of *Russkaya Mysl*. This is a Black-Hundred and Cadet periodical. The author of the article, too, is a counter-revolutionary, which means that he is a witness partial to the landlords rather than to anyone else. He has discovered in Samara Gubernia an uyezd (Novouzensk) which has made "tremendous" progress in "land distribution", more than fifty per cent of the householders having been allotted land in one piece.

Nevertheless, the conclusion which the author *had* to draw was this:

"As regards the immediate results of the new agrarian reform ... they can hardly be considered encouraging at all.... A considerable amount of allotment land has passed for a song from peasant semi-proletarians to well-to-do peasants and speculating buyers-up.... Rents have increased.... The difference in cultivability between integral farms and communal strip holdings is quite negligible.... The new law ... has helped to aggravate the contradictions between the conditions of economic activity and its inner content.... Perhaps the minds of the peasants are now working harder than they did at the height of the recent revolution."

It is no use at all asking the liberal of *Russkaya Mysl which way* the minds of the peasants are working. It is not for nothing that he has left out altogether the question of feudal farming on the landed estates.

But it is worth giving some thought to the conclusions drawn by the liberal landlord. All the contradictions have become sharper, exploitation has increased, rent has risen, and progress in farming is *quite negligible.* Not "perhaps" but quite certainly the minds of the peasants are working.

Pravda No. 45, February 23, 1913   Published according
Signed: *V. I.*   to the *Pravda* text

THE HISTORICAL DESTINY
OF THE DOCTRINE OF KARL MARX

The chief thing in the doctrine of Marx is that it brings out the historic role of the proletariat as the builder of socialist society. Has the course of events all over the world confirmed this doctrine since it was expounded by Marx?

Marx first advanced it in 1844. The Communist Manifesto of Marx and Engels, published in 1848, gave an integral and systematic exposition of this doctrine, an exposition which has remained the best to this day. Since then world history has clearly been divided into three main periods: (1) from the revolution of 1848 to the Paris Commune (1871); (2) from the Paris Commune to the Russian revolution (1905); (3) since the Russian revolution.

Let us see what has been the destiny of Marx's doctrine in each of these periods.

I

At the beginning of the first period Marx's doctrine by no means dominated. It was only one of the very numerous groups or trends of socialism. The forms of socialism that did dominate were in the main akin to our Narodism: incomprehension of the materialist basis of historical movement, inability to single out the role and significance of each class in capitalist society, concealment of the bourgeois nature of democratic reforms under diverse, quasi-socialist phrases about the "people", "justice", "right", and so on.

The revolution of 1848 struck a deadly blow at all these vociferous, motley and ostentatious forms of *pre*-Marxian socialism. In all countries, the revolution revealed the various classes of society *in action*. The shooting of the workers by the republican bourgeoisie in Paris in the June days of 1848 finally revealed that the proletariat *alone* was socialist by nature. The liberal bourgeoisie dreaded the independence of this class a hundred times more than it did any kind of reaction. The craven liberals grovelled before reaction. The peasantry were content with the abolition of the survivals of feudalism and joined the supporters of order, wavering but occasionally between *workers' democracy and bourgeois liberalism*. All doctrines of *non*-class socialism and *non*-class politics proved to be sheer nonsense.

The Paris Commune (1871) completed this development of bourgeois changes; the republic, i.e., the form of political organisation in which class relations appear in their most unconcealed form, owed its consolidation solely to the heroism of the proletariat.

In all the other European countries, a more tangled and less complete development led to the same result—a bourgeois society that had taken definite shape. Towards the end of the first period (1848-71), a period of storms and revolutions, pre-Marxian socialism was *dead*. Independent *proletarian* parties came into being: the First International (1864-72) and the German Social-Democratic Party.

II

The second period (1872-1904) was distinguished from the first by its "peaceful" character, by the absence of revolutions. The West had finished with bourgeois revolutions. The East had not yet risen to them.

The West entered a phase of "peaceful" preparations for the changes to come. Socialist parties, basically proletarian, were formed everywhere, and learned to use bourgeois parliamentarism and to found their own daily press, their educational institutions, their trade unions and their co-operative societies. Marx's doctrine gained a complete victory and *began to spread*. The selection and mustering of the forces of the proletariat and its preparation for the coming battles made slow but steady progress.

The dialectics of history were such that the theoretical victory of Marxism compelled its enemies to *disguise themselves* as Marxists. Liberalism, rotten within, tried to revive itself in the form of socialist *opportunism*. They interpreted the period of preparing the forces for great battles as renunciation of these battles. Improvement of the conditions of the slaves to fight against wage slavery they took to mean the sale by the slaves of their right to liberty for a few pence. They cravenly preached "social peace" (i.e., peace with the slave-owners), renunciation of the class struggle, etc. They had very many adherents among socialist members of parliament, various officials of the working-class movement, and the "sympathising" intelligentsia.

III

However, the opportunists had scarcely congratulated themselves on "social peace" and on the non-necessity of storms under "democracy" when a new source of great world storms opened up in Asia. The Russian revolution was followed by revolutions in Turkey, Persia and China. It is in this era of storms and their "repercussions" in Europe that we are now living. No matter what the fate of the great Chinese republic, against which various "civilised" hyenas are now whetting their teeth, no power on earth can restore the old serfdom in Asia or wipe out the heroic democracy of the masses in the Asiatic and semi-Asiatic countries.

Certain people who were inattentive to the conditions for preparing and developing the mass struggle were driven to despair and to anarchism by the lengthy delays in the decisive struggle against capitalism in Europe. We can now see how short-sighted and faint-hearted this anarchist despair is.

The fact that Asia, with its population of eight hundred million, has been drawn into the struggle for these same European ideals should inspire us with optimism and not despair.

The Asiatic revolutions have again shown us the spinelessness and baseness of liberalism, the exceptional importance of the independence of the democratic masses, and the pronounced demarcation between the proletariat and the bourgeoisie of all kinds. After the experience both of Europe and Asia, anyone who speaks of *non*-class politics and *non*-class socialism, ought simply to be put in a cage and exhibited alongside the Australian kangaroo or something like that.

After Asia, Europe has also begun to stir, although not in the Asiatic way. The "peaceful" period of 1872-1904 has passed, never to return. The high cost of living and the tyranny of the trusts are leading to an unprecedented sharpening of the economic struggle, which has set into movement even the British workers who have been most corrupted by liberalism. We see a political crisis brewing even in the most "diehard", bourgeois-Junker country, Germany. The frenzied arming and the policy of imperialism are turning modern Europe into a "social peace" which is more like a gunpowder barrel. Meanwhile the decay of *all* the bourgeois parties and the maturing of the proletariat are making steady progress.

Since the appearance of Marxism, each of the three great periods of world history has brought Marxism new confirmation and new triumphs. But a still greater triumph awaits Marxism, as the doctrine of the proletariat, in the coming period of history.

Pravda No. 50, March 1, 1913
Signed: *V. I.*

Published according
to the *Pravda* text

BIG LANDLORD AND SMALL PEASANT
LANDOWNERSHIP IN RUSSIA

In connection with the recent anniversary of February 19, 1861,* a reminder of the present distribution of land in European Russia will not be out of place.

The last official statistics of land distribution in European Russia were published by the Ministry of the Interior and date from 1905.

According to these statistics there were (in round numbers) about 30,000 big landlords owning over 500 dessiatines each, their total land amounting to about 70,000,000 dessiatines.

Some 10,000,000 poor peasant households owned the *same amount* of land.

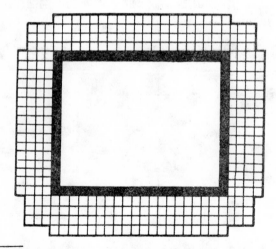

* Anniversary of the abolition of serfdom in Russia.—*Tr.*

It follows that on the average there are about 330 poor peasant families for each big landlord, each peasant family owning about 7 (*seven*) dessiatines, while each big landlord owns about 2,300 (*two thousand three hundred*) dessiatines.

To show this graphically, we have drawn the above diagram.

The large white rectangle in the middle stands for the estate of a big landlord. The small squares around it represent the small peasant holdings.

Altogether there are 324 squares, and the area of the white rectangle equals 320 squares.

Pravda No. 51, March 2, 1913

Published according
to the *Pravda* text

FALSE NOTES

Mr. Milyukov's Duma speech on universal suffrage was of outstanding interest because he had to touch on a number of subjects of prime importance to democrats.

Our press in general, including the liberal press, is becoming more and more addicted to the abominably unprincipled habit of disposing of Duma speeches by commenting on them in glowing (Mr. Litovtsev in *Rech*) or abusive terms, without *ever* analysing their *ideological* content!

The workers do not believe in bourgeois political chicanery. They want to *learn* politics. In response to this desire of theirs, we shall attempt an analysis of Mr. Milyukov's speech.

"You," said Mr. Milyukov, addressing himself *all the time* to the Octobrists, "are not linked with authority either by specific commitments or even by gratitude",

for the elections, you say, were rigged against you.

Mr. Milyukov, one of the most educated Cadets, a professor, editor, etc., put forward this argument in the most earnest way, and even added:

"Apparently there is no social stratum in Russia supporting the present government policy..." (*Rossiya* No. 2236).

The falsity of this argument is glaring. None other than Mr. Milyukov himself went on to quote the Frenchman Chasles, who very justly says that the "*crux of the matter*" "*is the agrarian question*".

"To obtain a conservative Third Duma," says Chasles, "the majority had to be shifted from the peasants to the landlords.... The landed proprietors and the aristocracy of wealth can form a bloc of five-eighths of the votes [in the elections to the Duma under our electoral law] and the minority can literally be crushed: the peasants, the middle classes and the town democrats are invited by the legislator to look on at the elections and not make them, to attend but not participate in them."

The reactionary Chasles argues cleverly and correctly. We thank Mr. Milyukov for his interesting quotations which *defeat* Mr. Milyukov's phrase-mongering! In Russia there evidently *is* a social "stratum" (the class of landlords—feudal lords or feudal-minded landlords) which supports the policy of the government and is linked *"with author-ity"* by the bonds of class interests. As for being linked by "commitments" and "gratitude", it is perfect nonsense. Remember that, learned Cadet!

In our next article* we shall show how this learned Cadet circled—like a cat round hot milk—about the *"crux of the matter"* (i.e., the agrarian question), which the reactionary Chasles correctly pointed out.

Pravda No. 55, March 7, 1913
Signed: *V.I.*

Published according
to the *Pravda* text

---

* See pp. 590-91 of this volume.—*Ed.*

"THE CRUX OF THE MATTER"

We have seen that Chasles, the French reactionary quoted by Mr. Milyukov, correctly considers that the agrarian question is the "crux of the matter" confronting Russia.*

Mr. Milyukov quoted a clever statement by a clever reactionary but he does not understand it at all!

> "Can the peasant whom you [i.e., the Octobrists and the government, for it is *to them* that Mr. Milyukov talks!] have brought into this body with your own hands be made dependent? After all, he speaks of the land from this rostrum, and he says the same thing as the independent peasant said in the First and Second Dumas. There is no element in Russian life, gentlemen, more independent or more stable than the Russian peasant." (Applause on the right and voices: "Hear, hear".)

Those handclaps must have come from the hypocritical Cadets alone, for everyone knows, firstly, that in the Third and Fourth Dumas the peasants have been saying *not quite* "the same thing" but something weaker than they said in the First and Second Dumas; and secondly, there *is* in Russian life an element that is more independent and more stable. Mr. Milyukov himself was *compelled* to admit in his speech that it is the *workers* who have done "most" for political liberty in Russia. Or can "independence" be measured with a different yardstick?

But this is not the point. The point is, can the interests of 130,000 landlords and of the mass of the peasantry be reconciled *now*? Mr. Milyukov "talked round and round" this question *to evade an answer.*

---

* See pp. 588-89 of this volume.—*Ed.*

But Mr. S. Litovtsev, hired by *Rech* to praise P. Milyukov, wrote that Milyukov's speech had

"dispelled the fog shrouding this sharp and debatable question. To many people, universal suffrage is still a sort of bogey, the height of revolutionism".

There you have yet another specimen of phrasemongering!

Learn from the reactionary Chasles, liberal wind-bags! The crux of the matter lies in the agrarian question. Can the interests of 130,000 landlord families and 10,000,000 peasant families be reconciled on this question *now*? Yes or no?

That is the *"crux"* of the matter as far as universal suffrage is concerned, Mr. Milyukov, while you *corrupt* the political consciousness of the people by *muddling up* with phrases this main point, which is obvious to any intelligent person.

If your answer to the question is *yes*, I shall refute you by means of *your* own admission that the peasants in the Third and Fourth Dumas have been saying (if less emphatically) the *"same thing"* as they said in the First and Second Dumas.

If, however, your answer is *no*, then *all* your talk about the conciliatory, non-*"one-sided"* character of universal suffrage in the Russia of today falls to the ground.

And your learned references to Bismarck are sheer childishness, for Bismarck "granted" universal suffrage at a time when the bourgeois development of Germany *had already reconciled* the interests of the landlords and all the well-to-do peasants, and even a section of the middle peasants.

The shrewd reader may ask: does it not follow that universal suffrage is impossible in Russia? No, we will answer the shrewd reader, it only follows that a reformist point of view is impossible in Russia.

Pravda No. 56, March 8, 1913
          Signed: *V. I.*

                                        Published according
                                        to the *Pravda* text

LIBERAL EMBELLISHMENT OF SERFDOM

Mr. Milyukov, a liberal historian, leader of the Cadet Party, wrote in a recent leading article in *Rech*:

> "Social inequality in Russia [serfdom] turned out to be more fragile and accidentally established than anywhere else in the civilised world. It gave way without resistance [!!!] at the very first stroke of the pen. Milyutin and Solovyov accomplished without difficulty something the feasibility of which Count Stroganov predicted as long ago as the reign of Alexander I."

We are used to seeing all liberal and some Narodnik historians embellish serfdom and the serf-owning state power in Russia. But not all went to the length of such disgraceful "gems" as the one we have just quoted.

Serfdom and the serf-owning landlord class in Russia were not fragile and accidentally established but much "stronger", more firm, powerful and omnipotent "than anywhere else in the civilised world". It did not cede even a small part of its privileges "without resistance", but did it with the greatest resistance. Or perhaps the liberal gentleman could point out in the "civilised world" examples comparable to the fate of Chernyshevsky?

Milyutin and Solovyov *themselves* upheld the privileges of the feudal landlords and the exceedingly onerous "*compensation*" for these privileges. By saying nothing about this, Mr. Milyukov distorts history, which testifies to half a century of "tenacious" feudal privileges, omnipotence and unlimited power after Milyutin and Co., after "*their*" feudal reform.

Why do liberal historians embellish serfdom and feudal reforms? Because they see in the activity of the makers of such reforms a servility to the feudal lords that is gratifying to them, a fear of democracy that they find encouraging, a desire for a bloc with reaction that they appreciate, and an embellishment of the class struggle that is familiar to them.

The question relates to the distant past. And yet the attitude to the class struggle adopted then and now by the liberals (liberals "without and bureaucrats within"[210]) is a phenomenon of one and the same nature.

By embellishing serfdom, Mr. Milyukov has splendidly portrayed his own self, his party and all Russian bourgeois liberals, who class themselves among the democrats in order to fool simpletons.

Pravda, No 57, March 9, 1913
Signed: *I.*

Published according
to the *Pravda* text

A "SCIENTIFIC" SYSTEM OF SWEATING

U.S. capitalism is ahead of all. The greatest development of technology and the most rapid progress are facts which make old Europe emulate the Yankees. But it is not the democratic institutions that the European bourgeoisie is borrowing from America, nor political liberty, nor yet the republican political system, but the latest methods of exploiting the workers.

The most widely discussed topic today in Europe, and to some extent in Russia, is the "system" of the American engineer, Frederick Taylor. Not so long ago Mr. Semyonov read a paper on this system in the assembly hall of the Railway Engineering Institute in St. Petersburg. Taylor himself has described his system under the title of "scientific", and his book is being eagerly translated and promoted in Europe.

What is this "scientific system"? Its purpose is to squeeze out of the worker three times more labour during a working day of the same length as before. The sturdiest and most skilful worker is put to work; a special clock registers—in seconds and fractions of a second—the amount of time spent on each operation and each motion; the most economical and most efficient working methods are developed; the work of the best worker is recorded on cinematographic film, etc.

The result is that, within the same nine or ten working hours as before, they squeeze out of the worker three times more labour, mercilessly drain him of all his strength, and are three times faster in sucking out every drop of the wage slave's nervous and physical energy. And if he dies young? Well, there are many others waiting at the gate!

In capitalist society, progress in science and technology means progress in the art of sweating.

Here is an example from Taylor's book.

Speaking of the operation of loading cast iron on to hand-carts for further processing, the author compares the old and the new, "scientific", system :

	Old	New
		system
Number of workers engaged in loading	500	140
Average number of tons loaded by one worker (a ton equals 61 poods)	16	59
Average earnings of worker (rubles)	2.30	3.75
Expenditure incurred by factory owner per ton of load (kopeks)	14.4	6.4

The capitalist cuts his expenditure by *half* or more. His profits grow. The bourgeoisie is delighted and cannot praise the Taylors enough!

The workers get a wage increase at first. But hundreds of workers get the sack. Those who are left have to work four times more intensively, doing a back-breaking job. When he has been drained of all his strength, the worker will be kicked out. Only young and sturdy workers are taken on.

It is sweating in strict accordance with all the precepts of science.

Pravda No. 60, March 13, 1913
    Signed: *W.*

                                    Published according
                                    to the *Pravda* text

OUR "ACHIEVEMENTS"

The Minister of Finance, in his explanatory note on the Budget, and all the government parties assure themselves and others that our Budget is firmly based. They refer, among other things, to the "achievements" of industry, which indubitably has been on the upgrade in the last few years.

Our industry, as well as our entire national economy, has been developing along capitalist lines. That is indisputable, and needs no proof. But anyone who limits himself to data on "development" and to the smugly boastful statement that "there is an increase of so-and-so many per cent" *shuts his eyes* to Russia's *incredible* backwardness and poverty, which these data reveal.

The output of our entire factory industry was worth 4,307 million rubles in 1908 and about 4,895 million rubles in 1911, says the Minister of Finance exultantly.

But see *what* these figures *mean*. In America a census is taken every ten years. To come upon a figure *similar* to ours, we must go back to 1860, when America still had Negro *slaves*.

In 1860 the output of America's manufacturing industry was valued at 3,771 million rubles, and in 1870 it was worth as much as 8,464 million rubles. In 1910 its value was already as high as 41,344 million rubles, i.e., almost *nine times* as much as in Russia. Russia has a population of 160 million, while America had 92 million in 1910 and 31 million in 1860!

In 1911 the Russian factory worker earned an annual a erage of 251 rubles, or 8.2 per cent more (in terms of the wages total) than in 1910, exults the Minister of Finance.

In America the average pay of the industrial worker in 1910 was *1,036 rubles*, i.e., more than *four times* that of his Russian counterpart. In 1860 it was *576 rubles*. i.e., double the *present* amount in Russia.

Twentieth-century Russia, the Russia of the June Third "Constitution", *is in a lower position than slave-owning America*.

In Russia, annual productivity per factory worker was 1,810 rubles in 1908, while in America it was 2,860 rubles in 1860 and 6,264 rubles in 1910.

These few figures suffice as a brief illustration of *modern* capitalism and of the medieval oppression of serfdom which fetters it, and which accounts for the sorry plight of the bulk of the peasantry.

As a matter of fact, the plight of the peasantry is inevitably reducing the home market to miserable dimensions and dragging down the worker, who in 1911 earned half the amount earned by the American worker in the period of slavery. Besides, the conditions of the world market confront Russia with the alternative of either being crushed by competitors among whom capitalism is advancing at a different rate and on a truly broad basis, or of getting rid of all the survivals of serfdom.

Pravda No. 61, March 14, 1913
Signed: *V.*

Published according
to the *Pravda* text

AGREEMENT OR SPLIT?

CONCERNING THE DIFFERENCES
WITHIN THE SOCIAL-DEMOCRATIC DUMA GROUP

Social-Democratic opinion is alarmed by the threat of a split in the group that sounded in the letter of the seven deputies. The matter has justly aroused keen interest among the workers. It is essential to make an accurate and clear-cut appraisal of the situation.

On one side are all six deputies from the worker curia, i.e., representatives of the vast majority of Russia's working class, as everyone realises. On the other side are the remaining seven deputies, who command an accidental majority of one vote inside the group.

On the face of it, the point at issue is that the seven deputies want to force the other six to become contributors to the newspaper *Luch*, and declare for merging *Pravda* and *Luch*. These demands of the seven deputies seem to us simply unreasonable, to put it plainly. Can anyone be compelled "by a majority vote" to contribute to a newspaper whose trend he does not share? (It goes without saying that any self-respecting editorial board would refuse to have "contributors" who have been dragged in by force, against their will.) Can one speak seriously of merging *Pravda* and *Luch*?

Of course *not*! And we declare plainly that we should consider it a *betrayal* of the proletarian cause for *Pravda* to renounce its struggle against liquidationism, and hence, for *Pravda* and *Luch* to be merged, *so long as* Luch *has not renounced liquidationist propaganda—against the "underground"*, *against political strikes*, etc. A serious Social-Democrat would hardly believe it if he were told that *Pravda* and the six workers' deputies had decided to commit suicide merely because *Luch* insisted on it. That is out of the question, and the seven deputies will do well to cease harking back to their absolutely unacceptable and unrealistic "plan"

However, this does not exhaust the issue of the differences within the group. Everyone senses that behind the outward dispute over the forced collaboration with *Luch* there is some other, more serious and important dispute. The point of this dispute is *the attitude of either section of the group to liquidationism.*

And we think that in this matter the workers are entitled first of all to insist on the seven deputies *stating their attitude to liquidationism—in plain, precise, clear and definite terms.* It is the duty of the seven deputies to do this as openly as the six workers' deputies did it. In the Third Duma group, the overwhelming majority of the deputies were *Mensheviks.* But their attitude to liquidationism was markedly *negative.* Now what is the attitude of the seven deputies today? They have themselves raised the question of *Luch*, i.e., of liquidationism. They are, therefore, doubly obliged to say openly and exactly what they think of the propaganda of *Luch* against the underground (see *Luch* No. 101 and other issues), against political strikes, against the hegemony of the working class in the emancipation movement, etc. Unless this is done, not a single step can be taken towards finding a way out of the situation.

We say plainly: if the Social-Democratic group were found to include even one deputy who would make speeches from the Duma platform like the article in *Luch* No. 101 (which said that the growing sympathy for the "underground" was a "deplorable" fact, etc.), *a break with that deputy would be unavoidable.* And any Social-Democratic deputy who did not get up and say that that speaker did not express the opinion of the Social-Democrats would fail in his duty towards the working class.

Are we right or wrong in expressing this opinion? We shall calmly leave it to the workers to answer this question.

In view of the serious differences between the two halves of the group, unity can be preserved only *if both sides alike strive for agreement.* To "settle" questions bearing on the Party Programme by an accidental majority of one vote means *inviting a split.* That is obvious to anyone. People who are earnest in their desire for unity will never adopt this way of "settling" questions.

Is such an agreement possible in the group as it now stands? Until recently it *was*. The declaration of the group, read at the beginning of the Fourth Duma's work, is an example. The group rejected liquidationist claims, and thus made an agreement between the two sections possible. Given goodwill, and provided the seven deputies are not preparing for a split, this *will be* possible in the future as well on all important political questions.

The declaration is an example of *what should be done* to avoid a split. On the other hand, the example of "cultural national autonomy" is an example of *what should not be done*, to avoid a split. To put forward this demand, as did Comrade Chkhenkeli, means *cancelling* the Social-Democratic Programme. Hitherto the liquidators have asserted that this demand "does not contradict" the Programme, but now they have been exposed even by the Bundists themselves, who (see *Die Zeit* No. 9[211]) congratulate Chkhenkeli precisely for having "abandoned the rigid standpoint of official theory on the national question". To cancel the Programme by seven votes to six *means* paving the way for a *split*. That is obvious to any class-conscious worker.

And so, the alternative is *agreement or split*!

What do *we* propose? *Agreement*!

Is agreement possible? Yes!

Is it desirable? Yes!

What is needed to bring it about? What is needed is not to cancel the Programme, not to revile the "underground", to remain loyal to the old banner! Our demands are modest, as the reader will see.

For agreement between the seven and six, against a split! This is what all class-conscious workers should demand.

Pravda No. 62, March 15, 1913
Signed: *B. B.*

Published according
to the *Pravda* text

"SPARE CASH"[212]

The government newspapers, headed by the sycophantic *Novoye Vremya*, are extolling our government for the splendid results achieved by the national economy. Just think: 450 million rubles of "spare cash"! Bringing money into the house and not taking it out—that, please note, is how "we" manage our household.

And *Novoye Vremya*, newspaper of the Black-Hundred landlords and Octobrist merchants, comes to the conclusion that there is no risk at all even in waging war when you have such a nest-egg as 450 million rubles.

Let us, however, look at the explanatory note of the Minister of Finance to the Budget for 1913. Perhaps we can find in it, besides self-praise (of which the note is chock-full!), *exact data* on the origin of the vaunted "spare cash"?

We open the Minister's explanatory note and read (Part I, p. 15) that in the five years from 1908 to 1912 *loans* brought the Treasury 339,500,000 rubles. During the same period, loans were paid off to the value of 252,100,000 rubles.

Hence loans have *increased* by a total of *87,400,000 rubles*. There you have the first "source" of the "spare cash". It is a simple one, as you see.

But to proceed. It is known that *on October 1, 1908*, the price of state-monopoly vodka was raised to the limit, that is, from 8 rubles to 8.40 per vedro* (meaning the standard vedro, for the price per table vedro went up from 11 to 12 rubles).

As a result of this "financial measure", the price of state-monopoly vodka in the five-year period 1908-12 averaged 8.48 rubles per vedro, i.e., exactly *42 kopeks* more than in the previous four years (in 1904-07 it was 8.06 per vedro).

---

* Twenty-one pints.—*Tr*

Altogether the Treasury sold 440,500,000 vedros of 40% vodka in five years (1908-12). The 42-kopek increase in profit per vedro added up to *185 million rubles.*

There you have the second source of the "spare cash"!

The third source—the state railways—yielded in four years (1908-11) *53 million rubles* of "net profit", *if one leaves out of account* payment of interest and amortisation of Treasury capital expenditure, which totalled 2.250 million rubles!! Let us assume that in 1912 this "profit" was as high as in 1911, i.e., 105 million rubles. We get a "profit" of *158 million rubles* during the five years. Obviously, a national "economy" in which interest and amortisation on thousands of millions spent are not taken into account is more like national juggling. Let us note that it was not some "Left-wing journalist" (God forbid!) but the *State Control itself* that estimated at *397,600,000 rubles in four years* (1908-11) the interest and amortisation on the investments made by the Treasury in the railway system. In terms of the five years from 1908 to 1912, it adds up to *500 million rubbles!* This is a specimen of *predatory economy.*

We shall now sum up the three sources of the "spare cash":

(1) Loans	87,400.000	rubles
(2) Increased price of state-monopoly vodka	185,000,000	"
(3) State railways (*leaving out of account 500 million rubles interest and amortisation on capital expenditure*)	158,000,000	"
Total	430.400,000	rubles

This would seem to be enough. No need to indicate the less important "sources".

Is it not clear that our feudal-minded landlords are the greatest financial geniuses? Borrowing money, raising the price of vodka, "leaving out of account" interest and amortisation on thousands of millions spent (on the "economy")—are not these indications of genius?

Are not they proof of the "stability" of our Budget?

Pravda No. 62. March 15, 1913
Signed: *V.*

Published according
to the *Pravda* text

NOTES

[1] This refers to the shooting of unarmed workers in the Lena gold-fields, Siberia, on April 4 (17), 1912.

The gold-fields were owned by British capitalists, and their partners were Russian capitalists, members of the tsar's family, and tsarist dignitaries. The owners made a profit of about 7,000,000 rubles annually. The gold-fields being situated in a region of taiga forests, almost 2,000 kilometres from the Siberian Railway, the capitalists and their helpers committed the worst excesses: they paid the workers niggardly wages for their back-breaking toil, supplied them with rotten food, and outraged the workers' wives and children. Unable to bear the oppression and outrages any longer, the workers went on strike early in March 1912. The strike was led by the Bolshevik group formed in the gold-fields in the autumn of 1911. On March 4 (17), 1912, a central strike committee was elected with the Bolsheviks occupying a leading position on it. The demands to be presented to the management included: an eight-hour working day, a 10 to 30 per cent wage increase, abolition of fines, organisation of medical aid, improvement of food and living quarters, etc. The Board of Lenzoto (Lena Gold-Mining Company) rejected these demands and decided to dismiss the strikers, stop supplying them with food on credit and evict them from the gold-fields barracks, which meant dooming the workers and their families to death by starvation. The workers did not allow the police to carry out the evictions. The strikers held their ground and resisted all attempts at provocation and intimidation. The strike was peaceful and organised.

At the instance of influential British and Russian shareholders of the company, the tsarist authorities decided to use arms against the strikers in order to intimidate workers in Russia. During the night of April 3-4 (16-17) some of the members of the Central Strike Committee were arrested. In reply, on April 4 (17) about 3,000 workers marched to the Nadezhda Mine to lodge a complaint against the unlawful actions of the authorities and hand the Procurator a petition for the release of those arrested. Captain Treshchenkov of the gendarmerie ordered his men to open fire, with the result that 270 workers were killed and 250 injured.

The news of the bloody drama on the Lena aroused the furious indignation of the workers throughout Russia. Protest demonstrations, meetings and strikes took place all over the country. The Social-Democratic Duma group interpellated the government on

the Lena shootings. The insolent reply of the tsar's Minister Makarov—"So it was and so it will be!"—added to the workers'
indignation. Strikes protesting against the Lena shootings involved
about 300,000 workers. They merged with the May Day strikes in
which about 400,000 workers took part. "The Lena shootings,"
Lenin pointed out, "led to the revolutionary temper of the masses
developing into a revolutionary upswing of the masses." (See
p. 103 of this volume.)   p. 17

² The *Duma* was a representative assembly which the tsarist government was forced to convene as a result of the revolutionary events
of 1905. Nominally it was a legislative body but it had no real
authority. Elections to the Duma were neither direct, nor equal,
nor universal. In the case of the working classes, as well as of the
non-Russian nationalities of the country, the suffrage was greatly
curtailed, a considerable section of the workers and peasants lacking any voting rights. Under the electoral law of December 11
(24), 1905, one landlord vote was made equivalent to three votes
cast by representatives of the urban bourgeoisie, 15 peasant votes
and 45 votes cast by workers.

   The First and Second Dumas (April-July 1906 and February-
June 1907, respectively) were dissolved by the tsarist government.
On June 3, 1907, the government carried out a coup d'état and
issued a new electoral law which still further curtailed the rights
of the workers, peasants and urban petty bourgeoisie and guaranteed the complete supremacy of the reactionary bloc of the landlords and big capitalists in the Third and Fourth Dumas (1907-12
and 1912-17).   p. 17

³ The *Taurida* (Tavrichesky) *Palace* was the building in which the
Duma held its sessions from 1906 to 1917.

   Kazanskaya Square—in front of the Kazan Cathedral in St.
Petersburg—was the scene of frequent revolutionary demonstrations.   p. 17

⁴ See pp. 151-52 of this volume.   p. 17

⁵ *Russkoye Bogatstvo* (*Russian Wealth*)—a monthly published in St.
Petersburg from 1876 to the middle of 1918. In the early 1890s
it became a liberal Narodnik organ. In 1906 it virtually became the
mouthpiece of the semi-Cadet Popular Socialist Party.   p. 17

⁶ *Sovremennik* (*The Contemporary*)—a literary and political monthly
published in St. Petersburg from 1911 to 1915, around which were
grouped Menshevik liquidators, Socialist-Revolutionaries, Popular
Socialists and Left liberals. It had no links with the masses of the
workers. In 1914 Lenin described its trend as a hybrid of Narodism
and Marxism.   p. 17

⁷ *Black Hundreds*—monarchist bands which the tsarist police formed
to combat the revolutionary movement. They murdered revo-

lutionaries, attacked progressive intellectuals and organised anti-Jewish pogroms.   p. 18

[8] *Zaprosy Zhizni (Demands of Life)* —a weekly published in St. Petersburg from 1909 to 1912. Contributors to it were Cadets, Popular Socialists and Menshevik liquidators. Lenin called it a "liquidationist-Trudovik-*Vekhi*" periodical.   p. 18

[9] *Rasputin, G. Y.* (1872-1916)—an adventurer who enjoyed great influence at the Court of Nicholas II. "Rasputinism" most strikingly expressed the obscurantism, fanaticism and moral decay typical of the ruling upper stratum of tsarist Russia.
  Treshchenkov, N. V. (1875-1915)—Captain of Gendarmerie, one of those who led the shooting of the Lena gold-miners in April 1912.   p. 19

[10] This refers to Article 129 of the Criminal Code of the Russian Empire, which envisaged severe punishment, including penal servitude, for public actions and dissemination of writings against the tsarist system.   p. 19

[11] *R—kov*, N. A. Rozhkov—historian, Social-Democrat, one of the Menshevik liquidators.   p. 19

[12] *Zhivoye Dyelo (Vital Cause)*—a legal daily newspaper published by the Menshevik liquidators in St. Petersburg in 1912. Sixteen issues appeared.   p. 20

[13] Lenin is referring to the *"initiating groups of Social-Democratic functionaries of the open working-class movement"* which the Menshevik liquidators formed from the end of 1910 onwards as a counter to the illegal Party organisations. The liquidators regarded those groups as nuclei of the new, broad legal party they were advocating, a party within the framework of the June Third, Stolypin regime. They succeeded in forming "initiating groups" in St. Petersburg, Moscow, Yekaterinoslav and Konstantinovka (Donets coal-field) in the shape of small groups of intellectuals dissociated from the working class. These groups opposed the strike movement and revolutionary demonstrations of the workers, and fought against the Bolsheviks in the Fourth Duma elections. The guiding centres of the "initiating groups" were *Golos Sotsial-Demokrata*, which the liquidators published abroad, and *Nasha Zarya* and *Dyelo Zhizni*, legal liquidationist organs published in Russia.   p. 20

[14] *Dobrolyubov, N. A.* (1836-1861)—outstanding Russian revolutionary democrat, literary critic and materialist philosopher, one of the forerunners of Russian Social-Democracy.   p. 20

[15] *Nasha Zarya (Our Dawn)*—a legal monthly published by the Menshevik liquidators in St. Petersburg from 1910 to 1914. It was the centre for the liquidationist movement in Russia.   p. 20

[16] This refers to the Sixth (Prague) All-Russia Conference of the R.S.D.L.P., held January 5-17 (18-30), 1912.   p. 22

[17] *Bulgarin, F. V.*—a reactionary journalist and publisher of the first half of the nineteenth century who engaged in denouncing and slandering progressive magazines and writers of his day. He was notorious for his denunciations of Alexander Pushkin.

Burenin, V. P.—a journalist who contributed to the reactionary newspaper *Novoye Vremya*. He engaged in vicious attacks against representatives of all progressive social and political trends.

Lenin uses these two names as synonyms for individuals who resort to dishonest methods of conducting polemics.   p. 22

[18] *Vorwärts (Forward)*—central organ of the German Social-Democratic Party, published from 1891 to 1933. The slanderous articles against the Prague Conference of the R.S.D.L.P. which appeared in *Vorwärts* were written by Trotsky.   p. 22

[19] This refers to the Organising Committee set up by the January 1912 meeting of liquidators representing the Bund, the Caucasian Regional Committee and the Central Committee of the Social-Democrats of the Lettish Territory. Among those who took an active part in the work of the Organising Committee in addition to the non-Russian Social-Democratic organisations were the editorial boards of the Vienna *Pravda* and of *Golos Sotsial-Demokrata*, the *Vperyod* group and representatives of the liquidators' St. Petersburg "initiating group". Trotsky was the virtual head of the Organising Committee, which was officially entrusted with convening the August 1912 anti-Party conference.   p. 22

[20] The *Vperyod* group was an anti-Party group of otzovists, ultimatumists, god-builders and empirio-monists (adherents of the reactionary, idealist philosophy of Mach and Avenarius). The group was formed in December 1909 on the initiative of A. A. Bogdanov and G. A. Alexinsky. It published a printed organ called *Vperyod*. In 1912 it united with the Menshevik liquidators to form a general anti-Party bloc (the August bloc) against the Bolsheviks. This bloc was organised by Trotsky. Failing to gain support among the workers, the group virtually fell to pieces in 1913-14. Its final disintegration occurred in 1917 after the February Revolution.

The *Golos* supporters were Menshevik liquidators grouped around *Golos Sotsial-Demokrata* (P. B. Axelrod, F. I. Dan, L. Martov, A. S. Martynov, A. N. Potresov and others), which was published from February 1908 to December 1911 first in Geneva and then in Paris.

The *pro-Party Bolsheviks* were a group of Bolsheviks who took a conciliatory view of liquidationism and otzovism. Most of the conciliators opposed the Lenin bloc of Bolsheviks and pro-Party Mensheviks. They urged unprincipled unification of the Bolsheviks with various groups that had no support among the masses but sought to exert influence in the Party.

The *pro-Party Mensheviks* were a small group of Mensheviks led by Plekhanov. They had broken away from the Menshevik liquidators, and opposed liquidationism in 1908-12.   p. 23

[21] *Pravda* (Vienna)—a factional newspaper published by the Trotskyists from 1908 to 1912. Its first three issues were published in Lvov, the rest in Vienna. Twenty-five issues appeared in all.

With the exception of its first two issues, which appeared as the organ of the Ukrainian Spilka (Union), the newspaper represented no Party organisation in Russia and was described by Lenin as "a private undertaking". Its editor was Trotsky. Under cover of "non-factionalism", the newspaper opposed Bolshevism from the outset, and upheld liquidationism and otzovism. It advocated the centrist theory of "co-operation" between revolutionaries and opportunists within one and the same party. Following the January 1910 Plenary Meeting of the Central Committee it took a frankly liquidationist stand. It also backed the anti-Party *Vperyod* group of the otzovists and ultimatumists.

In 1912 Trotsky and his newspaper were the initiators and chief organisers of the anti-Party August bloc.   p. 23

[22] *Za Partiyu (For the Party)*—a sheet which the pro-Party Mensheviks and conciliators published at irregular intervals in Paris from April 16 (29), 1912, to February 1914. Five issues were brought out. Among those who wrote for it were G. V. Plekhanov, S. A. Lozovsky and A. I. Lyubimov. It was disseminated chiefly abroad and expressed mainly the views of the Paris group of Plekhanov's supporters.   p. 24

[23] The *Bund* (The General Jewish Workers' Union of Lithuania, Poland and Russia) came into being in 1897, at the founding congress of the Jewish Social-Democratic groups in Vilna. In the main, it comprised semi-proletarian Jewish artisans in the west of Russia. It represented nationalism and separatism in Russia's working-class movement.   p. 24

[24] *Biron, E. I.* (1690-1772)—all-powerful favourite of the Empress Anna Ivanovna. He came from the petty nobility of Courland and was not a Russian subject. But while holding no official position, he exerted great influence on the domestic and partly the foreign policy of Russia. He established a terroristic regime and followed a policy of Germanising the state apparatus. He took advantage of his position to rob the Treasury, take bribes and engage in speculative deals. After the death of the Empress he became Regent for a while. He was overthrown in November 1740 as the result of a coup d'état.

Arakcheyev, A. A. (1769-1834)—one of the most reactionary representatives of the tsarist autocracy, Minister of War in the reign of Alexander I. A man distinguished by brutality and cruelty, he exerted tremendous influence on Russia's home and foreign policies. His name is associated with a long period of reaction and police tyranny, brutal militarism, spying, bribery, corruption and soulless, petty formalism, comprising what became known as the "Arakcheyev regime".   p. 25

[25] *Manilov*—a character in Gogol's *Dead Souls*. A sentimental, amiable landowner, Manilov personifies pipe-dreaming and empty talk.   p. 25

[26] *The men of December 14* were Russian revolutionary noblemen who fought against serfdom and the autocracy. They revolted on December 14, 1825.   p. 25

[27] Lenin is quoting from Alexander Herzen's *Ends and Beginnings*.
                                                                                       p. 25

[28] The passage is taken from Herzen's letters "To an Old Comrade" (the fourth and second letters).   p. 27

[29] The *village commune* in Russia was the communal form of peasant use of the land, characterised by compulsory crop rotation, and undivided woods and pastures. Its principal features were collective liability (compulsory collective responsibility of the peasants for timely and full payments, and the fulfilment of all kinds of services for the benefit of the state and the landlords), the periodical redistribution of the land, with no right to refuse the allotment given, and prohibition of its purchase and sale.

The landlords and the tsarist government used the village commune to intensify feudal oppression and to squeeze land redemption payments and exactions from the people.   p. 27

[30] The *"peasant Reform" of 1861* abolished serfdom in Russia. As a result, the landlords were able to cut off for themselves over one-fifth, or even two-fifths, of the peasants' land. They retained possession of the best parts of the peasants' allotments (the "cut-off lands", woods, meadows, watering places, grazing grounds, and so on), without which the peasants could not engage in independent farming. The redemption payments imposed on the peasants for their allotments were nothing short of plunder by the landlords and the tsarist government. To pay off their debts by instalments to the tsarist government, the peasants were granted credit for forty-nine years at 6 per cent interest. Arrears on redemption payments grew from year to year. The former landlord peasants alone paid the government 1,900 million rubles by way of compensation, while the market price of the land transferred to the peasants did not exceed 544 million rubles. The peasants had in effect to pay hundreds of millions of rubles for their land, which led to the ruin of the peasant households.

Lenin described the "peasant Reform" of 1861 as the first act of mass violence against the peasantry for the benefit of rising capitalism in agriculture, as a "clearing of estates" for capitalism by the landlords. (See present edition, Vol. 13, p. 277.)   p. 27

[31] *All-Russia Peasant Union*—a revolutionary-democratic organisation founded in 1905. Its first and second congresses, held in Moscow in August and November 1905, drew up its programme and tactics. The Union demanded political freedom and the immediate convening of a constituent assembly. It favoured the tactic of boycotting the First Duma. Its agrarian programme included the demand for abolishing private landownership and transferring the monastery, church, crown and state lands to the peasants without compensation. Its policy was half-hearted and vacillating. While insisting on the abolition of the landed estates, the Union was agreeable to partial compensation for the landlords.

The Peasant Union was persecuted by the police ever since it came into being. It fell to pieces early in 1907. p. 28

[32] *Kolokol* (*The Bell*)—a political periodical, published under the motto of *Vivos voco!* (I call on the living!) by A. I. Herzen and N. P. Ogaryov at the Free Russian Printing Works established by Herzen. The periodical was published in London from July 1, 1857 to April 1865 and in Geneva from May 1865 to July 1867. It was a monthly, but occasionally it was brought out twice a month. In all 245 issues appeared.

In 1868 *Kolokol* was published in French (15 issues appeared), with an occasional supplement in Russian. It had a circulation of 2,500 copies and it was disseminated throughout Russia. It exposed the tyranny of the autocracy, the plunder and embezzlement practised by the civil servants, and the ruthless exploitation of the peasants by the landlords. It issued revolutionary appeals and helped to rouse the people to the struggle against the tsarist government and the ruling classes.

Kolokol was the leading organ of the revolutionary uncensored press and the forerunner of the working-class press in Russia. It played an important role in the development of the general-democratic and revolutionary movement, in the struggle against the autocracy and against serfdom. p. 28

[33] *Polyarnaya Zvezda* (*The Pole Star*)—a literary-political symposium. Its first three issues were published by A. I. Herzen, and the subsequent ones by Herzen and Ogaryov, at the Free Russian Printing Works in London from 1855 to 1862. The last issue appeared in Geneva in 1868. Altogether eight issues appeared. p. 28

[34] The *raznochintsy* (literally, men of various social-estates) were educated members of Russian society drawn from the small townsfolk, the clergy, the merchants and the peasantry, as distinct from those drawn from the nobility. p. 28

[35] *Turgenev, I. S.* (1818-1883)—a famous Russian writer who did much for the development of the Russian literary language. His writings reflected the typical contradictions of Russian society. While protesting ardently against serfdom, he put forward moderate liberal demands. Lenin said that "Turgenev ... was drawn to-

wards a moderate monarchist and nobleman's constitution, ... was repelled by the muzhik democracy of Dobrolyubov and Chernyshevsky" (see present edition, Vol. 27, "The Immediate Tasks of the Soviet Government").　　　　　　　　　　　p. 29

[36] *Narodnaya Volya (People's Will)*—an illegal organisation of the revolutionary-minded intelligentsia, the Narodniks, founded in 1879 to combat the tsarist regime. It was active until the second half of the 1880s.　　　　　　　　　　　　　　　　p. 31

[37] *Zvezda (The Star)*—a Bolshevik legal newspaper published in St. Petersburg from December 16 (29), 1910, to April 22 (May 5), 1912, at first once a week, from January 1912 twice weekly, and from March onwards three times a week. Among its contributors were N. N. Baturin, K. S. Yeremeyev, M. S. Olminsky and N. G. Poletayev, as well as Maxim Gorky. The pro-Party Mensheviks (Plekhanovites) were associated with *Zvezda* until the autumn of 1911. Ideologically the newspaper was led (from abroad) by Lenin, who contributed about 30 articles to it. Thanks to his guidance, it was a militant Bolshevik organ upholding the programme and tactics of the illegal Party. It had an extensive section for workers' correspondence, and kept in constant close touch with the workers. The circulation of some issues was between 50,000 and 60,000 copies.

The authorities were constantly taking repressive measures against *Zvezda*; they confiscated 30 and fined 8 out of a total of 69 issues. *Zvezda* prepared the way for the publication of the Bolshevik daily, *Pravda*; it was closed down by the government on the day the first issue of *Pravda* appeared.　　　　　　　　p. 36

[38] The *Trudovik conference* met in St. Petersburg in March 1912. It dealt chiefly with the Fourth Duma election campaign. Lenin assessed its decisions in his article "Liberalism and Democracy" (see present edition, Vol. 17, pp. 569-78).　　　　　　　　p. 41

[39] *Vekhi (Landmarks)* —a Cadet symposium published in Moscow in the spring of 1909. It contained articles by N. Berdayev, S. Bulgakov, P. Struve, M. Herschensohn and other spokesmen of the counter-revolutionary liberal bourgeoisie. In their articles on the Russian intelligentsia the *Vekhi* writers calumniated the revolutionary-democratic traditions of the foremost representatives of the Russian people, including V. G. Belinsky and N. G. Chernyshevsky. They smeared the revolutionary movement of 1905 and thanked the tsarist government for having with "its bayonets and jails" saved the bourgeoisie "from the fury of the people". *Vekhi* called on the intelligentsia to serve the autocracy. Lenin compared its programme both in philosophy and in political writing with the programme of the Black-Hundred newspaper, *Moskovskiye Vedomosti*. He called the collection *"an encyclopaedia of liberal renegacy"* and *"a sheer torrent of reactionary mud turned upon the democratic movement"* (see present edition, Vol. 16, pp. 123-31).　　　　　　　　　　　　　　　　　　　　　p. 41

[40] This refers to the unification of Germany which the German ruling classes undertook "from above" by means of the policy of "blood and iron", and through diplomatic intrigue and wars. The Prusso-Austrian war of 1866 resulted in the formation of the North-German Union, and the Franco-Prussian war of 1870-71 led to the formation of the German Reich.   p. 45

[41] *Svet* (*Light*)—a bourgeois nationalist daily published in St. Petersburg from 1882 to 1917.

Golos Moskvy (*Voice of Moscow*)—a daily newspaper published by the Octobrist Party, a counter-revolutionary party of the big industrial bourgeoisie and big landlords. It was published in Moscow from 1906 to 1915.   p. 47

[42] *Council of the United Nobility*—a counter-revolutionary organisation of the feudal landlords founded in May 1906 at the first congress of the delegates of the gubernia societies of the nobility. It functioned till October 1917. Its main objective was to defend the autocratic system, the big landed estates and the privileges of the nobility. The Council was headed by Count A.A. Bobrinsky, Prince N. F. Kasatkin-Rostovsky, Count D. A. Olsufyev, V. M. Purishkevich and others. Lenin called it the "council of united serf-owners".

The Council virtually became a semi-governmental agency which dictated to the government legislation designed to uphold the interests of the feudal landlords. A considerable number of its members were also members of the Council of State and the leading centres of Black-Hundred organisations.   p. 47

[43] This refers to the tsar's Manifesto of June 3 (16), 1907, dissolving the Second Duma and amending the electoral law. The new law greatly increased the proportion of members of the Duma representing the landlords and the commercial and industrial bourgeoisie, while reducing several times over the proportion of peasant and workers' deputies, already small. It was a gross violation of the Manifesto of October 17 (30), 1905, and the Fundamental Law of 1906, under which all legislation introduced by the government was subject to approval by the Duma.

The new Regulations entitled the landowner curia to elect one elector for every 230 persons, the first urban curia one for every 1,000 and the second urban curia for 15,000, the peasant curia for every 60,000 and the worker curia for 125,000. The landlords and the bourgeoisie elected 65 per cent of the electors, the peasants 22 per cent (instead of the former 42) and the workers 2 per cent (as against 4 per cent in the past). The law disfranchised the indigenous population of Asian Russia and the Turkic peoples of the Astrakhan and Stavropol gubernias, and cut by half the proportion of representatives of the population of Poland and the Caucasus. All those who did not speak Russian were disfranchised throughout Russia. The Third Duma elected under this law was convened on November 1 (14), 1907. It was Black-Hundred and Octobrist in composition.

The June Third coup d'état ushered in the period of Stolypin reaction.   p. 47

[44] The *Council of State*—one of the supreme organs of state government in pre-revolutionary Russia, established in 1810—according to a draft submitted by M. M. Speransky—as an advisory legislative body whose members were appointed by the tsar. Under the law of February 20 (March 5), 1906, it was reorganised and authorised to approve or reject Bills after they had been discussed in the Duma. Nevertheless, the tsar retained the right to amend fundamental legislation and issue certain laws of special importance.

From 1906, one half of the Council members were elected representatives of the nobility, clergy and big bourgeoisie and the other half were dignitaries appointed by the tsar. Hence it was an extremely reactionary assembly which rejected even moderate Bills passed by the Duma.   p. 48

[45] *Zemstvos*—so-called local self-government bodies dominated by the nobility. They were set up in the central gubernias of tsarist Russia in 1864. Their jurisdiction was restricted to purely local economic and welfare matters—hospital and road building, statistics, insurance, etc. They functioned under the control of the provincial governors and the Minister of the Interior, who could suspend decisions that did not suit the government.   p. 49

[46] Lenin is referring to the speech which P. N. Milyukov made at the luncheon given by the Lord Mayor of the City of London in June 1909, during the visit of a delegation from the Third Duma and the Council of State. Milyukov reaffirmed the Cadets' allegiance to the tsarist autocracy and stressed that as long as Russia had a Duma "the Russian opposition would remain an opposition of, not to, His Majesty".   p. 51

[47] Lenin is referring to the decree of November 9 (22), 1906, on "Additions to Certain Regulations of the Existing Law on Peasant Land Ownership and Land Tenure", drafted by Stolypin and named the law of June 14, 1910, upon its enactment by the Duma and the Council of State. On November 15 (28), 1906, another decree was issued—"On the Granting of Loans by the Peasant Land Bank on the Security of Allotment Lands". The two decrees granted the peasants the right to take over their allotments as personal property and the right to withdraw from the village commune and settle on *otrubs* or *khutors*. *Khutor* and *otrub* peasants could obtain subsidies through the Peasant Bank to buy land. The Stolypin agrarian legislation aimed at making the kulaks the new social mainstay of the autocracy in the countryside while preserving the landed estates and forcibly destroying the village communes.

The Stolypin agrarian policy speeded up the capitalist evolution of agriculture in the extremely painful "Prussian" way, with the feudal landlords retaining their power, property and privileges.

It intensified the forcible expropriation of the bulk of the peasantry and accelerated the development of the peasant bourgeoisie, whom it enabled to buy up the allotments of the peasant poor at a nominal price.

Lenin described the Stolypin agrarian legislation of 1906 (and the law enacted on June 14 [27], 1910) as the second step, after the 1861 Reform, towards transforming the feudal autocracy into a bourgeois monarchy.

Although the government vigorously advocated the withdrawal of peasants from the village communes, only some 2,500,000 peasant households withdrew from them in European Russia over nine years (1907-15). The right to secede from the village commune was used above all by the rural bourgeoisie, which was thus enabled to strengthen its farms. Some of the poor peasants who wanted to sell their allotments and end their connection with the countryside seceded too. The small peasants, crushed by want, remained poverty-stricken and backward.

The Stolypin agrarian policy did not remove the main contradiction between the peasantry as a whole and the landlord class. Moreover, it brought further ruin to the mass of the peasantry and aggravated the class antagonisms between the kulaks and the peasant poor.   p. 53

[47a] The Polish *Kolo* (Circle) was an association of Polish deputies to the Duma. In the First and Second Dumas, its leading core was composed of National-Democrats, members of the reactionary, nationalist party of the Polish landlords and bourgeoisie. The *Kolo* backed the Octobrists on all major tactical issues.   p. 55

[48] The article "A Questionnaire on the Organisations of Big Capital" appeared in *Prosveshcheniye* Nos. 5-7.

Prosveshcheniye (Enlightenment) was a socio-political and literary monthly published by the Bolsheviks legally in St. Petersburg from December 1911 to June 1914. It was founded on directions from Lenin to replace the Bolshevik periodical, *Mysl* (Moscow), closed down by the authorities. Lenin, who was abroad, guided *Prosveshcheniye* by editing articles for it and maintaining a regular correspondence with the members of its Editorial Board. The periodical published "The Three Sources and Three Component Parts of Marxism", "Critical Remarks on the National Question", "The Right of Nations to Self-Determination", and other works by Lenin.

The Editorial Board of *Prosveshcheniye* included M. A. Savelyev, M. S. Olminsky and A. I. Yelizarova. The art and literature section was edited by Maxim Gorky. The circulation reached 5,000 copies.

Prosveshcheniye was closed down by the authorities on the eve of the First World War. In the autumn of 1917, however, it resumed publication, but only one (double) issue was brought out; it contained Lenin's works "Can the Bolsheviks Retain State Power?" and "Revision of the Party Programme".   p. 56

[49] *Gushka, A. O.*, and *A. Yermansky*, mentioned further on in the article, were pen-names of O. A. Kogan, a Menshevik liquidator.
p. 56

[50] *Article 87* of the Fundamental State Laws authorised the Council of Ministers during the Duma recesses to submit Bills directly to the tsar for approval.
p. 63

[51] *Brentano, Lujo* (1844-1931)—a German bourgeois economist, one of the main exponents of "professorial socialism", who advocated renunciation of the class struggle and held it possible to resolve the social contradictions of capitalist society and reconcile the interests of the workers and capitalists by organising reformist trade unions and introducing factory legislation. On the agrarian question he upheld the reactionary theory of the "stability" of small-scale agriculture and the pseudo-scientific bourgeois "law of diminishing returns". In the closing years of his life he was an outspoken apologist of imperialism.

Sombart, Werner (1863-1941)—a German vulgar bourgeois economist, a prominent ideologist of German imperialism. One of the theoreticians of "social-liberalism" in the early period of his activity, he later became an open enemy of Marxism and described capitalism as a harmonious economic system.
p. 68

[52] *Kit Kitych*, or *Tit Titych*, a character in Alexander Ostrovsky's play, *Shouldering Another's Troubles*. He typifies an uneducated, stupid and barbaric petty tyrant.
p. 69

[53] *Rech (Speech)*—a daily newspaper, the central organ of the Cadet Party, published in St. Petersburg from February 1906. It was closed down by the Military Revolutionary Committee under the Petrograd Soviet on October 26 (November 8), 1917.
p. 71

[54] *Nevskaya Zvezda (The Neva Star)*—a legal Bolshevik newspaper published in St. Petersburg from February 26 (March 10) to October 5 (18), 1912. Twenty-seven issues appeared. At first the newspaper appeared simultaneously with *Zvezda*, which it was intended to replace in the event of the latter's closure or confiscation. After April 22 (May 5), 1912, it was published instead of *Zvezda*, which was closed down by the authorities. It published twenty articles by Lenin.
p. 74

[55] *Winter hiring*—the hiring of peasants for summer work, practised by the landlords and kulaks during the winter, when the peasants were badly in need of cash and compelled to accept shackling terms.
p. 75

[56] See Note 30.
p. 75

[57] *"Composite labour service"*—a form of labour service and of peasant renting of landlord land on onerous terms in post-Reform Russia. Under this system the peasants committed themselves—for money,

a loan for the winter, or for the land rented to them—to till with their own implements and horses one dessiatine of the landlord's spring crop, one dessiatine of his winter crop, and sometimes also one dessiatine of meadowland.   p. 75

[58] *R. B.*—R. M. Blank, a Cadet publicist.   p. 80

[59] See Note 46.   p. 81

[60] This refers to the tsar's Manifesto of October 17, 1905, published at the height of the All-Russia October political strike. The Manifesto promised "civil liberties" and a "legislative" Duma. It was a political stratagem of the autocracy designed to gain time, split the revolutionary forces, foil the strike and suppress the revolution. It was a concession wrested from the tsarist regime by the revolution, but that concession by no means decided the fate of the revolution, as the liberals and Mensheviks claimed. The Bolsheviks exposed the real meaning of the Manifesto. On October 18 (31), 1905, the Central Committee of the R.S.D.L.P. issued its appeal "To the Russian People" revealing the spurious nature of the Manifesto and calling for a continued struggle. "We still need the strike," said the appeal, "to show our enemies that they cannot appease us with a mere slip of paper, and that we want genuine rights and genuine strength." (*Leaflets of the Bolshevik Organisations During the First Russian Revolution of 1905-1907*. Part I, Moscow, 1956, p. 185, Russ. ed).   p. 81

[61] This refers to the Party of Peaceful Renovation, a constitutional-monarchist organisation of the big bourgeoisie and the landlords. It took final shape in 1906, following the dissolution of the First Duma. It grouped the "Left" Octobrists and Right Cadets. Among its leaders were P. A. Heyden, N. P. Lvov, P. P. Ryabushinsky, M. A. Stakhovich, Y. N. and G. N. Trubetskoi, and D. N. Shipov.

The Peaceful Renovators' programme was close to the Octobrist programme. It defended the interests of the commercial and industrial bourgeoisie and the landlords who conducted their farming on capitalist lines. Lenin called the Party of Peaceful Renovation a "party of peaceful plunder". In the Third Duma this party merged with the Party of Democratic Reform into the Progressist group.   p. 81

[62] *Utro Rossii (Morning of Russia)*—a daily newspaper published in Moscow from September 1907 to April 1918 (with a break in 1908). Although it called itself a "non-partisan democratic publication", it reflected the interests of the Russian imperialist bourgeoisie. It was a Progressist mouthpiece subsidised by Ryabushinsky's bank. It was closed down early in April 1918 for slanderous statements against Soviet rule. From the middle of April to July 1918 it was published under the title of *Zarya Rossii (Dawn of Russia)*.
                                                                    p. 81

[63] See Note 1.   p. 86

[64] *Russkiye Vedomosti (Russian Recorder)* — a newspaper published in Moscow from 1863 onwards by moderately liberal intellectuals. Between the 1880s and 1890s contributors to it included writers of the democratic camp—V. G. Korolenko, M. Y. Saltykov-Shchedrin, G. I. Uspensky and others—and it also published articles by liberal Narodniks. In 1905 it became an organ of the Right wing of the Cadet Party. Lenin pointed out that the newspaper "provided a unique combination of Right Cadetism and Narodnik overtones" (see present edition, Vol. 19, p. 135). In 1918 it was closed down along with other counter-revolutionary newspapers.   p. 86

[65] *Nevsky Golos (Neva Voice)* —a legal newspaper of the Menshevik liquidators, published in St. Petersburg from May to August 1912.
                                                                      p. 87

[66] In Russian political writing, the term "diehard" (*zubr*, literally, aurochs) was applied to the extreme Right-wing representatives of landlord reaction.   p. 91

[67] See Note 47.   p. 91

[68] *Temporarily bonded peasants*—serfs who after the abolition of serfdom in 1861 were obliged to perform certain services for the landlords, i.e., do corvée service or pay quit-rent. The temporarily bonded status of the peasants continued until they had, by agreement with the landlords, acquired their allotments by paying compensation. It was only under the decree of 1881, which discontinued the "obligatory relation" between the peasants and the landlords as from January 1, 1883, that the landlords were obliged to accept compensation.   p. 95

[69] In 1889 the tsarist government introduced the administrative office of *rural superintendent* to strengthen landlord rule over the peasants. The rural superintendents, who were selected from among the landed nobility, were vested with vast administrative and also judicial powers over the peasants, including the right to arrest peasants and subject them to corporal punishment.   p. 96

[70] The article "The Revolutionary Upswing" was published early in June 1912, after Lenin had made, at a meeting of the Paris section of the R.S.D.L.P. Organisation Abroad, a report on developments in Russia (April 26 [May 9], 1912) and read a paper entitled "The Revolutionary Upswing of the Russian Proletariat" (May 31 [June 13]). A printed notice issued by the Paris section of the R.S.D.L.P. Organisation Abroad gave a detailed outline of the paper coinciding with the main propositions of this article.
                                                                      p. 102

[71] *Sotsial-Demokrat (The Social-Democrat)*—the Central Organ of the R.S.D.L.P., published illegally from February 1908 to January 1917. In all 58 issues appeared. The first issue appeared in Russia,

and then publication was transferred, first to Paris and afterwards to Geneva. By decision of the Central Committee of the R.S.D.L.P., the Editorial Board consisted of representatives of the Bolsheviks, Mensheviks and Polish Social-Democrats.

Sotsial-Demokrat published more than eighty articles and other items by Lenin. On its Editorial Board Lenin upheld a consistently Bolshevik line. Two members of the Board—Kamenev and Zinovyev—took a conciliatory view of the liquidators and tried to defeat Lenin's line. Another two members, the Mensheviks Martov and Dan, obstructed the work of the Board and at the same time openly defended liquidationism in *Golos Sotsial-Demokrata*.

Lenin's uncompromising struggle against the liquidators resulted in Martov and Dan resigning from the Editorial Board in June 1911. From December 1911 the newspaper was edited by Lenin.   p. 104

[72] The leaflet mentioned by Lenin was printed in St. Petersburg and circulated at the factories before May 1, 1912. It called on the workers to hold meetings and demonstrations in Nevsky Prospekt on May Day, under the slogans put forward by the Sixth (Prague) All-Russia Conference of the R.S.D.L.P.: "A constituent assembly, an eight-hour working day, and confiscation of the landed estates." The leaflet ended with the militant appeals: "Down with the tsar's government! Down with the autocratic Constitution of June 3! Long live a democratic republic! Long live socialism!" It was signed: "Meeting of Representatives of All Organised Workers of St. Petersburg", "Social-Democratic 'Unity' Group", "City Central Social-Democratic Group", "Group of Worker Socialist-Revolutionaries", "Group of Worker Social-Democrats of St. Petersburg", and "Representatives of May Day Committees".

On June 4 (17), 1912, the full text of the leaflet was published in the news section of *Sotsial-Demokrat* No. 27.   p. 104

[73] *The December uprising* was the armed uprising of the Moscow workers against the autocracy in December 1905. For nine days the workers, led by the Moscow Bolshevik Social-Democrats, fought gallantly on the barricades against the tsar's troops. The government did not succeed in crushing the revolt until fresh troops arrived from St. Petersburg. It dealt with the insurgents with monstrous cruelty; the workers' districts ran with blood, and thousands of workers were killed in Moscow and the vicinity.   p. 107

[74] The *Okhrana* was an agency of the secret police in tsarist Russia, in charge of political investigation. It was under the jurisdiction of the Police Department.   p. 108

[75] See Note 1.   p. 108

[76] On January 9, 1905, the tsar ordered his troops to fire on a peaceful demonstration of St. Petersburg workers who were marching to the Winter Palace with the priest Gapon at their head to submit

a petition to the tsar. The atrocious shooting of the defenceless workers gave rise to mass political strikes and demonstrations all over Russia under the slogan of "Down with the autocracy!" The events of January 9 were the starting-point of the revolution of 1905-07.
p. 113

[77] *Budushcheye (L'Avenir)* — a liberal bourgeois weekly published in Paris from October 1911 to January 1914 in Russian (some items were published in French). It was edited by V. L. Burtsev and Mensheviks and Socialist-Revolutionaries contributed to it. p. 113

[78] Lenin is referring to the decision of the liquidators' Organising Committee to invite the Left wing of the P.S.P. to the August liquidationist conference.

Polska Partia Socjalistyczna—the Polish Socialist Party (P.S.P.), a reformist nationalist party founded in 1892. In 1906 it split into the Left-wing P.S.P. and the chauvinist Right-wing P.S.P.
p. 118

[79] *Zionist-Socialists*—members of the Zionist-Socialist Workers' Party, a Jewish petty-bourgeois nationalist organisation founded in 1904. They sought to isolate the Jewish workers from the revolutionary struggle of the world proletariat, and advocated a compromise with the bourgeoisie with a view to bringing about the establishment of a Jewish state.
p. 118

[80] The *Lettish Social-Democratic Union*, founded abroad in the autumn of 1900, put forward demands that were close to those of the Russian Socialist-Revolutionaries. It was imbued to a considerable extent with nationalist tendencies. In 1905 it gained some influence among a section of the peasantry, but it was not long before the Lettish Social-Democratic Labour Party superseded it. Subsequently the Union ceased to play any appreciable role. p. 118

[81] The Fourth (Unity) Congress of the R.S.D.L.P., held in Stockholm on April 10-25 (April 23-May 8), 1906, decided to merge the R.S.D.L.P. with the Social-Democratic Party of the Kingdom of Poland and Lithuania and with the Lettish Social-Democratic Labour Party. They became part of the R.S.D.L.P. as territorial organisations working among the proletariat of all nationalities in the territories concerned.
p. 118

[82] Lenin has in mind the Menshevik liquidators' plan to liquidate the illegal Party and replace it by a "broad", petty-bourgeois labour party without a programme, a party similar to the British Labour Party, with a supreme body in the form of a "labour congress" in which Social-Democrats, Socialist-Revolutionaries and anarchists alike would be represented. Lenin exposed this exceedingly harmful attempt of the Mensheviks to liquidate the Social-Democratic Labour Party and dilute the vanguard of the working class with petty-bourgeois elements. This idea of the Menshevik liquidators amounted to renunciation of the dictatorship of the proletariat.
p. 119

[83] *Dnevnik Sotsial-Demokrata (The Diary of a Social-Democrat)*—
a non-periodical organ published by G. V. Plekhanov in Geneva
from March 1905 to April 1912, at considerable intervals. Altogether 15 issues appeared. Publication was resumed in Petrograd in
1916, but only one issue appeared.   p. 120

[84] In February 1912 T. O. Belousov, a Menshevik liquidator, member
of the Third Duma for Irkutsk Gubernia, withdrew from the Social-Democratic Duma group. See Lenin's article "Deputy T. O.
Belousov's Withdrawal from the Social-Democratic Group in the
Duma" (see present edition, Vol. 17, pp. 521-26).   p. 120

[85] *Khlestakov*—a character in Gogol's comedy *The Inspector-General*,
typifying a reckless braggart and liar.   p. 121

[86] The *Organising Commission Abroad* (O.C.A.) for the convening
of a general Party conference was established by a meeting of members of the Central Committee on June 1 (14), 1911, and consisted
of representatives of the Bolsheviks, conciliators and Polish Social-Democrats. The other organisations and groups abroad which
had been invited to join the Commission did not send their representatives. The O.C.A. sent a group of Party functionaries to
Russia, including its authorised representative G. K. Orjonikidze,
to help in making preparations for the planned conference. It also
issued an appeal "To All Social-Democratic Party Orgnisations,
Groups and Circles", calling on them to set about electing members
to the Russian Organising Commission (R.O.C.). But as soon as the
O.C.A. was set up a majority in it was gained by the conciliators
and the Polish Social-Democrats who backed them. The conciliatory majority pursued an unprincipled policy aimed at continuing
talks with the *Vperyod* group and Trotsky, who had refused to send
their delegates to the O.C.A. The conciliators' publications accused the Bolsheviks of factionalism. They used their predominance
on the O.C.A. to hold up the dispatch of Party money to Russia
and obstructed preparations for the conference.
    As a result of the work done by the Bolsheviks, the Russian Or-
ganising Commission was set up. At the end of October the O.C.A.
discussed the Notification which the R.O.C. had adopted concerning its establishment and its resolutions by which it assumed
full powers for the convening of the conference while the Organising
and the Technical commissions were to be subordinated to the
R.O.C. After the conciliatory majority of the O.C.A. had refused
to submit to these decisions the Bolshevik representatives withdrew from the O.C.A. On October 30 (November 12) Orjonikidze,
who had arrived in Paris, made a report to the meeting of the
O.C.A. on the activities of the R.O.C. , whereupon the O.C.A. was
compelled to recognise the leading role of the R.O.C. Nevertheless,
it was not long before the O.C.A. began an open fight against the
R.O.C. On November 20 (December 3) it issued a leaflet entitled
"An Open Letter to the Russian Organising Commission" accusing
the R.O.C. of factionalism. The anti-Party actions of the O.C.A.

were exposed by Orjonikidze in a letter to the Editor published in
Sotsial-Demokrat No. 25, on December 8 (21), 1911. The entire
work of convening the Party conference, held in January 1912,
was carried out by the R.O.C., which had rallied all the illegal
Party organisations in Russia.   p. 121

[87] This refers to the following facts:
    In October 1910 F.A. Golovin, a member of the Third Duma,
announced that he was resigning his powers as a deputy, and shortly afterwards took an active part in a railway concession.
    In March 1912 V.A. Maklakov, another member of the Third
Duma, in spite of his status as a deputy, acted as defence counsel
for Tagiyev, a big oil industrialist of Baku charged with
manhandling Bebutov, an engineer employed by him.   p. 130

[88] By "*political babes*" Lenin means here the Bolshevik conciliators
who had their little groups in Russia and abroad.
    The "*seasoned diplomats*" were the few liquidators grouped
around Trotsky's Vienna *Pravda*, and the Bund leaders.   p. 133

[89] Lenin is referring to the law of December 11 (24), 1905, on elections to the Duma. That law divided the electorate into four curias
—landowner (landlords), urban (the bourgeoisie), peasant and worker. It granted the suffrage to persons who had reached the age of
25 years. With regard to the landowner and urban curias, it established property qualifications; in the peasant curia, only householders had the right of suffrage, and in the worker curia, only persons who had been working on their job for at least six months.
The elections were unequal. One landlord vote equalled 3 capitalist, 15 peasant and 45 workers' votes. The law debarred from elections women, agricultural workers, unskilled workers, handicraftsmen, students and servicemen. In the case of the worker curia, the
suffrage was granted only to those in factories employing at least
fifty male workers. Factories employing over a thousand workers
elected one delegate for every full thousand. Elections were multi-
stage: two-stage for the landlords and capitalists, three-stage for
the workers and four-stage for the peasants.
    For the law of June 3, 1907, see Note 43.   p. 138

[90] See Karl Marx, *Theories of Surplus Value*, Vol. II, Part Two. These
propositions of Marx's were set forth and explained by Lenin in
"The Agrarian Question in Russia Towards the Close of the Nineteenth Century" (see present edition, Vol. 15, pp. 139-42). p. 145

[91] *Gazeta Robotnicza* (*Workers' Newspaper*)—an illegal organ published by the Warsaw Committee of the Social-Democratic Party of
Poland and Lithuania from May to October 1906. Publication was
resumed in 1912. The split among the Polish Social-Democrats
in 1912 gave rise to two parallel Party committees. There were two
Warsaw Committees and two newspapers bearing the same title
of *Gazeta Robotnicza*, one of them being published by the supporters

sia, appeared as a supplement to *Sotsial-Demokrat* No. 26. It constituted a militant policy document calling for a struggle for the revolution. Lenin attached special importance to the election platform of the Party and exposed the liquidators' attempts to put forward a legal, opportunist platform "for the elections".

In sending to *Zvezda* a copy made from the leaflet "The Election Platform of the R.S.D.L.P.", Lenin marked it as follows: "This platform is being sent only for the *information of all*, particularly the *compilers* of the platform. It is time to *cease writing* platforms when there already *exists* one confirmed and published by the Central Committee. (A leaflet *has already been issued* about this in Russia, but as we possess only *one* copy, we cannot send it, but are sending you a hand-written copy.)" (See present edition, Vol. 17, p. 513.) p. 237

[115] *S. V.*—Stanislav Volsky, pseudonym of A. V. Sokolov, one of the organisers of the *Vperyod* group. p. 239

[116] *L. M.*—L. Martov, one of the Menshevik leaders. p. 241

[117] *The man in a muffler*—the chief character in Chekhov's story of that name, a man typifying the narrow-minded philistine who dreads all initiative and all that is new. p. 244

[118] *"Letter to the Swiss Workers"* was written by Lenin in connection with the following events:

In July 1912 the Menshevik liquidators' bureau of the united organisation of the R.S.D.L.P. in Zurich sent a letter to the Executive of *Die Eintracht* (a Social-Democratic organisation) and to the Swiss Workers' League. In the letter the bureau declared itself to be the sole representative of the R.S.D.L.P. groups in Zurich On July 27 (August 9) the Bolshevik Swiss Section of the R.S.D.L.P. Organisation Abroad held a meeting which was attended by representatives of the Zurich, Davos, Berne, Lausanne and Geneva Bolshevik groups.

The debate at the meeting ended in the adoption of resolutions (1) on the situation in the Party, (2) on the state of affairs abroad, and (3) a protest resolution against the liquidators' bureau. The three resolutions were published in the form of hectographed leaflets, the first and second being in the Russian language and the third, which was published along with Lenin's present letter, in German. p. 245

[119] The *International Socialist Bureau*—the permanent executive and information agency of the Second International. The decision on its formation from representatives of the socialist parties of all countries was adopted at the Paris Congress of the Second International in September 1900. G.V. Plekhanov and B. N. Krichevsky were elected to the Bureau as representatives of the Russian Social-Democrats. Lenin was a member of the Bureau representing the R.S.D.L.P. from 1905 on. In 1912 the Sixth (Prague) All-Russia

Party Conference re-elected Lenin to the Bureau as representing the R.S.D.L.P. On the Bureau Lenin fought resolutely against the opportunism of the leaders of the Second International. The Bureau ceased to function in 1914.   p. 245

[120] This refers to the investigation of Russia's factories carried out by the Industrial Department of the Ministry of Finance in 1908. Preliminary data on the results of the investigation were published by V. Y. Varzar in an article "The Manufacturing Industry of the Empire at the Beginning of 1909" in *Vestnik Finansov, Promyshlennosti i Torgovli* No. 50, on December 11 (24), 1911. Lenin cited data from the summary table in that article,   p. 256

[121] This refers to *A Summary of Factory Inspectors'. Reports for 1910*, St. Petersburg, 1911, p. XXXVII.   p. 258

[122] Lenin is referring to the miners' strike in the spring of 1912, which involved about a million miners. See pp. 467-68 of this volume for details.   p. 270

[123] Lenin took the figures from *A Summary of Factory Inspectors' Reports for 1910*, St. Petersburg, 1911, p. XV.   p. 272

[124] *Rossiya (Russia)*—a reactionary, Black-Hundred daily published in St. Petersburg from 1905 to 1914. From 1906 it was the official organ of the Ministry of the Interior.   p. 281

[125] The *Bulygin Duma*—an advisory "representative institution" which the tsarist government promised to convene in 1905. The Bill to establish an advisory Duma, and the Regulations on elections to the Duma were drafted by a commission under Bulygin, Minister of the Interior, and made public on August 6 (19), 1905. The Bolsheviks proclaimed and carried out an active boycott of the Bulygin Duma. The government was unable to convene it, and the October general political strike swept it out of existence.   p. 286

[126] *Pravda* appended to the article *"The Liquidators and 'Unity'"* a critical survey of the charges made against the newspaper by the liquidators. This section of the article was written by M.S. Olminsky.   p. 290

[127] *Oblomov*—the chief character in Ivan Goncharov's novel of that name. He was a personification of routine, stagnation and inertia.   p. 293

[128] *Zemshchhina (Land Affairs)*—a Black-Hundred daily newspaper, the organ of the Right-wing members of the Duma, published in St. Petersburg from 1909 to 1917.   p. 298

[129] The *sapient minnow* personifies the craven philistine in M. Saltykov-Shchedrin's fairy-tale of that name.   p. 308

[130] *Adherents of the old rites*—followers of a Russian religious movement against the official Orthodox Church. The movement arose in the mid-seventeenth century following the alteration of church rites by Patriarch Nicon. In tsarist times it was subjected to persecution. p. 311

[131] *Russkaya Mysl (Russian Thought)*—a liberal bourgeois monthly published in Moscow from 1880 to the middle of 1918. After the revolution of 1905 it became the organ of the Right wing of the Cadet Party. At that time Lenin called it *Chernosotennaya Mysl (Black-Hundred Thought)*. p. 312

[132] Lenin is quoting from Nekrasov's poem, *Who Can Be Happy in Russia?*

The quatrain quoted in the text further on is taken from Nekrasov's "To the Unknown Friend Who Has Sent Me the Poem 'It Cannot Be'". p. 313

[133] This refers to the "Letter to Gogol", dated July 3, 1847, in which V. G. Belinsky most vividly expressed his revolutionary-democratic ideas. Lenin described the "Letter" as "one of the finest productions of the illegal, democratic press" (see present edition, Vol. 20, p. 244). p. 313

[134] Lenin borrowed the phrase *"conformably to villainy"* from "The Liberal", a satirical fairy-tale by M. Saltykov-Shchedrin. p. 314

[135] *Zubatovism*—the policy of "police socialism", so named after Colonel Zubatov, chief of the Moscow Secret Police, on whose initiative legal workers' organisations were formed in 1901-03 to divert the workers from the political struggle against the autocracy. Zubatov's activity in this field was supported by V.K. Plehve, Minister of the Interior. The Zubatovists sought to direct the working-class movement into the narrow channel of purely economic demands, and suggested to the workers that the government was willing to meet those demands. The first Zubatovist organisation—the Society for Mutual Assistance of Mechanical Industry Workers—was set up in Moscow in May 1901. Similar organisations were founded in Minsk, Odessa, Vilna, Kiev and other cities.

The revolutionary Social-Democrats, in exposing the reactionary character of Zubatovism, used legal workers' organisations to draw large sections of the working class into the struggle against the autocracy. The growing revolutionary movement in 1903 compelled the tsarist government to abolish the Zubatovist organisations. p. 315

[136] *Judas Golovlyov*—a sanctimonious, hypocritical, serf-owning landlord portrayed in M. Saltykov-Shchedrin's *The Golovlyov Family*. p. 316

[137] *Russky Vestnik (The Russian Herald)*—a political and literary periodical published between 1856 and 1906. From 1856 to 1887

it was issued in Moscow, with M. N. Katkov as its editor and publisher. Originally it had a liberal trend but in the 1860s it became an organ of feudal reaction. After Katkov's death it was issued in St. Petersburg from 1888 to 1896, in Moscow from 1896 to 1902, and again in St. Petersburg from 1902 to 1906.   p. 317

[138] See Note 87.   p. 320

[139] The first quotation is taken from Frederick Engels's *The Berlin Debates on the Revolution* and the second from Karl Marx's *The Bill for the Abolition of Feudal Labour Services* (see Karl Marx, Friedrich Engels, *Werke*, Band 5, Berlin. Dietz Verlag, 1959).
                                                                              p. 331

[140] See Karl Marx, *Critique of the Gotha Programme* (Marx and Engels, *Selected Works*, Moscow, 1958, Vol. II, p. 33).   p. 343

[141] This refers to the following fact:
     A. A. Voiloshnikov, a member of the Social-Democratic group in the Third Duma, speaking on December 2 (15), 1911, at the Thirty-Fifth Sitting of the Duma in the debate on the Bill to amend the Rules on Military Service, described the tsarist army as a police force and called for the standing army to be replaced by the arming of the whole people. On account of this speech the Chairman of the Duma moved that Voiloshnikov be excluded from the next five sittings. Following Voiloshnikov's second speech at the same sitting the period of exclusion was increased to fifteen sittings. The Cadets voted for the original motion of the Chairman.
                                                                              p. 346

[142] Said by Liza, the maid, in Alexander Griboyedov's comedy *Wit Works Woe*.   p. 349

[143] Milyukov met Sazonov, Minister of the Interior, in September 1912 to discuss the Balkan policy of the tsarist government.   p. 351

[144] The expression is taken from the letter appraising the Paris Commune which Karl Marx wrote to L. Kugelmann on April 12, 1871 (Marx and Engels, *Selected Works*, Moscow, 1958, Vol. II, p. 463).
                                                                              p. 356

[145] Lenin is quoting from Frederick Engels's preface to the first German edition of Karl Marx's *The Poverty of Philosophy* (Foreign Languages Publishing House, Moscow, pp. 12-13).   p. 357

[146] The reference is to the battle in the Mukden area in February 1905, the last major land engagement of the Russo-Japanese war of 1904-05. The Russians lost about 89,000 men, and the Japanese about 71,000.   p. 372

[147] *Dyelo Zhizni (Life's Cause)*—a legal periodical published by the Menshevik liquidators in St. Petersburg from January to October 1911. Nine issues appeared.   p. 395

[148] *The Polish Social-Democrats' "territorial conference"* met on August 11-17 (N. S.), 1912. All the participants were supporters of the Executive Committee of the Social-Democratic Party of the Kingdom of Poland and Lithuania (Zarzadists), which took a conciliatory position in regard to the liquidators and opposed the Rozlamists, who upheld the Bolshevik standpoint. The Conference approved the activities of the Executive and resolved to dissolve the Party organisations that supported the Rozlamists. It declared for a tactical agreement with the Bund and the Left wing of the P.S.P. in the Fourth Duma elections. It also adopted a decision—analysed in this article—concerning the attitude of the Polish Social-Democrats to the R.S.D.L.P.   p. 405

[149] In 1608 Russia was invaded by Polish interventionist troops under Dmitry II the Impostor, an agent of the Polish feudal lords (he was made out to be the youngest son of Tsar Ivan the Terrible). The invaders drew near Moscow and camped in the village of Tushino. The Impostor formed a government with its own Court as a counter to the Moscow government. Some of the Russian noblemen and boyars deserted alternately to the Moscow and the Tushino governments in an effort to safeguard themselves in the event of the victory of either side. It was those deserters that were nicknamed "Tushino turncoats".   p. 408

[150] *Luch (The Ray)*—a legal daily newspaper published by the Menshevik liquidators in St. Petersburg from September 16 (29), 1912, to July 5 (18), 1913. In all, 237 issues appeared. The newspaper was supported chiefly by donations from the liberals. Ideologically it was directed by P. B. Axelrod, F. I. Dan, L. Martov and A. S. Martynov. The liquidators used it to oppose the Bolshevik's revolutionary tactics. They advocated the opportunist slogan of founding a so-called open party, opposed revolutionary mass strikes, and sought to revise the major provisions of the Party Programme. Lenin wrote that *"Luch* has been enslaved by a liberal policy" and called it a renegade organ.   p. 410

[151] The term *"Austrian" federation* refers to the Austrian Social-Democratic Party's organisation on the national principle. The Vienna Party Congress in 1897 abolished the united party, and replaced it by a federation of six national "Social-Democratic groups": German, Czech, Polish, Ruthenian, Italian and South Slav. These groups were all united by a joint congress and a common Central Executive. The Brünn Congress in 1899 reorganised the Central Executive into a federal body composed of the executive committees of the national Social-Democratic parties. Organisational federalism resulted in the break-up of the integral Social-Democratic Party of Austria.   p. 412

[152] Lenin's theses *"Concerning Certain Speeches by Workers' Deputies"* formed the basis of a declaration by the Social-Democratic group in the Fourth Duma. The manuscript has survived only in part.

The adoption of the declaration was preceded by a bitter fight of the Bolshevik deputies against the seven Menshevik members of the group. A. Y. Badayev, a Bolshevik member of the group, wrote in his recollections: "Our group devoted a number of meetings to the declaration, which it began to discuss before the Duma opened. The debate was exceedingly heated and often lasted till late into the night. On either side not only deputies but also Party functionaries then in St. Petersburg took part in drafting the declaration.... After a long and stubborn struggle and a number of heated clashes with the Mensheviks we at last had all the fundamental demands of the Bolsheviks incorporated in the declaration." (A. Badayev, *The Bolsheviks in the Duma. Recollections*, Moscow, 1954, p. 67, Russ. ed.)

In accordance with Lenin's directives, the declaration included nearly all the main provisions of the minimum programme. Nevertheless, the Mensheviks succeeded in getting the demand for cultural national autonomy included in the declaration. On December 7 (20), 1912, the declaration was read in the Duma.

On December 8 (21), 1912, *Pravda* carried a verbatim report of the Duma sitting together with the text of the declaration. This *Pravda* issue was confiscated for publishing the declaration, and its editor brought to trial. p. 413

[153] *The Extraordinary International Socialist Congress of the Second International* took place in Basle on November 24-25, 1912. On the opening day there was a large anti-war demonstration and an international protest meeting against the war. On November 25 the Congress unanimously adopted a manifesto calling on the workers to use the organisation and might of the proletariat for a revolutionary struggle against the war danger. p. 414

[154] This refers to the unrest among the political prisoners in the Kutomara and Algachi prisons. It began in August 1912 owing to the Transbaikal Military Governor's order introducing military rules of treatment of political prisoners in Nerchinsk penal-servitude prisons. In protest, the political prisoners at Kutomara declared a fifteen-day hunger strike. The prison administration retaliated by mass torture. Some of the prisoners, driven to despair, committed suicide. Similar events took place in Algachi prison. The summer and autumn of 1912 saw unrest among political prisoners elsewhere in Russia. In response to these developments there were protest strikes of workers in St. Petersburg, Moscow, Warsaw and Riga. On behalf of the Social-Democratic and the Trudovik groups in the Fourth Duma, an interpellation was made concerning the outrages against the prisoners. Discussion was postponed by a majority vote but was never resumed. p. 417

[155] This refers to the land Bill which was introduced by (non-party and Right-wing) peasant deputies in the Third Duma on May 10 (23), 1908. The Bill provided for the compulsory alienation, at average market prices, of landed estates not tilled by their owners themselves. For carrying out the land reform, it was proposed that local land committees should be set up to be elected by a general vote. Lenin appraised the Bill in his article "The Agrarian Debates in the Third Duma" (see present edition, Vol. 15, pp. 302-16). p. 418

[156] The document "Concerning the Workers' Deputies to the Duma and Their Declaration" was the draft of a declaration of the Social-Democratic group. It was copied by N. K. Krupskaya and sent to the Bolshevik members of the Duma from Cracow on November 13 (26), 1912. The draft was intercepted by the tsar's police. p. 420

[157] The demonstration was organised on the initiative of the Bolshevik representatives of various districts and factories of St. Petersburg. A few days prior to the opening of the Fourth Duma a leaflet was distributed in the factories calling on the workers to organise a one-day political strike on November 15 (28), 1912, and to march to the Taurida Palace. The liquidators, writing in *Luch*, opposed the idea of a march. On November 13 (26) the Social-Democratic group called a meeting of representatives of the St. Petersburg Committee, the Editorial Board of *Pravda*, the liquidators' leading centre—the Organising Committee, and the liquidationist *Luch*. At the meeting the Bolsheviks supported the workers' proposal to mark the opening day of the Black-Hundred Duma by a strike and demonstration. The liquidators emphatically opposed it. After the meeting the Social-Democratic group published in the press a politically erroneous statement in which they took a negative stand on the proposal for a strike. Despite the opposition of the liquidators and the political error of the Social-Democratic group, tens of thousands of workers struck on the day the Duma opened. In a number of factories short meetings were held at which the workers decided to boycott *Luch*.

After the demonstration the Bolshevik members of the Duma admitted their error at workers' meetings. p. 424

[158] Lenin is referring to the speech which Rodzyanko made upon his election to the chair of the Fourth Duma. Rodzyanko signified his "unshakable devotion" to the tsar and his support of a representative constitutional system. p. 424

[159] Lenin's letter was sent from Cracow to Stalin in St. Petersburg on November 28 (December 11), 1912. It had been copied by N. K. Krupskaya in invisible ink. On the way the letter was intercepted, decoded and copied on a typewriter by the police. The copy of the letter was found in the Police Department archives. Some of the words could not be decoded and there are omissions in the text. p. 427

¹⁶⁰ *Jagiello, J. I.*—a member of the Polish Socialist Party (P.S.P.), was elected deputy for Warsaw to the Fourth Duma. The Bolsheviks strongly objected to Jagiello's admission into the Social-Democratic group because he had been elected to the Duma thanks to the support of the bourgeoisie and the bloc of the P.S.P. and the Bund. When the issue was first put to the vote, the group split, six Menshevik deputies voting for and six Bolshevik deputies against Jagiello. With the arrival of the Right Menshevik Mankov, deputy for Irkutsk, the Mensheviks gained a majority and Jagiello was admitted into the group. But under pressure from the Bolshevik deputies his rights within the group were restricted: he was granted a voice but no vote on all inner-Party questions.
p. 427

¹⁶¹ *Dyen (The Day)*—a name given to the newspaper *Pravda* to evade the censor.   p. 427

¹⁶² There is an omission in the text of the document. The *Collegium* was the Bolshevik section of the Social-Democratic group in the Fourth Duma.   p. 427

¹⁶³ Several words are missing in the letter. "P."—N. G. Poletayev, a Bolshevik member of the Third Duma. The liquidationist "M."—apparently Y. Mayevsky (a pseudonym of V. A. Gutovsky), one of the contributors to the liquidationist *Luch.*   p. 429

¹⁶⁴ The delegates from the worker curia of St. Petersburg Gubernia for the Fourth Duma met on October 5 (18), 1912, with 50 delegates present. Of the six electors elected by the delegates, four were Bolsheviks.
    The tsarist government was afraid that the Social-Democrats might win in the worker curia and therefore it cancelled the election of delegates in twenty-one St. Petersburg factories. In reply, the St. Petersburg Committee of the Bolsheviks called on the workers for a one-day political strike. The strike involved about 100,000 workers. The government had to give in and announced supplementary elections. At all the factories where these elections were held the workers adopted a "Mandate of the St. Petersburg Workers to Their Workers' Deputy". On October 17 (30) the Mandate was passed by a new gubernia meeting. But during the second election of electors the vote was not taken by platforms, with the result that three Bolsheviks and three liquidators were elected. The Bolsheviks proposed to the liquidators that lots should be cast to decide who was to be nominated for election to the Duma for the worker curia. The liquidators rejected the proposal. The gubernia meeting of electors elected A. Y. Badayev, a Bolshevik, for the worker curia of St. Petersburg Gubernia.   p. 429

¹⁶⁵ N. K. Krupskaya copied the letter to J. V. Stalin in invisible ink, writing it between the lines of another letter. The letter was discovered in the files of the Police Department, among other letters that had been secretely inspected.
    Vasilyev—pseudonym of J. V. Stalin.   p. 430

166 The *leaflet on the occasion of January 9, 1913*, "To All Working Men and Women of Russia", was written by J. V. Stalin in December 1912 on the basis of the directives given by V. I. Lenin, and was brought out over the signature of the Central Committee of the R.S.D.L.P.   p. 430

167 This refers to the Right-wing Menshevik I. N. Mankov, a member of the Fourth Duma. See Note 160.   p. 430

168 Lenin is referring to the composition of the delegates to the Fifth Congress of the R.S.D.L.P.   p. 437

169 Lenin is referring to the composition of the Social-Democratic group in the Second Duma.   p. 437

170 *Balalaikin*—a character in M. Saltykov-Shchedrin's *A Modern Idyll*, personifying a liberal windbag, impostor and liar. p. 440

171 *Russkaya Molva (Russian News)*—a daily newspaper published by the Progressist Party in St. Petersburg from December 9 (22), 1912, to August 20 (September 2), 1913.   p. 441

172 *Shemyaka's trial*—an unjust trial (from the title of an old Russian folk story).   p. 442

173 *Slovo (The Word)*—a daily newspaper published in St. Petersburg from 1904 to 1909. From November 1905 to July 1906 it was an organ of the Octobrist Party. Subsequently it became an organ of the constitutional-monarchist Party of Peaceful Renovation. p. 442

174 *The Meeting of the C.C. of the R.S.D.L.P. and Party functionaries*, called the "February" Meeting for conspiratorial reasons, was held in Cracow from December 26, 1912 to January 1, 1913 (January 8-14, 1913). Participants in it included Lenin, N. K. Krupskaya and the Bolshevik deputies to the Fourth Duma: A. Y. Badayev, G. I. Petrovsky and N. R. Shagov. It was also attended by delegates from the illegal Party organisations of St. Petersburg, the Moscow Region, the South, the Urals and the Caucasus.

The preparations for the Meeting were made by Lenin himself, who also presided over it. He spoke on a number of items and wrote the "Notification and Resolutions of the Meeting".

The Meeting adopted decisions on major issues of the working-class movement. It discussed reports by delegates on the state of local Party organisations, and the work of the editorial boards of *Pravda* and *Prosveshcheniye*.

The resolutions of the Meeting were endorsed by the Central Committee and were hectographed. In the first half of February they were published together with the Notification as a separate pamphlet in Paris. In April 1913 the Central Committee Bureau Abroad circulated a letter to the Party organisations, delegates of the C.C. and individual Party functionaries, calling on them to discuss the decisions of the "February" Meeting in their committees, Party nuclei and groups. In a letter to Maxim Gorky, Lenin pointed out that the Meeting "was a great success and will play a definite role".   p. 447

[175] This refers to the statement which A. I. Chkhenkeli, a Menshevik member of the Duma, made on the government declaration at the Duma sitting on December 10 (23), 1912.   p. 461

[176] The formulation rejected by the Second Congress of the R.S.D.L.P. was the proposal made by Goldblatt, a Bundist, for incorporating in Clause Eight of the Party Programme—on "the right of all the nations included in the state to self-determination"—the following addition: "and to the establishment of institutions guaranteeing complete freedom of their cultural development".   p. 461

[177] At the fourteenth sitting of the Duma on December 15 (28), 1912, following the debate on the Government Declaration, the Cadets, Progressists, Trudoviks and nationalists proposed draft formulas of procedure to the next business. The Progressist formula was carried by majority vote. It expressed confidence that the government would implement the Manifesto of October 17, 1905. Members of the Social-Democratic group voted for this formula. Afterwards they admitted their vote to have been ill-advised. p. 461

[178] The unpublished clauses (7, 8 and 9) of the resolution on the work of the Social-Democratic Duma group called on the Bolshevik deputies to achieve equality in the group with the seven Mensheviks, strike their names off the list of contributors to the liquidationist *Luch* and rally together for Party work. The text of these clauses has not been preserved.   p. 461

[179] *The Bureau of the Central Committee*—the Russian Bureau of the C.C. of the R.S.D.L.P., the Bolshevik Party's practical centre for leading revolutionary struggle in Russia. It was established by the Sixth (Prague) All-Russia Conference of the R.S.D.L.P. in January 1912. Among its members were members of the Central Committee G. K. Orjonikidze, Y. M. Sverdlov, S. S. Spandaryan and J.V. Stalin, and alternate members of the C.C. M. I. Kalinin and Y.D. Stasova. Later on, owing to frequent arrests of Party functionaries in Russia, the composition of the Russian Bureau underwent changes more than once, new members being co-opted to replace those who had dropped out.

The Russian Bureau was led by the Central Committee of the Party headed by Lenin. Its tasks were to carry out the decisions of the Prague Conference of the R.S.D.L.P., rally the local Party organisations to the Central Committee ideologically and organisationally, strengthen Party unity, and combat opportunist trends. The Bureau did a great deal in the way of publishing and distributing Bolshevik leaflets, appeals and other illegal literature. It was an important connecting link between the Central Committee and local Party organisations. It ceased to function after the February bourgeois-democratic revolution of 1917.   p. 461

[180] Lenin is quoting from the workers' song which Georg Herwegh, a German poet, wrote in 1863 for the General Association of German Workers.   p. 467

[181] *Bremer Bürger Zeitung*—a Social-Democratic daily published from 1890 to 1919. It was under the influence of the Left Social-Democrats of Bremen until 1916, when it passed into the hands of social-chauvinists.   p. 469

[182] Before the delegates from the worker curia of St. Petersburg Gubernia held their congress (October 5 [18], 1912) to elect electors to the Fourth Duma, the government gave a so-called clarification on twenty-one of the forty-four factories that had taken part in the elections, saying that the election of delegates at those factories had been found null and void. In reply to this government move, the workers in a number of St. Petersburg factories called a political strike. The strike, which soon spread to every district of St. Petersburg, was accompanied by mass meetings and demonstrations. See also Note 164.   p. 471

[183] This refers to reports from Riga and Moscow about workers' strikes and demonstrations, published in *Sotsial-Demokrat* No. 30, on January 12 (25), 1913. On November 11 (24), 1912, the Riga workers organised a protest demonstration against the death sentences on a group of sailors of the battleship *Ioann Zlatoust* passed by a court martial in Sevastopol, against the torturing of political prisoners, and against the war that had begun in the Balkans. Over 1,500 workers marched through the streets of Riga singing revolutionary songs and carrying red flags. They were received sympathetically by the population. On November 12 (25) many large factories in the city began a political strike. On November 8 (21) the workers in a number of Moscow factories went on strike in protest against the Sevastopol executions. There was also a demonstration but the police soon dispersed it.   p. 473

[184] *V. A.*—V. M. Abrosimov, a Menshevik liquidator, subsequently exposed as an *agent provocateur*.
    F. D.—F. I. Dan, leader of the Menshevik liquidators.   p. 477

[185] The manuscript has no title. The title given here has been supplied by the Institute of Marxism-Leninism under the C.C. of the C.P.S.U.   p. 478

[186] *Avgustovsky*—pseudonym of S.O. Zederbaum, a Menshevik liquidator.   p. 483

[187] The article *"On Bolshevism"* was written by Lenin for the second volume of N. A. Rubakin's book *Among Books*. On January 12

(25), 1913, Lenin sent the article to Rubakin in Clarens, Switzerland, with a letter stipulating that the article "should *not* be altered *in any way*" (see present edition, Vol. 35, Russian ed., p. 45). The article was published in full.   p. 485

[188] *Iskra (The Spark)*—the first all-Russia illegal Marxist newspaper. It was founded by Lenin in December 1900 abroad, from where it was secretly sent to Russia. It played a tremendous part in uniting the Russian Social-Democrats ideologically and paving the way for the unification of scattered local organisations in a revolutionary Marxist party. After the split into Bolsheviks and Mensheviks that took place at the Second Congress of the R.S.D.L.P. in 1903, *Iskra* passed into the hands of the Mensheviks (beginning with No. 52) and came to be called the "new" *Iskra* as distinct from the "old" *Iskra*, edited by Lenin.   p. 485

[189] The *Zemstvo campaign* was conducted by bourgeois liberals between the autumn of 1904 and January 1905. It consisted of a series of congresses, public meetings and banquets at which speeches were made and resolutions passed in support of moderate constitutional demands. Lenin sharply criticised the Menshevik attitude of support for the campaign in his article "The Zemstvo Campaign and *Iskra*'s Plan" (see present edition, Vol. 7, pp. 497-518).   p. 485

[190] *Machism*—a reactionary, subjectivist-idealist philosophical trend which became widespread in Western Europe in the late nineteenth and early twentieth century. It was founded by Ernst Mach, an Austrian physicist and philosopher, and Richard Avenarius, a German philosopher.

Machism was particularly dangerous to the working class as a trend of bourgeois idealist philosophy, for while professing to be opposed to idealism it referred to contemporary natural science, a circumstance which gave it a "scientific" semblance. In Russia, Machist influence was strong among a section of the Social-Democratic intelligentsia. It was particularly widespread among the Menshevik intellectuals, such as N. Valentinov and P. S. Yushkevich. Some Bolshevik writers, too, including V. Bazarov, A. Bogdanov and A. V. Lunacharsky, adopted the standpoint of Machism. Under the pretence of developing Marxism, the Russian Machists tried to revise the fundamental tenets of Marxist philosophy. Lenin in his book *Materialism and Empirio-criticism* exposed the reactionary nature of Machism. He upheld Marxist philosophy against revisionist attacks and elaborated dialectical and historical materialism in the new historical conditions.

The defeat of Machism struck a powerful blow at the ideological positions of the Mensheviks, otzovists and god-builders. p. 486

[191] *V. Ilyin*—one of Lenin's pseudonyms.   p. 486

[192] *The Republican Party of Radicals and Radical-Socialists*—a French bourgeois party which took organisational shape in 1901. In reality

it has existed since the 1880s. Before the First World War it represented mainly the interests of the petty and middle bourgeoisie. Between the First and the Second world wars the big bourgeoisie increased its influence in it. Its leaders have repeatedly headed French governments. p. 487

[193] Lenin is quoting from D. Davydov's poem, "The Song of an Old Hussar". p. 491

[194] This refers to the following statement of the Communist Manifesto: "The executive of the modern state is but a committee for managing the common affairs of the whole bourgeoisie." (Marx and Engels, *Selected Works*, Moscow, 1958, Vol. I, p. 36.) p. 492

[195] Lenin is quoting from Karl Marx's *Zur Kritik der Hegelschen Rechtsphilosophie* (K. Marx, F. Engels, *Werke*, Bd. 1. S. 379. Berlin. Dietz Verlag, 1958). p. 492

[196] See Note 47. p. 495

[197] See Note 40. p. 495

[198] By *"Ropshin-like experiences"* Lenin means the reactionary ideas and decadent sentiments which became widespread in the years of reaction among the Socialist-Revolutionary intelligentsia and found a particularly vivid expression in the writings of Ropshin (B. Savinkov). p. 497

[199] *F. L—ko*—a pseudonym of Lenin. p. 507

[200] This refers to the Fourth Duma elections in Riga and Yekaterinodar, where the Cadets voted with the Right-wing Black-Hundred parties against the Social-Democratic candidates. p. 510

[201] *Pochin (L'Initiative)*—a Narodnik-liquidationist periodical published by a group of Socialist-Revolutionaries. Its only issue appeared in Paris in June 1912. p. 514

[202] This refers to the decisions of the Fifth All-Russia Conference of the R.S.D.L.P. held in December 1908 and of the enlarged editorial board meeting of *Proletary* in June 1909 (see *"The C.P.S.U. in Resolutions and Decisions of Its Congresses, Conferences and Plenary Meetings of the Central Committee*, Russ. ed., Part One, 1954, pp. 195-205, 212-32). p. 518

[203] *A. V. P.*—pseudonym of A. V. Peshekhonov, one of the leaders of the Popular Socialist Party. p. 524

[204] *Nikolai —on*—pseudonym of N. F. Danielson, an ideologist of the liberal Narodism of the 1880s and 1890s. p. 524

[205] The article *"To the Social-Democrats"*, intended only for Party members, was published in Cracow as a hectographed leaflet.
p. 529

[206] *Azef, Y. F.* (1869-1918)—one of the founders of the Socialist-Revolutionary Party, became a secret police agent in 1892. He made preparations for and carried out several acts of terrorism to win the confidence of the S. R. leadership. On the other hand, he betrayed members of the S. R. Party to the police. He was exposed in 1908.
p. 532

[207] A line seems to be missing in this passage in *Pravda*. The draft resolution analysed by Lenin proposed hanging up posters of *The Daily Herald* as well as of *The Daily Citizen*, which was in the hands of opportunists, on the premises occupied by Party organisations.

The Daily Herald was founded in April 1912 by George Lansbury as a Left-wing Labour newspaper. In 1922 it became the organ of the British Labour Party.
p. 548

[208] *The wild landlord*, a character in M. Saltykov-Shchedrin's fairy-tale of the same name.
p. 551

[209] The explanation offered by Kasso, the Minister of Education, in the Duma was prompted by a question of forty-four members of the Duma tabled on December 14 (27), 1912, regarding the arrest of thirty-four secondary-school pupils in St. Petersburg during a meeting at Witmer's private gymnasium. The pupils were suspected by the secret police of being members of an illegal political group. The question was discussed at five sittings of the Duma. On February 6 (19), 1913, the majority voted for a formula of procedure to the next business that considered the tsarist Minister's explanation unsatisfactory.
p. 571

[210] The words quoted by Lenin are a paraphrase of two lines in N. Nekrasov's "Cradle Song", which read as follows:

You will be an official without
And a scoundrel within....
p. 593

[211] *Die Zeit (Time)*—a daily newspaper published by the Bund in Yiddish in St. Petersburg from December 20, 1912 (January 2, 1913) to May 5 (18), 1914.
p. 600

[212] In the present edition, the article "Spare Cash" includes—between the phrase "national juggling" and the sentence "This is a specimen of predatory economy"—an insertion discovered in 1941, which was missing in the text of the article as it first appeared in *Pravda* No. 62, on March 15, 1913, and in the second and third editions of Lenin's *Collected Works*.
p. 601

THE LIFE AND WORK
OF
V. I. LENIN

Outstanding dates
April 1912-March 1913

1912

April-latter part of June (N.S.)	Lenin lives in Paris

April 22 (May 5)

The first issue of *Pravda*, a legal Bolshevik daily, is published.

April 25 (May 8)

Lenin's articles "The Fourth Duma Election Campaign and the Tasks of the Revolutionary Social-Democrats", "The Liquidators Against the Party" and "In Memory of Herzen" are published in *Sotsial-Demokrat* No. 26.

April 26 (May 9)

At a meeting of the Paris section of the R.S.D.L.P. Organisation Abroad, Lenin reports on the Lena shootings, on strikes in Russia and on the Party tactics necessitated by those events.

May 6 (19)

Lenin's article "Landownership in European Russia" is published in *Nevskaya Zvezda* No. 3.

May 8 and 9 (21 and 22)

Lenin's article "The Trudoviks and the Worker Democrats" is published in *Pravda* Nos. 13 and 14.

May 10 (23)

Lenin's article "Political Parties in Russia" is published in *Nevskaya Zvezda* No. 5.

May 22 (June 4)

Lenin's articles "The Essence of the 'Agrarian Problem in Russia'" and "Some Conclusions To Be Drawn from the Pre-election Mobilisation" are published in *Nevskaya Zvezda* No. 6.

May 31 (June 13)

Lenin reads the paper "The Revolutionary Upsurge of the Russian Proletariat" at the Salle de l'Alcazar, at a meeting organised by the Paris section of the R.S.D.L.P. Organisation Abroad.

Lenin's article "Economic and Political Strikes" is published in *Nevskaya Zvezda* No. 10.

June 8 (16) Lenin's article "The Problem of Resettlement" is published in *Nevskaya Zvezda* No. 11.

June 4 (17) Lenin's articles "The Revolutionary Upswing", "The Slogans of the All-Russia Conference of the R.S.D.L.P. in January 1912 and the May Day Movement", "The Liquidators Oppose Revolutionary Mass Strikes" and "'Uniters'" are published in *Sotsial-Demokrat* No. 27.

Lenin reads a paper on "Revolutionary Upswing in Russia" in Leipzig.

Latter part of June (N.S.) Lenin moves from Paris to Cracow to establish closer ties with Russia and give greater guidance to the Bolshevik Duma group and the Editorial Board of *Pravda*.

June 10 (23) Lenin's article "The Nature and Significance of Our Polemics Against the Liberals" is published in *Nevskaya Zvezda* No. 12.

June 17 (30) Lenin's article "Capitalism and 'Parliament'" is published in *Nevskaya Zvezda* No. 13.

June 21 (July 4) Lenin in Cracow moves to 218 Ul. Zwierzyniec.

June 24 (July 7) Lenin's article "The Elections and the Opposition" is published in *Nevskaya Zvezda* No. 14.

End of June Lenin writes the article "The Situation in the R.S.D.L.P. and the Immediate Tasks of the Party". The article was published in *Gazeta Robotnicza*, the "Rozlamist" opposition newspaper of the Social-Democratic Party of Poland and Lithuania, No. 15-16, on July 3 (16).

July 1 (14) Lenin's articles "The Significance of the St. Petersburg Elections" and "A Comparison of the Stolypin and the Narodnik Agrarian Programmes" are published in *Nevskaya Zvezda* No. 15.

July 6 (19) Lenin writes a letter to *Pravda* exposing Trotsky as a liar and intriguer.

Not later than July 8 (21) Lenin writes the item "A Reply to the Liquidators" for *Pravda*, insisting on a more determined fight against the liquidators at the Fourth Duma elections.

July 11 (24) Lenin writes a letter to *Nevskaya Zvezda* emphatically condemning the editors' fear of polemics against the liquidators.

July 12 (25)	Lenin's article "In Switzerland" is published in *Pravda* No. 63.
July 12-15 (25-28)	Lenin writes the article "The Results of Six Months' Work" and sends it to *Pravda* with directions on how it should be published. The article appeared in *Pravda* Nos. 78 to 81, on July 29 and 31 (August 11 and 13), and August 1 and 2 (14 and 15)
July 15 (28)	Lenin's article "Democracy and Narodism in China" is published in *Nevskaya Zvezda* No. 17.
	Lenin's articles "The Italian Socialist Congress" and "'Freedom of Speech' in Russia" are published in *Pravda* No. 66.
July 17 (30)	Lenin drafts a letter for the C.C. of the R.S.D.L.P. in reply to the inquiry of the Executive Board of the German Social-Democratic Party on the convening of a meeting of R.S.D.L.P. "centres", organisations and groups with the aim of achieving unity at the Fourth Duma elections. The letter formed the main content of the pamphlet *The Present Situation in the R.S.D.L.P.*
July 19 (August 1)	Lenin writes to *Pravda* insisting on an answer as to the editors' intention to introduce into the newspaper an anti-liquidationist section devoted to the Fourth Duma elections.
	Lenin writes to Maxim Gorky to inform him of the revolutionary movement in Russia and of the publication of *Pravda,* a workers' daily newspaper.
July 20 (August 2)	Lenin writes to *Pravda* pointing out the necessity for "launching polemics" against the Cadet press before the elections to the Fourth Duma.
	Lenin's article "Capitalism and Popular Consumption" is published in *Pravda* No. 70.
July 22 and 29 (August 4 and 11)	Lenin's article "How P. B. Axelrod Exposes the Liquidators" is published in *Nevskaya Zvezda* Nos. 18 and 19.
July 25 (August 7)	Lenin's article "Liberals and Clericals" is published in *Pravda* No. 74.
July 26 (August 8)	Lenin's article "Cadets and Democrats" is published in *Pravda* No. 75.

July 28
(August 10)

Lenin's article "The Liberal Campaign" is published in *Pravda* No. 77.

July 30
(August 12)

Lenin's articles "Revolts in the Army and Navy", "On the Eve of the Elections to the Fourth Duma", "Can the Slogan 'Freedom of Association' Serve as a Basis for the Working-Class Movement Today?" are published in *Rabochaya Gazeta* No. 9.

July 31 (August 13)

Lenin's article "Questions of Principle" is published in *Pravda* No. 79.

Late July-early August

Lenin's "Letter to the Swiss Workers" is brought out as a hectographed leaflet in German in Zurich.

August 5 (18)

Lenin's article "The Last Valve" is published in *Nevskaya Zvezda* No. 20.

August 8 (21)

Lenin's articles "A Little Explanation" and "Workers' Earnings and Capitalist Profits in Russia" are published in *Pravda* No. 85.

August 9 (22)

Lenin's article "The Strike Movement and Wages" is published in *Pravda* No. 86.

August 11 and 12 (24 and 25)

Lenin's articles "The Working Day in the Factories of Moscow Gubernia", "In Britain" and "Concentration of Production in Russia" are published in *Pravda* Nos. 88 and 89.

August 12 (25)

Lenin's article "The Working Day and Working Year in Moscow Gubernia" is published in *Nevskaya Zvezda* No. 21.

August 18 (31)

Lenin's article "A Career" is published in *Pravda* No. 94.

Lenin writes the letter "To the Secretariat of the International Socialist Bureau" protesting against the letter of the Executive of the Social-Democratic Party of Poland and Lithuania by which the I.S.B. was informed of the split among the Polish Social-Democrats.

August 19
(September 1)

Lenin's article "The Cadets and the Agrarian Question" is published in *Nevskaya Zvezda* No. 22.

August 21
(September 3)

Lenin's article "A Poor Defence" is published in *Pravda* No. 96.

August 22
(September 4)

In Cracow, Lenin moves to an apartment at 47 Ul. Lubomirskiego.

August 24
(September 6)

Lenin's article "The Liquidators and 'Unity'" is published in *Pravda* No. 99.

August 26
(September 8)

Lenin's article "A Talk on 'Cadet-Eating'" is published in *Nevskaya Zvezda* No. 23.

August 29
(September 11)

Lenin's article "The Workers and *Pravda*" is published in *Pravda* No. 103.

August 30
(September 12)

Lenin's articles "Before and Now" and "The International Congress of Judges" are published in *Pravda* No. 104.

August 31
(September 13)

Lenin's article "In Switzerland" is published in *Pravda* No. 105.

Late August

Lenin writes an introduction and an afterword to the pamphlet *The Present Situation in the R.S.D.L.F.*

September 2 and 9 (15 and 22)

Lenin's article "Yet Another Anti-Democratic Campaign" is published in *Nevskaya Zvezda* Nos. 24 and 25.

September 5 (18)

Lenin's article "The Unity of the Cadets and *Novoye Vremya*" is published in *Pravda* No. 109.

September 15 (28)

Lenin's article "Concerning N. S. Polyansky's Letter" is published in *Pravda* No. 118.

September 16 (29)

Lenin's article "The Political Line" is published in *Nevskaya Zvezda* No. 26.

September 18 (October 1)

Lenin's article "The Successes of the American Workers" is published in *Pravda* No. 120.

September 28 (October 11)

Lenin's article "The End of the Italo-Turkish War" is published in *Pravda* No. 129.

Second half of September

Lenin writes a letter to Maxim Gorky informing him of the progress of the Fourth Duma elections and asking him to write for *Pravda*.

Lenin's pamphlet *The Present Situation in the R.S.D.L.P.* is published in German in Leipzig.

October 4 (17)   Lenin's article "A Game of Chance" is published in *Pravda* No. 134.

Lenin writes to Maxim Gorky suggesting that he should become a permanent contributor to *Pravda*.

October 5 (18)   Lenin's article "The Priesthood in the Elections, and Elections with the Priesthood" is published in *Nevskaya Zvezda* No. 27.

October 6 (19)   Lenin's article "Mr. Milyukov's 'Position'" is published in *Pravda* No. 136.

October 13 (26)   Lenin writes to *Pravda*, insisting that the Bolsheviks' election platform be propagated with greater determination prior to the congress of the delegates from the St. Petersburg worker curia, that lists of the Bolshevik candidates for the office of elector be published in full and that a special issue of *Pravda* be devoted to the Duma elections.

October 16 (29)   Lenin's articles "Deputy of the St. Petersburg Workers" and "The Balkan Peoples and European Diplomacy" are published in *Pravda* No. 144.

October 18 (31)   Lenin's articles "The Fox and the Hen-Coop" and "A Disgraceful Resolution" are published in *Pravda* No. 146.

October 19 (November 1)   Lenin's article "A Cadet Professor" appears in *Pravda* No. 147.

October 21 (November 3)   Lenin's article "A New Chapter of World History" is published in *Pravda* No. 149.

October 24 (November 6)   Lenin's article "Cadets and Nationalists" is published in *Pravda* No. 151.

October 28 (November 10)   Lenin's article "The Horrors of War" is published in *Pravda* No. 155.

October   Lenin writes the article "Debates in Britain on Liberal Labour Policy". It was published in *Prosveshcheniye* No. 4, 1913.

Lenin writes the article "Two Utopias".

Early November   Lenin writes the theses "Concerning Certain Speeches by Workers' Deputies" as a guide for the drafting of a declaration of the Social-Democratic group.

November 4 (17) Lenin's article "Truly Russian Morals" is published in *Pravda* No. 160.

November 5 (18) Lenin's articles "The Platform of the Reformists and the Platform of the Revolutionary Social-Democrats" and "The Illegal Party and Legal Work" are published in *Sotsial-Demokrat* No. 28-29.

November 7 (20) Lenin's article "The Social Significance of the Serbo-Bulgarian Victories" is published in *Pravda* No. 162.

November 8 (21) Lenin's article "Regenerated China" is published in *Pravda* No. 163.

November 9 (22) Lenin's article "The Results and Significance of the U.S. Presidential Elections" is published in *Pravda* No. 164.

November 13 (26) Lenin sends the Bolshevik members of the Fourth Duma his draft of a declaration of the Social-Democratic group.

Latter part of November Lenin writes the article "Concerning the Event of November 15. An Undelivered Speech".

November 28 (December 11) Lenin sends to *Prosveshcheniye* in St. Petersburg a questionnaire for the Bolshevik deputies to sum up the results of the elections for the worker curia.

November 29 (December 12) Lenin's article "The Disease of Reformism" is published in *Pravda* No. 180.

November 30 (December 13) Lenin's article "Impoverishment in Capitalist Society" is published in *Pravda* No. 181.

November Lenin holds a meeting of the Central Committee to discuss the financial crisis in the *Pravda* Editorial Board.

 Lenin writes the article "The 'Vexed Questions' of Our Party. The 'Liquidationist' and 'National' Questions". The article first appeared in August 1913 in *Pismo Dyskusyjne* No. 1, published by the Warsaw and Lodz committees of the Social-Democratic Party of Poland and Lithuania.

December 12 (25)	Lenin's article "The Working Class and Its 'Parliamentary' Representatives" is published in *Pravda* No. 191.
December 15 (28)	Lenin's "article The 'Reconciliation' of the Nationalists and Cadets" is published in *Pravda* No. 194.
December 22 (January 4, 1913)	Lenin's article "The National-Liberals" is published in *Pravda* No. 200.
December	Lenin writes the theses "On the Attitude to Liquidationism and on Unity" for the "February" Meeting of the C.C. of the R.S.D.L.P. and Party functionaries.
December 26-January 1 (January 8-14, 1913)	Lenin leads the "February" Meeting of the C.C. R.S.D.L.P. and Party functionaries. The Meeting adopted resolutions drafted by Lenin: on the revolutionary upswing; the strikes and the tasks of the Party; the building up of the illegal organisation; the Social-Democratic group in the Duma; illegal literature; the insurance campaign; the attitude to liquidationism, and unity; the non-Russian Social-Democratic organisations.

At the Meeting Lenin outlined a series of steps to improve the work of the *Pravda* Editorial Board.

Lenin holds a meeting of the Central Committee and Bolshevik deputies to discuss the activities of the Bolshevik group in the Fourth Duma.

1913

Early January	Lenin edits the resolutions and writes the Notification on the "February" Meeting of the C.C. of the R.S.D.L.P. and Party functionaries.
January 1 (14)	Lenin's article "The British Labour Movement in 1912" is published in *Pravda* No. 1.
January 6 (19)	Lenin writes the article "Better Late Than Never". It was published in *Pravda* No. 8, on January 11 (24).
January 12 (25)	Lenin's articles "The Development of Revolutionary Strikes and Street Demonstrations" and "The Split among the Polish Social-Democrats" are published in *Sotsial-Demokrat* No. 30.

Lenin writes to *Pravda* demanding a reorganisation of its Editorial Board.

Lenin sends his article "On Bolshevism" for the second volume of N. Rubakin's book *Among Books*.